"A GOVERNMENT OF OUR OWN"
THE MAKING OF THE CONFEDERACY

William C. Davis

THE FREE PRESS

New York   London   Toronto   Sydney   Tokyo   Singapore

The Free Press
A Division of Simon & Schuster Inc.
1230 Avenue of the Americas
New York, N.Y. 10020

Printed in the United States of America

printing number

  2 3 4 5 6 7 8 9 10

Library of Congress Cataloging-in-Publication Data

Davis, William C.
A government of our own : the making of the Confederacy / William C. Davis.
    p.   cm.
Includes bibliographical references and index.
ISBN 0-02-907735-4
1. Secession. 2. Confederate States of America—Politics and government.
I. Title.
E459.D274   1994
973.7'13—dc20   94-15205
                                                                         CIP

For Alice and Charles Shewmake,
who introduced me to the Montgomery of today
and showed me that it is every bit as interesting as
the one of yore

We have pulled a temple down that has been built three-quarters of a century. We must clear the rubbish away to reconstruct another.

—ANDREW P. CALHOUN
South Carolina Secession Convention
Charleston, December 20, 1860

CONTENTS

ACKNOWLEDGMENTS

I HAVE RECEIVED KINDNESS and assistance literally all across the South in the research for this book. Understandably, my first and foremost debt is to the city where it all took place. The staff of the Department of Archives and History in Montgomery, Alabama, went leagues out of its way to be of aid, and not just by making their outstanding collections available. Director Ed Bridges and archivists Norwood Kerr and Rickie Louise Brunner dealt quite happily with what must have seemed an endless string of questions and requests. Without their aid and resources, this story could not be told. Similarly, special mention must be made of the continuing kindnesses of Anne Lipscomb of the Mississippi Department of Archives and History, in Jackson, and old friends Guy Swanson and Corrine P. Hudgins at the Museum of the Confederacy in Richmond, Virginia.

For assistance in making their manuscript holdings available to me, I am also indebted to Clark Center of the Hoole Library, University of Alabama; Mary Giles in the archives of the stunning Charleston Museum in Charleston, South Carolina; Lynda Crist of the Papers of Jefferson Davis project at Rice University, Houston, Texas; Pamela Williams of the P. K. Yonge Library of Florida History, University of Florida, Gainesville; Melissa Bush at the Hargrett Rare Book and Manuscript Library, University of Georgia, Athens; Karen E. Kearns at the Huntington Library of San Marino, California; Michael Musick, friend to all researchers at the National Archives in Washington, D. C.; Toby Gearhart at Philadelphia's Historical Society of Pennsylvania; Henry Fulmer at the South Caroliniana Library, University of South Carolina at Columbia; I. Bruce Turner, Dupree Library, University of Southwestern Louisiana, Lafayette; Ralph Elder at the Center for American History, University of Texas, Austin; my old friend Wilbur Meneray at Special Collections in the Howard-Tilton Memorial Library, Tulane University, New Orleans; Richard J. Sommers of the incomparable Archives Branch, United States Army Military History

Institute, Carlisle Barracks, Carlisle, Pennsylvania; and Gordon Cotton of the Old Court House Museum in Vicksburg, Mississippi.

Several friends are also due thanks. Jerry Russell of Little Rock, Arkansas, rummaged through newspapers when he should have been doing other things. Warren Rogers offered counsel based on his own forthcoming history of Montgomery during the entire course of the Civil War. Robert Krick offered more than one helpful suggestion, and T. Michael Parrish of Austin, Texas, repeatedly turned my eye to sources I might otherwise have missed, and in a couple of cases simply sent them to me. Michael Hammerson of London, England, spent many an hour exploring the vagaries of the William Gladstone Papers in the British Museum in search of a source that, alas, remains yet undiscovered. Rick Joslyn allowed me to share in his research on his relation Robert Josselyn, that poor unappreciated dogsbody to Jefferson Davis. Miriam C. Jones of Montgomery helped me to settle at last several nagging questions about just where buildings were located in 1861, and Captain John Culver of Portsmouth, New Hampshire, shared with me the brief but very worthwhile memoir of his ancestor William W. Culver, as well as the photographer's own print of his historic image of Davis's inauguration.

Sylvia Frank gave time above the call by turning her keen editorial eye to a very rough manuscript, and Dr. William J. Cooper of Louisiana State University most graciously read a more finished version and offered myriad questions and criticisms. Most of all, to Alice and Charles Shewmake of Montgomery I owe eternal gratitude for their inordinate hospitality and delightful company on many occasions during the course of work on this book. This project is done now, but I fear they are stuck with me all the same, for they and—thanks to them—Montgomery are now permanent fixtures on my Southern itinerary.

PROLOGUE, MAY 1861

———— ● ★ ● ————

IN MAY 1861 an English journalist took a seat beside one of the fluted Corinthian columns supporting the viewers' gallery in the Alabama House of Representatives and turned a keen eye on the proceedings before him. Some half a hundred men from their thirties to their seventies, tall and short, lean and fat, were making a nation. Indeed, exactly three months earlier they had first met in this same building, framed a constitution, elected a president, and started the turnings of the ponderous wheels of government.

He could see that they were men of much pride, and some prejudice, of intellect, and generally of at least moderate affluence and property. Most of them owned slaves, and even more either were or had been practicing members of the bar. They had come some distance from their homes, and much farther from their origins, and here they were, staking all they had on founding a new nation.

Interesting enough, the Englishman heard echoes in that hall, not just of the voices present, but distant reverberations of words spoken by other men, in other halls, and in another time. Indeed, as he looked at them now, with a war on their hands, with the charter of their new freedom as yet untried, in the midst of a crisis that could quite literally take their lives, their fortunes, and perhaps even their honor, he thought of another assembly bravely embarking on a new nationhood and an uncertain future with nothing but courage, patriotism, and a sure conviction that they were in the right. With the dispassionate eye of a neutral, he entertained few hopes for that future. The odds against them were so great. But then, so had been the odds against those other Americans some four score years before. Yet *they* succeeded.

But for the venue it could have been a reenactment of the hot summer days of 1776 in Philadelphia, he thought. The clothing was wrong. Yet garb these men in the raiment of a century before, he

1

decided, and he might well be sharing the floor with the Founding Fathers themselves. Had his visit lasted longer, and had he taken time to know more of them, he might have discovered that in fact and in spirit, that is just who they were.

They, too, heard distant echoes.

CHAPTER ONE

WELD THEM TOGETHER WHILE THEY ARE HOT

————•★•————

For generations North and South glared at one another across Mason and Dixon's line. Hand in hand they began the American adventure, but unknowingly they walked from the first toward a shore that promised to part them in violence. Hand in hand they waded ever deeper in their pride into waters they did not know and could not fathom. And now the waves were rising, with a wind behind them. Up to their necks in the seething foam, North and South loosed at last their grasp upon each other and held their hands before them, one poised to strike at a brother become a foe, and the other raised in a futile hope of holding back the oncoming flood. What Episcopalians among their number knew as "the deep waters of the proud" were about to overwhelm them.

Many saw the wave coming. All seemed powerless to halt its relentless course. Their fathers set it in motion at the founding, albeit unknowingly and without malice. A host of lesser breakers foretold its crest. The tug of industrialism against agrarian interest. Discriminatory internal tariffs. The growth of a more powerful centralized government in Washington versus the sovereignty of the individual states. Beneath these lay the yet broader issue of power, who should have it, and the fate of the minority that did not. But driving the flood, the current from which every wave inevitably drew its own momentum, was a single motive force.

Slavery. Generation after generation it loomed ever higher. Angrily, and without deep conviction, North and South built floodwalls to contain it—the Missouri Compromise in 1820, the Compromise of 1850, the Kansas-Nebraska Act of 1854. But none of them could hold it back. The black tide was too powerful. Confined exclusively to the South, it became the region's "peculiar institution," and as a result was

misunderstood and misrepresented in the North. Yankees cried abomi-
nation at the idea of one man owning another, conceived visions of
cruel hardship, bestial tortures, and worse, and pleaded against this
degradation of humanity, white and black. All the while, behind their
sanctimony, Northern leaders also saw in the issue of slavery a tool, a
lever to power. Using it, by 1860 the new Republican party in a scant
six years elevated itself from inception to domination in the North.
The nation was growing, new territories in the West were applying for
statehood. Keep slavery out of those territories, and the states to come
must inevitably be "free." Every new free state only plunged the slave
states deeper into minority, locking the Northern, Republican grip on
power in Washington.

Across that invisible line dividing the sections, slavery meant something much different. Certainly it provided labor for the fields and plantations, a labor essential to the economy of the agrarian South.
Moreover, the four million slaves in 1860 represented an enormous capital investment, at least $4 billion or more. Southern bookkeepers kept
their accounts almost perpetually in red ink. In just the six states of the
deepest South, South Carolina, Georgia, Florida, Alabama, Mississippi,
and Louisiana, by 1860 the public debt reached $32,653,448.[1] On top of
that the prospect of abolition or enforced emancipation coming out of
Washington would mean nothing less than ruin.

Moreover, an unspoken subtext ran beneath Southern protestations.
They feared social ruin from abolition as well. What would they do
with four million free blacks in their midst? Who would feed and
clothe them. How would they find employ with few skills other than
field labor, and with cash-poor planters unable to hire them? Long-held
patriarchal affection led to genuine concern over the slave's probable
fate as a freedman; deep-seated conviction of the negro's inability to be
responsible without white control produced ugly visions of rampant
squalor, degradation, and crime. And only whispered was the pervading
fear that if millions of whites and blacks lived together in freedom—if
not equality—inevitable pollution must ensue, the dreaded specter of
racial "amalgamation."

Much of this the South could not, or would not, say. Rather it
argued the benevolent nature of slavery, of how it uplifted the ignorant
black out of barbarity, fed and housed him, gave him some skills suitable to his abilities, and brought him Christianity. Quite rightly white
Southerners pointed to the living conditions of free blacks and factory
workers in the North, and claimed those of their slaves to be better.

Most of all, they sought refuge in the Constitution. It recognized slavery. At the very least, they said, this meant that no administration in Washington could touch it where it already existed. Beyond that they argued it to be their right to take their slaves with them into the territories, which were, after all, the property of all the people of the nation. And thus they might have at least a chance of seeing more slave states enter the Union. So doing might not preserve a true balance of power, but at least it could prevent the free states from achieving the three-to-one majority that would enable passage of any constitutional amendments actually abolishing slavery.

Thus, ironically, the South must extend slavery even into regions where it could *not* flourish in order to preserve it where it *did*. But to the North this looked like a true attempt to spread slave influence, and perhaps even force it eventually upon the free states. At the same time, while most Republicans neither proposed nor intended to attack slavery in the South, their increasingly strident declarations in the movement to contain it there and keep it from the territories only fed slaveholders' paranoia that, given the chance, the abolition mob would strike at the institution in its homeland. As 1860 arrived, section viewed section through waters distorted by its own fears and ambitions, each seeing the other not in its true intent, but rather as a reflection of its own apprehension.

It needed only a Republican victory in that fall's election to turn those waters into a tidal wave. Months before the balloting thoughtful men in the South saw what might come. Many hoped to prepare for it. The Republicans were exclusively Northern. How could the South live in a Union dominated by a sectional minority? Yet the old Democratic party, the only truly national organization left, suffered the same fragmentation and faction over slavery and the territories as the Union itself. More and more Southern leaders saw their only remaining protection in secession, withdrawing from the Union. Always regarding the Constitution as a compact, they never questioned a state's ultimate right to leave the Union when it felt its interests no longer served. But what could one state do, or even several, acting individually and without leadership? The prospect of failure, and worse, disgrace, loomed over such an attempt. Martin J. Crawford, a forty-year-old congressman from Georgia, saw the problem mirrored in the spring contest for the speakership of the House of Representatives. "We have the men of sufficient nerve to bring this matter to a bloody issue," he told his friend and fellow Georgian Alexander H. Stephens, "but we haven't got anyone who has the confidence of the country." With some guiding figure or coordinated purpose "we might possibly be supported by the public judgment, but as it is I fear the people would be disgusted and we should be disgraced."[2]

As the summer came and the party conventions met, events forced more and more to share Crawford's views. The Democrats, meeting in Charleston, South Carolina, fell apart in a fatal split. Eventually they fielded two candidates, Stephen Douglas at the head of those opposed to Congress intervening to protect slavery in the territories, and John C. Breckinridge, the sitting vice president, leading a Southern rights wing. A coalition of moderates, dedicated chiefly to calming the sectional controversy, formed the Constitutional Union party and nominated John Bell of Tennessee. And the Republicans, as feared, nominated Abraham Lincoln of Illinois. The South knew little of Lincoln other than that he was a Republican, that he opposed the extension of slavery beyond its current limits, and that it did not like him. Despite Lincoln's and his party's repeated declarations to the contrary, Southerners felt certain that upon taking office if elected, he would repudiate his promises and move against slavery in the South itself.

As the campaign wore on through the hot summer and fall, rumors, exaggerations, and hysteria swelled in the slave states. By September stories circulated of a thousand vials of strychnine being supplied to slaves by whites inciting them to rise up and kill their masters. In Alabama residents believed that wealthy Northerners enticed credulous blacks to murder whites indiscriminately, and hasty lynch mobs began to hang black and white upon little more than rumor and gossip. The same news came from Texas, and in every case the stories, real or exaggerated, seemed to crystallize the feelings of men who wavered. In fact, seeing that every new story made more of the hesitant into secessionists, extreme Southern rights men began to hope that such episodes would occur in states like Georgia that, as yet, seemed too slow to approach disunion.[3] Inevitably, when such outrages failed to emerge, those more ardent than honest invented them. In Alabama that fall, Jabez L. M. Curry, a thirty-five-year-old Alabama congressman, declared that immediately after a Lincoln election, an abolition army of half a million Republicans planned to invade the South, lay waste its fields, free its slaves, and worst of all, "amalgamate the poor man's daughter and the rich man's buck-nigger."[4]

Impelled by fears and events, real and imagined, Southern leaders could not wait. The Democratic split virtually ensured a Lincoln victory.

In South Carolina, at the forefront of extremism for more than a generation, Governor William H. Gist decided to be prepared. Yet he feared that his state might act alone and find itself isolated and without support from sister states of the South. Early in October he addressed fellow governors to ask what they felt should be the response to a Lincoln victory, and clearly hinted that he did not want to be the first to secede. The replies came in through the next month, and showed more trepidation than unity of resolve. John Ellis frankly admitted North Carolina's reluctance. From Alabama Andrew B. Moore said his state would go out, but not by itself. John Pettus suggested that Mississippi would want a council of the Southern states first, in order that all should act in concert. Louisiana's Thomas O. Moore said the same thing, but then added that he doubted harmony could be achieved. Georgia would not secede on her own without some overt act of aggression by Lincoln, but Joseph E. Brown added his voice to the call for a convention. Only Milton Perry showed some inclination to adopt a less passive stance. His Florida would not secede on her own, but she would follow South Carolina or any other state. Moreover, he said, "if there is sufficient manliness at the South to strike for our rights, honor and safety, in God's name let it be done before the inauguration of Lincoln."[5]

Perhaps Governor Perry wrote with special urgency because, unlike the others, he waited until after the election to respond. On November 6, as expected, Lincoln won the presidency with a mere forty percent of the vote. That die, at least, was cast. Now the South must decide how to throw the other. Disunion was inevitable, claimed Georgia attorney Thomas R. R. Cobb. Thinking it for the best, he at once began working for secession. He believed the rumors of Yankees inciting slaves to murder and insurrection. "These people hate us," he told his wife Marion. "They are a *different* people from us, whether better or worse and *there is no love between us.*"[6] His brother Howell Cobb, then secretary of the treasury for lame duck President James Buchanan, heartily agreed. Lincoln's election mandated secession. "An intense mutual hatred," he told the president, made separation "a necessity which could not be avoided."[7]

Quickly leaders and citizens alike acted to meet the emergency. The day after the election the Stars and Stripes came down in a host of cities, replaced by state flags as a sign of defiance to Lincoln. Two days later the South Carolina legislature issued the call for a special convention to meet on December 17. They would force Governor Gist to face the issue of being first to go out. That same day, November 10, Governor Moore addressed a citizens' meeting in Montgomery, Alabama, and declared that he now saw no alternative but secession. Moreover, he declared that the state should not act alone, but join with others in forming "a Southern Confederacy." Already one of his citizens, in defense of "the religious institution of slavery," had asserted that if so few as four states seceded together, the North would not attempt to coerce them back into the Union. Two weeks later Montgomeryites formed a Central Committee of Safety, to meet every Monday and work to induce Alabama to secede in consultation with, but not necessarily controlled by, her sister states.[8]

Cooperation became the word of the moment. Even as more state legislatures issued calls for conventions to meet in January, the governors appointed special commissioners to the several capitals, charged to represent the views of their states, as well as to send back information on the course of the secession conventions.[9] Georgian Benjamin H. Hill worried over the possibility of states seceding individually, and suggested to former Governor Herschel V. Johnson, Douglas's unsuccessful running mate, that the South ought to secede as a unit.[10] Yet others regarded cooperation as almost peripheral. The aged weakling Buchanan would do nothing for the remainder of his term, and Lincoln could not take office until March 4, 1861. By then, whether singly or together, the slave states would all be out. That in itself would be enough to force England and Europe to guarantee their security against coercion. A Montgomery editor proclaimed the reason. "The Southern States have the power to say what peoples of the earth shall purchase cotton and profit by it," he wrote.[11] When Senator James Chesnut resigned his seat in the United States Congress on November 10, along with colleague James H. Hammond, he was already telling people that the fear of having its supply of cotton cut off by trouble in America would lead Europe to force Washington to let the South go in peace.[12]

Howell Cobb, to whom many across the South already looked for leadership, saw clearly the wisest course. Lincoln's election called for immediate secession. Any appointment of a Southern convention promised only to waste time. "After the secession is effected," he counseled, "will be the time to consult," and the action must be taken before March 4. Moreover, he foresaw less certainty than Chesnut and others about the ease of success. Southerners should press their cotton crops, get them shipped to the markets abroad, and the money in their hands before Lincoln took office. An embargo on cotton could well coerce foreign powers in the South's favor, but their help might not be immediate. Southern planters were always short of cash. If Lincoln imposed a blockade to halt cotton shipments after he took office, the resulting financial strain in the South would risk widespread popular distress just when the secession movement most needed the enthusiastic support of all.

And once all this was accomplished, Cobb advised, then was the time for a Southern convention. Not just a meeting to talk and counsel, however, but a gathering of delegates "empowered to *act*," and whose actions would bind their states behind them. Howell Cobb was talking about a government.[13]

Throughout December and on into January one state after another held elections for delegates to their secession conventions. South Carolina would meet first on December 17. Florida would follow on January 3, with Mississippi and Alabama convening theirs four days later, Georgia on the 16th, Louisiana the 23d, and Texas on the 28th.[14] As the movement progressed, men once hesitant grew more sure of themselves and their actions. Widespread Union sentiment still dwelled in substantial sections of the South, especially the higher country in north Georgia and Alabama, and in rural sections of all the Southern states where neither cotton nor slavery reigned. But still the secession men felt mounting confidence. Soon to be Alabama's commissioner to the Georgia secession convention, jurist John Gill Shorter told his daughter early in December that "the Union will be dissolved." As an afterthought, to calm her fears—and perhaps his own—he went on to say "and there will be no war."[15]

Just days after Shorter wrote to his daughter, all Southern eyes turned to South Carolina. The initial call for a secession convention came at a caucus of legislators meeting in Charleston immediately after Lincoln's election. Robert Barnwell Rhett, Jr., editor of the Charleston *Mercury*, sounded the tocsin.[16] At once the campaigning commenced for the election of delegates to the special convocation, and immediately a strange phenomenon emerged for the first time, to be repeated in greater or lesser degree in each of the other Southern states. South Carolina, the hotbed of secession for two generations, revealed an alarming degree of conservative sentiment. Moreover, having allowed themselves to be led emotionally by a very highly charged group of men right to the brink of secession, the voters now suddenly revealed a hesitance to entrust those same men with power.

They called them the "fire-eaters." The name arose during the decade past, applied to a small group of rabidly outspoken advocates of secession. They sprang up in all of the Southern states, but from the first their most ardent representative was Robert Barnwell Rhett, Sr. The sixty-year-old senior Rhett owned the newspaper that his son edited, and prided himself on having guided South Carolina to this historic moment. Rhett exhibited every manifestation of the high-toned Southern aristocrat, yet much was pretense. Behind his high forehead, dignified whiskers, and calm blue-gray eyes, lay a mind narrow, obstinate, and more than a little vain. Twenty-three years earlier he changed his surname from Smith to Rhett because the latter sounded more noble. Wholly committed to secession since 1850, he had been one of the most extreme proponents of Southern rights since he first stepped into the state legislature in 1826. Thereafter as a congressman, and then senator, he pushed steadily for disunion. By the late 1850s he recognized that its best hope—and his—lay in a Republican victory in 1860, and toward that end he turned the pages of the *Mercury* against his own Democratic Party. Rhett's ravenous appetite for controversy matched his gluttony at table, and he did his work well. Through his son he conducted his own survey of leading men on what should be done if Lincoln won. One respondent, Leroy Pope Walker, told him what he wanted to hear. "Your policy is to go out *now*," said the Alabamian. "If secession is ever to be the remedy it must begin *now*."[17] Even though Rhett lost a bid that fall for the governorship to Francis W. Pickens, he rejoiced in an even greater victory, the call for the secession convention. "This is his hour of triumph," wrote one South Carolinian, "and the triumph is more properly his than that of any other man now living."[18] As a matter of course, Rhett expected greater personal triumphs to come.

But Southerners somehow instinctively understood that deep flaws ran through the characters of men like Rhett. The fire-eaters were political renegades, men who worked outside the system to foment discord within it, and with no responsibility or accountability to the body politic. They were controversialists, dismantlers not builders. For all his efforts to take emotional issues like slavery and property rights and cloak them in abstract constitutional terms, men of sense saw that he was only once more changing Smith to Rhett.[19] Seasoned statesmen and the more discerning electorate recognized that such men promised only ruin if entrusted with real power.[20] Rhett impressed most as a ranting extremist. Thus it was that he showed a poor third to Pickens for the governorship, and then on December 6 he suffered another blow. He won his seat in the secession convention, but only after placing seventh in the balloting.[21]

Ahead of him were other men, more moderate, more temperate, men like Chesnut and Christopher G. Memminger. Theirs was the influence that would start to tell now, and not only did they differ with Rhett, some detested the man. William Porcher Miles, handsome, well bred, considered himself just as solid on secession. But after resigning his seat in Congress and winning one as a convention delegate, he quickly tried to distance himself from any suspicion of being under the fire-eater's influence.[22] Echoing Miles's sentiments, a friend lamented that "we have done a bad business in electing him, for he is so damned impractical that I am afraid he will kick up hell."[23]

Still Rhett got his secession. December 17, the day they convened, the delegates voted unanimously. Three days later they signed the formal ordinance. While waiting for the document to be inscribed they addressed other business. Now that South Carolina was leaving the union, her military affairs needed attention, especially since Federal troops occupied Fort Moultrie on Charleston Harbor. A committee had to address foreign relations for the independent republic. All the concerns of a nation confronted the state now, and well before the convention met, its delegates had nationhood on their minds.

The fire-eaters always advocated separate state action, being too doctrinaire to cooperate even with each other from state to state.[24] But now they joined with the moderates in recognizing the need for some coordination of action with other states expected to secede. The first resolution proposing a confederation came on December 19, a day before the delegates signed their own document, and the next day Rhett himself called for invitations to be sent to sister states to convene for forming a new Southern union.[25] A few days later, possibly at the suggestion of his son, Rhett further proposed that the convention be held before February 13, 1861, and that it meet in Montgomery, Alabama.[26] Rhett's initial motion died, but on the last day of the year the convention adopted his proposition, excepting only the suggested time and place. At the same time the delegates approved an election of commissioners to go to the other states to propose a general convention before Lincoln's inauguration. Each should send delegates equal to their recent number of representatives in Congress, though balloting in the convention itself should be on the basis of one state, one vote. Further still, the commissioners were to propose that the new Southern confederation adopt the old United States Constitution as a basis for their own provisional government.[27]

On January 2, 1861, the convention selected its commissioners, and the next day they met in caucus before departing for their destinations. Coordination seemed essential. Among themselves they decided to adopt Rhett's suggestion of Montgomery as a meeting place, but advanced the date to February 4. That would allow a month to put a provisional government in operation and to get started on a permanent constitution before Lincoln took office and could act against them. That done, the commissioners scattered, like disciples, to spread their faith. They were a first step, but still the message they carried was chiefly one of consultation. Like the host of commissioners from all the states now criss-crossing the South, their power extended only to talk, and the suggestion of more talk in February.[28] Nevertheless, now the call was out to the other states. South Carolina had chosen the time and place. Like their Revolutionary forebears in 1776, now they had to see who would come.

Before it adjourned on January 5, the South Carolina convention performed one last task. It elected from among its own membership the eight delegates to represent it in Montgomery if the other states agreed to convene. This time, to his delight, Rhett led the balloting, but he and dashing, long-haired young Lawrence M. Keitt were the only true fire-eaters so honored. Miles was not far behind, but the rest, Memminger, Chesnut, Robert W. Barnwell, William W. Boyce, and Thomas J. Withers had been slow to come to secession during the past decade.[29] Significantly, while Rhett considered himself the head of the delegation, the rest, including Keitt, regarded him with feelings that ran from suspicion to loathing, and looked on his cousin Barnwell for what little leadership they desired. Barnwell himself treated Rhett with care, and newly installed Governor Pickens seemed to regard the much younger Miles as being loosely in charge. Having just finished their work of dividing the Union, the South Carolinians would go to Montgomery almost as seriously divided among themselves.

By the time the South Carolina convention adjourned, Southerners looked to Washington for what was to happen next. Senators and congressmen from the states about to consider secession were already there, and South Carolina's action seemed to demand that they act in concert in anticipation of the proposed Montgomery meeting. It was not for them to make policy for their states, but their actions now could influence future events.

In particular, eyes focused on the senators, and on none more so than Jefferson Davis. The lean, fifty-two-year-old, ramrod straight Mississippian had been a war hero in Mexico in 1847, and then as senator, secretary of war, and senator once more, a firm, though not extreme champion of Southern rights. Many saw him as the inheritor of the mantle of John C. Calhoun, the patron saint of secession. Yet Davis's record appeared cautious to many, and to a few equivocal. In 1856, when the Republicans fielded their first presidential candidate, one Southerner urged Davis to use his authority as secretary of war to concentrate arms in the South in case a Democratic defeat led to secession and a new Southern nation. Shaking his head at the suggestion, as well as at the notion that he might be the president of such a new combination, Davis would have none of it.[30] Yet after he returned to the Senate in 1857, critics charged that as head of the military affairs committee he managed to dilute army bills in anticipation of secession.[31]

The picture only clouded more in the summer of 1860. Briefly spoken of as a possible Democratic presidential nominee, Davis made a brave but futile effort to reunite the splintered factions of his party in order to defeat Lincoln. That summer Washingtonians saw Davis's dark, plump wife, Varina, wearing a badge on her clothing that said "Jeff Davis no seceder."[32] And as late as December 17, while South Carolinians voted to secede, Davis spoke of the possibility of reconstructing the Union thus sundered.[33]

The action of South Carolina and the calls for conventions in their states virtually forced Davis and others to go on record. On January 5 they met: Davis and Albert G. Brown from Mississippi; John Hemphill and Thomas Waul of Texas; Louisiana's influential and eloquent John Slidell and Judah P. Benjamin; Alfred Iverson of Georgia; Floridians David Yulee and Stephen R. Mallory; Robert Johnson of Arkansas, and Clement C. Clay from Alabama.[34] Most of them regretted coming to secession. Ironically, the only ardent proponent of disunion in the group was Clay. Neither Georgia's Robert Toombs nor the more outspoken Louis T. Wigfall of Texas attended. Still those present quickly agreed with Davis that no other remedy for the South's dilemma remained.[35] Consequently they prepared a set of resolutions suggesting that their states should secede as soon as possible, and asked their legislatures if they should themselves resign immediately, or remain in Washington in the Senate in order to hamper any hostile legislation as long as possible. And having heard by telegraph of the action of the

South Carolina convention, they called as well for a meeting in Montgomery no later than February 15 to form a new confederacy.[36] Years later, bitter, jealous, and disappointed, Rhett would invent the story that they went even farther, conspiring to parcel among themselves the highest offices in the new nation to be.[37]

This done, they all went about what they knew would be their last days in Washington. Despite a growing illness that confined him to his bedchamber for days at a time, Davis conferred widely with other Southerners in Washington, met with Buchanan to sound his intentions, and sent information and impressions on what the government would do about the forts and garrison in Charleston to Pickens.[38] Receiving instructions from Governor Pettus to resign his seat, Davis made his last speech in the Senate on January 21, offering in a tearful farewell testimony to his own anguish over events seemingly beyond control.

Even political foes like Stephen Douglas paid tribute to his address, though the most ardent secessionists liked little enough to see him weep at leaving the Union.[39] His tears fell not so much over secession itself as from his conviction that it would lead to civil war.[40] But he had thrown his die now, too. It was time to pack, to leave Washington for good, and return to Mississippi. Before leaving he succinctly characterized the situation before them to the brother of his one-time father-in-law, President Zachary Taylor. "You are at one end of the rope, colonel, and we are at the other," he said. "Let us see which of us can pull the longest and the strongest."[14]

Well before Davis returned home, Mississippi moved. Throughout December telegrams flew from Jackson to Washington and Charleston.[42] Governor Pettus, like Gist before him, sent commissioners to other states in the vain hope of achieving some concert of action, but another representative, this one sent by Arkansas to Mississippi, laid Pettus's best course before him. The policy of "Bark and *not* bite" should be abandoned, he warned. Mississippi must act on its own and leave cooperation for later.[43] On January 7, just as the secession convention met in Jackson, Senator Brown wired from Washington that any remaining hope of staying in the Union was dead. The House of Representatives had voted in approval of the action of the Federal garrison in Charleston, which moved by dark of night from its exposed position in Fort Moultrie, to the seemingly impregnable Fort Sumter in the middle of the harbor. Southerners took it as a blow in the face. "Today is the darkest yet," wired Brown. "Secede at once."[44] Two days later an ordinance passed and William S. Barry, president of the convention, announced that Mississippi desired "a new union with the seceded States" on the basis of the old Constitution.[45]

Even before passage Pettus sent agents to purchase arms and equipment for his state militia. The day after secession he issued orders for raising companies for the emergency. The state forces sat in severe disarray, one of their brigadiers complaining to the governor that virtually every other Southern state enjoyed better organized militia than Mississippi.[46] Pettus knew how to solve that problem, however. There was a Mississippian then on his way home who knew as much about organizing and leading soldiers as any man in the South. Meanwhile, the convention, without bothering with nominations, cast ballots for its seven delegates to the proposed Montgomery meeting. Wiley P. Harris would lead them. Barry would go, along with Josiah A. P. "Jap" Campbell, Alexander M. Clayton, James T. Harrison, and William S. Wilson, lawyers and Democrats all. A lone Whig, Walker Brooke, received enough votes to join them, representing those in the convention who voted for secession in the face of the inevitable, but who still hoped for sectional reconciliation.[47]

Florida followed on January 10. So small as to be an afterthought on the national scene, she assumed much greater importance if the proposed scheme of one state, one vote took hold in Montgomery. Well did Governor Perry know that, and he promptly sent not only copies of her secession ordinance to his fellow governors, but also Florida's hearty assent to the proposed convention in February.[48] Recognizing this new importance, South Carolina quickly moved to ally Florida to her interests.[49] The convention in Tallahassee failed to agree on its three delegates after two ballots, leaving it to Perry to appoint the men. He chose James Patton Anderson, a Democrat and former congressman, James B. Owens, a minister and also a Democrat, and the planter Whig Jackson C. Morton. Even before they left for Montgomery, rumors floated about that they were resolved to follow South Carolina's lead.

Inevitably all eyes turned toward Georgia when her convention met on January 16. She stood at nearly the center of the cotton South, a keystone tying east and west, the Atlantic and the Mississippi, by her great railroad hub in Atlanta. She had manufactories, raw materials, and the biggest population, white and black, of any of the Deep South states. This alone meant that her representation at Montgomery, based on her recent congressional delegation, would be the largest there. But looming over all were her three giants on the public stage, Howell Cobb, Robert Toombs, and Alexander H. Stephens.

Stephens came more slowly to secession than most. Until the very end he maintained hope that North and South would cooperate to find a way to save the Union and Southern institutions at the same time. For unlike Cobb and Toombs, he doubted the possibility of peaceable disunion, and coupled that with a belief that nothing good was ever achieved by war.[50] "We are without doubt on the verge," he told a friend after Lincoln's election, "on the brink of an abyss into which I do not wish to look." More than irreconcilable sectional issues, he saw disappointed ambitions behind the crisis, looking chiefly at fire-eaters like Rhett and William L. Yancey of Alabama.[51] If only South Carolina would wait to see what Lincoln did when he took office, Stephens believed that the rest of the South would delay as well. But he knew the Palmetto State would not wait, not with Rhett and others fanning rather than dampening flames. "The odds are against us for peace & Union," he told a friend at the end of November. "I am not confident, or even sanguine in my hopes."[52]

It did not help that perhaps Stephens' closest friend had become one of those ultra men whom he believed genuinely did not want to see a sectional settlement.[53] He and Robert Toombs enjoyed a devoted comradeship that dated back for years, an odd pairing considering the bluff, hearty, intemperate Toombs, and the frail, reclusive, introspective Stephens. Toombs was master of the *bon mot*, center of attention wherever men met, a man impatient of lengthy deliberation. "Send for Cromwell!" he shouted whenever a legislative session went too long for his span of attention. He, like Stephens, stood by the Union far longer than many. Even into the spring of 1860 he resisted the attractions of secession. He joined Davis in trying to patch the split in the Democratic Party that summer, and still applied to men like Rhett his definition of a fanatic as "one of strong feelings and weak points."[54]

But finally Toombs went over to the other side, and typically did it without subtlety. Lincoln's election clinched his conversion. Just two weeks before he had invited "Dear Stephens" to spend a week or two with him on his plantation.[55] Barely two weeks afterwards they were all but estranged, and secessionists and reconstructionists who knew both of them rejoiced alike that each seemed at last free of the influence of the other.[56]

Despite Stephens's warning that "we shall become demons, and at no distant day commence cutting one another's throats," Georgia elected convention delegates on January 2, and convened two weeks later.[57] Both Stephens and Toombs attended, and each spoke his stand. "This step, secession, once taken, can never be recalled," the diminutive "Little Aleck" warned. "We and our posterity shall see our lovely South desolated by the demon of war."[58] But talk of war held no terrors for Toombs. "I ask you to give me the sword," he shouted to the hall, "for if you do not give it to me, as God lives, I will take it myself."[59] Toombs spoke for the majority, though the vote on the afternoon of January 18 proved nothing like the virtual landslides in South Carolina, Mississippi, and Florida. Secession won by 166 to 130, a solid victory that still revealed the deeply troubled minds of many Georgians like Stephens.[60] But even some of the ardent secessionists felt less than sanguine. "I have no belief in peaceable secession," said Francis Bartow. "There will be some sharp work, before this business is over."[61] And the next night, when Stephens reminded an audience of Toombs's belligerent declaration of taking the sword, Toombs himself shouted out "I will," and the crowd went mad with enthusiastic cheers.[62] "I then saw the shadows 'coming before,'" he moaned.[63] Given to melancholy already, Little Aleck slipped quickly into a depression that gripped him for weeks thereafter.

Immediately upon the vote being taken, Eugenius A. Nisbet, who had himself come to the convention opposing secession, proposed that all present should sign the ordinance. Disunion was no longer the question for them, he argued. Now it was merely a matter of being for or against Georgia. It proved a powerful argument, one that was heard and heeded in every secession convention, and a neat stratagem to diffuse the Union men or "cooperationists" and their followers. Even Stephens signed.[64] That done, they showed their solidarity with the other states by forwarding copies of the ordinance, and also affirming attendance at the Montgomery meeting.[65]

Not yet yielding secret hopes for reunion, Stephens moved on January 28 that Georgia's delegates to Montgomery be instructed to move for a permanent Southern government modeled on the Constitution. It passed, as it did in the other states, showing at the outset that these men were no revolutionaries, tearing down the old to erect the new. What they wanted was what they believed they had all along, or what the Founding Fathers intended for them, before sectionalism and the Republicans perverted the old Union. And he still hoped quietly for reunification, under a constitution that included guarantees to protect the South and slavery. But he was a Georgian, too, and with

enough state rights concern that he also suggested that no new constitution formed in Montgomery should be binding upon the state until
this convention gave its approval. He would not see them flee the
thorns of the old compact, just to hurl themselves on more in a new
one.[66]

Nor did the convention's choice of delegates to Montgomery leave
him sanguine. Secessionists predominated, led by Howell Cobb, his
brother Thomas, Toombs, the firebrand Bartow, Congressman Martin
J. Crawford, and the recent convert Nisbet. Relations with the two
Cobbs, especially Tom, were polite, but hardly cordial. He had no use
for Bartow at all. But Crawford was a good friend, and Nisbet a man of
sense. And at least Toombs and he were speaking again. With secession
now a fact, the reason for their split disappeared, and Toombs made
generous and warm overtures to which Stephens inevitably responded.
Unfortunately, he got on better with Toombs now than with one of the
three other cooperationists besides himself who were chosen. Stephens
stopped speaking to Benjamin H. Hill in 1856, when the two came
close to a duel. But he enjoyed good relations with Augustus R.
Wright, and applauded silently the defiance of Augustus H. Kenan,
who signed the secession ordinance along with the rest of those who
opposed it, and then contemptuously threw away the pen.[67]

But Little Aleck was not happy with the delegation as a whole, and
probably he was not alone.[68] Now Georgia, the most powerful state in
the potential new confederation, presented like South Carolina a delegation deeply divided both by personality and policy, thereby hazarding
its influence. He spent several days considering whether or not to
decline his election. Friends implored him to accept, including even
some of the secessionists like Toombs and Crawford, and in the end he
did so only reluctantly, and after the convention adopted his January 28
resolution. "Nothing but an earnest desire to avert evils if possible and
to render the country in this emergency all the aid I could induced me
to accept the trust," he told a friend a week later.[69] Perhaps there was
something more—just the faintest glimmer of ambition . . . or hope.

Louisiana would be next, her issue never doubted. The climate
turned freezing in early January as the elections approached. Alexander
De Clouet, a fifty-eight-year-old planter from Lafayette Parish, teased
that "you have to be a candidate (or a wild goose) to be outside in such
weather," but campaign he did, confidant that a heavy majority of
secessionists would go to the state convention. He proved correct, and
it took the convention only three days to pass an ordinance on January

26, by a vote of 113 to 17. The excitement was intense. "One is ready for anything," De Clouet told his son.[70] The Pelican flag went up in New Orleans, cannon boomed, bands played, and the convention turned to selecting delegates to Montgomery, a post of honor.[71] Only one of them, Charles M. Conrad, was a firm Democrat, the rest being Whigs, yet all except Conrad were secessionists going into the convention. Conrad himself was the most distinguished, a veteran of the Senate, and one-time secretary of war to President Millard Fillmore. John Perkins had also been to Congress, while De Clouet, Duncan Kenner, Henry Marshall, and Edward Sparrow all served terms in the state legislature. Moreover, all but Conrad ran plantations, and between them they owned a startling 1,749 slaves. That alone explains why so many former Whigs, moderates everywhere else on the secession issue, became such ardent Southern rights advocates.[72] Reposing high trust in the six delegates, the convention gave them no immediate instructions, relying on their patriotism, good judgment, and no doubt their own heavy investment in Louisiana's welfare.[73]

Now all of the seceded states had endorsed the South Carolina plan for a meeting, and the suggestion of her commissioners for February 4. The wisdom of it became quickly apparent with some forty-eight commissioners roaming from capital to capital among the several slave states, both those in and out of the Union.[74] Confusion inevitably followed. Commissioners appeared at state houses not knowing if secession conventions were planned, or even if the current legislature was in session. States like Kentucky, to whom commissioners proposed secession, responded with their own suggestions that the Montgomery convention merely agree upon constitutional guarantees within the existing Union, while Virginia went no farther than to say that if all attempts at reconciliation failed, then perhaps she ought to unite with the seceded states.[75]

The lesson of Aesop's fable of the sticks became more and more urgent. Easily snapped one by one, they became unbreakable when bound together. William Trescott of South Carolina saw it plainly enough. "A revolution works its way through the blindness of those who attempt to direct it," he told Howell Cobb. "The condition of weakness and confusion which will result from four or five states floating about is indescribable." They must set up a government, elect a president of their own, and thus be ready to meet Lincoln head on.[76] Pickens of South Carolina agreed. The states must take direct action when they met in Montgomery, and select officials who were honest and firm in character. Otherwise he thought just who filled those offices rather unimportant for the moment. The real urgency was to choose a military commander to see to their defense.[77] Even crusty Governor Joe Brown of Georgia saw the necessity. "Conciliation and harmony among ourselves are of the most vital importance," he told John G. Shorter of Alabama. They must unite and cooperate to form "a more perfect union."[78] All this required much more than consultation, or even agreement on some new constitution to send back to the legislatures for ratification. It required decisive action. "Weld them together while they are hot," Trescott told Cobb.[79] Montgomery must be their forge.

If South Carolina had a sister state in secession, it was Alabama, and Rhett heard his most outspoken brother in extremism in the voice of the titan William Lowndes Yancey. A Georgian by birth, he grew up in South Carolina. He stood out as a prominent Unionist in his youth, but after moving to Alabama in the late 1830s, and especially after the Mexican War, he rapidly shifted his position toward sectionalism. Finally he even broke with the Democratic Party in his overriding commitment to secession from the Union. In 1860 he led Alabama's delegation to the Democratic convention, and precipitated the split that doomed the party in the fall. Ostensibly he practiced the law, though men close to him saw that he did not care for it much, and did it only for the money, of which some reputed him overfond. Still they agreed that as a criminal lawyer he was most elegant. But his real profession was secession, and to that he devoted his best talents. Tall, powerfully built, he was a born mover of men. "He has no smoothness or elegance in his mien," observed one Alabamian. "He has only massive strength and fiery earnestness."[80]

That earnestness and intemperance infected a host of others in central and southern Alabama, and especially in Yancey's town, Montgomery. Months before even the 1860 nominations, the legislature—prodded by Yancey—resolved that a Republican victory ought to impel the governor to call an immediate special convention.[81] Other less prominent but still influential men, like Thomas H. Watts of Montgomery, added their voices to the call for secession,[82] and the editor of the Montgomery *Mail* declared that if Alabama failed to secede he would leave in disgust and move to California.[83]

The election day passed in strange quiet in Montgomery, but almost immediately afterward the turmoil began.[84] Rumors of planned slave insurrections surfaced again, reminding Montgomery of the days in

1856 when similar stories—never sustantiated—circulated and led to the True Blues, a local militia company, patrolling the streets at night.[85] Now billiard parlors and barrooms echoed to darkly told tales of plans to murder white men when they went to the polls on election day, and of worse outrages in store for the women. Fearful of the growing hysteria among whites, a few slaves started running away, knowing that sooner or later the talk must turn to action.[86] One Montgomery merchant actually used this to argue against secession, for if Alabama left the Union he predicted she would soon battle the North in her front, and a slave uprising in her rear. Should that happen, he warned, "slavery is doomed." More than that, some feared that in seceding, the Southern states would only finish by fighting among themselves.[87]

But secession was in the wind, fanned by the powerful influence of Yancey, and heartily backed by the governor. Andrew B. Moore was not entirely a happy man. With less than a year of his term left to serve, he lived in the governor's mansion with his son and two daughters. His wife stayed in the new state mental asylum in Tuscaloosa that he, himself, had seen through construction. Lonely, and to some a "scary" man, he made up in determination for what many felt he lacked in personality.[88] He stood solidly for secession. He sent representatives to all of the other Southern states in December, long before his own special convention met on January 7, and some of them at least went armed with the suggestion that in any new confederacy Alabama would like to see Yancey made president.[89] In December, too, he sent agents to the North to start buying weapons.[90]

The deep divisions in Alabama showed in the contest for delegates to the special convention. Just one county in the southern half of the state favored cooperation, while only Calhoun County in the north voted for the secessionists.[91] The feeling spread through much of the state that in the crisis the extremists were not to be trusted, and that moderates—what one rather ironically called *"conservative secessionists"*—should be elected.[92] In the end, when the convention met on January 7, the truly rabid disunionists held only a slim majority of six or seven over the moderates and outright cooperationists. Yancey was the key, and he quickly assumed dominance over the gathering.[93]

Under cloudy skies turning toward rain, the delegates walked and rode up Market Street to the state house. The weather was in a turmoil. Below freezing the day before, the noon thermometer now looked almost summery at sixty degrees, and remained there until after nightfall.[94] It gave the Union men little lift, however, as they saw the odds, and Yancey, arrayed before them. It hardly helped that an armed guard of militia stood around the capitol, thanks to a recent attempt to burn the building that all assumed to be abolitionist inspired. Only those armed with a countersign gained entrance.[95] Once inside, almost to a man the north Alabama delegates spoke against secession, joined by Montgomery's Henry Hilliard, a one-time congressman and for twenty years Yancey's antagonist. They should wait for the North to perform some overt act first, he argued.[96] Yancey and his followers scarcely listened. Looking upon them, Unionist Robert Jemison concluded that "a sett of restless, rash, reckless politicians have laid ruthless hands on the pillars of the finest, noblest temple of political liberty ever erected."[97] That night, seeing the direction of things, one Unionist delegate, a clergyman and a slaveholder, went back to his hotel room at Montgomery Hall and wept.[98]

Montgomery prided itself on its well-lit streets. In just the past year the city council spent $5,271.38 on gas lamps and posts.[99] But when it stayed warm all that first night, and with a heavy rain as well, dense fog greeted the city on the morning of January 8 and stayed with it most of the day.[100] Remaining lit, the gas lamps barely coped, instead casting a sickly glare that matched the mood of the cooperationists as they stumbled through a superabundance of mud and slush on their way up Market Street.[101] This day would be no better for them. John C. Calhoun's son Andrew arrived as a commissioner from South Carolina, and now he addressed the convention in advocacy of united action, bringing South Carolina's invitation that all the states should meet in a provisional body to make a constitution and form a future government. As bait, he also dangled before them the suggestion discussed by his fellow commissioners of making Montgomery the meeting place. It was centrally located, had fair rail and steamboat communications, offered seemingly ample accommodations, and was a good secession town. Moreover, it was the lair of Yancey.[102]

By the time they adjourned for the day the fog cleared and the evening sky turned fair. It was still warm.[103] On the walk back to their lodgings the delegates and the rest of Montgomery gazed into the western sky to see a peculiar white cloud shaped rather like a goose quill, its milky hue standing out against the deep blue as it stretched a good twenty degrees across the horizon. These were hours when men craved omens. Some thought it a sign of peace, like a weary dove with an olive branch. Secession would bring no war. But to others it meant calamity, a symbol of the pens with which they would soon sign their doom, condemning themselves, like the cloud, to disappear forever in the winds and darkness.[104] That night, again, the clergyman cried.

The remaining debates took on an increasingly bitter tone. Yancey accused the cooperationists of treason against Alabama. His opponents invited him and his followers to bring their arguments into the Unionist hills of north Alabama where the difference of opinion could be settled by guns instead of words. Watts, almost as ultra as Yancey himself, actually stepped in to chastise the fire-eater, who never could control the groundswell of his own arguments. But throughout the remainder of the deliberations, the only outcome in doubt was the size of the majority for secession. When the vote came at half past two in the afternoon on January 11, it passed 61 to 39, the smallest margin of secession victory in any of the states so far. A number of those who voted for it did so only in the face of the inevitable, and to give the appearance of unity. Moreover, when delegates suggested that it be submitted to a popular referendum, the secessionists attacked and killed the resolution, fearing the possible result. In a last act of defiance, twenty-four of the delegates refused to sign the document.[105]

At once after the vote, men rushed from the chamber to spread the word. Montgomery was ready, and so was Yancey. He had already engaged ladies of the town to make a huge sixteen-by-twenty-foot blue flag depicting the goddess of Liberty holding aloft a sword in one hand, and a "lone star" flag for Alabama in the other. "Independent Now and Forever" it proclaimed. The reverse displayed a cotton plant, the state seal, and a rattlesnake.[106] Members now brought it forth, to a speech by Yancey, and then erected it in the chamber. Soon it flew from the capitol dome. Across town businesses closed and the church bells rang, first the Catholics', then the Baptists', and finally all of them. Governor Moore wept in front of the convention. So did delegate Jeremiah Clemens, though out of anguish. Others embraced, whether from joy or heartbreak, and outside Miss C. T. Raoul touched off the first shot of a one-hundred-gun cannon salute. Watts ran home to fly a blue lone star flag of his own, while out on the Alabama River steamboat whistles and calliopes screeched, the Montgomery & West Point engines rang bells and blew whistles of their own, and scores of boys lit firecrackers in the streets. "Take it altogether it was one of the most stirring— enthusiastic & thrilling scenes I ever witnessed," one visitor wrote that evening.[107]

The cacophony went on without cease through the afternoon, and the barrooms filled with the celebratory and the sad. The Reverend

Basil Manly of the First Baptist Church, himself an unsuccessful candidate for the convention, sat listening to it all. "Of course I rejoice," he told his wife, "but I feel more serious than joyful."[108]

It was well into the evening before the noise subsided. Revelers stumbling home tramped the day's streamers and confetti into the muddy streets, and hardly needed the gaslights to find their way. The capitol, the Montgomery Theatre, the telegraph office, Montgomery Hall, the Madison House, the Campbell House, the Exchange Hotel and other hostelries, as well as private homes and the four newspaper offices, all put out illuminations. Fireworks sprinkled the streets and the night sky while the ever-present speakers droned on and on from the steps of Montgomery Hall.[109]

Back in their rooms, the convention delegates—those still sober— put their thoughts in letters to their wives. Listening to the occasional cheers and shots still disturbing the streets, secessionist H. L. Clay crowed that the people *are in advance of their leaders* & prepared for anything."[110] William R. Smith, who opposed the ordinance, looked out his window at the frantic rejoicing and sensed the unthinking mind of a mob. "I am trembling with the scenes around me," he told his wife.[111] Henry Semple ignored the general illumination and kept his windows dark in protest, predicting that they would all be mourning within a year.[112]

Over in Montgomery Hall, while the politicians made speech after speech outside, photographer William Culver of Vermont, only recently arrived, shared a room with the weeping reverend. Tonight he cried again, then meditated, and confessed that he felt less fear at losing his slaves than he did of a bloody war. Downstairs in the sitting room Culver found others anxious to talk. A former Episcopal bishop of Alabama confessed that fears of secession and disunion dogged him for years as he traveled his state. But another delegate dismissed the idea of secession resulting in war. The North was too cowardly, and far too penurious, to go to the risk and expense of war. And the Yankees were too divided themselves. "Now that secession is a fact," he told Culver, "all we have got to do is to go on and form a government of our own."[113] Men like Clemens felt less certain by far. "God knows where all this is to end," he cried that night. He saw all too well the storms gathering, but not how Alabama was to weather them. "If we are not already involved in war, we soon will be."[114] And that other delegate, so proud of the people leading rather than being led, had to agree. H. L. Clay actually feared civil war within Alabama between its factions, but that was only a small part of his vision. In pride and awe he wrote to Clement C. Clay that "a tempest has been raised that is already beyond control."[115]

During the ensuing days the convention continued in session, even on the Sabbath, in the rush to complete its business. "God *made* a nation and *rested* on Sunday," lamented Smith. His colleagues "destroyed a nation and work on Sunday."[116] They incorporated an invitation to meet in Montgomery on February 4 into the secession ordinance, and sent copies to all of the slave states, including those not yet seceded. Governor Moore appointed new commissioners to take the copies to his fellow governors, to consult with them on the best means for mutual protection, and to press for the speedy formation of a provisional government, with a permanent one to follow.[117] Moore called Leroy Pope Walker to come from Huntsville and be a commissioner to Tennessee. A friend of Yancey's, and leader of the Alabama delegation at the abortive Democratic convention the year before, Walker had been expecting secession and a new Southern nation at least since 1857. He was glad to serve, and already wondered if there might be a place for him in the future government.[118] The governor also looked to continuing postal routes and contracts in the state once he took them over from United States agents, and he ordered $200,000 in coin to the credit of an agent authorized to buy more arms and munitions, while commencing the sale of state bonds to raise more capital.[119]

There was so much to do, and after January 13 they did it with the huge new flag flying atop the state house. Down in the Exchange Hotel at the foot of Market, convention delegate L. R. Davis looked out his room window and saw "the nasty little thing floating in the breeze." He mourned the passing of Old Glory like the death of an old friend. "I would scream one loud shout of joy could I now see it waving in the breeze although I know the scream would be my last."[120]

It only remained to choose delegates to the February 4 meeting. Jemison protested against the convention itself naming the men. They were already too polarized. Their choices must inevitably reflect the divisions and distractions of party and faction, yet this would be their very first step toward the formation of a new government that they hoped would be without party.[121] In a final desperate move to prevent this, and hoping conservative voices might still be heard in the new convention, the cooperationist element proposed that the delegates should be elected in a popular canvass across the state. This, at least, would ensure that some who shared their views would be chosen from the northern counties. But the secessionists tabled the motion, and there it died.[122] A dejected Smith told his wife that "the majority of the convention will elect their own favorites."[123]

He proved a poor prophet. Incredibly, once again, as in South Carolina, men who had just taken a radical step retreated from placing themselves any longer in the hands of radicals. Neither Yancey nor Watts received enough votes to join the new delegation, nor, but for two, did any other men then present. Instead they chose William P. Chilton, Montgomery lawyer and one time state chief justice; Thomas Fearn, a Huntsville doctor; young Curry from Talladega; the Eutaw lawyer Stephen F. Hale; another lawyer, David Lewis of Moulton; Colin J. McRae, an influential cotton factor from Mobile; John Shorter, the Mobile lawyer; prominent cooperationist Robert H. Smith; and Leroy Walker's brother Richard, then an associate justice on the state supreme court. Of them all, only Curry—the youngest—had been a life-long Democrat. The rest were, or had been, Whigs. All but Fearn and McRae were lawyers, and only Curry, Shorter, and, recently, McRae, strongly advocated secession. From a convention dominated by one of the most extreme men in the South, Alabama would send the most conservative delegation of all to Montgomery on February 4. Johnson J. Hooper, editor of the Montgomery *Weekly Mail*, and himself the most ardent of secessionists, could not help but express his dismay. The best he could say for those chosen was that they appeared to be men of ability and personal worth.[124]

Yancey's distress showed. Men found him mortified at the rebuff. He had expected that he would be able not only to lead the new delegation, but to dominate the convention to follow, and enough people around were suggesting his name as a probable Southern president that the thought could not have been far from his mind. But he was too like his counterpart Rhett, too unpopular even with men who shared his views. "He has great talent in some things," wrote one friend to McRae just after his election, "but his temper is unpredictable & he makes few personal friends."[125] Indeed, Yancey often seemed not to recognize people he had known for some time, habitually forgot names, and projected austerity rather than affability. Even his friend Watts admitted that "*he* seemed to know nobody,"[126] and Yancey's own wife would bitterly confess that "no man knew my husband."[127] Yet he put the best face on it all. Besides, not being a member of the provisional meeting might even work to his advantage. Being outside its debates, and probably arguments, he might loom all the more presidential when the time came.

As for those elected as delegates, friends soon swamped them with advice, especially McRae, who reportedly considered declining his appointment. He must accept, one told him. "I am more and more disgusted with mere *talking men* the more I see of them. What we want is *good sense & prompt action*." Moreover, McRae supposedly possessed the widest knowledge of history and foreign and domestic commerce of any man elected. The new confederacy would need that. McRae knew the international cotton trade. European powers wanted Southern cotton "*& they will have* it."[128] "You possess the Talisman to obtain within ninety days the recognition of your government," said another. "An embargo on the export of cotton, brings the world at your feet."[129]

So now they were six, the heart of the slaveholding South had withdrawn from the Union. They expected Texas to join them soon, and hoped for the so-called Border States as well—Arkansas, Missouri, Tennessee, Kentucky, North Carolina, Virginia, Maryland, perhaps even Delaware. But their leaders and people were conservative, sifted through with Union sentiment, hesitant. They would take time, though in the end they must come. Meanwhile, these six were enough for a bold beginning. Indeed, even before the delegates could convene in Montgomery, the first of a torrent of office and place seekers began littering their mails with applications for favor and influence. Stephens and Howell Cobb received the first trickle of the coming flood from those wanting commissions in new armed services, or positions with the provisional convention. Others like Bartow began making recommendations of their own. A new government was like a new administration, and surely there would be spoils.[130]

The leaders of the new movement faced much greater matters than filling as yet nonexistent offices. As each state seceded—and sometimes before—her sons seized Federal arsenals, customs houses, and even fortifications, all of them either unguarded or else peaceably released by vastly outnumbered occupants. But two glaring exceptions pressed against the pulse of Southern rights men. At Pensacola, Florida, a small garrison declined to leave Fort Pickens, so placed that it would take a small army to drive them out. More galling still was Fort Sumter at Charleston. From the moment of secession, South Carolinians flocked to growing militia companies. Steadily they built batteries ringing the fort on the islands and mainland surrounding the harbor. But they were enthusiastic rustics for the most part, untrained and wanting for knowledgeable leadership.

Moreover, Governor Pickens did not feel at liberty to do more than attempt to negotiate with Washington to get the garrison out of the fort. To blast them into submission would be to take military action that he and other governors agreed ought to await their new government's assumption of military direction. If he opened fire but failed in the attempt, humiliation would cloud the entire South. Even when an inventive, if unprincipled, South Carolinian proposed that they fire exploding shells filled with strychnine into the air over Sumter during a rain, Pickens demurred. The falling water, contaminated, would run down the fort's roofs and into the cisterns from which the garrison took its drinking water, "poisoning the whole concern," said this first proponent of chemical warfare, but that would surely inaugurate war.[131] No, for the moment he must continue peaceful efforts.

But he needed to be prepared, and like everyone else in the South he looked to the region's greatest living military hero, Jefferson Davis. Even before Davis left the Senate he repeatedly counseled Pickens by telegraph. "My quiet hours are mostly spent in thoughts of Charleston harbor," he told Pickens, but over and over he advised against overt action. The tiny garrison inside Sumter offered no threat, and for the moment pressed only on a point of pride. Soon they would have a new Southern confederacy, and *then* would be the time to make forceful demands for evacuation, or more. As for Fort Pickens in Pensacola, Davis told Florida Senator Stephen R. Mallory virtually the same thing. Neither fort, at this juncture, merited a drop of blood.[132]

Once Davis resigned, and despite his deplorable health, Pickens and others begged him to come to Charleston on his trip home, though it was hundreds of miles out of the way.[133] For a time Davis considered going, but Mississippi called urgently. He left Washington on the morning of January 22, and the very next day, as he traveled west on his train, the state convention passed a military bill that named him major general to command the "Army of Mississippi."[134] When finally he arrived in Jackson on January 28, dressed in a homespun suit, though sad, sick, and weary, he put up in a boardinghouse for a few days and began the work of organizing an army for the state.[135]

His heart was not in it, and to everyone with whom he spoke, and especially in his discussions with Wiley Harris and the other delegates to Montgomery, he reiterated his tragic conviction that war with the North was inevitable. Moreover, he made it clear to Harris that when war did come, he preferred not to be the head of the Southern army. His old friend Colonel Albert Sidney Johnston, now commanding

Federal troops out on the Pacific coast, was the man for that, and he expected Johnston to join with them.[136] And when another delegate, Alexander M. Clayton, sent him a message stating that he believed Davis would or could be the choice of the coming convention for president, and asked if he would accept, the Mississippian showed even less enthusiasm, and some equivocation.[137]

He foresaw several scenarios. If the Border States joined with the Deep South, he believed the size and solidarity of the new nation would be a guarantee against Northern aggression and war. Then government service would be the only field for men to contribute to the public good. But if the cotton states already seceded had to proceed on their own, war was inevitable, and patriots would be needed in the armies more than in the halls of legislation. Of course, if the provisional convention drafted a constitution that made the president also commander in chief, as in the old Constitution, then a president could act either a civil or military role, depending on circumstances. That said, and unable to foretell the future precisely, he could not say where best he might serve. As a president, he told Clayton, "I have no confidence in my capacity." Unsaid, but implied, was his reluctance to be placed in such an office where he might be kept from military command in case of war. As a general he would feel more sure of himself. To Clayton, as an old friend, he confided that he would prefer neither position. He wanted to return to his plantation, tend his roses and his cotton fields, and pray that somehow the forthcoming tragedy might be halted. But nowhere in his reply did Jefferson Davis say "no."[138] Two days later, on February 1, Davis and Varina returned to their home at "Brierfield," below Vicksburg, to rest, and wait.

In those last days before February 4 speculation and activity redoubled. The Alabama senate unanimously adopted a resolution offering its chamber to the new convention, to what it called the "Southern Congress."[139] Yet ominous signs of discord haunted the fringes of unity, and in the northern part of the state Unionists burned an effigy of Yancey in defiance. Men worried over the situation in Pensacola, and Keitt told Governor Pickens that Sumter was unlikely to give up peacefully. "It will ultimately have to be taken."[140] Ominously, throughout January Northern states passed measures and resolutions for protecting the Union and sent copies to the seceded states, raising fears that the Yankees would fight. One of Miles's South Carolina friends forthrightly declared that they should simply start a war now. It would give them the advantage over the still-dithering North, and also make it impossible for Southern cooperationists in Montgomery to back away.[141]

Meantime speculation mounted on who should lead the new government, in peace or war. In Washington rumor said it would be Robert M. T. Hunter, senator from Virginia, which had not even seceded as yet, and might not. In Georgia some suggested Governor Pickens, but in Charleston itself others spoke of Davis, as did the New York press. Others mentioned Toombs or Rhett or Yancey, while legions expected that it would be Howell Cobb. Even Little Aleck Stephens, the unionist to the end, found himself touted as one who could unite the extremists and the conservatives within the new nation.[142]

All the while the bands played on, the cannon boomed their salutes, the crowds kept cheering. Men with confidence in the cause and their future counted on the gathering delegates "to do just as they think best," and that would be security enough. As the day of the meeting approached they scarcely contained their enthusiasm to hear from Montgomery.[143] Yet others felt a different emotion. "Now our sun is to go down at noon," lamented Henry Hilliard; "the sky that overreaches us is lurid, with ominous fires."[144] In South Carolina, where it all began, the wife of a delegate coming to Montgomery confided in anger to her diary that "we are divorced, North from South, because we hated each other so."[145]

CHAPTER TWO

A NICE, TIDY LITTLE SOUTHERN TOWN

———— •→ ★ ←• ————

ONTGOMERY'S WAS THE PECULIAR HISTORY of a score of small inland cities, part accident, part luck, part irony, and like them it never expected to be drawn into the very center of national and world events. It sat in the center of the state on a height called "Chunnanugga Chatty" by the local Creek Indians, and later changed to High Red Bluff or Hostile Bluff or Thirteen Mile Bluff depending on which white man was talking. The edge overlooked a gorgeous deep bend in the Alabama River some hundred miles and more upstream from Mobile. When the whites came they found only old Indian mounds. Arthur Moore settled there first in 1814, joined three years later by Andrew Dexter, an ambitious man who foresaw the spot as a future capital when statehood came. He laid out a town he called New Philadelphia, and on a rise west of the bend called Goat Hill he set aside grounds for a state house. But when Congress admitted Alabama as the twenty-second state in 1819, the capital went to Tuscaloosa, and infant New Philadelphia came to be called derisively "Yankee Town" for Dexter's pretensions.

Perhaps in admission of defeat, Dexter put up no fight later that year when a move proceeded to merge New Philadelphia with several other small villages nearby like Alabama Town and East Alabama into a single frontier municipality. A hero of the Revolution, General Richard Montgomery fell in battle at Quebec in 1775 fighting the British. Irish by birth, and a resident of New York, Montgomery had not a single discernible connection with the tiny Alabama settlements or their inhabitants, but all the same they named their town for him, and finally saw it incorporated as Montgomery on December 23, 1837.[1]

Growth came slowly for the town until cotton and the steamboat converged at the foot of High Red Bluff. The first vessel chugged up the Alabama in 1821, and within a few years they ran daily to and from

31

Mobile and Selma to collect and ship the exploding bounty of fluffy white gold. First in sacks, and eventually in huge five-hundred-pound bales, the cotton came into the town by wagon from surrounding counties, to be rolled down the steep bluff and onto the waiting steamboats by slave laborers. Every bale brought new wealth to central Alabama, and to Montgomery. Not surprisingly, in its wake came gambling, fighting, and lawlessness, giving the town a reputation for being rough-edged even in the 1820s. But its economic advance continued unabated, and that, plus its central location, finally induced the legislature to realize Dexter's dream by relocating the capital in 1846. There, on Goat Hill, they built the new state house, only to see it burn three years later. Undeterred, they erected another by 1851—large, white, imposing if somewhat ill-proportioned, and dominated by a huge dome. Business took a giant boost, new stores and hotels opened, and the prominent of the state quickly flocked to the city on the bluff, men like Yancey and Hilliard and Watts. The next year the city council contracted with the Cincinnati firm of John Jeffrey & Co. to provide lamps, posts, and lines for illuminating the main streets with gas. Montgomery was on its way to becoming a proper capital.[2]

As 1860 dawned it gave the visitor a view of "a nice, tidy little Southern town."[3] There were 4,341 white citizens, just slightly outnumbered by the 4,502 slaves living with them. Yet those whites also largely owned or controlled real estate in the surrounding Montgomery County, chiefly cotton fields, valued at more than $51 million, making it per capita one of the wealthiest cities in the South. Moreover, while the slave population of the city roughly equaled the white, in the county at large slaves outnumbered the whites by two to one.[4] At least 130,000 bales a year passed through Montgomery now, believed to be the highest trade in ratio of population of any city.[5] Steamboats paid $5 per day to tie up at Francis M. Gilmer's Planters' Wharf below the bluff to disgorge passengers and take on cotton, and inevitably the railroad had to come.[6] The Montgomery & West Point was completed in 1851, and in 1860 Gilmer and other partners began building the South & North Alabama into the interior not served by river traffic. The Alabama & Florida connection to Mobile needed only a few months' work to completion, while another line to Eufaula lay partially complete.[7] The city may not have been a boom town, but it rested on a solid base of cotton, transportation, wealth, and politics.

Still, visitors found it an oddly rural kind of town. One of Yancey's friends thought it "not at all a political centre, . . . nor was it a Pharos, whose political light was flashed out over the South."[8] Mayor Andrew Noble and twelve aldermen ran the city council, and they appointed and elected the public officers necessary to run the city—captain of police, marshal and deputies, a clerk to oversee the city market, a "wharfinger" who looked after the river wharves and collected landing fees, and more. Noble met with his council every Monday to determine granting hack licenses and market stalls, assess fines for violations of the city code, and deal with civic improvements like gas lighting or caring for the streets. Just now sewers occupied their attention a good deal. Montgomery sat on hills, and when hard rains came as they did that winter, they roared down the sandy streets leaving them deeply rutted, and caved in the banks alongside the gutters. Clayton Street was especially susceptible. A main avenue leading into the city, it deserved beautification. They were working on it.[9] Meanwhile, the council also looked after the city's two artesian wells, long since expanded into basins in the middle of Commerce Street, and surrounded by ornamental iron fences. Here the city shone, for few visitors came to Montgomery without experiencing what a New Orleans journalist called "the purest and best water I have ever drank."

But everyone complained about the streets. The layout of the town bewildered many of a newcomer. Commerce Street started down at the city wharf, climbed up the steep bank to the top of the bluff, crossed the Montgomery & West Point tracks, and ran in a wide boulevard back some three blocks, past Water, Tallapoosa, and Bibb streets, to open onto a wide triangular space called Court Square despite its shape. In its center sat the main artesian basin. Calling a triangle a square provided a fair hint of what was to come in Montgomery's street plan, for hereafter it became a jumble. Commerce and Montgomery streets formed the right angle of the "square," but then Court Street made the diagonal on the east, and virtually all of the street plan from there eastward formed rectangular grids based on Court. The main thoroughfare here was Market, another wide avenue that ran east six blocks, past streets named for heroes of the young nation—Perry, Lawrence, McDonough, Hull, Decatur, Bainbridge—to terminate on Goat Hill and the capitol. Beyond the state house ran Union and a few other lesser streets to the outskirts.

Meanwhile, to either side of Market the streets honored more American immortals. Monroe, Madison, Jefferson, Columbus, and

Randolph ran off to the north, while on the other side lay Washington, Adams, and Alabama. Here came one problem at once. Montgomery had two Washington Streets, this one, and another parallel to Commerce and one block south, and they did not connect. Indeed, but for Market meeting Commerce at the square and Monroe meeting Coosa, one block north of Commerce, none of the streets in the two grids interlinked. Moreover, where Jefferson did extend west of Court Street, its name changed to Scott. And the situation on the opposite side of town was no better. The streets intersecting Commerce ran southwest past Washington, Molton, Catoma, Wilkinson, and State, to bump abruptly into yet another diagonal street, Goldthwaite, that ran parallel with Court on the other side. The same thing happened to the southeast where Molton, Catoma, and the rest came to an end in a series of triangular blocks formed by their junction with Clayton, which soon changed its name back to Alabama on this stretch and eventually extended across Court and then ran directly alongside the other Alabama Street.

Small wonder then that visitors complained, some acidly remarking that Montgomery must have been laid out before the invention of the surveyor's compass, while others warned that a stranger could lose his bearings and wind up in Georgia or Mississippi.[10]

People groused not just about the layout of the streets, either. Despite the city ordinance prohibiting throwing trash or filth into the roads, they generally looked a mess. Paving was a rarity, and most were just sandy soil that easily washed away in rain, or else stayed where it was and turned into mire. In late January, after winter rains, the street to the post office sat knee-deep in mud, and in a section unilluminated by street lamps. Two weeks before the great convention assembled, Hooper at the *Mail* worried that such conditions might "give to strangers a most unfavorable impression in regard to our city," and he was right.[11] One reporter from Georgia scarcely arrived before sending back a report that the city looked woefully undeveloped, and that "it needs some candid, impartial and fearless man to speak the truth and tell this people wherein they are derelict."[12]

Yet Montgomery offered much to admire. A visitor in 1855 gloried in the pretty cottages perched on its hills, the stately capitol, and the profusion of gardens. Seemingly every home sported plantings, flowers, shrubs, and wide shade trees, making Montgomery in springtime especially fragrant. Downtown along the principal streets most of the businesses and homes were brick, testimony to lessons learned from a number of fires over the decades. The elegant mansions of the wealthy like Watts, Judge Benajah Bibb, Gilmer, Charles Pollard, president of the Montgomery & West Point, and more especially impressed the eye. So, too, did their occupants. "This place is made up of the sharpest and shrewdest men in the world," said one visitor. "The accumulated point of a diamond is no sharper than their wits." They offered a cultivated and agreeable society, while their women showed more than the ordinary beauty. If there was a complaint, it lay in the way Montgomeryites displayed their considerable wealth. More than thirty of the leading men held estates valued at $100,000 or more. It showed in their houses, and on their wives, who wore a profusion of jewelry that some thought in bad taste, and silk and satin dresses that cost upwards of $100. Looking on, one stranger quickly concluded that "this is a decidedly fast place."[13]

Thus newcomers found much on which not to agree. To some Montgomery could never hope to be a major city, nothing more than a "great inland village," while others still found that "on the whole, the effect of Montgomery upon the newly arrived was rather pleasing."[14]

Once there, whether at the landing or the depot, a twenty-five cent ride in a hack took the visitor to one of several hotels, the most imposing being the great Exchange at the corner of Commerce and Montgomery, facing Court Square and the artesian basin. It accommodated at least three hundred guests on its three upper floors, the ground level being given over to shops and stores. Lodging cost $2.50 a day including meals, and amenities included a barroom, reading and smoking rooms, and a ladies' entrance on Montgomery Street for those who preferred not to enter by the main doors through the Oriental Billiard Parlour at 98 Commerce, beneath a great red lamp. The dining room offered some of the best fare in Montgomery—oysters, turkey, lobster salad, cakes, fruits and nuts, candies and confections of all kinds, and an extensive and international wine and champagne cellar.[15]

Less elegant, and not so well regarded, was Montgomery Hall at the corner of Market and Lawrence, its accommodations for 150 more subdued, but its rates the same. John Floyd kept a good bar, and was known to put on a fine spread for special dinners occasionally, but newcomers complained of the high prices when they saw the ill-kept and dirty rooms. Many of Floyd's and partner Hugh Watson's guests were semipermanent residents, clerks, storekeepers, omnibus conductors,

stagecoach drivers, country merchants, and livestock men, with a smattering of attorneys. For the more genteel, Montgomery Hall offered at
best a second choice when the Exchange register was full.[16]

A block away, at Market and Perry, stood the Madison House, with
beds for another 150. Smaller still were the American Hotel on
Tallapoosa and the Campbell House on Commerce, just down from
the Exchange, run by South Carolinian J. D. Campbell. For those planning longer stays, and wanting both economy and less bustle, about a
dozen boarding houses like the Dillehay House at Bibb and
Washington, Josephine Scott's on Perry, Stoudenmier's at Tallapoosa
and Court, and Mrs. Cleveland's on Montgomery offered room and
board at around $30 a month[17]

Handsome stores in solid brick buildings lined the main streets,
chiefly Commerce and Market. The Great Wardrobe on Court Square
offered the finest in ready made clothes, and as well proclaimed itself
"the Pioneer of Low Prices," to set it apart from the fourteen other
clothiers in town. Phister and White sold books beneath the Exchange,
as did Ben Davis, and not far away on Commerce was Giovanni's
Confectionery for the sweet toothed. Along with the four other candy
makers in town, Giovanni indirectly provided plenty of custom for
Montgomery's three dentists, and a steady demand for oil of clove and
other pain killers from the half-dozen druggists.

Joseph Pizzala's restaurant at Montgomery and Washington consistently garnered the highest praise, but three other downtown eateries
did a fair business, and for the residents who dined at home some thirty-four grocers provided fresh fruit and produce, while butchers added
their wares, and both grocers and fishmongers sold virtually the freshest in seafoods, especially oysters, brought daily from Mobile.

For entertainment, four billiard parlors presented heavy slate tables,
and sold cigars and newspapers as well. Ale houses and lager saloons
clustered around Court Square and the hotels, and along the streets
coming into town from the depot and wharf. The Hutchinson Brothers
Gym at Market and Perry gave the ambitious a place to sweat away the
beer and whiskey or Giovanni's candy, while elsewhere the more seden-
tary could sit for their portraits. J. Massalon painted in oils, but instan-
taneous images came from the cameras of the photographers. Davis
and Gerrish operated their studio on Court Square near the Exchange,
while A. B. Hutchings took portraits upstairs at 23 Market. M. J.
Hinton opened a new "Sky-Light Gallery" above Belshaw and Co., jew-
elers, across from the Exchange, and offered "ivorytypes" for $3.

The largest share of the sittings went to Montgomery's premier photographer, A. C. McIntyre, established there since 1849. Like the rest, he kept his studio on Market Street on a second floor where a skylight provided sufficient illumination for his exposures. He offered the new "Mahanotype" process for $5, and kept his gallery open from morning until the sun went down. Moreover, thanks to the painting skills of his assistant, young Culver from Vermont, he could offer lifelike tinting on portraits. Townspeople all knew his black servant Henry, who went to the artesian basin every morning for water. They would see him return, leading a procession of black water bearers, women with tubs on their heads, and children carrying pails. A more than clever fellow, Henry gave them praise and flattery, and the youngsters marbles, in return for carrying his water. At McIntyre's he also cajoled the other servants into doing most of his work for him. The photographer hired him from his real owner, and often gave him considerable responsibility by leaving him in charge of the studio when called away. As he could, the mulatto saved extra bits of cash until he could buy his freedom for $1,000—from his own white father.[18]

Of course Montgomery was a slave town. Four dealers kept sales rooms and living quarters for blacks in the city, most of them on Market between Lawrence and McDonough. Bernard and Co., Mason Harwell, and Thomas Powell all acted both as dealers and auctioneers, as did S. N. Brown at Perry and Monroe. The negroes, with little to do, generally lounged about inside the auction rooms, or sang to the tune of their rude instruments. One visitor thought they actually enjoyed remarkably little restraint from their dealers until he remembered how truly difficult escape would be here in the midst of the slave South.[19] When a prospective buyer appeared, however, they quickly returned to benches lining the walls, ready to be inspected. Most went as field hands, bought by planters come to town on market day, but now and then the wealthy city folk found domestics here as well, and at least one with, apparently, a touch of American royalty. In 1855 one of the dealers advertised a "nice, plump, modest little girl" of just fourteen. Rumor said she was the daughter of the late President Zachary Taylor.[20]

Advertisements for slaves and a great deal more ran regularly in the city's press. Montgomery was a very literate community, and to all appearances its newspapers thrived. The *Confederation*, the *Post*, the *Mail*, and the *Advertiser* all published both dailies and weekly editions, and competition ran keen. All charged about the same rate, $8 for the daily for a year, and $3 for the weekly—$5 for a tri-weekly edition. But after that they differed considerably. The *Confederation* never entirely kept up with the others, not least most recently when its editor supported the unpopular candidacy of Stephen Douglas in 1860. J. F. Gaines's *Post* did only a little better, not helped by its 1860 backing of the pointless Constitutional Union Party. The real sheets of record were the other two, both staunchly Southern rights in character, and outright secessionist in the case of the *Mail*.[21] George Shorter, a slim, gentlemanly Georgian just twenty-three years old, entertained great hopes for his *Advertiser*. Behind his wide-rimmed gold spectacles he calculated the prospect of becoming the official organ of the new government to be formed in Montgomery. That could bring a prosperity that at the moment eluded him, and might even make it possible to move out of restauranteur Pizzala's home and into one of his own.[22] As for the *Mail*, "Jonce" Hooper shared the editorship with Henry Coyne and J. F. Whitfield, but he was always the guiding light of the sheet. He, at least, had his own home at the corner of Monroe and Lawrence, but it was mostly for show. Montgomery thought him delightful, a comical figure who wore a shabby hat and shirts with no collar, only accentuating a prodigiously bulging Adam's apple. He bore a physique that reminded some of the hated Lincoln, and showed a wit to match, but behind his perpetual smile lurked impending hardship. Despite renting quarters in his building to a baker, and having his own steam printing press, Hooper's *Mail* was going broke. The only way to keep the newspaper and himself afloat was to find a supplemental job somewhere.[23]

Hooper, like most men in Montgomery, belonged to at least one of the host of clubs and societies in town. Several volunteer private military companies paraded at the fair grounds and on the streets from time to time, the True Blues, the Mounted Rifles, the Independent Rifles, and more. Some got their impetus from the fledgling Montgomery Military Academy, and the flower of the city's young manhood filled their ranks.[24] For those disinclined to the uniform and march step, seven Masonic lodges and three Odd Fellows groups offered male comradeship.[25]

Then there were other pursuits. Known as a lawless town in the 1820s, Montgomery still retained elements of the raw frontier edge even by 1861. The criminal dockets were always heavy. Violence never lay too far under the surface. Fistfights, drunken brawls, pistol duels, and more happened often enough that they held no novelty for the residents, though some complained that certain elements still behaved as if this were the edge of the frontier, not a prosperous state capital.[26] In

1860 Alabama as a whole ranked ninth of the thirty-four states for the number of murders, and Montgomery saw its share.[27] Less violent misdemeanors abounded, drunkenness most of all, despite a $5 fine for being on the streets inebriated, and double that for saloons that got too rowdy.[28] And the pleasures of the flesh had their merchants. Only a few blocks from the state house sat the city's best-known brothel, the Macon House, which more than once saw fighting and violence erupt. The mayor's court even had to deal with what Hooper called two "fair, frail, fat and fancy" prostitutes for plotting the death of a third. Not so frail after all, apparently.[29]

Withal, dust and mud, wealth and squalor, pure water and less than perfect street plan, Montgomery watched the approaching sectional storm as did most other Southern cities, and could not avoid being drawn into the vortex. Being a trading center, it attracted a number of Northern merchants, and as Lincoln's election became more and more a certainty, some of them took fear of a backlash and went home.[30] Yet there was no violence. Indeed, the only real outburst came just before the election, on November 1, when Stephen A. Douglas brought his candidacy and his appeal for the Union to the South. As he stepped out of the Exchange and into his carriage, unseen hands threw three or four eggs at him, prompting Hooper to condemn the hooligans despite his own aversion to Douglas.[31]

When the election itself came, the fever that was always there mounted. Citizens called a secession meeting of their own at the capitol on November 17, and within days renewed rumors of Yankees inciting slaves to flee or, worse, murder their masters, flew from lips to ears.[32] That overwhelming two-to-one ratio of slave population to white in the county came dramatically to mind now. Local statutes already provided a drastic fine of $500 from any planter found not properly feeding and caring for his slaves, and more than humanitarian motives lay beneath. Unhappy, ill-fed, or badly treated slaves thieved from other plantations what they did not get on their own. Worse, it made them resentful, and mindful that they had little more to lose by open revolt.[33]

It took but a week after the election before specific rumors of a plot came out in Pine Level, just twenty miles away in the southwest part of the county. Details were sketchy at first, but substantial enough for locals to organize themselves into the Line Creek Sentinels, a vigilante committee armed with revolvers and shotguns. One by one they began interviewing the slaves on neighboring plantations.[34] Grimly one of the

Sentinels wrote that "we are now whipping the negroes taking them as they come," and soon the outline of the plot emerged, though none could say how much was real and how much invented to stay the lash. First reports said two white men incited the blacks to rise at Christmas, kill their masters and their families, divide any moveable property and livestock, and disappear into the hills, awaiting the march of an abolition army from the North when Lincoln took office.[35] A few days later, on December 16, more came out. The leader was a "nominal" white man named William Rollo—or Roller or Rolan, none could agree—abetted by his brother, and now it appeared that they meant the slaves to march on Pine Level after doing in their masters, killing indiscriminately as they went. Any blacks who refused to join them were to be murdered as well. Eventually the army would march on Montgomery itself, where the optimistic—if impractical—Rollo would distribute $500 and land and livestock to each slave, and then open a store so they could trade with him!

The vigilantes hanged a mulatto and one slave on December 16, then executed Rollo and four more two days later, but not before they extracted the most damning evidence of all. Quite probably the terrified blacks simply read into the Sentinels' questions the answers the vigilantes wanted to hear. Knowing themselves doomed anyhow, they just invented in order to halt the whips. In addition to the broad outline of the plot, they said, they intended to kill all children but only the old or ugly women. They would spare *the young and handsome* white women *for their wives.*"[36] Then on Christmas itself another plot came out, this in Autaugaville twenty miles west. Planters took handmade pikes from the hands of nineteen slaves and two white leaders, and found strychnine that a local miller purportedly intended to put into flour to sell in Montgomery. The day after New Year's the miller and two blacks swung.[37]

Throughout December and January new rumors abounded. Usually no source ever appeared, but hysteria supplied all the verification most needed.[38] The week before Christmas Hooper warned his readers: "Be on the alert—remember that fire, poison and the knife are supplied to bad negroes, by our pious brethren in the North."[39] They must keep strangers off their plantations, especially free blacks. Moreover, the usual Christmas festivities for slaves ought to be canceled, and Lincoln should be blamed to dampen spirits and any notion that he would try to free them. And whenever a white man was found inciting the slaves to unrest, "*hang him* to the first tree."[40]

In this highly charged atmosphere a negro named Elias saw a thin trail of smoke curling up from the capitol on the evening of November 29. Going inside and climbing to the third story, he found some smoldering wood leaning against a door and extinguished it before a blaze could start. Hooper quickly published his conclusion, based upon no evidence at all, that "some lurking abolitionist" did the deed. He demanded an investigation "and prompt judgment in the case of every man of doubtful fidelity, among us."[41] While the editor and others set neighbor looking warily at neighbor, and endangered the safety of any strangers in town, Culver and a few others suspected that secessionists had actually set the fire to produce just such a response, and to incite the people. An arsonists really intending to burn the building would have started a blaze on the bottom floor, not the top.[42] If extremists did set the little fire, it worked to their advantage. Mayor Noble already had authority in the city code to hold all males between eighteen and forty-five liable for watch and patrol duty, and now he used it. Moreover, for weeks to come an armed guard stood post at the doors to the state house.[43]

The resulting panic, coming as it did just before the secession convention, helped to persuade the wavering, and embitter the rest. At Montgomery Hall Culver boarded next to a woman who kept a loaded shotgun at the head of her bed, a butcher knife and a revolver beneath her pillow, and still she did not sleep, warning that "the niggers might come fooling around any night."[44] Hooper, already an extremist, turned almost apoplectic. "On all sides we have insurrectionary plots, instigated by the North," he screamed to a friend. The hangings, though necessary, destroyed thousands of dollars worth of negro property. The attempt at poisoning typified Yankee perfidy. "I *am* bitter towards them and I often regret that I cannot in some way help to destroy them. I hate them instinctively—I hate the race and the blood from which they spring." He would teach his two sons to hate them as well, and if resistance to Northern tyranny ever failed after his own passing, he would make them leave their homeland despoiled before surrendering.[45]

Amid the mounting tension and paranoia the people of Montgomery still managed to enjoy themselves. A large New Year's celebration dinner was served at Estelle Hall on Market and Perry, and a few days afterward George Christy's famous minstrels commenced a series of concerts. Drama and farce, always popular in town, flourished at the Montgomery Theatre, with a rather overacted *Hamlet* opening on January 17 and running nightly.[46] But even the drama now felt the tinge of politics. The summer before Daniel Emmett had come to town with Bryant's Minstrels to perform at the theater. Among their repertoire was Emmett's own composition "Dixie's Land." When the theater's orchestra conductor Harman Arnold asked for a copy of the score, it turned out that Emmett had never written it down. There, as the composer hummed the tune, Arnold scratched the score with charcoal on a backstage wall. He copied it the next day and arranged the first band score of the tune that now came increasingly to be the anthem of secession. All the while the fading charcoal transcription remained on the wall.[47]

It was still there when the rising actor John Wilkes Booth came to the theater in December to join celebrants of the local St. Andrew's Society in an annual dinner at the Post Office Restaurant where they toasted "Bobbie" Burns, the haggis, and "The Southern Confederacy."[48] And it was there a few days later on December 19 when a huge audience tramped through the muddy streets and the rain to see Maggie Mitchell, Montgomery's favorite actress, perform in *The Cricket on the Hearth*. The play done, she stepped out for her bows and the manager Sam Harris presented her a new lone star flag of Alabama, praying that beneath its folds beauty and innocence might "carol upon Southern soil the lays of the pure and the brave." By prearrangement, immediately afterward she sang a new song, "The Southern Marseillaise," backed by a chorus that formed a tableaux with flags. In honor of South Carolina's vote to secede two days before, she wore a blue cockade, and as she sang she strode across the stage, grasped the Stars and Stripes where it hung from a box, and ripped it down to trample it beneath her feet. The crowd roared.[49]

They cheered almost daily now, and the flags appeared everywhere. Maggie Mitchell gave hers to Hooper to hang in front of the *Mail* office at 94 Commerce Street. The next day the proprietors of the Exchange set out a huge blue, yellow, and black banner with fifteen stars on one side and the lone star on the other, made for them by their wives. The day after Alabama's secession, when the steamboat *Le Grande* arrived at the wharf flying an eighteen-by-twelve-foot flag of blue with a six-foot silver star, local ladies secured it to present to Hooper as well, in honor of his pen's efforts toward the glorious occasion. In the center of the star sat a huge scarlet letter "A" for Alabama. Apparently Nathaniel Hawthorne was not popular reading in Montgomery.[50]

Already the muddy streets sounded the splash of boots. On January 10 the True Blues, the Metropolitan Guards, and the Independent

Rifles left on the still-incomplete Alabama & Florida for Pensacola and the growing force facing Fort Pickens. The Montgomery Rifles and the Montgomery Greys departed the next day for Mobile.[51] In the growing ferment of euphoria and fear, and from his own commitment to annihilation before subjugation, Hooper suggested opening a shooting gallery to teach Montgomery's women marksmanship, and thereby "double our force of effective *fighting-men*."[52] Even Montgomery's black population felt the stir of their blood. After all, they may have been slaves, but the South was their home, too. A slave named John contributed $10 of his own money to buy uniforms for the militia. Of course he could not go to Pensacola himself, but "his money, his hogs, his cows, and his corn, were all at their disposal."[53]

Those who stayed behind speculated, made great plans, and worried great worries. Taking the formation of a new government for granted, Hooper began suggesting that the infant nation be called "Washington," or perhaps "Columbia." Of course, Montgomery should be the capital, and under the new regime "no point has a finer prospect."[54] Amid all the bold plans and predictions, one boarder at Montgomery Hall felt less sanguine. While his wife continued to sleep fitfully surrounded by her arsenal, he grimly held any optimism in check. Montgomery might feel high hopes, but he had seen domestic disputes large and small before, and he knew better. "Did you ever know of a family feud or quarrel between brothers," he asked Culver, "that was not bitter?"[55] Just how bitter *this* family spat was to be would depend very much upon the two score and more of men even then readying their departure for Montgomery.

CHAPTER THREE

THEY ARE SELFISH, AMBITIOUS, AND UNSCRUPULOUS

————⋆————

THE FIRST TO ARRIVE actually came twice. Patton Anderson arrived in Montgomery from Florida on a cloudy, cool January 24 and easily found a room at the Exchange before the flood of visitors to come. Sent by Governor Perry as an envoy to Moore, he might have seen no sense in returning home when that mission finished, just to come back again as a delegate to the convention, but that is what he did, departing for Montgomery once more at the beginning of February.[1]

The following Tuesday morning Robert H. Smith boarded one of the Cox, Brainard & Co. steamers that daily departed Mobile, and after a trip of nearly forty hours up the Alabama, stepped off the landing stage on the evening of January 30, and onto a wharf so run down that even city officials thought it wretched.[2] He probably stayed in a private home with friends, being well acquainted in Montgomery. People liked Smith. Short, bald, dark complexioned, and stout enough to be called "chuffy," he projected agreeability, and a few even thought him handsome after a fashion. Despite his vote against secession, his colleagues easily selected him as a delegate to the provisional convention, and now that disunion was a fact, his loyalty lay with Alabama, as always.[3]

The next morning, a warm, fair, sixty-degree day, he walked up Market to the capitol to talk with Alabama's leaders in the legislature and the secession convention, both of which still sat. On the way he passed stores doing a brisk business in selling crude woodcut diagrams of Charleston and Pensacola, showing the growing numbers of batteries facing the Yankee-held forts, ample enough evidence of the growing interest and fear over what might happen there any day now.[4] All of the men he spoke with shared that interest; only a few yet seemed apprehensive. Most assumed that the coming meeting of delegates

44

would do no more than organize a temporary government, adopt a constitution, choose a president, and then go home, leaving the work of framing a permanent *working* establishment to await the secession of all the remaining slave states. On the one hand, it hardly seemed worth the bother, for what would they have accomplished? But when Smith pointed out the alternative of commencing at once to create a full, working government, the contemplation exhausted him. They had no treasury nor any machinery in place to raise revenue, no established national existence on which to pledge credit to borrow from other nations, no commerce for duties, no customs houses, and no navy to protect a nonexistent carrying trade. The forts they had seized would be all but empty with no army to fill them, and in the absence of a postal department there was no system in place for conveying the mails. Where to start? "I feel really like I was called on to build a great edifice in a short time without any tools or materials to work with," he mused that evening. "I do not yet see my way out." Still Alabama and the rest had taken their stand and there was no backing away now. A crisis confronted him and the rest of those on their way to Montgomery, and they had no choice but to meet that daunting prospect. "If any one has a fancy for such a position as I now occupy," he moaned, "he must be a very different man from me."[5]

Even as Smith sat lost in introspection that night in his room, at the Mills House in Charleston Rhett packed to leave on the morning train for Montgomery.[6] Despite the recent slaps of rejection from fellow South Carolinians and the state convention, he still stood at the head of his new delegation so far as he was concerned.[7] And with that as a base, he already had plans for exerting a dominating influence in Montgomery by being better prepared than the rest. Into his bags he put a fat notebook already prepared containing his proposed amendments to the old United States Constitution. Armed with this, he could preempt much debate by taking the high ground at once in the framing of a new provisional document, and that in turn must naturally form the basis of any permanent constitution. After exerting this kind of influence as a founding father, he could expect a cabinet post at the very least. His gaze sought a higher summit.[8]

Friday morning, February 1, Rhett and his kinsman Barnwell boarded the cars on the South Carolina Railroad for the long trip to Atlanta. With them came E. G. Dill, "phonographic reporter" for the *Mercury* who intended to transmit verbatim accounts of the debates to Charleston. Rhett meant for his people to watch his actions from afar.

Moveover, in any other editorial accounts sent back by the reporters, he could expect them, as his employees, to say what he wished. A few hours out, in Branchville, former Governor David Swaim and a team of commissioners from North Carolina boarded the train, and late that evening they reached Atlanta.[9] Already Rhett fretted. He felt nothing personal against Swaim or any other Border State men coming to Montgomery as observers. But he feared their moderation. They might try to delay declaring a new government in favor of the "wait and see" approach. They might even act as cooperationists, hoping to see the seceded states back in the Union.[10]

More delegates joined them in Atlanta for the overnight run to West Point, and these men looked exhausted. Wiley Harris and a few other Mississippians, Brooke, Harrison, and Wilson, were just then on the last leg of a virtual circumnavigation of Alabama. The heavy winter rains had washed out the rail bridge over the Tombigbee some days before, severing the most direct connection between Jackson and Montgomery. Instead, after conferring with Pettus and Davis and taking final instructions from their convention, the delegation—minus Clayton and Campbell—took the Mississippi Central north to Grand Junction, Tennessee, changed to the Memphis & Charleston to steam east to Chattanooga, then boarded the Western & Atlantic to head south again to Atlanta. Now, with Rhett and the rest, they nodded through the night on the Atlanta & West Point before finally catching the Montgomery & West Point at eight o'clock on February 2 for the last push through the morning rain to their destination. When they stepped onto the platform of the rather slovenly station, Harris and the others finished a trip of more than nine hundred miles while Jackson actually lay barely a third of that distance to the west.[11]

Montgomery in the rain did not impress them after they each paid their quarters for hack hire, and another for their baggage. Court Street was one continual slush. The mud covered horses and mules from head to tail as they drew their alarmingly rickety omnibuses.[12] Moreover, they saw no crossings for pedestrians, and the sidewalks, such as they were, appeared more dangerous than convenient. Gaping cellar doors threatened to swallow the unwary as walkers dodged around stacks of shipping boxes piled about indiscriminately. A reporter from the Charleston *Courier* mused that the city's attorneys must do a brisk business in suits for damages. Even Montgomery's innumerable dogs found it challenging to navigate the street. One leaped from a sidewalk to harass a passerby and almost immediately disappeared in the mire. It opened its mouth to bark, only to choke on the mud. As the hacks slowly passed on, the animal frantically wiped the mud from its head with a foreleg, then shook its head wildly to get the slime from its eyes. Dill saw in it a metaphor for the South trying to clear abolition muck from its own eyes.[13]

At the Exchange they all found rooms awaiting them, though some would have to share a bed. Rhett, of course, got a room to himself, number 6 on the first floor. Ironically, its previous occupant had been his absolute opposite, Unionist-to-the-last Robert Jemison, while a delegate to his state convention.[14] They sat out the afternoon in the hotel. At word of their coming, some of the Alabama delegates already in town, and those just now arriving, came down to the Exchange to greet them. Chilton already lived in Montgomery, but the rest, like Robert Smith, had more than enough friends and relatives in town to take more comfortable quarters in private homes and evade the bustle and expense of the hotels.[15] They passed the day in talk, speculation, and probing. Rhett must not have been happy to hear the Alabamians speaking of Yancey as the potential president.[16]

The evening train brought more South Carolinians, Boyce, Keitt, Memminger, and Miles, and they too came to the Exchange.[17] Keitt, for one, barely made it to Montgomery. Dashing but flighty, he was no listener, and far too cavalier. One of Miles's friends quipped sarcastically that Keitt could not remember a thing "half an hour after hearing it," and just five days earlier Keitt himself confessed he had forgotten when the convention was to meet. Once a heavy drinker, he refused liquor altogether now. He also talked too much, and too intemperately. "He is quick as a flash," said James Chesnut's wife, "always original and entertaining." Too quick for good sense, as it turned out, and too hot-headed. "He covers himself with words—the longest and the finest, as a garment," she went on. "No one gets the better of him." In the effort to reform his habit of speaking without thinking, his wife sent him to Montgomery under orders to keep his hair brushed and his mouth shut.[18] Thoughts of a sick child at home with his wife helped keep him quiet now.[19] Also, he detested Rhett and had little to say to him.

Boyce's head, too, seemed more hot than clear. A strong secessionist right up to the signing of South Carolina's ordinance, he then turned suddenly moderate and begged leaders to do nothing inflammatory toward the North. "After raising the Storm," complained a critic, "he tells it to blow gently."[20] The modest Miles, a handsome fellow despite his slight "student's stoop," and his eye for the ladies, still feared that others saw him as Rhett's foil, even though Pickens sent most of his official communications to the thoughtful, unassuming younger man in preference to anyone else.[21]

In fact, contrary to Miles's fears and Rhett's pretensions, the South Carolinians had no leader. If anyone, they looked to the fatherly Barnwell.[22] But despite the internal conflict already evident in this portion of the delegation, they remained cordial, and some of them at least still expected to wield heavy influence. That night as they took their rooms, they also rented a private parlor for an additional $5 per day, each to share the expense. Here they could caucus, entertain, cajole.[23] And here, perhaps, Rhett first learned that Memminger came prepared with a constitutional agenda of his own, and an actual draft of the document itself based on a plan he published anonymously in Charleston a few weeks before.[24]

That evening, and probably on the same train, the generally well regarded Nisbet reached Montgomery. He too went to the Exchange.[25] So did Howell Cobb, who arrived not from Georgia, but on a steamboat from New Orleans via Mobile where he had business. He came sporting a new haircut, and still chuckling good-naturedly over the quip of a Creole barber who ran his hands over Cobb's plump face and intemperately exclaimed, "by gar, you are a fat one. I be tam—but he fat."[26] A "fat one" he was, but liked even by his foes. "He was a man of amiable and conciliatory temper," said South Carolinian William Trescott, "with a clear head, very decided opinions himself but always willing to listen and combine the opinions of others for practical action." Curry of Alabama found in him "the docility of a child," suspecting him too fond of convivial company and cheer to devote himself to "severe application and midnight oil."[27] Cobb spent five terms in Congress, one of them as Speaker of the House. Ardent Southern rights men considered him a traitor in 1850–1851 when he supported the Compromise of 1850, and then went on to win the governorship the following year at the head of a Union party that he organized.

Sensing that estrangement from the Democratic party would mean his eventual political doom, Cobb tried to return to the fold in 1853, but only left both Unionists and state rights men suspicious. Not until 1856, when he firmly embraced the Southern rights platform, did Democrats grudgingly accept him once more. In Buchanan's administration he was the only Deep South man of influence, and served in the cabinet right to the moment of secession. In time Cobb felt his strength in Georgia renewing. By late 1859 he even dreamed of a presidential nomination, and only a bitter debate in the state party convention in March 1860 prevented his name from being put forward in Charleston that April. Still he supported the Southern rights candidate John C. Breckinridge in the campaign that followed, and when Lincoln won he quickly declared secession the South's only alternative.[28] Ambitious and opportunistic to be sure, Cobb still offered dignity, restraint, and common sense. He was a man of character to match his national reputation. Now an even bigger light than Yancey and Rhett shone in Montgomery. There was little enough bright other than these luminaries and their conversation that night. The drizzle continued all evening and the temperature fell in the darkening hours. Even the street lamps on Market cast only gloomy glows as time after time the delegates in the Exchange went to the windows. "Whilst the rain drops!—drops!—drops!" as the *Mercury* reporter watched, the men inside wondered just how they would make the half-mile trip up the street to the state house on Monday.[29]

The Chesnuts left their Camden home on February 2, changing at Branchville to run the same route as the rest of the South Carolina delegation. James Chesnut had just turned forty-six, boasted a Northern college education, and came fresh from almost eighteen years of service in the South Carolina legislature. Not even Rhett stood more dedicated to secession, though Chesnut was at once the smarter of the two, and the more practical. Elected to the United States Senate, he resigned even before secession came, in order to speed its arrival. Well before leaving home, he turned his thoughts to the course South Carolina should pursue at Montgomery, and decided it best that the delegation make no attempt to offer candidates for high office. Unity counted above all else now. Rhett was too extreme, and besides Chesnut liked him little if at all. His state had been the bully boy of secession from the beginning. It was time now to stand aside and put the new government into the hands of more moderate men, just as many of the states turned to moderates for their delegates. Speaking his mind to others in his delegation, he found that they agreed. That, in itself, was unusual. When he thought of the high offices, Chesnut thought of Davis and Stephens, and perhaps—though not definitely— in that order.[30]

The miles passed uneventfully as the Chesnuts steamed west across the Georgia line. Mary Chesnut was so far the only spouse to accompany a delegate. Where James was serious, uncommunicative, almost dour, she exuded vivacity. Mary Chesnut was not beautiful, though she wanted to believe men when they said she was. Yet she was remarkably intelligent and observant, quick and keen, possessed of a sure insight into character. Always a center of attention, she drew people to her in a way her husband never could. Even on this trip he remained reserved, as usual, and something of a snob, disdaining to ride in the same car with what he called "whiskey drinking, tobacco chewing rascals & *rabble*."[31] With them, too, came her uncle, old Thomas J. Withers. Family stories said that he talked too much as a child, and he simply never stopped, and where Mary might have wished that her husband be more communicative, she prayed that her uncle would shut up. A bundle of prejudices and resentments, he never let them die, nor others stop hearing them. "He had moral courage in a high degree," said a friend, "and cared not whom he pleased or offended."[32] While some thought him quaint, even amusing, in time most found him a dreary bore who thrust himself uninvited into the most pleasant conversation and immediately launched into diatribes that all had heard innumerable times before.

Thus it probably relieved the Chesnuts when their train stopped in Union Point, Georgia, very late on February 2, and among the boarding passengers they met Tom Cobb. He had left his home in Athens a few hours before, nursing a bad cold that the heavy rains did not help, and still felt dismayed that his own wife would not come with him to Montgomery. Indeed, he very nearly resigned from the delegation rather than be separated from her.[33] After seventeen years of marriage, he was just as much in love with Marion Cobb as when they wed. An odd mixture, this Cobb, and neither in character nor intellect the equal of his brother Howell. At birth he weighed a staggering twenty-one pounds, eight ounces! Superstition often governed him, from changing his wedding date that it might not fall on a Friday, to seeing the future in signs.[34] Super-religion narrowed his mind and judgment, to the point of advocating that trains should not run on Sundays. Hypocrisy blinded him to his own inconsistencies; tomorrow, Sunday, February 3, *he* would be riding a train into Montgomery.[35] And bald obstinacy and prejudice ruled his views of any who opposed him. Just thirty-seven, he showed himself an able lawyer, and a voluminous writer on political and constitutional subjects. His dedication to secession, as in all enterprises he adopted, was single-minded. Stephens believed that Cobb, even more than Toombs, bore the chief responsibility for Georgia withdrawing from the Union.

Still, he could be affable enough. Dressed in a homespun suit—with which he saw no problem in wearing kid gloves—he matched his brother for new haircuts, though friends said he looked better before the barber. Perhaps that was because the trim revealed a growing crop of gray not there even three months before. Cobb blamed current events. "The exciting anxiety of these times is telling on me," he wrote Marion.[36] Yet others found him youthful still, and admired his clean shaven face. Some thought him a man of brains.[37]

Before Cobb boarded he conversed politely with others awaiting the same train. Puffed up by his importance in Georgia's secession convention, Cobb *thought* he might be a giant in Montgomery. But two others waiting with him *were* giants, and on a national stage, and any cordiality between him and them reached no deeper than their forced smiles.[38] Little Aleck Stephens visited with his beloved brother Linton in Sparta for a few days late in January, then returned to his home "Liberty Hill" in Crawfordville to pack for the trip to Montgomery. Depression and second thoughts still gripped him, and on the very verge of departing he wrote to his brother that he almost wished he had refused his appointment. "It is with great reluctance I leave home." At least he felt well, for his health generally ran from poor to abominable, and even when fit his hypochondria persuaded him otherwise.[39]

Surely this was the tiniest "giant" ever to tremble Southern soil. In fact he stood five feet seven inches, an average height, but his body was so frail and perpetually emaciated that most at first took him for a boy.[40] "A more pinched up, misshapen, dead-and-alive specimen of humanity" could not be found, said one on meeting him.[41] He weighed as little as eighty pounds much of the time, and never got above a hundred. Arms and hands dangled long and bony, claw-like, the joints swollen from arthritis. He stood stooped thanks to a pinched nerve in his spine. Everything that could afflict man's internal organs attacked him, from angina to colitis. Migraine headaches incapacitated him. Pneumonia almost killed him three times. Diarrhea robbed his bones of their little flesh. Pasty, pale skin hung about his face, innumerable wrinkles emanating spoke-like from his eyes. Coarse, wispy, graying hair straggled loosely about his protruding ears. Only his blazing black eyes showed life. In nine days he would turn forty-nine, but many at first mistook him for a wizened old woman of eighty.[42] Typically, he described himself as "a malformed ill-shaped half finished thing."[43] And to a life dominated by physical pain, he added near-constant emotional turmoil. He fell in love one time, perhaps more, but for his freakish physiognomy there could be no hope of finding a mate. For him enduring love was restricted to his brother Linton, his dog Rio, and the South. Little Aleck made a most unlikely giant.

Yet he towered on the national stage. Stephens spent sixteen years in Congress, at first a Whig, then a Democrat. Though always a strong proponent of Southern rights at all times, he retained a firm attachment to the Union whenever compromise seemed possible. In 1850 he joined with Cobb in forming Georgia's Union party, and a decade later supported the Douglas candidacy as the only means to avert calamity. Unlike Cobb, his last-ditch stand against secession and grudging acquiescence in the inevitable cost him little good will among Southern rights men outside Georgia. His chief enemies were the Cobbs themselves, and the hotheads like Bartow. For the rest, friends and opponents alike regarded him as eighty pounds of intellect and principle. He held few hopes for this present mission. There seemed to him to be a "want of high integrity, loyalty to principle, and pure, disinterested patriotism" in the men running this movement." "My word for it," he told a friend the day he left, "this country is in a great deal worse condition than the people are at all aware of." He distrusted men like Rhett, fearing they would dominate the convention. "They are selfish, ambitious, and unscrupulous."[44]

The other giant with him seemed his absolute opposite. Robert Toombs, just six months older than Stephens, looked years younger. They had been friends for a quarter-century, a relationship grown into deep and abiding love as Stephens saw in Toombs the physical man he could never be, and Toombs rightly recognized a power of intellect greater than his own. This Georgian was a big man, six feet tall or more, of solid frame and broad shoulders. Long, shiny black hair rimmed a strong face, and flew about like a lion's mane as he shook his head while speaking. His face perpetually changed from smile to scowl, stopping at every intermediate expression, dominated always by brilliantly white teeth and lawless dark eyes that to Varina Davis betokened his character.[45]

Toombs invited superlatives. "Bob Toombs!" roared a train conductor who knew him. "His brain is as big as a barrel and his heart is as big as a hogshead." "Princely, royal, kingly, even god like," said another, "were the words with which men tried in vain to tell what they saw in him."[46] Stephens, usually objective toward Toombs in spite of their deep friendship, thought him one of the most extraordinary men he ever met. He proved a lightning quick study at whatever he undertook. During the 1850 compromise debates in the Senate, Toombs listened to the discussions with one ear, while reading a French play and roaring with laughter.[47]

Indeed, there lay his tragic weakness. Everything came too easily to him, and that combined with an impulsive nature work against him. Stephens deplored Toombs's lack of self-control and mental discipline. "He has brain enough, if its energy had been properly directed, to govern an empire."[48] Yet he reined neither ambitions nor passions, making his spontaneity both blessing and curse. "No one else has ever made such perfect and telling impromptus as Toombs," Stephens said, while a much younger friend marveled at his "brilliant snatches, his sudden uprisings, his thawing humor, and flashing wit." But these same friends saw as well his propensity to lapse into harsh language in the heat of debate, his indiscretion, and an instinct toward hyperbole even in pleasant conversation. He swore profoundly.[49] Then there was the drink. Stephens sipped alcohol by the tablespoon several times a day, thinking erroneously that it aided his health. All it did was turn him into a latent alcoholic.[50] Toombs's consumption was small by comparison with other sober men, but he could not handle the little that he drank.

He, too, joined with Cobb and Stephens in the Union party in 1850, and it did not hurt him. After one term in Congress, he won a Senate seat in 1852 and held it until he resigned on January 7, 1861, now convinced that compromise with the North was no longer possible. From that moment he became an ardent secessionist, and from that time dated his brief estrangement from Stephens. But the bond between them was too great to be broken even by disunion. As they boarded the train, they grew closer again with each day.

Tom Cobb disliked that closeness between two such powerful potential foes in Montgomery. But they were all polite, and during the ride, as he did whenever possible, Cobb bragged on his little one-year-old daughter Maria, and how she could walk, dance, play the toy drum, even talk—and of course pray.[51] Stephens talked of his plantation, or made gallant pleasantries and quips for Mary Chesnut's benefit. When the train stopped in Atlanta, he failed even to notice Patton Anderson boarding their car, now on his second trip from Florida to Montgomery in a week. The two served a term in Congress together a few years before, but a western sojourn left the modest Anderson much changed in appearance. During the balance of the trip he often looked at Stephens several seats away, but decided not to introduce himself for fear the great Georgian would not remember him.[52]

The next morning, February 3, about an hour out of West Point their train stopped at Opelika, Alabama, and Francis Bartow joined them in the last car on the train.[53] He was a bold, posturing, but light-weight politician. Thanks to being captain for the past four years of the Oglethorpe Light Infantry, a militia company composed of the cream of Savannah society, he fancied himself a military hero waiting to happen. Fully a month before Georgia's secession he told Governor Brown that he stood "ready for action" and that he and his men meant "to be taken at our word."[54] Here, at least, was an ally for Tom Cobb. They shared much the same stature, and they both disliked the giants.

In preference to Cobb and Bartow, Little Aleck and Toombs spent most of the trip talking with the Chestnuts. Mary believed that Southern prospects looked bright, and her husband expressed a conviction that there would be no war, especially if the Border States joined with them.[55] Stephens argued to the contrary. "I see great troubles ahead," he would say, and from the first he believed that secession must in the end lead to blood.[56]

From this their talk turned to the coming convention in Montgomery. Stephens and Chesnut spoke for some time on the pending organization of the new government, and especially the need to get the executive cabinet departments up and functioning as quickly as possible. Both agreed, as did Toombs, that the times demanded more than mere consultations, or simply drafting a constitution and then referring it back to the state conventions for ratification before putting a government into operation. That could take a month—even two months or more. The only way to meet the crisis was for the convention to draft a provisional constitution and thereby assume unto itself the powers of a congress, in expectation that the several states would later ratify their action. It would be a dangerous move. Beyond doubt it represented a usurpation of authority not specifically granted by some of the conventions. And should even one of the several conventions repudiate the actions of such a congress, there loomed the specter of a state or states going it on their own, seceding, as it were, from the seceders. The bundle of sticks would come untied, inviting disaster for them all. But they had before them the example of 1776, when another body of delegates went beyond its mandate. It had worked once. It could work again.[57]

One of the choices they faced was who should lead them. Chesnut told Stephens of the resolve of the South Carolina delegation—undoubtedly excluding Rhett—not to put forward anyone from their state for president or vice president.[58] He did not need to add that the same logic ought to preclude Yancey and any of the other extremists. They must to look to the middle ground, especially since Stephens and Toombs could testify to the deep divisions within Georgia. Part of their commitment to turning the convention into a congress immediately without waiting for state sanction was their fear that if a mere plan for government should be put to a referendum in their state, the widespread Union sentiment still remaining might vote it down.[59]

From that standpoint, the best candidates were obvious. The only remaining men of truly national stature in the seceded states were Davis and the three Georgia giants. Chesnut preferred Davis, though he may not have said so. But a widely held notion that the Mississippian preferred the chief military command, or ought to have it, could rule him out, and Chesnut may even have mentioned rumors that Davis positively did not want the chief executive.[60] In that case where else could they look but Georgia?

When he mentioned Georgia initially, Chesnut may have been thinking of the vice presidency. Stephens took him to mean the first office, and he suggested Toombs—his own preference—first, then added Howell Cobb, and one or two others of no real consequence. But Chesnut replied that he, and those members of the South Carolina delegation with whom he agreed, looked only to Toombs or Little Aleck himself. Again Chesnut may have been thinking of the vice presidency, since Stephens was his own choice for the office. But should Davis be out of the question, *this* Georgian would naturally be his next. Whether confused or not, Stephens at once disqualified himself. He came to secession at the last minute, he said, and unwillingly. They should look to someone identified with the movement much longer than he, specifically Toombs. There they let the matter rest, Stephens under the clear impression that he had removed himself from consideration for any office, and that Chestnut would turn South Carolina for Toombs. Unfortunately, the Palmetto State delegation being what it was, Chesnut could speak only for himself, and on later reflection felt uncertain of the result of his talk with Stephens. Toombs took no part in the discussion, perhaps knowing that his own name occupied much of their talk. More likely he was lost in thought and worry. Of his three children, an only son had died in infancy, and a daughter in 1855. Now his last child, Sallie M. DuBose, just twenty-five, lay abed expecting his first grandchild, and was already dangerously ill. For once Robert Toombs was not in a mood to be conversational.[61]

Interruptions occasionally silenced Stephens and Chesnut. A Toombs *bon mot* perhaps, or else one of Withers's snuff-induced thunderclap sneezes.[62] But if they were talking at 11:30 A.M. something else disturbed them. Alabamians took a little pride in the Montgomery & West Point Railroad. It snaked eastward eighty-eight miles to link the state capital with West Point, Georgia, and then met other lines wedding Alabama to Atlanta and on to the sea.[63] Two trains a day steamed east and west. The night run made the trip in four hours and fifty minutes. The daylight train took exactly five hours, and sometimes less.[64] Passengers coming from Atlanta on the Atlanta & West Point line expected speed, though some complained that forty miles an hour pushed the limits of safety.[65] The Montgomery & West Point engineers held their trains to just half that speed, and with good cause, but it stung their pride to hear the Georgians complain of the seeming snail's pace after the fast run to West Point from Atlanta. Sometimes an Alabama trainman relaxed his grip on the throttle to put on a bit more speed. He knew better.

The line was unsafe. While most Northern and many Southern engines ran on substantial wrought iron "T" bar rails, a number of Deep South companies still relied on ruder forms dating from the earliest days of railroading. The Montgomery & West Point ran for much of its length on the crudest variety of all, "strap and stringer" rail—nothing more than wooden "stringers" with a wrought iron "strap" attached to the upper surface. Moreover, nothing bound one of these "rails" to those before and behind. Track layers simply aligned them end to end without benefit of joints, and then spiked them to the wooden ties. The thin strap wore out easily. The wooden stringers cracked and split. A loose or ill-placed spike let the rails separate at their joints. Most often, under only moderate use, a rail simply broke, generally as a train passed over.[66]

The night train from West Point on February 2, 1861, reported a bad rail three miles west of Montgomery. Heavy rains had beaten the region for two days, driving away rather warm winter temperatures. The track crew, some of them slaves, went out before dawn the next morning in a miserable drizzle with the thermometer at forty-four and falling.[67] They had to replace the damaged rail before the eight o'clock train left for West Point. But it was cold and wet. They hurried. The gang leader failed to check the rail carefully for splits, or to ensure that the men drove their spikes well and that the ties were not softened by rot. Still, the morning train chugged over the path to West Point without incident.[68] Three and one-half hours later that rail met with Stephens's train. First they heard the engine whistle wildly blowing. Then came the screech of the locomotive's brakes. Finally a sickening jolt and shock. Stephens looked out the window to see chaos up ahead. Two baggage cars had jumped the rails, one of them now lying on its side and the other thrown directly across the tracks, which lay shredded for some forty yards or more. The front passenger car also derailed, and as Stephens, Toombs, Cobb, the Chesnuts, and the rest rushed from the two rear cars that still stood on the track, they saw people hurriedly climbing and crawling from the wreckage.

Soon there came a reassuring cry that no one was injured, but the mess before them looked frightful to Stephens, and for once Cobb agreed with him, thinking it "an awful smash up." A flock of chickens flew from one of the broken baggage cars and cackled over the fields. A horse jumped unhurt from another and now grazed quietly beside the disrupted roadbed. When curiosity replaced shock, the passengers looked about in wonder that there were no fatalities. Incredibly, a basket of eggs sitting beneath one seat revealed not a single one broken. Cobb spoke with the conductor and learned that the cause of it all was a new "strap and stringer" rail laid just that morning. The engineer spotted the weakness in it all right, but could not stop before the locomotive passed over, its weight displacing the rail to upset the cars following. If the passenger carriages had been immediately behind rather than the baggage cars, the result could have been tragic. "This comes from Sunday travelling," Mary Chesnut told Cobb. A Savannah reporter on one of the cars mused that this presented a bad omen for the new Southern confederacy, and another passenger, thinking of the preponderance of important men on the train, referred only half in jest to the South having "run off the track." He said more than he realized. But for chance, Stephens, Toombs, Chesnut, or all of them might have been disabled or even killed, with consequences beyond their foretelling.

As he walked about surveying the ruins, Stephens heard of someone hurt at the front of the train. He stepped forward to find samaritans lifting an old black man from the ruins. The Georgian's body servant Pierce, with him for years, thought he recognized the man as a hack driver they knew in their days at Washington. Stephens saw that he was right, and talked for some time with the fellow, who proved to suffer nothing more than a bruised leg. Meanwhile the engine went off to Montgomery, less than five miles away, to bring back cars to carry the passengers the rest of the trip, and on its return Stephens and Cobb joined the injured slave in a baggage car, chatting cheerfully with him while they smoked. Finally, at 1:30 they pulled into the depot, two hours late.[69]

The night's rain and the morning drizzle left Court Street as much a mess as the day before.[70] Stepping out of the ill-kept station, they all engaged hacks, Withers and the Chesnuts for Montgomery Hall, and the rest for the Exchange.[71] Some climbed into the shaky Montgomery Omnibus Company hacks, and others went for Wade's Independent One Price Accommodation Line carriages. Both cost the same quarter per rider, baggage extra.[72] The three-inch cab numbers painted on their running lamps stood out in the mournful gray light as the vehicles started on the short trip to the hotels. While Stephens's hack splashed down the right side of Court Street he might have occupied himself reading the driver's rates and provisions posted inside.[73] More likely he looked out the window as they passed a succession of saloons, then turned right into Court Square, past the artesian basin and the old ceremonial signal cannon "Little Texas" standing nearby, and pulled up at the Exchange.[74]

Withers and the Chesnuts reached Montgomery Hall to find De Clouet of Louisiana, the only man of his delegation yet arrived.[75] When the rest joined him, they would make a most congenial group. Culver, the photographer boarding in a nearby room, soon enjoyed their company, Montgomery Hall, with its limitation to about 150 guests, being smaller and more conducive to intimacy than the mammoth Exchange.[76] So would the commissioners from Virginia who, like Swaim and the North Carolinians, intended to listen and press for peace and forbearance.[77]

Howell Cobb and Nisbet greeted Stephens and the others when they reached the Exchange, but Little Aleck cared little at all for what else he found waiting. Having sent ahead to engage a room, he discovered now that the hotel was filling so rapidly that he would have to share with two others, and that did not suit him at all. Fortunately, Stephens had foreseen this possibility and earlier asked an old friend to inquire about private lodgings in one of the boardinghouses. Seaborn Howard met him at the hotel now and delighted the Georgian with news that he had found the ideal place, and only a few minutes away. Stephens quickly agreed to return to the hotel shortly to dine and talk with other delegates, then another carriage and another quarter or so took them two blocks south on Montgomery to Catoma Street and Mrs. Elizabeth Cleveland's commodious two-story frame house on the southeast corner of the intersection.[78]

Stephens took the apartment immediately. It included a bedroom and a parlor with a fireplace. Better yet, he could have a private outside entrance, and the place was quiet, there being only two or three other boarders at the moment. Howard assured him that most of the other boardinghouses in town were both full and rather ill-maintained. Mrs. Cleveland, on the other hand, kept a clean house. Two servants helped her with the place and kept her five children out of the way. Her dancing master husband had disappeared some time before after squandering most of her small fortune, but the thirty-four-year-old landlady remained most genteel and agreeable.[79] Little Aleck would be quite content there. But for now he had a luncheon date.

Francis Gilmer, builder of so much else in Montgomery, originally started the Exchange in 1846, and after more than a year under construction it opened in November 1847. Almost immediately it became one of the premier hostelries in the South, *the* place to stay when in the Alabama capital. Eight years later Sidney C. Lanier assumed its management, joined shortly by A. P. Watt of North Carolina.[80] The massive edifice stretched three hundred feet down Commerce, and one hundred feet back on Montgomery, its exterior wearing a smooth coat of plaster over the brick to give the appearance of granite. Open balconies sat in the middle of the two street sides, ornamented by massive columns that rose three stories to the roof. When Stephens walked up the steps from the grand entrance on Commerce Street and passed between the pillars, he entered a vestibule crowded with guests lounging and smoking cigars. Most of the men he sought were in the bar. There Toombs, the Cobbs, Bartow certainly, and the rest, enjoyed an afternoon julep beneath the plate glass ceiling of the old English wood-paneled room.[81]

The Montgomery Hall delegates certainly came over this afternoon as well, though still only about twenty of the expected delegates had arrived.[82] "The crowd is not large here," Tom Cobb observed,[83] but already it attracted much attention from the other hotel guests and townspeople who came in increasing numbers to see the gathering of notables. After every new arrival passed through the vestibule and into the office to sign the guest list, he scarcely went on his way to his room before groups of the curious rushed to peek at the ledger for his name.[84] The extravagant welcome from forty-three-year-old Watt and his wife Jane only added to the atmosphere of expectation for the onlookers. Watt's jolly round face glowed with congeniality, and suited his squat "Dutchmanish" physique.[85] Eight Irish and Scottish hall and

parlor maids added to the bustle as they scurried about with the linens
and piles of the very best stationery sent over by Governor Moore for
the use of the delegates.[86]

More than just locals and the idle curious paid careful heed to the
distinguished guests. Newspaper reporters and editors from all across
the South gathered to report on the forthcoming proceedings. Rhett
brought Dill from the *Mercury*, and in his wake came a host. Many
were already here, and within a few days journalists represented four
South Carolina papers, ten from Georgia, two from Louisiana, several
from Alabama besides the four Montgomery papers, and scattered
newsmongers from Virginia, Tennessee, and even New York. Moreover,
for those states like Mississippi and Florida who could not send
reporters thanks either to the distance or the washed out bridges, and
to serve smaller sheets unable to afford their own reporters, W. H.
Pritchard checked into room 37 of the Exchange representing his
Southern Associated Press. By telegraph, his reports could appear in
newspapers in every state North and South.[87]

The correspondents and the curious alike watched the delegates'
every movement, especially the South Carolinians'. After all, these
were the men who started the revolution. It did not take long to see
that Rhett's notion of being leader was a fiction to which only he subscribed. Keitt scarcely concealed his dislike. Miles stayed distant, as did
Memminger and Boyce. Old Withers was too erratic to count.[88]
Chesnut, at least, stayed polite, regarding Rhett as bold and frank, if
dangerous.[89] Some thought Chesnut exerted the most influence with
his colleagues, while Barnwell, looking the very image of Mr. Pickwick
behind his round-rimmed spectacles, exuded a mien of calm benevo-
lence and character that led most except his cousin to look to him for
rational counsel.[90] Rhett just turned to the dining room. He, like
Barnwell, looked Dickensian enough with round gold spectacles of his
own, and just now a plaster covering an annoying pimple on his nose.
Already other boarders at the Exchange wondered how long Watt and
Lanier could make a profit at $2.50 a day for meals the way Rhett laid
into the boiled turkey and oyster stuffing. One of the Alabamians
thought his gluttony ought to be "a caution to tavern keepers."[91]

Harris of Mississippi also attracted some notice, not least for his
habit of audibly talking to himself.[92] An attorney of considerable
repute, he blamed his baldness on having worn his head out "rubbing
against the books in the library."[93] He also suffered from terrible eye-
sight, a result perhaps of too much study, but his standing put him eas-

ily at the head of his delegation.[94] Old former Governor Swaim also became something of a curiosity, too talkative to listen, and too deaf to hear. Tom Cobb immediately thought him "a plain good old man, but by no means a *great man*."[95] But they all behaved most cordially to him, even though the other delegates regarded the Tarheels largely as cyphers.[96]

Nevertheless, Swaim did his best to convince them this afternoon that North Carolina definitely would secede, though granting that it would take time.[97] That was all very fine, but it did nothing for the convention about to convene on the morrow. Better news, great news, came with confirmation this same day that the Texas convention voted for secession two days earlier. Unlike the other states now out, Texas planned to put this move to a popular referendum later in the month, but no one doubted the result. Now they would be seven, and the larger their nucleus, the more inevitably the laggards like North Carolina and Virginia must yield to their gravity.

The dining and drinking out of the way, and the spectators kept at a distance, the delegates turned the Exchange lobby into a "conversational parliament." In pairs and groups they traded views, both their own and those of their conventions. Significant differences emerged. Mississippi had already delegated its recent United States congressional delegation to be its representatives in any new Southern government. Consequently Harris and his colleagues believed they should adopt the old United States Constitution as it stood, choose a president, and leave it at that. And Mississippi's choice for president, not surprisingly, was Jefferson Davis. This done, the convention ought to go home and leave the other states to elect their representatives. After all, Harris argued, this meeting was a *convention*, not a *congress*.[98]

Louisiana, too, offered some embryonic ideas. De Clouet suggested that they frame immediately a provisional constitution and government on the basis of the old Constitution, select a provisional president and vice president, and then put together a permanent constitution and refer it back to the state conventions for ratification. But he did not say who should form that first provisional government once the constitution was completed. Some argued for immediate elections of provisional representatives, and later ballots for delegates to the permanent congress once the constitution was ratified.[99] De Clouet was a man of wealth, influence, and a good sense. He knew where the powerful intellect in this meeting lay, which is why he and other Louisianians brought with them letters of introduction to Stephens.[100]

De Clouet's proposal came close to the Georgian's own notion of what should be done, but he would go farther. He and the rest of his delegation came armed with the most comprehensive plan of all, endorsed by their convention at Stephens's behest. They argued for this very convention immediately assuming to itself for up to one year the full legislative powers of a unicameral congress, including the ability to raise taxes, create offices, confirm appointments, frame the provisional and permanent constitutions, and choose a president and vice president. Following state ratification of the permanent document and formal elections of senators and representatives, this provisional congress would then pass out of existence.[101]

Smith and another of the Alabama delegates endorsed the Georgia plan, and with good cause. They feared putting any question before their people in a referendum. The cooperationist sympathy was too great, and still growing in some counties. The delegates here or coming to Montgomery, even former Unionists like himself, stood committed now to Southern unity. But if getting a government into operation were to be postponed until another election for representatives took place, the possibility of a disruptive number of their opponents being elected loomed very real, and could prove disastrous in any ensuing legislature, perhaps fatal. Stephens, Toombs, and the other Georgians heartily agreed.[102]

It all shocked Rhett and some of his delegation. Every proposition affronted the very principles of independent state rights and determination that impelled them to secession in the first place. "Words are certainly very shadowy in their meaning," he concluded.[103] South Carolina had one thing in mind when it invited other states to meet with it in convention. Even though they used virtually the same words in accepting, Georgia, Louisiana, and Alabama meant something else entirely. Worse, one of the South Carolinians listening this afternoon suddenly proposed going even further, that the convention assembling here should not itself act as a legislature, but that it should elect the representatives from each of the states to form the permanent congress. Rhett regarded that as "a monstrous commentary upon representation in government." Thereby, Georgians and Alabamians would be voting upon, and influencing the election of, representatives from South Carolina![104] As the afternoon wore on, Rhett could see that it was all getting out of hand even before they were started. His defenses went up, his hearty paranoia more alert than ever. There were enemies here, threats to the South, and to himself.

The Charleston convention empowered its delegates to do no more than make alterations to the existing Constitution, submit them to the states for ratification, and then adjourn. Upon ratification, each state convention should then hold elections for senators and congressmen, and also cast ballots for the chief executive offices. The new, lawful congress could assemble before the end of February, count the presidential ballots, and then declare the victors, all without any usurpation of power such as Georgia and the rest proposed.[105]

This convention had no power to elect anyone, Rhett argued. As for the Mississippi plan, if this body did elect a president and vice president, the men would be powerless puppets without a congress. They could not raise money, conduct foreign policy, or even get the executive departments functioning without a senate to advise and consent on appointees. And if the state conventions were to elect senators and representatives anyhow, as Harris proposed, then why should they not ballot for president and vice president at the same time?

Rhett saw the dreaded specter of reconstruction behind this, the fear that if he and others were not careful, they would find themselves reunited with the North under the old Constitution, perhaps with some guarantees covering slavery, but still yoked to their mortal enemies the Yankees. By taking the Constitution as it was, Harris of course spoke for the essential conservatism of all of them. They were not rebelling to erect some radical new shrine founded on principles of their own devising. They were withdrawing from the influence of the corrupt priests of the North who had perverted the existing temple, and they hoped to re-erect it here. Their argument lay not with the Constitution, a document of unparalleled perfection, but with those who interpreted it in ways never intended by the Founding Fathers. Thus Harris and the Mississippians saw no need for altering the existing document. In the hands of responsible Southerners its sanctity would be inviolate.

But Rhett expected that when the Border States withdrew from the Union to join with their equivocal stand on slavery, it would be impossible to put through any amendment limiting statehood to slave states. Moreover, Maryland, Kentucky, and Missouri were tainted with approbation of high protective tariffs and congressionally funded internal improvements, both issues anathema to South Carolina. Inevitably the Deep South and Border States would have a bitter struggle over those issues. And meanwhile, in theory, the old Constitution would allow the remaining free states of the old Union to join with them, thus effecting virtual reconstruction. "After all, we will have run around a circle, and end up where we started," Rhett protested.[106]

The fire-eater felt no great regard for the "Georgia project" as he called it. Clearly it represented a usurpation of power, though he felt forced to admit that it was more practical. While the Mississippi scheme made it impossible for this convention to accomplish anything, the Georgia plan did provide for some form of working government getting under way at once. Since all of them came here as elected representatives of their states, at least they stood closer to being an expression of the will of their constituents than would any senators and congressmen they might themselves select, as suggested by one South Carolinian.[107]

All through the afternoon and on into the early evening the talking continued, and the longer it lasted, the more the weight of logic argued in favor of the Georgia project, aided by the persuasive Georgians themselves. Harris and the Mississippians soon yielded, and gracefully, agreeing to the paramount necessity for speed.[108] Alabama already stood behind Georgia. De Clouet and Anderson, still the only members of the Louisiana and Florida delegations present, could hardly argue. And despite Rhett's protests, South Carolina finally came over. Even Keitt agreed, convinced that the feared repudiation of the movement by any popular election in Georgia and Alabama might be fatal to them all.[109] Barnwell clinched it. The situation here in Montgomery looked so completely different from what he came expecting to find that the necessity justified for him the resort to more radical steps. He feared that they all looked forward too much to the Border States joining them, and felt too prone to modify their positions in order not to put off Virginia and the rest. But that was a matter to handle later. When the respected Barnwell gave his nod, most of South Carolina came with him.[110]

Reporters lurked on the fringes of the discussion all afternoon, hungry for news, here and there picking up the broad outline of the debate. Something quite different struck many of them, however. Most impressive of all was not what the delegates said, but how they said it. Those here present comprised every possible past political cast—Democrats, Whigs, Union party people, Douglas men, Breckinridge followers, even members of the old nativistic "Know Nothing" group. In Congress halls and on the hustings they had often spoken long and harshly against each other in decades past. But now all manifestation of party feeling seemed evaporated "What a man was, is not once alluded to," observed a New Orleans journalist. "What he is is the only question discussed."[111] And even Dill of Rhett's *Mercury* felt impressed. No finer body of statesmen could be put together anywhere in the South, he decided. "What they do, they will do thoroughly."[112]

They settled it then and there. The convention meeting tomorrow would form itself into what so many already called it, a congress. That decided, they turned to more specific matters of what should be done in these first days. Most agreed that all but the most inconsequential of their debates ought to be conducted in secret session.[113] Facing at least the possibility—most thought it no more—of war with the North, they would be foolish to publicize or allow general access to deliberations that touched on their security and defense. Rhett felt outraged. He intended to shine in these debates, and wanted the world to read his words. One more cord of his self-fantasized domination of the convention slipped from his grasp.

There must be a president of the convention, equivalent to a house speaker. Even as he commented himself on the "disposition to unite and harmonize" among his fellow delegates, they rapidly united on Howell Cobb as the best choice. Cobb himself began hearing this from the moment he arrived in Montgomery the day before, and regarded it with a little pride mixed with more suspicion. He offered a natural choice. Besides his distinguished recent career, he had served as speaker of the house during the Thirty-First Congress. But he suspected that among the South Carolina and Mississippi delegates talking up his name on February 2 there also lay an expectation that making him president of the convention would exclude him from consideration for a higher presidency, whenever *that* election should come.[114] Harris, of course, wanted Davis, and the rest of his delegation stood with him. Some of the South Carolinians still distrusted Cobb for his defection from the Southern rights movement in 1850, and Rhett, of course, had ambitions of his own. Sensing this, his brother Thomas today, along with Bartow, advised him to decline the appointment. But Howell disagreed. And besides, the presidency of the new confederacy, he wrote his wife that night, "is an office I cannot seek and shall feel no disappointment in not getting."[115] Still, in deciding to accept one presidency, Cobb never specifically said that he would decline another if offered.

By the time the afternoon discussion wound down, the feeling for making Cobb convention president was virtually universal.[116] Even before coming to Montgomery, some of the hangers on, like journalist William Browne from Washington, foresaw that Cobb would be a

power in any new concern, and armed themselves with letters of recommendation from him.[117] It was agreed. Cobb should be nominated
president. Significantly, Rhett agreed to put forward the nomination.[118]

Before they broke apart for their supper, the delegates also settled
much of the rest of the procedure for the morrow. Hundreds of citizens
would be watching, and through the reporters they would be under the
gaze of the world. Everything must run smoothly and give an impression of complete and effortless unity. Rhett dominated here, suggesting one item of business after another, and in return they designated
him to introduce them before the convention. That suited him perfectly. He brought his own correspondent, and he wanted his name
prominently featured in the published debates.

Someone raised the matter of a secretary of the convention, to oversee recording its debates, and the candidate was firmly fixed in the
minds of a host of them even before they came to Montgomery.
"Jonce" Hooper's friends, and probably Hooper himself, wrote to delegates from several of the states throughout January lobbying for them
to give him the position.[119] Hooper was broke, his newspaper barely
staying afloat and already for sale for some time now.[120] Worse, one of
his partners lay deathly ill, and the other had enlisted in a militia unit
and left town, so Hooper had to run and edit and write for the paper by
himself. The forty-five-year-old North Carolinian was wearing himself
out.[121] Even his friendly competition over at the *Advertiser* offices could
see him going downhill, and added their voice to the clamor for the
appointment.[122] The first gift of government patronage settled easily on
the ungainly editor, Stephens told his brother, "all according to previous arrangement."[123]

Indeed, the scramble for offices commenced even before the first
delegate set foot in Montgomery. The first piece of mail addressed to
an official of the anticipated new government came from Tennessee on
February 1, when Gideon Pillow of Tennessee addressed a plea for a
command to the "President of the Convention or Congress of Seceded
States," having no idea who that officer might be.[124] Pillow would have
to wait until there was someone to receive his letter. On the same train
with Stephens, Toombs, and the rest, came four other Georgians intent
on putting their names at the head of the list for secretary of the convention, doorkeeper, sergeant at arms, and messenger. "We had not the
face to ask these places for them," Tom Cobb admitted that night.
After all, Georgia had already just won the first tug over turning the
convention into a congress, and seeing his brother made its president.

The delegation must not appear too demanding. They sent three of the men back before they could unpack, and kept one for whom they got an appointment as assistant to Hooper.[125] Meanwhile, as Georgia disposed of these first faint hints of a future scramble for patronage, South Carolina's delegates sat unaccustomedly silent. "We prefer that our course should suffer no imputation of selfishness," one of Miles's friends said. South Carolina would seek no office for its delegates nor press any of her other public men.[126] "How different!" a cynical Tom Cobb declared that night.[127] But then he could not see into the mind of Robert Barnwell Rhett. Neither did he look very deeply inside his own.

By the end of the long day's discussions, Stephens clearly saw another obstacle that needed early settlement. Three of the state conventions, South Carolina, Mississippi, and Louisiana, instructed their delegates to vote as a bloc; the others had not. How could any ballot be taken in such a fashion? Voting must be all one way or another. Then too, as he observed the afternoon's discussions, Stephens concluded that despite a lot of legislative experience at the state and even national level being congregated here, most of these men were "green" when it came to making a congress actually run. No one knew what to do first. He suggested to Howell Cobb that one of their first acts on the morrow should be the appointment of a committee to draft rules of order governing their debates. Cobb agreed at once, but said nothing when Stephens asked that he not be appointed to the committee himself.[128] Then they went their separate ways to their rooms, their suppers, and their boardinghouses, some, like Tom Cobb, confidant that with things running so smoothly, they would get through their work, adjourn, and be back home in a fortnight.[129] This business of creating a nation need not be so difficult as they feared.

Behind them in the Exchange bar they left the newspapermen and other onlookers speculating wildly on the one subject not addressed, and cornering the remaining delegates to get their views. Who should be president? A New Orleans journalist heard more than enough for him to conclude that the man would certainly come from Georgia—a common expectation—while the second spot would go to Louisiana or Texas. The names Toombs, Cobb, and Stephens dominated the discussion, and several thought it would be a master stroke of policy to turn to Little Aleck. In fact, some of the South Carolina delegates—probably Keitt, Withers, and maybe Chesnut—even told him they favored Stephens. Such a move would be bound to conciliate the fears of the Border States, while bringing into the fold the conservative cooperationist element in all of the states. Perkins of Louisiana seemed a popular suggestion for vice president.[130]

An Atlanta reporter, obviously talking to different delegates, found it generally conceded that Howell Cobb should be the president, though he probably confused the presidency of the convention with that of the new nation itself.[131] But certainly some did speak of Cobb as a possibility for the chief executive, especially Boyce, Keitt, Withers, and even Rhett. Tom Cobb and Bartow also spoke loudly in his favor.[132] Toombs, too, garnered much mention, though chiefly from Georgia, and especially among Stephens, Crawford, and Nisbet. Keitt, too, thought well of him, as he seems to have thought well of almost everyone but Rhett.

Smith and the other Alabamians present were divided, and therefore not as vocal. The old line secessionists of their number favored native son Yancey, but then he was simply too radical for the Border States to swallow. Governor Moore's commissioners sent to Virginia back in December reported to him that Senators James Mason and R. M. T. Hunter of the Old Dominion actually feared that war must come from a Yancey presidency, even though Yancey himself never believed that secession would lead to conflict.[133] The more moderate delegates originally looked to Toombs, and perhaps a majority still did. But the ubiquitous F. M. Gilmer, Moore's chief commissioner to Virginia, also reported that Mason and Hunter were most impressed with another former Senator. Jefferson Davis's farewell speech from the Senate on January 21 made a profound impression, both for its conservatism and pacific intent, and by its moving, tearful eloquence. Also friends in the legislature in Richmond asserted that the commonwealth was looking to Alabama for direction.[134] Gilmer got the hint, if the senators intended one. "If Virginia wanted Davis for President," he concluded, "we wanted Davis." He sent word to Governor Moore, who told Yancey and the state convention, and the delegation. Those pledged to Yancey were freed by the fire-eater himself, though of course he still hoped that the convention as a whole might turn to him. Those more interested in Toombs were asked to be flexible.[135]

Thus Tom Cobb went to his room that night to write Marion that the "strongest current" appeared to be running for Davis, with Mississippi assertively behind him, several of the Alabamians tending in that direction, and Barnwell definitely in his favor, with Chesnut, Memminger, and Miles sounding friendly.[136] Anderson of Florida, though not vocal, also appeared to look to Davis.[137] Dill of the *Mercury* concluded the same, stating his belief as a positive assertion, and backing it by the fact that so many also talked of Davis for general-in-chief of a new Southern army that might have to retake Sumter and Pickens from their Federal garrisons. The forts would elect him.[138]

But nothing was certain this early, especially with so many delegates, chiefly in South Carolina and Alabama, not entirely settled, several speaking well of a number of candidates. "There seems to be a good deal of difficulty in settling down on any person," Tom Cobb observed.[139] Moreover, most of the delegates from Louisiana and Florida, and several from Mississippi and Alabama, had yet to arrive, and winds could shift with their coming. Up in their rooms in the Exchange, and back at Montgomery Hall, a small army of pens scratched the day's impressions on Governor Moore's best stationery. Mary Chesnut told her diary that "we are here in Montgomery to make a new confederacy,"[140] yet she felt anything but optimistic as she looked about at the delegates present. "Sleeping deadheads," she called them, men long forgotten or passed over. Instead of young and energetic nation builders, she feared that the state conventions had sent only worn out politicians trying to garner places for themselves.[141] As if continuing her thoughts, the reporter of the New Orleans *Daily Picayune* went on to say that "what may be the result of the gathering time will show."[142] Howell Cobb punctuated their musings by saying that "I feel confidant all will work out well in the end."[143]

Over in room number 6 at the Exchange another delegate saw it all differently, and drained his anger through his pen. The convention had no authority whatever to turn itself into a congress, much less to select presidents or any other officers. Only the states in their sovereignty could do that. Then there was the idea of taking the Constitution unaltered. It all reeked of reconstructionism. Mississippi did not even send any of her best statesmen to the meeting, and their proposal in the very first discussion that Davis should be president was an insult—though Rhett thought "it was but natural"—a clear attempt to preempt the field from other, more deserving men.[144] Besides, Davis was hardly sound on Southern rights, so far as Rhett was concerned. "Jefferson Davis and Mississippi have acted very meanly," he fumed to his son. "Instead of being here to give all their weight to the proceedings of the convention, they cook up offices for themselves, and send tools here to carry out their selfish policy," He doubted that any of the other delegations even thought of suggesting a man this early (certainly not South Carolina, he could grumble). He smelled great danger to the whole movement. Moreover, though they appeared solid on secession, he feared that

Toombs and Howell Cobb might be in on the reconstruction scheme, too. He even suspected some in his own delegation. "The poor South!" he exclaimed. "If I had no trust in God, I would despair, utterly."[145]

Terrified of the dreaded apparition of reconstruction, having finally taken the momentous step toward independence after all his years of struggle, Rhett saw the dashing of his own ambitions, and looked ahead to fear that "we will only have changed masters."[146] Already the night before their first convening, Rhett saw dangerous divisions on vital issues. They all came supposedly devoted to the ideal of a government without faction, but with the first gavel not yet sounded, a second "party" was born in the disappointed ambitions and fears of this one South Carolinian. It was yet to be seen if he would remain a party of one, or if more would be drawn to his opposition stance, as well as just how "loyal" that opposition would be. If in the end they did just change masters, no man as conservative as he could forget the admonition of an earlier president. Government was like a blazing fire, warned George Washington, "a dangerous servant and a terrible master."

CHAPTER FOUR

WE ARE A CONGRESS

———— ◄ ★ ►————

EVERY DAY AT DAWN Charles Barrell stepped outside his house to record the weather. He hardly needed instruments to tell him that the sky looked cloudy, nor that the temperature had dropped dramatically over the weekend, some twenty degrees since Saturday. This morning, Monday February 4, the thermometer registered thirty-four degrees, just above freezing. It was going to be a cold week.[1]

Little Aleck Stephens awoke after a wonderful night's sleep at Mrs. Cleveland's, helped perhaps by a good supper there late the evening before. He sat down to an excellent breakfast and then returned to his rooms to write letters. Montgomery's city code prohibited burning the fireplaces before nine o'clock, but now Pierce laid a jolly fire for his master.[2] Sitting with his feet to the flames and his pen in his hand put Stephens in a rosy mood as he passed the morning.[3] Soon enough came eleven o'clock. The convention was to meet at noon. Time for him to go.

The Georgian always presented an apparition in the winter. He donned a huge woolen overcoat that reached practically to his feet, and then almost disappeared beneath its great folds. When he stepped outside, as was his wont he wore his top hat pushed forward on his head and slightly to the left, which most people found gave him overall a remarkable appearance.[4] With the temperature up to forty degrees by now, his weak breath cast vapors of steam as he stepped out onto Montgomery Street and down a few doors to the post office to send his daily letter to brother Linton.[5] Then he turned around and started the half-mile walk to the state house. Once in Court Square, he stopped at the office of the Southern Telegraph Company on the second floor of the Winter Building, at Court and Commerce, to send a wire to Governor Brown. He was recommending a young man for a captaincy in the Georgia militia. Little Aleck played the patronage game, too.[6]

He found wide Market Street sandy and badly paved, but level at first, requiring no great effort until it began to incline at Perry. Thereafter with each succeeding block the walk grew steeper, but he hardly minded. The clouds had given way to bright sun, and on the clear, crisp air, he heard the hubbub of voices from every street corner. Clusters of townspeople gathered in the squares and at the intersections, and more people from the outlying country came in to join them, all abuzz over the historic meeting about to commence. By the time Stephens began puffing up the steepest part of Market past McDonough, streams of spectators walked beside and beyond him on their way to the state house.[7] It all set the city's innumerable dogs howling and barking in a canine chorus that announced their coming well before they crossed Bainbridge and climbed up the bank onto the ill-kept capitol lawn.[8]

As he climbed the steps of the front portico of the capitol, Stephens, like everyone before him, could look off to his left to see the flooding Alabama in the distance, and the steamers plying the river, one of which had delivered yet more of the Mississippi and Louisiana delegations this morning.[9] The Reverend Basil Manly, walking that same portico, looked out to see the whole bend in flood. "Our old river is honoring the occasion by exhibiting a specimen of what it can do," he quipped.[10] Stepping into the entrance hall, Stephens saw the doors that led to the supreme court straight ahead before he turned left and climbed the twenty-seven steps up the winding stair to the second floor. There he turned left again into the rotunda, looked up to see the underside of the dome two floors above, and saw the lower house hall to his right. He turned left once again, looking past anterooms on either side of the corridor leading to the north wing and the senate chamber now set aside for the provisional convention.[11] He strode across the unfinished wooden floor of the lobby, stained by more than a decade of tobacco juice, and through the doors.[12]

The chamber formed an elongated octagon, with the speaker's rostrum sitting directly across the hall from the only entrance.[13] Five days earlier, when the Alabama Senate adopted a unanimous resolution tendering their room to the convention, they instructed their doorkeeper to provide sufficient seating for delegates and visitors, and otherwise to make the room comfortable.[14] He did his work well. Ordinarily the white plaster walls lay bare and unornamented, but now they fairly flowered with patriotic hangings. Immediately to the left of the door hung a memorial listing the names of the Palmetto Regiment of

Mexican War fame, in honor of South Carolina. Next to it hung a painting of Washington's first inauguration, and beyond that another tribute to South Carolina and secession in a portrait of Calhoun. Next came one of Alabama's own, a picture of state historian Albert J. Pickett, followed by a favorite legislator, Dixon Lewis. Immediately behind the rostrum hung the prize, an original Gilbert Stuart portrait of George Washington on loan from the mother of one of the city's leading citizens. Alexander B. Clitherall. Andrew Jackson came next, then Yancey, Henry Clay, another nod to South Carolina with a scene of Francis Marion and his men in the swamps, and finally, to the far right of the door, Washington once more.[15] The local ladies of Montgomery had done their best to make the hall comfortable, too, by providing two tables groaning with fruit, bread, and cold meats. They intended to replenish the buffet every day while the convention sat, and the food was there for any and all, including spectators.[16]

Long before noon the crowd started gathering, mostly men, but with a good representation of well appointed ladies as well, and fortunately very few of the small boys who usually turned any public meeting into a clatter of rolling marbles and croaking frogs.[17] The doorkeeper knew to expect crowds. After all, besides this new convention, the legislature still sat, and so did the state convention, as well as the supreme court. Many of those other statesmen would be here on the opening day to watch, too.[18] Most, especially the ladies, climbed up to the third floor gallery that almost completely ringed the hall to sit on wooden benches behind its cast iron rail. The rest of the crowd shared the floor with the delegates themselves, and to keep them from interfering with the proceedings, the doorkeeper erected a low screen along the gilded Corinthian columns that supported the balcony, separating them from the statesmen.[19] The reporters clustered below the speaker's desk, their number now swollen to more than twenty, while out on the floor a fair proportion of the spectators had the look of office seekers about them.[20]

In the last minutes before noon the delegates moved about from desk to desk, shaking hands, exchanging smiles, renewing old acquaintances. Patton Anderson approached Stephens to introduce himself at last, and of course the Georgian remembered once he looked at him carefully. "A very inter[est]ing clever gentleman," Stephens at once recalled.[21] James Harrison from Mississippi finally arrived after the overnight trip upriver from Mobile. With the Tombigbee bridge still out it had taken him two days longer than necessary to get here, and two more of his delegation were still absent.[22] Tom Cobb, chatting with Barnwell, and ever the devout Baptist, claimed that today's proceedings owed their inception to a denominational convention back in 1844 when the Southern Baptists finally split away from their Northern brethren.[23] As the greeting and conviviality progressed, they lost track of the clock above the speaker's desk until finally the gavel called them to order at almost twelve-thirty.

So now it was to begin. Thirty-seven of them sat out on the floor. The Georgians were all there. So were the South Carolinians. Alabama missed two of its number, old Thomas Fearn and David Lewis. Florida still waited for Jackson Morton to arrive, but James B. Owens now sat beside Anderson. Louisiana needed only Charles Conrad to complete its complement, and Mississippi missed "Jap" Campbell and Alex Clayton.

By any conceivable measurement, they composed a remarkable assembly. When complete they would include forty-three men of substance and stature. Alabama fielded both the youngest and the oldest—Curry at thirty-five and Fearn at double his age, seventy-one. When the thirty-one-year-old Campbell arrived he would take the honors for youth. In age they averaged just over forty-seven. Thirty-three of them were lawyers, including every member of the Georgia delegation. Seventeen were planters, some combining that with the law or other professions. One practiced medicine, and three others held professorships. A startling thirty-nine of them looked back to some form of university education, and most held degrees. Two came from Harvard, three each from Yale and the College of New Jersey at Princeton, four from the University of Virginia, and nine from the University of Georgia. All but eight were slave owners, from Toombs who reported owning none to the 1860 census, but now brought a servant with him, and Colin McRae with a mere two, to Duncan Kenner's small army of 473. Interestingly, among those owning none were some of the most outspoken slavery men like Keitt, and Miles, whose father owned several dozen, however.

Not surprisingly, most of them were Democrats, twenty at least and there were six old-line Whigs. The rest were from the intermediate parties between that came and went during the 1850s. Reflecting most eloquently of all the complexion of their constituents, only twenty-four of them had been pro-secession prior to their states going out of the Union. The remaining nineteen either favored moderation and cooperation, or else opposed secession outright. Most telling of all was their

accumulated experience in public affairs: six judges, twelve state legislators, twelve congressmen, seven senators, one governor, and two cabinet secretaries.[24]

Never in its history had the South seen such an assembly of brains,
accomplishment, statesmanship, and property. Rarely if ever was a
greater diversity of opinion represented nor, at the same time, a firmer
resolve for unanimity and harmony. Here as spokesmen for a movement grown out of an unwillingness to look for further compromise
with the North, almost to a man they coveted compromise with each
other. The days ahead would also reveal their ambitions, the scheming
of some, and the would-be demagoguery of a few. But taken in their all,
they were the flower of Southern culture and society. If *they* could not
build a government, none could.

It all went according to the program set the night before. As leader
of the host delegation, William P. Chilton took the chair to call them
to order, and then moved that Barnwell be made acting president of
the body. After unanimous approval, Barnwell assumed the rostrum,
offered a few remarks of thanks for the honor thus conferred, and then
called on the Reverend Manly to bless their proceedings.

Manly approached full of dread. It was the most difficult task he had
ever performed. Through much of the previous night he struggled with
his words, thinking it improper and somehow unpious to prepare his
prayer ahead of time, and yet fearful that words might fail him should
he speak extemporaneously. In the end, he wrote, and now as they
bowed their heads, he raised his aged voice to "thou God of the uni-
verse." He granted that if somehow, in what they were about to do,
they stood in violation of any binding compact with the North, then
they could not hope for His blessing. "Oh, thou heart-searching God,
we trust that thou sees we are pursuing those rights which were guaranteed to us by the solemn covenants of our fathers, and which were
cemented by their blood." In tones sometimes scarcely audible he
begged that they have wisdom, calmness, and soundness of mind, and
perhaps looking at many among the spectators, added the prayer that
they might not yield to the lust for spoils and patronage. So long as the
sun and moon should last, he begged that the "Union of these States"
might exist. "Let truth, and justice, and equal rights be decreed to our
government."[25] The "Amen" said, Manly returned to his seat, convinced that he had failed to capture the spirit of the moment, when in
fact he was the first to sound a recurring peal in this body when he proclaimed that they were not revolutionaries, not rebels, but reformers.[26]

Barnwell declared it time for them to establish their permanent organization. They chose a temporary secretary, and then each of the delegations came forward alphabetically by state to present their credentials to the secretary and sign a roll of the convention. Now it was Rhett's turn to take the floor to call for the election of their permanent president. On behalf of his delegation he offered Howell Cobb and moved that his election be by acclamation. Immediately upon the unanimous acceptance, applause rippled through the hall and the gallery as Rhett, Walker, and Anderson walked to Cobb's seat for the formality of notifying him of his election, and to escort him to the chair.[27]

As he stood to make his acceptance speech, Cobb impressed one of the reporters present as "a fat, pussy, round-faced fellow, who, although he has been Secretary of the Treasury, looks much more like spending money for the comfort of the inner man, than finding out where it comes from."[28] His remarks, thought Manly and others, were brief and pertinent.[29] They all knew why they sat before him today. He had no need to rehearse for them the causes that brought them there. It sufficed merely to say that the separation now made from the old Union "is perfect, complete and perpetual." Applause roared across the hall before he could continue. Now they must extend their hands to their remaining sister states still in the Union, those "identified with us in interest, feeling and institutions." At the same time, they must strive for peace and amity with their one-time colleagues in the Union now behind them, as well as with the world at large. "Our responsibilities, gentlemen, are great," he concluded. Speaking squarely to those like Rhett who yesterday opposed doing anything more than consulting, he went on to admonish them all to "assume all the responsibility which may be necessary for the successful completion of the great work committed to our care." Doing that, and convinced of the justice of their cause, "we will this day inaugurate for the South a new era of peace, security and prosperity."[30]

That done, and after the applause quieted, Cobb turned to electing a permanent secretary. Chilton nominated Hooper, and Toombs moved that it be approved by acclamation, all according to program. The ungainly "Jonce" marched forward to his desk and nearly tipped it over when he sat down. If any chuckled, it would not be the first time he made men laugh. Those here who did not know him personally still knew him by reputation as one of the South's most popular humorists, all for a shifty character he had created years before named "Simon

Suggs." Everyone present now saw what an observer called "one of the ugliest phizes" in creation, animated by a constant chewing on a plug of tobacco. Once he got the quid out of his mouth and some *"quid pro quo"* in it, though, they expected him to suit just fine.[31]

That left only the appointment of a doorkeeper and messenger, and then Stephens arose for the first time to move for the appointment of a committee of five to prepare the rules of the convention. The motion carried, but then Cobb ignored Little Aleck's request of the night before by putting him in charge of the group, to include Keitt, Curry, the newly arrived Harrison, and John Perkins of Louisiana. They adjourned. Until they had their rules of conduct, there was nothing else for them to do.[32]

As soon as the gavel came down, the spectators flocked around the delegates, who themselves arose to congratulate one another on getting through the first day, though it took barely an hour. One Alabamian in the audience complained that this was "only a great conference," not the congress he expected to see, but applauded the earnestness and solemnity of the delegates.[33] Cobb felt genuinely touched when even some of his old foes like Stephens, Hill, Wright, Kenan, and others, came to compliment him on his brief address. The unanimity he felt gave him added heart.[34] The reporters rushed out in what one called "a regular *hades* hurry" for the Southern Telegraph office on the second floor of the Winter Building on Court Square to get accounts of the proceedings on the wires. Already some suspected that the day's session smelled a bit choreographed, too arranged for the interest of appearance. Pritchard worried that the real debates to come would be kept largely behind closed doors, and vowed to go to war to get them made public.[35]

For most of the delegates, it was back to the Exchange for the balance of the day, much of it to be spent in renewed discussion in the lobby and bar. An ill Charles Conrad arrived in the afternoon to complete the Louisiana delegation, while others thought they began detecting an assumed dominance by the ten-member Georgia group, the largest in the convention.[36] A South Carolinian visiting in Montgomery recognized their strength, and heard more of it from Chesnut.[37] Tom Cobb positively bubbled with hubris. "The Ga. delegation has already the most powerful influence in this body," he boasted to his wife. The "Georgia project" had won—or bullied—its way past the objections of Rhett and others, brother Howell held the presidency of the convention now, and stood a good chance of taking the national chief executive when the time came. Inflated with self-importance, he assured Marion that he and his delegation "will undoubtedly control the concern."[38]

Cobb would have felt a little less confidant had he sat in on some of the conversations then buzzing in the hotel corridors. The names of Cobb, Toombs, Stephens, and Yancey slipped from the speculations of hundreds. South Carolina was to get the vice presidency, said one.[39] Others still spoke of Davis, even though word continued to spread that the Mississippian would not want the presidency. From far-off South Carolina influential men wrote to Howell Cobb and others repeating what they heard—though not from Davis himself—that he preferred to be general-in-chief.[40] Stephens heard such expressions everywhere around him, and believed he saw a universal desire to respect that preference.[41] Yet others thought differently. That afternoon Dill of the *Mercury* mailed a report that "I think there is no doubt that the Hon. JEFFERSON DAVIS will be chosen the President of the Confederacy,"[42] a sentiment already being echoed that same evening in far-off Mississippi and elsewhere.[43]

The appearance of contentment and harmony wore thin as the afternoon progressed. With all of the Alabama delegates now present but Fearn, and having time to speak to members of the state convention and legislature, the rest began to appreciate the dangerous divisions in the state. Many spoke of a sullen minority still opposed to secession, and now those divisions showed in the Alabama delegation itself. "A very bad state of things," lamented Tom Cobb. Then there was South Carolina. All afternoon Rhett and others raised major and minor technicalities over the powers of the convention, and even over their privileges as delegates. Rhett argued strenuously against conducting any deliberations in secret session. Others hinted that the convention should assume military powers even before there was a president, and take control of the growing confrontation in Charleston harbor. "The breakers ahead of us are beginning to appear," Cobb groaned, "and I fear we shall not be as harmonious at the beginning as We expected."[44] Their thin veneer of unanimity was curling at the edges, and starting to show some cross grain beneath.

Aleck Stephens had no time for listening or grumbling. After appointing an hour for his colleagues on the rules committee to meet him at Mrs. Cleveland's, he went back to his rooms to start work on a draft. Fortunately the Georgian knew the rules of the old House and Senate in Washington pretty much by heart, though he may well have brought copies with him. Working from these and a manual written by Thomas Jefferson he produced a simple set of thirty-one articles before the committee arrived.

To get around the problem of some state delegations being mandated to vote as a unit, and the others not, he provided that *all* states should have one vote in all balloting. The yeas and nays might be demanded, but only for the record, and a simple majority should decide in all matters, which at the moment meant four out of the six states present. If a state's delegates split evenly on an issue, their vote was nullified, and in any tally of the states a tie meant defeat of the issue in question. Moreover, any number of delegates from any state could constitute a quorum for determining its vote, even as few as one. Members were to remain silent while others spoke, and each would be limited to speaking twice on any measure unless a majority of the members present allowed otherwise. When speaking, a delegate should stand at his desk, and be seated when finished. Cobb was to decide all points of order, and enforce the rules, but could participate in the debates himself if he wished. No one was to use objectionable language.

Stephens established the daily order of business by calling first for the reading of the journal for the previous day, the dispensing of old business, a call of the states alphabetically for presentation of memorials and other business, followed by committee reports, and then the day's calendar of business. Every measure should receive three readings before a vote, and amendments might be offered only after the second reading. As for privacy in their deliberations, he provided that Cobb should decide where newspapermen might sit during deliberations, and if at any point a member moved that they go into secret session, upon its seconding Cobb could immediately clear the hall of all but members and officers like Hooper. Anything relating to defense or foreign relations must be so handled. Disclosure to outsiders of anything said or done behind closed doors could bring expulsion.

Stephens felt some particular pleasure with his handling of the issue of the "previous question." He dispensed with it entirely, for it stopped debate, prevented any further amendment, and forced a vote on all the pending amendments to a measure in their order of appearance, and then a vote on the resulting measure itself. For it he substituted "the question," which when called and sustained by a majority, produced a vote on any motion currently in debate, without inhibiting further amendment, and saving considerable time.[45]

That evening Keitt, Harrison, and Perkins came to his parlor to go over the draft. Curry pleaded illness and did not appear, which failed to impress Stephens, who always felt ill to some degree yet still did his duty. Some discussion followed, and others proposed minor variations here and there, but virtually the entire set of rules met their approval. Well after half past nine they took a final vote as a committee, accepted the rules as drafted and amended, and Stephens bundled himself in coat and hat once more to walk down Commerce Street to the *Advertiser* offices of Shorter and Reid. From his own pocket he paid them to print and deliver fifty copies before noon the next day.[46] That done, he walked back to his lodgings, a fair day's work behind him and, he hoped, a good prospect before them. A few blocks away the Reverend Manly stared at his diary, stumbling for words to record the momentous day. "Thus has been inaugurated this important movement," he concluded. "May the Father of Lights guide the whole!"[47]

It dawned even colder, below freezing, the next morning, making Stephens appreciate his cozy fire all the more as he wrote his letters and occasionally peered out the frosted windows into the clear sunlight.[48] Well before noon a messenger came with the printed rules and, having them in hand, the Georgian again trudged up Market to the state house, this time well in advance of the hour of convening. Once in the chamber, he placed on each delegate's desk the tiny pamphlet somewhat redundantly titled "Government of this Congress, Rules for the government of this Congress."[49]

An even larger crowd poured into the chamber before noon today, many of them ladies come to see the anticipated first full day of debate and to hear some of the South's finest orators in action. From the balcony they blew kisses to some whom they knew down on the floor.[50] Other delegates walked up the steps to speak to them, while more greedily tore into the cold buffet before Cobb sounded the gavel. Following a prayer, the new rules became the first order of business and achieved a speedy passage with only insignificant alteration. Seated bent over his desk, shoulders contracted, his bony limbs outlined by his limply hanging clothes, Stephens struck those who saw him from the rear at first as but a boy.[51] A reporter looking at him thought of fevers, agues, swamps, and malaria. "What in the name of wonder did they send such a man here for," one wondered. Where *did* he come from?"[52] When he stood, and especially when he spoke, they could see that this apparition was a man—"every inch a man."[53] And now, in rising to address a question on one of the rules, he became the first to assert a *de facto* reality that Rhett and some others still wished to deny. "We are a Congress," he told them.[54]

There was little more to do. Nisbet suggested that the clergy of Montgomery be asked to provide a different minister each day to offer a prayer. Curry, well again, moved that they appoint Shorter and Reid their official printers. Stephens proposed that they set noon as their regular hour of meeting. And then, prepared for this moment, Memminger offered resolutions that Cobb appoint a committee to frame a provisional government, appointing two members from each delegation to the convention. (Quickly Little Aleck arose again to move that the word "convention" where it appeared in Memminger's resolutions be replaced with "Congress.") Bartow then stood to offer a substitute to Memminger's resolutions, and after him Barry of Mississippi suggested yet another. Sensing that a real debate was about to begin, and knowing of the serious current of division flowing beneath their calm public surface, Perkins jumped from his seat and moved that they clear the house and go into closed session.[55]

The clock barely touched quarter of one as the startled spectators filed out. They came for a show, and got less than an hour, none of it of real interest or consequence. The ladies especially grumbled audibly, virtually everyone expressing outrage.[56] The reporters made an even greater demonstration. "What a disappointment," cried a Mobile correspondent. Fearing that this might presage the future order of things, he suggested that all candidates for election to this body henceforward ought to declare themselves in advance as either for or against secret sessions.[57] Basil Manly, however, though disappointed, supported the decision. The delegates needed to be protected against the "army of *Reporters*," he said, and believed that by deliberating in secret men could exchange views, and change their positions, without fear of public recrimination.[58]

For the next four hours they sat with doors closed.[59] Now the motions came out. Tom Cobb sought passage of resolutions specifically declaring this congress a fully empowered legislative body for the new government until regular elections could be held, the so-called "Georgia program." Boyce tried to curb that with a counterresolution that stopped with a call for elections, and then Memminger managed to have Cobb's operative proposition eliminated entirely, with only Georgia and Louisiana supporting it. Cobb simply withdrew the remainder of his resolutions. Finally Memminger's original offering passed intact, only Georgia voting against. But Barry of Mississippi kept the door open for the plan that his delegation had joined Georgia in supporting during the Exchange conversations two days before. He offered resolutions, not for adoption by the congress, but only for referral to the new committee to be formed, and for their consideration. A provisional constitution should be framed based on the old Constitution. The Congress should select a president and vice president. This done, a convention should be called to frame a permanent constitution more at leisure, and subject to new circumstances presented by the possible joining of more states. Most importantly, he suggested that on the adoption of the provisional document, the several states should be asked to send regularly elected or appointed senators and congressmen, but that until they should convene, this body would assume to "take such legislative action as the public safety may require." Since there was nothing to vote on, South Carolina could not oppose Barry's resolves.

This done, they agreed to appoint official stenographers to record their debates, while Stephens moved the keeping of two separate journals, one for the public sessions, and the other for closed-door debates. Then, just before their five o'clock adjournment, each delegation put forward its two members for the provisional government committee. Alabama announced Walker and Smith. Anderson and Owens—the only delegates present from their state—represented Florida. Georgia selected Stephens and Nisbet, while Louisiana put forward Perkins and Kenner. Mississippi offered Barry and Harris, and South Carolina appointed Memminger and would have added Rhett had he not been ill that day. Fortunately, Barnwell would go in his stead.[60]

Now they were making progress. Even the *Mercury* noted their high spirits, and Tom Cobb felt much better. "I am more hopeful of harmony today," he wrote Marion. "I think we shall go through the ordeal with a bold and united front." "There will be no wavering."[61] Even Boyce agreed with him there. No one spoke of compromising with the old Union, or of going back. He expected a new constitution almost exactly like the old one. "Independence is the only thing thought of," he said that evening. "We will act promptly & vigorously." Looking back on his years in the old House of Representatives, he almost gleefully declared that "I cant describe to you how much pleasanter it feels to sit in a Congress where you are surrounded by friends."[62]

Predictably, not everyone felt so joyful. Bob Smith thought the use of secret session fully justified, agreeing with Manly that it allowed for frank and full discussion, free from the fetters of previous opinions, and prevented posturing for the galleries.[63] But over in room number 6 the mood was black, and not just because Rhett felt ill.[64] *He* should have been appointed to the constitutional committee, not Barnwell. The sudden profusion of schemes for organization, one today even from another South Carolina delegate, left him more than chagrined. "Why are all these expedients brought forward?" he ranted.[65] Then, worst of all, was this secret session business. Conscience, duty, and policy all demanded that the people be kept informed. He would battle this secrecy as if it were a living enemy. For the furtherance of his reputation and ambitions, it *was* his enemy. Almost with disgust he wrote back to Charleston that night that "it is very doubtful whether you have not committed a great error in proposing any Provisional Government at all."[66]

For the constitutional committee, the workday was just beginning. After a hurried dinner at six o'clock they convened in the parlor at Mrs. Cleveland's and worked until midnight. There was much with which they could dispense, all being agreed that the United States Constitution was to be their model, indeed, their ideal. Their reverence for the document approached a religion for most. Indeed, in seceding from the Union *they* were the keepers of the original flames of 1776 and 1787. The overwhelming majority of that sacred charter could be adopted *verbatim* and they need not lose time on those portions. But even before coming to the changes necessary, they had to address the issue that so quickly sent them into secret session that afternoon. Just what were *they* to be—a constitutional convention or, as Stephens so insistently called them, a congress. It was the February 3 Exchange debate once more, now brought out by the afternoon resolutions by Tom Cobb and Stephen Hale. Harris, among others, argued Mississippi's position once more that they lacked any authority to constitute themselves a legislature. Indeed, the instructions from their state convention quite specifically limited what they could do.[67] Anderson of Florida argued the opposite, supporting Stephens and Nisbet in asserting that time demanded they take definitive action now.[68]

Then Smith of Alabama joined the discussion persuasively. "The required Provisional Government could only be framed, so as to respond to the high purposes aimed at, by the exercise of legislative powers," he argued. Framing a constitution was only one part of a government. Someone must be able to make laws, and in the crisis facing them, they could not wait for ratifications and elections. "To be effectually done it had to spring into strength," he went on, "and to spread as if by magic touch, confidence to the pursuits of our people." For his part, he felt no doubt at all of their warrant to assume those powers.[69]

Smith's may have been the most forceful arguments of all, and once more they were backed by both Alabama's and Georgia's knowledge of the deep divisions within their peoples. Stephens, Nisbet, Smith, and Walker united in arguing that they simply could not afford to risk an election at home.[70] Members from the other states, too, knew those fears, especially Mississippi. Only the South Carolinians expressed no anxiety about taking their government before the people in the polls.[71]

Finally at some point in their discussions, and perhaps by a majority vote, they settled the question. "We yielded to the necessity," said Harris.[72] They began wording Article 1, Section 1: "All legislative powers herein granted shall be vested in this Congress now assembled, until otherwise ordained."[73] The greatest hurdle lay behind them, at least for this committee, and Cobb and Hale, when they found out, could be pleased that parts of their resolutions survived in spirit.

By contrast, the rest was, while not easy, hardly as charged. Memminger brought out his plan for a constitution as already published, and with that and the Constitution before them, they proceeded article by article.[74] It was exhausting. At midnight they adjourned, to meet again the next morning at ten o'clock, and Little Aleck stumbled to bed. "I shall wear myself out here," he told Linton. He feared that it might not do any good. "I do regret having come."[75]

His mood was not much improved the next morning as he scrambled to answer a few letters after breakfast. "These are revolutionary times," he mused. "We are now perfectly at sea and enveloped in fog." He hoped to get the new government under way and based on sound constitutional principles, but feared to speculate on its fortune. That depended far less on the ship of state than upon its crew, "and particularly those in command." "*There*," he lamented, "*lies the trouble.*" It was the leaders who drove the old ship on the rocks, and he had seen more than enough of the Rhetts and the Yanceys and even the Cobbs—Tom at least—to fear it could happen again. "We have more to apprehend from the ambition and selfishness of our public leaders than from all other sources combined." Those other sources worried him, too, of course. "We shall have a collision with the North," of that he was certain. "How it will come I do not see. But . . . it will come. . . . "[76] As he slowly walked up Market toward the capitol, the enormity of what they were about seemed overwhelming.

Others awaking with fewer responsibilities—or a lesser grasp of affairs—saw only the beautiful, crisp sunny day before them. With the whole morning ahead before the congress convened at noon, Tom

Cobb shopped for a dress in the tiny dot pattern that Marion liked so much. He missed her terribly, and resolved never to leave her again for any congress or convention. The shopping and the beautiful day cleared his mind of some of its apprehension of the day before. Moreover, the streets teemed with people who continued flocking to Montgomery for the congress, not knowing how little of it they would be able to witness. A flurry of excitement swept every main street,[77] and one native reporter declared that "a dog fight, a scared horse, a smoking chimney, or a runaway negro, is all that is necessary to put the people in a stir."[78] The streets and hotels also showed the influx of office seekers that increased every day, and already attracted the disapproving notice of citizens, correspondents, and congressmen alike.[79] Still Cobb's mood remained optimistic. "I cannot help feeling that the Giver of Light smiles kindly on our efforts," he said.[80]

The constitutional committee met at ten o'clock and continued their discussions until the delegates and the crowds gathered for the noon session.[81] Among those walking into the hall was another delegate, Jackson Morton of Florida.[82] That completed the state's delegation, and left the Congress as a whole missing just Clayton and Campbell of Mississippi.[83] Morton need not have hurried, for this day's public session proved even shorter than the day before. Indeed, the opening prayer ran longer than anything else. The North Carolinians presented their credentials and took seats on the floor as observers, and then Memminger asked for and received permission for his committee to absent themselves from the public sessions while they continued working on the constitution. He expected to be able to finish with it that day and present it to them on the morrow. There was nothing more to do, not even a secret session, for without a constitution they really did not exist.[84]

Now and long into the evening, with only a break for supper, the so-called Committee of Twelve continued their work on the provisional constitution. As they got to know each other better in the total immersion of these long hours, impressions formed among the seven Democrats and five former Whigs.[85] Balding, genial Harris at once impressed Stephens and the others. He spoke rarely, and when he did never for more than a few minutes, "but every word is a ball that seldom fails to have effect." "When he spoke," said a colleague, "he had something to say that was worth hearing." Once prone to intemperance, Harris had given up the drink, making his insights all the sharper.[86] His colleague Barry spoke more often—too often. Considered by other Mississippians as more brilliant than profound, his arguments suffered from too many words and too little substance despite his fascinating manners.[87]

Kenner stood out. Little Aleck found him sharp and shrewd. He never spoke without having a point. Moreover, he showed system and method in presenting his views, making them the more cogent.[88] He kept an eye to the Border States in all his suggestions, and on the need for the new confederation to include *all* of the slave states if it were to be strong and prosperous. Moreover, he fully appreciated the delicacy of the slavery issue not only to Virginia, Kentucky, and the rest, but even to the seceded states. Louisiana's wealth came from sugar and from the river trade, both of which bound her more closely to other river states than to those here represented. With them she shared only slavery.[89] Though they disagreed on the issue of war, Kenner being confident of peace when he arrived in Montgomery, Stephens still concluded that he was "a very superior man in [every] way." And Kenner was starting to change his mind about that war business.[90]

Stephens thought Memminger a man of intelligence and good sense, though rather prone to make too many mistakes through carelessness. But everyone loved Barnwell. "I like him very much," Stephens confessed. The South Carolinian showed tact, precision, candor, and best of all, brevity. He was a diplomat. Everyone had seen already that he alone of his delegation could really get along with his cousin while avoiding any acknowledgment of Rhett's presumed leadership.[91] "Mr Barnwell is one of the nicest old gentlemen that ever I met with," said one of the Mississippians,[92] and Tom Cobb found him to be "full of politeness and modesty."[93] Even among his own troubled delegation Barnwell enjoyed respect for his character, his self-effacing manner, his calm and sense of balance.[94] Barnwell returned the compliment so far as Little Aleck was concerned. "I like Stephens," he said, "better than anyone of them." Barnwell thought him courageous and frank, though he also found him "rather changeable however in his movements and not without a spice of policy, which seems engrained in a Georgian."[95]

In their work today they blocked out the form of their provisional constitution. Regarding it from the first as a temporary document designed only to get the government functioning, they scarcely worried about the organization of its constituent parts as they sifted through the old United States Constitution. Theirs would have but six articles, each taken as literally as possible from the Constitution. Only in

Article I did they do heavy violence to the older document. Recognizing the exigencies of their own existence, they virtually eliminated all of the lengthy Sections 2 and 3 regarding congressional organization, eligibility, and elections. That could wait for the permanent constitution. At Stephens's urging they scratched from Section 5 the prohibition against members of Congress also holding cabinet positions, a pet notion of Stephens, who much admired the British parliamentary system in which all cabinet ministers also sat in the Commons.[96]

They made changes in fiscal policy. Congress was to be prohibited from enacting taxes or duties in order to promote any particular industry. Moreover, import duties on goods from foreign nations were to be capped at fifteen percent except in time of war, but with the proviso that Congress could change that and regulate export duties on Southern goods as well in a "most favored nation" policy. Europe and King Cotton were on their minds. And Stephens introduced another paragraph to address an old wound in the South. Under the Constitution, appropriations had to originate in the House, and in past decades this had been abused by Northerners appropriating funds for so-called "internal improvements" that seemed to favor only certain states, at the expense of all. In this constitution, Congress could make no appropriation except on the request of the president or his cabinet heads.

Then there was the matter of slavery. They prohibited the African slave trade. The prohibition came from no opposition to slavery itself, but rather from a long held belief that with some four million slaves in the South now, more than a sufficient population existed to provide for any future needs in such property. Having no carrying trade of their own, Southerners also resisted becoming dependent upon Yankee merchants for providing them with anything, including slaves, and moreover feared that the introduction of more blacks from outside only served to reduce the value of those already held. As a gloved fist raised toward the Border States, they also decided to empower Congress to prohibit trade with other slave states not members of this confederation. It was probably with no sense of irony at all that immediately after the slave provisions, they appended the old Bill of Rights along with the Eleventh Amendment.

Pointedly they left out the next amendment that fixed the method of selecting a president. Considerable debate among the members turned around whether to have an electoral college or not, and even on the advisability of general elections for the presidency, some preferring selection by Congress or by the legislatures. This one they put off for

the permanent constitution. Meanwhile, the provisional president
would be selected by the delegates here, one state, one vote, as in all
other matters, and here they also fixed his salary at $25,000 annually.
His appointive powers remained intact, though instead of requiring
consent of a senate—which did not yet exist here—the Congress as a
whole would ratify his choices. All of the new Article II covered the
president and his powers, but included a most significant addition.
The Congress, by a two-thirds majority, should have the power to
declare a president unable to perform his duties, and a vice president
as well, and in that event appoint an officer to act as president temporarily. Clearly they felt that the power of the executive could grow
too large, and wanted Congress to be able to remove him by means
other than impeachment. On the other hand, faced with the example
of the pathetic Buchanan, they also needed a mechanism that allowed
them to remove immediately a man truly unfit for the office.

Their third article embraced the judiciary and adopted the model
almost *verbatim*. Suiting their actions to the moment, they also provided that Congress could legislate to transfer actions then pending in
United States courts to its own jurisdiction. They added paragraphs
that designated each state a judicial district, with a presidentially
appointed judge to supervise both the district and all its lower circuit
courts. Appeals to the Supreme Court could be taken directly from the
circuit bench, bypassing the district level, every trial lawyer's dream.
Not surprisingly, ten of the twelve on the committee were lawyers.
Moreover, the district judges would compose the Supreme Court.
Significantly, that court could sit only when and where called upon by
Congress. Just as they sought to limit the power of the president, the
Committee of Twelve also looked back on bitter past experience with a
Supreme Court that interpreted law against Southern interests.

Article IV dropped the old provision regarding persons in service
escaping to other states, and replaced it with a strong fugitive slave law
modeled on the provision in the Compromise of 1850. Any escaped
slave must be given up on demand to the party from whom he fled.
And in the case of abduction or "forcible rescue" of a slave, the state in
which it took place must make full restitution to the owner. At the
same time, it also eliminated completely the mechanism for admitting
new states and territories, an issue that caused much of the turmoil
that led them all here in the first place. Even now disagreement on
who should be admitted, and how, divided them. Some even wondered
if free states from the old Union might not apply for admission. The

fear of reconstruction coming in by the back door, through their own constitution, haunted many delegates. They must leave this matter for the permanent constitution.

Virtually cementing the powers of this congress, they limited their Article V to a single provision. Only Congress, by a simple two-thirds vote, could amend this constitution at any time. There would be no ratification by the state legislatures.

Finally in the sixth and last article they addressed themselves to the practicalities of their immediate situation. Any debts incurred by the states in the act of severing ties with the United States should be assumed by the confederacy. That government itself should also attempt immediately to settle all outstanding differences with the old Union over property and debt—Forts Sumter and Pickens lay uppermost in their minds—and they declared their intention to do so fairly and in good faith. They also provided that "until otherwise provided by the Congress" Montgomery should be the capital. And then they closed with an invitation to other slave states to join with them.[97]

By the time the committee adjourned, close to midnight, the document was complete—hardly perfect, but sufficient until a permanent constitution could be framed at more leisure. Many of the provisions in Memminger's original plan did not make inclusion, particularly one calling for the congress to elect a general-in-chief. Indeed, all of the members of the committee found some pet notion left out, but they had fulfilled their mandate, and done it well.

The Committee of Twelve missed more than a fair, almost balmy evening as they met into the night. With no secret session to keep them after the adjournment, the rest of the delegates were free to give themselves to Montgomery society, and many of the more distinguished citizens stood well prepared to vie for their company. Few could match John G. Winter, owner of the Winter Building among others. Builder of roads, an iron works, a mill, owner of a bank, the agreeable, white-haired old man was almost a millionaire, and set a delightful table.[98] So did Tom Watts, the forty-two-year-old attorney worth nearly half a million, whose shining black eyes and perpetual smile betokened his geniality.[99]

Colonel William Pollard gave excellent dinner parties, though with a certain South Carolinian smugness, Mary Chesnut thought she could do better.[100] He even kept seven acres of grapes under cultivation south of the city for making his own Madeira and still catawba wines.[101] James Ware offered dinners to whole state delegations at his Perry and High

Streets mansion.[102] And then there was Judge Bibb. Benajah S. Bibb—affectionately dubbed Titus Pomponius Atticus Bibb by a newsman who thought his attire dated at least to Roman times—sooner or later entertained everyone. He and wife Sophia were especially fond of the Cobb family, old friends, but the sixty-five-year-old judge opened his doors and larder to all.[103] Tall, dignified, cleanly shaven, he wore a frilled and ruffled shirt, white cravat, a high-pocketed coat almost from the era of George III, knee breeches and short boots with dangling tassels. One visitor marveled that "he has not the pig-tail and cocked hat to complete the costume."[104] He may have looked a bit peculiar, but with a fortune of over a quarter million, he was no fool, and made excellent company.

Moreover, Montgomery society boasted all the amenities for entertaining dignitaries like these newborn congressmen. Their halls, vestibules, and parlors exhibited beautiful frescoes by Mr. F. Schmidt of Market Street.[105] Their pantries bulged with the finest foods and delicacies available, especially since everything fresh came daily on the Mobile steamer. Half a dozen stores offered seafood barely a day out of the water, and fresh oysters in Montgomery quickly attracted almost religious adoration from the delegates, appearing in every dish conceivable.[106] Best of all were the spirits. Glackmeyer and Robinson, the druggists down on Market—Mr. Schmidt kept his studio on their second floor—stocked only the very best domestic whiskies and even finer imported vintages. His champagnes featured Moet et Chandon, Mumm, and Heidsick, while his Bordeaux surpassed anything available elsewhere: Chateau Margeaux, the even better Chateau Latour, and several cases of sublime Chateau Lafitte 1834.[107]

No wonder the delegates seldom refused an invitation. In the offing, Montgomery took a close look at the men about to govern it and the rest of the South. Miles of South Carolina seemed at once the most aristocratic, his manners flawless, his appearance perfect despite the stoop, and his attention to the young ladies most gallant.[108] His colleague Boyce, by contrast, paid hardly a care to his dress.[109] The entire Louisiana delegation impressed Montgomery, both for their manliness and their tolerant views of the opinions of others. Best of all, at table they found something other to talk about than the day's work in the state house.[110] Instead, parlor talk could revolve around the coming cotton or sugar crop, old times in Washington, their families—especially Tom Cobb's brilliant daughter. For their part the Montgomeryites brought to the talk their own local insights, and occasionally the bit of juicy gossip, or lurid tales like the previous week's dreadful tragedy when William English of Baldwin County went mad, slit his children's throats, then killed himself.[111]

Mary Chesnut complained that too many of them were Baptist and Methodist ministers. "A bad mixture of trades," that and politics, she muttered.[112] But townspeople and visitors alike saw personalities emerge that characterized the delegations. The Alabamians were the most reserved, they said, and the Louisianians the most "excited." The South Carolinians, not surprisingly, struck people as the most bellicose, while at the other end of the scale, the poor Florida delegation seemed "too few to be noticed." Mississippians, they said, were "the most braggartish," and the Georgians by far "the most boisterous."[113]

But perhaps people really only thought of two of the Georgians when they called them so. Certainly neither priggish Tom Cobb nor wizened Little Aleck struck anyone as "boisterous." But there was Bartow, who drank too much, and blustered with as much belligerence. Especially there was Bob Toombs. Almost every evening, if not a guest in one of the homes of the civic elite, he held court in the Exchange bar, surrounded by fellow congressmen, delightedly repeating old stories for new faces whenever asked, in those rolling tones that perfectly rounded off even "bar-room periods." "What a jolly rotund celebrity Toombs is," mused one reporter.[114] Listening to the "Bibacious Georgian," no constable or alderman would have thought of holding *him* liable for the mandatory $10 fine for loud or disorderly conduct in a saloon, or for his prodigious profanity.[115]

No, while they played at their billiards or drank, they all gathered round Toombs. Already speculation rose in Montgomery that *this* might be the Georgian for the presidency. Certainly delegates from other states discussed his name, while Stephens and Crawford made no secret that they believed him the best man.[116] Stephens himself declared his friend the superior even of Webster, Clay, and Calhoun in debate, surpassed for raw power only by Niagara Falls.[117] The dapper Miles regarded him as absolutely sound on Southern rights and the very antithesis of a reconstructionist.[118] Yet others found him too impulsive in address. "What I say, I mean," Toombs admitted, "sometimes perhaps with too much plainness of speech."[119] Even close friends like Herschel Johnson and Crawford attested to this, but the latter went on to maintain that Toombs's apparent rashness was only in conversation.[120] "When anything is *to be done*," said Crawford, Toombs was a different man. "Notwithstanding all he may say in the highway, he is the wisest and safest man *in counsel*."[121]

Wise, that is, until he drank. Almost every day now in Montgomery Stephens saw both Toombs and Bartow "mellow" after dinner.[122] Toombs's was no insane thirst, nor was he an alcoholic as Stephens may have been. Despite his robust size, his system simply could not handle liquor in any quantity.[123] Friend Pleasant Stovall saw how even the smallest indulgence affected him. "When he measured himself with others, glass for glass, the result was distressing, disastrous."[124] During the Georgia secession convention Toombs had met with the foreign relations committee that he chaired shortly after his election to the Montgomery delegation. As he went back and forth from the table to two bottles of champagne on the sideboard, his speech became ever more expansive and imaginative. Finally he told of receiving a telegram from Governor Pickens announcing that Charleston batteries had opened fire on Fort Sumter. It was pure invention, and Stephens had later to explain to members of the committee that when his friend drank with something important on his mind, he became wildly fanciful. "I have studied him closely," said Stephens, "and sometimes feared he would become a monomaniac; but these fits wear off very soon and tomorrow he will have no recollection of what has occurred."[125]

Such a performance hardly instilled confidence in people seeking a president. With still no outward signs of electioneering, and with no candidates yet announced, the subject of who should be chief executive nevertheless crossed most lips every day, and dominated much of the talk over those bounteous dinner tables. Most of the speculation still centered around the Georgians and Davis. Toombs especially seemed gaining in support, and some Georgia colleagues understood that Alabama was yet behind him, notwithstanding the suggestion from Gilmer that Davis would most please Virginia.[126] After his discussion with Chesnut, Stephens clearly believed that South Carolina backed his friend as well, and Florida's determination to follow the choice of the Palmetto State was by now an open secret, though one not perfectly understood. One Floridian—probably Owens—told Rhett that his state "would go with South Carolina; and that she *expected South Carolina to nominate a candidate.*" More to the point, he said, they expected the state to nominate Rhett.[127] Mississippi, of course, wanted Davis, though even some of her delegates wavered because of the belief that he preferred a generalship instead. Louisiana remained an unknown, though it hardly mattered. With South Carolina, Florida, and Alabama behind Toombs—if indeed they were—all Georgia need do was unite on him as their candidate to decide the election.

Toombs took dinner this evening with Stephens and others as they enjoyed a brief break from their evening's work in finishing the provisional constitution. As he ate, he drank. The camaraderie was good, and it helped him forget his worries about his only child's health. Unfortunately he drank in proportion to his anxiety. The meal done, he got up unsteadily to leave for a party at Montgomery Hall being given by Chesnut. Stephens watched him leave *"tighter* than I ever saw him—too tight for his character & reputation by far."[128]

At the party that evening, attended by many of the delegates not involved in the Committee of Twelve, the wine and wit flowed freely, and Toombs partook of both in equal measure.[129] The result, as Stovall had said, was disastrous. Some suddenly found Toombs "flighty." Others saw in him irrationality, even foolishness. All week they had seen Toombs a bit tipsy in the evenings, and even those who missed his displays no doubt heard stories of earlier episodes, such as the evening after the secession ordinance passed in Georgia. How could they place their trust, and the fortunes of their new nation, in a man so apparently unable to control himself? At best a convivial glass or two of wine over luncheon with some dignitary or diplomat risked severe embarrassment. At worst, in the event of war a tipple too much at the wrong moment could cost them far, far more. Men who came to Chesnut's party intending to support Toombs left severely shaken in their confidence, and some with their minds changed.[130] Where Bob Toombs was concerned, Stephens told his brother, "I think that evenings exhibition settled the Presidency."[131]

Even as the bluff Georgian's star began to flare out—without his knowing it, or much else, that evening—virtually all of the delegates still felt themselves united in the opinion that everything was going wonderfully. While privately admitting that they were encountering both delays and difficulties in their work,[132] Crawford sent word to Atlanta that "great unanimity and the best of feeling prevails."[133] Admittedly that reflected the public face the delegations wanted to put on their meeting, but in private they also felt much the same. *"Harmony prevails,"* Tom Cobb wrote to Marion, underscoring the words almost as if they surprised him.[134] Brother Howell agreed, admitting differences of opinion, but predicting unanimity and looking forward to complete success. The secret sessions provoked anger and disappointment, of course. Scrupulously delegates refrained from divulging anything in their letters home, though there was little yet to keep secret. The public complained, including Ben Hill's wife, now come to join him. The press moaned at their exclusion, and increasingly resorted to even the wildest rumor in order to present at least something new in reports to their papers.[135] When a reporter could get $2.50 to $3.00 for each letter he sent to his editor, he had to say something, and those people at home hungered for any morsel they could get. The editor of the Augusta *Chronicle & Sentinel* even begged Stephens to find him a correspondent, and hinted that the delegate himself would be quite acceptable.[136]

Indeed, many found this half-finished little man acceptable, and their number started growing just now. A former governor advised the Louisiana delegation that they must eschew extremists like Yancey, whom he doubted to be as adept at building "as he has shown himself expert in pulling down a government." No, the sort of man to ask for leadership was a moderate, one who appealed to the Border States—a man like Stephens.[137] On almost all sides men still conceded that the presidency should go to Georgia "in deference to the Empire State," as a Charlestonian correspondent suggested.[138] With Toombs effectively out of the running now, more and more eyes looked down a few inches to find Little Aleck. He bore, said one, "no stain of the prevalent corruption," meaning ambition and ardent disunion. "With Stephens at the helm (for he has brains) Georgia and the South are safe."[139] On the streets this evening, before the night boat left for Mobile with daily letters to their papers, some of the correspondents heard unnamed delegates speaking confidently of Stephens being elected. Men favorable to him claimed that the delegations from South Carolina (Rhett excepted), Georgia, and even Mississippi stood willing. Certainly a strong minority supported him in the first two, and especially after Toombs's exhibition, of which the correspondents could yet know nothing, and about which they remained silent if ever they did learn.[140]

And yet, others still spoke of Howell Cobb, though without the enthusiasm shown for Toombs or Stephens. Likeable, affable, able, he struck a middle note between the highly intelligent yet reclusive Little Aleck and the ebullient but intemperate Toombs. Just now he beamed with pride over his new son, only a few days old, and named for his brother Tom, though family advised him that the little Cobb "would take a premium at any fair for ugly." With five bottles of gin sent by an older son in congratulation, Cobb was ready to start celebrating today with his friends.[141] Yet where men seemed not to object to Toombs or Stephens because of their involvement in the Union party in Georgia in 1851, for some reason they did not forgive Cobb. Perhaps it was because he so quickly, and rather cynically, turned his back on his new party when he saw that his political future had looked better with the old one. His brief defection cost the Southern rights element of the Democratic party an embarrassing setback in Georgia then, and his quick reconversion smacked too much of expediency and too little of principle. That did not sit well with many here in Montgomery, men who admired a principled foe far more than a fair-weather friend. Many expressed their objections to Cobb vocally.[142]

Cobb himself professed no interest in the presidency, and asked his friends not to suggest his name when discussions turned to possible nominees. He preferred not to be considered, he said. "All that I have seen & learned since I got here has satisfied me that it is a most undesirable position," he told his wife this same evening.[143] But he did not say that he would refuse if asked. Protestations of modesty, of lack of ambition for high office formed part of the political ethic of the time. No man sought high office; the office must seek him. Every president since Andrew Jackson had denied wanting the position prior to his nomination; not one refused it when actually offered. Brother Tom actually seemed surprised at the thought that Howell might be sincere, and as events of the next forty-eight hours revealed, he did not take him seriously.[144]

As yet, the only perceived aggressive movement for any man appeared to be coming from the Mississippians. Rhett and his *Mercury* correspondent seemed convinced that they came armed with a single order to "get Davis elected President."[145] Certainly Wiley Harris admitted his own opinion being influenced by Davis's experience in military affairs. If war came, what better chief executive than one who could also serve knowledgeably as commander-in-chief? All or most of his delegation probably agreed, though some still felt uncertain that Davis wanted the top position, or that he would accept it if tendered.[146] Kenner of Louisiana detected a "general inclination" running in Davis's direction among some delegates from other states as well.[147] The *Mercury* reporter concluded this evening that Davis would probably get the office, and that the second place would go to Cobb or Toombs, noting that some of the South Carolina delegation actively pushed the names of men from other states rather than any of themselves.[148] But any thought that the Mississippians as a group tried to press Davis on the rest existed chiefly in the mind of Rhett, who saw everyone as a rival. More than anyone else, former Senator James Hammond back in South Carolina thought of Rhett this very same day when he bemoaned that *"big-man-me-ism* reigns supreme & every one thinks every other a jealous fool, or an aspiring knave."[149]

One thing that both Cobb brothers agreed on this evening was that no electioneering was evident, that in the desire for harmony all of the delegations showed commendable restraint.[150] The Mississippians agreed with them, but appearances deceived. Mississippi saw no electioneering because no one would try to win their votes, believing they came committed to Davis and to swaying the votes of others toward him. As for Georgia, who would try persuasion there, since so many conceded that Georgia herself would select the president? Because the men from these two delegations saw no intriguing did not mean there was none to be seen. It was about to come out into the open.

CHAPTER FIVE

THE MOST MOMENTOUS EVENT
OF THE CENTURY

———•★•———

T HE GREAT, THE SMALL, the ambitious, and the self-effacing, all
assembled at eleven o'clock February 7, anxious to dispense with
the obligatory open session. About the worst-kept secret in Montgomery at the moment was the completion of the report of the Committee
of Twelve the night before, and members chaffed to see the charter of
their new government.[1] First must come the formalities and at least a
little show for the gallery. It was not much. In fact, almost immediately they adjourned for an hour. The constitution was still at Shorter and
Reid's, where the committee had left it the night before, but they
expected its delivery at any moment. After the visitors stood to
stretch, and came down to empty the tables of fruit and meat, the delegates reconvened. Old Withers moved a complimentary granting of
seats on the floor to Governor Moore and members of his legislature as
a recognition of their patriotism in that day offering the loan of up to
$500,000 to the congress. Then, after barely an hour and a quarter,
Memminger himself moved that they close the doors. He was ready to
present his constitution.[2]

Rhett wanted a word first. Despite not getting to help frame the
Provisional Constitution, he had certainly learned its provisions from
Memminger or others, and knew already he did not approve of some
items. Thus, even before the document's presentation to the congress,
he now moved that a new Committee of Twelve be appointed to start
work on the permanent constitution. Moreover, to ensure that he got
onto this committee, he proposed that each state's representatives be
nominated by the delegation itself. After Rhett's motion went on the
calendar for early consideration, Memminger took the floor and proceeded to read the "Constitution for the Provisional Government of
the Confederate States of North America."

As the congress quietly listened, Memminger carefully read from a handwritten draft, his Charlestonian tones hardly betraying his German birth. "In the name of Almighty God," he began, showing the influence of several who had suggested to the committee that the deity ought to be recognized in their efforts.[3] Article by article, section by section, he read on. Little if anything surprised his audience. This was what they had expected—indeed, desired. But when he finished they were all dismayed to hear Stephens immediately arise and move a postponement of any debate on the constitution. The printers still labored over it, and would not be ready with the hundred copies ordered until at least seven-thirty that evening. At first agreeing to adjourn until then, they decided in the end to wait until the next day. After hearing a proposal from Atlanta offering itself as the seat of a future permanent government, they left.[4]

Rhett fumed. The whole day was lost for want of a speedier printer, he grumbled.[5] Interestingly enough, as the delegates spent the rest of the day in other pursuits, or in making notes on what they remembered of the reading of the constitution, reporters in Montgomery sent fantastic dispatches announcing that the delegates meeting in secret session actually deliberated some five hours over the document and finally voted to adopt it, their only change from the United States Constitution being the addition of free trade with foreign powers.[6] Meanwhile, others rumored that behind the secret sessions lay an attempt to hide the discord and disagreement that actually characterized congressional sessions, putting the lie to the false face of harmony presented in open sessions.[7] Certainly Rhett felt so, and vowed to resist anew any attempt to conduct the debates on the permanent constitution in secret. He meant to take the lead in crafting that charter, and he intended that the South should know his every word in its making.[8]

Unoccupied by constitutional deliberations that evening, more and more the delegates played the presidential game, and with each hour the intensity of it escalated. Stephens's name suddenly vaulted nearly to the front. Word came from Washington that Southern sympathizers there expected Little Aleck to be the new president.[9] In Charleston more and more reports suggested the Georgian would take the office.[10] The press all across the South, as well as in Montgomery, carried word of the telegram sent to the delegates by fire-eater Louis T. Wigfall, still remaining in Washington to aid the cause. Elect Stephens, he said. It would conciliate the conservative element, bring in the Border States, and ensure unity.[11] "All for the cause, and the best man for it," Wigfall and others supposedly proclaimed, and that meant Stephens. Davis they demanded be made general-in-chief.[12] By the evening of February 7 the wires from Montgomery carried "verbal assurances" to some editors that Stephens was to be the choice.[13]

Such stories caused no little distress in certain quarters. Trescott in Charleston spoke of surprise and dismay, and with it an admonition to the South Carolina delegates that the people of the state expected either Howell Cobb or Davis.[14] The rumors were more than enough for Barnwell to redouble his recent efforts. He favored Davis for the position, but his colleagues, as in all things, lay divided, and hardly spoke to one another on the issue. Keitt and Boyce loathed Davis personally. Rhett did not know him, but did not like what he heard about the man. Withers held an old grudge going back some years. Miles, on the other hand, seemed favorably inclined to Davis. Chesnut, if still attracted to Stephens, felt no objections to the Mississippian, and Memminger entertained no fixed opinions as yet, and lay open to persuasion. To Barnwell the situation, though hardly promising, looked possible. Steadily taking advantage of the influence that his character and demeanor gave him with most of the delegation, he worked on Miles, Memminger, and Chesnut, and—through Chesnut—Mary's uncle Withers. And Barnwell started to call repeatedly on his cousin Rhett.[15]

Active support for a Stephens candidacy now emerged from an entirely unexpected quarter, Ben Hill. Four years before the two traded insults over disagreements growing out of the election of 1856. Words escalated until Stephens issued a challenge, but Hill refused to accept it, and worse, made Little Aleck look a fool in the process. Stephens took the affray public, calling Hill a liar and coward in the press and daring him to fight. Hill only responded that dueling was no measure either of gentility or of manhood, and moreover he had a family to support and his own soul to save, "while Stephens has neither."[16] They had not spoken since. Seeing Toombs effectively out of consideration, detesting Cobb, and distrusting Davis, Hill now set aside his own animosity—considerably less virulent than Little Aleck's—and decided that his fellow Georgian was the best choice. He made his feelings known to selected press in Georgia, prompting one editor to advise Stephens of Hill's support and to beg him not to refuse the office if offered.[17] Moreover, he started politicking within the Georgia delegation. The two Cobbs were out of the question, of course, and so was Bartow, who proclaimed a "perfect contempt" that surprised Stephens but which soon became mutual.[18] However, Crawford, Kenan, Nisbet, and Wright were all friendly, though one or two preferred Toombs, as did Stephens himself. It was too soon after Chesnut's fatal party for any to realize that Toombs's standing was on the decline with other delegations, but still Hill rightly assumed that if the Georgians did not unite on the mighty Bob, then he would himself gladly support his friend Stephens in preference to Cobb, whom he disliked considerably. Quietly Hill started urging friendly fellow delegates to think of Stephens when the time came.[19]

Less than friendly Georgians inevitably heard of Hill's efforts. When not in the capitol, Tom Cobb busied himself with his praying, boasting on his daughter, and indulging a growing delusion that he cut a large figure in Montgomery. Proud of the fact that a man of his standing had been too busy as yet even to set foot in the Exchange parlor, or to meet proprietor Watt, Cobb yet found time this evening to go to a party at Judge Bibb's with brother Howell and Bartow, though only after keeping their hosts and the supper waiting an hour and a half, and afterward complaining that he wore white kid gloves with his homespun suit and in such formal attire arrived to find that they were only having tea.[20] A big fish in the small secession pond at Milledgeville the month before, he did not realize that here, surrounded as he was by a school of the greatest in the whole Southern sea, he now ranked somewhere between the minnows and the plankton. He had already decided that he would be offered a cabinet post by any new president, probably attorney general, and spent much of that day telling those around him that he had no intention of accepting any position proffered, no doubt much to their amusement.[21]

Part of his expectation arose from the assumption that brother Howell could still become president, despite his *pro forma* disavowal of any such ambitions. But now came these rumblings from Hill and the other signs of growing support for Stephens. Tom Cobb could hardly decline a cabinet appointment from a president unlikely to offer him one. The movement for Stephens had to be stopped, and so, too, any tendency toward Toombs, though a few glasses of wine had already done that little job unbeknownst to Cobb. The only certain support for Howell in the delegation was Bartow and the two Cobbs themselves, assuming that Howell would in the end consent to be put forward. All the rest, if divided upon which candidate they preferred, united in opposition to Cobb, with only Wright and perhaps Nisbet persuadable. Even with them there would be no majority. Clearly, to stop Stephens and promote Howell, Tom Cobb would have to go to work outside his delegation. In the end, if he was clever, he could achieve both ends: get the other states to force Howell to stand for election, and force Georgia to get behind him.[22] This same evening, if not before, he and Bartow began talking to South Carolina, Louisiana, Florida, and Alabama.[23] However clever their intent, subsequent events showed them hardly subtle.

Late that same afternoon or evening Alexander Clayton finally arrived from Mississippi, detained by the heavy rains to the west and the washed-out bridges. He went straight to his delegation's rooms at the Exchange, only to be met by hasty greetings and the exclamation that "Georgia wants everything."[24] First there was the morning's suggestion that Atlanta should have the permanent capital, not to mention the presence in Montgomery for some days of men lobbying behind the scenes in Atlanta's behalf.[25] Following as this did the persistent assumption that Georgia would get the presidency, Tom Cobb's early arrogance at his delegation's influence, Hill and others' politicking for Stephens, and Cobb's and Bartow's countermaneuvers, Clayton needed to hear little before he concluded that, indeed, there was a bit too much Georgia in evidence in Montgomery.

From his pocket the Mississippian drew a blade that just might cut the Georgian knot. He showed the other delegates Jefferson Davis's recent letter responding to questions about the presidency. Indeed, he brought it with him for just this purpose. Certainly Davis uttered the obligatory protest that he did not desire the office, but he did not explicitly forbid its consideration, and quite clearly did say that he felt it his duty to serve in *any capacity* to which his countrymen called him.[26] Moreover, this very afternoon the other Mississippians heard the answer to the only substantive objection that Davis raised. Though their printed copies of the proposed provisional constitution were not yet in their hands, they could hardly forget that in Article II, Section 2 the framing committee followed the old Constitution to the letter: "The President shall be commander in chief of the Army and Navy of the Confederacy, and of the militia of the several States." Clearly in this new government, as in the old, Davis as president could also direct the armies, even assume field command if he chose.

In that moment, the Mississippians solidified. Whether some came supporting Davis for general and others for chief executive, they all united now on the single purpose that Rhett accused them of pursuing from the first. As such, they stood now the only delegation in Montgomery united in support of a candidate, and the only delegation *with* a candidate whom they were determined to put before the others. Almost certainly they wired Governor Pettus in Jackson to let him know their intent, and perhaps to suggest that Davis should be near at hand just in case. Pettus himself now sent a wire to Davis via Vicksburg. "We need you here," said the governor. "Come prepared to go to Montgomery."[27]

At his fire the next morning, expecting a long day in closed session, Little Aleck nursed a cold and reflected as he did so often on what they were doing and what lay ahead.[28] "We are now in the midst of a revolution," he wrote in one of his uncountable letters. "It is bootless to argue the causes that produced it, or whether it be a good or a bad thing in itself. The former will be the task of the historian. The latter is a problem that the future alone can solve."[29] Much of that future depended upon what was to happen this day and the morrow, for now they must settle their constitution and choose their president.

The weather smiled on Stephens as the bundle of little bones in the great coat walked up Market. The frost was gone and the day promised to be warm and fair, already nearly sixty degrees as he walked along the short blocks. With him at almost every step were the growling, yelping dogs that kept up a constant chorus at passersby. One man counted thirty-seven of them howling at him in a distance of five blocks, and a Charleston reporter, showing off his Greek, quipped that this city of dogs ought rightly to be called "Kunopolis."[30]

Arrival at the capitol revealed something new. The crowds of spectators seemed lessened. In fact, the daily resort to secret session, and the pallid business conducted with open doors began to discourage those who came for the show, and now they were leaving.[31] But the lobbyists still remained, and the office seekers seemed to grow in numbers. The congress grew slightly this morning, too. Clayton presented himself, and so, at last, did Fearn and Lewis of Alabama. Old Dr. Fearn, seventy-one now, would rather not have been here, both for his ill health and for the fact that he opposed secession until the very last minute. At least it afforded him a chance to see again his son-in-law, Barry of Mississippi.[32]

Preliminaries and the routine of the open session were by now a bore. Credentials from new members, Alabama's tender of the use of its supreme court library to the members, a resolution of thanks to the state for the $500,000 loan, and more occupied but a few minutes. Then the spectators went out, and the congress went to work.[33]

On each of the small walnut "student" desks sat a copy of the proposed constitution. Most of the members studied it during the brief open session, and more still came with notes and suggestions based on yesterday's reading. As a result, there was no wasting time now. With barely any preliminaries, they went straight to the document. After days of threatening to quit and go home if they did not *do* something, Tom Cobb could finally say that "we are hard at work *at last.*"[34]

Stephens started the process of amending with the very title itself. A host of names had been suggested for the new nation—Alleghenia, Chicora, Atlanta, the Georgia Confederacy, and more.[35] The committee settled on "the Confederate States of North America," but now Little Aleck proposed that the word "North" be removed, to which all agreed. Thus they would be the Confederate States of America. In the next breath he addressed the invocation of the Almighty and suggested that it be removed, but, slightly reworded, it remained. Tom Cobb tried to rewrite the entire preamble, and in the process impose a name of his own on the nation, calling it the "Republic of Washington," and suggested February 22—Marion's birthday as well as Washington's—as its date of inauguration. Like everything else he had proposed in the congress to date, his motion lost, not even Georgia standing behind him.[36]

Then came the first of the hurdles that the framers feared. Harris of Mississippi and his delegation tried one more time to honor their convention's instructions to do no more than frame a constitution, and avoid this congress's taking on legislative powers. The rules under which they operated seemed especially dangerous to the Mississippians. On the basis of one state, one vote, and with any number of men in a delegation forming a quorum, it was theoretically possible that just four men, one per state, could constitute a "majority" and exercise legislative power.[37] Harris now moved to strike out that part of Article I that gave to this congress all such power, his delegation united behind him.[38] Florida agreed. This very morning Patton Anderson and his colleagues received by certified mail a resolution from their state convention instructing them to oppose any such attempt.[39] But on the vote, Florida and Mississippi stood alone. Too many of these members, like McRae of Alabama, had received urgent appeals not to waste time, but to act. "The condition of the country is beyond ordinary political panaceas," they were told. "The body politic is diseased . . . & hence the hopelessness of a cure by usual remedies."[40] "Delay, eternal delay, has been the bane of the South in the Union," warned another. Any more would be fatal.[41] Even South Carolina stood with the majority.

Stephens and the others breathed their first sighs of relief. Now they were not just a congress, but *the* Congress.[42]

Undeterred by his first rebuff, Tom Cobb tried for a Georgia power play now in proposing to change the voting provision so that each delegate got a vote, and a majority of all delegates should decide issues rather than a majority of states. Georgia, with ten delegates, constituted twenty percent of the whole congress, and by Cobb's measure could virtually dominate most legislation. Once more he lost, and not surprisingly. Withers then tried to counter Stephens's provision allowing cabinet ministers to be appointed from congress, and to continue holding their seats in the body, but Memminger managed to table the amendment for the moment.[43]

When they turned to fiscal matters the debate escalated. No one seemed to object when Bob Smith of Alabama proposed giving the president a line item veto on appropriations, but when they came to Section 6 dealing with taxes and duties, disagreement emerged. As written, the section provided for import duties of up to fifteen percent. Kenner of Louisiana represented a state vitally tied to world commerce, and many of whose constituent groups were committed to the ideal of free trade. As well, he kept his eye to the Border States, most of them heavily tied to the Mississippi, and themselves also free trade in persuasion. While Stephens looked on, admiring Kenner's intellect and his inability to be boring on any subject, the Louisianian proposed eliminating all wordage dealing with duties on foreign goods, or with congressional authority to impose such levies.[44] He knew that he had Georgia and Alabama behind him. The challenge came from South Carolina. "We are all against it," Keitt said of free trade. Without import duties, seaport states would have to raise their revenues through direct taxation, and that would ruin them. "Each of our people would sooner give ten dollars which they have never seen, than one they have had in their pockets."[45] In the end, however, South Carolina's delegates split evenly on the amendment, nullifying their vote, while all of the other states went with Louisiana. Free trade would be the order of the day, at least for the time being, and Little Aleck concluded that Duncan Kenner was one of "the shakers" in this congress.[46]

To everyone's relief, they sailed through the next sixteen paragraphs without substantial amendment or even discussion. Late in the afternoon McRae moved the addition of a clause specifically giving this congress full executive powers until a president should be inaugurated, and after passing that they adjourned around four o'clock for supper.

Tom Cobb spent the recess writing to his wife, his delight at their progress swallowing any disappointment at his failure to have any impact on the work thus far. Several of the members regretted that they would miss a gala party being given in town that night, but since they expected to be working until midnight at least, there was no choice.[47]

Out on the streets, the townspeople knew something was happening, and in a general fashion expected that it had to do with the constitution. A Mobile reporter told people that he had gone to the *Advertiser* office the night before, knowing that even then Shorter and Reid were at work into the late hours printing the draft. But all his pleas for a look at it got him nowhere. Sworn to secrecy, and with their congressional business in jeopardy if they violated their trust, the printers closed the door on him.[48] Consequently, like people throughout the South, Montgomeryites had to rely upon speculation. Indeed, after four days in session, these delegates showed an adherence to their oath of secrecy unaccustomed among politicians. In South Carolina friends complained of the meager news from Alabama.[49] This same afternoon all that the reporters could get out on the wires was that the delegates were locked in session, and that they expected important results late that night or the next day.[50] For any other news, Montgomery and the world must continue to rely on a lady Jonce Hooper called "Madam Gossip." "Let her 'rip,'" he suggested. "She has not a very enviable reputation for veracity, at best."[51]

At half past seven they reconvened and by the light of a massive eighteen-globe oil chandelier and several wall sconces they immediately jumped into the most divisive issue of all, the banning of the African slave trade. At once Rhett proposed eviscerating the clause with wording granting only that congress "may" enact such a prohibition. For once agreeing with Rhett, Chesnut suggested an entire rewording that achieved the same effect. Both objected to the implied stigma on slavery, but in the end South Carolina stood alone.[52] Alabama and Georgia, the two states whose base of public support seemed the most tenuous, specifically instructed their delegates to oppose reopening the trade. And they and the rest also recognized that the prohibition would be popular with the Border States. When Bartow called for the question, both Rhett's and Chesnut's amendments failed five to one.[53]

Smith of Alabama and Keitt both opposed the clause preventing any appropriations except on application of the president or a cabinet head. The South Carolinian feared a situation in which congress might declare war, but the president being opposed to it might simply refuse to submit appropriations. "I don't want the safeguards to break us down," he complained.[54] Their efforts failed. Passing on into Article II, the mode of electing the provisional chief executive by the one state, one vote means passed without obstacle, as did the provision that he must be a natural born citizen, or else for fourteen years a citizen of one of the states at the time of the adoption of this constitution. His salary of $25,000 per annum went through without opposition, though with a stipulation that he receive no other "emolument" from the country while serving.[55]

By late that evening there came a feeling of relief that they were going to get through with it all, and that the major potential obstacles had been passed. Certainly division and disagreement manifested themselves, and once or twice emotions may have appeared, but dissenters steadily yielded to the majority and the work pressed on.[56] Stephens reflected on the men around him as he now saw them engaged in real action for the first time, and he felt impressed by what he saw. Of all the deliberative bodies in which he had served, he decided, "I never was associated with an abler one."[57] Indeed, the debates were going so smoothly now that Little Aleck decided to ignore one particularly windy and pointless speech and spend a few minutes writing to Linton. "I have many things I wish to write to you about," he scribbled. "Had I leisure to do it I would fill twenty sheets."[58] He would have a lot more information to fill them with before long.

Even while Stephens approvingly observed others in the hall, many of them turned careful eyes toward him, none more so than Lawrence Keitt. He thought the Georgian looked like a spider in its web, quiet and waiting as he observed and listened to the debates. But when he arose to speak, said Keitt, "his speech is the concentrated sense of that whole house—the brains of Congress double-distilled."[59] He and Little Aleck had known each other for years back, and the personal regard was mutual, Stephens thinking the South Carolinian too much a speaker of the "Spread Eagle order," but adding that, unlike others of that ilk, "Keit[t] I believe."[60] Thus when Keitt walked across the floor and asked him to step out into the rotunda for a moment, the Georgian happily obliged.

Keitt asked if he would accept the presidency. While a stunned Stephens listened, his friend explained that South Carolina looked to Georgia for the man, and that it must be either Stephens or Toombs. Personally, Keitt felt great affection for Toombs, and probably preferred him until the dinner episode of two nights before.[61] Keitt also liked Cobb, as did Boyce and Rhett, but too many of the rest both in the South Carolina delegation and in congress as a whole simply would not accept Howell. Toombs and Cobb being out of the question, the only remaining top contenders were Davis, whom Keitt disliked, and Stephens. Keitt well knew that Barnwell was pressing hard in his delegation to go for Davis, and thus acted now on his own to attempt to cut those efforts short. Disingenuously he told Little Aleck that South Carolina preferred him.[62] In fact, besides Keitt, probably only Chesnut and Miles could have been persuaded easily to rally behind him on a first ballot, while Withers and Memminger were still undecided.[63] Keitt's own regard for the Georgian, whom he called "the peer of the loftiest in worth and intellect," was well known.[64] And, like many others, he may have assumed that Stephens's influence with Toombs was such that the smaller man could control the larger.[65] If Toombs was past consideration, then a Stephens presidency could still bind to it the best talents of the bluff Georgian thanks to their friendship.

Keitt could count on support from other states, as well. Especially in Louisiana did Stephens enjoy a strong following. Kenner, returning Little Aleck's approbation, found now that Stephens's correctness of views and warm Southern patriotism won his confidence.[66] Conrad also seemed well disposed, and as Little Aleck himself would note, those two men really guided the Louisiana delegation.[67] The chief reason that Davis figured strongly in their speculations was his military experience, but with him as general in chief, the South would have that anyhow.

Keitt played a long shot, but his calculations could work. Mississippi was probably lost to Davis, and very possibly Alabama, too. But if Georgia put forward Stephens, and if Keitt could use that to move a couple of men in his own delegation, there was a chance—if Florida made good on its expressed intent to vote with South Carolina. Presented with a bloc of three decided states, Louisiana would need little persuading—if any at all—to make the majority.[68]

It all depended at this moment on Stephens. Just a year earlier he told a friend that "if there is anything particularly disgusting to me it is a scramble among Presidential aspirants." "My nature looks not that way for objects to gratify my outgoings of spirit."[69] But now, so close to the actual election, and after some days of hearing his name increasingly associated with the office, Little Aleck did not return a categorical "no." After all, the fact that men like Keitt from South Carolina even considered him showed just how far away from the fire-eaters and extremists the movement had turned. The only slightly bumpy ride the provisional constitution was taking through congress that day also affirmed that the "revolution" was no revolt at all, but a sound conservative enterprise safely in the hands of moderate men like himself. Stephens still favored Toombs, and then reiterated for Keitt the reasons against his own selection that he had given to Chesnut, but in preference to Cobb he would take the post himself if his election were to be unanimous, and if he could select a cabinet of his own choosing who harmonized with him on the political course he determined to follow.[70] He might still be able to avert the calamity that he so strongly believed lay ahead. And Little Aleck was no stranger to flattery or ambition, and immune to neither.[71]

When they walked back into the chamber, Stephens believed that Keitt, Chesnut, and the rest still favored Toombs first, but he had left them an alternative if they wanted one.[72] Sitting down beside Crawford, Stephens told him what had happened, and then explained that he still felt it impolitic for him to be a candidate. To make him president, he said, would be tantamount to "taking a child out of the hands of its mother and giving it to a step-mother." "Someone who has been identified with the cause should be chosen," he concluded, his diffidence returning. Whomever it should be would have his support.[73]

Stephens and Keitt certainly did not walk out of the debate nor return without being noticed, especially by Tom Cobb, who might have guessed what lay afoot. "Stephens is *looming up* for President since Howell's name has been almost withdrawn," he wrote to his wife from the chamber. At that moment he believed that Jefferson Davis stood the best chance of election,[74] but more and more he feared what he saw first as Hill tried to persuade fellow Georgians towards Stephens, and now the huddled exchange with Keitt. Moreover, the "*enteinte cordial*" as he put it, between Little Aleck and Toombs was restored. Tom Cobb had come to Montgomery determined to be a leader, but now he had to admit that he, Howell, and Bartow constituted a minority in their own delegation.[75] Seeing overt efforts to put Stephens in the presidential chair was too much for him.[76] His and Bartow's efforts thus far having failed, there was one more stratagem left.

First they must finish with the constitution. The last matters passed with only minor amendment, chiefly in their wording. Harris tried to insert a significant amendment declaring all laws of the United States currently in force to be effective in the new Confederacy as well, thus immediately giving the new nation a body of law, but his amendment failed. However, he succeeded in throwing out another provision that obligated the new government to adopt the debts the several states incurred in the act of separating from the Union. Meanwhile, Stephens succeeded in getting the word "North" eliminated wherever the name of the new nation appeared, well conditioning the delegates to being the Confederate States of America, while Miles of South Carolina, asserting the doctrine of localism, managed to throw out the word "national." Between them, Harris and Chesnut adjusted the paragraph covering admitting new states so as to leave all details on the proce- dure for later, simply asserting congress's power to grant admission.[77]

That finished it. Hooper read the revised and amended constitution for a last time, and then the came the vote. At midnight, after a total of nine hours in secret session, the states approved the document unanimously.[78] Immediately Memminger moved that they all take the oath prescribed by the new Constitution in open session the next day. This time, for a change, they could give the public a good show. Then Boyce of South Carolina proposed that they set the time for the elec- tion of their president at noon on February 9. Before a vote could come, Miles stood and moved instead that they vote immediately. But then someone suggested that the delegations needed time to confer first, and thus Boyce's motion carried. They would vote in twelve hours, and do so in secret session.[79]

They all made their way back to their boardinghouses and their hotels in a hard rain that came down in sheets.[80] At first their talk cen- tered on the hard day just completed. Keitt proclaimed the provisional constitution a good one, and in a few hours Clayton would declare that "this is the most momentous event of the century upon this conti- nent."[81] But Southern Associated Press reporter Pritchard found some who seemed less pleased. Wandering the lobby and corridors of the Exchange, he heard complaints that the document did not go far enough. Already the defeated, like Rhett, planned to redress battles lost in this debate when they framed the Permanent Constitution.[82] The *Mercury* correspondent said frankly that "I see no little dissatisfac- tion on some faces," by which he meant South Carolina faces.[83] There was too much disposition to cater to the Border States, thought Rhett, and of course the nagging sore of the secret sessions pestered him con- stantly. "I have spoken a great deal," he told his son, and fumed that no press accounts could support him.[84] Others still felt that the document went too far, there now being no check on the federal authority of congress, since only South Carolina of all the states had enacted a specific resolution to deny it military and diplomatic powers.[85]

Five of the delegations reassembled as soon as they got to their rooms, to caucus on their presidential support. Georgia decided to meet in the morning. Perhaps rather smug in face of the continuing belief that everyone else would get behind whomever they put forward, the Georgians assumed that their decision could wait and need not keep their weary heads from their beds. One of them did not sleep, not just yet.

For Tom Cobb the arithmetic of election was easy. By common consent, the delegates intended that to the public their choice should be unanimous. Privately that meant that any candidate getting the vote of four states would be the winner, and the other two would change their secret ballots for the appearance of unanimity.[86] That simple math revealed to him a way to accomplish a number of goals. He still feared that when they met in the morning, the majority in his delegation might go for Stephens, and that, worse yet, could determine the election. But if at least three other states stood already united on another candidate from Georgia, then his colleagues would risk great embarrassment by refusing the compliment offered to one of their number by insisting on another instead. How to unite those other states first on someone besides Little Aleck? Simply by visiting them tonight and telling them that Georgia had already decided on her candidate. That done, he could rely on the belief that the other states would willingly accept whichever man Georgia put forward to settle the presidency.

And so Cobb made his visits—to South Carolina's Barnwell, to Alabama, to Florida, and probably to Louisiana. He told them all that Georgia had already made her decision. Tomorrow at noon she would nominate Howell Cobb. Naturally they would follow her lead. Being Thomas R. R. Cobb, and the brother of the future president, he probably made his announcement with just the wrong mix of hauteur and self-importance. Be that as it may, now it was up to them to do as they were told.[87]

If Cobb took that tone with South Carolina—and he probably did—he misjudged his audience, just as he continued to misjudge his own influence. All the talk of Georgia getting the presidency as a matter of course offended Barnwell, and so did rumors abroad in the past two days—fostered by the Atlanta lobbyists, perhaps—that if Georgia did not get the president, then she expected the permanent capital.[88] Cobb's failed attempt to dominate the debates on the constitution that afternoon only further aggravated his irritation. "I am not however much of a Georgian," Barnwell would tell a friend in a few hours; "they are able but intensely selfish."[89] And now here came Tom Cobb, telling him that the Georgians wanted Howell for president.[90]

Matters were difficult enough inside the Palmetto delegation without Georgians trying to bully them. While outside delegates expressed admiration for the discrete and self-effacing public demeanor of the South Carolinians, those who knew them more intimately could see that they were "all Ishmaelites amongst themselves," as Stephens observed. "No two of them agree. They are all jealous of each other— no news—there is no harmony or cordiality among them—always respectful in debate but they talk about and against each other."[91] Even now so far apart did they keep from one another that they did not meet in caucus like the other states, nor had they met at all to discuss the presidency. Rhett, indulging the delusion that he led them, claimed that he never called them together. He explained their failure to hold such a meeting by saying that it did not "become me to urge one," his delusion being that by his calling a caucus, his associates would be obliged to nominate him.[92] The fact is, if he had called, most would not have come.[93] In spite of that, he seems to have made no attempt to influence others' opinions in the matter now at hand. Instead, they all made their decisions independently. Despite free and frank discussions between them when one delegate encountered another, "everyone determined his own course for himself," said Miles.[94] Rhett, of course, still hoped that somehow his own name would be the one on their lips, though he afterward most disingenuously claimed that "I preferred Mr. Thomas Cobb of Georgia—a man pious, honest, earnest, able and brave—altogether I thought the best man in the Congress."[95]

No other delegation stood so evenly divided. Some wanted Davis, and others wanted Cobb, with no majority in sight just yet. Boyce detested the Mississippian, and his almost violent opposition to Davis was well known in Montgomery.[96] "I never thought Davis was the man," he said, and held to his view implacably.[97] Keitt, discouraged after his talk with Stephens, and probably finding little encouragement among his South Carolina colleagues, went into the Cobb camp in preference to Davis, whom he always opposed strenuously.[98] On the other hand, Barnwell supported Davis strongly, and Chesnut, like Keitt, by now abandoned any flirtation with Stephens and accepted—perhaps uneasily— a place in the Davis camp.[99] Miles also preferred Davis to Cobb.[100] That left Memminger still undecided, and Rhett and Withers both leaning against Davis, if not for Cobb. Indeed, this may account for Miles's seemingly strange motion to go to an immediate ballot that night. Knowing that Davis enjoyed a plurality, if not a majority, within his delegation, Miles may have hoped that a vote at that moment would preempt any last minute change among his colleagues. Barnwell had been working on Memminger and Rhett, and Chesnut on Withers. Forced to it at this moment, they might be moved to give Davis the majority. With Mississippi already for Davis, and Alabama leaning that way, and if Florida followed South Carolina's lead, Davis would have it.

The postponement until February 9 only meant that Barnwell and Chesnut must now redouble their efforts, and here the dreadful state of communications between the delegates worked to their advantage. None was entirely sure of where the others stood, said Keitt; "they did not understand one another."[101] Chesnut approached Mary's uncle Judge Withers and worked his persuasions. The garrulous old fellow held a grudge of several years standing going back to Davis's days as secretary of war. Withers imagined that the secretary had been rude to him, and perhaps he had.[102] Chesnut now asked him to overlook his private grievance in favor of the public good. Davis certainly offered a preferable alternative to Cobb, and in the end, under heavy pressure from Chesnut, Withers grudgingly agreed.[103] Barnwell also made some four calls on Withers to persuade him.[104] One vote for Davis.

Barnwell took on his cousin. Having called on him twice so far to press Davis as a candidate, he came to him once more this night. Until now Rhett leaned toward Thomas Cobb, or so he said. He opposed brother Howell, thinking him inconsistent and unpersistent after sounding the Georgian's views on Southern policy some three months before.[105] As for Davis, Rhett could not forget the 1858 speech in which reporters—inaccurately—credited him with saying that the Union could never be dissolved. He did not like the way Davis and New England took to each other during a vacation there that year. And he did not at all like Davis's reply to the same questions put to Cobb back in November 1860, in which the Mississippian advised caution and expressed doubts that Mississippi would secede if South Carolina alone went out of the Union. Worst of all, when delivering his farewell speech in the United States Senate in January, Davis wept at leaving the Union. *That* sort of man did not suit Robert Barnwell Rhett, Sr.[106]

When Rhett told Barnwell of his distrust of Davis's principles, his genial cousin agreed in part. "His temper is not good & his record in politics is not quite clear," conceded Barnwell. "I think him however the man for the time and place."[107] Davis might not be a man of great ability, said Barnwell, but he was "a fair, just and honorable man." Besides, he added with a twinkle of humor behind his spectacles, if Rhett held out for a man whose past career met his every requisite as criteria for the presidency, "*he* might vote for nobody."[108] Barnwell's persuasions began to work on Rhett, especially when he led the fire-eater to believe—or did not discourage his false impression—that a majority of the rest of the delegation had declared for the Mississippian. Another vote for Davis.[109]

That decided the matter for South Carolina. Even with Memminger undecided—though he probably gave way to Barnwell's persuasions, too—the majority seemingly overwhelmed Keitt and Boyce, and Barnwell may have won over Keitt, too, by telling him that all the rest of the delegation stood for Davis, and Keitt would thus waste his vote on a vain opposition.[110] And as voted South Carolina, so went Florida.[111] Davis enjoyed generally good opinions in this tiny delegation anyhow. Both Patton Anderson and James Owens had lived in Mississippi in the 1840s, and Anderson at least knew Davis from service in the Mexican War and later as an appointee in the Pierce administration. Jackson Morton served part of a term in the Senate with Davis. However, Morton, a lifelong Whig and opponent of secession, might have preferred one of the Georgians, while Owens, a committed secessionist and rigid Southern rights advocate, leaned toward Rhett, or his choice.[112] Combining Anderson's views, Morton's acquaintance, and the influence of Rhett on Owens and South Carolina on all of them, a decision for Davis came easily. Tom Cobb's planted story may not have driven them to Davis, as it helped to do with South Carolina, but it certainly brought them nowhere near his brother Howell.

Mississippi, of course, presented a foregone conclusion, especially after Clayton arrived with Davis's letter in his pocket. The notion most or all of them held that Davis only wanted a generalship and would not accept the position dissolved, and now to a man they stood united.[113] As they caucused they presented the only delegation in Montgomery completely unanimous, needing neither internal politicking nor Tom Cobb's backfiring stratagem to put them in the Davis camp, where they had been all along. Their unity was sufficient that no one else even approached them about another candidate, misleading Harris and Clayton into thinking that no electioneering took place at all.[114]

Louisiana, too, finally gravitated in that direction. In fact, at this late date Stephens still figured prominently in their deliberations, especially with the leader Kenner.[115] But the news that Georgia would put forward Howell Cobb was more than enough to move their thoughts elsewhere. Louisianians already felt some faint distrust of being too much under the thumb of the cotton states. Economically and socially their ties were to the river states, especially Mississippi. Influential men even suggested to Kenner that Louisiana might be best off in a smaller confederacy composed only of states bordering the mighty Mississippi.[116] Georgia lay far to the east, and answered different interests and needs, and Howell Cobb himself could be expected to listen to them first. Besides, his past career worked against him, and more recently, as secretary of the treasury, complaints accused him of poor management of the public funds. Louisiana lived by her commerce and could ill afford a president deficient in financial sense. Davis, on the other hand, was their neighbor, a man who understood the river and its trade, and one not under the influence of the overbearing Georgians. And of course, he brought military attainments that might be very much needed. After a very brief session during the rainy night, the Louisianians made their choice.[117]

Alabama vacillated among several candidates during the past week, including native son Yancey, whom Hooper supported strongly in his newspaper, with other editors following his lead.[118] Privately Yancey told his brother barely a week earlier that "I have no idea of ever again returning to public life," but it seems likely he simply penned one of those necessary signs of self-effacement and modesty that ambitious politicians felt obliged to give in deference to prevailing practice.[119] No real support for Yancey ever developed, and even his closest friends in the delegation, like his law partner Chilton, concluded rather early that they must look elsewhere. Seemingly Yancey agreed, but privately he still hoped.[120]

Toombs had been their next choice, but his behavior eroded that support, and the word from the commissioners to Virginia that the Old Dominion seemed to like Davis diluted it even further.[121] Correspondents from Mobile and elsewhere urged Davis on the delegates, as well.[122] And when Tom Cobb came to them with his story, they discussed Howell, only to reject him out of hand.[123] This was the most conservative delegation in Montgomery, men convinced that the future of the Confederacy, if it had one, demanded that the Border States come in with them. As evidenced by the word from Gilmer in Virginia, Davis looked good to those states. Cobb, more outspokenly associated with secession than Davis, might not appeal, while his seesawing policy of ten years before and his association with the discredited Buchanan administration disturbed the stronger Southern rights elements within the delegation. A combination of the rumor that Georgia would present Cobb, along with Virginia's preference for Davis, turned them toward the latter, though the majority may have been as slender as a single vote.[124]

So it stood when they all finally went to a much-needed rest on that almost summery night.[125] Tom Cobb went to sleep thinking he had set in motion wheels to stop Stephens and carry his brother to the presidency, hardly imagining the effect of his actions. But when he awoke on a cloudy Saturday morning it began to hit him like a five-gun volley. Already the press had rumors of an expected consensus. Men leaving for Atlanta on the morning train took with them word of an expected Davis victory, and the *Mercury* correspondent, writing early, stated that only Davis and Cobb would be nominated, and that Davis would win.[126] Barnwell felt confidant this morning. "Davis will be elected," he said, "though with out much zeal."[127] And in the Mississippi delegation, James T. Harrison confidently wrote that "Col. Jef. Davis of Mississippi I have no doubt will be elected President."[128]

The Georgians met at the Exchange, where all but Stephens, Hill, and Wright lodged, and with the last two not in attendance.[129] It was ten o'clock, and six of the eight of them present came expecting to choose the first president of the Confederacy. Bartow and Tom Cobb came not knowing what to expect, however, for earlier that morning they canvassed the other delegations and discovered that the Howell Cobb ruse had gone terribly wrong. Probably stunned and uncertain, they sat quietly at first.

Stephens still thought that South Carolina was behind Toombs, in spite of Keitt's conversation of the night before. Moreover, he believed that Louisiana and Florida also favored Toombs, and now he immediately opened by stating the case for his friend and asked if he would accept the nomination. Toombs expected this all along, and responded that he would accept "if it was cordially offered him."[130] That was the only name put on the floor. With Hill absent, no one spoke of Little Aleck, and Stephens did not expect it.[131] Nor did anyone speak for Howell Cobb. His brother and Bartow now knew that it was pointless, and certainly he could not do so for himself, nor would he, his resolution against the presidency now well fixed.[132]

The support for Toombs was strong. Besides Stephens, Crawford stood close behind him, regarding Toombs as a natural leader for the past year or more.[133] Kenan agreed, and Nisbet now sided against the Cobbs-Bartow faction. That decided it. But before they took the actual vote, Tom Cobb spoke up. They were about to put Toombs "in a false position," he said. He had learned that Alabama, Florida, and probably South Carolina had already declared for Davis. Everyone knew where Mississippi stood. When Bartow chimed in to agree, the rest were stunned.[134] How could it be? Everyone, *everyone*, had taken it as a given from the first that Georgia's choice was to be followed by the rest.

Toombs met the news with surprise and incredulity. No doubt Stephens had told him of the discussions with South Carolina, and the assumption that she would go for this Georgian. Everyone knew that Florida would follow along, and the earlier commitment of Alabama he still assumed to be good. Georgia behind him would make the majority of four states. But now it seemed he had none but Georgia. It was too much to believe, and Toombs said so. So did Stephens.[135]

Both Cobb and Bartow insisted that there was no mistake, and Toombs suggested that the other delegations be canvassed before Georgia took further action. If Davis did already command four or more states, then Georgia would put Toombs in the awkward position of balking the decision for unanimity by even nominating him. They asked Crawford to act as a committee of one to go to the other delegations, directing him first to South Carolina and Florida. If they had not gone for Davis as reported, but showed the disposition toward Toombs that he and Stephens still believed existed there—Florida, again, being assumed to ape South Carolina—then he should announce to them that Toombs would be nominated, and Georgia would do so.[136] Thus Toombs would have three states and could bargain for the one more needed, probably Alabama. However, if Crawford found that four of the other states stood for Davis, as reported, then the issue was futile, and Toombs stated that he would not allow his name to be presented.[137] Georgia should join the swell for Davis.[138]

Before Crawford left, Toombs suggested that if the story were true, then Georgia certainly deserved the vice presidency, and he suggested Stephens for the post. Immediately Kenan and Nisbet spoke to second the idea.[139] "What do you say, Aleck?" Toombs asked his friend.[140] Stephens did not want the job, as some of his friends well knew.[141]

Moreover, his objections to being considered for the presidency applied to the second position just as strongly. Not a leader in the movement, but an opponent up to the last minute, he felt himself a poor choice. But Toombs and others pointed out that rather than being divisive, his name ought to help bind the more conservative elements in the Confederate States to the government, and serve as an inducement to the Border States as well. Stephens saw the point. His selection might achieve harmony. Moreover, as between the two executive offices, he rather preferred the second spot. It would be less taxing, and when a permanent constitution created two houses of congress, he would preside as president of the senate, which he expected to have considerable influence.

And so he agreed, but with the proviso that Crawford should mention his name as he canvassed the other states. He would only accept if the response proved unanimous.[142] As he spoke, the two Cobbs and Bartow sat still and quiet as death. It was bad enough to see the plans that two of them had laid go so perversely awry. All three shuddered that Stephens, who had opposed their movement from the first, should receive any honor such as this. Howell Cobb kept his disgust to himself. He could see the majority for Stephens within the delegation. The only way to stop him would be to go before the other delegations himself as a candidate for the office, but that he would not, could not do. Even while he saw the sound policy behind putting a man *like* Little Aleck in the second spot, he could not stomach Stephens. Comforting himself with the thought that it was an empty compliment since "the Vice President has nothing to do," Howell Cobb stood and walked out of the room without saying a word.[143]

"We saw they had us," Tom Cobb reflected as he watched Howell leave. Bartow rose and left next, with the brother Cobb right behind him.[144] With the remaining five delegates united in feeling, they finally voted on the proposal to nominate Toombs, and did so unanimously. In the contingency that Toombs could not be put before the congress, they voted unanimously again to nominate Stephens.[145] That done, they adjourned and Crawford left on his mission.

It did not take him long. With most of the other delegations headquartered at the Exchange, he had but to walk the corridors, from room to room, and one by one he learned that support had swung to Davis. He called on Clayton of Mississippi last, knowing by then that Davis's election was an accomplished reality. Telling Clayton the result of his survey, and expressing satisfaction that Mississippi should now have the presidency, he asked if Stephens would be acceptable for the vice presidency. Clayton assented readily.[146] So did all the others, agreeing with Chesnut that Stephens was a man of high character and ability, and that it would be "right & just" for Georgia to have the second office.[147] Crawford found Toombs, probably at the bar, and gave him the news. Putting as brave a face on the situation as he could, the Georgian immediately called for the rest of his colleagues to honor the agreement to drop his name and unite on Davis. From there it was but a five-minute walk to Mrs. Cleveland's to notify Little Aleck that he was to be vice president.[148]

The Georgians must have been bewildered. At ten o'clock that morning when they first met they were the largest and most influential group in Montgomery, and they expected to choose the president. A scant hour later, as they assembled with the other delegates at the capitol, they were reduced to settling for a vice president put forward by half of their members, not even a majority of the delegation. Crawford understood how it happened, or most of it. "Toombs, Cobb and Stephens were all from the same state, and the political waters were too shallow for them to turn in without injury to each other."[149] Had they come united on one of their number from the first, the presidency was theirs. But by waiting until the last moment—modestly and prudently, so they thought—they only succeeded in fragmenting support for the three of them among the other delegations, and allowed Mississippi to gain ground by offering a single candidate. Moreover, Stephens had told too many people that he did not want the job, and so had Cobb, though both would have taken it if chosen. In the days ahead delegates from other states would tell Stephens that support for Cobb was never strong, thanks to lingering prejudice against his behavior ten years earlier.[150] In short, Stephens turned down his chance at it, Cobb in fact never had one, and Toombs simply squandered his. Still, had they not complacently waited until the morning of February 9 to decide on their candidate, Toombs might still have taken the spot but for the chicanery of Tom Cobb, who helped drive other delegations to Davis out of fear of a Howell Cobb candidacy and an understandable resentment of the haughty Georgians.

With the sun shining brightly and the air approaching seventy degrees they walked to the state house and up the steps to their chamber.[151] Once there, before Howell sounded the gavel, the Cobbs and Bartow learned that Stephens would be vice president. They could do nothing about it now. "We placed ourselves right," Tom Cobb smugly noted, "then let it rock on."[152] The Reverend Manly, who seemed

Montgomery, Alabama, as sketched in February 1861. The statehouse appears at left, the spire of St. John's Episcopal Church in the center. *(Harper's Pictorial History of the Civil War)*

The Alabama firebrand William Lowndes Yancey, founding father of secession. *(Alabama Department of Archives and History)*

The Montgomery & West Point Rail Road depot was where most of the delegates first set foot in the new capital. *(Alabama Department of Archives and History)*

Montgomery, as viewed from atop Montgomery Hall, ca. 1870 with the statehouse in the distance. Monroe Street runs past in the foreground. *(Alabama Department of Archives and History)*

Court Square shortly after the Civil War, looking past the artesian basin up Market Street to the statehouse. *(Alabama Department of Archives and History)*

The Exchange Hotel at left, and in the center Commerce Street leading to the river. From the Commerce-side balcony of the hotel, Davis and others made their speeches. (*Alabama Department of Archives and History*)

The Alabama statehouse, first capitol of the Confederacy, shortly after the war. (*Alabama Department of Archives and History*)

Fat, affable Howell Cobb was trusted to be president of the convention, but not of the Confederacy. (*Museum of the Confederacy*)

Robert Toombs of Georgia wanted the presidency, and perhaps could have had it but for a fatal flaw. (*National Archives*)

Governor A. B. Moore welcomed the Confederates to his own capital, but soon proved a bore to some of his guests. *(Alabama Department of Archives and History)*

William P. Chilton received the convention on behalf of Alabama and sounded the first gavel. *(Alabama Department of Archives and History)*

William Waud's sketch of an early session of the Confederate Congress in February 1861. It was one of those rare moments when the galleries were packed before the doors were closed. *(Museum of the Confederacy)*

"Little Aleck" Stephens, though a half-finished man with the body of a boy, had the mind of a giant. *(Library of Congress)*

…Iarket Street on February 8, 1861. Already the militia parade. *(Harper's Pictorial History of the …ivil War)*

The man and the hour met when Jefferson Davis addressed Montgomery from the Exchange balcony on February 16, 1861; from a sketch by Waud. *(Museum of the Confederacy)*

The only portrait of Jefferson Davis almost certain to have been taken while he was President, probably made in 1861, maybe even at the time of his inauguration. *(Alabama Department of Archives and History)*

always on hand for the most important occasions, delivered the opening prayer. Chief Justice Richard Walker stepped forward from his seat with the Alabama delegation, held a Bible for Howell Cobb's hand, and administered to him the oath prescribed by their new Constitution. When he finished, Cobb took the Bible and called up Walker's colleagues. As he did so, all of the other delegates in the chamber stood at their desks. A Georgia reporter found a "death-like stillness" in the crowded room as the Alabamians raised their hands and repeated after Cobb their oath.[153]

Thereafter, alphabetically, state by state, they came forward and repeated the oath: "You do solemnly swear that you will support the Constitution of the Provisional Government of the Confederate States of America, so help you God."[154] As he finished, each delegate bent forward and kissed the Bible in Cobb's hand. The spectators saw "no signs of fear or trepidation" on their faces as they took their oaths—Alabama, Florida, Georgia, Louisiana, Mississippi. Finally came South Carolina, and for Rhett the culmination of nearly a life's work. With his oath he became a citizen of a new Southern nation. To all who watched, it presented an "impressive and solemn scene."[155] The only act to mar it came at the very end when Withers, who added agnosticism to his other peculiarities, refused to kiss the Bible. While Tom Cobb seethed at his seat, conceiving an immediate disgust and loathing for the man, brother Howell, the ceremony at an end, put the Bible in his pocket to keep as a memento.[156]

They all appeared to breathe easier when it was over, a certain tension gone from the floor.[157] Immediately following came the call of the states for memorials. Anxious to get to the election, none presented any until Memminger stood for South Carolina to present two designs for a flag for the new nation. He showed them a blue cross of seven stars on a red field, and declared it to be inspired by the Southern Cross constellation (which, ironically, could not be seen in their hemisphere), then somehow even managed to include the poet Dante and the explorer Humboldt in his speech. On this solemn occasion, he mused, "the debt of the South to the cross should be recognized." But in presenting the second design, he suggested a hope for the future, for it contained fifteen stars, one for every slave state, emblematic of the prayer that one day soon they would all be together "in the glorious constellation of our Southern Confederacy."[158]

The galleries loved it, and broke out in applause, not realizing that before long, "flag" speeches were about all they would get in open session, and far too many of them at that. Miles moved that a committee undertake the selection of a design, and that Memminger's be referred to it, which the chair approved. Then Stephens rose to turn to more substantive matters, proposing that Cobb appoint standing committees on foreign affairs, finance, military and naval affairs, judiciary, postal affairs, accounts, engrossments, patents, and printing, each to consist of five members. Congress adopted his resolution, and that done, Crawford moved them into secret session for the election.[159]

It took but half an hour.[160] Knowing what was to happen and thinking it improper that he should participate, Stephens got up and stepped out with the spectators.[161] On the call for nominations, Mississippi alone stood and presented the name of Jefferson Davis.[162] Alphabetically by states, with Curry and Miles acting as tellers, the chairman of each delegation arose to cast its vote.[163] As they did so, a flood of thoughts and emotions passed through some who sat quietly on the floor. Those few who still favored Yancey showed their chagrin, and Toombs's mortification at this moment seemed evident, at least to Tom Cobb. Trying to conceal his emotions, the Georgian told those around him that he had not really wanted the office.[164] But his closest friends, then and later, sensed what one said, that "Toombs regarded this as the great miscarriage of his life."[165]

From his seat in front of Rhett, Chesnut turned and commented with something like resignation, "Uncle! I suppose I must vote for him." Of course, he had already done so, and the comment now was purely rhetorical.[166] The words intruded upon the bitter thoughts in Rhett's mind. Now, for once, the South Carolinians willingly acknowledged him as their leader as they let him stand to cast their state's vote.[167] It cruelly punctuated for Rhett his disappointment that these votes now cast were not for him. Two days later he would moan that "life is nothing but a continual series of disappointments."[168] After his years of struggle, *he* deserved this office. *He* was the man to lead the new Southern nation. As if to thrust a needle into the wound already so deep, when the balloting was through and Cobb proclaimed Davis the victor, he appointed Rhett to the formal committee charged with notifying the Mississippian. Without ever meeting Jefferson Davis, Rhett began to hate him.[169]

Bitter, too, was Tom Cobb, and as the house turned next to the balloting for vice president, he pointedly ignored the whole proceeding and sat at his desk writing a letter to Marion. It was all too much. As the delegations voted he poured out his frustration. "So is the world, the man who has fought against our rights and liberty is selected to wear the laurels of our victory." Granting that Stephens's election might conciliate the border, he feared that it would deflate true Southern rights men. It was a "bitter pill," he lamented, made the worse by his unspoken realization that he had contributed to it by his bungled maneuver. Instead of electing Howell, he cost Georgia the presidency entirely, thus reducing the influence of which he was so proud. And while he helped stop any movement for Stephens for the office, such as it was by then, his action indirectly led to Little Aleck's choice for the vice presidency. *"I wish I was at home,"* he complained. "I have felt like a whipped dog."[170] Within days he would be complaining to her of all "the daily manifestations of selfishness, intrigue, low cunning, and meanness" in his fellow congressmen, conveniently forgetting that of all of the mean, low, selfish intriguers, he had been the first.[171]

Someone given to flights of fanciful speculation might now have remembered that train wreck only six days before. If the train had been going faster, or if the passenger cars had been in front where they would have run off instead of the baggage wagons, the potential results were incalculable, he might muse. Toombs and Stephens, two top contenders for the presidency, were aboard. With them either killed or seriously injured, only Howell Cobb would remain as a potential Georgia candidate. With Anderson on the same car, the chief mover for Davis in the Florida delegation could have been eliminated. With Chesnut and Withers aboard, two votes that gave Davis a slim majority in South Carolina stood in jeopardy. And with Tom Cobb possibly out of the way by the same accident, the principal source of resentment against Georgia would be removed, not to mention the mover of the botched play for his brother Howell. Eliminate the one-vote majorities for Davis in Florida and South Carolina, eliminate two anti-Cobb votes from the Georgia delegation and with them his only opponents for the nomination itself, and the whole picture of the election changed. South Carolina could have gone to Cobb, and Florida with it. To whatever extent Tom Cobb's cunning drove other delegations toward Davis, that influence would have been removed. Georgia, with only one candidate of presidential stature left, would have had little choice but to put forward Howell Cobb, and without waiting until the last minute. And even if Georgia did take its time, other states, acting on the prevalent assumption that Georgia should have the nomination, would have had no one to turn to but him.

A little more speed, a different arrangement of the cars, and the one potential candidate who never had a real chance here in Montgomery might have taken the presidency.[172]

CHAPTER SIX

GETTING ALONG WITH SEVEN-LEAGUE BOOTS

———— ◆●★●◆ ————

THE WHOLE CITY WAITED. Moments after the applause exploded in the galleries at the announcement, Montgomery itself went wild.[1] Over at the Montgomery & West Point depot the locomotive whistles shrieked.[2] The steamboats on the Alabama and down at the wharf joined in, and in anticipation of a result, militia brought cannon onto the grounds of the state house. At three o'clock a young lady of the town touched off the first shot of a salute that burned fully a hundred pounds of powder before it ended, oblivious of the city ordinance prescribing a $5 fine for firing a gun in the town limits.[3] As the smoke from the cannon rose in the still afternoon air, it encircled the Alabama independence flag flying above the state house.[4] Cynics, by now jaded on fireworks and demonstrations, smirked that "we will probably have an apology for an illumination tonight."[5]

The telegrapher down in the Winter Building sent a steady stream of terse, but exultant messages over the wires, especially to the Border State governors and their conventions.[6] Meanwhile members of Congress penned their thoughts, many writing even while they returned to a brief secret session after announcing the election. Miles hastened to scribble a note to Governor Pickens, and virtually all who wrote attempted to spread the impression of unity.[7] "We are getting along with great harmony," said Keitt, adding that the election of Davis and Stephens only enhanced their singleness of purpose. "We have started a govt," he wrote, "and I do not see any thing to mar our unity."[8] Toombs sent out word that "there is no difference of opinion here."[9] Even the Texas delegates, who having no vote as yet, took no part in the intense politicking of the past two days, tried to spread the word of unanimity.[10] While a few might grumble that their new name for themselves, "Confederate," sounded less than distinctive, others

thought it hit the mark exactly.[11] "The word Confederate truly expresses our present condition," Harrison wrote to his wife in Mississippi.[12] It
spoke to their unity of mind and purpose. Only Vice President-elect
Stephens, writing immediately after the election and while still in
secret session, hinted at the grain beneath the veneer. "I have a great
deal to say to you about this and other matters," he told Linton. But it
would have to wait until they could speak face to face.[13]

While the celebration spread outside, the Congress went on to other
important work. Unyielding in his hostility toward these secret sessions, Rhett moved that members be allowed at least to tell their state
conventions of their actions in the forming of the Constitution—
which meant that he wanted South Carolina to know what *he* had
done, and what he had opposed. He got his wish. Congress also acted
immediately on his motion to appoint a new committee to draft the
permanent constitution. Given a few minutes to deliberate among
themselves, the several states announced their appointees: Walker and
Bob Smith, Morton and Owens, Toombs and Tom Cobb—an unlikely
pair just now—De Clouet and Sparrow, Clayton and Harris, and Rhett
himself and Chesnut.

Harris moved, and the body passed, a resolution declaring all eight
volumes of the current United States statutes to be immediately in
force in the Confederate States, unless or until amended or repealed.
Only South Carolina voted in the negative. Rhett, of course, was
incensed, for those statutes included the 1857 tariff, passed chiefly by
Northern votes, that continued to stand in the way of free trade. The
Confederacy was going to need money, however, and now Memminger
passed a resolution for the finance committee to report as soon as possible a revenue tariff of their own. The house assigned Shorter, Chilton, and McRae to a committee to investigate suitable buildings in
Montgomery to house the executive and its departments, and report
on the anticipated expense of fitting them out for business, and Miles
closed the session by suggesting that the flag committee also consider
devices for a great seal, arms, and a motto.[14] It was a lot to set in
motion in a single day. Even the *Mercury* correspondent had to admit
that "we are getting along with seven-league boots."[15]

The "apology" for an illumination that night set the city to sparkling. In the unseasonably warm evening, several hundred gathered at
the Montgomery Theatre at seven o'clock, where hastily printed handbills earlier in the afternoon had announced a procession would form.
Following Mr. Canning's "accomplished brass band" playing "Dixie,"

the crowd marched up Perry to Market, down Market to Court Square, then up Montgomery to Mrs. Cleveland's, gathering numbers along the way. Once there, they found even more waiting in anticipation of an entertainment. As Canning led his men in the "Marseillaise," a committee called on Stephens and offered congratulations. As they spoke, the crowd outside began to cry for Little Aleck to come out. The people were hungry for speeches, and would not be denied.

Stephens stepped out onto the portico of the house, where Judge Samuel A. Rice introduced him to the crowd. He felt unwell—as usual—and apologized that his voice and the night air prevented him from giving them as much as they wanted. Calling them "fellow citizens," for surely they were all once more citizens of a common country, he congratulated them that on this day "the Confederate States of America has been ushered into existence, to take its place amongst the nations of the world." Their future as Confederate citizens rested now with themselves. He expected that in time the remaining slave states would join with them, and then that republic might expect a bright future if they all showed virtue, intelligence, integrity, and patriotism. He called these the "corner stones" of liberty. For themselves they enjoyed a climate that produced staples treasured around the world, and in slavery they had a labor system ordained by God himself. Toward others they should hold out the hand of peace and friendship. If conflict came, they must not strike the first blow. "We ask of all others simply to be let alone," he said, each allowing the other, in the spirit of friendly competition, to develop "the highest qualities of our nature."[16]

Amid wild cheers, Stephens went back indoors, and the band struck up "Dixie" once more, leading the procession back down Montgomery to the Exchange. Shouts of "Toombs," "Keitt," "Barry," "Clitherall," and "Perkins" rang out, and one by one they stepped onto the second floor portico to address the gathering. Each in turn made a few remarks, Keitt forgetting his wife's injunction to keep his mouth shut and speaking the longest. "We have taken our household gods from the old temple which our fathers built," he told them, "and we will never carry them back."[17] "The old Union is dead; its body has been carried to its last resting place; its honors and decorations have been laid upon the coffin." The Border States must inevitably come to make common cause with them. "But, gentlemen, come they quickly, or come they slowly, or come they never, our separation is final, absolute and eternal."[18] Still stunned from the day's disappointment, Toombs

seconded Keitt's flourishes, only admonishing the crowd that they
must be prepared to defend themselves. "Liberty, in its last analysis,"
he said, "is but the blood of the brave."[19]

After Clitherall made a few humorous remarks, the band and the
crowd moved on, down to Montgomery Hall. Their blood up, they
wanted more, and more. From the street they shouted out the names:
"Ben Hill," "Cobb," "Both Cobbs," "Bartow," "Wright," "Withers."
Exasperated when no one answered the summons, they started shouting simply "somebody." Part of the problem, of course, was that the
Cobbs, among others, boarded at the Exchange, not Montgomery Hall.
Finally Judge Rice went inside looking for speakers, and came out on
the portico with the sad news that he could find none. The crowd
started to grumble, one of them protesting at "not having been fed
with half enough big speeches."[20] But finally Chesnut stepped out from
his room and gave them half an hour that renewed their frenzy and
ably capped the evening.[21]

Not everyone in Montgomery shared the elation. In room 6 at the
Exchange, Rhett remained indoors while the speakers held forth outside. No one had called *him* out. Instead he fumed over the secret sessions still, noting especially that Article I, Section 3 of the new provisional Constitution called for Congress to publish its proceedings from
time to time, excepting only those portions absolutely requiring secrecy. He would keep that in his pocket as a weapon in his cause if needed. "Conscience and the Constitution, duty and policy," he felt, dictated that the people should know what he—they—had to say.[22] As for
this Constitution the fools outside were celebrating, he now regretted
"that any Provisional Government was formed at all." The acceptance
of the 1857 tariff, if only until the finance committee presented a better one, affronted him. "Free trade is the true policy of the Confederate States," he insisted. He bristled that any such "stigma of illegiti-
macy and illegality should be placed upon the institution of slavery" as
the prohibition of the slave trade. England imported its coolies and
France used unpaid apprentices, all of whom thereby competed unfair-
ly with Southern labor, to his mind. Only slavery allowed planters to
even the balance for cheap labor. These and other ills he resolved here
and now to redress in the permanent constitution.[23] Also among those
ignoring the festivities, Tom Cobb went to a Saturday evening prayer
meeting in company with Nisbet. Once in the church he felt more at
home, his head still swimming with the day's events and the influence
of his own actions upon them. Howell at least tried to cheer him with

an offer of the chairmanship of the new judiciary committee, but Tom wisely declined. It smacked too much of favoritism.[24]

For the rest, it was the grandest night yet seen in Montgomery. They had a government, a president, and they confidently hoped and expected that their fair city would become the permanent capital of the new nation. It only required what some called "the proper public spirit and judicious liberality."[25] Certainly no one could fault their spirit this night. Indeed, the enthusiasm so carried away all of them that the keepers of the state house forgot to bring down their proud Alabama flag with Liberty holding her sword and banner. As a warm gale came up during the night, the high winds began to rip it apart.[26]

As the evening crowd dispersed, and the illuminations in Montgomery's windows winked out one by one, other lights burned late some 250 miles west at Brierfield plantation. Jefferson Davis was packing. That afternoon, immediately after the close of the secret session, Toombs sent a telegram signed by Rhett and Morton as well. "We are directed to inform You that You were this day unanimously elected President of the provisional Government of the Confederate States of America, and to request you to Come to Montgomery immediately."[27] Probably learning from Clayton that Pettus had already asked Davis to come to Jackson, they sent multiple copies, one to Jackson, and another to Vicksburg for delivery to Davis's home. Moreover, they now dispatched Davis's old friend the newspaperman William M. Browne to take a copy of the notification to Davis by hand.

Speedy as the wires could be, the telegram still had to be relayed from office to office, sent and resent as it made its way west. It was five in the afternoon or later when finally telegrapher Lee Daniel in Vicksburg heard the great news clicking out at his desk. Vicksburg was ready for this. Just the day before the Vicksburg *Sun* had put the name of Jefferson Davis on its masthead, anticipating his election.[28] Now as Daniel realized what had happened, he discussed it with others and they soon engaged a messenger to ride to Brierfield, nearly twenty miles downriver, to inform Davis.[29] Swiftly the horseman pounded off down the river road.

Still recovering from his recent illness, Jefferson Davis came back to Brierfield expecting to spend some time with his dog and his parrot, and what was to him "the most agreeable [*sic*] of all labors planting shrubs & trees and directing the operations of my field." Home only a few days, he already had his slaves at work plowing the ground for the new cotton crop. He held no illusions. He knew that he would likely be called away from home in his capacity as major general commanding Mississippi's militia, and the telegram from Pettus on February 7 summoning him to Jackson only confirmed his expectation, however much it disappointed his inner wishes. "I feel the strongest desire to pass the remainder of my days in the peaceful useful toil of my little cotton field," he told a friend the day Pettus's telegram arrived.[30]

In the warm evening air of February 9 Davis and Varina turned their hands to their neglected garden. He grew up at Woodville, Mississippi, surrounded by the scent of the roses his mother Jane grew in hedges around their modest home, "Rosemont."[31] Now he kept his own, and had new rose cuttings in his hand when he saw the rider approaching on a well-lathered horse. As he read the telegram, Davis' face grew stern, then showed dismay, even grief. Looking on, Varina thought the message must bring news of a death in the family, until he spoke to her after a few silent moments. "As a man might speak of a sentence of death," she said, he told her he was to be president.[32]

He did not want this, though he had feared it. The letter to Clayton, he thought, took him out of consideration, but now he realized that he had been too equivocal. "Notwithstanding my years of political service," he would say, "I had no fondness for it and felt always a distaste for its belongings."[33] But now, in the crisis at hand, and with his expressed sense of duty and willingness to accept whatever task the South set him, he could not refuse. "O God spare me this responsibility," he confided to his brother Joseph. But he could not spare himself.[34] That same evening he called together his slaves and told them he would be leaving the next day for Montgomery. He packed. He looked around his beloved Brierfield. And he sent back by the same rider a brief note of acceptance.

By one o'clock on February 10, his response surged eastward on the wires to Montgomery,[35] where at the end of an almost frantic week the delegates took off their seven-league boots for a Sunday of rest. Clitherall and others noticed the torn flag atop the state house and brought it down, now too damaged ever to fly again. They sent it to Governor Moore as a treasured relic of the state's brief period of independence. As temperatures rose above seventy degrees and the air turned humid on a cloudy, windy day, they went to their several churches.[36] George Petrie had offered Stephens the use of his family pew, number 10, at the Presbyterian church, and Little Aleck accepted.[37] He already felt even more ill than the day before. The close night air and a mind troubled by the enormity of his new position robbed him of all but a little sleep.[38] Now on his arrival he discovered that Petrie had invited others from the Georgia delegation, as well. He sat through a service with Hill at his side, the venue allowing each an excuse not to speak, even though Stephens was beginning to learn of Hill's advocacy during recent days.[39] A few blocks away Tom Cobb and others sat for the Baptist Basil Manly's sermon, this one drawn quite appropriately from Daniel—"Now when Daniel knew that the writing was signed . . . he kneeled upon his knees three times a day."[40] In the afternoon he sent valentines home to his wife and children, presents to him from a bookstore operator anxious for delegates' business.[41] Brother Howell indulged himself—as he often did—with oysters, fresh fish, and succulent oranges, and the hope that with everyone now anxious to go home, he could hold them there until their work was truly done.[42] That night Little Aleck went to bed early and for a change enjoyed a good night's sleep, untroubled by coughing.[43]

The rain came down again all through that night and into the morning, offering a bleak portent for Stephens's swearing-in scheduled to take place in the afternoon. But when he awoke, he saw a bright, clear blue sky, cheering him as he wrote his remarks for the occasion and committed them to memory. The delegates reassembled at eleven, with the chamber and its galleries thronged with spectators come for the event.[44] They transacted only a little business first, Conrad commencing the authorization of the executive departments by suggesting a committee to prepare a formal establishing bill. Stephens suggested further that the military and naval committee be split in two, with the addition of further committees on territories, public lands, and Indian affairs. Both propositions carried, and then they went into a brief secret session before a half-hour recess. At one o'clock they returned and opened the doors for the ceremony.[45]

Cobb announced Stephens, who arose and walked toward the rostrum. It was Little Aleck's birthday—the forty-ninth—and the coincidence of the two occasions strangely troubled him. More disturbing still were the myriad doubts that stepped forward with him. He felt a temptation simply to run away from the responsibilities before him, and an even greater aversion to making any sort of speech now. Yet they expected something from him, and he could not disappoint.[46] He could feel himself on the edge of the dark side of his temperament. "I have in my life been one of the most miserable beings, it seems to me, that walked the earth," he confided to his friend Richard Johnston, "subject to occasional fits of depression that seemed well-nigh bordering on despair. Without enjoyment, without pleasure, without hope, and without sympathy with the world."[47] He could feel it now.

Standing at the rostrum, with the two flag models presented by Memminger hanging above him, he spoke.[48] Despite having carefully prepared his remarks, he used no text or notes and feigned that it was extemporaneous. Fearing in advance that he might disappoint, he proceeded to do so. He sounded almost apologetic at accepting the high office proffered him, and gave clear evidence that he only accepted because he thought no man had a right to refuse when called to a public trust. That said, he declined to comment on their present condition, their relations with the former Union, or the potential dangers ahead, since all of that was better left for the president-elect on his arrival. Until then, he suggested that they should use their time profitably, get to work establishing their postal arrangements and customs houses, and decide on their tariff duties. He suggested ten percent. Above all, they must proceed without delay to the permanent constitution.[49]

While Stephens spoke, Tom Cobb once again studiously ignored him, and instead lifted the top of his desk to take a sheet of writing paper. Spreading it on the green felt desk surface, he penned his wife a self-serving account of the confusion among the Georgians the morning of the election, with no mention of his own less than honorable role in the affair, and offering the outright lie that brother Howell was the choice of the delegation. If Little Aleck felt depressed, so did Cobb. "I am so tired of this place and this life," he moaned.[50] There, at least, he and his enemy now taking the oath of office felt as one.

Stephens's fears that he would disappoint proved prescient. Capable of searing eloquence, he met the occasion with tepid banality. Disappointment swept through the galleries, and some vented their anger as Congress adjourned and they filed out. Basil Manly decided earlier not to attend. "I did not think it worthwhile to go," he said, and he was proved right.[51] Throughout Montgomery went the word of Stephens's poor performance. The people expected theater, drama, and flights of oratorical patriotism. The Georgian gave them only diffidence, evasion, and mundane advice.[52]

That evening some of Montgomery's leading citizens took a matter into their own hands. Knowing of the committee appointed to investigate quarters for the executive departments, they met at Estelle Hall and decided to offer the upper floor of the Montgomery Insurance Building at the northwest corner of Commerce and Bibb. Huge, comprising more than twenty rooms, and only a block from the Exchange, it seemed ideal. That done, they promised also to start looking for an executive mansion for Davis when he arrived. These men made no pretense of modesty at all in their desire that the permanent capital should be their city.[53] While citizens looked toward housing for the president and his government officers, some of the congressmen sought better shelter for themselves. Montgomery hotel prices quickly grew exorbitant with the influx of men of means and influence. Mrs. Cleveland having some empty rooms, Crawford moved from the Exchange this evening to join his friend Stephens, and Toombs promised to come in later in the week. When he checked out of the hotel, Crawford learned from the proprietor that, as he was a congressman, there would be no charge for his room and board. But then the smiling hotelier added, as Crawford put it, "that I might if I chose leave them $40—for the servants." Having stayed there just eight days, that worked out to $5 per day, almost double the standard room and board.[54]

While Crawford and Stephens stayed up late, the former shaking Little Aleck out of his mood with an inexhaustible fund of witty stories and recollections of their old days in Washington, Southern response to the election finally started to come in, since most newspapers could not announce the news until their Monday editions.[55] In Washington, Wigfall greeted the announcement with joy. "Now, Lord, let thy servant depart in peace," he prayed for Yankee ears.[56] Governors Pickens and Brown declared Davis a great choice.[57] Prominent statesmen gave much the same reaction, though one not unmixed with second thoughts. Herschel Johnson of Georgia approved Davis, but thought Little Aleck the better man. "On some accounts Davis is well enough for the Presidency," he said on learning the news. "He has courage and military instinct. But I never thought him a Statesman of the first order." He feared Davis was only a conservative when it came to his own reputation, and only an ultra when he gave way to his vaunted "fiery impulses."[58]

Alabamians disagreed. A supreme court judge pronounced Davis the ablest man for the presidency since his namesake Thomas Jefferson,[59] and Curry sent out the word that no better selection could have been made.[60] Linton Stephens thought Davis a safe choice, but a "mean" one,[61] while Hammond in South Carolina scarcely concealed displeasure. "He is not the man ever to forgive," grumbled Hammond; "he is as malignant as the Devil." Moreover, he found it unthinkable that a man who tried so hard to hold the Democratic party together a year before, and thereby the Union, should now be so honored with the first office among secessionists.[62] Others also took Davis's moderation as a possible sign of his being a reconstructionist, which some thought might hurt the cause in the Border States.[63] Even Wigfall's wife complained that "eleventh-hour men" like Davis and Stephens seemed to reap all the rewards, but others countered that they thought better of men who acted not rashly, but stopped to think.[64]

Considering how little news got out of Montgomery as yet, the editors reacted with vigor, and near-unanimous approval. The New Orleans press spoke as one in praise, only the *Bee* suggesting that Stephens might have been a wiser choice, while the *Daily Delta* predicted that Davis might also become the permanent president when the provisional government expired in a year.[65] From South Carolina came word of general satisfaction, and derision at the thought that Davis might be a reconstructionist.[66] Seconding the dismissal of questions on Davis's soundness, even the Nashville press hailed the election.[67] What few complaints came out centered on technicalities, like dissatisfaction with the name of the new nation. To some "Confederate States of America" implied rather too much nationality. In preference, and to stress the sovereignty of the individual states, they suggested changing the name to "League of Nations," "The Allied Nations," or "Allied Republics." One even suggested "The Six Nations," presumably entailing a name change every time another state joined the confederation.[68] Most common of all were responses like that of the Grove Hill, Alabama, *Clark County Democrat*: "Three cheers and a tiger for the new Government."[69]

Men close to the decision makers in Montgomery recognized that behind the euphoria and the speech making there still lay peril and uncertainty. The times called for an end to the rashness that precipitated so many of them into secession originally. They would "lay our tyrants as flat as pancakes," said a friend of Chesnut's, if only they observed caution.[70] A South Carolina reporter found among the delegates a universal determination "to sink or swim, to perish or succeed, with an independent Government."[71] Hooper heard not one voice raised in favor of returning to the Union in any fashion, and Cobb and Stephens agreed.[72] "There is no compromise that the seceded States would accept," Howell declared. Not one member had advocated it in his hearing, but instead he heard around him that "the idea of going back to the Union is ridiculed."[73] Little Aleck agreed, reporting that "no person here thinks of any compromise or of returning to the old Government on any terms."[74] The idea of reconstruction simply did not abide in Montgomery.

Even fears of coming to blows over separation did not take deep hold. Tom Cobb believed the signs argued against any collision—at least anything major—and in a few days thought his assumption universal, and fear daily diminishing.[75] Bartow believed it probable there would be no war,[76] and Curry argued now that the interests of both sides so favored peace that "war can hardly be unnecessarily attempted."[77] Wilson of Mississippi saw in many hopes that the entire success of the movement might be achieved without blood,[78] and even Rhett, speaking through the *Mercury*, proclaimed that "there will be no war," his correspondent saying that fighting would be something dwelling only in the poetry section of the newspaper.[79] Clayton put it simply: "A hundred thousand bayonets was the strongest argument for peace."[80] Yet some still worried. Nisbet thought he saw a pervading opinion that some kind of low-scale conflict loomed before them, and confessed that "what *that* may result in no one can tell."[81] No one trembled more than Stephens, whose belief that this would all end on the battlefield never left him. Incredulously, he watched others blithely dismiss talk of war, or else speak gaily of it as a grand adventure, sure to whip the Yankees in one glorious battle. Still in the grip of his depression, he told housemate Crawford that if their efforts went down to defeat in conflict, he prayed not to survive the cause.[82]

In fact, some here in Montgomery already heard the rattle of sabers, and contributed to the din. "There are a few," Wilson complained the night of the election, "who believed in nothing but the Logic of Cannon and Ball,"[83] and a Georgia journalist lamented that "some of the members are quite rampant, and seem possessed with a mad desire to rashly precipitate the country into a bloody collision."[84] Predictably, they were the hotheads like Bartow and the South Carolinians. The *Mercury* reporter almost struck a man on the street who asked him with a smirk "when are you going to take those seventy men in Fort Sumter."[85] The embarrassment of the tiny Yankee garrison glaring defiantly at all of the armed South Carolinians ringing Charleston Harbor dug at her delegates like a knife. Even mild-mannered Barnwell complained of Governor Pickens's folly and cowardice in irresolutely waiting and watching. Moreover, it hurt them here in Montgomery. "We are much weakened in influence here by the unfortunate condition of things in Charleston," he complained.[86]

Yet when Pickens appealed to Miles before the Constitution's adoption to create immediately a strong government and take control of military affairs, Miles counseled restraint.[87] Any move now to take Sumter could plunge the whole Confederacy into a war, which South Carolina had not the right to do. The Palmetto State had already demonstrated its courage repeatedly in the past. Here in Montgomery men more often questioned her wisdom and good sense. The Confederacy was not ready to take action, and the South Carolina delegation must be careful in pressing the matter. "We cannot," said Miles, "seem to implore our brother delegates." Rather, "it is for them to suggest action of some sort, not for us."[88]

Toward that end, Miles and probably Keitt, who expressed his own anxiety for Congress to do something immediately about the forts,[89] met with Toombs to ask him to tender a resolution on February 11 officially asking Charleston not to start hostilities. That would relieve Pickens of his embarrassment, and the South Carolinians of theirs. But they ran up against the perversity of Rhett, who felt that South Carolina was "disgraced already," and did not deserve to be relieved. "No reasoning on Earth can satisfy the people of the South that in these two months a whole State could not take a fort defended by but 70 men. The effort is absurd. We must be despised." Somehow he persuaded Toombs against making the motion "to get the miserable imbeciles in Charleston out of their disgraceful position." Moreover, in disgust Rhett predicted that when Davis took office, he would not force the issue, but would attempt to negotiate.[90] Not content with attacking everyone else, Rhett as an opposition party of one would just as soon strike out at his own state.

While Toombs backed off, others took the matter away from Rhett. Clayton heard rumors that Pickens was preparing unilaterally to launch an attack, and Toombs undoubtedly told his Georgia colleagues of his thwarted resolution.[91] After an inconsequential open session February 12, during which the standing committees got their appointments and more flag designs came forward, they closed the doors and went to work. Chilton introduced a resolution to send a commission to Washington to ask for recognition and settle all disputes over the forts and arsenals, and then Kenan, Bartow, and Clayton, with Chesnut's help, fashioned among themselves an acceptable resolution whereby the government immediately assumed charge of all disputes over forts and other public installations. It passed at once.[92] Howell Cobb immediately wired the news to all governors, and coincidentally a telegram came from Davis strongly advising against any overt action toward Fort Sumter.[93]

It was hardly a crisis averted, but in such a delicate matter as the possibility of war the new Confederacy simply could not afford to be guided by a blind doctrinairian like Rhett, and especially with promising news coming from other quarters. Wigfall wired now from Washington that the French minister said that France would certainly grant formal recognition to the Confederacy at once. Former Senator John Slidell soon wrote to Howell Cobb from New Orleans confirming the same news.[94] There was the vital first step. If France recognized, Great Britain and the rest would surely do the same. That done, independence set assured, for any attempt by the North to coerce the Confederacy back into the Union would then be viewed as an aggression against a member of the family of nations, and European needs for cotton would decide its choosing of sides. Even now Tom Cobb discussed a "cotton scheme" with his colleagues, an embargo to coerce Europe into recognition or face a cutoff of their supply. It seemed that this Cobb always thought in terms of schemes and crafty maneuvers, but his colleagues all told him to forget it, at least until other nations actually refused to acknowledge their independence.[95] The good news about France suggested there might never be a need for an embargo. Besides, foreign policy like this belonged to presidents, and not to increasingly disliked and discredited congressmen.

After the heavy rains of the weekend, the delegates saw a sheet of water for miles along the Alabama as they daily walked up Goat Hill to continue their work of building and organization.[96] Day after day they gathered, impressing one correspondent as "plain farmer looking, serious men, invested with a sort of unaffected revolutionary simplicity."[97] A friend of Chesnut's who watched their daily proceedings concluded that these men intended to accomplish so much as to make any future Congress little more than a caretaker.[98] Howell Cobb himself spoke the tone that animated most of them. "It is a good rule in big and little things," he said this week, "that what is worth doing at all, is worth doing well, whether applied to dressing up a great government or a little doll."[99] If anything, the men sitting on the floor of the chamber feared that their work would last too long. Tom Cobb, pining for his wife and children, worried that the session might go another two weeks or longer,[100] and Wilson lamented, "God knows when we shall get away." He wanted to resign and go home as soon as he could, and so did others he knew. Yet he feared framing a permanent constitution might take up to three months. Most of them came expecting quick work and a speedy departure. With men like himself and others planning to resign, he wondered if the permanent constitution and even the Congress itself might not in the end lie in the hands of a small committee of those willing to remain.[101]

Meanwhile they worked. They set their hour of convening back from eleven o'clock to noon, to allow the committees extra time in the mornings to work on their recommendations. Brooke and Clayton often arrived in the hall first, half an hour before time, and sat at their desks writing. Hooper, of course, came early to prepare for the day's stenography, his ever-present pipe ringing his "ugly mug of a countenance" with pungent smoke. Reporters gathered early in the perpetual triumph of hope over experience, praying each new day that something would actually happen in open session besides the increasingly interminable presentation of flag designs.[102] "Keen as briars" they appeared every morning, wrote one of the scribblers, only to return home to their lodgings "as dull as bricks."[103] When the delegates themselves arrived in the forenoon, many already sagged from weariness. Each sat on as many as three committees, the first meeting right after breakfast, the next subsequent to the adjournment of Congress around four o'clock, and the third following supper from seven-thirty until ten or later. The round of parties and socials that filled the first week in Montgomery now seemed a distant memory.[104]

Their effort came at a price. Already depressed over the election, Tom Cobb could not take his mind from Marion, even in secret session during the debate on an important bill. When she wrote that she would not come to the inauguration of Davis and suggested that her husband was accomplishing more without her there, his anxiety only increased.[105] Keitt pined like a lovesick schoolboy, and in the expected romantic language of his culture. "Here I am in the midst of pageantry, cheers, enthusiasm and waving kerchiefs, more completely alone and lonely than I would be by the dead sea," he moaned. "What do I care for all these banners and sensations and shouts while you are not with me?" When he saw a pretty view, it grew dull because Susan was not there to share it with him. He would do his duty, he determined, but as soon as they finished their work "I may justly give way to my soul's longings, and fly right back to you."[106]

As yet they knew not what the policy of the new government would be. That awaited Davis's arrival and assumption of office.[107] Until then they strove to have a government ready to act. Every day after the rou-

tine open session show of presenting memorials and petitions from citizens, flag designs, reporting new bills, and reading engrossed and
passed acts, they closed the doors and got started. Matters military
commanded immediate attention. Bartow, at the head of the Military
Affairs committee, presented a resolution for organizing the army of
the Confederacy, while a much more energetic Conrad led Naval
Affairs in reporting bills and resolutions to establish the navy, purchase
warships, hire naval experts, and in accepting the services of naval officers recently resigned from the old United States Navy. Others proposed inquiry into establishing armories and powder mills, and Wright
presented a letter from an iron founder in Etowah, Georgia, offering to
convert his works to the casting of ordnance. With a bit of dithering as
they felt their way through legislation, they first wanted to refer
armories to Finance, and then to a select committee, before they finally sent it to Military Affairs where it belonged.[108]

Wisely they decided not to pursue Memminger's original suggestion
that the provisional constitution empower Congress to elect a general-
in-chief.[109] By common assent, they believed that Davis should make
that choice himself, with only Rhett and Barnwell in strong disagreement. Suspicious of the powers of a chief executive, still they did not
want to cripple him, especially a sound military man like Davis.[110]
Bartow, too, finally retreated from a strident resolution introduced that
would have called on Davis to attack and take Fort Sumter if the
Yankees did not surrender it on demand. Cooled by sounder heads, the
final resolution simply *authorized* the president to do so.[111]

Hand-in-hand with military preparations went their efforts at peaceful separation. Nisbet suggested that Davis be directed to send a peace
commission to Washington as soon as he took his oath, and Chilton
went even further, with specific instructions. Rhett's Foreign Affairs
committee took those recommendations and turned them into a resolution that requested the president to do so.[112] In domestic diplomacy
he was content, apparently, not to meddle with the executive's prerogatives. Besides, by not giving Davis specific instructions, he could allow
Charleston's embarrassment to continue a little longer. But on international diplomacy a different Rhett emerged. All agreed with Keitt when
he declared that "we must get before the world."[113] Walker of Foreign
Affairs moved and passed a resolution that the committee itself should
investigate sending commissioners to Britain and the European powers. The next day, February 13, Rhett actually tried to preempt the constitutional prerogatives of the president by reporting a resolution that

Congress itself elect a commission of three men to go abroad at once, subject to the instructions of Congress until Davis took his oath. Seeing the threat, Perkins, Boyce, and Withers all moved to dilute the measure and leave the appointments to Davis. Since Davis would be here and in charge in a bare few days, there would be no time for Congress to act in the matter anyhow, but many would not forget what Rhett attempted.[114]

The other committees showed equal vigor. Proposals for admission of new states came forward, Chilton's Postal Affairs people reported a comprehensive plan for establishing a system that would pay for itself by raising rates and cutting costs, Toombs moved making the secret journals of Congress available to the president at all times, and with a view to promoting public spirit, they granted Hooper permission to publish a facsimile version of the Provisional Constitution with their signatures. They also appointed Clitherall as an assistant to Hooper, and with further attention to the needs for secrecy, required Shorter and Reid to print all congressional material in a private and locked room. Reporting on behalf of the committee to find a government building, John Shorter told of the tender of the Montgomery Insurance Company building on Commerce, offered by the citizens of the city free of charge. Deeming his committee unauthorized to accept a gift, he went on to negotiate with the owners of the same building a lease for a year at $6,000, to which the Congress readily agreed.[115]

"Slow and painful is the growth of a good man—still more so that of the great Nation," Keitt mused, but in fact they moved with considerable speed and energy.[116] Even without access to records of the secret sessions, the press could tell that much was taking place. As rapidly as possible, Congress subsequently announced acts done behind closed doors when they did not threaten security, and most of the delegates happily talked with the reporters about their efforts. Until the journalists asked what happened in closed session, that is. Then, complained the scribblers, the congressmen to a man went "dumb."[117]

In the chamber they proved more than talkative enough to make impressions on each other. Campbell of Mississippi still had not arrived, and Brooke had to ask for an extended leave of absence for him. It began to appear that he would not be here for this session at all. Some of the Texans started coming in, John Gregg arriving February 15, but neither he nor his colleagues could actually take the floor until a popular referendum February 23 accepted or rejected their convention's secession ordinance.[118] For the rest, the floor was theirs, and on it they showed of what they were and were not made. Boyce impressed some as most able, though Stephens thought him wordy and too prone to the "spread eagle" school of debate. Perkins of Louisiana seemed among the most steady and staunch.[119] His colleagues Marshall, De Clouet, and Sparrow all impressed the new Vice President as sensible men of good education, and while Conrad "frequently *bores*, Kenner never." Harris of Mississippi, of course, stood very high in Little Aleck's estimation, while his associates Barry and Harrison spoke rather too much to little point, and even Wilson appeared sensible, but too wordy.[120]

"*Meminger* [sic] is as shrewd as a Yankee," thought Tom Cobb, but he rated his abilities rather low.[121] Among the Alabamians, everyone agreed that the youngster of the group, Curry, simply talked too much. While Williamson Oldham of Texas appreciated his common sense and thought him quite eloquent, the rest tired of hearing him.[122] Stephens had known Curry in Washington a few years before and there thought his speeches in Congress "decided hits." But in open debate now, without the benefit of prepared remarks, he showed weakness and too much resort to meaningless flourish. Stephens thought Chilton just as "windy" as Curry, with Hale and Walker superior to both, and Smith clearly peerless,[123] though Chilton certainly worked as hard as anyone there.[124] Little Aleck stood judgment with the rest, most feeling considerable awe of his mental and legislative abilities. But Tom Cobb, at least, thought he saw the new Vice President turning arrogant, prone to proclaim in "oracular announcements" what Confederate policy should be. More than once in secret session, in words judiciously left out of even Hooper's journal, Cobb took occasion to "let the Congress know that I for one would not yield to any such assumption."[125]

They kept their little feuds and petty squabbles to themselves. While Cobb complained to his wife that "this political arena gives the darkest picture of frail humanity that I ever witnessed," completely overlooking his own hefty contribution to that frailty, the rest guarded their public image.[126] Brother Howell claimed that "in all our debates there has not been a single unpleasant word."[127] "This Congress is the coolest assembly and the most elevated I have ever seen," Hooper boasted.[128] Nisbet believed that "this Congress is honestly bent on doing right." If he thought the general run of the members less able than others found them, still he saw their sound patriotism. There were "ultras & some impracticables," to be sure, and even a few he thought reckless demagogues, but their own radicalism weakened them with the rest. "They are thus far held in check."[129] One of those Nisbet had in mind was Rhett, yet it would have surprised him to hear the fire-eater saying at the same time that in general he applauded the quality of his fellow members, "highly pleased" at their patriotism and determination.[130] Stephens wrote to everyone that Congress worked harmoniously, and as expeditiously as possible. "I am not without hope," he said, "that all will end well." "We will do the best we can."[131] Only to Linton did he confide uncertainty as to just how long the harmony might last.[132] One of the Louisiana delegation gave an interview to a New Orleans reporter that said what all wanted the public to think. "Animated with a harmony of thoughts and unity of action seldom before exhibited in a deliberative body, while a system of mutual concession and forbearance is manifested," he said, "there is every disposition to do what we need to do and get back to our constituents."[133] There spoke a politician.

The press remained always suspicious, and resentful of the secrecy. "Nothing leaks out," complained a Georgia reporter, and from that some decided that the Congress in fact did very little.[134] "We are only left to conjecture and surmise what is being done," complained another,[135] and a specially cynical Virginian decided that the delegates "locked themselves from the newspapers that they might drink whiskey and give their votes, excluded from the observations of the world."[136] Despite the secret sessions, the crowds of spectators and journalists kept coming, sometimes gathering in the chamber and the galleries more than an hour before the announced convening.[137] With each passing day, more reporters arrived, this week coming from Charleston, Savannah, Augusta, Washington, Mobile, New Orleans, and elsewhere.[138] Every arrival only added to the chorus of complaint.[139] The congressmen themselves made virtually no effort to mollify the newsmen, other than a feeble gesture by Curry, who praised the local *Advertiser* as "about as good a weekly newspaper as I know of," and said he hoped that people would spread "good newspapers" through the country.[140] All the reporters could do to get even was crowd the free lunch in the chamber, and once they and the growing mob of office seekers steadily cleaned out the buffet tables set for the congressmen, the ladies of the town stopped replenishing them after the first two weeks.[141]

There were few quiet hours. "Never was I so overwhelmed with business & calls," Stephens complained. Visitors besieged him at Mrs. Cleveland's from the moment he rose from breakfast until he left for the capitol, and then again upon his return home and late into the evening, sometimes to midnight and beyond.[142] Some wanted nothing more than to say hello or to bring him gifts, including one fellow who made the Vice President the grand present of a button.[143] The rest of the time he dealt with his mail, by now running to more than thirty letters a day, all requests for everything from autographs to jobs in the new government.[144]

Members like Stephens stood constantly at risk of being challenged by disgruntled citizens and correspondents over the closed door proceedings, and at the most awkward moments. The evening of February 13, managing a brief escape from their labors, Little Aleck and Howell Cobb attended a dinner party in town, only to be accosted at once by ladies who complained of the secret sessions. Tongue planted firmly in cheek, Cobb told them with a straight face that the Congress had decided to have one flag speech each day for the public, mentioned that Brooke of Mississippi made one that morning—which he had—and said that the program called for Keitt to be on the next day, "according to order."

"No, you mistake Mr. President," interrupted Stephens, taking the tease right away. "Dont you recollect that Mr. Keit[t] got excused . . . upon the grounds that his wife had put an injunction on him to keep his mouth shut and his hair brushed." Boyce had agreed to replace him.

"Oh yes . . . I did forget it is Mr. Boyce," Cobb replied.

Of course, there was no such program in effect. Stephens and Cobb chuckled over their little joke until the next day when, with their victims in the galleries anxiously awaiting, Boyce actually got up and made a real "spread eagle" flag speech. Howell's and Little Aleck's eyes met during the harangue and both broke out laughing, as did Keitt and Boyce when let in on the story.[145]

The members took what fun they could amid the rush of business, and managed to attend to some more serious personal matters as well. The Stephens-Hill situation caused embarrassment in the Georgia delegation, and now as vice president, Stephens could not afford to indulge old animosities with members of Congress. Their surprise seating in the same pew at church the previous Sunday may have opened a slight thaw on Little Aleck's part, while Hill's support of his antagonist for the presidency itself revealed an earnest desire to erase their differences. This same day that the Boyce speech put Stephens in a good mood, Kenan and Toombs approached him and Hill and asked to be allowed to mediate their differences. Both agreed. The arbiters suggested that all unkind and offensive remarks of the past be considered as withdrawn simultaneously. There need be no face-to-face apologies on either side. Again both agreed.[146] Shortly afterward, quite by accident, the two met on the street, each spoke a greeting, and they soon found themselves engaged in a long and pleasant conversation, Hill especially complimenting Stephens on some good shots delivered against Bartow and Tom Cobb in a recent secret session.[147] Within a couple of days Tom Cobb and others saw that the two former antagonists were "thick as brothers."[148]

This was one reconciliation that everyone welcomed. Little Aleck still wandered in and out of depression, his thoughts turning sometimes morbid. "All is temporary," he said. "The great object of life is to prepare for death."[149] Fortunately Crawford boarded at Mrs. Cleveland's now. Little Aleck loved his "rich vein of humor," and the other Georgian knew well how to find fun in any little incident, cheering Stephens greatly. Better yet, the same evening of the Hill rapprochement, Toombs moved out of the Exchange and into the boarding-house. The three Georgians immediately made a jolly "mess," enhanced considerably by Toombs's servant Bob. Light enough to pass for white, he had once been a free man but voluntarily sold himself into slavery to raise money for a former master in trouble. Fat and lazy, Bob already enjoyed quite a reputation for drinking Toombs's liquor and smoking his cigars at the Exchange, spending the bulk of his time playing cards, all of which Toombs smilingly indulged. Having his life-long friend Toombs with him, their former estrangement now completely forgotten, brought great peace to Stephens's troubled spirit.[150]

In their precious idle hours others felt scarcely more at peace. Affable to all on the face of it, Howell Cobb worried over his son Howell, Jr., who now stood at the verge of expulsion from the University of Georgia. "You treat all my advice & counsel with such contempt that I have no heart to say more," the father complained.[151] And Toombs, who did so much to ease Little Aleck's mind, took delight in adding to Cobb's burden. At a party, in front of others, he started on what sounded like a compliment as he congratulated Cobb on doing more for secession than any other man. Barely could Cobb start to appear smilingly humble than Toombs went on to say that as secretary of the treasury, Cobb had left the Yankee government so impoverished that, far from being able to buy munitions of war, they could hardly afford two quarters to put on Buchanan's eyes when he died. As a chagrined Cobb walked away, Toombs just kept pouring it on. "He never lets Cobb pass without giving him a lick," said Stephens. Delighting in pouring salt in the open wound, Toombs seemed "determined to run in the salt even when the skin was off."[152]

Nor was the brother Cobb any happier. While Stephens and Hill made up, and Toombs persecuted his brother, Tom Cobb bedeviled himself. Struck in the face with what little he had accomplished, and how scarcely anyone acknowledged his anticipated influence, he turned morose. "I magnified myself," he confessed to his wife. "I overestimated the *importance of my presence* in this Congress." Having expected to be a dominating force, he faced the fact that he had been no force at all, and was not needed.[153] His dejection showed visibly enough for others like Stephens to see it. "Tom Cobb has utterly failed to impress the House," Little Aleck crowed. "He came here puffed up. He is now on the other extreme."[154] Unfortunately, dejection produced no humility in Tom Cobb, only resentfulness, and envy—ideal requisites for an opposition.

So, too, Robert Barnwell Rhett, Sr. In every revolutionary movement, even a conservative revolution like this, the most dangerous potential enemies of the new order are the disappointed ambitions of its early ideologues. For two weeks now, outvoted, overruled, ignored, the South Carolinian drank from the same bitter cup as Tom Cobb. Even now as the first rumors of cabinet appointments fluttered through the delegations, few if any spoke of him. Memminger might be secretary of state, said one.[155] Crawford could get War, and Conrad Navy, perhaps. One did speak of Rhett for Treasury, but it was only street talk.[156] Besides, he knew he would have no support even in his own delegation for any appointment. Barnwell was his only friend, but being uninterested in office himself, he would do nothing for his cousin either. Keitt and Miles were avowed enemies, and the rest indifferent to him. "I expect nothing therefore from the delegation, lifting me to position," he moaned to his son the day Stephens took his oath. "I have never been wise in pushing myself forward to office or power, and I suppose never will," he went on. "I will do my duty as the occasion requires, and leave office to be intrigued for by others." In the clutch of self-pity, he advised his family to "prepare for disappointment."[157]

Significantly, the one delegate in Montgomery who had the most to say for Rhett was Tom Cobb. "*Rhett* is a generous hearted and honest man," he said, but then went on to add, "with a vast quantity of cranks and a small proportion of common sense."[158] He might have added to that a pettiness and spite bordering on the infantile. Already his Charleston *Mercury* assumed the leading—almost solitary—role in press opposition to the government still forming, reflexively gainsaying virtually every act. "The Provisional Government may be useless," it warned in response to the Constitution that Rhett so disliked.[159] "The fruit of the labors of thirty odd long years, in strife and bitterness, is about to slip through our fingers," it went on, charging the Congress with not knowing what sort of government it wanted. "Vague dreads of the future, and terrors of the people, and in some degree a want of statesmanship, paralyze all useful and essential reform," said the *Mercury*, "and weaken men into inaction." It labeled the prohibition of the slave trade an act of "terrorism," and warned the Palmetto State's people to prepare their minds for failure, "for South Carolina is about to be saddled with almost every grievance except Abolition."[160]

Already rumors flew in South Carolina that the *Mercury's* petulant editorials sprang not from its Montgomery reporter who signed himself "Reviewer," but from Rhett himself. Trescott wrote to Miles this week that he would not even mention the ravings of the *Mercury* "because if report speaks the truth, you are much nearer its source of inspiration than I am."[161] The stories became so widespread that "Reviewer" himself noticed them and wrote a strong denial. Unfortunately he then proceeded to show sufficient inside knowledge of the deliberations of the permanent constitution committee headed by Rhett that if it was not the fire-eater himself writing, then certainly he advised his reporter, and in the process violated his oath of secrecy.[162] Denials or not, Rhett repeatedly wrote directly to his son, coaching him in opposition to the acts of the government.[163]

Throughout the country Confederates witnessed the embarrassment that the editorials caused to the movement. From Washington Wigfall sent Barnwell a scathing letter, demanding that it be read to Rhett himself, and wrote as well to President-elect Davis, pleading with him to find some way of controlling the *Mercury*. "It is doing us immense harm."[164] Other Southern press joined the chorus, charging Rhett's paper with being "always discontented and grumbling, arrogant in tone, flippant in judgment, intolerant of any opinion but its own."[165] Even before Jefferson Davis arrived in Montgomery to take his oath, Rhett and the *Mercury* poised to attack. Old Robert Barnwell knew his cousin more than well enough to see through all the protestations of policy and principle. Rhett began gainsaying even before the government had time to do wrong, he told Mary Chesnut. "He felt he had a vested right to the leadership," the wiser South Carolinian went on, and the anger he was about to direct at the new president was not so much with Davis himself, as with "anyone being put in what [he] considered Barnwell Rhett's rightful place."[166] The Georgia press expressed satisfaction that "moderate men held in check ambitious rival aspirants."[167]

Above these swirling undercurrents of wounded pride and shattered aspirations, the rest of Congress and Montgomery anxiously counted the days until Davis should arrive, following his progress in the newspapers as he made the long circuitous trip from Mississippi. Miles of South Carolina spent his free hours in the Exchange parlor talking smoothly to the young ladies as he leaned against the piano.[168] Harrison of Mississippi could hardly think of young women, very astutely telling his wife that Montgomery had no females to compare with her.[169] The signs of patriotic and military panoply blazed everywhere. Mobile steamboats like the *Southern Republic* landed at the wharf with calliope screaming and a Palmetto flag flying.[170] Montgomery's Independent Rifles paraded and drilled Tuesday and Friday evenings at seventhirty, to the delight of assembled crowds.[171] Tuesday evening the audience at the Montgomery Theatre howled as an infant extra in "Wept of the Wishton-Wish" completely upset Maggie Mitchell's best scene by going into uncontrolled screams, and the performance had to be halted until a quieter child could be found.[172]

Townspeople gawked at Mary Todd Lincoln's two sisters who came to visit, strong secessionists both, but still eyed suspiciously.[173] Indeed, a rising ripple of paranoia haunted many. Authorities briefly arrested William R. Waud, a sketch artist for *Frank Leslie's Illustrated Newspaper* of New York, simply on a drunken rumor that he might be a spy,[174] and Tom Cobb suspected that Marion did not receive his letters—which she did—and blamed Montgomery's postmaster, a Yankee. Imagining that all of his vitally important expressions of gall and lovesickness were being sent straight to the enemy in Washington, he stopped using the mails and began sending his letters by Adams Express, which carried congressional materials free of charge.[175]

If men like Cobb imagined some threats, real ones surrounded them all the same. "It really seems as if half Georgia was here after office," Howell Cobb complained, "& the other half were at home writing letters." He walked to the capitol every morning with a pocket filled with mail from applicants.[176] Men looking for positions hounded the congressmen wherever they went, filling the galleries sometimes, and never letting up. Crowding the lobbies of the hotels and the barrooms, they

generally protested in public that they were too modest to ask for anything, but behind the scenes they pulled every available wire.[177] Some
badgered delegates to get their governors to send a recommendation
directly to Davis when he arrived.[178] Others like Pierre G. T. Beauregard,
just then a captain in the United States Army, sent congratulations
that Davis would find on his arrival, and along with them strong hints
that they would like commissions in the new Confederate Army.[179]

The sheer cheek in their demands showed far more of opportunism
than patriotism. They used family relationships to get an ear.[180] One
asked "what I can expect from the South in the way of encouragement," adding as a persuasive afterthought "my sympathy as you well
know is with the South."[181] Some hinted none too subtly, like the man
asking McRae "how will your Postal arrangements be formed?"[182]
Others simply came out and asked directly for what they wanted, a foreign consulship, a judgeship, an office in the executive branch.[183]
Seventy-one-year-old Flag Officer William Shubrick of South Carolina
wanted to resign and join the Confederacy, but he feared there might
be no employment for a man of his age in the new navy. He asked for
some assurance before he left the United States Navy and his only
means of employment. Expedience defeating conscience, he finally
stayed with the Union and became a rear admiral.[184] Even cities joined
the swell, Atlanta continuing to petition for consideration as the permanent capital, and offering as inducement its good railroad communications, freedom from summer fevers, ample access to abundant supplies, and peanuts. "As for 'goobers,' an indispensable article for a
Southern Legislator," they said, "we have them *all* the time."[185]

Even as Montgomery felt the swell of all the hungry and the wire-
pullers swarming to her hotels and boardinghouses, she knew that this
boom would burst if a city like Atlanta got its wish. Citizens met to
take subscriptions to pay the rent for the Insurance Building for the
government, and began discussions on building a new capitol building
for the Confederacy at a cost of $1 million or more. "Our Montgomery
people don't do things by halves," a civic leader proclaimed.[186] A South
Carolinian attending their meeting suggested that if they really wanted
to keep the Congress there, however, they should do something about
the rivers of sand and mud that passed for streets, either by paving "or
else furnishing them with draw-bridges or passenger steamboats."[187]

Montgomery could ignore the wags and cynics. For now she had the
capital and she would work to keep it. Moreover, within days the greatest event in the history of the South would take place on her wide—if

muddy—streets. On Valentine's Day the city council called a special meeting to appoint a committee to work with the Congress. They were going to inaugurate the first president of the Confederate States of America.[188]

CHAPTER SEVEN

THE MAN AND THE HOUR
HAVE MET

———◦★◦———

W HEN THE FAMED Mississippi steamboat captain Tom Leathers
brought his stately *Natchez* around Davis Bend on the morning
of February 11, he saw a rowboat manned by blacks pull away from the
upper end of an island just approaching. A white man on the boat
hailed him, and the paddlewheeler's slow headway upstream made it
an easy matter for the rowboat to come alongside. Jefferson Davis, still
weak from illness, climbed aboard in a suit of blue-gray homespun and
began his passage to the presidency.[1]

He reached Vicksburg that afternoon, word of his coming preceding
him. Thousands lined the levee, cannon boomed salutes, echoed by
musket volleys and the cheers of spectators. A parade of citizens and
militia ushered him from the boat and across town to the Southern
Railroad depot. After making a brief speech in which he promised to
die for their cause if need be, he was off to Jackson.[2] Once there he
remained for three days to clear pending business in his briefly held
command of the state militia, and then resigned his commission.[3]
Already he confessed to friends that the new mantle did not rest comfortably upon his shoulders. He hoped that it would be only temporary.
After all, he was *provisional* president. Within a year when the permanent constitution was in effect and a properly elected congress sat in
Montgomery—or wherever—the people would then elect a regular
chief executive, and he might then to return to his uniform in Mississippi.[4] There was little time for reflection, however. While in Jackson
he received yet another telegram urging him to come to Montgomery
as quickly as possible. The government could not proceed without
him.[5]

With the railroad bridges still out on the most direct route to
Montgomery, Davis boarded cars running north toward Holly Springs

on Valentine's Day, writing a brief note to Varina before he left. Gone from them barely three days, already he confessed that "I miss you and the children even more than usual."[6] That was the tender face he only showed to his family. To those in Jackson bidding him farewell, he revealed a different visage that sternly warned they all faced the prospect of "long and bloody" war.[7] Thereafter he followed a grueling circuitous route north, then across Tennessee and northern Alabama to Chattanooga, then southeast to Atlanta. At almost every stop people stood gathered to see their new president, calling him out to address them. Davis himself lost count of the speeches made, though he said much the same thing in all. When he could sleep at all, he slept in his clothes to be ready for the next speech.

It was past four in the morning February 16 when he pulled into Atlanta, and still a throng of citizens waiting for him expected a speech later that morning. Standing on the verandah of the Trout House hotel, leaning on a cane, he told them their destiny was independence.[8] Moreover, he suggested that the old doctrine of Manifest Destiny should now be revived, and that Cuba, the West Indies, and northern Mexico must inevitably become a part of their constellation of stars one day. As for the North, he preferred peace, but he would accept war if he must.[9] While some in the audience thought his tone and manner seemed too restrained, "not the man for the occasion,"[10] others fretted at the bellicosity. They remembered his days as a war hero in Mexico, and worried now that perhaps he too much coveted military fame and glory.[11]

That afternoon he left on the Atlanta & West Point for the Alabama line, still in his homespun.[12] Adorning either end of the car in which he traveled were two new flags with six stars in a circle, surrounding a larger seventh in the center. Along the way Davis chatted amiably with a Yankee from Rochester, New York, leaving him with the impression that the president-elect's bland manner concealed a hard determination beneath.[13] The travel told on him now. When he got off at West Point to board the special car waiting for the last leg of his journey, he left his cane behind. The Yankee picked it up.

When he left Jackson, Davis telegraphed ahead to Montgomery that he expected to arrive February 16 or the next day, and then kept friends in the capital apprised of his movements during his two-day trip to Atlanta.[14] That gave Montgomery more than sufficient time to plan a welcome. Governor Moore asked several local dignitaries, including Yancey, Watts, Pollard, Shorter, Mayor Noble, and more, to serve as a welcoming committee. Pollard had fitted out for the occasion a special car recently built in his shops in Montgomery,[15] stocked it with the best food and wine available, put his own slave man Charles aboard to serve, and had it waiting at West Point when Davis arrived.[16] Pollard himself actually met Davis several miles east of West Point and accompanied him for the last part of his run through Georgia. When they got to West Point, the entire welcoming committee were ready.[17]

The buffet table in the car brimmed with fresh mutton, ham, tongue, chicken salad, wine, whiskey, and more. Indeed, the welcomers spent some time at the food and drink before Davis reached West Point, practicing their toasts with rather too much gusto. As he boarded the special car, Davis made yet another brief speech from the rear platform, and then they were off amid the thunder of a musket volley and the flutter of hundreds of white handkerchiefs in the hands of the ladies.[18]

Tired as he was, Davis enjoyed the final sprint to Montgomery. Again there were the brief stops, the hasty speeches. At Opelika the Columbus Guard boarded the train as military escort, hoping to fire twenty-one guns, but the conductor protested that they were already running half an hour late. The salute could wait until Montgomery.[19] As the gentlemen talked, mostly of what lay ahead, Charles served them from the table, pouring the wine and whiskey. Davis took but a single glass, and when the black said to him "Mr. Jeff, won't you take a drink?" Davis simply said "No, sir, I thank you," and resumed his conversation. The slave stepped away with a head swelled by pride that the lofty man had spoken so politely to him.[20]

While Charles beamed, Davis and Watts spoke for some time on more serious matters. Weary, and anxious that no one believe that he had wanted this office, Davis told him as he would tell many others that he would have preferred to be a soldier for the Confederacy. Watts confessed his own belief that secession would lead to war, and Davis agreed, though promising to try to avoid conflict. When Watts asked who should lead their army in the field, Davis already had an answer waiting for him. "There is one man above all others," he said. "He is now in California—I have written to him—I believe he is with us— that man is Albert Sidney Johnston."[21] Watts may not have known him, but Jefferson Davis certainly did. They had been friends at the United States Military Academy at West Point more than thirty years earlier. Davis had few close friends, but those he trusted without question. Already he thought to turn to them.

It was late evening when the train stopped a few miles outside Montgomery. The official greeting delegation from Congress boarded the train, along with more civic authorities, headed by Frank Gilmer, now back from Virginia.[22] Amid greetings all around, they informed the Mississippian of the ceremonies awaiting his arrival. At ten the train finally rolled to a stop at the depot. Even before Davis stepped down, the crowd awaiting him shouted, cannon boomed repeatedly, and the city's church bells pealed again and again. Montgomery was getting used to celebrations like this. The reception committee walked down the long platform to his car, followed by a cheering throng. The Columbus Guard formed in front of Davis, and the procession marched to the front of the depot, his perfect military step matching their own. Finally they fired their salute, and after an introduction, Davis spoke to the crowd. He called them "fellow citizens," for now surely they were all brothers, whether from Mississippi or Alabama, or any of the other new states, united by their new freedom, and their determination to defend the old Constitution in its new framing "to the last extremity with Southern blood and Southern steel."

That was the kind of speech the crowd liked to hear. Caught up in the enthusiasm, Yancey embraced Gilmer before leaving and congratulated him on his role in bringing about this moment, despite the disappointment to his own ambitions.[23] As the cheering rose without letup, Davis and Yancey stepped into a four-horse coach and rode, with a procession of carriages and citizens on foot following, toward Court Square. On both sides of the street Davis saw doors and windows brilliantly illuminated. Fireworks sputtered and boomed overhead in the cool evening drizzle.[24] In a few minutes he stepped into the Exchange with Yancey and the rest, accompanied by the shouts of yet another and larger crowd gathered outside the hotel. Indoors Tom Cobb believed that "the whole city is agog." Ladies blocked the parlor, while men filled every passage and corridor, and the streets outside.[25] Shouts of "Davis" and "Yancey" rose to a deafening roar.[26]

At quarter to eleven Davis stepped out onto the second floor portico, between the massive columns overlooking Commerce Street. "Now we are brethren," he told them, "men of one flesh, of one bone, of one interest, of one purpose." He hoped that they would live in peace. Storms might hazard their infancy, but could not dampen their spirit or their determination. And if war should come to test their resolve, they would show themselves worthy inheritors of the heritage of 1776. He was tired, he said. He had no more to say to them that night, and his voice was nearly gone from all the speeches made in the past week. He promised to meet the duties of his office faithfully, and thanked them for their faith. Moreover, he hoped that this same trust might meet him should he be called upon in future to serve them in another role, as general. Jefferson Davis made no pretense of his belief—or his hope—that this matter of the presidency should be only temporary.

That said, he went inside, where proprietor Watt showed him to room 101, a corner accommodation with a large parlor.[27] As Davis began to unpack, and finally took off his homespun suit, the crowd outside called for Yancey, their hometown favorite. He came out and congratulated them on having found the right man, a patriot, states-man, and soldier. "Fortunate, thrice fortunate, are the people of the South," he said, whipping the crowd into repeated applause with his oratory. "They have found the man as well as the principles," he shout-ed, "a man in whom are combined in so eminent a degree the wisdom of the statesman, the skill of the soldier, and the incorruptibility of the patriot." This was their defining moment as Confederates, he told them. "The man and the hour have met."[28]

The cheering was so great that people inside the Exchange could not hear the speakers outside.[29] Nor did the ovations stop at the doors. The Exchange fairly bulged with visitors in addition to the congress-men and other officials already boarding there. Now in anticipation of the inauguration, even more flocked to the hotel. In just a ten-day period, 1,140 people scratched their names in its register.[30] Of their number a small host came not to serve, or even to watch, but to be served. "It seemed as if from every part of the land the crows had flocked together to share in the anticipated feast," carped a cynical observer. Office seekers filled every corner of the Exchange and the other hotels, and more actually came on the train with Davis. "Most of these men," said one lady, "had little or nothing to lose, but hoped to gain a good deal."[31] Other men already here in Montgomery, saw visions of appointments going far beyond the mere civil service dreams of this rabble. Davis was here. In two days he would be president. There would be cabinet posts. Now people spoke of Toombs for State. Yancey's name and that of Louisiana Senator Judah P. Benjamin fig-ured prominently. Tom Cobb still detected hints that the attorney gen-eralship could come his way. He still intended to refuse.[32]

February 17, a frosty Sunday, the exhausted president-elect remained abed in his room until well after ten o'clock unable even to receive a call from his vice president-to-be Stephens.[33] When he arose, he set to work preparing his inaugural, while those outside speculated on its content.[34] Rumors of his being a reconstructionist still persisted, and if he did not come out boldly now for no retreat, Tom Cobb expected that Congress itself would denounce him "or we shall have an explosion here."[35] Others in town just then thought the inauguration of rather secondary importance, suggesting even that it be postponed until February 22 and the propitious anniversary of Washington's birth—not to mention Marion Cobb's. "For the present, let our attention be directed to the *business* of organizing, maintaining and perfecting a Confederacy on the basis of *liberty, equality and independency for white men, and slavery for negroes*," said the *Advertiser*.[36] The notion of the cementing of the faith in the new nation took stronger hold everywhere. "There will be no halting or backing down," Harrison of Mississippi wrote that day. Reconstruction was an idea whose time never would come. He prayed that they achieve their independence with peace, but with or without, they would be free. "We may be kept down by force of arms," he said, "but the cement has not been discovered that can make whole the broken vase of the Union."[37]

In room 101 that day Davis struggled for the words to express the meaning of what they were about. Sadly, his was not the eloquence of the poet, but more the conventional, competent, but uninspired, prose of the politician. Stephens would have called him one of the "spread eagle" sort, full of cliched metaphors about the "ship of state," repeated allusions to their ancestors and the glorious days of '76, and far too many words to say much too little. Sadder still, Davis himself felt deeply the import of what he had to say, and what an occasion like this demanded. He felt the right things, but he could not impart them in a manner to inspire. But that, as so much, lay in the nature of the man.

Many men held acquaintance with Jefferson Davis. Few truly knew him. Born in Kentucky in 1808, he lived a restrained childhood with a painfully austere father, secured a good education for one reared on the Mississippi frontier, and hoped to be a lawyer when he entered Transylvania University before his father's death. Thereafter he answered the dictates of his older brother Joseph, whom he idolized, and who insisted on his attending the Military Academy at West Point. During the ensuing years that he spent in the Army, Davis claimed ever to dislike the service, yet once he resigned his commission he rarely stopped looking back on his military days as his happiest. He married the daughter of future President Zachary Taylor, only to be widowed tragically a few months later, and then spent nearly a decade as a semi-recluse.

Occasionally he broke free of his plantation home at Brierfield to look into railroading, for a flirtation with politics, or even to attempt another stint at the supposedly despised life of the Army, but mostly he stayed at home and studied and planted his cotton fields. Only with his remarriage in 1845 to Varina Howell and his emergence in local Democratic politics, did Davis really return to the world.

He came back a changed man. At West Point his fun-loving and carousing nature had brought him twice to court martial, and almost dismissal. Now people looked in vain to find fun in the man. Always priggish and punctilious to a fault, he scarcely survived another court martial when serving on the frontier, and found his conditional acquittal so embarrassing that he rarely if ever spoke of it afterward, even to his wife. He early developed an almost blind trust in close friends like Sidney Johnston and Lucius B. Northrop, to the point that faults in them evident to other men never occurred to him. Always proud and willful even in youth, he now displayed a pride that undercut much of the good that he sought to do. He would not explain himself when questioned or misunderstood, and took questioning to be not curiosity or uncertainty, but perverse and malignant in purpose. His obstinacy had been questioned even on the floor of the Senate, for when Davis decided that he was right on a matter, he stood immutable, and all who opposed him were not just of differing opinions, but wrong. Compromise did not dwell comfortably within him.

This last was hardly a sound attribute in a career politician. Maintaining that he disliked public life, Davis seemed unable to stay off the political stage. He saw brief service in Congress before the Mexican War. When he returned as a hero after his performance at Buena Vista, he took a Senate seat from Mississippi, resigned it for an unsuccessful bid for the governorship, and then served as President Franklin Pierce's secretary of war from 1853 to 1857 before going back into the Senate once more. Like most Southern statesmen of his time, he authored no legislation of his own and saw his role chiefly as one of opposition to measures introduced by Northern Whigs, and then Republicans, all supposedly aimed at the South and her institutions. Calhoun served as his ideal, though Davis, who never did anything to extremes, always stood as a moderate on the sectional controversy, upholding Southern rights, but preferring that they be respected by the North so that the South could remain in the Union. He was no Southern nationalist and never had been. Few of them were. Not yet.

For all of the obvious and hidden personality flaws in the man, an obverse existed that few saw, but those who did could love. Women and children were drawn to him, to his warmth and gentleness, and so were blacks, free and slave. He could be open to them. They posed no threat to his pride, for in 1861 all stood socially inferior to a white adult male. Varina stood up to him him repeatedly in their early years together, but after he left her once and threatened to do so again, she gave in to his view of the proper role of a woman and challenged him no more. No one doubted his intelligence or his application. He could master any topic by intense study and then surround an opponent in debate with walls of facts and data. But he could not always take that accumulated knowledge and use it to think creatively. Rather, the weight of his learning bound his imagination. Having studied a subject to exhaustion and formed a single conclusion, he was capable of no more than one, and thereafter his pride became obstinacy as he clung unswervingly to that one in spite of all persuasions otherwise. His was a wonderfully open intellect, driven by a very closed mind. Unable or unwilling to change his own conclusions, he distrusted others when they did.[38]

No one worked harder, but many accomplished more. Davis put in Herculean hours at his work, methodically exhausting himself at any task, and ideally doing everything himself, while making little or no distinction between the essential and the irrelevant. He never truly learned the difference between doing business and simply being busy. Yet in some matters he possessed very clear vision, and fewer illusions than many of his peers.

He knew sadness. The death of his first wife, the one great love of his life, nearly struck him down. The death of his first son in infancy again almost prostrated him, and still the sound of a crying child could unnerve the man. Dogged by a wide strain of indecision, he spent much of his life answering the wants of others rather than his own, perhaps because for the most part he never really knew what he wanted for himself. In the Army he hated it; out of it, he wanted back in. Despising politics, he never said no to the offer of an office. He often said he would have liked to go into the law, yet his temper could be so ungovernable, and the groundswell of argument so easily shoved him to intemperate utterance, that considering the times in which he lived, courtroom debate would inevitably have led him again and again to the dueling field. As it was, by 1861 his temper and his priggishness and pride got him involved in more than half a dozen arguments that stopped just short of shots at dawn, including near affrays with Toombs and Benjamin.

"You were terrible sometimes," his friend Northrop told him of their years together in the Army.[39] Even Varina, who knew him best, admitted that his pride and his reticence were "unusually developed,"[40] and Davis himself, in rare moments of self-understanding, confessed his excess of pride and self-confidence in his youth, not realizing that they never went away.[41] On top of that, the man simply would not communicate if he did not have to, and made no effort to ease for others the task of understanding him. "Your penetration made you always hard to talk with," Northrop told him.[42] He refused to relax in public. No matter how ill, he would not come to the breakfast table in his dressing gown, even with his own family. He read no light literature, but instead crammed himself with history, biography, and political science.[43] It gave precious little lightness or humor to his conversation, but then he would not speak in such vein to most people anyhow. Outside his family and a few close friends, he uniformly showed to others a close-mouthed, stern face that neither gave nor encouraged conviviality.[44] On first meeting he greeted some with an austerity that was positively forbidding.[45] Varina found "his personal self-denial" most unusual. Well aware of the comforts available to him, he partook of few, rarely made known any personal want, and refused most of what friends and family proffered.[46] He told people that "all men are not built like martyrs," and then tried repeatedly to make one of himself.[47]

Jefferson Davis dressed not foppishly, but immaculately, preferring dull browns or grays in his suits. He never left his home looking unkempt, and always made certain that his hands and fingernails were clean. Fancying himself a keen judge of character, he took a lack of neatness in others to be a sign of mental messiness as well.[48] He allowed himself a thin wispy bit of beard beneath his chin, but otherwise wore his iron-gray hair rather short. None of the flowing locks of a Toombs for him. His grim mouth showed a smile only for the ladies when they met, but to the sterner sex he turned a sterner visage, one made the more forbidding by the discoloration in his nearly blind left eye.[49] His intimidating anger when aroused was widely known. As a result, his life could be measured in part by his friendships lost. The one besetting sin to which he confessed was profanity.[50] He promised Varina to try to curb his oaths when in his wrath.[51]

For all of his flaws and foibles, Jefferson Davis presented an altogether logical choice for president. For one thing, many of the men who voted for him had never met him and knew him only as they did most national statesmen, from the newspapers. He stood soundly on the issue of Southern rights, but was no fire-eater, making him an ideal compromise candidate to bind the skittish Border States to the more radical cotton South. His reputation as an able administrator in the old United States War Department promised that he could manage the tasks of a chief executive, though few really knew what a peacetime secretary of war actually did, or how much of his department's inconsequential minutia occupied Davis's time. And his standing as a military hero—the South's foremost—gained him many a vote that might otherwise have gone for Stephens or Toombs. No one knew or cared to question that his reputation derived solely from a hasty and unconventional maneuver involving a scant two hundred men, and that but for the stupidity of a Mexican opponent, it could well have resulted in disaster. This is how Americans chose their presidents, and by their standards, Jefferson Davis was a wise choice.

All day he labored over the inaugural, writing, revising, and then attempting to commit it to memory.[52] When he looked out the window of his room he saw the growing numbers of men and women coming to town for the ceremonies on the morrow.[53] He heard the growing hubbub in the Exchange itself, and when he went to his meals he found it hard even to walk through the hotel to the dining room.[54] Having said himself that secession represented "the separation of the sheep from the goats," he might have wondered that the flock all seemed to be here in Montgomery.[55]

Three days before, once they knew definitely when Davis would arrive, Congress had set the date and time, Keitt moving that the president take his oath at one o'clock on February 18.[56] The next day Chilton, at the head of a committee, reported the plans for the ceremony agreed upon in conjunction with committees representing Alabama and Montgomery, and the Congress gave their approval. Managers contacted the owners of the finest carriages in the city. Mayor Noble hired a brass band. The proprietors at Estelle Hall told Dr. David Grieve of Louisville that his lecture on phrenology, including the examination of heads from the audience, followed by the inflation of miniature hot air balloons for the amusement of all, would have to be postponed so that the Hall could host the president's inauguration evening levee.[57]

It dawned one of the coldest mornings of the month, barely thirty degrees with frost covering the ground and clouds obscuring the heavens.[58] At nine o'clock young Ellen Noyes, a basket on her arm, walked down Catoma Street, past Mrs. Cleveland's, to the spacious yard of John Garrett, dealer in hardware. She cut bunches of pink, red, crimson, and variegated japonicas, white and purple hyacinths, small white spring magnolia blossoms, and dark green arbor vitae and boxwood. Filling her basket, she went back home to start weaving an intricate wreath.[59] Out at the fairgrounds the Columbus Guards, bivouacked on straw bedding inside their tents, arose early, polished their brass, brushed their uniforms and started the short march into the city.[60] Jonce Hooper looked out the *Mail* window on Commerce Street to see men, women, and children gathering already in their best holiday attire, while businessmen unable to close their stores looked out shop doors wistfully at those who would get to witness the great event that afternoon. "Presently the drums will beat, the soldiers will 'form company,' the procession will be arranged and all will be off for Capitol Hill," mused Hooper. He closed the *Mail*'s doors and put out his Monday edition early so that he and his employees would not miss a moment of the grand day.[61]

Hours before one o'clock the city's main streets bustled with clumps and crowds of expectant spectators, delighted that the day was rapidly warming. Scores of carriages stood beside the sidewalks, their occupants hoping for a better view of the parade, and augmenting their own warmth from well-stocked hampers and jugs.[62] Flags broke out from windows and porches all up and down Market and Commerce. Fireworks crackled sporadically in the streets, and the army of dogs set up an infernal howling, so confused by the mass of people that choosing an individual target for a bark or a growl almost defeated them.

Pulses quickened when the militia companies came into sight, heading for Court Square. The Columbus Guards arrived first, cleared a space on Commerce in front of the Exchange, and thrilled the crowd for several minutes with complex evolutions at close-order zouave drill. "They move like machinery," exclaimed onlookers.[63] Their sky blue pants and smart red coats seemed almost a blur as they moved, while local bands started playing, and the cannon by the artesian basin boomed. Pritchard of the Southern Associated Press gazed at the thousands of people lining the streets, standing on porches and balconies, even roofs, and wondered at the enormity of the day. He was smart enough to have gotten to the capitol portico early in the morning, where he would wait for hours with many another reporter, to be certain of seeing and hearing everything. Now he looked down Market and saw that "thousands and thousands were moving up to the capitol, with about as little chance of hearing the inaugural address as they were capable of flying."[64]

As the Guards finished their exhibition, other military companies arrived, and about eleven o'clock six white horses pulling a beautiful open barouche, with a "veteran whip" in the seat, stopped at the Commerce Street entrance to the Exchange. Colonel H. P. Watson, chief marshal for the day, emerged from the hotel with his six aides and began composing the parade. Mr. F. Arnold's brass band took position at the front, to be followed by the militia companies. The barouche was next, followed by the committees from Congress, the state, and the city, and then a succession of commissioners from other Southern states, governors, supreme court judges, and local ministers, all in carriages. Behind them would come townspeople in coaches, and then more on foot.[65]

Finally Davis emerged, accompanied by Stephens, who had come to the Exchange earlier in the morning to be ready. They stepped into the barouche and sat in the rear seat facing forward, Davis on the right and Little Aleck next to him. The Reverend Basil Manly, who once more found himself in attendance on a great day, sat in the front seat opposite the president-elect, despite the efforts of Henry Hilliard to urge his own minister, the Methodist Lovick Pierce, for the honor. Pierce, unfortunately, held avowedly antisecession views, and they would not do for today.[66] Captain George Jones, Davis's military escort, sat next to Manly. It was noon. A salvo of guns signaled the start of the procession.[67] At once Arnold's band blared forth, determined to earn the $40 that the city council was paying them. They played "Dixie."[68]

Several blocks up Market Street the Congress came to order just as the procession commenced. Even through the thick brick walls of the capitol the delegates heard the fanfare and the cheers, the firing of the guns, and the faint tinny strains of the band. They had a solemn formality to perform. Shorter, chairman of the Engrossments committee, reported that a carefully prepared copy of the Provisional Constitution now awaited their signatures. It lay draped across a table in front of Cobb's rostrum, nine sheets of parchment pasted together and measuring 19 3/4 inches wide and 121 inches long.[69] Howell Cobb stepped down and signed first, then called the states in geographical order from east to west. As called, the delegates filed forward—South Carolina,

Georgia, Florida, Alabama, Mississippi, Louisiana. Most signed with their own pens. Each must have had in his head visions of a painting of an earlier historic signing in 1776. Many, like Tom Cobb, determined to put aside the pens they used that day as mementoes.[70] That done they went into secret session for some quick business before the parade reached the state house.[71]

The procession moved slowly, first around the artesian basin, then onto Market. The temperature just broke fifty degrees and after a cloudy morning the sun glinted through the overcast as Davis passed the Winter Building on the right. It cast his shadow to the left as he made the gradual slope up to Perry Street. Looking down the side street he saw the spire of St. John's Episcopal Church a block away. On another block then, and by now the crowds lining the street were moving along with the procession, a single mass of humanity gathering size at every step. Smiling and cheering faces beamed down at Davis from every open window and balcony.[72] Then he crossed Lawrence, the bluffs above the Alabama visible off to his left. Market Street grew steeper now. Up to McDonough. Then steeper still to Hull, and across Decatur. The roar of the crowd grew in intensity with each block, and now he could see the crowd of five thousand or more that awaited him on the capitol grounds.[73] Above them loomed the west portico of the capitol itself.

Finally the head of the procession reached Bainbridge. The military companies drew up in line along the street, oblivious of young Culver setting up one of McIntyre's cameras off to the left.[74] Then the barouche stopped in front of the steps leading up the bank onto the capitol grounds, and Captain Jones alighted to clear a way for Davis and the others through the crowd to the portico.[75] As Arnold's brass struck up, the "Marseillaise," Davis stepped down amid renewed cheers.[76] Now came Rhett and the rest of the congressional welcoming committee. By now Rhett had learned that Barnwell misled him on the unanimity of the other South Carolina delegates in voting for Davis. He believed now that his own vote may have been the one that clinched the state for the man approaching him from the carriage, and with it Florida, of course. Had he but held out, and had Georgia voted for Cobb—as he still assumed to have been that delegation's intent—there might have been no majority for Davis, and thereby a chance for another candidate. Who but him?[77]

His face showing nothing of what he may have felt inside, Rhett stood on the President-elect's left and offered his arm, while Chilton moved to his right. Flanked by the congressmen, his arms linked in theirs, Davis started up the steps and walked through the cheering crowd, which by now spilled completely over the grounds and even around to the opposite side of the state house on Union Street. Behind Davis came the other dignitaries. As the Montgomery committee passed through the corridor of spectators, Ellen Noyes stepped out and handed to Tom Watts the wreath she had made from that morning's harvest of flowers. She told him it was for the president, and gave him a bouquet for Stephens as well.[78]

When Davis and his escort climbed the final step and stood out on the portico itself where all could see, one giant shout went up from the ten thousand voices assembled below. Thousands of ladies waving handkerchiefs created a fluttering sea of white from which brilliant meteors of color erupted as many threw forward small bouquets of fresh flowers.[79] With barely a stop, Rhett led Davis into the main lobby and up the stairs to the Congress chamber, where he escorted him to the rostrum. There he introduced the president-elect to the assembled delegates, most of whom stared amid their applause at this, their first meeting with Jefferson Davis. Tom Cobb sat at his desk and wrote a letter to Marion. "All is excitement," he admitted, "but my thought and my heart turn to you and home."[80] Old Withers seemed unimpressed, too. He saw Davis coming up the hill, and he did not like the look of those six white horses drawing him—altogether too kingly and pretentious. He may have voted for Davis, but he did not have to like him.[81]

On a motion from Chilton, the secret session adjourned temporarily to go outside for the inaugural ceremonies.[82] The delegates formed in line and walked downstairs and out onto a platform erected around the portico steps where they took their seats along with other dignitaries, state and local, including one woman, the wife of former Senator Ben Fitzpatrick.[83] At last Davis stepped out, walking now with Howell Cobb, Stephens, and the Reverend Manly behind them. The crowd sent up one grand cheer, the militia fired a salute of artillery, and then the president-elect took his seat near a table on which sat Ellen Noyes' wreath and a Bible from the governor's office.[84]

Before him sat his new fellow citizens, from the six-year-old girl clinging to her father's hand out of fear of the stern-looking militia, to the slave barber Jim Moore, who paid $50 of his own money to help raise a militia company, and then came on his own all the way from Tennessee to witness the inauguration.[85] Davis could see out over the city to the Alabama, where the steamboat *King* had just put into the wharf with four hundred people from Mobile, all now too late to see the ceremonies.[86] On the platform before him he looked directly into the faces of the men who put him here—some of them reluctantly. Barnwell had as much to do with it as anybody, and now he looked back, struck by the enthusiasm of the crowd, the gay, upturned faces of the ladies making "a variegation which was very striking & very beautiful."[87] William B. Ochiltree, delegate from Texas just arrived to join his colleague Gregg, found the scene "grand, solemn and impressive."[88] Even the by now jaded reporters agreed that, all in all, it was "the grandest pageant ever witnessed in the South."[89]

Davis sat between the center columns on the portico, Cobb seated on his left, and Stephens on his right, with Captain Jones standing behind him.[90] Then, just a few minutes prior to one o'clock, Manly stepped up to deliver an invocation. He addressed the "Great Spirit! maker and Lord of all things," who made rulers tremble and senators become students. He offered thanks for the peaceful birth of this new Confederacy, for the unanimity of their councils, and for providing this man to "go in and out before us, and to lead thy people." Praying that Davis might enjoy a sound mind in a sound body, he asked also for a blessing on the Congress sitting before him. "Let the administration of this government be the reign of truth and peace," he said, and "put thy good Spirit into our whole people." As for the North, he begged that the Almighty "turn the counsels of our enemies into foolishness." "We ask all through Jesus Christ our Lord," he concluded; "Amen."[91]

With the hands on the great clock above the portico at one minute before one, Howell Cobb introduced Jefferson Davis. He stood beside the table, looked over the crowd, and began to speak. Not then nor later did he ever give a sign that the irony of the moment occurred to him. About to embark on a journey meant forever to divorce them all from their old antagonists in the North, he stood here now making an inaugural speech in a city once called Yankeetown. Preparing to lead them all in their flight from the old flag, he faced west down Market, with his back literally turned to Union.

As young Culver took the cap from his lens for a few seconds to capture the scene forever on a glass negative, Davis addressed the Congress, his friends, and fellow Confederates. He spoke of his feeling of inadequacy to the task before him, but trusted in the wisdom and patriotism of all assembled to give him guidance. He hoped that they would be allowed to pursue their course of independence in peace. After all, they did nothing more than follow the time-honored American tradition of government resting upon the consent of the governed, and now that Washington no longer represented their interests, but rather threatened them, they were taking their peaceful and rightful alternative. In the spirit of true conservatism, they merely emulated their fathers of 1776. "The impartial and enlightened verdict of mankind will vindicate the rectitude of our conduct," he promised. Secession was an inalienable right. To call them revolutionaries was to abuse the language.

They sought no invasion of the rights of others; merely the protection of their own. And should war come as a result, he trusted that posterity would acquit them of responsibility. "Doubly justified by the absence of wrong on our part, and by wanton aggression on the part of others, there can be no cause to doubt that the courage and patriotism of the people of the Confederate States will be found equal to any measures of defense which honor and security may require."

At every emphatic point, as he finished a tribute to their courage and determination, the crowd sent up cheers and applause.[92] His clear voice carried wonderfully, even to the outer reaches of the gathering, where the parade marshals sat on horseback to get a better view.[93] On the platform Ochiltree felt inspired. "God bless the man!" he would say in a few hours, "for he is every inch a man."[94]

"Our true policy is peace," Davis continued, "and the freest trade which our necessities will permit." They did not want war. The difference between the agricultural pursuits of the South and the industry of the North ought to make the two sections complementary, not antagonistic, each needing the produce of the other. For decades the South had tried every peaceful means to see its rights honored, but in vain, and now they took this step "as a necessity, not a choice." He appealed to the old Union to let them go in peace, that they might not have to resort to "the final arbitrament of the sword." Meanwhile, war or peace, they had much to do. They must perfect their government, establish their executive departments, and commence relations with other nations. They must build an army and a navy stronger, more efficient, and better equipped than the existing militias. And they must also be prepared to grow, as more states of like interests left the old compact to join the new. But to all he made it clear that he, and he believed the people before him, rejected utterly any idea of reconstruction of the whole Union. Hard experience had proven that they could not yoke themselves to those who did not share their interests and institutions.

Time after time cheers interrupted him as he spoke, and midway through the speech the excitement spread to some of the citizens of "Kunopolis," gathered like the rest to witness the occasion. Off on the fringe of the crowd a Newfoundland and a much smaller bull terrier commenced a snarling, growling tussle that attracted attention. Some might have thought to look at the numbered collars that the city sold to owners for ten cents, intending to report the offenders to the police.[95] But several boys from the local military academy quickly lost all interest in the inaugural, dropped their antiquated flintlock muskets, and ran to watch the dogfight. In moments it was over, the smaller dog's pluck and spirit quite intimidating the larger. As the Newfoundland sullenly trotted away, the boys saw in the brief spat a hopeful symbol of what would happen if the North should attempt to test the courage of the Confederate underdog.[96]

Davis hardly noticed the brief scuffle. In fact, he seemed unable to escape his repeated refrain of pleading the desire for peace, then following with the threat of a harsh retribution should the North attempt coercion. "The suffering of millions will bear testimony to the folly and wickedness of our aggressors," he declared, and if the Union did attack them, he promised to retaliate against its ocean commerce as well as on the battlefield. The Confederacy would advance to the fray armed with the Constitution of their fathers, interpreted now as their fathers intended it to be understood. For himself, he asserted yet again that he did not seek this position, nor did he want it. Now that he assumed its powers, he promised unfailing zeal in their behalf, hard work, and a reliance on the people to forgive him his errors. "I may disappoint your expectations," he said, but no one should ever have cause to fault him for trying.

"Obstacles may retard," he concluded, "they cannot long prevent the progress of a movement sanctified by its justice, and sustained by a virtuous people." With the blessing of the Almighty, and with virtue, honor, and the right on their side, "we may hopefully look forward to success, to peace, and to prosperity."[97]

It took him eighteen minutes to deliver his address. As the applause subsided, Howell Cobb stood, took the Bible from the table, and held it out. Resting his left hand upon it, Davis raised his right, and commenced his oath. "I do solemnly swear that I will faithfully execute the office of President of the Confederate States of America, and will, to the best of my ability, preserve, protect, and defend the constitution thereof."[98] He repeated the words as Cobb said them. When Cobb added "So help me, God," Davis raised his eyes skyward amid a deathly hush in the crowd. With tears welling in his eyes, he repeated the words, then said them again, and bent down to kiss the Bible in Cobb's hand. It was done.[99]

"O, that you could have looked upon him when he took that solemn oath," Tom Cobb would say in a few weeks, briefly elevated from his customary disapproval of everyone and everything.[100] "I think I never saw any scene so solemn and impressive," said a lady in the crowd.[101] Many wept openly, one man confessing that "I never before or since that hour so experienced the ecstasy of patriotism."[102] Hearing it as he sat next to Davis, Howell Cobb had to agree that the speech was most satisfactory, and the occasion itself more impressive than any other he ever witnessed.[103] The President's declaration against any thought of reconstruction reassured him and others that there would be no thought of going back.[104] Barnwell agreed that "his taking the oath was very solemn & very impressive." He thoroughly approved of the address, thinking it well suited to the occasion and "markedly well delivered." Already his few doubts about Davis were beginning to melt.[105]

The people on the platform stood and began to reenter the hall to conclude their secret session. Watts handed Davis Ellen Noyes's wreath, and the President slipped it over his arm, then began catching flowers and petals tossed down at him by women leaning from the upper balconies and windows of the state house.[106] Distracted as he was, he may hardly have noticed when one of the *Advertiser* editors stepped up and practically grabbed the text of the inaugural from his hand. Other journalists had asked for copies the day before, but Davis sent them word that it was yet unfinished. Now Shorter and Reid intended that theirs should be the first paper in the land to print the inaugural.[107]

As he accepted the compliments of those around him and walked toward the door with Stephens, one woman, Mrs. Fitzpatrick, rather ostentatiously poked him in the back with the tip of her parasol to get him to turn around and notice her.[108] Once all the dignitaries disappeared into the building, the crowd still remained. It happened too quickly. They did not want to leave. They wanted to savor the moment. A reporter from Mobile, standing among them, thought that they "felt like him of old, that it was good to be there."[109] It was good for young Culver, too, who passed through the crowd taking orders for prints of his photograph.[110]

Again inside the Congress hall, Davis and Stephens sat on Cobb's right as the delegates conducted their final business of the day, ordering the printing of five thousand copies of the inaugural.[111] The President felt somewhat stunned by the enormity of the occasion. "Upon my weary heart were showered smiles plaudits and flowers, but beyond them I saw troubles and thorns innumerable," he told Varina. Still, "I do not despond and will not shrink from the task imposed upon me."[112] As they left the hall at the adjournment, Davis asked Stephens to come to his room at the Exchange at four o'clock. Similar requests went to Yancey and Barnwell. He would begin his work right away.[113] With the crowd outside dispersing, Cobb joined Davis and Stephens in the barouche for the ride back to the Exchange, and within minutes the Congress hall lay empty but for Tom Cobb, finishing his letter to Marion.[114] Davis spent the next few hours receiving callers, but this Georgian would not be one of them. "I hate toadyism so much," he told his wife, especially when rumor associated his name with a cabinet post. Strangely, no one seems to have heard or repeated that gossip except Tom Cobb himself.[115]

Handbills and the press announced during the day that at eight o'clock Estelle Hall and the Concert Hall would both hold levees in honor of the new president, with the general public invited to attend.[116] An hour or more beforehand, as the sun went down, illuminations sprang up all along Market, Commerce, Court, Perry, Monroe, and Montgomery streets. Public and private houses alike shone a blaze onto the thoroughfares, so that Jonce Hooper found he could almost read his own newspaper by their light.[117] A committee from Estelle Hall went further by shooting overhead from either side of Commerce a steady stream of rockets and "bengal lights" throughout the evening.[118]

Montgomery came to the levees well prepared. Rumor said that ladies of the town ordered more than $30,000 in jewelry to be shipped in from Tiffany & Company in New York just for the occasion,[119] and what New York did not sent, the Harris & Hoyt Jewelry Shop at 44 Market Street, just below Montgomery Hall, obligingly supplied. Men and women appeared in every manner of attire, from the ornate black velvet trimmed with lace and pearls on Mrs. Fitzpatrick, to simple shawls on other women. The men wore everything from patrician black broadcloth to populist homespun.[120] The walls of Estelle Hall held wreaths of arbor vitae circling the names of the states, while at one end evergreens spelled out "Davis—South—Stephens."

Davis himself stood beneath an arbor of evergreens intertwined with flowers as the multitude filed past him. Watts made the introductions as the men shook Davis's hand and exchanged words of well wishing, and the ladies gave him seemingly endless kisses. "Every body and his wife were there," said Tom Cobb, who most certainly did not attend, but stayed in his hotel room working on congressional bills well into the night.[121] While watching the ladies in hoop skirts trying to navigate their way gracefully through the crush of men, crinolines, walls, and other obstructions, the newsmen in town stood in a group and kept an eye on the President, envying him the ladies' attentions and "attitudinations."[122] Before long, however, the crush in the hall became simply too great. "Oh the crowd," Ellen Noyes exclaimed the next day. She met Davis herself eventually, and got in return for her wreath a handsome compliment from the President as the crush of people jostled them. A twinkle in her eye, she promised that when the Confederacy built him an Executive Mansion, it would surely have more room for receptions than Estelle Hall.[123] Mary Todd Lincoln's two sisters came through the receiving line, making a point of telling Davis that their relationship was to Lincoln's *wife* and not himself. But their blood relationship to Breckinridge, they added, ought to atone for any matrimonial mistakes.[124] Finally many, including the reporters, could take the crowd and the rising heat no more, and left early. Those who remained eventually went to the Concert Hall for a dance that lasted until well after midnight, and from which more than a few young couples did not get home until the coming of dawn.[125]

Every new nation could dream of such a natal day. Inspired by the event, ladies of the city proposed that the council rename Market Street as "Davis Avenue."[126] A proud couple, looking on their new baby boy born just as the President uttered his inaugural, named the infant for him.[127] Word of Davis's stand against reconstruction quickly went out to commissioners in Baltimore and Richmond and other border capitals, while the text of the inaugural itself was on the wire to Washington within hours of its delivery.[128] That same evening came word from Wigfall that Southern sympathizers in the Federal city received the address with enthusiasm. "It has the ring of the true metal," he crowed, and promised to help the cause immeasurably.[129] At McIntyre's studio, young William Culver made his first prints from the glass negative developed earlier that afternoon, and found captured in the image one of the most historic moments ever yet recorded in a

photograph. As he filled the orders for copies, he made one to send
north to the editors of *Harper's Weekly*, the Union's most influential
and widely read illustrated newspaper. Once their artists finished making a wood block engraving from it, the portrait of the dignified and
imposing ceremony could be published all across the country, to proclaim to the world itself that the Confederate States of America was
ready to join the fraternity of nations.[130]

CHAPTER EIGHT

WE ARE AT WORK

———•★•———

CAPITALS DRINK GOSSIP and dine on rumor. Even before Davis took his oath, stories flowed through Montgomery like the spirits in its bars, and more often than not the one came out of mouths even as the other went in. Davis intended to appoint everyone, it seemed. State would go to Yancey or Herschel Johnson, Toombs or Robert J. Walker of Mississippi. Memminger was to get Treasury, but then so was Toombs. The War portfolio went to Bartow, or John Forsyth, while Navy should be given to Mallory of Florida, or perhaps Perkins of Louisiana, or even merged into the War Department. Judah Benjamin should have the attorney generalship unless it went to Montgomery's John Elmore, and John Hemphill of Texas, not yet arrived as a delegate to Congress, should be postmaster general. Interior was certain to go to Porcher Miles, while Davis already wanted Keitt as minister to Spain, and Wigfall as one of his major generals. Moreover, a host of other names flowed with the wine, attached to no particular office— Rhett, Conrad, Henry Jackson, Henry Benning, Hammond of South Carolina. Almost the only name not mentioned for anything was Tom Cobb.[1]

It was all the sort of talk that always surrounded the building of a government, though in this case the speculation grew so rife that within two days of the inauguration one reporter declared that he could write a new column every day and fill it with the latest prognostications. They were doing more than inaugurating a new administration; they were starting a new nation, and the filling of its offices now would portend much of its future, and whether or not it had a future. Already rumor said who would *not* be in the cabinet, as well, especially Toombs and Howell Cobb, both certainly known to have turned down offers.[2] Cobb himself confessed to being entirely unaware of Davis's intentions, and without knowing if Davis even thought of giving him one,

169

made it clear that he would not accept any post.[3] Inevitably, some thought they knew better than the others, and in one of the conversational parliaments of Montgomery during the first couple of days after Davis took his oath, one man claiming intimate knowledge of the President, his character and his habits, shouted to a group of lounging speculators, "You are all wrong. I know exactly."

"Pray tell us," implored his auditors, and happily he obliged.

"For Secretary of State, Hon. Jeff. Davis of Miss.; War and Navy, Jeff. Davis of Miss.; Interior, ex-Senator Davis, of Miss.; Treasury, Col. Davis, of Miss.; Attorney General, Mr. Davis, of Miss."[4]

Davis of Mississippi would not have been amused, but his austere air, coupled with his reputation for pride and unshakable certainty in his own convictions, invited such jibes. Then too, there was his penchant for doing everything himself, to make certain it was done right. Some others gave him more credit in his judgment of men, however. His old West Point roommate Crafts Wright told Northerners that "he will surround himself only with those who are competent," and Davis himself told Varina of the need for advisors of strength of character and decided opinion.[5] "I can trust my own methods so far," he said, "that they are humanitarian, and, I feel sure, honest—but I want the standpoint of other honest eyes, single to the good of our people and of the country." He admitted the possibility that he might see only one side of an issue.[6]

Davis came to Montgomery with his cabinet on his mind, but few firm decisions yet planted. At least he came with no debts to pay, or friends to reward, since he neither sought nor wanted this new office. He liked to think that he also saw no enemies to punish.[7] One political reality did face him, however. Six states composed the Confederacy just now, and each must have one cabinet post. That was only politic. Moreover, in all appointments he must be careful to spread them evenly among the states without favoritism.

Yet there were obligations, philosophical if not personal. The state conventions and the provisional congress almost completely ignored the guiding lights of secession in their elections. Yet in the service of unity, these men must receive something, and at the same time the positions, if carefully chosen, could remove the hotspurs from arenas where they might still make trouble. Davis could do nothing about Rhett. He held a congressional seat now and the President simply had to hope that he did nothing too volatile or destructive. But then there was Yancey. No more than a couple of hours after the inauguration,

Davis met with him at the Exchange, his first interview in forming his government. He offered the fiery Alabamian his choice of cabinet posts.[8] Then, perhaps before Yancey could answer, the President went on to suggest placing him at the head of a commission to be sent to the courts of Europe to sue for recognition. Yancey had not the temperament for a cabinet minister, and Davis probably did not really want him there. On the other hand, turning a hothead like Yancey into a diplomat was an absurd notion, explainable only by Davis's belief that Britain, France, and the rest must automatically pay court to King Cotton, therefore making foreign ministers largely cyphers. Yancey left promising to make a choice in the next few days.[9]

Barnwell kept an appointment next. In his only fixed cabinet decision made before reaching Montgomery, Davis wanted the South Carolinian for secretary of state. He knew and trusted Barnwell, and besides, the Palmetto State, as long-time leader of the movement now culminating, deserved the most prestigious spot in the cabinet.[10] Now he made the offer. Barnwell felt truly flattered, his earlier reservations about Davis momentarily disappearing in a surge of esteem and regard. But he declined, politely, yet firmly. He wanted no more of politics when his term in Congress ceased. In the brief minutes they spoke, exchanging only a few sentences, Barnwell suggested that Howell Cobb would make an excellent secretary of state, then went on to add that in looking for an appointment from South Carolina, he thought Davis would do well to put Memminger in at Treasury. Reluctantly Davis accepted his refusal, but then asked him to keep their conversation confidential, as it would be an embarrassment to the future secretary of state to have it known that he was not first choice.[11] The secret lasted only hours before Barnwell told Keitt, and he started telling others.[12] Within a week the *Mercury* made it public thanks to Rhett, in whom Barnwell also foolishly confided.[13] Keitt and others testified to Rhett's disappointment that Davis did not make the disastrous mistake of turning to him instead of his cousin.[14]

Thus matters stood when Little Aleck arrived for his four o'clock appointment. Stephens freely confessed to others that he would employ his influence in the interest of sound appointments, as he saw them.[15] To his adversaries like the Cobb brothers, that meant getting offices for Toombs and perhaps Herschel Johnson. The former they could stomach—indeed, they could hardly deny him. But Johnson, whose running on the Douglas ticket in 1860 stood as a repudiation of Southern rights, they would not stand. On the basis of rumor only, the

Cobbs gave Little Aleck and others to understand that they would oppose any Johnson nomination when it came to the Congress for confirmation.[16] They need not have worried, for Stephens said nothing of Johnson. Davis asked him what place best suited Toombs. Little Aleck suggested giving his friend his choice, while secretly he hoped to see him in the War office. Davis, on the other hand, really wanted to put him in at Treasury, but he could not refuse Barnwell's request that Memminger have that post. Consequently, putting the best face on it, the President suggested "the highest compliment" by proposing the Georgian for State.[17]

It was a start, though a modest one. Davis had taken care of South Carolina and Treasury. A quick meeting with Memminger brought an immediate acceptance,[18] and when Stephens left him Georgia and State looked like a pair. But scarcely did Little Aleck return to Mrs. Cleveland's to broach the matter to his housemate before an urgent telegram arrived from Georgia. Toombs's daughter had gone into labor and was gravely ill. He must come at once. His last and only child could die. The news unnerved Toombs almost completely. With no more talk of cabinet posts, he rushed to pack and barely got to the West Point depot in time to catch the evening train east.[19]

As he awaited the legislation from Congress formally creating the cabinet departments, Davis kept confidential his preferences and his appointments, consulting only Stephens with any regularity. He did not invite any of the state delegations to put forward candidates, and they did not presume to do so, though some potential appointees' friends made efforts to get to Davis to argue their cases.[20] Inevitably, men not consulted turned resentful, especially Rhett and Howell Cobb. Tom Cobb must have been coming out of his depression, for he, too, complained that the President was not consulting *him*.[21] "Davis acts for himself," he grumbled, "and receives no advice except from those who pass their advice unasked."[22]

Early on February 19 Memminger sent a message for young Henry D. Capers of South Carolina to come to his room in the Exchange. The treasury secretary-designate knew the fellow's father, and had some fleeting acquaintance with him when Capers taught anatomy at the Atlanta Medical College.[23] Moreover, the young man held the right views, serving in a militia company in Charleston until two weeks ago when he came to Montgomery. Just yesterday he was an assistant parade marshal representing his state. If some thought him erratic, even impulsive, Memminger believed him the right man to be his first appointee.[24] He asked him to be his private secretary for the moment, which really meant that Memminger wanted Capers to be his *factotum* in organizing the department.

Memminger gave simple enough instructions. *"The world must know at once that we are at work,"* he told Capers, *"and that we are in earnest."* To that end he ordered a notice to be published that same day in the local dailies announcing their business hours as nine to three commencing the following day. It should also include the location of their offices, though here Memminger confessed a small difficulty. While he certainly knew that the committee of Congress had found a building for the executive departments, he did not yet know just where it was. Capers would have to find it for himself.[25]

As Capers began his search for the government building, President Davis continued a hunt of his own. While he enlisted Alexander Clitherall to help him temporarily as private secretary, he pressed on with filling his cabinet.[26] That morning he sent a telegram formally proffering the State premiership to Argus, Georgia, where Toombs sat at the bedside of his sick daughter. At the moment only his child commanded his attention. He shot back an immediate reply. "I cannot," he said. He would better serve the country in Congress. It was not the reply Davis wanted. He scribbled a note on the bottom of the telegram asking Stephens to call on him that same morning and sent Clitherall off with it to Mrs. Cleveland's. When Little Aleck arrived Davis asked him how he might influence Toombs to reconsider, and Stephens himself composed another telegram, this one calling on him to heed his country's call. Then they waited.[27]

Later this same day Yancey called on the President once more. He gave no answer to Davis's offer, but instead gave the recommendation that Leroy P. Walker would make an excellent choice for secretary of war. Davis had already wired to his old friend Clement C. Clay of Alabama tendering him the War portfolio, but Clay declined on grounds of poor health.[28] Still thinking that Yancey himself would accept yesterday's offer of a position in the government, Davis now replied that "I have offered you a seat, I cannot grant two Cabinet positions to Alabama, one state." "Give it to my friend," Yancey answered. "I desire the appointment of Mr. Walker." It was his way of declining a position for himself.[29] The Alabamian had concluded that he could not accept a cabinet seat in a government now completely in the hands of moderates and conservatives, and still "maintain a dignified position" with his extreme Southern rights party in Alabama.

However, he gave at least a conditional acceptance of the European mission.[30]

Though he had never met Walker, Davis knew his name, for this Alabamian actively pulled wires in hopes of securing such a post. Besides enlisting Yancey's aid and recommendation, he also secured Clay's blessing. Three weeks earlier, with the future organization of the provisional government still uncertain, Walker talked of seeking a seat from his state in the Senate. When the provisional constitution came out with a unicameral legislature, and no positions available until elections late in the year, Walker then came directly to Montgomery to start politicking for a cabinet post instead. With him he brought endorsements from Clay, and a promise that Clay would telegraph Davis directly to recommend him. City rumor already suggested him for attorney general.[31]

With Walker near at hand, an interview took but a few minutes to arrange. When the Alabama lawyer called at room 101, the President saw a tall, lean, slightly stooped man with bright eyes, a dark beard, and a quid of tobacco ever in his mouth. One caller pronounced him "a profuse spitter."[32] The son of a one-time senator from Alabama, Walker accumulated some small fortune in law practice in Huntsville, and in the process demonstrated considerable accomplishment in classical studies.[33] In fact, Hooper regarded him as "one of the giant intellects of the South," praising his method and logic.[34] Walker spoke well in public, impressing people with his mild manners and gentlemanly deportment, and an apparently unassailable character. Some thought him more like a church elder than a statesman,[35] and his own son confessed that "in truth he was *no* politician." In private he struck people as cold and aloof despite his kind and charitable nature, with the result that men often misjudged and misunderstood him.[36]

Davis knew little of this as he spoke with Walker now. He did know that he needed an Alabamian in the cabinet, and that several influential men in the state spoke on behalf of the man seated with him. He also realized, or surely learned very quickly, that Walker knew literally nothing of the military, nor had he any experience at administration. Such matters, unfortunately, played too small a role in the President's thinking about his cabinet appointments. Of his offers made so far, only Memminger possessed any suitable background for the position tendered. Davis was paying political debts, not of his own, but of the Confederacy itself to its constituent states. When Walker left the room, he took the job with him.

Putting South Carolina and Alabama out of the way with Treasury and War, and expecting Toombs to take care still of State and Georgia, Davis sent telegrams to the rest of his first choices, none of them then in Montgomery. He knew Stephen R. Mallory of Florida well, and knew too that he had served knowledgeably on the Naval Affairs committee in the old Senate. He should have the Navy Department if he wanted it. From the Senate, too, Davis knew Judah P. Benjamin of Louisiana. Indeed, a few years earlier some hot debate, combined with Davis's ungovernable temper, nearly resulted in a duel between them before intermediaries settled the dispute. Friends since, Davis knew of Benjamin's reputation as legal scholar. He wanted him for attorney general. Having no need or intention to establish an Interior Department just yet, this left Davis needing only to match Mississippi with the postal service, which no one had any idea how to run. He settled on Henry Ellett, a noted attorney and state legislator. That done, he spent the rest of the day consulting with congressmen on their necessary first legislation and waiting to hear from Toombs.

Capers, too, enjoyed some success in his quest. He found local attorney and civic leader James H. Clanton and got from him the keys to the Montgomery Insurance Building. Now armed with the actual location of the offices, he sat down beside a dry goods box and composed his advertisement, the first official act of any of the Confederate executive departments.[37] At eight the next morning, under cloudy skies, he walked to Commerce and Bibb, and there on the northwest corner found "a great, red brick pile" that Montgomeryites soon called Government House.[38] The three story building ran one hundred feet along Commerce, and another hundred feet back down Bibb and, ironically, sat just a block away from the Exchange and on the same side of Commerce, despite Memminger's not knowing where the building was.[39]

Even before taking occupancy the government decided to fill the ground floor, too. When Capers opened the Commerce Street door and stepped in, he found the building absolutely empty, not a stick of furniture to be seen, a thick film of dust covering the floors, and cobwebs in every corner and window. Four large rooms composed this floor, each twenty-five feet by a hundred, and Capers immediately claimed the first for the Treasury. The other departments could fend for themselves when they moved in.[40] Now, with barely an hour before he must open his doors for business, he wasted no time. He commandeered a passing black on the street to help him sweep out the room and act as ersatz office boy.[41] Meanwhile he ran to the furniture store of

John Powell at 8 Perry Street nearby, explained his predicament to the proprietor's son, and minutes later had Charles Powell assisting him in carrying a walnut table, a small desk, and a set of office chairs into the newly swept room. While he arranged the furniture to his liking, Capers sent the black down the street to Pfister and White's Book Store under the Exchange, to fetch stationery. By nine o'clock with everything ready or so it appeared, he wrote "Treasury" on a piece of cardboard and tacked it to the door. Then he waited. The Confederate government was open for business.[42]

Congress acted quickly to help. Bill after bill, printed triple-spaced on blue foolscap, each line numbered for reference and amendation, appeared on the delegates' desks.[43] This same day it passed bills formally organizing State, Justice, Treasury, War, the Post Office, and finally Navy, another allowing the president a private secretary, and yet one more setting the salaries of cabinet heads at $6,000.[44] Davis himself signed his very first bills, one of Bartow's to provide for munitions of war, and the other the legislation authorizing his secretary. Anticipating the latter, he already had old friend Robert Josselyn near at hand. The fifty-year-old Massachusetts native had spent the past quarter-century in Mississippi, some of it in the legislature, and went to Mexico in Davis's regiment in 1846. Recently resigned from a job in Washington with the Treasury Department there, he returned to Mississippi where his round, ruddy face and perpetual smile made him well liked as a "Prince of Good Fellows." Fat, jolly, graying, a bit too fond of the bottle, he added poetry to his other talents, and with a measure of literary license somehow managed to go from service as a private in Mexico to being called "captain" these days. He would earn his $100 a month.[45]

As Josselyn relieved Clitherall, the President struggled on to finish his cabinet. A long telegram, followed by a letter, brought Toombs's second refusal. He protested that his experience in public affairs lay entirely in the legislative arena. He knew nothing of administration. Moreover, he regarded framing the permanent constitution as a paramount concern, especially the amendments necessary to suit it to their situation. Having a place on the framing committee, he would be weakened in advocacy if his time were divided between Congress and cabinet. And expecting Virginia and North Carolina to join soon, he thought that Davis would want to give one of them representation on his highest council.[46] What Toombs did not say was that he regarded a cabinet post as an empty and somewhat insincere compliment, a meaningless bone tossed to a man who might himself have expected to be the one choosing secretaries.[47] Besides, it was an office job with little to do. Rumor in Montgomery speculated that, if anything, Toombs would have preferred the more active role of foreign minister to some nation.[48]

After stating all his objections, and probably in response chiefly to the urgings of Stephens, Toombs concluded by saying that he would be willing to take the office temporarily until Davis found someone else when one of the Border States joined the Confederacy. That was enough for the President. Word went out from the Exchange to continue the illusion of complete harmony and selfless dedication, and when Toombs returned to Montgomery on February 24, his daughter's crisis passed, he heard on the street and in the press that his acceptance of the State portfolio had been "unhesitating."[49]

Certainly one person in the capital felt less than harmonious. Having lost the presidency, Rhett wanted the State Department job. South Carolina was due the top cabinet post, and as "the prime mover of secession," as his own *Mercury* called him, he was the South Carolinian who should have it. But not a single member of his delegation would go to Davis and recommend him, not even cousin Barnwell.[50] Worse, Memminger, who got the state's one slot, was in Rhett's eyes too soft on secession before the fact. He would not have recommended him for Treasury, and soon took pains to make that known publicly.[51] Indeed, he claimed that now Memminger "never made a single suggestion of any value whatever, with respect to our finances."[52] Of course, Rhett told his family days before to expect disappointment, so there was no surprise in his being passed over. It was just one more reason to harbor bitterness toward the man who now sat in the chair that should have been his. Now, the same day that he learned of Toombs's appointment, news came from home to add wormwood to his gall. His daughter had died. Considering his duty with the constitutional committee paramount, he would not try to go back for the burial. He could only send word of his grief to Charleston, bury his ambition's disappointments in his personal anguish, and cry of "my poor bleeding heart."[53]

Davis wasted no time. The next day, February 21, he returned the signed bills creating his executive departments, and then submitted to an executive session his nominations of Toombs, Memminger, and Walker. Congress consented unanimously.[54] Word quickly spread to the street, and the news met a favorable reception, despite some surprise at first that neither Yancey nor Rhett appeared on the list. Soon enough it became known that the former had refused his offer, and the other simply never received one.[55]

Finally young Capers got some business. He had spent most of the day before fidgeting, reading the newspapers, walking to the door occasionally to see if anyone was coming, and teaching his office boy the proper way to receive visitors. Midday had come a note from Memminger saying that he could not leave the capitol and would not come in that day. Capers went to Powell's again to get a mat for the floor and a few other things, sat until closing time, and went home. The next morning, expecting much the same, his heart jumped when he heard a step outside the door and then a knock.[56]

"My name is Deas, late of the United States Army," said the tall, handsome military man who stepped into the office.[57] Looking around the largely empty room with but a single person in it, he asked for the office of the secretary of the treasury, only to be told that this was it, and Memminger was at the Capitol.[58] Somewhat skeptically he said that he came with an order from Davis for funds to buy blankets and provisions for one hundred men just arrived at the West Point depot to offer themselves to the new army. Certainly Davis knew that Alabama had pledged money to the new government, and that other states were about to do the same, but he should also have known that the Provisional Constitution made it quite clear that Congress could not appropriate a penny without a request from a cabinet head. Memminger only got his confirmation this same day, and had no time yet to draft an appropriation request. In short, the Confederate government did not have a cent, as Capers all too painfully had to confess. He pulled his last five dollars from his pocket and showed it to Deas. "I have been on considerable of a frolic in Montgomery for the last two weeks," he shrugged. "Beyond the small amount in my pocket, if there is another dollar in this office, I am not informed of its existence."[59]

Deas swore at first, but soon they laughed together over the improbable situation, and then went to the state house, where Capers managed to get a message to Memminger then in secret session. The secretary gave Capers a letter to the president of the Central Bank of Alabama pledging his personal credit, and armed with that they got Deas his money. It was a small start, and an odd one at that, but the government was working.[60]

In the anxiety to complete his organization, Davis made other small mistakes. Without waiting for acceptances from all of his other nominees, he sent their names to Congress on February 25.[61] Benjamin agreed to come to Montgomery, though he may not have known yet the exact post Davis had in mind for him.[62] On Washington's birthday he made a rousing speech in New Orleans while presenting a flag to a military company, and predicted to them that "our independence is not to be maintained without the shedding of blood." He hoped he might be wrong, but if not, they could look upon it like the fire that purges a landscape for planting anew.[63] After conferring with Slidell and other prominent New Orleaneans on the commercial and trading interests that so concerned them all, he left on the February 27 boat for Mobile and beyond.[64]

An interesting man stepped off the paddlewheeler in Montgomery. Medium height, rotund, with glistening black eyes not quite square with each other, dark hair and beard, Benjamin seemingly wore a perpetual smile on his lips, and an everlasting cigar stuck between them.[65] He spoke with a slight lisp and something of a French accent, betraying his birth in the West Indies to Sephardic Jewish parents. Many a story went around about him, from rumors that he left Yale after being caught stealing, to his shrewdness in building a fortune as a Louisiana planter. In the Senate he made an effective spokesman for state rights, and anti-Semitism, while generally lurking in the background in the Old South, seemed not to have impeded his rise to influence. Though his addiction to cards may have threatened his prosperity, it aroused little gossip, but perhaps that was because tastier rumors dogged Benjamin, the most popular of all being about his peculiar marriage.[66] In 1833 he wedded a sixteen-year-old Catholic girl from New Orleans. After ten years together, she moved to France, though he continued to support her apparently profligate ways. In 1859 she came back to join him in Washington in a new house, but immediately unsubstantiated rumors of her infidelity flourished, and suddenly she left again for Paris, never to return.[67] Perhaps she was unfaithful. Yet stories also persisted that the problem might lie with her husband, that he was, as one put it, "only a quarter man." "J. P. B. should rather have kept himself unto himself in single blessedness," hinted a reporter who observed him closely and did not like him. "Nature had made him the safest of creatures, in manly mould." He might, said one, have made an excellent harem guard.[68]

Regardless of his sexual orientation, Benjamin made the most companionable of fellows, and Little Aleck and the other Georgians happily welcomed him to Mrs. Cleveland's.[69] Less welcome, so it seemed, was Stephen R. Mallory. After returning to Florida upon resigning his

Senate seat in January, he studiously avoided going to Montgomery to observe or participate in forming the government, chiefly because he feared it would appear that he was trolling for an office. Then came the telegram from Davis. It being only a short trip from Pensacola, he came to Montgomery to decline in person and explain his reasons to his old colleague, but when he arrived early on February 27 he discovered that the President had already sent his name to Congress. Worse, he learned that while Benjamin and Ellett received immediate and unanimous approval, his name did not. Worst of all, it was Morton of his own state who held up his appointment by referral to the Naval Affairs committee.[70] Now he could hardly decline the appointment in the face of such a slur and still retain his honor.

In the old United States Senate Mallory had served on the Naval Affairs committee himself, hence Davis's interest in him for the new Navy portfolio. Thanks to his position he was privy to confidential information in the growing crisis of December 1860 and January 1861, and of special interest to him had been Federal plans for Fort Pickens. Initially he advised secessionist forces at Pensacola to seize the fort from its garrison, but warned them that it could only be done by fighting. Later, he changed his mind, saying that at the moment its possession did not warrant a drop of blood. When the Union planned to send warships to reinforce the fort's tiny garrison, Mallory persuaded Buchanan to call it off, and then got the Pensacola commander to agree not to try to take the fort so long as Buchanan did not attempt to land troops for its defense. Bloodshed was averted, the Pickens garrison remained unaugmented, and an uneasy peace remained.[71]

Unfortunately, long-time opponents of Mallory seized on his change of policy as a sign of being less than committed to the cause, and even erroneously charged him with preventing the taking of Pickens, when in fact all he avoided was a bloody attack, and possibly war. Moreover, Morton's "chuckleheadedness" toward Mallory, as he put it, really derived from friction in the mid-1850s when Morton joined the rabidly nativistic Know-Nothing party and Mallory effectively opposed him on the stump. Evidence of how quickly men followed the fortunes of their states, Morton himself stood against secession in 1860, and yet now charged Mallory with being soft on the movement.

Most people liked the short, roly-poly Floridian. When he took a room at Montgomery Hall they met a pleasant, witty sort of fellow, definitely very pro-British, and even to some ears affecting an English accent. He pronounced "clerk" as "clark," and the like, and dressed his chubby frame in the British fashion.[72] Some rumors followed him just as they did Benjamin. The more snobbish said that his mother had been a mere washerwoman. Withers, staying at Montgomery Hall, took a liking to Mallory immediately, and probably out of sheer perversity since others did not. "She taught him not to go with the great unwashed," he said in defending Mallory. "Cleanliness next to godliness, you know"; an interesting quip from a most ungodly and not particularly fastidious man.[73] More serious were the stories of his behavior. Mary Chesnut heard him described as "notoriously dissolute." Merely being seen with him, some claimed, could compromise a woman. Frequent attacks of gout confirmed for many his drinking habits.[74]

The holdup of Mallory's confirmation embarrassed both the nominee and the President. While the Floridian appeared saddened to those around him, and Rhett and his reporter jumped on him in the *Mercury*, Davis faced the very first challenge to his judgment from Congress.[75] On February 28 the naval committee reported a recommendation that Mallory be confirmed, but Owens of Florida, a member, filed a minority report not exactly opposing Mallory, but saying he could not support the nomination until he heard more from his state.[76] Patton Anderson happened to be in Florida at the time, and when he returned he threw his support in favor of the nomination. At the same time Mallory himself politicked a bit, getting an introduction to Ben Hill from Mary Chesnut, and in particular appearing to curry old Withers, who already had a liking for him. "Designs upon a man," clucked Browne as he watched Mallory courting the old South Carolinian. "That is not in his way?"[77]

Finally on March 5 the nomination came to a vote, and Mallory won confirmation handily. Five states voted for him, and only two against, one of them Texas, which finally gained admission four days before after a popular referendum upheld secession. Embarrassing for Mallory was that the other "nay" came from Florida. In a voice poll of all the delegates, thirty-six stood with him, and seven against.[78] Still, it was an overwhelming repudiation of the rumors.

Meanwhile, Davis encountered the greatest trouble where he might have expected the least. No one, it seemed, wanted to be postmaster general. Congress confirmed Ellett before the President got a response to his offer, and when he did, it proved negative. Immediately the rumor-makers suggested that the President would turn next to Washington Chilton of Texas, but instead Davis sent a telegram on February 28 to Wirt Adams of Mississippi.[79] He was a trusted old friend, and actually prepared to leave for Montgomery before he changed his mind at the last moment and declined. "It is certainly the most undesirable position in the Cabinet," a reporter noted just then, and the President was about to agree.[80] The only person who seemed to want it was the annoying Mrs. Fitzpatrick, who thought her husband should have a spot in the cabinet.[81]

As it happened, more delegates from Texas were arriving to join Gregg and Ochiltree. First came Thomas Waul, and then Williamson S. Oldham and John H. Reagan arrived on March 1, the day before their state's formal admission.[82] John Hemphill and Wigfall had also been chosen as congressmen, and would come in time. Now that he had a seventh state, Davis naturally looked to Texas to fill the troublesome postal void. Mississippi already had the presidency and could hardly feel slighted by omission from the cabinet.

For some reason he turned to Reagan, most likely because the Texan simply took the trouble to make a courtesy call on him when he arrived. They might have had some slight acquaintance in Washington during Reagan's two terms in Congress while Davis served in the Senate, but otherwise nothing in the background of this rough-and-tumble looking frontier character suggested the administrator. Planter, Indian fighter, surveyor, lawyer, and judge before he turned statesman, Reagan spoke with a rude drawl, used quaint and often crude expressions, and habitualy whittled at a stick with a pen knife. Sometimes he absentmindedly twirled the knife on its blade point on his finger. He had common sense, and he was tough. Davis decided immediately to make Reagan, at just forty-two, his last and youngest cabinet minister.

Twice the Texan turned him down. It was, as one observer said, "a reputation-tearing office," and Reagan knew it. No one had ever satisfactorily filled it in the old Union, and there was every reason to think the job even more difficult and thankless in this new and ill-prepared Confederacy.[83] Maybe Davis turned to him in part because Reagan indirectly flattered the President during his call. He said he would not have voted for him as President, but continued to explain that he preferred Davis at the head of the South's army. Confessing that "we are to have war," Davis sadly agreed that his own desires lay elsewhere than the executive office.[84] Compliments to his military vanity almost always endeared a man to Jefferson Davis. But still Reagan refused. Finally the President asked Waul and Curry to come to his office on March 5, bringing Reagan with them. There all three worked to persuade him to reconsider. Protesting that he felt no great desire to be a martyr, still in the end the Texan yielded.

When he left he felt something akin to depression, but already his mind worked on the problem before him. On the way to his room at Montgomery Hall he encountered Mary Chesnut's cousin H. P. Brewster. Reagan asked if he would make a trip to Washington on vital business, and when Brewster agreed, told him to come to his room that evening before the train left for the East. When he called, Brewster took from Reagan letters to Wigfall and other Texans still in Washington, along with notes addressed to six of the chiefs of bureaus in the United States Post Office. Reagan offered them jobs, and asked that if they came, they bring with them copies of all the postal forms then in use. In his direct frontier manner, he reasoned that the best way to create a postal service from nothing was to steal one.[85] By the next day, when Davis submitted his nomination to unanimous approval, Reagan's depression disappeared. "I shall enter on my new duties with some distrust of my capabilities—the more so as I shall be charged with the organization of the Department and have to commence its organization with an empty Treasury," he confessed to a friend. But still, "I shall have the pleasure of being associated with a president and cabinet of no ordinary men."[86]

Ordinary they were not. How capable they would be as cabinet ministers remained to be seen, but at last the first step in organizing the government was taken. Davis himself felt pleased—and no doubt relieved that after more than two weeks of cajoling, he had finally filled all the places. Despite the imperative of representing every state in the group, he thought otherwise that he acted from the best motives. Only the exclusion of Rhett might have smacked of personal animus. Certainly Davis knew of the South Carolinian's attempt to preempt a foreign policy initiative in appointing commissioners to Europe before his inauguration and making them subject to instructions from Congress, and this was a president who would never forget any challenge or infringement on his executive prerogatives.

Later Davis boasted that none of his appointments went to personal friends, and there he was right.[87] Memminger and Walker he had never even met before. He chose them purely on the recommendations of Barnwell and Yancey and Clay.[88] Their appointments hardly paid any political debts, and sprang more from the desire to appease influential leaders in Alabama and South Carolina than from any knowledge of the appointees' abilities. Only Mallory and Benjamin brought backgrounds well known to Davis to their portfolios, yet neither belonged to the small inner circle of his friends before secession. Indeed, Davis nearly fought duels both with Benjamin and Toombs in the 1850s, which hardly qualified them as bosom companions, though the ingratiating Benjamin would soon become a close confidant. Davis gave Toombs a spot out of necessity and expediency, and Reagan got his because no one else would take the job.

Predictably, the new cabinet got mixed reactions, and few approved of all of them. The *Mercury* liked Benjamin, but remained silent as to the rest.[89] Tom Cobb thought the appointments strong and generally approved, but another observer expressed no confidence in any including Davis, dubbing the cabinet "a one-sided affair" since all of the appointees were secessionists. Calling Toombs "the great I am," he actually thought the Georgian capable of leading a palace coup.[90] The greatest criticism came from those who saw too much sameness of political complexion in the cabinet. "It is objectionable on the score of its exclusive party character," said one critic. In 1860 all the nominees supported the Southern rights Democrats led by Breckinridge, though Reagan and Mallory seemed less dedicated than the others. The more conservative Douglas wing of the Democrats should be represented, they argued, and even the Constitutional Union party led by John Bell deserved a place. For all their impetus to be reformers rather than rebels, the Confederates embraced one truly revolutionary, even idealistic, ambition. By common consent, the statesmen here in Montgomery desired the eradication of all party allegiance, having seen just how destructive such influence could be. Some applauded Davis's selections, seeing that in them "the last vestige of party is being rapidly swept away."[91] Yet others saw in these same appointments the signs of a "partisanship that appears to have influenced their own selection."[92] In any political setting, even one determined to eschew party politics entirely like the Confederacy, all it needed for isolated views to coalesce into cliques and eventually merge with others into parties was an issue or issues to unite them.

These men were approaching their new system with a wonderful kind of innocence that they should have been able to see, but did not. They thought that by leaving the old Union and leaving behind all of the issues that *had* divided men along party lines—the tariff, the territories, slavery—they would thus escape future divisiveness among themselves, not realizing that the lesson of politics since the dawn of time was that when one issue died, another sprang to life. Moreover, in proclaiming their desire to see the abolition of party and partisanship, they neglected to see that individually that meant that every former Whig hoped to see abolished the partisan views of the Democrats, while the latter wanted to see no more of the partisanship of the former. For so many, starting with Rhett and beginning to seep into the other delegations gradually, the new nonpartisanship meant everyone else should agree with *him*. The harmony that all in Montgomery so publicly proclaimed in spite of their private disagreements already showed a crack before the cabinet announcements, in Rhett's frustrations. Now, and in spite of the unanimous confirmations of all but Mallory, Jefferson Davis unwittingly gave the discontented their first wedge to widen that split, and the first real glue to cement themselves together—himself.

With the secretaries appointed, organization of the departments moved as rapidly as the energy of their heads allowed. For some there was next to nothing to do, none more so than Benjamin. The physical needs of his domain were so slight that the first descriptions of the offices in Government House failed even to include the Justice Department. The attorney general had but to nod a formality approval of the President's appointments for the state district judgeships before they went to Congress, and otherwise, as one wag put it, devise "means for agreeably spending the time with the fair sex until his legal lore should be called into requisition."[93] While Memminger and Reagan sweated often into the late hours, this dapper little rotundity spent his afternoons and evenings walking the promenade along the bluff above the Alabama, usually in company with ladies who, gossip said, had nothing to fear from him thanks to the odd reasons behind his marital split.[94] Very quickly, having so little to do, Benjamin started serving Davis as a host, sparing the President's pressed time by undertaking to entertain visiting dignitaries for him, not an altogether disagreeable task.[95]

Jonce Hooper complained the day after the first confirmations that Davis worked hard, but some of his appointees did not.[96] Writing before Benjamin's appointment, he could not have meant him, nor Toombs, who had yet to return from nursing his daughter. But Walker must have to come to his mind. Not for want of desire, but simply from not knowing what to do, the Secretary of War made a slow start. Yet he showed some sense. He was the first to attempt to fill his departments by pirating staff from Washington, sending off his first solicitations the very day of his confirmation, and he continued doing so in the weeks ahead.[97] As recently resigned Southern officers from the old United States Army came to Montgomery, waiting for the new service to give them commissions, he commandeered some and put them to work briefly in his second floor chambers at Government House.[98]

He also revealed a common failing among these amateur administrators by trying to do too much himself, and at tasks he did not understand. His first day in office he summoned to Montgomery Pierre G. T. Beauregard of New Orleans, until recently superintendent of the Military Academy at West Point. When the Creole walked into the War Department four days later on February 26, he found the secretary puzzling desperately. "Just in time to assist me out of a great dilemma," Walker jumped up to exclaim. He was trying to calculate the weight of some heavy cannon being shipped to Pensacola and Charleston, despite the fact that he probably had never seen a siege gun in his life. Beauregard helped him with the figures, then suggested that Walker get department bureaus set up and staffed quickly on the model of the War Department in Washington. The Alabamian agreed, and asked him to write to men he knew in the Federal service who might take their charge.[99] Meanwhile, with the assistance of the Military Affairs committee, bills went through Congress establishing the several offices and bureaus in the department—adjutant and inspector general, quartermaster general, commissary general, and surgeon general—on the day Beauregard called. The Engineer Bureau and Indian Affairs followed in March, with Ordnance to follow in April. Realizing that paperwork moved armies as much as mules and trains, Walker contracted with the local printer Barrett, Wimbish and Company to print the library of record books he would need.[100]

Unseen as yet was the hand of Jefferson Davis. Already some suspected that he accepted Walker for the War Department precisely *because* the Alabamian knew nothing of the task. Rumor said that the President wanted merely a pliant agent to do his bidding, while Davis himself really ran things.[101] He *had* been a secretary of war himself, after all. He fancied his own military acumen, and it was in his nature to think that he knew more about some matters than anyone else. Back home in Mississippi the press comforted the people with the notion that despite Walker being in the War office, "with Jefferson Davis at the head of the Government, we may feel sure that everything pertaining to our military affairs will be properly and vigorously conducted."[102]

When Toombs returned to Montgomery and took over his third

floor office directly above Davis, he showed so little disposition to over-work himself that he earned Hooper's displeasure.[103] In fact, since Davis would formulate foreign policy and choose commissioners to other nations, Toombs had literally nothing to do until they got there and began sending back their reports. He needed no bureaus or other offices, but only an assistant secretary and a clerk to handle the mail. William Browne, called "Constitution" by friends thanks to his former editorship of the Washington *Constitution*, would become assistant secretary in March. At the same time Toombs made William Alexander, husband of his daughter who died in 1855, his chief clerk.[104] That done, there was little else for him. Besides, he still sat in Congress, and the new constitution kept him especially busy. He would leave Browne to do most of the work. For himself, he was no office man and, disdain-ful of his essentially powerless position, quipped to all who listened that he carried the business of the State Department around with him in his hat.[105]

Hooper saw no fault with the men in Treasury, however. Long after sundown the gas lamps in their offices cast light out onto the streets.[106] Only the day after Memminger's confirmation, Barnwell made a motion to excuse him from committee duties because of his more urgent cabinet business.[107] Memminger set an excellent example, always on time or early into his own office, and watching carefully to make certain that every employee worked his full day without lounging or loitering. "No extravagance will be permitted," he told his staff. In handling public funds they must show frugality to retain the public trust. He kept office furniture to a minimum, stressed that clerks show courtesy to all visitors who came on business, made all financial records confidential, and strictly enforced a code against any corresponding with newspapers or otherwise allowing department business to leak outside the building.

Memminger's management style, accentuated by his abrupt manner and occasionally sanctimonious attitude, quickly antagonized some staff as his department grew.[108] Within two weeks he installed Edward C. Elmore as treasurer, Clitherall as recorder, Lewis Cruger as controller, Bolling Baker as auditor, and Commander Raphael Semmes, late of the United States Navy, as chief of the Lighthouse Bureau. An even dozen clerks assisted them all and Chief Clerk Capers, and in a few weeks Philip Clayton joined them as assistant secretary of the treasury.[109]

Clayton was the main problem, though many of the clerks, lured away from Washington offices as with other departments, also had complaints. In the Union Treasury they had taken their time, talked with friends, observed irregular hours, and generally lived the less-than-frantic life of the civil servant of all times. These rules of Memminger's chaffed. As for Clayton, he came highly recommended, and no little full of himself. He could add huge lists of figures in his head in an instant, knew all the forms and system of the old Treasury, and even brought copies of its official documents with him, as did others. Garrulous in the extreme, he complained about all of Memminger's "restraints" and "exactions" as he called them. Friction between the two almost immediately arose and never lessened.[110] Worse, Clayton proved divisive thereafter by accusing other subordinates in the department of conflicts of interest, even dishonesty, taking his complaints not to Memminger, but Howell Cobb.[111] Still, the treasury secretary allowed his bureau heads a wide latitude, especially in choosing their own subordinates, requiring only that applicants apply in writing, not in person, in order not to interrupt daily business. Those sending endorsements by prominent businessmen received priority.[112] That was sound management.

Now if he just had some money. "The treasury had not funds to pay for the table on which the secretary was writing," Memminger lamented.[113] A large vault sat in one corner of his ground floor office, its open doors showing an embarrassment of emptiness.[114] Of course, the government had available to it the half million pledged in loans by Alabama, and that would last them a little while, but it made a pittance compared to their anticipated needs, especially if war erupted.

The day after Memminger's confirmation Barnwell introduced an attempt at a comprehensive bill to raise money for the government. Some proposed that their states simply make outright contributions, Barry suggesting to Finance that they could raise $2 to $3 million in this way. Barnwell believed that South Carolina alone could find $1 million in its state defense fund that it would not need when the Confederacy assumed control of defense. Barry went further to argue that Mississippi, for instance, might raise $1 million of its own by taking loans from citizens in return for state promissory notes. "The more money we have to begin with the more ease we shall have in acquiring more," argued the Mississippian, "and the chances are we shall need all we are likely to be able to get." Yet others like Marshall of Louisiana countered that they would not need much now because as soon as the government went into regular operation it would be raising its own money from conventional sources like duties and tariffs. No one wanted to talk about taxes just yet.[115]

After discussing duties on cotton and even a tax on slaves, the Congress almost inevitably found its way back to the Alabama precedent as the quickest way to raise money. On February 28 they authorized Memminger to print and issue ten-year loan certificates bearing eight percent interest, to an amount not to exceed $15 million. Citizens purchasing the certificates in effect loaned money to the government, the interest and principal to be paid back to them out of income derived from a cotton export duty of one-eight of a cent per pound, or about $5 per bale. It was left to Memminger's discretion, and public needs, to determine how much of the issue to sell at any given time.[116] Moreover, recognizing the scarcity of hard cash, the legislation allowed subscribers to pay only six percent of their loan in specie at the time of subscribing, with the balance due by May 1.[117]

Days later, and before the first of the loan subscription was even announced, Congress took the next step, though a modest one, in authorizing the issue of up to $1 million in Treasury notes. They conceived these not as a circulating currency, but rather as additional promissory notes from the government, bearing 3.65 percent interest, that citizens could use in paying duties and any taxes. In the end, under the March 9 legislation, they would issue just over $2 million in notes with denominations of $50 and higher.[118]

All of this required a lot of printing, and high quality bank note paper to prevent counterfeiting. Of that the Confederacy had not a sheet. On his own private credit Memminger sent abroad for English note paper, though it would never reach him. Fortunately, an agent of the New York based American Bank Note Company passed through Montgomery just now, hoping to find business with the new government, and Memminger quickly gave him a contract. With no skilled engravers available in the South, Memminger had then to look to the North as well for his engraving and even printing, finally striking a deal with the same company for those services, too. Yet it all teetered on the edge of war. The end of the uneasy peace would undoubtedly mean a cutoff of any such supply from the old Union. Viewing their unfortunate reliance on Yankee firms to provide their notes and currency, one Confederate in Montgomery shrugged that "we can't be altogether independent in a moment."[119] In his Lighthouse Bureau, where Semmes had responsibility for ship's registry as well, they did not even have a stamp for their registration certificates. Inventive by nature, Semmes took a wooden type block from the *Advertiser* office and carved a crude seal of his own with his pocket knife.[120]

A few serendipitous one-time sources of revenue also provided hard cash, chiefly money seized from United States agents and depositories in the seceded states. On March 6 Memminger sent broadcast an order to all Union officers in the Confederate States to surrender funds in their hands at once, stating that he would then make an accounting with Washington. The next day he issued a similar confiscation order for all customs houses to turn over their accounts. In the end, between specie and bullion at the closed United States mints and the customs houses, he collected over $700,000.[121]

Other resources awaited exploitation. On March 5 Memminger assumed control of all public lands formerly owned by the United States, and henceforth revenue from them would go into his Treasury.[122] Even before he took office, others suggested that in the produce of the land itself lay the richest source of revenue. The government should simply buy cotton from the planters, and then itself act as exporter, the assumption being that patriotic cotton growers would accept Treasury notes and loan bonds for the staple. Even before Memminger took office some suggested that cotton might also be turned over to the government in lieu of specie for loan certificates.[123] Such matters went considerably beyond Memminger's current authorization from Congress, however. Besides, feeling the pulse of public reaction to the $15 million loan, he anticipated that he could fill the government's needs entirely from that for the moment. Even blacks, free and slave, evidenced eagerness to invest, and the whole subscription might be taken up in a single day.

Memminger and Capers often beavered away by their gas light until midnight and beyond preparing the loan and Treasury certificate issues, and gradually putting enough in their vault to justify locking its doors. Meanwhile another more questionable wealth flowed into Montgomery.[124] Where there was a government, and especially a new administration, there were jobs and favors. With the announcement of the creation of the executive departments, and even before, thousands of would-be officeholders disembarked from the trains and steamboats. Certainly they took the new regime as an accomplished fact, and risked their money on train and boat tickets in the expectation of manifold returns. The first rush came from Washington, which as far back as February 2 some leaders conceived as the best source of experienced clerks for the anticipated new government.[125] Immediately aware of the press for places, men expressed hopes that jobs should go out only on the basis of competence rather than the "corrupting doctrine" of past political stance.[126] Indeed, the subject even engaged Davis and his cabinet in an early meeting, where they decided that in filling vacancies in their departments the pre-1861 political divisions should exert no influence in selecting candidates.[127] Eventually nearly one hundred of the Washington clerks found jobs.[128] "Every body wants office," Mary Chesnut groaned, "& every body raises an outcry at the corruption of those who get the offices."[129]

But any sort of influence, including old political friendships or debts, came into play in the competition for positions. Some worked on the congressmen, like the presumptuous South Carolinian who told Chesnut that "I wish for a place that will *pay*" and declined to accept anything less than a consulship or a top bureau position at $5,000 per annum.[130] The hunters dogged cabinet officers, especially Walker, who would have the most positions, and even after he filled all of his clerkships, they continued to call as he politely tried to introduce them to other cabinet ministers who might still have vacancies.[131]

Most of all, anyone with any sort of entree to Davis tried to enlist his assistance. Impatient at the best of times, the President quickly wearied of their importuning. Just two days after he took office the man who picked up his cane in the car on the West Point train called to return it. He found the Exchange packed with office seekers, and Davis already in a mood to give them a cool reception. "It seems that he would rather see a man, who proposes to fight for his country and firesides, than one who seeks for spoils of office," said the Samaritan.[132] It became especially aggravating when men resorted to obvious flattery, like the author who announced that he wished to dedicate his new book to Davis and Stephens—and then asked for a clerkship.[133]

Before long more than three hundred letters a month came across Davis's desk asking for some kind of profferment. At first he tried to answer many himself, offering no assurance of a place thanks to the volume of applicants.[134] Even that kind of attention quickly turned impractical, and he shoved the bulk of the inquiries over to Josselyn, simply docketing them himself with a few words of instruction. The President still gave personal attention to some requests from dignitaries, marking them "special attention" and directing them to the appropriate cabinet secretary, and sometimes when the appeal came from an old friend he took time to hint not too subtly to his ministers that he would be pleased to see something done for them.[135]

When the first influx of office seekers hit Montgomery, citizens and the press saw it as evidence that "the race of patriots has not yet died out."[136] But within days the mood changed as the numbers swelled and they showed their obvious self-serving motivation. "I thought we had left all that in Washington," Mary Chesnut grumbled. "Nobody is willing to be out of sight. And they take any office."[137] Soon reporters chuckled at the legion of aspirants rushing from one office to another trying to get endorsements and recommendations. One Mobile newsman predicted that all of the Confederacy's anticipated offices for the next twenty years could be filled from the men just then thronging the cabinet offices. Some, in their anxiety for a position, developed the notion that current officeholders would soon resign and make way for others out of pure patriotism, while the incumbents themselves seemed to think it more patriotic to hang on.[138] Others wondered at the bother. The government paid low salaries, as little as $500 and no more than $1,200 a year for its clerks, and Montgomery's prices rose dramatically with the increased demand of so many people. Who could live on a clerk's wage? And yet, so great was the press for office that some found applicants who would have worked for nothing at all but board.[139] Perhaps that was because the arriving aspirants filled every corner and bed in the city, making any accommodation scarce by early March.[140] A job that provided a bed and no pay was better than no bed at all. The desperation of some of the job seekers even raised fears that these men actually wanted a clash of arms. "This is the class of men who will precipitate us into war, if they are not carefully watched," William Smith warned as he condemned the "feverish inclinations of the rabble of loafers who seek war for the sake of *employment*."[141]

Their desperation led to gullibility, and the exasperation of locals in stumbling over the office seekers in every lobby and corner soon found an outlet. Early on the morning of February 27 a notice appeared on the wall of the city post office announcing "Twenty-five good accountants wanted immediately by the Secretary of the Treasury. Apply at Room No. 10, Treasury Buildings, between the hours of 9 and 11 o'clock A.M." Word spread through the legion of aspirants like a virus. In a swell they mobbed the barber shops for shaves and haircuts, rushed the bootblacks for shines, and bought or borrowed clean white shirts. By ten o'clock most of the city noted the mass of them walking to Commerce and Bibb, jostling each other aggressively to be first in line. When they came to the stairs leading into the building, a final rush for the lead got them to the closed door of the department. Hats off, panting heavily, they formed a line along the wall and waited. Two hours passed, and then they simply opened the door themselves and tried to enter, pressed on by a corridor literally crammed and seething with applicants behind them. The clerk inside shoved them back out, protesting that he knew nothing of the advertised positions, and then locked the door not only to the seekers but to all callers. For a while longer they stood waiting in the hall until a voice in their midst suggested that "it might, after all, be a hoax." Suddenly the realization hit all of them at once, and silently, sheepishly, they filed out, to spend the rest of the day hearing all Montgomery laugh at the joke, and to see it in the afternoon papers as well. None seemed willing to admit that he had been a part of the crowd of gullibles. Meanwhile Capers, frustrated to distraction with the annoyance, refused even to admit a genuine messenger from Congress who came on important business, mistaking him for another applicant and angrily grumbling that Memminger had "suffered enough already from these chaps."[142] Even by the end of March, when it became evident that all of the executive departments must expand to meet the growing press of business, word went out that no new applicants need apply. The departments already had more than a hundred applications for every opening, and finally hired a special clerk charged to do nothing but handle the files.[143]

By the end of March the small army of clerks working in Government House overflowed even that substantial building, and the departments sought more space.[144] Reagan moved his offices into the second floor of a building at the northeast corner of Perry and Washington. Then the rest spread into the Noble and Brothers building across Commerce from Government House, and also engaged the twenty-four-room second floor of the Figh building immediately adjacent on Bibb.[145] George M. Figh, local alderman, also happened to be in the brick contracting business, and he built these "great block buildings," as locals called them, as offices for the city's thriving cotton trade, but they suited the government nicely.[146] There were even plans to take another floor in one of them by April 15 and move Reagan's department back with the other offices.[147] However, the mess attendant to their conversion did not suit the city officials, who spent weeks fielding complaints about the piles of lumber, shingles, and the like that almost obstructed the sidewalks at busy Commerce and Bibb.[148]

Reagan needed his extra space, for he worked fast once he got going. On March 9 Congress authorized organization of his domain on the model of the United States Post Office Department. In the end, all but two of the Washington postal officials he contacted came to Montgomery. He made Washington Miller chief clerk, and chose Henry St.

George Offutt to head the contract bureau, charged with securing mail route carriers, stamps, mail bags, and other necessary equipment. John L. Harrell took charge of the finance bureau to manage receipts of postal monies and distribute stamps, as well as pay contract carriers. The decisions on establishing and discontinuing post offices and routes rested with Benjamin Clements in the appointment bureau.

By the end of March all of Reagan's bureaus stood in place, and well staffed. Thanks to pilfering from Washington, he had all the form and route map models that he needed to produce his own, and long before then—even before Reagan took office, in fact—Congress started the machinery of setting rates and services. On February 21 they debated their first postal act, setting rates for a half-ounce letter at five cents up to a distance of five hundred miles, and ten cents thereafter. Packages traveled at double the letter rate per half ounce, and special rates applied to advertising materials, periodicals, and newspapers based on their frequency of publication. To correct an abuse that had infuriated Southern statesmen for generations, the legislation abolished the franking privilege for everyone but the postmaster general, his deputy if any, the auditor, and chief clerk.[149]

Meanwhile, Congress also authorized Reagan simply to adopt the postal field force then in the employ of the United States. On March 15 he notified all postmasters and carriers that they were to continue in their positions until the department was prepared to assume full control of the postal service, and might then make other arrangements. In effect, in a single act he pirated the entire postal establishment in the seceded states. Anticipating that United States stamps would no longer be available, and wanting in any case to have his own postage, Reagan, like Memminger, searched for paper, engravers, and printers. In the end Treasury and the Post Office Department used mostly the same suppliers. But until he secured stamps, Confederates would have to pay for their postage in coin and postmasters would simply mark the letters paid.[150]

Reagan's mandate to make his department self-supporting inevitably resulted in higher rates and reduced services. Complaining of the increased cost of simple postage, one reporter determined to write a year's worth of letters all at once and get them in the mail before the change took effect.[151] Newspaper publishers muttered over anomalies in the rates that resulted in a higher rate to mail a paper five miles across a state line than two hundred miles within a state.[152] But despite the grumbling, Reagan met no serious opposition, and when he summoned to Montgomery the presidents of most of the major railroads in the Confederacy late in April and appealed to their patriotism to carry the mails at lower than their customary rates, and accept payment in notes and bonds rather than hard cash, they willingly agreed.[153]

Some wondered just who did the work in the department. The lower level clerks seemed to be a lazy lot—an "insufferable set of 'understrappers'" one associate called them. Some came unable even to spell or write simple sentences. Offut appeared equal to whipping them into shape.[154] Indeed, a few suspected that Offut was the motive force behind the department. Neat, tidy, precise, the forty-year-old seemed the very opposite of Reagan.[155] Montgomery knew Reagan chiefly from seeing him sitting on the bluff at the end of Commerce Street in the evenings, whittling away with his knife, or else at his desk in the department, feet propped in another chair, fiddling idly with his blade. His laughter, though abundant, sounded to most like some strange Indian mumble, and those taken by surprise might have seen in his deep-set brown eyes, high cheekbones, brawny shoulders, and rough hands, cause for apprehension. "No position in life, no stretch of art, can give the man even the semblance of good breeding," said one of his employees.[156] And yet, facing a task so daunting that two men before him refused it, Reagan, by ingenuity, common sense, necessity, and theft, stood poised to make good on the mandate given him by Davis. Unlike the President, he was a natural born executive with the gift of delegation and the ability to make it all look easy.

By mid-March, barely five weeks after the delegates first convened in Montgomery, the skeleton of the government stood virtually complete, with the mechanisms in place to assume those remaining operations and services not yet in hand. They had a constitution, a president and a congress, a little bit of money, and on March 16 when Memminger announced that the first subscription for up to $5 million of the authorized loan would open on April 17, they were ready to put some flesh on those young bones. What remained to be seen was how much of their blood they might have to give.

CHAPTER NINE

MAKE UP YOUR ACCOUNT FOR WAR

———————•★•———————

H IS OLD FRIEND AND POLITICAL FOE William H. Seward, about to become Lincoln's secretary of state, maintained that without Jefferson Davis there could have been no Confederacy. No one else had the courage or the intellect to make it work.[1] Certainly he had the industry it required. Organizing a government was only the beginning for him, of course. That done, he had to get it working, and he showed at once that he would take far too much of that work on himself, while not a few others to whom he entrusted responsibility would prove to be poor choices, indicative of his own very fallible judgement in men.

Anywhere Jefferson Davis sat became immediately the executive office. Business even followed him to the breakfast table in the Exchange. Invariably Toombs, Cobb, Yancey, or some of the other influential men in Montgomery sat with him. While sometimes their talk turned to wit, Davis himself specially liking to reminisce about earlier days in the army on the frontier, inevitably the government and the impending crisis with the North absorbed them, even when congressmen like Patton Anderson made a nuisance of themselves by squiring visitors over to the table for introductions.[2] Most of the time, especially in the first weeks in Montgomery, Davis used his suite upstairs as residence and office combined. Visitors found his parlor-reception room rather too plain, though it seemed to afford "a kind of winning republican appearance." Stephens thought he could not have stood to live there for a day, but others, looking at the bed shoved in the corner, thought it almost invited them to lie down for a nap after shaking the President's hand.[3] In the center of the room stood a table with a simple oil cloth draped over it, manuscripts standing atop it in piles along with books, maps, samples of military cloth, hats, swords, buttons, and all other manner of military paraphernalia. A lounge, a sofa, a few simple chairs, a mirror in one corner, and a few landscapes and portraits of Henry Clay, Daniel Webster, Calhoun, and Napoleon completed the furnishings.[4]

Callers first presented their cards at the desk beside the lobby, where a clerk acted as the first line of resistance. He took the cards to Josselyn, who received instructions from Davis as to whom he would see and in what order. At every hour of the day men congregated around the door to room 101, on the left side of the first corridor, or sat in the always filled chairs against the wall. Others constantly passed in and out as Josselyn first called their names, and then escorted them back to the corridor.[5] "Captain" Josselyn himself sat at a desk in the parlor attending to his correspondence or his callers, while cabinet members passed freely in and out with no announcement to speak a few words with him or the President. They talked in whispers with strangers present, and Davis in any case kept his replies brief and to the point. To the innumerable office seekers who called, he was courteous but did not encourage tarrying.[6] If he needed Josselyn, especially when working in the other room, he summoned him with a bell. Despite their old acquaintance, when frustration tried the President's patience, he sometimes took it out on his secretary. The captain, in turn, found solace with spirits.[7]

Once Government House provided furnished quarters, Davis spent more and more of his work day there, though his Exchange rooms continued to be an informal Executive office as well. When he stepped out of the Exchange onto Commerce Street in the morning, he could see the building to his left at the intersection with Bibb. With his trained military stride, a scant 250 paces took him to the door in barely two minutes. Then it was into the whitewashed hall, past a few bustling clerks, and up the stairs to the second floor where three rooms overlooking Commerce, each twenty-five by thirty feet, held his offices. A plain cardboard sign tacked to the door of the center room said "Pres'd't."[8] Once in the plain, as yet unadorned room, a ring of his table bell summoned Josselyn from his office to the left, or if meeting with his secretaries he turned to the cabinet room to the right. By this time the War Department occupied most of the rest of this floor, while Navy and State filled the third story.[9]

Davis actually held his initial cabinet meeting on March 4 in room 22 at the Exchange, before his ministers moved into Government House.[10] From the first he tried to set the tone for those to follow, asking his advisors to be absolutely frank with him in expressing their opinions, just as he promised to do the same. Moreover, he told them to select whomever they chose to run their bureaus, submit the names to him, and he would approve, though he charged his associates that he would hold them responsible for the conduct of their subordinates. Some thought him a civil service reformer of sorts, and indeed he was. Sitting in Franklin Pierce's cabinet he found himself unable to effect some reforms in the War Department by moving out superannuated old bureau chiefs grown indolent—if not senile—in their chairs. Now as a president himself, he could try to keep the same thing from happening in the Confederacy.[11]

At that first cabinet session Benjamin reiterated the conviction of a long and bloody war that he expressed a few days earlier in New Orleans.[12] Going further, he advised that they would need a great deal of money and tens of thousands of weapons, and that immediately shipping large quantities of cotton to Europe for sale by the government could achieve both ends, with any unsold balance to be kept there for future credit. The cotton policy itself appealed both to Toombs and Stephens, but Memminger objected that under current legislation it was unconstitutional for the government to go into the cotton business. Both Stephens and Davis agreed that war was likely, if not inevitable, but most of the others present seemed to dismiss the idea, especially Walker, who had boasted earlier that he would sop all the blood shed as a result of secession with a handkerchief. Memminger agreed, and even if there were a war, most expected it to be very brief, assuming the Yankees simply would not fight once they found what it would cost them. The meeting ended with no action on Benjamin's suggestion, but the discussion had centered on the three principal issues that dominated cabinet meetings for a long time to come—the Confederate relation to Europe, the possibility that the crisis of the moment would lead to war, and the need in that event to raise and equip a large army.[13]

As he pondered his policy on these critical issues, Davis went about his old habit of overworking himself. Even on his evening walks—when he took them—a congressman always seemed to be tagging along, pressing for appointments and lobbying for a bill.[14] In his late hours when alone, he lay awake—often insomniac—and made lists of the problems, real and potential, confronting him: free navigation of the Mississippi, oaths to support the new Confederacy, indictments against prominent Confederates for treason in the North, regulation of imports, enlisting volunteers, the potential of having to deal with prisoners of war, and more.[15] He had before him constantly the evidence of the enmity of many in the North. Just recently a Yankee editor had sent him a pen holder made from a rafter in Benedict Arnold's birthplace, sarcastically saying that Davis was continuing the work of treason that Arnold had begun.[16]

He tried to do everything at once. Callers found him invariably holding a sheaf of letters in one hand as he spoke with them, and just as often standing rather than sitting as they talked. Expansive at one instant, he could turn quite reticent the next.[17] Occasionally, when he needed prolonged discussion with someone, he simply had them sit with him as he dealt with the endless string of visitors, saying that ideas would occur to him between interviews.[18] When he listened for any period of time, he closed his eyes as he concentrated on their words,[19] and contracted his brows at anything serious.[20] He saw them all to the door when done, offering each his hand and thanks "in the name of the Government."[21] Never in robust health in recent years, he pushed himself so hard now that old acquaintances felt shock when they first saw him again. Alabamian William Smith thought the President looked twenty years older than when he last saw him seven years before.[22] Thomas C. De Leon, a young protege of Davis's, arrived from Washington to see him looking thin from emaciation, sickness, and overwork. The creases in his face had grown deeper, the stern expression fixed on his face seemed all the more intimidating, while he clamped his jaw tight from tension, hardening his already stern visage.[23] Yet in some part, people saw what they wanted to see in Jefferson Davis. Mississippian William Barry reported to Governor Pettus after Davis had been three weeks on the job that "the President is worked hard, but bears up under it well, and grows continually on the people here."[24]

While Congress worked on completing the organization of the government, addressing a body of laws for the new nation, and framing a permanent constitution, Davis moved at once to exercise the powers assigned to him under the Provisional Constitution. Almost his first attention spent itself on foreign policy. He, like so many others, sensed that independence depended to a great deal—perhaps critically—upon recognition and support from Britain and France in particular. Like so many others, he saw cotton as a political tool to encourage—or coerce—that support. And like far too many, he thought that this was all that would be needed.

Given the importance of French and British support, Davis could hardly have chosen less worthy men for his diplomats. After turning down a cabinet post, Yancey agreed to take a foreign mission. He did so against the advice of his brother, himself a one-time diplomat, who believed that England, much opposed to slavery, would never recognize the Confederacy so long as the institution existed, while France was too weak and indecisive to make any move but to follow England's lead.[25] Now that doctrinaire hothead, champion of secession and slavery, the most undiplomatic of men, would be going to the courts of Europe to play the ambassador. The idea was ridiculous on its face, and it got no better. While everyone seemed to know that Yancey would be going almost as soon as he agreed, his co-diplomats remained a subject of some speculation.[26] Some thought Toombs himself would go, though clearly that was out of the question.[27] Envisioning Yancey centering his efforts on England, Davis very naturally looked to Louisiana for a second diplomat, perhaps under the urging of men like De Clouet, who pointed out that "because of 'racial' sympathies, someone from that bastion of French culture in the South would be ideal."[28] He turned immediately to his old colleague in the Senate, John Slidell, nearly seventy, but a man of sense.

That would have been fine but for the third man selected. In areas he did not intimately understand, Jefferson Davis often mistook experience for ability, and showed it now when he turned to Ambrose Dudley Mann for his third commissioner. The Virginia native, sixty years old, had spent almost ten years in Europe for the United States State Department, and was an assistant secretary of state when Davis ran Pierce's War Department. Davis and Mann became close friends. Knowing nothing of diplomacy himself, Davis could hardly judge it in others, and mistook Mann's fawning, flattering ways as qualifications for foreign service. Never able to look at his friends very critically, the President now simply could not see that Mann was an impractical, bombastic lightweight—windy, wordy, ineffectual, and sometimes silly. Slidell saw it, however, and as soon as he learned that Mann was to be on the commission, he declined his own appointment. "If there had been no other objection," he told Howell Cobb, "the association with Mann would have been sufficient." He hardly approved of Yancey, either, and then showed his own egotism by declaring that "I am a great believer in one man power." "I am not willing to share either the responsibility of a failure or the credit of a success with others."[29] With Slidell's refusal, Davis stuck with the determination for a Louisianian and turned to Judge Pierre Rost, a French native who brought no diplomatic experience, but who did have a wide acquaintance among influential men in his native France. In the end, this completed his triumvirate of diplomats, and a trio of poor choices at best.

While a public and a press just as inexperienced at diplomacy as Davis tended to hail the appointments to England and Europe, he attempted to deal with other nations.[30] But the same "big-man-meism" that afflicted Slidell stood in his way. Charles Gayarre contemptuously turned down the appointment to Berlin, Sardinia, and Denmark because "the position would not be sufficiently elevated to tempt me." If he could not have France or Spain, he would accept nothing.[31] Then there was the Confederacy's only non-English speaking neighbor. Davis hoped that Mexico would recognize the Confederacy, but he was himself on the record as saying that expansion into its northern provinces lay in the South's destiny, hardly a good opening bid for friendly relations. Hints came to him that his neighbor might consider recognition, but only if the Confederates promised to respect the territorial integrity of their country.[32] In the end, Davis simply waited to deal with Mexico. It was just concluding a long civil war of its own, its future leaders and policy looked in doubt, and it stood so overwhelmingly in debt that he could expect no material assistance. At best, he needed to stay friendly enough to use Mexican harbors within reach of Texas, in case the United States blockaded Confederate ports.

Davis also hoped that Mexico might cooperate in controlling the marauding Indian tribes of the border region. At the same time, Confederates began contemplating diplomatic efforts to woo some of those tribes into alliances. In part they could capitalize on old feuds to use one group to neutralize the other, and at the same time enlist them to protect the Confederacy's western borders against possible Yankee intrusions. "They are strong and afford as good material for war as any people," a Mississippian declared.[33] Because of the great distances involved, and poor communications, negotiation would take weeks, even months. Meanwhile, looking to other borders, he sent commissioners to the remaining slave states not yet seceded, including even tiny Delaware, all in the hopes of at best securing their secession, but at the very least encouraging bonds of trade.[34]

In fact, trade represented the only active foreign policy initiative Davis had to offer. On February 25 he signed an act declaring free navigation of the Mississippi, an attempt to reassure states like Arkansas, Tennessee, Missouri, and Kentucky that they would have unfettered access to the port of New Orleans for sending their goods abroad. The extended hand of friendship just might tip the balance in their own secession discussions. Allowing even Northern states to use the river for shipping sent a powerful message that the Confederacy felt no hostile or spiteful inclinations.[35] "The Mississippi will be kept a highway," Curry told a friend.[36] Moreover, Congress repealed navigation laws that restricted internal coastal trade. Such measures produced an unexpected backlash in Louisiana, where some shippers claimed that being too conciliatory to the upriver states could hurt their own business, but friends like Benjamin and Slidell kept a close watch on affairs there, and the fears soon subsided.[37] They needed such a policy as a lure to other states tied by commerce to the river. In fact, on March 2, with Arkansas meeting in convention, Davis asked Stephens to go to Little Rock to promote secession interests. Little Aleck pleaded poor health and suggested Tom Cobb instead, probably just to get him out of his hair in Montgomery. Cobb, too, declined, unwilling to leave important constitutional deliberations in Congress.[38]

Looking beyond internal diplomacy, Davis offered the inducement of reduced tariffs and duties. "We have to change our tariff and navigation policy," said Curry, "so as to make our commerce and trade as free as possible to all nations."[39] They altered the prevailing tariff concept from one of protection of domestic goods against foreign competition to a strictly revenue-raising measure that allowed for markedly lower rates. Within days of Davis's inauguration, Congress published long lists of items exempted from duty, including everything from bacon to gunpowder, though they could not cover everything at first.[40] Soon afterward importers hounded Montgomery for more specifics, one man even confronting the President with a demand for clarification of the duty on hooped skirts.[41] Once more they aimed at reform, not revolution.

Taking the next step—or contemplating it—the Confederates also looked at taking an active part in the foreign carrying trade. John Forsyth proposed establishing a steamship line between Mobile and the Mexican Gulf ports. "Our new political relations have enhanced the importance of this enterprise," he urged Alabamian McRae.[42] A representative of an English iron firm came to Montgomery just now to propose establishing a steam line between Mobile, New Orleans, and Liverpool, and offered to provide half the necessary capital.[43] Early in March there was even talk—perhaps only rumor—of a commission of delegates including Keitt, Waul, Anderson, Chilton, Harris, and Sparrow, taking a steamer to Antwerp to arrange direct importation of goods for Southern merchants.[44] This, the Confederacy's first and only foreign Congressional junket, never came to pass.

But for foreign policy, a step toward free trade is all that Davis and the Congress offered, and here the President differed with his secretary of state and with many others as well. Toombs leaned much more toward active inducements like "most favored nation" status in order to lure foreign nations into recognition and assistance. Moreover, he seemed to feel some leanings toward Spain, chiefly because of her retention of slavery still in some of her colonial provinces. But as one wag said at the time, if it would aid the Confederacy Toombs "was for an alliance with Satan himself."[45] Here, for a change, men like Rhett agreed. The fire-eater wanted Davis to offer European powers rock-bottom import duties guaranteed for twenty years and free entry into Southern ports in return for recognition and military alliances both offensive and defensive. Indeed, he and others took it for granted that this is what Davis empowered the Yancey-Rost-Mann mission to do.[46]

Thus he met a startling surprise when Rhett and Toombs bumped into each other on the stairway at the Exchange toward the end of the second week of March. Holding the chair of the Foreign Affairs Committee certainly entitled Rhett to ask of the secretary of state the nature of the instructions given to the commissioners, but when Toombs replied that nothing like Rhett's assumptions existed in those orders, the South Carolinian turned almost apoplectic.[47] Immediately he went to Yancey's house on Perry Street just a few blocks away, and the Alabamian confirmed that his instructions did not include any power to conclude commercial treaties. His official orders came from Toombs, but certainly reflected the president's views. They were to plead the justification of the South's cause in seceding, point out that they were not revolutionaries, show that they possessed the physical and spiritual wherewithal to establish and maintain their independence, and stress that theirs was a movement conceived in peaceful intent. Behind each statement was to lie the hint that there was commercial and strategic advantage in two separate North American nations.

To Rhett this appeared as nothing but nonsense, the sort of stuff they expected Mann to say. It meant nothing. Where was the inducement to England and France? Nations, like individuals, acted from self-interest. He demanded to know just what Davis relied on to persuade other powers to get actively involved in aiding Confederate independence. "I suppose on our cotton," said Yancey rather vaguely. "He says that 'cotton is king'."[48] In fact, the instructions contained the indirect hint that the supply of cotton might be cut off by a Yankee blockade, and that would wreak havoc on British textile mills and world trade. Since the South lacked a merchant fleet of its own, Europeans would have to come to the Confederacy to get their bales, and that meant breaking any such blockade, and thereby conflict with the Union. But recognition of the Confederacy now could forestall an attempt at coercion by the North, preserve peace, and ensure the flow of cotton across the Atlantic.

"You have no business in Europe," shot back an angry Rhett. Generally blinded by prejudice and ambition, Rhett in this case saw to the heart of an issue. In probably his first overt act to thwart Davis, and the first outright effort of an "opposition" that Confederates still dreamed would not exist, Rhett sought to force his own policy on the President. "You carry no argument which Europe wishes to hear," he said. Offering nothing, the Confederacy could expect nothing. Now he took it upon himself to "make" policy by persuading Yancey not to pursue Davis's unproductive course. "If you will take the advice of a friend," he told Yancey, "do not accept the appointment. You will meet nothing but failure and mortification." He should demand that Davis give him powers to accomplish something, or stay at home.[49] For reasons he kept to himself, Yancey decided not to withdraw. He resigned his seat in the Alabama Convention, collected Treasury drafts from Memminger totaling $6,500, put $40 in cash in his pocket, and left on March 15 for the long journey abroad.[50] To others not as much in his confidence as Rhett, he displayed no doubts. Indeed, unschooled in diplomacy and zealously convinced of the righteousness of their cause as he was, he may have felt none of the doubts expressed by Rhett. Saying farewell to friends, he expressed complete confidence in his success, vowing that when he returned again, it would be to the arms of "a victorious and independent government."[51] Porcher Miles, for a change agreeing with Rhett, lamented that "our unfledged Confederacy—with no footing at any foreign court, can scarcely be said to have framed any 'foreign policy' whatever."[52]

Davis had to formulate two kinds of state policy: one for Europeans, and the other for fellow Americans only recently become "foreign" in his eyes. Even before the President took office, the Congress discussed sending emissaries to Washington to treat for peaceable separation, but then waited until the new President could direct such efforts. The morning of February 21 Davis met with Memminger, and when their business concluded he asked the treasury secretary to see Stephens when he returned to the state house and ask the Vice President to call. When Little Aleck arrived, Davis said he wanted him to head the commission to Washington to negotiate with the Union authorities.

There was some good sense in asking Stephens. As vice president, by his own admission, he had almost no duties, and would not until a Senate were created for him to preside over. As a conservative, among the last to come to secession, he enjoyed the good opinion of most of the Democrats in Washington, and even some of the Republicans, not least his old friend President-elect Lincoln. But now Davis encountered yet again an unfortunate quirk in the Georgian's nature. Almost invariably he resisted even attempting to do anything with which he disagreed, and his means of resistance invariably involved his health. Usually sickly anyhow, he become conveniently too ill whenever asked to do something that, in reality, he simply wished to avoid. He believed that any commission to Washington was foredoomed to disappointment, anyhow, thinking that Buchanan would only stall and leave any decisions for his successor. Now he prejudiced its chances by removing himself from participation. Given his attitude, he simply may have wanted not to associate himself with an anticipated failure.

Davis took the Vice President's refusal since he had no choice, but may have wondered at the Georgian's refusal to the President's second request in a row. It hardly put the Georgian in league with Rhett, but the fact is that for reasons of his own now Stephens, too, offered an obstacle to Davis's plans. Stephens went on to suggest others for the commission, thinking that it should be representative of the three divisions in 1860 now represented in the Confederate body politic. Henry Hilliard of Montgomery should represent the John Bell supporters, Herschel Johnson of Georgia the Douglas faction of the old Democratic Party, and Benjamin the Breckinridge wing.[53]

He offered sensible suggestions as to the first and last, but Stephens never grasped just how Southern rights men felt about Johnson. Already the President had heard from Howell Cobb and others that they would oppose Johnson for a cabinet post. Davis had to assume he would get the same response to any other Johnson appointment. As for Hilliard, Davis did not know him as yet, and Benjamin was already on his mind for the attorney generalship. So he would make other choices, and did so without consulting Stephens, who left thinking that Johnson had a chance, especially after Martin Crawford added his voice in favor. Three days later when Davis submitted his nominees to Congress, Stephens found to his dismay that none of his recommendations appeared on the list. Instead of Hilliard representing the Constitutional Union people, he saw former Louisiana Governor Andre B. Roman. Looking for Benjamin on the list, Stephens found instead Mobile newspaperman John Forsyth, a one-time envoy to Mexico. And there was no Herschel V. Johnson. Rather, a stunned Stephens saw that Davis had nominated Martin Crawford, and without even asking if he would accept. Crawford himself only learned of it an hour earlier when Toombs mentioned it to him. He, for one, did not want it, yet found himself in an embarrassing position when the Congress gave immediate assent to the nominations. He decided in the end that he had no choice but to go, and resigned his seat in Congress on March 1.[54] Stephens grumbled. He did not like his advice being ignored. He probably bristled at not even being consulted. He would miss Crawford's conviviality at Mrs. Cleveland's. "I think the appointments injudicious," he muttered that evening. "I fear that the appointing power will not act with sufficient prudence, discretion, and wisdom."[55] It was not quite cause to resent Davis, but it predisposed Little Aleck's thinking toward the President in future.

Once Davis made his choices, plans for getting the commissioners to Washington commenced. Crawford immediately prepared to leave. So did Forsyth, who was in Montgomery anyhow covering the government for his newspaper, the Mobile *Register*, though like Slidell, he also grumbled about being part of a commission. "Such work as that is better done by one," he complained.[56] Unaccountably, Toombs waited two days before telegraphing to Roman to inform him of his appointment, and another three weeks before sending him a draft for his $1,000 salary to cover expenses.[57] It was time not to be wasted, for with every day the war talk became louder.

"Make up your account *for war*," came the word from Senator James Mason of Virginia even before Davis took office.[58] Hooper, while feverishly trying to keep up the journal of the debates in Congress, anticipated that "the vigor of our Govt. will necessitate some action on the part of the U.S.,"[59] and the son of John C. Calhoun, haunting the Government House departments just then, found a general opinion that war would come, adding that "the people here are ready."[60] Echoing the sentiments that citizens and press heard around his cabinet ministers, Davis continued to predict that they would see fighting, adding now that he believed most of it would come in Virginia.[61]

Regardless of where the bulk of the battles might come, everyone expected that the first shots would be heard either at Pensacola or, more likely, Charleston. On top of that, within hours of the inauguration it looked as if fidgety militia and a worried governor might initiate hostilities there without waiting for the President or Congress. "If the attack on Sumter is delayed a week our harbor may be in the possession of a fleet," a panicked Isaac W. Hayne wired Davis just hours after he took his oath.[62] The South Carolina delegates wired back asking when Charleston forces would be ready to strike at the Yankee garrison, only to be told that "we are not ready & never will be, but delay beyond Monday would be more dangerous than an attack."[63] In Congress, even the ordinarily mild Barnwell declared that "if I were President I should order an attack on Sumter." He doubted that Davis would do it, expecting instead negotiations, which the subsequent appointment of the commissioners in a few days confirmed. But either way, Barnwell expected war.[64]

More and more it appeared that South Carolina was about to act unilaterally. Such a move could be disastrous. Even though Davis believed that war would come, he also thought that it did not have to if Lincoln would back down when he took office. A slap in the face like bombarding Sumter first would leave the Union no ground for retreat without humiliation. Further, it would compromise the Confederates' attempts to present themselves to the world as wanting peace. Startled on the day he took office to find these nervous hotspurs threatening to usurp to themselves a decision that affected all of the Confederate States, he commenced at once to try to calm.[65] He worked on several fronts. Writing directly to Pickens he emphasized their unreadiness for war. "Valor is ours and the justice of our cause will nerve the arm of our Sons to meet the issue of—unequal conflict," he said, "but we must seek to render the inequality as small as it can be made."[66] That required time, time they would not get if Charleston precipitated them into a war now. Two days later on February 22, while starting to form his commission to Washington, Davis had again to appeal to Pickens to keep a rein on his state militia.[67]

Even Yancey, normally the hothead, begged Pickens not to go too far. "It will produce a confusion—an excitement—an indignation & astonishment here in the Confederate Congress," he warned on the same day that he resigned from the state convention, "that will tend to break up the new government."[68] His strong words, combined with Davis's soothing assurances that the crisis was not yet so great, helped to quell the growing panic in Charleston, while Miles and others on his delegation did their best to act as intermediaries between Pickens and Davis. If the governor could get a good engineer officer to supervise construction of his batteries, then he could keep up with whatever the Yankees were doing in Fort Sumter, and be ready to meet any feared attack by a relief fleet. Under those conditions Pickens could keep his subordinates pacific a while yet.[69] At once Davis started casting about for an engineer, meanwhile trying to relieve Pickens of the fear of personal disgrace in case they held their fire now, and failed later. "I am prepared for the criticism which the rash often bestow upon necessary caution," Davis told him, "but if success follows and the blood of the brave be thus spared, I will be more than content to have the censure which in the mean time may be encountered."[70]

Then on February 25 a so-called "peace" convention meeting in Washington came to an end after three weeks of largely ineffectual debate in which none of the seceded states participated. Few had any hopes of its solving the sectional dilemma, and hope disappeared entirely when the meeting's recommendation of reinstating the Missouri Compromise line and extending it clear to the Pacific went down to an easy defeat in the United States Congress. So insignificant was the convention that when Thomas De Leon arrived in Montgomery a few days after its adjournment to hand Davis a report of the proceedings, the President simply threw it aside and asked instead for a quick verbal account.[71]

This made it all the more important to get the commissioners to Washington and to work. Roman did not help, pleading ill health and asking to be relieved even before leaving, but Davis insisted for a change, and the Louisianian did not fight him.[72] Meanwhile friends in the Yankee capital provided a steady flow of intelligence and rumor. Two days before Lincoln's inauguration, word came that the Republican was expected to sound peace notes in his speech and follow it with a conciliatory policy.[73] The next day Crawford arrived, and assumed—both by his being the first to come, and also his natural bent—that he would lead his commission. At once he wired Davis not even to bother with Buchanan. "He is as incapable now of purpose as a child," said the Georgian. They must see what Lincoln had to say.[74]

The new President's inaugural did not please the Confederates. His soothing words about "mystic cords of memory" binding them together could not conceal his firm promise to protect and defend Federal property as his oath required. Further, the announcement of a cabinet of mostly hard-core Republicans convinced some like Wigfall that war was inevitable.[75] Crawford went immediately to work, joined March 5 by Forsyth. They spoke to everyone who would talk with them, but had to use intermediaries with new Secretary of State William H. Seward. He could not meet with them officially for fear that it might be construed as a recognition of the Confederacy. In a memorandum, Crawford proposed to Seward that the Confederacy would allow the Union time to get the new administration up and going by taking no overt action against Sumter or Fort Pickens for twenty days if the Union agreed not to attempt to disturb the status quo by sending reinforcements. Then they should meet formally to discuss peace, establish diplomatic relations, and negotiate the turnover of the forts and arsenals, and settlement of any disputes over compensation that arose. Crawford thought such a moratorium worked to the South's advantage by buying time, and Seward thought the same, though he believed that a breathing period would make it easier for the seceded states to calm and return to the Union.[76]

In Montgomery, Davis and Toombs watched the unfolding dance in Washington through Crawford's dispatches. Seward presumed to be speaking for the new administration, yet seemed to retreat from one promise and deadline after another. Unable to meet directly with him, Crawford got the assistance of John A. Campbell of Alabama, a justice of the Supreme Court, but it did not avail to get anything more definite out of the administration. "It is clear to us that this Government has not yet made up its mind what to do," Crawford and Forsyth wrote Toombs on March 8. Every time they pressed for some definite statement of Yankee policy and intent, Seward only asked for more time. At the same time, he led them to believe that he, not Lincoln, was able to set policy, and intimations even came their way at one point that Fort Sumter would be evacuated on March 20. The day came and went and nothing happened. Seward pleaded for more time, and Campbell sided with him, pointing out that governments, especially one in office only two weeks, could not act on such a great matter with "bank accuracy." Again the commissioners agreed to wait a little longer. Finally, after the Confederates received assurances through a Russian diplomat that Seward was sympathetic, and even that he would let the seceding states go if they really persisted in their independent course, the secretary of state agreed to having a staged "accidental" meeting with them on the evening of March 28 at the Russian's home. At last, it seemed there was a chance of a face-to-face discussion that could lead to something.[77]

To some in Montgomery, all of the nonnegotiating in Washington merely confirmed what they already believed. Kenner pronounced Lincoln's inaugural "an unqualified declaration of war."[78] "The general opinion here now is that war is almost certain," Stephens wrote to his brother. "I see great troubles ahead."[79] So did Davis, and not content to wait for what might happen towards peace in Washington, he commenced preparations for war in his own capital. On February 20 Congress empowered Davis to contract for arms and munitions a full day before it formally created the War Department.[80] The very next day Davis commissioned Semmes to go North with funds for buying powder and arms.[81] One of the difficulties the President faced immediately was a lack of information on the war materiel then in the hands of the several states, a problem immediately apparent the next day when he shipped cannon powder to Charleston for its artillery aimed at Sumter, but then had to confess that he did not know if it would be suitable since he knew nothing of the size and model of the weapons there emplaced.[82]

Day after day from then on, people saw Davis privately engaged with Bartow of the Military Affairs committee, crafting the various legislation needed to get a military establishment going in as little time as possible.[83] On February 26 he asked for authorization to transfer all arms and munitions from the former Federal arsenals and armories now in state hands to the Confederate service, along with all of the forts and navy yards.[84] Immediately notification went out to the several states when Congress approved. Secretary of War Walker demanded a full statement of all arms and munitions, promising that they would be put in the hands of a new Provisional Army to be raised for the common defense as quickly as possible.[85] As if to give evidence that the Confederate war machine was in earnest, these were the first letters to go out on new War Department stationery.

Even as Davis took his oath, a first "victory" of sorts came in Texas when General David E. Twiggs, commanding Union forces on that frontier, agreed to surrender his command and its arms in return for the safe passage of the men back to the North. Old, ailing, and feeble in spirit, Twiggs yielded almost too easily, but then no one expected him to resist. A Southerner himself, his sympathies lay entirely with the Confederacy, and as soon as his men were taken care of, he offered his services to the new nation. It was a humiliating blow to the Union, one whose emotional impact far exceeded the minimal importance of a few hundred soldiers on the frontier. A number of them, like Twiggs,

also threw in with the new concern, and some in Montgomery expected to see command of the new army given to Twiggs, the highest ranking field officer from the so-called "Old Army" to give allegiance to the
new.[86]

The issue of commanders occupied much of the President's thought
from the moment he took office. Indeed, it seems to have been in his
thinking for at least a month, well before he had an inkling of his election, and when he still hoped to be a general himself. One of his final
acts before leaving Washington in January had been to return a number of books to the Library of Congress. The last one he sent back was
Charles M. Gardner's *Dictionary of all Officers . . . in the Army of the
United States.*[87] He knew most of the higher ranking ones anyhow, but
must have been studying the records and state origins of many more in
case a need for them arose, as now it certainly did. In fact, right after
taking office he wrote to Wigfall in Washington sending a list of ranking staff officers who he hoped could be induced to resign and take service with the South.[88]

On February 25 Congress authorized a general staff and Davis
immediately set about filling the vacancies.[89] Good news came when he
learned that his old friend Samuel Cooper, adjutant and inspector general in the Old Army, was coming to Montgomery to assume the same
post.[90] He arrived on March 14 and took office immediately with the
rank of brigadier general.[91] Davis approached another old friend,
Richard Johnson of Kentucky, wanting him to be quartermaster general, but Johnson remained loyal to the Union.[92] Instead, Davis appointed Abraham C. Myers with the rank of lieutenant colonel. For commissary general, responsible for feeding the army, Davis turned to an even
older friend, Lucius B. Northrop, with whom he had served in the army
on the frontier in the 1830s. Knowing that Northrop had been on more
or less permanent sick leave from the Old Army for years, Walker asked
if his health would allow him to serve. Northrop lost no time in assur-
ing that "no delay shall spring from me."[93]

Other departments needed to be filled, but they could come later.
These first were the ones that could get an army on its feet and keep it
moving. Cooper, "the great functionary" one called him, was elderly,
slim, stately, polite, but sometimes querulous, perhaps because Davis
imposed upon him.[94] Interestingly, just a few weeks earlier, when both
still wore the Union blue, he engaged in an acrimonious letter exchange
with Myers when the latter turned over Federal property in New
Orleans to the Louisiana authorities "in anything but a commendable

spirit." Myers shot back that Cooper's statement "shows a splenetic spirit and contains offensive language from a source personally irresponsible."[95] Yet now, when both arrived in Montgomery, they actually rented a house together that soon became something of a general staff hostelry. When Davis appointed David De Leon surgeon general, he moved in with them, as did brother Thomas. So did the imposing Captain Deas. Before long their house, called the "Ranche" by Deas, became a center for military discussion over cigars on the piazza in the evenings, and every newly arrived former officer looking for a position inevitably "happened" by.[96] Deas, now assigned to Cooper's department, became known in Montgomery as the ideal "carpet-knight," a soldier sufficiently fond of his comforts that he remained content with "Bureau-cratic soldiering" instead of going into the field.[97]

They must have soldiers to make an army. Before Davis took office, Chesnut told the Congress that "a speedy and thorough organization of an adequate army" must be effected, suggesting that from the several state militia they could raise 60,000 men and equip and drill them as volunteers, whereas raising a standing professional or "Regular" army could cost $10 million that, at the moment, they did not have.[98] Just the day after Davis's inauguration—and perhaps after speaking with the President—a Georgia delegate told a friend that "we intend to put the strongest force in the field which can be raised," even while complaining that as yet Congress had done nothing to that end. "We are delaying much time over the most trivial matters." He predicted that Davis would accept all state militia companies offered, with their officers, while he would try to get as many Old Army officers to lead them as he could.[99]

Wright of Georgia introduced a bill on February 22 to form a "Volunteer Division" as a means to take advantage of companies already formed that wanted to become a part of the Regular Army, but the idea did not take hold.[100] Davis, consulting with Bartow, wanted his forces patterned on the old Union's. The Regulars were to be a standing army, and the volunteers raised only for specific times and then discharged when no longer needed. Finally, on February 27, Bartow introduced and saw passed without opposition a bill to organize "provisional forces," a volunteer army.[101] From the first, Davis expected this to be the reliance of the Confederacy for the immediate future, as volunteers could be raised speedily.[102] Bartow's committee called on Davis and proposed that the volunteers authorized be called for only six months' service. Expecting that the emergency before them would last far

longer than that, the President argued in turn for three years or the
duration of the war, if any. Bartow reasoned that just the six months'
call would produce so many men that there would be no war, but Davis
persisted.[103] In the end he settled for one year, Bartow saying that the
Congress would not approve any longer period.[104]

From the time the first volunteer act passed on February 28, Davis,
Bartow, and Congress continued to refine the shape of what they called
the Provisional Army, the President sometimes nitpicking over the
wording of army bills, and often summoning Bartow for conference.[105]
He could accept existing state units, or private companies that volunteered with state consent, and all would be received with their officers
and retained intact as companies or regiments. The President would
appoint all general officers, however.[106] A week later Congress set the
limit on volunteers at 100,000, and Walker sent a request to all governors that they transfer all state units who volunteered right away to get
the army going.[107]

Davis and Walker decided that initially the best way to work would
be to make specific calls on each state, according to its means. On
March 9 they sent out their requests for volunteers: 2,000 from Alabama, 2,000 from Georgia, 1,500 from Mississippi, 1,700 from Louisiana, and 500 from Florida. South Carolina already had several thousand manning the batteries at Charleston. It was a small force to start
with, and they decided to apportion them where the danger seemed
greatest: 5,000 to Pensacola; 3,000 to Charleston; 1,000 to Mobile's
Fort Morgan; 1,000 to the Texas frontier; 1,000 to Fort Pulaski outside
Savannah; and 700 on the upper Mississippi.[108] It was a lot of territory
to cover with a very small army, but the situation was not as bad as it
looked. After all, and as Davis knew as well as anyone, the entire active
duty United States Army at the moment numbered barely more than
13,000, at least half of them spread over a myriad of distant frontier
posts in the West. In the very first response from the governors, he
could expect near parity with the North, and *his* troops would mostly
be within reach of where he needed them. Consequently Davis felt no
unease at turning down Reagan's suggestion in cabinet that he send
men into Kentucky to raise volunteers there. He would get enough
from his initial calls, and besides, Kentucky was a friendly Border State.
Until she came into the Confederacy, their troops could not set foot on
her soil without themselves being invaders.[109]

Almost immediately Davis and Walker encountered something they
had not expected. The governors balked and started trying to set up

their own conditions. In the spirit of state rights, they argued that the new government had no right to accept volunteers directly, and that only men proffered through the governors themselves should be allowed to take service. Moreover, since some private military companies carried arms supplied by the states, the governors further refused to allow them to take their weapons with them if they did volunteer directly. Not surprisingly, the problem first appeared with Georgia's Governor Joseph Brown, a petty, niggling, knee-jerk controversialist constitutionally unable to see beyond immediate expedients to greater ends.[110] Brown would furnish regiments, meeting the call for 2,000, but only if he appointed all officers himself.[111] At almost the same time he virtually warned Montgomery not to attempt recruiting volunteers in Georgia directly, nor to accept any who volunteered except through his office. Louisiana's Thomas Moore felt the same.[112]

The situation only got messier when it came to the state officers. Congress's legislation only authorized receiving complete regiments of about 1,000 men, and with them their officers from colonel on down. But Brown created officers first, then sent them out to recruit their companies. In responding to Walker's call for 2,000, he offered instead two regiments only just begun, but with a full complement of officers already in place. Walker declined to accept the officers without commands and mere portions of companies, but soon Toombs and other politicians got into the fray, and in the end forced Walker to bend the rules, though only after at least nine letters passed between them. "Technicalities must not stand in the way of harmony," he said. It was a hint entirely lost on Brown, who lived for technicalities, and in the end held up these troops for nearly two months.[113] It set a bad precedent, for thereafter Brown was only more querulous. Meanwhile, even Governor Moore of Alabama became a little difficult, demanding clarification on what would happen to his twelve months' men if there were no war, or it concluded sooner. Walker assured him that his men would be released as soon as peace seemed secure.[114]

While trying to placate and cajole the difficult governors, Davis and Bartow planned ahead for their Regular Army as well, showing just how permanent they thought their new nation would be. Bartow introduced the bill on March 2, and when it passed it provided for the creation of a standing force of 10,745 officers and men, exclusive of medical and general staff officers. There should be a corps of engineers, one regiment of artillery, six regiments of infantry, and one of cavalry.[115] As with the Confederate Constitution, the Regular Army was to be an echo of the Old Army, even to the authorization for Davis to appoint four brigadiers.

This matter of appointing commanders for his army, whether volunteer or regular, Davis kept exclusively to himself. Partly it was his duty as President. But for the most part he trusted no one else's judgment so much as his own. Because he kept his thinking so much to himself, cynics claimed that he was in fact paying off old debts from Washington with his commissions. Rhett objected to this in public during debate on one of the military bills. "Let him have his way," shot back another. "This is one of the President's hobbies. If we have war, of course, his system will be blown away."[116]

From the first Davis determined to get as many West Point-trained officers as possible, and it was sound policy. In an era when everyone—especially politicians—thought anyone could lead troops and that professional soldiers were costly and faintly dangerous to the republic, he knew better. The best men to lead in a war were men trained for war. On February 23 he got a bill introduced to accept resigned United States officers—virtually all West Pointers—into his new army, and Conrad soon followed with a resolution suggesting that in commissioning his own officers, he should give priority to such men.[117] Two weeks later, to clarify matters of seniority—always important to officers, and to Davis—Congress further provided that in the case of these resigned officers, their appointments in the new Regular service should all bear the same date, so that their seniority would be determined by their rank in the Old Army, thus preserving their relations to one another.[118]

Of course, the opening of the army only resulted in another mad scramble for places. "I always thought we were a military people," said a South Carolinian looking at the rush for commissions, "but we cannot all be officers."[119] Patton Anderson believed that he saw "a *thousand* applications for each of the army offices,"[120] and even Davis mildly complained that "we find it difficult to gratify them all.[121] William Dorsey Pender, just arrived in Montgomery on March 13, went to the War Department to ask about a captaincy and was told that he "got here in the nick of time." First place in the line for appointments was going to Military Academy graduates.[122]

Naturally, this hardly pleased the host of other would-be Bayards who crowded the hotel lobbies and corridors of the Exchange, not to mention Government House. Sons of senators, financiers, favorites of Davis's from the Old Army—anyone with some claim to extra attention made a bid.[123] Former adventurers like the Nicaraguan filibuster

Karl Henningsen appeared to be extensively lionized, even though he was so far "gone," according to Chesnut, that men he met one day, he forgot the next. Davis had the good sense to put him off, leaving him to entertain drinkers at the Exchange bar with his one-handed cigarette rolling.[124] Of course the hopefuls pulled every wire they could find. Some worked through congressmen like Perkins, or Yancey before he left. More went for Walker, one even enlisting the secretary's wife to get him a commission.[125] The seed of the patriarch of secession tried as well. James Calhoun engaged recommendations from Keitt, Toombs, Miles, Pickens, Chesnut, and others, in his quest. Chesnut himself was often seen walking with Davis in the evenings lobbying for commissions for South Carolinians, while his hopefuls waited anxiously. "It requires much patience to wait here to learn my success in office-seeking," Calhoun confessed. "I think if a person ever forms a *taste* for it, it must be acquired—it is certainly not natural."[126]

In an attempt to expedite processing the inundation of requests for commissions, Davis developed a shorthand docketing to tell Josselyn how to handle them. Some he merely marked "referred" so they might be passed on to Walker. Others in which he took a more personal interest he annotated as "special" or "special attention." The most important he actually wrote notes on, giving specific instructions. Inevitably misconceptions spread, what with all the wire-pulling. In South Carolina, some thought that only men who asked for commissions could get them, which Pickens found troubling, "for many delicate and sensitive gentlemen of the highest merit will not apply personally."[127] Walker quickly disabused him of the notion.[128] Even when men did get their commissions, Davis and Walker had then to deal with complaints of the rank being too low.[129] Brigadier General Milledge L. Bonham of the South Carolina militia suggested that he and his fellow state brigadiers should all be taken into the Provisional Army at their same rank, though pointing out most humbly that he would "cheerfully report" to the superiors Davis might appoint.[130] Worse by far was the behavior of Texan Horace Randal. Believing he had been promised a captaincy in the Regulars, he went to his assignment at Pensacola and there received an actual commission as a first lieutenant. Back he went to Montgomery, stormed into Cooper's office, "expressed his opinion in a forceful manner," then tore the commission to bits and left the room.[131]

For pure petulance and "big-man-me-ism," however, none could touch W. H. T. Walker of Georgia. Early in March he came to Montgomery after resigning his United States commission as a major. Secretary Walker offered him the colonelcy of a new regiment, but in a huff the other Walker refused. "They have insulted me by the rank they have offered me," he declared. His "brother Georgians" would be offended if he were not made at least a brigadier general, especially when he saw one Louisianian, always his junior in the Old Army, now made a brigadier. "If this is the way the Confederate States are commencing to treat Georgia," he wrote to Governor Brown, "it is wise for us to be on our guard." He went on to plant rumors in Brown's already fertile paranoid mind that Davis would not accept the officers *he* appointed, and then vowed that if he could not be a general, he would not serve at all. "We are in the same boat," he told the governor. "It is very important that the rights and dignity of Georgia should be maintained in this *scuffle* at Montgomery."[132] The only dignity at stake was Walker's, and it shrank by inverse proportion to his conceit. "This began a War of Secession," Mary Chesnut said bitterly. "It will end a War for the Succession of Places."[133]

Fortunately thousands of young Confederates of larger character and smaller ego stepped forward at the call. They came into Montgomery by companies on trains and steamboats, marching outside town to the fairgrounds where many camped without even tents, sleeping under wagons.[134] G. W. Lee brought a company to town the very day of the inauguration, offering them to Davis that same afternoon, and it was for them that he gave Deas the order to buy blankets.[135] That same day another company of seventy-five presented themselves, and every day thereafter the number of volunteers increased.[136] Companies like Montgomery's True Blues, the Montgomery Grays, and the rest, came out as soon as they returned from Pensacola. A dispatch from New Orleans said that five hundred crack zouaves were being raised, and even from Washington came word that Wigfall secretly enlisted sympathetic men there for the National Volunteers.[137] From everywhere they came, the flower of Southern youth, reminding Davis of his comment to Wiley Harris in Jackson in January that "society cannot support the loss of such men."[138]

While the building of the army occupied most of Montgomery's attention just then, a navy claimed some of their thoughts as well. Resigned United States Navy officers like Duncan Ingraham joined the influx to the capital, while others like Semmes were already there consulting with Congress on river and harbor defense before Davis sent him north.[139] While Naval Affairs early split from the Military Affairs committee, Congress took its time about actual organization of a navy, waiting until March 11 to pass the bill, and only after considerable prodding from Rhett, who for a change admitted that he used the columns of the *Mercury* to press his views.[140] Yet even before the official organization took place, and well prior to Mallory's confirmation, Naval Affairs began looking ahead. The South had no navy whatever other than the steamer *Fulton* captured in drydock at Pensacola, and she carried but four guns and would need at least $10,000 in repairs.[141]

Chilton moved first that the Congress investigate building gunboats and at least two ironclad warships capable of protecting their harbors. The ironclad was a popular new fancy, a few having been built in Europe, but none had ever been used in combat as yet. A concept born to equalize odds, it offered great hope for an underdog Confederate naval service, and quickly ideas and designs began to arrive in Montgomery.[142] On March 14 an actual bill passed directing the purchase or construction of ten gunboats, and Mallory, now in office, soon began investigating the sources, virtually all of them abroad.[143] Meanwhile a small fleet appeared almost instantly as officers commanding revenue cutters once belonging to the United States government now turned them over to the Confederates. It came not without some pain, however. Memminger's department had no intention of inaugurating a revenue service, and so the ships would be turned over to Mallory, but he had naval officers to appoint to commands, which meant that the officers on the cutters would lose their positions and their commissions. One disgruntled revenue officer complained that "we have got to fight the Navy influence backed by the Secretary of the Navy," else he and his comrades would be "put aside for others no way our superiors."[144] Worse, the ever-troublesome Brown ordered the seizure of some Yankee vessels in Georgia without authorization from Montgomery, arousing a howl of protest even in the South, and resulting in Congress, behind closed doors, venting no little steam over what Howell Cobb frankly called his "follies & blunders."[145] In the press, too, Brown caught a beating. Separate state action was fine before there was a government. Now they were all Confederates, however, and there must be nothing but "Confederate action."[146] It remained to be seen whether Brown would learn the lesson. Those who knew him held little hope.

Such minor internal conflict hardly concerned Mallory as much as his Navy itself. By late March he had the *Fulton*, which might not be ready for sea until August 1, a tug and another steamer each mounting a single cannon, five revenue cutters carrying among them a mere nine guns, and a couple of unarmed vessels, most of them sail powered.[147] It was not a very imposing force with which to meet a threat, even from a disorganized but still infinitely better equipped Yankee fleet. Rhett later claimed that Davis expressed himself as unconcerned with building a Navy, recognizing enemy superiority, and feeling he would only be building ships for the Yankees to capture or sink.[148] Still Mallory immediately sent agents to the Confederacy's major ports to buy whatever vessels could be had for conversion to war needs, and at the same time began enlistments for a Marine contingent.[149] And every new arrival among the resigned officers from the old Navy met a battery of questions on the state of the Federal service and the intentions of other prominent officers of Southern birth. Sometimes Mallory and Davis interrogated the men together in their anxiety to learn more.[150]

Ships presented the least of Davis's weaponry concerns, however. He was building an army that needed arms, ammunition, clothing, and the whole mountain of other supplies necessary to keep men in the field. At the moment, between guns captured from the Yankee arsenals and armories, and what state militia had in their own armories, he could count about 300,000 of all calibers in the Confederacy. But many of those dated back two wars, while others rusted from neglect and overlooked repair.[151] Even before he took office, Alabama cooperated voluntarily with South Carolina, shipping 500 barrels of cannon powder to Charleston, while Memminger, though serving in the Congress, also acted as a purchasing agent in securing another 30,000 pounds for his state.[152]

Clearly these were only stopgap measures. While Wright and Bartow debated in Congress on whether or not they were ready for a war, and when it would come, the former also pressed for the building of a Confederate armory so they could manufacture weapons to their own needs. Going further, he began championing designs for modern breech-loading cannon, and no doubt took advantage of the presence of Joseph R. Anderson in Montgomery.[153] Director of the Tredegar Iron Works in Richmond, Virginia, the South's only foundry capable of casting heavy ordnance, Anderson came to the new capital looking for a contract.[154] In a week he left with an order for thirty seacoast cannon.[155]

Until the Confederacy could buy or cast new big guns, Davis and Walker had to shift about those already available to them. As soon as he formed an idea of what the several states had, he started moving heavy ordnance from the interior to Savannah, Charleston, and Pensacola, as well as Mobile and New Orleans.[156] Showing the urgency of the situation, the scarcity and importance of any weapon, and Davis's own penchant for involving himself in even the smallest details, he personally directed efforts to acquire three field pieces from St. Louis.[157]

It was to be the same in most other areas of supply. Until the army general staff were all in place and functioning, acquisition of any item came about more by improvisation than system. As they tried chiefly to get their soldiers through the states, so did Davis and Walker primarily solicit their arms and equipment in the same fashion. Otherwise, and with Anderson a notable exception, Walker seemed to close the door on most contractors who proposed to manufacture things for the government, whether firearms or foot powder.[158] There was some sense in the approach, especially if war never came. With thousands of arms and scores of cannon already in state hands and more or less available to him, the problem seemed more one of distribution than supply, especially to one with Walker's almost complete absence of military experience. Besides, weaponry was expensive. He had his instructions from Davis and Congress as to the size of the army he was to administer, and appropriations matching his requests for their equipping. To go beyond the immediately necessary risked straining the already meager treasury.[159]

So many other demands came forward for those funds. Uniforms must be designed and made. Rhett's son the editor sent the department a series of colored plates of European patterns that he hoped might provide a model.[160] Money had to be spent just to transfer ordnance from one post to another. They needed new Drummond searchlights to help illuminate the Mississippi channel below New Orleans at night, in case of hostile naval approach.[161] Then there were the actual purchases. Indicative of Walker's inexperience, Davis's interference, and the general lack of coordination in the first days, they sent two agents to the North to buy firearms, Semmes and George W. Morse. Inevitably the two crossed paths, and purposes, causing some embarrassment.[162] Worse, they found themselves competing with agents sent out by the governors, who sometimes expected that Montgomery would pay for the weapons in the end.[163] Only by the end of March, with Northern suppliers all but cut off to them at last, did they make plans to send agents abroad.[164]

It was a sketchy start, yet one that promised to put a huge dent in the proceeds from the $15 million loan and other revenue sources. Walker sent his first expense estimates to Davis on March 4, but by the time they passed a week later in a larger military appropriation bill, his anticipated needs mushroomed to $7,183,995.17. The lion's share of the appropriation was intended for raising the Regular Army. A mere $1,323,766.72 was to be used to maintain 3,000 soldiers at Charleston for twelve months, with $880,228.45 included for an additional 2,000 more men if needed. No other volunteers were provided for, not even those already at Pensacola and elsewhere, showing either a startling oversight or a considerable myopia, but the legislation wisely allowed money for the Regulars to be used for volunteers if necessary, and it included everything from apprehending deserters to the costs of horseshoes and nails.[165] Supplementary bills followed within days providing an additional $5 million for volunteers on March 12, and a further $110,000 four days later for cannon and musket powder that Walker neglected to include in the original legislation. To save money elsewhere, Walker began getting promises from the Confederacy's railroad companies to carry men and munitions free of charge.[166] He was learning.[167]

By the middle of March, unaware of the oversights and the occasional cross-purposes, observers seeing only the constant activity at the War Department concluded that they had their man in Walker. While bewailing a "mushroom confidence" in peace among the citizenry, they complimented the secretary's "thus far manifested efficiency and energy."[168] Certainly everyone approved of the first steps taken to coordinate the gathering of men and materiel under a commander empowered to do something with it all. Responding to Pickens's repeated pleas for an engineer officer to supervise his batteries and defenses, Davis sent W. H. T. Whiting to Charleston on February 23 to perform an inspection of its readiness for active operations. When the officer returned to Montgomery a few days later, he reported that he thought rather too much attention had been paid to offensive operations against Sumter, and not enough to defending Charleston itself, and Pickens continued to say that he wanted the Federal garrison out of the fort as quickly as possible.[169]

Davis knew the man for the job. Even before he sent Whiting on his way, the President telegraphed to New Orleans for Beauregard to come to Montgomery. When the Creole arrived on February 26 he first called on Walker, from whom he learned that he might be sent to Charleston. Maps of Charleston and its defenses were plentiful in Montgomery just then, and Beauregard got one before he went to the President's office, exchanged pleasantries for a few minutes, then got to business.[170] Davis showed him Pickens's letters and a copy of Whiting's preliminary report, and asked what he knew of Charleston. For the next several hours they poured over the chart and made plans. At the very least the President hinted strongly that he would assign Beauregard to Charleston, and the Creole had to have been purposely thick not to surmise the same. The next day, however, meeting as usual with Bartow, Davis told him he intended to do so. When Bartow mentioned it to Beauregard that same day, the officer met the news with the false modesty that characterized most of the great egotists of the day and pretended then and ever after that it came to him as a surprise.[171]

Beauregard himself spent that day sending telegrams to officers in the North whom he thought might "go South" and help Walker with the War Department, unaware that the Federals were now intercepting wires that passed through Northern offices.[172] He also called on members of the Louisiana congressional delegation, telling them of his orders, despite their being a "surprise."[173] Then on March 1 Davis formally nominated him to be brigadier general in the Provisional Army, and wired to Pickens that he was sending him a man of "zeal and gallantry." Unable to restrain entirely a little strain of jealousy that he was sending another to a duty that he would have preferred himself, the President held out the possibility that he might himself come to Charleston "when public duties here will permit." It would be his first, and certainly not last, hint at being a commander -in- chief in more than name only.[174] He told Beauregard to go immediately.[175]

Now Davis turned his eyes to the other hot spot, Pensacola. He knew Braxton Bragg from their days in Mexico, though they had not been close, and Bragg actually feared that the President would overlook him in apportioning command now. But the cranky, irascible, and occasionally unstable Bragg had been cool under fire, and he came immediately to Davis's mind for the forces and works facing Fort Pickens. On March 7 he sent Bragg's nomination for a brigadiership and without waiting for its confirmation had the War Department order him to Pensacola.[176] In the days immediately following, lending support to the fear that conflict, if any, could start here rather than over Fort Sumter, the department forwarded some 12,952 rounds of ordnance shot and shell, everything from eight-inch exploding shells down to grape-shot. Days later a large reinforcement of volunteers from Mobile and Montgomery started on their way for Pensacola, and excitement swept the city amid rumors that the fighting was to begin and the capital's sons were to commence it. In Pensacola itself the anticipation mounted. It might be war at last, after all.[177]

Fort Pickens or Fort Sumter? None could tell. Wigfall reported from Washington that some Republicans believed that Sumter would be evacuated by March 16, but then the day before the event Walker got rumors that Major Robert Anderson's garrison would mine the fort and blow it up as they departed. The secretary suggested that if the Yankees did march out, Beauregard ought to keep one of their officers in the fort awhile as surety of no foul play. "Do not slacken for a moment your energies," he urged.[178] For his part, Beauregard seemed suddenly more concerned with his rank, asking if he couldn't be made a brigadier in the Regulars instead of the volunteers. "I care more for the success of our arms and of our cause than for the honor of being in command here," he said of course.[179] But there was no harm in asking.

Always there came the speculation of war. In Montgomery talk went the rounds that Davis would himself take the field and leave Stephens in charge of the government, a rumor that soon spread all across the South, and even to the North where by mid-March the press reported that Davis would march at the head of 50,000 to take Washington itself if Lincoln meddled with the Confederacy.[180] "I hope you will not have occasion to take the field," his friend David Yulee wrote from Florida, "but if there is a war, . . . you have the example of Napoleon before you."[181]

Still the issue of war seemed not entirely out of men's hands. People coming into Montgomery from Washington thought the chances of conflict diminishing, and Davis himself resolved to continue with peace efforts even while Beauregard set about strengthening Charleston's works.[182] Davis, Toombs, and Benjamin, at least, expressed the belief that Lincoln would try to hold onto the forts in the end.[183] If so, then the Mississippian's conviction of impending conflict would be realized, even as one of Governor Moore of Louisiana's friends predicted that, despite the uneasy truce with the Buchanan administration, "that of Lincoln will be a bloody one."[184] Davis could avoid a war, it seemed, but only if Lincoln backed down, abandoned the forts, and agreed to let the South go. They could not glare at each other across Charleston Harbor indefinitely, and Lincoln, when he took office, could only avoid conflict if Davis and the Confederacy remained quiescent. Even then, in the end Lincoln would have to try to get them to abandon their "rebellion." To do less would be to violate his oath of office. But then, almost word for word, Davis took the same oath, and with it the same obligations. Neither could win the tug without the other losing. Their only hope—and that a slim one—lay in negotiation, yet it appeared that neither could yield an inch without sacrificing a mile.

CHAPTER TEN

A MATTER OF RESTORATION

———•★•———

B Y THE TIME THE PRESIDENT saw military matters taking a semblance of organization from all the confusion, Congress fought a battle of its own. On February 28 the Committee of Twelve reported its draft of the Permanent Constitution. At the suggestion of others on his delegation—one of the occasions when they did speak to him—Rhett first moved the formation of such a committee three weeks earlier, and immediately after the adoption of the Provisional Constitution Howell Cobb appointed the dozen framers.[1] The committee had some strengths. All but three were college graduates. Nine were lawyers. All served in some kind of state or national legislature, and four had judicial experience. Moreover, Harris, Owens, Walker, and Smith also served on the Provisional Constitution committee, though chairman Rhett, not at all happy with that first document, might have regarded this last as a poor qualification.[2]

There were weaknesses, too, or rather imbalances. South Carolina and Georgia had very forceful representation in Rhett, Chesnut, Toombs, and Tom Cobb. Smith of Alabama was strong, and Harris of Mississippi stood out anywhere. But the other half of the committee— Clayton, DeClouet, Sparrow, Morton, Owens, and Walker—lacked force. The men from the cotton states would dominate.

Everyone expected much from the permanent document. Toombs thought it more important than anything except their actual independence, while Rhett—speaking through the *Mercury*—asserted that now was their chance to right all the old wrongs of the original Constitution. In fact, they had few if any objections to that original document as framed and *intended* by the Founding Fathers. Unhappily, it had fallen into the hands of men who increasingly shaded and changed its meaning through "interpretations." To Southern minds, the Constitution, like the Gospels, was a fixed and literal fact, requiring and admitting of no interpretation, and most especially where it regarded the sovereignty and rights of the several states. Generations of Yankee politicians had twisted it to allow them to spend Southern dollars on Northern projects, turn Federal money to the advantage of selected industries, and worst of all curtail the rights of slaveholders to take their slave property with them wherever they chose. If a South Carolinian's money could go to build a canal in Ohio, why could not his slaves go there, too? If there was any problem with the old Constitution, it was that it left too many doors unclosed, making itself susceptible to the shading of unscrupulous men. In preservation of their rights, in the very act of defining who they were and why they were taking this stand now, these men in Montgomery had to close those doors. They were not going to repudiate the Constitution. They were going to save it, to resuscitate it, to help it rise phoenix-like from the ashes of the Union, reframed in perpetuity in its original intent. Here most of all the world would see that they were not rebels. They were reformers.

They could make a document "closed against constructive usurpations." "We do not want doubt, dissatisfaction or revision here, in order to please others," an obvious reference to the Border States and the tendency here in Montgomery to try to soften their stance in order not to scare them away.[3] Indeed, Rhett already feared that some would try to delay debating and adopting the permanent document in order to allow those states time to secede and join, but he intended not to let that delay *him*. "A failure now," said his reporter, "will probably be a failure forever."[4] Some others not on the committee, like Curry of Alabama, rather thought that it would be better for the provisional status to last longer, but most agreed with Stephens that they must show the world their true intent as quickly as possible, and reveal themselves not as revolutionaries, but as conservatives and reformers. The Permanent Constitution offered the perfect opportunity.[5]

The committee started its meeting on Monday, February 11, and Rhett immediately took the high ground by putting before it the draft that he brought with him from Charleston.[6] They should use this as a model, he suggested, and throughout their deliberations he kept it before them.[7] The Alabama and Georgia committeemen came already instructed by their state conventions to use the old United States Constitution as their inspiration.[8] In the end, while they certainly borrowed from Rhett's document, the Committee of Twelve agreed overwhelmingly to start with the Constitution and amend from that, making only the most necessary changes to produce a result that Rhett himself would call "a matter of restoration, than of innovation."[9] After all, he said, "the South was always satisfied with the Constitution of the United States" so long as the North did not pervert it by interpretation.[10]

They worked every night from seven until eleven or later.[11] Rhett, assuming once more that he would dominate the proceedings thanks to coming prepared with a complete draft of his own, predicted the day they started that he would be able to report a new document by February 16 after only five days' work.[12] He soon learned otherwise. Cobb had ideas of his own, and so did some of the others. First they went at the Preamble, Walker actually striking out "Confederate States" from their name and making it, instead, "the Federal Republic of America" which Toombs adopted in future suggestions of his own. Predictably, Cobb put in a line to invoke divine favor, to which no one argued.[13]

Then they got to the meat of the matter. Sounding a consistent theme throughout, they sought to protect the document against all interpretation by weakening the national bond, and to some extent by weakening the presidency. Powers should not be "granted" to Congress, as in the old document, but only "delegated," said Chesnut. Going further into Article I, Rhett tried a gambit that would have resulted in states like South Carolina getting a higher proportion of representatives, and thereby power in the new Congress. Under the old system, for apportionment purposes, slaves were counted as three-fifths of a person in determining population. Now Rhett proposed instead that all persons be counted whole, but his motion failed. The best he could do was get agreement that states should get a representative for every 50,000 in adjusted population, rather than the existing 30,000. This still worked to his purpose, in that if any of the Border States later joined, their much higher ratio of white to black inhabitants would not give them undue representation.[14]

Night after night they went on as rapidly as they could, but Rhett soon saw that they would not finish as quickly as he hoped. Too much presented itself, and there were too many ideas. Stephens's pet notion of requiring the President to appoint his cabinet ministers from among the members of Congress lost despite Toombs's strenuous efforts, but at least Sparrow did get through wording that allowed Congress to grant cabinet members seats in the body if it so chose.[15] Rhett sought to control Congress's power to raise revenue by limiting it to allow only for payment of debts and defense, but Smith of Alabama actually enhanced presidential power—in the interest of fiscal restraint—by inserting a line item veto. With no opposition at all Toombs proposed that the Post Office Department must be self-sufficient by March 1, 1863, and continuing the concentration on matters financial, Smith inserted a proviso that Congress could not appropriate money except for its own expenses, unless requested by a cabinet head through the President, or unless two-thirds of both houses approved. Cobb moved from this a strict prohibition against extra appropriations or bounties to contractors beyond an agreed-upon price. There would be no cost overruns.[16]

After three days the committee got through its first examination of the old Constitution, paragraph by paragraph, and now even Cobb thought they might finish by the end of the week.[17] But then they hit the thorny issues. Walker moved a prohibition of the African slave trade, and proposed further that Congress could also prohibit the introduction of slaves from other slave states not members of the Confederacy. His motions got into their draft, but not without time-consuming opposition from Rhett and a few others who still reacted hotly at any stigma being attached to slavery.[18] Then they came to the President. There had not been a two-term President since Andrew Jackson, and while they admired him as a Southerner, still they looked askance at the assumption of power that characterized his second term. These men believed in the paramount authority of Congress as a reflection of the will of the states. They wanted no imperial Presidency, and one way to curb the possibility was to limit any man's tenure. Rhett suggested holding him to a single six-year term, and proposed that he could not succeed himself, but might be reelected after an intervening term, the same restriction applying to the vice president as well. The committee incorporated his proposal, but then snagged on the manner of electing the chief executive.[19] They considered having presidential electors chosen by the state legislatures, and even by the House of Representatives, but in the end could think of nothing to improve on the old system. That knotty problem they would leave for the debates in Congress to settle.[20]

February 16 came and went, and still they talked. "I never was so sick of any place or business in my life," Tom Cobb complained four days later. "My *heart is not* in the work." Every night he urged hurry so that he could get home to see Marion.[21] He had actually planned on leaving his place and going home earlier, but then came the word that Toombs must go to his ill daughter, and the other Georgians in

Congress implored Cobb not to go, too, and leave the Empire State unrepresented on the committee entirely.[22] As unofficial secretary of the committee, Cobb made a draft of each article as they concluded their deliberations, and by February 21 he was able to hand the first third of the proposed document to Shorter and Reid for them to commence setting type. The committee moved faster by this time, having passed the most troublesome waters, and he hoped they might report it to the whole Congress on Monday the twenty-fifth.[23]

On they worked, Rhett now at least comforted by his second wife's coming from Charleston to join him and ease the grief over his daughter's death.[24] Back in their deliberations the committee wrestled with civil service reform, a pet of Rhett's, and the judiciary.[25] The only serious obstacle remaining was the matter of admission of new states. Cobb wanted statehood open only to slave states, but Clayton alleviated Cobb's fear that free states might one day outnumber the slaveholding ones again and threaten the institution, by inserting a clause guaranteeing protection of slavery throughout the "Republic," regardless of state legislation on the subject. Walker then added a further protection by proposing that a two-thirds vote in both House and Senate should be necessary for admission.[26]

They were almost through. Rhett suggested a new means of amending the document by directing that when any three states, by their conventions, should demand of Congress a convention of all the states to consider amendments, such a meeting must be called. Any amendments that it proposed must then be approved by two-thirds of the states, either by their conventions or their legislatures, in order to become law. He also suggested that it require the action of five of the states to ratify the document.[27] The evening of February 24, even though his wife Mary returned to Montgomery after a visit to relatives, Chesnut stayed up working well past midnight while she lay on the sofa listening to the scratch of his pen.[28] In a distant echo of Calhoun a generation before, Chesnut prepared a resolution that the doctrine of nullification be recognized in an amendment as a right, but the rest of the committee voted him down. They were conservative enough to withdraw from the Union themselves, but no one here wanted to plant seeds of a secession from the Confederacy. Then there came a final run through, and upon reflection Walker changed his mind on his original change in the Preamble, and the rest went along with him. What had only briefly been the Federal Republic went back to being the Confederate States of America.[29]

By gaslight in his room at the Exchange, Cobb worked away up to five hours some evenings, incorporating all of the changes into a final version. To get the work done faster, he enlisted Smith to draft a few pages as well, and by February 25 Rhett could report to the Congress that they were nearly finished and might have it in the delegates' hands in another two days.[30] In fact, Rhett announced the document completed the next day, and added that the committee preferred to report it formally in secret session.[31] It seems an odd request for Rhett, who declared after the Provisional Constitution passed that they must certainly debate the permanent document in open session in order to correct the evils that got by, and also, of course, so that South Carolina could see in the newspapers what he was saying.[32] But the rest of the committee probably overruled him. Moreover, some favored postponing the debate for several weeks, or after a recess allowed them all to go home, while the rest favored finishing the work as quickly as possible. Until they decided which course to pursue, secret discussion seemed most judicious.[33]

They were all anxious to get away from Montgomery. "I am bored to death with company and calls," Little Aleck complained a few days earlier.[34] Howell Cobb actually feared the anxiety of some of the members to go home, and worried that they would leave important business unfinished. Whenever a proposal came onto the floor to adjourn, he opposed it strenuously, and thus far did so successfully, determined that they must finish with the Permanent Constitution first.[35] Some of the members, on the other hand, positively looked forward to seeing and molding the document. "I intend to make it an instrument worthy of all acceptation," Harrison of Mississippi told his wife.[36] Nisbet promised Stephens's brother that they would approach the old Constitution "very guardedly" in making their changes.[37] They revered the document, and meant not to overturn it, but give it new birth. The Vice President himself heaved a sigh of relief when Rhett reported the document ready for consideration, and even hoped that they might get through with the debates and adopt it in a matter of only three or four days. He wanted to go home and see Rio. He should have known better.[38]

Congress certainly found plenty to do while waiting for the committee to report its new document. Every day the President sent in new legislation for the War Department as he organized the military, while the members themselves introduced everything from patent protection for the inventors of new cannon to authorization to pay for the services of Shorter and Reid that prescribed in minute detail the fees by the page.[39] They embarked on initial discussions of the form of a supreme court, and worked through their tariffs and duties, despite Toombs's somewhat drunken comment to a reporter that the Confederacy would practice entirely free trade with the world.[40]

If there were any novelty remaining after the first euphoric week for the Congress, it wore away rapidly now as the tedium of routine, and for many overwork, set in. Poor Jonce Hooper did not manage a meal with his family more than twice, despite having by now three or four capable assistants to help him with the journal of the Congress. Worse, one of his partners in the *Mail* was ill and the other had joined a militia company then gone to Pensacola, so he was running the newspaper entirely on his own, unable to edit, or even to read what his reporters put into the issues.[41] The tall, gangly, and undeniably homely editor made quite a sight as he wearily trudged the streets of the city, his head covered with a disreputable cap that was more a tile than a hat. Walking up Commerce past the Exchange one afternoon, he heard "Church" Churchill yell at him to stop. The hatter walked out into the street, whispered something about it being hard times for publishers in Hooper's ear, and then shoved a new hat from Paris on what Jonce's own paper would have called his "cocoanut."[42]

For those delegates not swallowed in the nightly deliberations of the Committee of Twelve, social life provided about the only release from the growing tedium of the days' sessions. Stephens ate his breakfast precisely at eight o'clock every morning, wrote his letters, attended the debates, and then went to the dinners and parties in the evenings when he felt well.[43] For men like Tom Cobb, the only society of the day came at the Exchange breakfast table, where President Davis often sat with him and tried to be more "chatty" and agreeable than came to him by nature. "He is not great in any sense of the term," thought Cobb, who yet recognized that the Mississippian had achieved much by the sheer force of his will.[44]

Even the pleasures of the table waned as the congressmen considered the rapidly rising prices and the correspondingly flagging quality. Rumors of congressional salary abuse already bounced from ear to ear in Montgomery, some thinking that the delegates were drawing salary for a full session in advance, whereas they were paid only to date, and with pro rata deductions for any days missed.[45] And at $8 per day, they were not getting rich in any case. Howell Cobb joked that they kept their pay small intentionally "for fear the Hotel keepers may demand it all."[46] Tom Cobb complained in the middle of his committee's deliberations that the rates at the Exchange were becoming exorbitant, while at the same time the hotel looked increasingly unkempt and filthy. The meals put him off so much that he sometimes did not bother to eat until late in the day. "The filth at the hotel is almost starving me," he lamented. Only the oysters failed to disappoint.[47]

No one suffered from the food more than fastidious Porcher Miles. He liked soup, and that served by Messrs. Watt and Lanier came to the table cloudy with grease. He blamed it for his heartburn and his unsettled dreams at night, and complained to friends as far away as South Carolina. They could not fail to sympathize, even if a bit tongue in cheek. Speaking of the offending cook and his broth, one friend responded, "how great then are the responsibilities of that important officer to the Montgomery Convention!" A delegate needed cool judgment and sound digestion. "Who can fairly appreciate the rights of others whose soup is bad and who has the heart burn in consequence?" He even suggested that if the Founding Fathers in 1776 had a better cook in Philadelphia, then the offending phrases in the Declaration of Independence like "all men being born equal" would not have come about. As for the cook who catered the Constitutional Convention of 1789, with all the ills it begat for which they now sought remedies, well, "what has not that man to answer for!" Clearly the men in Montgomery should not too much mirror the experience of 1776.

Either the convention in Montgomery or the Congress itself should hire a good cook. "Miles it should be attended to!" said his friend. Else the danger was too great. "A constitution under the influence of greasy soup, conceived in dispepsia [*sic*], shaped into portentious form by the visions of night oppressed dreams cant do otherwise than produce a flatulency which will blow up the whole concern!"[48]

Of course the Congress had trouble enough with wind without the Exchange's bad food. "The debates in this body are becoming a great bore," Stephens complained the day after Rhett presented the new draft. Rarely did anyone say something of interest.[49] A bit of humor, often at the expense of each other, lightened the tedium. Onlookers enjoyed the sight of Nisbet's young daughter tossing a bouquet from the balcony to Tom Cobb, whose face beamed only briefly before it turned embarrassed when she whispered that it was for the handsome Bartow seated next to him.[50] The Vice President always put down his pen to listen when Harris spoke, especially when his caustic wit was aimed at the more sanctimonious like Cobb. When a delegate humbly suggested that the hand of the Lord inspired his efforts, Harris replied that he feared "any man who avowed that he considered himself an instrument in the hands of Providence," like the bull that hid his horns beneath straw.[51]

Old Withers constantly amused Stephens, though few others, as he interrupted their debates with snuff sneezes into his red bandanna so loud that some swore they could be heard at the other end of Market.[52] The Vice President, considering the South Carolinian "a perfect impracticable," still found that he sometimes said "some very good things," especially when he harped on about public expenditure. "Too much money is dangerous to private virtue," Withers carped when discussing appropriations; "to public it is absolutely fatal."[53] The house roared when Withers and Tom Cobb got into a debate February 27 over an increase in pay to Shorter and Reid. At first Withers argued for economy, but then Cobb declared that his motion would cost the government even less than the existing contract provided, whereupon Withers announced that "I am opposed to it more than ever." When the laughter subsided, he explained that "it would be derogatory to the reputation of this government to want work done for less than it is worth."[54] Yet in the same breath he would go too far. Withers ranted constantly about Congress trampling its own Provisional Constitution, and became so fixated on the business of the six white horses in the inaugural, together with Congress's provision to provide an executive mansion, that his niece Mary Chesnut thought him "certainly crazy on the subject of Jeff Davis."[55]

No one provided more mirth to the rest than old Rhett, undoubtedly because he took himself so seriously. All wearied at his being constantly on the floor both in open and closed session, and so humorlessly doctrinaire and self-important when he spoke. By now Conrad of Louisiana so tired of it that almost automatically he rose after every Rhett speech to argue against him. The two were "always at words," Mrs. Chesnut noted, "everlasting speakers and wranglers."[56] Tom Cobb saw quite plainly that "Old Conrad 'sets' for Rhett and never allows him to speak without answering him at once."[57] The idle pens of bored stenographers needed little stimulus to turn themselves to ridicule.

On February 21, through a confusion, a minister failed to appear to open the public session with a prayer. Howell Cobb asked Hilliard, observing on the floor for the Alabama convention, if he would ask a blessing, but he declined. The congressional clerk Robert Dixon then had an idea that may not have gotten to the chair, but certainly found its way to the ear of one of Hooper's waggish scribes, and from thence into verse.

> No Preacher is on hand today,
>   And Cobb is filled with care,
> For want of some one used to pray,
>   Soon as he takes the chair.
>
> He calls on Hilliard to perform,
>   Who smilingly refuses.
> Tis not the mission at this time
>   Which the Ex-Belgian chooses.
>
> Bob Dixon then the Georgia clerk,
>   Fun flashing from his eyes,
> When Hilliard thus the prayer did shirk,
>   Proposed this compromise.
>
> The place left vacant by the priest,
>   Just call on Rhett to fill,
> And if the Lord dont answer him,
>   Conrad of Louisiana will.[58]

The bit of doggerel soon circulated throughout the Congress, Howell Cobb himself sending a copy to his wife, while Rhett's own colleagues delighted in the poem, Barnwell and Miles carrying it about with them to read aloud in drawing rooms and parlors.[59]

These interludes helped to pass the time, but did nothing to keep the members' interest for more than a few minutes. With each day private conversations in the chamber grew louder as more men simply ignored the speakers on the floor. "I am bothered to death almost with the din of noise about," Stephens complained on the very day Rhett reported the Constitution ready.[60] The lack of decorum and deteriorating behavior did not escape the notice of visitors in the galleries during open session. "The lawmakers of the Confederacy looked little like poets," young Thomas De Leon thought. Rather, he saw them as a reversed image of the Congress in Washington, as if viewed through the wrong end of a telescope. There was no dignity, no solemnity. He saw too much indolence as members sat in the sessions with their hats on their heads and their feet up on their desks, chewing unlit cigars, and buzzing constantly among themselves.[61] The scene sufficiently disturbed one Montgomery lady that she complained the Congress lacked dignity, and needed to adopt form and ceremony, like the English Parliament, if it wanted to gain respect and stature.[62]

All it took to shake the congressmen from their lethargy was an issue, and predictably the old bugbear of slavery gave it to them. On February 22 Clayton reported from the Judiciary committee a bill to abolish the slave trade. The following day they debated it in closed session longer than any other issue yet before them. Immediately Barry of Mississippi tried to dilute the bill by making persons caught practicing the trade guilty only of a "high misdemeanor" rather than a felony. It failed, though only because Georgia was divided, while South Carolina and Florida backed him unanimously. Then Barry tried again by moving to strike out the stated punishment of ten to twenty years, replacing it with a much reduced sentence or a fine. Again he failed. Next Chilton went at it, as well as others. Tom Cobb put up much of the opposition, and was so wearied by it at the end of the day that he had a headache.[63]

The bill came up again two days later, and resulted in an even more disputatious session lasting all afternoon. They tried to deal with how to handle slaves illegally imported when discovered, and decided that the President should deliver them either to the United States, or else ship them back to Africa if it could be done at no expense to the government. Failing that, he was to have them sold to pay the costs of their apprehension and detention, and the balance split between the informant who reported them, and the Treasury. Throughout the debates, Barry sought to weaken both the coverage and the punishments in the bill, but generally without success. Just as consistently, South Carolina opposed him, but in the end his own state was sufficiently dissatisfied with the bill to stand alone in voting against its passage.[64]

Congress invested a lot of time and effort in crafting the bill, and thus it came as a shock to some when three days later Davis sent it back with his first veto. He cited the provision in the Provisional Constitution that prohibited the importation of blacks, and pointed out that by providing that the President should send illegally imported slaves to the Union or sell them in the Confederacy for costs, they were allowing a *de facto* importation to take place after all.[65] Tom Cobb turned livid. After all his effort, to have the bill vetoed on a technicality shook him to the core. "I shall strive hard to pass it over his head," he said to his wife in his fury, "it will do my very soul good to *rebuke* him at the outset of his *vetoing*."[66] Indeed, so irrational did it make him that he violated his oath of secrecy in telling Marion what had happened, and two days later wrote to beg her not to tell anyone, fearing embarrassment if his indiscretion should become known. That same day, March 2, Congress failed to override the veto, with only Florida, Georgia, and South Carolina voting in favor, and a voice vote of fifteen for and twenty-four against. Cobb again flew into a fury, and made a long speech in which he demanded that the veto be made public, along with the results of that day's vote, and his own intemperate speech. "I was *hot* in my heart," he confessed that night. "I think I convinced the Presdt's friends that I did not look to that quarter for office or favor." Cobb foolishly took pride in having alienated Davis, or so he thought, and thus put himself close to the small but growing group of the dissatisfied, united by their growing hostility to the President. Stephens quickly managed to defeat his motion to take it all public. It would reach the people soon enough, and when it did, some, especially the South Carolinians, would condemn it roundly and hint that Davis secretly favored emancipation.[67]

The debate on the bill offered an ill omen, coming as it did just as they were about to start on the Permanent Constitution. Symbolic of the heating passions, the day before the veto two reporters from Charleston got into a fistfight when they argued over which was to get the first copy of Hooper's handouts for the day. One wound up confined to his room with injuries, and talk of a duel circulated through Montgomery.[68] How easily passions drew battlelines, and in the slave trade debate some coalitions—it was too soon to call them parties yet—began to emerge, chiefly the more radical eastern cotton states versus the western Gulf and Mississippi states. What remained to be seen was the true underpinning of the coalitions, especially ones that could put Rhett, Toombs, and the Cobbs all in the same camp. It may have been Jefferson Davis himself. Barely a week earlier, one reporter had complimented the Congress for "the dignity, the moderation, the promptness, and the wisdom with which it has acted, has solved that most difficult of all problems—satisfying everybody. So may it continue."[69] There were a number of men in the state house who were not so happy just now. Ambitions were being stunted, too. Tom Cobb stewed over the press failing to give him credit for introducing bills on cotton export duty and management of Confederate courts, and began toying with notifying the papers of his accomplishments himself.[70] Who could tell what impact that dissatisfaction might have in the deliberations about to begin on the very charter of their independence?

Wednesday, February 27, Mary Chesnut made the steep walk up Market to the Capitol, and then up the flight of stairs and into the chamber, but barely caught her breath before Howell Cobb announced that the doors were closing.[71] Nothing whatever of interest transpired except the introduction by Wright of Georgia of a resolution calling for debate on the Permanent Constitution to be held publicly. His colleagues did nothing about it in the secret session that followed, but Kenner proposed that starting on the morrow the new document should be the special order for each day thereafter until they concluded the work. Rhett then offered what seemed at first an odd amendment, suggesting that consideration not commence until the following Monday, without actually specifying the date. It would be March 4, the day of Lincoln's inaugural. Despite his earlier anxiety to report the Constitution as quickly as possible, he now hoped to hear the Yankee program spelled out first, no doubt thinking that if it were confrontational enough, it would help solidify support for this document and pass it through all the more quickly. Not a single state stood with him, not even South Carolina.[72]

That night Judge Bibb held a large party for all of the government dignitaries. Both Davis and Stephens felt too unwell to attend, much to the host's disappointment, but many of the other luminaries went, to be dazzled by three rooms, each with two long tables filled with meats, oysters, cakes, and more.[73] They all needed a night out, more than they realized. Even Tom Cobb relaxed enough to allow himself a good time. None knew just what was going to happen when they started on the constitution on the morrow. Amid the fine wines, the wonderful oysters, and the convivial babble of Montgomery gossip, there was an air of anticipation and apprehension. In his room the next day Little Aleck, always the pessimist, was to confess that "I think we have great troubles ahead."[74]

"Our Congress is inclined to go forward," DeClouet told his son the next morning. Informally they had decided not to postpone consideration of the new Constitution.[75] After convening at eleven they spent little more than an hour listening to the usual flag presentations and memorials from constituents before President Cobb cleared the house, and as soon as the doors closed moved a standing order that henceforward whenever the open session completed its regular routine, they should automatically go into secret session. Morton followed that with a resolution that at noon every day the Congress should resolve itself back into its functions as convention to consider the Constitution. Waul of Texas, whose delegates were to be allowed participation and a vote in the debates even before Texas's March 2 admission, then proposed keeping a separate journal of the constitutional debates. All of these preliminaries out of the way, at noon they went into convention and started work.[76]

On his desk each member of the convention found a copy of the proposed Constitution as reported out of committee. As Hooper read the document aloud, they followed along over the twenty-seven pages of legal sheets, the lines triple spaced to allow for extensive editing and emendations.[77] There was to be no debate until the first reading was completed. Harris, who often mumbled to himself during debate, sat silent as Jonce read. Most now knew that this meant Harris intended to rise to speak.[78] As soon as Hooper finished, the Mississippian stood and commenced the discussion with proposing to eliminate the preamble that his own committee had decided on, and suggesting a substitute. It presaged much of the debate that would follow, for it addressed semantically their concept of themselves and just how much they were *Confederates* and how much Georgians or Alabamians. "We, the people of the Confederate States, each State acting for itself," it now began. Harris, seeking a more nationalistic sense, moved to strike out the "each State acting for itself." Withers, on the other extreme, wanted that phrase retained but moved to eliminate the "We, the people," thinking it implied too much homogeneity. Hill wanted the whole thing changed to enumerate each of the states. They spent half of their first day at it, perhaps not realizing that they were fighting not over words, but their concept of themselves. In the end they settled for "each State acting in its sovereign and independent character" after the "We, the people." As Stephens said, it stressed that this was the action of individual states, and not of a collective people.[79]

At once they turned to Article I, which comprised fully half of the document, and would in the end occupy more than half of their debate. The first section delegating all legislative powers to Congress passed without comment. But when they came to the next section on citizenship and eligibility to serve in Congress, debate ensued that lasted the rest of the afternoon with no resolution. At half past four they still had no decision, and despite Stephens's motion that they convene again in the evening to continue, they adjourned for the day.[80] It was not a lot of progress for their first day—ten lines of the document covered, and more than four hundred to go. Those like Stephens who hoped for a speedy adoption went back to their lodgings considerably sobered.

Realizing that it was going to take time, Congress agreed to set its hour of convening an hour earlier, to meet at ten o'clock, but the next day, March 1, many of them forgot, or overslept. Withers loped up to the state house grumbling about the early hour, and even when the clock above the portico hit ten, a third of the delegates had yet to arrive. Portly Howell Cobb was among the tardy, huffing and puffing and sweating up Market Street looking like a man in a hurry to see a doctor.[81] As soon as he called those present to order, Cobb had Hooper read the journal of the day before, then announced that there was no business on their public calendar for that day. "Whereas our transactions are considered Treason by the late so called United States," he announced, "it becomes my duty to request all visitors to retire."[82] After an equally speedy secret session, Congress once more went into convention.

A full day's session until half past four once again failed to get past more than ten lines, and with little resolution. Citizenship remained unsettled and tabled for the moment, the clause specifying that representatives must be twenty-five years of age or older and citizens of the Confederacy got by unchanged, and then they logjammed on apportionment. Once again South Carolina raised the issue, this time Keitt proposing that slaves be counted at their full number.[83] Uninterested in much of the petty debate, some members ignored it. When the younger Cobb spoke, Stephens wrote letters "with Tom smoking," or else joked with Withers who quipped that if he did not escape from all these politicians soon he feared he would start stealing. Indeed, the day before, he told Little Aleck, he stole a piece of ribbon from Chesnut. "I must get away from here soon Sir," he declared, "or I shall be stealing on a larger scale. I feel it Sir." Stephens just joked that his petty theft was a sign that Withers was a good Democrat.[84] Ten lines was far as they got, and again Stephens could not get them to agree to an evening session, even with Tom Cobb backing him.[85]

The slowness of it all and the spirit being manifested by some left Stephens increasingly uneasy. He happily saw that harmony and good temper still prevailed, but weaknesses manifested themselves. "We lack statesmanship of what I consider of the highest order," he lamented that night. "We have but few if any of real forecast." None seemed to agree with him on the great dangers before them, and to realize that unity for the greater purpose should take precedence over pettifogging at technicalities. Only "great patience forbearance and patriotism," he said, could see them through.[86]

Unable to gather much of what happened behind the closed doors, the public relished the next day's open session, which gave them the first real day of interesting and lengthy debate since the delegates first met. It started with Harris presenting a resolution that the Finance Committee be asked to revise the tariff in order to enlarge the list of duty-free items, and reduce the rates on the rest. He pointed out that it was his original motion that adopted the entire body of laws then extant in the United States, which included the offensive 1857 tariff. Now it was time to remedy that. Toombs, as head of Finance, responded that he and his committee had been working on that very problem fully a fortnight, and resented a resolution instructing them to do what they were already about. Moreover, he pointedly told them that they must raise an army and a navy, and money had to come from somewhere. If not from the tariff, then where? Reduce it drastically, and despite the political and diplomatic attractions of free trade—with which he was quite familiar as secretary of state—they risked the internal strength needed to maintain their independence. "Such a reduction would be unwise in the last degree," he declared. But Barnwell, Miles, and then Withers all chimed in to support both Harris's resolution, and the healthy cut in rates that Toombs so feared. Only when someone erroneously announced that Finance would deliver a report in two days did Harris withdraw his resolution, but even then the passions were up and Toombs, Withers, Miles, Rhett, Harris, and others continued the debate despite its being declared out of order. Finally the public got a show, and one of discord that broke through the carefully cultivated veil of harmony. Everyone in Montgomery by that evening knew that the tariff was dividing the delegates.[87]

At least the congressmen all felt they accomplished something in their regular secret session when Stephens moved the admission of Texas, which passed immediately.[88] Waul, Oldham, and Reagan took their formal seats at once, with Gregg and Ochiltree already present, and all of them grateful for the warm welcome they received from their new colleagues, and from Montgomery itself.[89] Texas did not come easy into the fold. Indeed, the results of its referendum would not be known for two more days, but the state convention acted without waiting. Very quickly Governor Sam Houston would be forced from office for his opposition to secession. "Houston is not, nor will be, a favorite name in the Confederacy," he lamented, and the delegates now sitting in the Congress felt a bit embarrassed by it all.[90]

Once the convention session began at noon, Keitt's motion arose once more, and Stephens started a process that they would use again and again. He simply moved that they skip over the apportionment issue and postpone it until all the rest of the document had been settled. By putting aside matters too divisive or thorny until the end, they could get through much of the rest of the Constitution with more expedition. Secretly, Little Aleck probably supposed as well that after several days of long debate, they would be too tired at the end when the postponed matters arose once more to drag them out long. The plan would work well.

They moved swiftly through the rest of Section 2 and clear to Section 6 of Article I before adjournment. Early in the afternoon debate stalled on impeachment of judicial or federal officers residing and working solely within a single state. Finally Stephens got so tired of it that he demanded the question twice to halt further proposed amendments on the subject, and then called for a vote on another amendment allowing state legislatures to impeach by a two-thirds majority in such cases. Chilton asked for a vote by states, but Hill, opposed to the amendment all along, said there was no need as they could easily defeat the measure by a voice vote. Yet when the ballot came in, seven states supported the amendment, and not one stood by Hill. The hall erupted in laughter, and after looking what Stephens thought "perfectly blue" for a few moments, Hill joined in the mirth at his own expense. They needed these light moments, few as they were. "So on we go," mused the Vice President. "No body looking on would ever take this Congress to be a lot of Revolutionists."[91]

Despite a number of motions and proposed amendments, no further changes in Article I arose before they went back into secret session, and then adjourned for a dinner break. That night they met again until past ten. Though Montgomery knew few specifics of what happened behind those closed doors, the amount of work itself was apparent. "It is hardly to be expected that your regular Congress will average with this body in ability," a South Carolinian wrote that evening.[92] Talking with one delegate, young Calhoun learned that despite their slow progress to date, they expected to move much faster in the days ahead.[93] Rhett still hoped they would finish with the Constitution that week, but pessimistically told the Mercury reporter to write to his readers that "your members are fighting hard for a Constitution such as the people of South Carolina will approve of, but it is doubtful if they will succeed."[94]

They needed Sunday March 3 to relax away from the state house. Stephens dined with the Louisiana delegation, stayed out well past midnight, and thoroughly enjoyed himself. It put him in a mood to compliment his fellow members on their good behavior, even fibbing a bit to say that "not the slightest discourtesy has been shown in debate." Despite his gloomy judgment of just the Friday before, now he concluded that "upon the whole this Congress taken all in all is the ablest, soberest, most intelligent and conservative body I ever was in."[95] Moreover, despite complaints that men spoke too long and wandered from the subject, he also praised the debates for their brevity, precision, and force of argument.[96] In short, Little Aleck's judgment of their doings vacillated in step with his mood from day to day. Most of the other delegates felt pleased enough. At Montgomery Hall, where the food now seemed even worse than at the Exchange, the Chesnuts and their usual "mess," including Withers, Mallory, Wright, and others, enjoyed a cheerful Sunday dinner, Mary Chesnut perceiving that much of their good cheer was due to "all having spoken in Congress to their own satisfaction."[97] And people kept outside those closed doors felt increasingly good about the men working behind them. "The Congress now in session here is composed of good material," Alabamian William Smith wrote to his wife, "much superior, generally, to the body at Washington."[98]

Montgomeryites felt even more contented with their Congress on the following day, March 4, for the delegates gave them a show. Finally the time was at hand for a new flag. During weeks of what De Leon called "windy dissertations on the color of the flag,"[99] everyone offered his own ideas. Brooke actually suffered accusations of treason when he argued to retain the old Stars and Stripes because they were used to loving it. The flag did not wrong them—Yankees did. He even suggested adopting Francis Scott Key's "Star Spangled Banner" as their own anthem.[100] A surge of rebukes and the urging of friends persuaded him to withdraw his proposal.[101] Most of the congressmen took some interest in the matter, and Miles made an almost impassioned speech in open session February 13 to promote a new design.[102] Yet for his part, President Davis did not want a new national flag. He thought with Brooke that the old one suited very nicely.[103]

All through February and into March suggestions came from every quarter of the new Confederacy, virtually all of them submitted through congressmen. Withers received the first, or so he thought, but then quipped that he never had time to "manufacture resolutions" for bringing it to the house.[104] Tom Cobb probably presented the most, setting at least a dozen before his colleagues to refer to Miles's committee.[105] The variety and ingenuity—not to mention the frivolity—of some of the designs staggered the delegates. A Phoenix shooting out of flame and ashes with the motto "We Rise Again." Seven stars and seven stripes. A yellow Southern Cross on a field of red, with the Palmetto in the upper corner. A globe displaying their hemisphere with the Confederacy highlighted that it might be "instructive." Best of all was the one showing seven rattlesnakes tied by their tails, with a bale of cotton on one side and a jug of whiskey on the other. One Montgomery editor thought its designer showed pure genius and deserved a government office.[106] In the end more than 120 designs appeared, and the committee had to engage a draftsman to translate all of them into suitable sketches for consideration.[107] Bartow served with Miles on the flag committee, and visitors to his room at the Exchange often found models draped over the furniture while the committeemen engaged in lively discussion, most echoing Bartow's desire to stay as close to Old Glory as possible, while still creating something distinctive.[108]

Eventually the committee decided that none of the designs submitted suited the case. They divided them into two basic groups, those that to some degree emulated the Stars and Stripes, and the more elaborate or "fantastical," as Miles termed them. Substantial objections nullified both. The first for the most part looked *too* much like Old Glory, and could lead to confusion. Besides, looking at flags of the world, the committee found that the banners of the black colony of Liberia and the Sandwich Islands in the Pacific both borrowed heavily from the Stars and Stripes. The Confederacy should have no desire to emulate "a free negro community and a race of savages," said Miles.[109]

Instead the committee proposed its own model, though the design did not originate with them.[110] Niccola Marschall lived in nearby Marion, Alabama, where he taught school to supplement his income as a portrait painter. Governor Moore's daughter Mrs. Napoleon Lockett also lived in Marion, and sometime during February she asked the artist to take a hand at a flag design. On a sheet of paper he rather quickly sketched three designs, of which the first showed three wide horizontal stripes of equal width, the inner white and the outer red. In the upper left corner he placed a field of blue, and in its center a circle of stars, one for each state. Somehow, almost certainly through Governor Moore himself, Marschall's design found its way to the committee and they settled on it as the best choice.[111] By March 2 the design leaked to the press, though it could hardly be classed as a state secret. It may well have gotten out thanks to Miles handing it to Hooper with orders to have one made. Being a newspaperman at heart, Jonce could hardly keep the news from fellow journalists. He took the design down Market Street to the Cowles sewing establishment with instructions to have it ready by Monday.[112] In fact, the committee deliberately delayed reporting it until March 4, to time the event to the precise moment that Abraham Lincoln delivered his inaugural in Washington.[113]

March 4 came warm and cloudy, sixty degrees by noon. Curry began the day by presenting Howell Cobb with an inkstand made of Alabama marble, and it was received with appropriate thanks.[114] Congress adjourned at noon and went into convention for some time, while the announcement of the event to come quickly brought a large crowd to the capitol grounds. Miles left organizing the formal ceremony to Hooper, and Jonce in turn put Commodore Ingraham and a Colonel Sayre in charge of the event. Given the choice of raising the first banner, President Davis gallantly passed the honor on to Letitia C. Tyler, the teenage granddaughter of former President John Tyler. Just after three in the afternoon, seven young ladies of the city climbed to the dome, each representing a Confederate state, and there they arranged the flag that Sayre unfurled for them while the band from Canning's Theatre played the "Marseillaise" and "Red, White, and Blue" below. Then Clitherall and others escorted Miss Tyler to the capitol dome, from which she looked down upon a throng on the grounds below. Clitherall handed her the halyard, and when the state house clock hit the last chime of four o'clock, cannon thundered, the crowd roared, and she drew the flag up its temporary staff as the band played "Dixie."[115]

The True Blues fired a seven gun volley that sent a circular cloud of blue smoke coiling up above the crowd, where it hovered in "a most beautiful and auspicious omen," and the cheering spectators went wild.[116] The Chesnuts, Curry, and Mallory stood on the balcony at Montgomery Hall, with an excellent view. While they watched, Chesnut leaned to Mallory's ear and gave him the good news that at last the Congress that afternoon had confirmed him as secretary of the navy. Saying nothing, Mallory simply smiled and bowed his thanks.[117]

Nearby George N. Sanders and his daughter watched, she thinking the crowd not at all sufficiently enthusiastic for such a moment. Mary Chesnut reminded her with some haughtiness that "our mobs are gentlemen."[118] For everyone the day was an unqualified hit. Few had even a momentary criticism of the new design. "The glories of the future will cluster round that flag," declared a South Carolinian.[119] The next day, when Miles delivered his formal report in open session, Brooke followed immediately after to endorse the design and remove any doubt about where his loyalties lay.[120]

Quickly word of the design went forth from Montgomery, Miles himself wiring it to South Carolina, where a banner went up over the Charleston customs house on March 6.[121] The next day the merchant vessel *Susan G. Owens*, just arrived in Charleston, ran up a makeshift version of her own to fly on the high seas, and within days the likeness of the national banner flew atop the mastheads of newspapers all across the Confederacy.[122] Within just weeks a frenzy of flag making spread around the new nation. Capers designed a variant banner for the Treasury's revenue service in case it should ever have one, and rumors flourished that the French government, though officially neutral, had given orders that the new Southern banner was to be accorded the same status "provisionally" as the old Stars and Stripes.[123] Miles ordered Hooper to have a larger version, twenty-eight by eighteen feet, made for the capitol, and when it arrived it proved so heavy that the staff required extra reinforcement to carry it in the breeze. Clitherall took care of it all, paying $90 out of his own pocket to the makers, and for the staff, halyards, and freight. It would take him two months to have it reimbursed.[124]

"Debate debate—no end of debate," Little Aleck complained the same day the flag appeared.[125] Their first act that day had seen the final defeat of Stephens's pet notion of having cabinet officers sit on the House floor. Toombs moved its inclusion once more, but withdrew it after a silly rambling speech by Withers. Then Little Aleck tried another way by moving to strike the prohibition, but his motion lost.[126] By the time Miss Tyler raised the banner, Congress had already spent five and one-half hours on the Constitution, and went back at seven that evening for another four.[127] Through all of it they only completed the balance of Sections 6 and 7 of Article I, giving the President the line item veto, and the first two clauses of Section 8 that dealt with taxes and duties. Setting aside his personal animosity toward Davis the man, Withers declared that their President should be a man of "back bone" with at least the power to defeat stuffing appropriations bills. He would get the line veto.[128] They devoted almost the entire evening to wrangling over an amendment proposed by Rhett to prohibit Congress from granting bounties from the Treasury, and excluding taxes or levies being imposed on foreign trade in order to foster any domestic industry. In the end he got his way, but only after hours of debate over wording. They barely reached the third clause before they adjourned.[129]

That evening most of them waited to hear what the wires said of Lincoln's inaugural. "It will affect no one here," Tom Cobb averred. "It matters not what it contains."[130] His brother thought the address a declaration of war, but still believed that Lincoln would in the end negotiate for a peaceful separation after any clash of arms. The first battle, if any, would be the last.[131] But if war did come, Cobb would be prepared. Colonel Samuel Colt of Hartford, Connecticut, obviously willing to sell guns to any who would buy, had sent Cobb a handsome cased revolver, and another for his wife, boxed to look like a book, bound in leather, and titled, *Colt on the Constitution, Higher Law & Irrepressible Conflict.*[132]

The fatigue told on the delegates when they assembled again March 5. Stephens smoked contentedly one of the thousand new cigars recently made for him, and in the open session Howell Cobb flirtatiously played Romeo and Juliet scenes for amusement with a young lady in the balcony, but the closing of the doors inevitably brought them back to the relentless seriousness of their work.[133] Now they hit their hardest day yet. It started with Toombs's amendment to the third clause of Section 8 covering regulation of commerce with foreign nations and among the several states. This is where Toombs proposed adding a prohibition of so-called "internal improvements."[134] It had been a hot issue in the South for decades, this notion of spending taxes and duties collected in one state to enhance or encourage the commerce of another. By and large, Southerners believed that work on Charleston Harbor should be paid for by South Carolina; Louisiana should pay for enhancements to the docks in New Orleans. Yet there were logical exceptions, such as navigational lights and buoys. It was so thorny a problem that Stephens came prepared to move its postponement until the end of their deliberations, and the rest agreed.

Better progress ensued as they moved on through naturalization, bankruptcies, coinage, and counterfeiting. The provision for the Post Office to be self-supporting passed unchanged but for the addition of Miles's proposed March 1, 1863, deadline. Patents and copyrights, lower courts, and more passed without much debate. But then they came to the first clause of Section 9, and it stopped them cold. "The importation of negroes of the African race, from any foreign country other than the slaveholding States of the United States of America, is hereby forbidden," it said, "and Congress is required to pass such laws as shall effectually prevent the same."[135]

They must face slavery, the gorgon that more than anything else brought them there. "Here we have in charge the solution of the greatest problem of the ages," Hammond of South Carolina had said a few days before. "We are here two races—white and black—now both equally American, holding each other in the closest embrace and utterly unable to extricate ourselves from it. A problem so difficult, so complicated, and so momentous never was placed in charge of any portion of *Mankind*. And on its solution rests our all."[136] When Hammond's friend Boyce first arrived in Montgomery he found that none of the delegates he met so far favored a reopening of the slave trade.[137] Indeed, Alabama, for one, specifically instructed its men to insist upon a prohibition of the foreign trade, and Yancey himself proposed it as a lure to Virginia and the Border States.[138] From all sides friends advised the delegates to place a prohibition in their Constitution.[139] Yet as Rhett and others argued, to do so implied a stigma on an institution of which they could be justly proud. Smith of Alabama pointed out that their slaves were a "civilized appendage to the family relation," while their African cousins still lived a brutish existence. "Improved, civilized, hardy and happy laborers," their chattels owed all of their elevation to an institution that took them from barbarity and gave them such of training and education as they were capable of absorbing, and at the same time fed, clothed, housed, and cared for unto the grave a people that their masters agreed would be incapable of caring for themselves.[140] The *Mercury*, speaking for Rhett, became almost rabid at the notion of a prohibition.

Now Rhett struck at the provision that he could not keep out of the draft, moving to eliminate and replace it only with a tentative assertion that Congress "may" prohibit. Chesnut offered a variant aimed at achieving the same thing, but the majority against them became immediately apparent when South Carolina stood alone in opposing both changes being tabled. Then Waul moved a variant of the prohibition, and that, too, went on the table. Faced by overwhelming force against their position, the South Carolinians gave up, but only after the debate grew more heated than in past days, and the engendering of some of the first truly harsh opinions. Tom Cobb declared the Texans conceited, then said the same of Harris of Mississippi, pronouncing his entire delegation the weakest there.[141] Despite their vows of secrecy, word of this debate got out, leading a somewhat tasteless New Orleans reporter to suggest that "the lover of 'scenes' would like the nigger question reopened on the floor of this Congressional Hall."[142]

If that were not enough for one day, next they faced the clause covering appropriations, and spent the rest of the day on it without resolution. Stephens complained of being "bored to death with long useless speeches," and worse saw feeling and temper exhibited on the floor.[143] Tom Cobb felt exasperated, too, and wondered that "Lord knows when we shall get through."[144] Hill was going on far too long now, and showing that tendency to get carried by the swell of his own arguments into increasing invective and spleen. Admiring his ability as a speaker, still Oldham of Texas felt troubled by Hill's "feelings and prejudices."[145]

"We are worked very hard, too hard to have time for anything but work," Barry complained that night. All of his writing he had to do in the chamber while the debates proceeded, and still his business piled up. At least his wife was with him there, but it was cold cheer for their son was deathly ill with measles. "We are all anxious to get home," he mused, but "when we shall be able to do so, is uncertain."[146] "I don't know what to do, I am worn out," Tom Cobb wrote. Already he had decided that when they finished he would not even stay around to sign his name to the Constitution, but would go home immediately. Despairing of when that might be, he advised Marion "don't look for me till you see me."[147] Brother Howell shared the exasperation. He gave up on finishing with the Constitution by the end of the week, a situation made worse by the heat, though only he felt it. The temperatures never rose above sixty degrees in fact, but with his girth and the long shuffle up Market every morning, the genial president of the Congress overheated.[148] Warmth of one kind or another seemed to be spreading in the Congress hall.

By now they all dreaded the march up Market. Sometimes only Howell Cobb seemed able to muster cheer. "Cobb bears himself proudly in the chair," said one reporter, "but there is a rollicking bullishness about him which suggests the presidency of a boxing club."[149] Given the timing of yesterday's hot debate on the slave trade, it was an inopportune time for Curry to introduce in open session a resolution to look into prohibiting slave trade with the United States except in cases of people moving into the Confederacy and bringing their blacks with them.[150] Yet the resolution passed, and in ten days the judiciary committee would report a bill making such a prohibition. In fact, even the ardent proponents of slavery in time agreed that it was a stern inducement to the Border States. If they did not join soon, they could be prevented from selling their slaves to fellow slave states,[151] though some warned not to push too hard just yet. "Virginia, to be moved at all," said one friend of the cause, "must not be threatened."[152]

Surprisingly, when they went into convention, the appropriation issue passed without undue trouble when Curry proposed a revised version that almost word for word repeated the original draft, except that any two-thirds vote to appropriate on its own volition must be done by voice vote, every man going on the record. A series of clauses cleared without incident after that, until Boyce arose to take up where Chesnut left off in the original committee. He moved a new amendment specifically recognizing the right of any state to secede from the Confederacy. Once again, the issue was too hot, and South Carolina stood alone in opposition when the other six states tabled the proposition.[153] Similarly an extremist proposal by Rhett that any Confederate state abolishing slavery should be expelled found itself on the table. With that, and the postponement of an issue of states collecting duties, they finally finished with Article I, after almost six days of debate.

But they were not yet done for the day. Now came that knotty problem of how to elect a president. Nothing in all their deliberations provoked more discussion with less resolution.[154] None liked the electoral college, and yet they also for the most part held a prejudice against direct popular election. Universal male suffrage cost time and money, thought secessionist Edmund Ruffin, and tended to empower an uneducated electorate easily duped by demagogues.[155] Curry thought popular elections actually encouraged the growth of parties, which they all professed a wish to see abolished.[156] Smith of Alabama confessed that reforming the existing system would be "nice and difficult."[157]

In the end, they gave up. After agreeing easily on a single six-year term for the two executive offices—Rhett's proposal for reeligibility after an interim term being defeated—the minute they hit the five clauses in Article II, Section 1 that covered election they stopped cold. Sensing an impasse, Stephens immediately moved that this issue, too, be postponed until the end, to which they agreed. That done, they easily covered a little more business on eligibility for the presidency, requiring that he be a natural-born citizen of one of the Confederate

States at the time of his election, or else a citizen of one of them at the time of adoption of the Constitution, thirty-five years old, and at least fourteen years a resident within the limits of the nation as constituted at the time of his election.

Before they finished, exhausted, the ever-perceptive Harris moved appointing a select committee of one member from each state to take in hand the several matters now postponed. It was evident that they could still logjam in their final deliberations with so many unresolved issues awaiting them. The committee might perhaps reach some solutions to put before the convention to save time. Everyone agreed.[158]

Curry thought the debate thus far "sparkling, earnest, learned," and found Rhett, Toombs, Hill, Smith, Tom Cobb, Little Aleck, and Conrad the most imposing and effective.[159] Rhett, despite his disappointments in several issues, confessed to his *Mercury* reporter that they were all working hard. "Perhaps no set of men ever applied themselves more diligently," the journalist wrote that evening. Rhett may also have intimated that he did not yet admit complete defeat on the apportionment issue, hoping still to get slaves counted for what he called "full representation."[160] Barry even wrote to Pettus to be ready to call the Mississippi convention within two weeks to work for a speedy ratification.[161] That evening, meeting informally, a number of the delegates with second thoughts discussed the postponed issues, and their uneasiness with risking what the select committee might present. They may have started evolving compromises of their own.[162]

While they congratulated themselves in their exhaustion, already some feared another issue due to arise soon, the matter of admission of new states. Everyone saw George N. Sanders, the New York political adventurer and journalist, in town. "A doubtful man," one observer called him, "always shifting with prevailing winds and generally found associated with the men of force and violence."[163] Heavily tied to Stephen Douglas, he came, they believed, to work for reconstruction of the Union under the new Confederate constitution. "A Wily, good natured politician, mixed up in everybody's business," one reporter said of Sanders. He turned up at every dinner, spoke casually with the President, knew congressmen intimately and flaunted his acquaintance, and shook all the right hands. Yet some thought him to be "cunning as a fox," and intent on influencing the government to admit free states.[164] Rumors already floated that New York and Pennsylvania might apply for admission.[165] Tom Cobb suspected now that Sanders was politicking members to get them to leave out any clause that might prohibit -

nonslaveholding states from applying. He believed that within his own delegation Toombs, Stephens, Wright, and Hill were for leaving the door open to such a possibility. The rest of the Georgians would oppose it, giving them a majority in the delegation. But he also believed that Davis himself favored the idea, and contemptuously dismissed the Mississippi delegation as "wax in his hands." There could be a hard fight on the matter. "I am much afraid of the results."[166] Howell Cobb, less fearful, quipped simply that the inept professional schemer Sanders had come "to take charge of the government."[167]

The morning frost dissipated long before the Congress went into convention once more on Thursday.[168] Immediately Keitt successfully moved that they drop Harris's motion for a select committee. That done, Hill then rose and tried to reawaken the issue of secession and nullification by jumping ahead to appending seven clauses to Article VII dealing with ratification. He proposed a strict denial of the right of nullification, but suggested that when any state challenged a law of the nation, its constitutionality should be tried by the Supreme Court. Withers and others bristled . The last thing they wanted was a high court once again "interpreting" a constitution. That was part of why they left the old compact.[169] Hill then suggested a remedy for states that could not abide some laws, and that was secession. Chesnut quickly stepped in with a revised amendment accomplishing the same thing, before both were cut off by the postponement of their proposal until Article VII came under consideration.[170] It had been a surprise move, perhaps intended as such, especially since secession had already been discussed and dispensed with earlier. They may have hoped to catch the convention off guard, but if so, they failed.

It was time to finish with the presidency, and they did so with the clause Rhett put into the report that allowed the chief executive to dismiss his cabinet officers at will, but guaranteed lesser employees four years in office unless the executive could show just cause to the Senate for dismissal. By restricting the president's power of removal they believed they could reform the remaining vestiges of the party-based spoils system.[171] Thus finishing with the president, they went on to several indecisive hours on the judiciary in Article III, and then Article IV covering public acts and some rights of citizenship.

Rhett and Withers bobbed up and down on the floor all day, considerably amusing Keitt and others. Complaining that the fire-eater wasted all his influence by making himself a nuisance and speaking too much while saying too little, Withers declared "why will he make such a fool of himself" as Rhett delivered yet one more speech. Sometime later, as Withers himself rambled on, Rhett commented to his colleagues, "Just listen to that old fool." The story passed quickly from ear to ear around the floor. "We have some fun even in our trouble," Little Aleck confessed, but still the endless debate wore on him and the rest. When Keitt came over to chat during the evening session, the South Carolinian quipped that he wished he could find a deaf man to put in his place. "If I could find a *"mute,"* Stephens shot back, "I should fall in love with him. Just look at Rhett now, speaking and no body listening."[172]

They all paid attention when it came to Section 2, clause 1. Here was their chance to eradicate forever the uncertainty that led to the famed Dred Scott decision just a few years before, when a slave sued for his freedom because his master had taken him to a state that did not recognize slavery. Hale, in one of the very few occasions he ever spoke in this chamber thus far, moved adding wording that protected a citizen's property in slaves, and his right to take it with him anywhere within the Confederacy. In the very next clause they enacted their own fugitive slave law, stipulating that any escaped black running from one state to another would not be free should that state not countenance slavery. Rather, all states were enjoined to assist in the apprehension and return of runaways. In these brief, uncontested clauses, the convention neatly dealt with two of the most divisive issues of the previous decade. The presence of either in the old Constitution, if adhered to, would have gone a long way toward shortcutting secession.[173]

Then they came at last to the subject of admitting new states. Miles made the very motion that Stephens and others feared, proposing that only states with slavery should be allowed admission. Immediately Little Aleck tried to stop the debate by having this matter postponed, but he failed. Harris successfully softened Miles's proposal by suggesting that nonslaveholding states could be admitted, but only by the unanimous vote of all other states in the Confederacy, but Rhett immediately got a vote to reconsider, effectively stopping Harris. Then, before the debate could gain heat, they adjourned.[174]

By now the journalists were almost frantic at the protracted closed-door sessions. On a typical morning they and some of the citizens gathered in Court Square and marched up Market to take their seats. They watched as the delegates came in, looking on the "boyish" face of Stephens, Toombs "glowing" from mirth or wine, Miles's "bright eye," and Howell Cobb's rotundity. But then Hooper would read the previous day's open doings—rather unintelligibly, thought one listener—a preacher said his prayer, and then a member declared that there was no business on the calendar and it was time for secret session. The spectators were barely warm in their seats before Cobb stood, pointed toward the doors, and sometimes playfully said that as they were "evidently designed as a place of entrance and exit," and since the visitors had used them for the one purpose, it was now time to use them for the other.[175]

Cobb's wit compensated little at all for their effort in coming there. "It's too bad," said the ladies, who grumbled the loudest as they trudged back down the stairs. More quietly, because of the ladies, the men groused that "it's a ——— shame."[176] It especially frustrated the newsmen. While granting that the secret sessions prevented posturing for the crowds, and probably discouraged "buncombe speeches and windy harangues"—Stephens and Keitt would have disagreed—they still chaffed at the absolute drought of news.[177] As a result, they could only guess. "I could give you a column every day of speculations," a Mobile reporter confessed, while others, forced to make up *something* to say, attested that "not a harsh word has been uttered in debate," or more perceptively, "if there be or has been, bickering and dissensions among the members of Congress, it is unknown to the outside world."[178] A desperate few like the reporter "Cato" working for the Cincinnati *Enquirer* did not even bother to make up news. He simply plagiarized his reports verbatim from the New Orleans *Daily Delta*.[179] Ironically, spurred by men like William Gilmore Simms not to "forget the interests of Literature," the Congress just the day before passed an international copyright law that Tom Cobb believed would protect them from "Yankee Literary Pirates." Maybe so, but it could not protect them against lazy or frustrated Northern journalists.[180]

March 8 proved to be no different for congressmen or spectators. The open session sped by in only minutes, followed by some work in secret session that included final settlement of congressional pay at $8 per day during sessions, and ten cents per mile for travel to and from home. Howell Cobb japed that they had to pass this in secret to keep it from local hotel keepers, who would otherwise adjust their daily bills to correspond exactly with the pay.[181]

Once into convention, they went immediately to statehood, commencing what Stephens would call the "Great Debate." The whole matter turned on the issue of whether new states could be free or only slave, and it got to the heart of the fear of reverse reconstruction that some thought George Sanders represented. To let free states join was to risk the slave states eventually becoming a minority once more, and even with a guarantee of slavery protection in the Constitution, once the free states were numerous enough they could enforce an amendment to the contrary. The South had not come all this way, surely, to create a framework in which within a few decades they could be back where they began?

The debate continued much of the day, Stephens himself making what he considered the best speech since his arrival in Montgomery, and carrying a slim majority with him on the motion involved.[182] Florida and South Carolina consistently struggled to keep the prohibition of free states in the document, and the rest just as consistently defeated them. It came as a great disappointment to Tom Cobb, because Kenan failed to attend that day's session—perhaps unable to make up his mind. His absence meant Georgia's delegates split evenly for and against, nullifying its vote, though it would not have mattered, for every time a clear majority of four states voted against the exclusion of free states. But it was closer than it looked. Texas consistently decided its vote by three-to-two voice ballots, and Ochiltree wavered back and forth. Had Kenan been present and sided with the Cobbs, and had Ochiltree come around, they would have had the four state majority necessary to enact the restriction. No wonder Stephens sat uneasy in his chair most of the day. "We had the most exciting debates of any in the convention," he said that night, yet he trembled for fear that someone would still move to reconsider before they finished with the Constitution.[183]

In the end they settled for almost exactly the same language that came from the Committee of Twelve. After the time spent on the statehood issue, the rest of the day seemed a whirlwind. They passed speedily over the rest of Articles IV and V, and all of Article VI but the final clause, and closed the evening at nine-fifteen with a resolution to appoint a committee of three to go over all of their changes to date with a view to proper grammar and punctuation, and have it printed for final revision.[184] Rapidly they all left but Hooper, Clitherall, Dixon, and the printer Reid, who sat at their tables working on their journals. Stephens alone remained of the delegates, waiting for the hack he had ordered for ten o'clock hardly expecting to finish early. In the dark and heavy rain he was not about to walk back to Mrs. Cleveland's. Instead he sat and ruminated over the day's debates. He still felt terrible anxiety, for fear that the statehood issue could explode again tomorrow when they turned their attention to the postponed matters—apportionment, internal improvements, the mode of presidential election, and a prohibition against states entering individually into treaties. He had seen so much disagreement on all of them, as well as a tendency by some to bring up other matters already settled. Howell Cobb ran the convention with a pretty loose hand, and it could all get out of control on the next day with so many divisive issues before them. Little Aleck prayed that night that there would be no debate on the morrow, just yea or nay votes. But he knew better.[185]

The morning of March 9 rumors flew through Montgomery that the Constitution might be finished that day, and the fair weather seemed to be a good omen.[186] Those looking for portents could find others, however, like the crumbling wrought iron fence around the capitol grounds, symbolic perhaps of disintegration ahead for their new nation if the document they debated were not well done.[187] The Vice President needed no signs and portents. He came into the hall with a knot in his stomach that remained all day, wondering if they would get safely through the Constitution.[188]

On every desk Hooper placed a draft printed overnight containing all of their changes to date, and as the delegates looked over it, the debates began anew.[189] They dealt quickly with a minor technicality in presidential eligibility, and then Keitt went after apportionment once more. Happily, with little debate the motion to switch from enumerating slaves at three-fifth to full representation lost quickly, and they spent the major share of their time then dealing with the determination of the number of representatives. The 50,000 figure finally stayed in, but only after much argument that they should go to 30,000 or even 70,000 or 80,000. South Carolina, always the prime mover in trying to gain greater representation, then sought to change the stipulation in the clause that specified the number of congressmen each state should have until the next census. Allowed six, Chesnut moved for a seventh, but lost. As a sop to the Palmetto State, Barry generously moved that they be given nine, which also lost. In the end, they left it as written and moved on.

That brought them to the matter of internal improvements. Toombs had the prevailing amendment on the floor, but agreed to drop it for one Rhett now proposed, and for which he had been politicking, thinking that he could produce the crucial vote of Alabama to give him the majority. In fact, he hardly needed to bother.[190] Except for the addition of language allowing Congress to appropriate money for navigational safety on the coastlines and to maintain harbors and keep river channels clear, Rhett's prohibition of spending to encourage industry sailed through with only Texas voting in opposition. To some it seemed a milestone. "This clause alone is worth all the sacrifice we may be called on to encounter in the great revolution in which we are engaged," declared Shorter and Reid.[191]

On prohibiting states from entering into treaties, Rhett had outstanding the last attempt to add an amendment expelling any state that should abolish slavery. At first he withdrew it, but only so Perkins could reintroduce it himself. Immediately Stephens moved to kill it by suggesting they table the amendment. Knowing himself a lightning rod for opposition, Rhett may well have agreed beforehand to back away personally from some of his pet issues in the hope that others might get them through unfettered by the personal animus he inspired. But it did not work this time, though thanks only to Florida and Louisiana being evenly divided, and thereby unable to influence the vote. Stephens's motion lost, but seeing the close margin, Perkins withdrew his amendment, and then one of Barry's to the same effect came to the floor. Now Stephens demanded the question and an immediate ballot without debate. The tardy Owens arrived in time for this vote, which put Florida in favor of the amendment, making it three states for and three against. Only the divided vote of Louisiana therefore resulted in the defeat of the measure. Little Aleck felt a little of his anxiety slip away. They were skirting the dangerous issues, though still only by dangerously slim margins. When statehood arose next, Shorter finally proposed a simple two-thirds vote in both House and Senate that passed without much debate, the Rhett forces having seen themselves so consistently defeated that there remained no point in pressing the exclusion of free states further.

Greatly to Stephens's relief—and surely that of others—the issue of electing the president did not come up at all. By common consent, they did not like the electoral college system, but they could devise nothing better. They simply let it alone, trusting that later, with more leisure, another convention might solve the problem.[192] Bob Smith confessed that it might simply be a necessary evil with which they must live.[193] Everybody wanted a change, he said, but "we hurried over the subject." He would not have minded going to a parliamentary system, or even a hereditary presidency.[194] Curry perhaps took it hardest of all. "It will surely breed mischief," he said, "and introduce anew some of the most obnoxious practices of former parties." He worried that in time the presidency might become "an object of greedy and unscrupulous ambition."[195] But of course, that would only matter if the Confederacy outlived its first president. With this out of the way, they were done. Though some wanted a vote on the final draft immediately, they decided to wait for the morrow and the printing of a new version incorporating all of the last changes.[196]

The day had been an agony for Little Aleck. "I am constantly suspended between hope and fear for the future," he confessed. Even now, he felt ambivalent about their final Constitution. He did not like all of its provisions, and lamented omission of some of his pets like seats for cabinet ministers. Privately he confessed that, all in all, he preferred the old United States Constitution. "I do not think we have improved upon it," he told Linton. In retrospect, he felt their main achievement may have been in keeping the new document from being even worse. And he could not but be disturbed by the tenor of some of the debate. He saw factions slowly starting to form, chiefly the hardline ultra slavery people and the extreme state rights element, though their memberships were not identical. For the moment, both centered around South Carolina, but each found adherents in the other delegations. The group dedicated to keeping the presidency as weak as possible drew membership from both, and with characters like Withers, Rhett, and Tom Cobb aboard, seemed clouded as to whether their stance was policy or just aversion to Jefferson Davis. Out of all this could grow what they all dreaded: parties. "There are some very bad passions and tempers beginning to develop themselves here," he mused. "I see many dangers and breakers ahead."[197]

In fact, what they achieved in the Permanent Constitution was a decidedly curious mix of looks backward, forward, and sideways. The general trend in the old Union had been toward expanding power of government and the presidency. Here they turned back the clock. In several of the articles curbs went up to halt the potential spread of usurpation. They explicitly prohibited internal improvements or the spending of public monies for the encouragement of industry, and solidified it by denying themselves the power to create appropriations. Here, too, they tied the president's hands in distributing—or more accurately *redistributing*—spoils. They limited him to one term to end any dynastic pretensions or the danger a single administration holding power long enough to start aggrandizing itself.

At the same time, however, they looked ahead, profiting by decades of experience under the old Constitution. They struck for civil service reform. They paid at least lip service to the parliamentary notion of granting cabinet heads a seat in Congress at their pleasure, and four years later would actually do so, thus to allow the president to make his views known, as well as to hold him—through his ministers—accountable. They enacted a positive reform with the line item veto, putting an end to bills loaded with pork barrel. They made at least a start toward free trade and the elimination of protective tariffs, and required that their post office pay its own way. And then there were the other areas in which they simply adopted the status quo. Unable to find a better way of electing their president, they kept the old one. They made property in slaves and the right to taken them anywhere emphatic parts of their charter, and with them a firm fugitive slave law.

And at the end, for all their reverence for the sanctity of a constitution, they made it easier to amend theirs than the old Constitution. A mere three states could call for Congress to summon a constitutional convention to address amendments, and after that only two-thirds of the states had to ratify for the amendment to become law. Significantly, Congress itself could not generate amendments. The old system required two-thirds of the states to get an amendment before Congress, and then three-fourths of them to ratify. But then, knowing that their work of reform was not complete in this first effort, the Montgomery framers expected to go back. Still, it is at least ironic that they put in place a mechanism to make their charter marginally more responsive to the needs of the moment than the one on which it was modeled. Taken altogether, considering the time in which they did it, and the pressures under which they worked, these men produced a strikingly good document.

The next day was almost anticlimax. Hooper delivered the final copies printed overnight by Shorter and Reid, who earned their $6 per page.[198] After an uneventful open session, they went into secret session, and then into convention. John Hemphill of Texas, a preacherish-looking fellow nicknamed "Gutta Percha" because of his leathery skin, finally arrived just in time for the vote.[199] But Tom Cobb, Bartow, and Keitt left that morning to go home, after getting permission for their affirmative votes to be recorded in their absence. Hooper read the final draft to them for the formal third time. Then came the vote, and Georgia asked that each man speak for himself. One by one, to a man, they stood and said "yea," and it was done.[200]

The word spread immediately. Barry wrote to Governor Pettus telling him to assemble the state convention as quickly as possible, promising that the new Constitution should give general satisfaction.[201] Quickly members leaked word of their action to the press, and even provided some details of the new features such as the six-year term, the curtailment of the spoils system, and the appropriations reforms.[202] Naturally the journalists complained that they could not get more just yet. "Politicians are very anxious that their speeches should be given to the public," said a Georgia reporter the next day, "yet how rare it is to find one willing to impart the result of his studies."[203] The full text of the Constitution finally reached the public on March 12, when Shorter and Reid provided their last, final version, and soon thereafter it appeared in newspapers all across the Confederacy.[204] Howell Cobb, quite the souvenir collector, kept the first copy from the press for himself.[205] At the same time he sent copies to all of the state conventions, who would now begin their deliberations on ratification. The whole process was not over just yet.[206]

Curry, sometimes guilty of saying foolish things, declared that "the new government sprang forth as if by magic."[207] Nothing could have been further from the truth. There had been nothing easy about it. They were all dog tired, and with at least several days of legislative work yet to do before adjournment, each counted the days.[208] "I have never seen more intelligent looking men," a visitor said of the Congress just finished with this great work.[209] One of the journalists from Atlanta agreed, and ascribed it to the fact that many of the delegates were bald. "This is an indication of talent," he asserted, noting the exceptions of the well-maned Toombs and Howell Cobb. "You will seldom find a man of much sense who is not deficient as to his capillary qualifications."[210] Whatever they had achieved came more from hard effort, compromise, and restrained passions than from tonsorial poverty, however. Only half in jest, Little Aleck complained to a friend of the "*big* work and *little* pay," and when an office seeker cornered him outside the Exchange begging for a remunerative position that required little effort, Stephens said he had none to offer, but if the man would like to have his job as vice president and member of Congress "it would be cheerfully bestowed."[211]

They rushed through their last work with speed that seemed driven by the wind compared to the endless constitutional debates. With all of the initial organization of the government behind them, Barnwell turned now to establishing a committee to revise the United States statutes that they had adopted wholesale earlier, intending to prepare a digest of those applicable to the Confederacy. They paid more specific attention to duties, revising those on some raw materials downward, and imposing one on importation of slaves from the United States. They touched on the matter of public lands, proposing that the states cede to the government as much of the former United States acreage in their boundaries as would be needed for timber for naval needs, but the big forest states defeated the motion. Some of their longest debates of the session came over judicial matters and the jurisdiction of the courts, which they resolved without incident. A boon came on March 11 when Louisiana turned over $369,267.46 from its state bullion fund, and another $147,519.66 in customs receipts since the first of the year in New Orleans. Feeling defensive that South Carolina could not do the same, Withers stood and apologized for his state.[212]

Indeed, such little humor as was left to them came from Withers in these last days. The day after the vote on the Constitution, he arose in public session to declare that the only thing he had been able to produce out of his own brains was a resolution to print the laws of Congress and give a copy to each member. To the accompaniment of guffaws from the floor he went on to add that by that means "I will be able to know what I have been doing since I have been here, for I cannot recollect it all without such assistance. I shall also have an opportunity to repent of my sins and iniquities, if I have committed any."[213] A few, perhaps, even got a mild chuckle out of religious zealot Tom Cobb's proposal that they abolish any carriage of the mails on Sundays. "May God help me if I am doing his Will," he declared, which no doubt prompted Harris to recall his suspicion of men doing the Lord's work. Kenner answered Cobb, however, and spoke persuasively of the American ideal of freedom of conscience and the separation of church and state, and that settled the matter.[214]

By March 13 many of the members were gone, on their way to their states to take part in the ratification conventions. Florida left entirely, and on that day fewer than twenty of the others sat in the hall.[215] "Our Congress to-day looked rather thin," observed one reporter, and when Waul delivered a long speech of little consequence, he did it to an almost empty house.[216] The legislation flew past those who remained: duties, appropriations, nominations to approve, the appointment of Clitherall as registrar of the treasury, appointments in the army and navy to confirm. On March 15 Davis signed twelve acts and one resolution, with fifteen more acts and three additional resolutions the next day.[217]

Good news came to those present on March 12 when the Alabama convention ratified the Constitution. Expecting it to be ready to consider earlier, the members had been in session a week waiting. The cooperationists, who said suddenly they found themselves under a new government, complained in amazement "who did this?" "They find themselves in the hands of a new Congress," they went on, "and exclaim—who elected this new Congress?"[218] But the issue was never in doubt. The night before convening to discuss the document, its friends in the convention caucused, counted votes, and knew they could push it through. The next day it passed by 87 to 5.[219]

Then came the last day, March 16. During the open session Hooper brought forward the enrolled Constitution written on parchment twenty-seven inches wide and twelve feet long. Cobb signed first, followed by the delegates in the same order as they signed the previous provisional document. Many were absent. Only two each from Alabama and Georgia signed today, and one from Louisiana.[220] Those missing would be allowed to sign later. Rhett moved Hooper should have a lithographed copy prepared to be sent to each of the states as soon as possible. He later applied for the publication of the journals of their debates on the document, but found himself once more in the minority. Their deliberations must remain secret, relaxing the confidentiality only on so much as they could use to help argue for ratification in their state conventions. Grudgingly he yielded yet again. South Carolina, it seemed, would never get to read what he was saying.[221]

Still, in a good spirit, and no doubt relieved to be going home, Rhett also moved a resolution of thanks to Howell Cobb for his performance as president of Congress. Cobb could not fail to be moved. "I have never seen such a body assembled as the one over which your partiality has called me to preside." He complimented them on their grueling work and dedication, and on their good behavior. "We rest for a period from our labors to receive the judgment of our constituents," he continued, pointing out that Alabama had already given her approval, and then his own Georgia just now. Well done, he said, well done. Following their secret session to approve last-minute legislation, it was time to adjourn. Congress would meet again on the second Monday in May.[222]

They evaporated from the city so fast that townspeople hardly noticed their passing. The journalists did, however. "There will be no business for editors and newspapers," a reporter observed.[223] They, too, could go home for awhile. Little Aleck packed his bags, took the free pass sent him by a railroad president, and with Pierce in tow went back to the Montgomery & West Point depot to start the trip east. Packed into his valise were more than two hundred letters he still had not found time to answer. Once at Liberty Hill, with Rio at his feet, he could get around to them.[224] Already, as the word spread of what they had done in that scant six weeks, the plaudits began. "All honor & glory to that wise & noble Convention," the crusty Hammond wrote from the even crustier South Carolina. And Howell Cobb, on his way home, could not resist a bit of prideful gloating as he wrote to his old friend, now ex-President James Buchanan. They had been "eminently successful," he said

"Providence has smiled upon us."[225]

CHAPTER ELEVEN

ONE MASS OF VULGARITY & FINERY & HONOR

———•—★—•——

"TELL ME WHAT SORT OF A PLACE Montgomery is," a South Carolina friend asked Porcher Miles the day before Davis's inauguration; "what sort of capital it will make,"[1] For all their anxiety to escape the evils of the old Union, the Founding Fathers of the Confederacy and the people who looked to them all shared a burning anxiety to retain much of what they left behind. They had a Constitution now, and one not markedly different from the old one. They had a president and Congress, too, the latter truly representative of the interests of the South, while even Rhett would have conceded Davis to be a sounder chief executive than Lincoln. Their government, though embryonic, progressed rapidly, and in virtually the mirror image of the old. But all across the new Confederacy men and women were curious about one other vestige of nationhood, their capital. Did Montgomery possess the dignity becoming of a city of state? With the nation still in formation, and with other states surely yet to come, would the capital even remain there, and should it? Could Montgomery escape all of the degeneration, political and moral, that in their imaginations so characterized Washington? A capital was a symbol to Americans. To these Southern Americans Washington symbolized the excesses and corruption of a broken down Union. Could Montgomery represent something better?

Miles's friend might better have asked his question of one of the citizens of the city, yet for them the fact of being a capital proved so unsettling that their answer might not have been any more perceptive than Miles's. "We can hardly realize our position; so suddenly, strangely, new," the Reverend Manly confessed. "Instead of being in the outskirts of creation, very near the point of *sundown*, we find ourselves just in the centre; & ourselves the object of attention every where."

Montgomery was accustomed to looking at the affairs of the great world from afar. "We are ourselves *making history*, & observing momentous issues so rapidly, that we hardly pay attention today, to the events of yesterday." Barely a week after he delivered the invocation at the inauguration, he thought that stirring day so distant that "we hardly remember much about it."[2]

Visitors formed differing opinions of the impact of Montgomery's new status. Some thought the city hardly seemed to "bustle" at all, contrary to prevailing stories.[3] "Montgomery is dull," complained a Charlestonian: "dull to the citizens, dull to the traders, dull to the strangers, and dull to everyone else but the hotel keepers and the heads of the various departments."[4] Another decided that "this is perhaps the dullest place about now in the Confederate States."[5] Others, by far the majority, saw nothing but activity. William Smith decided that "Montgomery is assuming the appearance of a Metropolis."[6] Others commented on the city being full of "strangers," as they called most visitors. Some few of those here still favored reunion with guarantees, but most professed absolute Southern independence.[7] Many of the arrivals wore the uniforms of their recent United States service, lending a martial air to the hotel parlors and barrooms.[8] But the small army of office seekers still composed the majority. The loitering about of the "lobby vultures" reminded townspeople of Lazarus of the Bible, who waited about a rich man's table for crumbs to fall. One hopeful joked that he intended to demand that Davis give him a juicy diplomatic posting to England. If refused, then he would tell the President to give him "an old suit of his clothes and let me go home."[9]

By the time Congress adjourned and the members departed, most of the office seekers left, too, yet still several hundred stayed, forlorn but hopeful fellows whom a New Orleans reporter found "principally occupied in affording consolation to each other."[10] With them remained the actual townspeople who also hoped to garner some kind of emolument, but already it was evident that the only locals destined to get positions were those enjoying influence with the politicians.[11]

The flood of people during February and March literally thronged the hotels, making worse the fact that financial reverses briefly closed the Madison House just at the time when it could have made a fortune matching the exorbitant rates of the others.[12] Of the major hostelries, then, only the Exchange and Montgomery Hall remained open, and bursting to their eaves. "Every nook and corner of the city affording bed-room space is literally jammed," complained a reporter.[13] Another viewed it more as "camping out" than genteel living, with hotels, boardinghouses, apartments, and even stables and—he swore—henhouses occupied. Travelers of the time expected to sleep two abed, but when it came to three on a mattress, one with his boots still on and the other drunk, it was a bit much.[14] Between February 11 and 22 the Exchange alone registered 1,140 arrivals, and on March 3 the clerks turned away nearly fifty would-be guests.[15] Every place Watt and Lanier could stick another bed, or cot, or mattress, they plugged more people into their establishment. Poor William Smith shared a room with Jemison who "snores like a steam-boat," he complained. But he was getting used to it, and warned his wife that when he returned home she might have to lull him to sleep at night "with a *coffee-mill* or some such musical instrument."[16]

The parlors, barrooms, corridors, and the lobbies teemed with a promiscuous mix of the great and the grimy. Politicians stood out readily amid the throng of naive would-be luminaries.[17] Even through the dead hours of the night the lobby still buzzed with the talk of those too excited to sleep—or unable to find a bed. They stood in groups and clusters everywhere, talking their real and imagined state secrets, their state and regional wants and dreams, their personal feuds and private ambitions. The halls reeked of tobacco fumes while the carpet underfoot turned soggy from the juice of the chewers. Watchful lobby "vultures" lurked everywhere, ears cocked for a hint of a job, while what De Leon called "a rank growth" of newspaper correspondents skulked the halls like jackals sniffing for any morsel. Amid the sea of smoking, chewing, teeth-picking, gossiping humanity, Jefferson Davis noted something interesting. They all seemed to look alike to him. "They assimilate," he said—long straight hair pulled back behind their ears, stovepipe hats, flared bottom trousers, natty boots, kid gloves, and gold or silver headed canes. Far too many of them struck some observers as "dressed up and deluding nonentities."[18]

One step into the Exchange bar or billiard room instantly engulfed the visitor in a hum of conversation. "What a buzz," wrote Charles E. L. Stuart, a journalist recently arrived from New York. "That is the place for lusty talk and thirsty crowds."[19] Toombs was usually there, and probably Bartow, with a smattering from the other delegations. "Drinking there was general and sometimes deep," said De Leon, and with it came the inevitable jockeying for place and position.[20] Posturing and boasting accompanied the cocktails, and here Stuart and others heard for the first time expressions like "the damned Yankees—mere trash, sir. One Southerner can whip ten of them."[21] In the nearby dining room the experienced staff barely clattered their plates and cups as they served, and if they did, the constant murmur of conversation over-whelmed the sound as everyone ate and talked quickly, as if waiting for the next exciting news at any moment. Then out came the cigars and the toothpicks, and afterward a retreat to the lounge or a walk down Commerce to the promenade along the Alabama bluff. Wherever they went, the conversation moved with them, uninterrupted.[22]

Those inclined to less political pleasures haunted the Exchange par-lor, where the ladies held court, and the young and lovely especially did not want for attention. Reagan's assistant Henry Offutt spent quite a bit of time here, especially paying court to George N. Sanders's hand-some daughter, while some would have liked to remind him that he had a wife and daughter at home. As Miss Sanders sang at the piano, Offutt competed for her favor with two young correspondents, E. A. Banks of the Montgomery *Confederation* and J. Calhoun Moses of the Charleston *News*, and for the latter two, anyway, the rivalry was becom-ing increasingly unfriendly.[23] All in all, men who had seen the comings and goings at the great hotels in Washington looked on here with a profound sense of *déjà vu*. "In the evening you might almost imagine yourself in Willard's Hotel," wrote one experienced reporter: "the same talk—men in the same groups, and many of them the same men."[24]

Montgomery Hall mirrored the Exchange, though smaller in size and certainly less well managed. Mary Chesnut loathed the place, "that den of dirt and horror." The bed linen was old and soiled and she could find no fresh cream for her coffee.[25] Constitution Browne's wife stayed there only because she feared "the unknown sea of troubles called Montgomery housekeeping" even more, and too much to risk boarding with the servants of other people. Instead, she kept to her second floor room with its "asthmatic hair sofa" and an old painted rocker.[26] Most of the congressmen whose wives came to join them boarded here, and Mary Chesnut soon found that "the Hotel women are curious crea-tures."[27] They seemed to live their lives entirely subject to the schedules and interests of their husbands, dining with their friends and political associates, listening to their conversations, and apparently unable—or unwilling—to break with the social bonds formed back in Washington. Here the first hints of Confederate "official" society appeared, very much in the mold of the old circles they left behind with secession. In the evenings the Chesnuts, the Hills, Mallory, old Withers, and a few others inevitably dined together, exchanging much the same conversation as before. Hill and Withers joked about their youthful flirtations, even though Mrs. Hill sat nearby. Mallory told the best stories, though sometimes rather too lurid for the ladies. Still his basic refinement left him second only to Chesnut in the wives' regard. Withers engulfed the conversation far too much, prattling on over his personal hatreds and jealousies, especially Jefferson Davis. "There was a spice of malice in his composition," said a friend of Withers, "and if he disliked anyone, he showed it in a manner not to be mistaken."[28] Chesnut stayed reticent as was his wont, yet occasionally his wife had to smooth ruffled feelings among the others when discussion led to disagreement.[29]

After dinner they retired to the drawing room, and the interminable political conversation continued. Governor Moore liked to call here, no doubt because of the wives, whom he already scandalized by spending far too much time in public with the actress Maggie Mitchell. Governors, judges, senators, generals, and a host of others passed through those doors to enliven the conversation, along with the occasional crackpot and unwise Unionist. On March 12, while they relished the relief of the finished Constitution and speculated rather loudly on the meaning of Lincoln's inaugural and whether or not the Union would risk a costly fight, a woman who spent the morning playing "Yankee Doodle" on the piano until Withers made her stop, now burst through the folding doors at one end of the drawing room to yell "Yankees are no more mean and stingy than you are. People at the North are as good as people at the South."[30]

The conversation grew stale at times, and the flowery gallantries of the gentlemen wore thin. Surgeon General David De Leon unconsciously repeated the same flattery to Mary Chesnut four times, leading her to question whether "in the thousand compliments I hear there is one *grain* of truth." "Some of these great statesmen always tell me the same thing—and have been telling me the same thing ever since we came here." Even Boyce in her own delegation she found "studied" in his compliments.[31] Sadly, stale compliments were more than she got from her husband. Amid the mingled excitement and boredom of Montgomery, she confessed that after twenty years of marriage she hardly knew him any better than when they wed. At best, occasionally they understood each other. "Then up goes the Iron Wall once more." Chesnut did not like parties and often refused to go. Wanting a full twelve hours' sleep, when he did go out they had to return early. If Mary then sat too long talking in the parlor after he retired, her husband stamped on the floor for her to come to bed. Her solace came in the private journal that she started keeping in February. Even that troubled her, for she found it too engrossing, capturing a world around her and reducing it to her pages, with her intimate self too much a part of the picture. "I think this journal will be disadvantageous for me," she wrote the day the Constitution passed, "for I spend the time now like a spider spinning my own entrails."[32]

Indeed, the wives rapidly tired of Montgomery, Confederate society, and the Congress, especially the increasing signs of factions and jealousies. Asked when she would return to South Carolina, Mrs. Chesnut often replied "when this thing breaks up," shocking some that she spoke so disrespectfully of her husband's colleagues. "The farther away they send us from this Congress, the better I will like it," she confessed. "We are abusing one another as fiercely as ever we abused Yankees. It it is disheartening."[33] She thought they had left that kind of behavior behind them in Washington. Her uncle's increasingly intemperate harangues bored everyone, especially when Withers began calling for a military despot. While Mary thought the members of the Alabama convention presented a generally shabby and common portrait of humanity, the judge still embarrassed her and others when he ridiculed members of the body over dinner one evening, not knowing that several of its members sat at the same long table. Then Governor Moore bored her interminably until she could hardly curtail her yawns. This capital, and especially in Montgomery Hall, offered nothing to the taste of these bored, ignored, and somewhat spoiled plantation wives. They wanted to go home even more than their husbands.[34]

Yet the stay in Montgomery did not prove entirely dreary for some. Tom Cobb, of course, loathed it, especially feeling his homesickness when he walked the streets and looked in the faces of the passing schoolgirls, wishing to see again the smiles of his own two children.[35] Brother Howell fared well enough, especially with occasional shipments of gin from his son in Georgia.[36] Bob Toombs rather quickly recovered any lost composure after the election, and delighted in the company of Stephens, Crawford, Benjamin, the Charleston *News* reporter Moses, and other boarders at Mrs. Cleveland's.[37] Expecting his wife to join him, he spent the little free time allowed by Congress and cabinet in looking for a house to rent. He found one advertised at $2,000 a year, but when he tried to engage it the owner suddenly pushed the price up to $5,000, claiming that she had a "charitable object" in view.[38]

Little Aleck, in the small time allowed, found Montgomery about as comfortable as did the others, and certainly more so than the hotel dwellers, though he visited often for dinner at the Exchange. A lady staying there thought he had "more the appearance of a dead than a living one, until he begins to speak, when you forget entirely how ugly he is."[39] The casual visitors exhibited almost as much curiosity about this "little, sallow, dried up looking fellow" as they did over the President.[40] People called often to see him for no real purpose, and Mrs. Cleveland's slave waiter Livy formed the unfortunate habit of ushering anyone, high or low, day or night, directly into Little Aleck's bedroom.[41] Friends sent him several gallons of expensive brandy to ward off his several ailments, and having by his own admission "no duties to perform whatever as Vice President," he could indulge his little free time in visiting with Toombs and other friends.[42]

Occasionally he shopped, only to confirm that "prices in this city are exorbitant for everything." Out to purchase an umbrella that should have run $2.50, he had no choice but to hand over $5.50 since he was shopping in the rain. When he wanted a bath, he sent Pierce into town to buy a $5.00 tin bathing tub, and learned it cost $8.00. Rather than be overcharged, he found an old washtub in a yard that he could use for nothing.[43]

Among the other delegations life in the new capital ran much the same. A New Orleans reporter found that the congressmen led "a sort of happy bachelor life," with most of them away from wives and family. The Louisiana delegation rented a pretty little cottage where they sat before a jolly fireplace at the end of the day, and chatted into the night hours. Conrad led them in fireside geniality, and DeClouet held his own in the fun, though he was dreadfully homesick.[44] He pined over letters from his wife and daughter asking him to come home. "I am tired of this Convention or Congress, whatever it is called," his wife complained, while his little girl told her daddy to come back. "It is time for you to return because all of us desire to see you and then so you can fix the hall's clock which does not run."[45] DeClouet himself wanted his son Paul to join him in Montgomery for company, but the boy could not come.[46] Meanwhile, the Louisianians entertained, often inviting Stephens, Chesnut, and others to come for dinner, and in their off hours doing the occasional good deed like helping photographer Culver through a low period when McIntyre did not pay him.[47] Being worth more than one and a quarter million dollars, Sparrow could afford a little generosity. About the only member of their band cut off from the hospitality, in fact, was their delegation's secretary, who did not fit in the cottage, and could only find a room in a part of the city so remote that a reporter thought it necessary to hire a guide to find him.[48] The South Carolinians all inhabited the Exchange except for Chesnut and Withers. Fittingly, Memminger handled the financial arrangements with Watt and Lanier for their rooms and their common parlor. Rhett for some reason paid only half his share when he left, but Memminger seemed not to mind. He echoed around in that parlor by himself, and wrote to Miles after the adjournment that "I feel quite lonely since you all have left."[49]

Montgomery society accepted rather uneasily most of the temporary dwellers from the Congress. While some of the reporters lauded the "sumptuous and unaffected hospitality" of its citizens, De Leon and others detected "a trifle too much superiority" in the attitude of some of the older families, and under their breaths most of the city elite grumbled about this business turning their town "topsy-turvy" and threatening their moral character. In time their grumbling grew louder and less discreet.[50] The Alabamians manifested unquestioned patriotism for the cause itself, but in their private views toward the Congress, thought De Leon, "they regarded the individuals connected with it as social brigands come to rob their society of all that was good and pure."[51] It was a place, some said, of "considerable culture, more hospitality, and still more ambition, social and civic."[52]

Nevertheless, dozens of the lovely Italianate houses of the wealthy and influential opened their drawing rooms and their spacious grounds to the delegates.[53] At the governor's mansion on Lawrence Street, Moore occasionally entertained, though Mary Chesnut complained that "the old sinner has been making himself ridiculous with that little actress Maggie Mitchell."[54] The Georgia delegation dined every Sunday as guests of the Wares on Perry Street, while historian Albert Picket, Ben Fitzpatrick, railroad magnate Pollard, and others put on lavish banquets. Tom Watts's hospitality became known for the luxury and variety of its refreshments, and Judge John Phelan entertained President Davis himself, putting away a bottle of the wine used that evening to save for his daughter's wedding.[55]

The fifty-two-year-old Henry Hilliard and his wife Mary entertained often, and people came despite the whispered rumors of his involvement with another woman, and his son's intemperance.[56] More embarrassing, perhaps, would have been his long opposition to secession, and even after the government came here he still took no part in it, though quite loyal in his Southern sympathies.[57] Perhaps that is why Hilliard sent to Stephens papers showing that their positions had been identical before and after secession.[58] Certainly the Vice President did not hold Hilliard's previous politics against him, and he, like many another, enjoyed the hospitality of the Belgian-style home on Washington Street, including Hilliard's novel conceit of displaying the evening's desserts before the meal, on a table surrounded by flowers.[59]

For conviviality, however, none surpassed Judge Bibb's Moulton Street residence. Simple yet elegant, it never failed to attract all invited. Toombs, both Cobbs, the Chesnuts, Browne, Curry, Stephens, and more all came. Mary Chesnut might turn up her nose at some of the decor, sniffing that "I did not know the art of portrait painting could get *so low*," but even she had to set aside her South Carolina hauteur to confess that Bibb's parties put to the lie the notion that Montgomery was a dull town.[60]

Montgomery etiquette proved baffling at first to some of the visitors. Party invitations carried an injunction to "R.S.Y.P." that neither Stephens nor Toombs could figure out, until the latter suggested that it might stand for "Reply if you please." Since French was not a widely spoken language in central Alabama, Stephens decided that Toombs's was as good an answer as any, whether right or not.[61] More puzzling was the matter of punctuality—or rather the lack of it. Stephens accepted two party invitations set for February 28, one at Colonel J. J. Siebels's home at five o'clock, and another at Hilliard's set for eight. Between parties he intended to meet a friend at his lodgings at seven, and then return home after the second affair to meet another caller at ten. Little Aleck may have been trying to cram a lot into a single evening, but then he was a busy man, and one who took appointments seriously. That is where he came up against the Montgomery ethic of fashionable lateness. The party at Siebels' did not in the end get started until six, and by seven o'clock only three courses had passed over the table linen. Stephens announced to his host that he must leave, as did Toombs, and when the guests of honor departed the poor colonel was crestfallen. Memminger joked with Little Aleck that *he* would never keep him waiting, and the Vice President left with the rather irritating announcement that his rule was "punctuality to the moment if possible."

Getting back to Mrs. Cleveland's, Stephens met his caller, smoked one of his new cigars, read his mail, and then left to arrive at Hilliard's at precisely eight. During the next two hours the rest of the company came intermittently, and still not a morsel had been served. At ten, once again accompanied by Toombs, Stephens announced his departure to a second distressed host, and as the Georgians left they took with them the distinct impression that the townspeople left behind regarded them as social ignoramuses or, worse, "crackers." "They were most certainly the *'crackers'*," concluded the Vice President.[62]

The capital society always turned out well gilded for their affairs. "The women here crowd on all sail," Mrs. Chesnut wrote somewhat disparagingly. She believed they wore their jewelry, especially diamonds, from breakfast until bedtime, though chances were the town ladies just put on their finery when expecting to meet people from the more genteel—and definitely more snobbish—eastern seaboard.[63] As for what they set on the table, even Mary Chesnut could not complain. By March 1, and the coming of somewhat warmer weather, the mint going into leaf made for the first juleps.[64] After their cocktails, the guests sat to tables laid with finest silver service and cut glass, decorated by arrangements of fruit and flowers. Soup came first, usually oyster, followed by the fresh oysters over which everyone raved. The Mobile boat brought them up the river every day, and Montgomery's cooks used ingenuity in their preparation. Then came fish salad and perhaps fried oysters, perhaps grated ham or beef and sardines with waffles, acorn-fed turkey, followed by four other kinds of meats, along with rice, vegetables, jellies, pickles and condiments. When the waiters removed the tablecloth and spread a new one, the desserts came out, almost always headed by charlotte russe, sliced oranges with coconut, syllabubs, calves' feet jelly flavored with wine, fruit, nuts, raisins, and champagne.[65]

Over that gargantuan fare flowed the conversation, stiff and tentative at first. The women—Mary Chesnut thought them "dowdy" and "common place"—invariably asked "how do you like Montgomery." Swallowing a sense of her own hypocrisy, and silently beaming in pride that her gowns were inevitably the best present, she invariably answered "charmed."[66] Talk naturally started at politics, an interest shared by all, and visitors soon found that Montgomery's women seemed rather more violent and ultra in their beliefs than their husbands.[67] As the conversation gradually turned to gossip, on which so many of the guests had thrived in Washington, the Montgomery wives looked on in mock horror. Mallory, especially, always unloaded a fund of stories about who had been sleeping with whom, speaking of his own attentions to the notoriously unfaithful wife of a prominent Alabamian in Washington with a manner that suggested to some a not entirely innocent flirtation.[68]

No wonder the local society dames cringed and prayed that Montgomery might not be the permanent capital, else the politicians would corrupt it as they had Washington. All the signs were there: legions of lobbyists crowding the hotels and saloons, thousands of place seekers scrambling for office, greedy congressmen politicking for favors and influence, and around their fringes the inevitable corruption of drunkenness, gambling, and no doubt worse. The financial, political, and sexual scandals that often characterized the old capital could hardly be long in coming, and from experience people here knew that once out, that kind of embarrassment became quickly publicized. Montgomery had its own secrets. It did not want more, and feared that in attracting the eyes of the nation by its new status, it would also be held up to ridicule just like Washington.

But then as the parties lasted into the later hours, the Montgomery gossip began coming out. There came the common knowledge that the wealthy planter, forty-three-year-old Colonel John Siebels, Governor Moore's adjutant, was the father of the baby carried even then by the wife of local attorney Elisha Fair.[69] More shocking still was the whispered word that when Eliza Mayo married Judge Mays, their first child did not gestate for the socially acceptable nine months after the wedding. The father, everyone knew, was Henry Hilliard, whose wife carried a burning hatred for Mrs. Mays. "Was there ever such a world," Mary Chesnut marveled. Listening to all the talk of Montgomery suffering corrupting influences from hosting the capital "in a place where I have *seen* & heard so much," she concluded that "it can't be injured." "The people, I thought one mass of vulgarity & finery & honor." Sometimes it was a relief when a bore like Withers or the insufferable Philip Clayton walked over to interrupt the gossip. "What a *party*," she chuckled to herself at the Wares' one evening, "when we are glad to see Mr. Clayton."[70] "Social life moves in its accustomed channels," concluded a Macon reporter.[71]

One visitor who complained of nothing in Montgomery was the President. He found it "gay and handsome" on his arrival, and predicted that it "will not be an unpleasant residence." As soon as possible he intended to look for a house for his family.[72] Until then he occupied his cramped suite at the Exchange, which Stephens thought almost uninhabitable.[73] Almost immediately after his inauguration, however, others took the matter of housing out of Davis's hands. On February 22 Congress debated a motion to buy an executive mansion. Quickly the question changed from purchase to lease, with a $5,000 per year limit, and though South Carolina especially opposed as unconstitutional any emolument other than Davis's $25,000 salary, the rest of the Congress approved.[74] They soon settled on a fine two-story frame house at the southwest corner of Bibb and Washington, less than two hundred yards down Bibb from Government House. Built in the early 1830s, the house belonged at the moment to Colonel Edmund Harrison, who worked for Governor Moore selling state bonds.[75]

Everyone thought the house a splendid acquisition, leased at the full $5,000 per year. It sat back from the street, facing down Bibb looking toward Government House, with gardens and shrubbery about.[76] Erected on a slight terrace, the house and its modest front porch afforded a near-bird's-eye view of much of the city looking north and west to the river.[77] Everything was within easy walking distance—Government House and the Exchange just a block away, and St. John's Episcopal Church, which Davis would attend, only three and one-half blocks north on Madison. Everything about it was perfect but for three things. It was not immediately ready. Harrison's wife would not move out for some weeks yet, and Davis could not take possession before early April.[78] Then there were the South Carolinians, especially Rhett and Withers. The house became a fetish for the latter, who never ceased ranting day and night about this additional symbol of a regal presidency. In Congress he denounced the arrangement "with no little warmth and indignation," according to Rhett, while Rhett himself more quietly added his voice.[79] His *Mercury* damned the expenditure as "enormous," and he concluded that in voting for Davis—who came expecting to rent his own home and had nothing whatever to do with leasing this one—he had committed one of "the greatest errors of his life." Moreover, having spoken in opposition to the house, Rhett now assumed that Davis's pettiness matched his own (in some matters he was right) and concluded that he could not henceforth approach the President on any business because of what he called the "hired house affair."[80] So simple a matter as the renting of a home had managed to lay another plank on the platform of the amorphous party gradually growing not around policy, but opposition to the President.

The final problem with the Harrison home lay in a neat bit of irony and an architectural feature. Back in his days as secretary of war for President Pierce, Davis assumed oversight of the extension of the Capitol building, including the design and erection of its massive new dome, even now still under construction. Being Jefferson Davis, he involved himself in every last detail, even to the statue of Liberty to crown the dome. He saw an immediate problem with her, for the designer had placed on her head a conical Phrygian cap, which in ancient Rome symbolized, as he put it, "freedom obtained by manumission—that is, of *freed slaves*."[81] He could not have that in a nation half of whose states embraced slavery and opposed manumission or any other form of black freedom. Davis redesigned the headgear himself. But now when first he looked at the Harrison house that he was about to inhabit, he could hardly fail to notice the lovely cornice just beneath the eaves on all four sides. Between ornamental brackets ventilation holes allowed the attic to breathe and cool the house. Instead of simple grates, the builder had installed in the holes a series of cast iron devices in a design not to be seen on any other house in the South so far as anyone knew. Phrygian caps.

Until he moved in, however, he remained at the Exchange, dividing his office hours between the parlor next to his bedroom and his office at Government House. There was little inaccessible about him at the Exchange. He answered the gong calling guests to meals along with everyone else. Watt and Lanier set aside a special seat for him, but often he sat at the "ladies' table" for his meals, or huddled with Samuel Cooper and other officers over the paltry breakfast he allowed himself. No applause or ceremony attended his appearance in the doorway of the long dining room. Guests just stared respectfully as he walked to a seat. Looking about, he nodded slightly to acknowledge smiles. Congressmen, too, composed his dining company, many of them old friends from days in Washington with whom he felt he shared a "cointelligence" that augured well for their working together.[82]

He lived a lonely life at the Exchange until the whistle on the *Le Grande* announced on March 1 that Varina was arriving.[83] She came somewhat depressed, fearing what lay ahead for the two of them. "I deprecated his assuming the civil position," she confessed. She knew his hypersensitivity to criticism, his phobia about being misunderstood while still disdaining to explain himself to others. After all, these very things led him to leave her twice in their early marriage until she controlled her own strong will and subordinated it to her husband's nature.[84] No one knew better than she just how ill-suited to the presidency was Jefferson Davis.

All Montgomery felt curious about the new First Lady when she arrived. That same day Robert Smith escorted Mary Chesnut to pay a courtesy call, and the old friends immediately lost themselves in two hours of chat and Washington gossip.[85] Those not sufficiently well placed to call or secure an introduction could only ask others. "Do you see your mulatto cook over there," journalist Stuart replied to one inquiry. "Isn't she a fine looking woman in her way? Now just refine her form a little, lighten her color a little, give her straight hair, but do not interfere with her lips or with any other features in her face—then you can picture to yourself Mrs. Davis." She was, in short, "a fine, portly, graceful woman." However much she may have subdued herself around her husband, however, others saw the spirit and strength in her. "She frequently says strong things in strong words," said an acquaintance, "but, then, she has a strong mind." Many observers believed that Varina's "somewhat masculine grasp of thought" undeniably exerted considerable influence on Jefferson Davis, even in public affairs.[86]

Mary Chesnut's was only the first call. The next morning Stephens and Toombs came together, partly on business, but while there Varina gave Little Aleck one of her favorite remedies for neuralgia. Stephens felt slightly surprised and touched to hear her affectionately address her husband as "Jef," and him calling her "My dear," when so many statesmen observed a rigid formality with their wives in front of distinguished company.[87] When Howell Cobb called, she addressed him as "Burrow," an old nickname between them, its origins long lost.[88] For his part, Cobb thought he still saw some of her earlier depression, and perhaps a longing for Washington with its broader and more varied society. Indeed, for as much as Montgomery's society feared becoming another Washington, the men and women like the Davises who had spent their public lives in the old city looked always back to its society for their model in this new capital. The only really bright smile he got from her came when he suggested that if Virginia should secede, their success would be unstoppable, and by Christmas next she would be sitting in the White House in Washington itself.[89]

Since the Davises could not move into their house right away, Varina remained only a week. Besides, the house required minor alterations and she needed to get to Brierfield and select furniture to ship to Montgomery, as well as visit New Orleans to purchase more. Still social obligations demanded that she hold at least one levee to introduce herself and greet the dignitaries then filling the city. On March 6 the great and near-great flocked to the Exchange in the morning, though many of Montgomery's society remained aloof, partly out of uneasiness, not knowing quite how to act with a First Lady, and partly from the same suspicion that they turned on the other outsiders.[90] To all who came Varina appeared bland, cordial, polished, and dignified. None commented on her beauty, but all applauded her manners.[91] "She is well received, and admired more as a true Southern lady than as the wife of our First President," said the *Mercury* reporter, perhaps displaying a little bit of Rhett prejudice.[92] Davis himself attended only briefly, and then just long enough for Mary Chesnut to run away from him when he approached, in spite of the fact that she was helping Varina as hostess. "I am afraid of him, a little," she confessed to her diary.[93] Davis had little taste for levees and parties, at least during working hours. He told his wife he could "do either one duty or the other—give entertainments or administer the government."[94]

Yet when Varina left on March 7, the President faced still more entertainments on his own, and some he could not escape.[95] An unrefusable obligation came on March 11. Earlier the Alabama convention passed a resolution desiring to pay its respects as a body to the new President. This morning the Constitution cleared the Congress, and this same convention would immediately consider ratification. Davis had to see them. Speedily a reception was arranged at the Exchange, and sometime before the appointed hour the members of the convention assembled in the hotel reading room. Their president instructed them on their expected behavior. "It was extremely rich," an amused William Smith chuckled. They were to go into the parlor arm in arm in pairs to meet Davis, who would be standing in the opposite corner. "I will introduce each member as he approaches," their leader went on, "but as I am forgetful of names, each of you as he approaches must announce his name then I will introduce him to the President." As Smith almost doubled over from laughter at the officious speech, their president left to meet Davis first and Jemison started forming them in their pairs. Worse, to get them in step, Jemison marched them around the reading room a couple of times for practice, and then they filed arm in arm in their twos out into the hall toward the parlor.

Ladies already occupied the few seats in the room, while reporters and gawkers jammed their heads through the doors opposite, leaving only one opening for the delegates to enter and exit. When the first half of their line strode in, they filled the room, with the rest hanging about outside in the hallway. Only as the introductions were completed and Davis made a brief address were the delegates able to start moving again to allow the other half to cram themselves through the doorway as those ahead of them passed back out. Davis impressed them with a calm, dignified address. The cabinet were present, too, Benjamin making quite an impression by his social skills. The earlier foolishness of the assembling soon disappeared around a well-laden table in the dining room where wine flowed, toasts echoed, and Stephens, Governor Moore, and Howell Cobb made further speeches. "Wit and humor" sparkled around the board, according to a lucky reporter who got into the room, and even Smith confessed that "the Great reception" proved most agreeable.[96]

In the main, for Jefferson Davis life in Montgomery meant much work and little leisure, making even a reception like this a break that he needed, whether he realized the fact or not. Otherwise, after breakfast in the Exchange dining room, generally spent talking official business, he went to his parlor or his office down the street at nine, and did not leave until at least six, and often much later, silent and exhausted.[97] By the time he put in a request for his first quarter's salary at the end of March, few could question that he earned it.[98] Lost without his family around him, he cared little what he did in his sparse leisure.[99] Though not yet a communicant of any denomination, on Sunday mornings he frequently went with Memminger and Walker down to the corner of Madison and Perry to St. John's Episcopal, where Mrs. Cleveland worshiped, as it happened.[100] In the evenings he liked to walk up Perry Street toward the depot, then along the river bluff, occasionally drawing the cheers of passing groups of schoolboys.[101] Now and then he stopped at the Montgomery & West Point depot itself to visit with president Charles Pollard, no doubt on official business. Once while there he encountered first a clerk who must have been the only man in Montgomery not to have seen Davis before. He mistook him for a planter in from the country, and seeing Davis's fine watch chain, reached over and yanked out the time piece saying "fine watch—how'll you trade?" Just then Pollard came into the room and addressed his visitor as "President Davis." The shocked clerk dropped the item in Davis's lap, fell backward over his desk, and dived into his bookkeeping once more, too terrified to look up.[102]

The clerk was a little like Montgomery itself, fascinated by the brilliance of this new government, yet a bit afraid when once it realized what it all could mean. Just a few days after he attended the Exchange reception, William Smith observed that "Montgomery is assuming the appearance of a metropolis."[103] That was not so bad, but others, the outsiders, saw the city becoming "Washington all over again," with all its attendant pursuit of spoils "somewhat enhanced by the freshness of the scent."[104] No wonder the older ladies of the town predicted that one year of being the capital would "demoralize the society beyond purification."[105]

But the rest saw a wonderful opportunity. By the end of March people could see already that the city was growing, with new buildings going up, and the money brought into town by the delegates and the hangers-on helping boost Montgomery out of a recent business slump.[106] "It would be folly," said one editor, "to presume that we are not interested in the welfare and expansion of our city."[107] Her well-lit streets—at a cost of $7 per day for gas—invited building smart new offices and warehouses.[108] Her wire connections via the Southern Telegraph Company were good, and the president of the American Telegraph line even now visited Montgomery to investigate expanding its network. The line that came in on the old Three Mile Branch Road, ending in the second floor office in the Winter Building on Court Square, connected the city with the rest of the world.[109]

Already citizens talked of erecting a massive new hotel across from Government House at Commerce and Bibb, touted to be "the largest and most magnificent structure in the Southern States."[110] Montgomery's business leaders applied to Congress to have their city declared a port of entry, with all of the commercial advantages that could entail.[111] Mayor Noble and his city council increasingly turned their attention—at the embarrassing urging in print of the editors at times—to the need to make Montgomery *look* like a capital. They hired thirty-one slaves to perform street and sidewalk maintenance and improvement under street overseer William Williamson, while ordinances against obstructions on sidewalks and throwing refuse in the thoroughfares came under enforcement. Williamson went after merchants to remove the packing boxes that commonly blocked pedestrian traffic outside their shops, attacked the piles of construction trash beside Government House, and started efforts to remove a number of broken-down carriages and wagons fit only to burn that owners had abandoned on Washington Street, from the new executive mansion up to Church Street. Unfortunately, having sold their owners licenses, there was little else the council could do about the "infernal legions" of dogs who still harassed walkers by day, and bayed them to insomnia at night.[112]

The city council cleaned the trash out of the artesian wells, enforced the regulations against bathing in them, and began work on refurbishing the wharves. They equipped their fire company with handsome

William Wirt Culver's own print of his historic photograph of the inauguration of Davis at 1 p.m., February 18, 1861. The President is one of two figures seen standing in the doorway between the two center columns at bottom. This print was retouched by Culver to make up for imperfections in the original exposure. *(Captain John A. Culver)*

The Rev. Basil Manly seemed to be on hand with prayer at every important moment. *(Alabama Department of Archives and History)*

James Chesnut of South Carolina, photographed in Charleston in 1861, was a stern husband, but a staunch friend of Davis even if he did not prefer him at first for the presidency. *(Museum of the Confederacy)*

Alexander M. Clayton of Mississippi brought with him to Montgomery the letter in which Davis did not say he would *not* accept the presidency. *(Mississippi Department of Archives and History)*

William P. Barry of Mississippi was a solid friend and supporter of Davis and the new Constitution. *(Mississippi Department of Archives and History)*

Alexander Clitherall of Montgomery made himself useful first to Congress and then to the President. *(Alabama Department of Archives and History)*

Old, irascible Thomas Withers of South Carolina helped start the opposition with his mania over a hired house and six white horses. *(Kirkland and Kennedy, Historic Camden)*

The man who would be king. Robert Barnwell Rhett, Sr., never forgave Jefferson Davis anything and blamed him for everything. *(Museum of the Confederacy)*

Lawrence M. Keitt of South Carolina, young, impetuous, romantic, was a last-minute would-be kingmaker. *(Museum of the Confederacy)*

The unhappiest man in Montgomery, Thomas R. R. Cobb, came to be a giant and left a dwarf. *(Museum of the Confederacy, photo by Robert K. Krick)*

The original Government House as it appeared in the early twentieth century, with Commerce Street on the right and Bibb Street on the left. *(Alabama Department of Archives and History)*

From the offices of the Montgomery *Advertiser* news of the new Confederates went to the world. *(Alabama Department of Archives and History)*

The ungainly "Jonce" Hooper was Montgomery's man of letters. *(Alabama Department of Archives and History)*

Martin W. Crawford, friend of Stephens, became an unhappy commissioner to Washington. (*Museum of the Confederacy*)

RESIDENCE OF MR. JEFFERSON DAVIS AT MONTGOMERY, CALLED "THE WHITE HOUSE."

The Harrison mansion at Washington and Bibb Streets, its nice full of the dreaded Phrygian caps, became the new ex tive mansion. (*Harper's Pictorial History of the Civil War*)

Benajah S. Bibb, patriarch of Montgomery society, made sure his dining room never failed to send congressmen home happy. (*Alabama Department of Archives and History*)

Sophia Bibb was one of the grande dames of Montgon who so feared the corrupting influences of its being a c tal. (*Alabama Department of Archives and History*)

Above left, Varina Davis, the new First Lady, liked Montgomery despite the heat, and struggled to get her husband to take time for meals. *(Museum of the Confederacy)*

Above right, Mary Boykin Chesnut's insight into men and events in Montgomery was keen. *(Museum of the Confederacy)*

Left, The blowhard Louis T. Wigfall, photographed in Charleston just a few days after Fort Sumter's fall sporting a soldier's hat. *(Museum of the Confederacy)*

The *Times* of London's correspondent William Howard Russell, though smugly superior, found the new revolutionaries in Montgomery fascinating. *(Library of Congress)*

Jefferson Davis's nemesis in the Georgia statehouse Governor Joseph E. Brown, made a better enemy even than Lincoln. *(Museum of the Confederacy)*

The Selma Independent Blues, parading in the street in 1861, were just one of the hundreds of volunteer companies that came through the capital on their way to the war. *(Alabama Department of Archives and History)*

new white leather helmets and speaking trumpets, enacted a $5 fine for driving buggies faster than a walk in the city, and by a host of other signs gave evidence that they were prepared to take this business of being a capital quite seriously.[113] Businessmen, too, treated it as an opportunity, especially considering the recent lull. Sales ran better now than they had in months.[114] In the public market, open a couple of hours until nine every morning, and all day on Saturdays, vendors did brisk business with all of the new mouths to feed, especially late in March as the first strawberries of the season arrived.[115]

Barely one of the city's merchants and professionals failed to profit by the government's presence, from the dentist charging $5 for a filling or "plug," to Gregory's Fashionable Clothing or Saulsbury & Co., clothiers, or Seelye's, where shoes increased in price almost sixty percent in two months. White and Phister sold both books and sheet music to an eager market anxious for the latest patriotic melodies, while McIntyre and others peddled their daguerreotypes and "Mahanotypes" hand colored by young Culver for $5 and more.[116] No question at all, everyone gained from being a part of the great new capital, and despite the grumblings of the city's older elite, the merchants and civic leaders wanted it to remain.

Repeatedly the citizens held meetings to consult on how to accommodate the government's needs. They all knew that tenure as the capital could be temporary. There had never yet been any formal legislation establishing this as the city of state, and Congress could relocate the government at any time. The people here must offer every inducement they could. Ironically, the city that complained of all the lobbyests now became one itself. "Let Alabama have the Capital," an editor proclaimed, "and let Montgomery be the city."[117] Without seeing or sensing it, they were become Washington in spite of themselves.

Certainly they tried. As the excitement over the doings of Congress waned in the face of interminable secret sessions, and then the adjournment, speculation on the site of a permanent capital mounted. Boosters like Hooper argued for the city's good railroad connections, inexpensive living, proximity to natural resources, and did not forget the fresh oysters.[118] Quickly other Confederate cities touted their own advantages. Augusta, Georgia, put itself forward, while Atlanta still aggressively lobbied.[119] Tuscaloosa, Alabama, somehow came into the discussion, William Smith presenting an eloquent bid for the town while making a speech at Montgomery Hall, and before long a citizens' deputation came from the city to do some lobbying of its own.[120] Soon more than a dozen cities stood in the ring, each with its advantages and disqualifications. Many thought Montgomery excellent. Atlanta looked good, "but those streets, and that mud, and that population," squealed the *Mercury*. Columbia, South Carolina was too damp, and when someone suggested Macon, Georgia, the *Mercury* simply responded, "for mercy's sake." Charleston would make the best capital, of course. "It is due to her," but even Charleston's most ardent supporters admitted that should Virginia and Maryland eventually come into the fold, then Washington itself must be their seat of government.[121]

Montgomery took all of this much to heart. The sprinkling wagons came out to settle the dust on the streets. Work gangs demolished derelict houses on what some already called "Davis Avenue," while other crews laid flagstones around the artesian basin to contain its muddiness. People brought to the state's attention the falling fence around the capitol and Hooper publicly shamed city authorities for allowing Bibb and Commerce to get so muddy that one could only cross safely by jumping over the street, as if that were possible. Worse, Bibb from Commerce to the executive mansion was just as bad. If Montgomery wanted to keep the capitol, it must earn it.[122]

Problems loomed beyond the city council's control. Contrary to Jonce's boast of low prices back in February, everything escalated by late March. Real estate prices soared as lot owners held their property, counting on even greater prices as the government expanded. Then there were the meal and lodging costs. Quickly some speculated that Montgomery's "high board and rather poor fare have turned the scale against her," and the cost of consumer goods like Stephens's umbrella did not help.[123] Ever the civic conscience, Hooper chided his fellow townsmen the day before Congress adjourned. "From the lack of hotel accommodations, and the *extreme rates* of board, a stranger might suspect that the city needed a Provision Government, rather than a 'Provisional one,'" he warned. "The allegory of the '*golden egg*' should not be forgotten."[124]

Responding in part to predictions like this, Watt and Lanier sufficiently cleaned the Exchange that a few days after all the congressmen left—and with them many of the office seekers—a visitor from Cincinnati found the hotel "one of the very best to be found anywhere in the South, for courtesy and kind attention to its guests, coupled with sumptuous fare, well furnished and cleanly rooms."[125] Most of the recently departed guests would have guessed the writer stayed at some other Exchange Hotel than the one they knew. Certainly Hooper was not fooled. "Can a first class hotel be speedily erected," he asked. "If not, this city may be considered *as finished*."[126] Others shared his fears, and by the first week of April local investors worked over actual plans for their mammoth new hotel, promising it would be an "astonisher." They found and bought the land, and expected to start construction by the summer.[127] Not to be left behind, the state legislature voted shortly after Congress adjourned to cede a ten-square-mile parcel of land for an independent capital on the model of the District of Columbia. Already some spoke of the District of Davis.[128]

No one in the Confederacy shared the patriotic fever of these days more than the townspeople, who increasingly revealed the intense reactions to public affairs that characterized the citizens of a capital. "A cheerful Sunday would be a novelty here," complained a sarcastic reporter. The church bells rang incessantly, birds chirped, and every now and then "Old Secession," a signal cannon placed outside the Government House, announced some great news. The people seemed almost too jolly and gay in the crisis.[129] Lincoln's inaugural only stirred them to more warlike positions.[130] "We may look out for interesting events in a few days," William Smith predicted, adding ominously that "the *end* of this thing is not yet come."[131] "We are all in good spirits and firm in the faith," wrote a Mississippian in town, even though rumor said that men like Stephens thought war inevitable.[132] Besides, others knew that Howell Cobb and Toombs and Robert Smith thought they could avert conflict, and when the noted Southern novelist Augusta Evans came to town to be lionized at the end of February, she left saying "I know most positively that there is to be *no* fighting."[133]

In their patriotic fervor the ladies of Montgomery proposed renaming Market Street "Davis Avenue" in honor of the President, though the city council found it inexpedient to do so. Undaunted, people suggested that surely Montgomery did not need two Washington Streets. "I think one is enough," one petitioner said, and a committee agreed to look into the matter.[134] Now and then a poor Yankee, unlucky enough to be caught in the wrong crowd, or foolish enough to utter Union sentiments too loudly, found himself carried to the artesian basin and well dunked.[135]

Militia displayed incessantly, and while it took place in half a dozen other Confederate cities in much the same degree, still this city throbbed with an extra beat, for being the capital, this was the heart from which these soldiers were to be pumped through Confederate veins everywhere. "One never hears anything but companies and arms and war," De Clouet's wife complained. "I would like to live in another time."[136] With every passing day the comings and going of volunteers increased. Montgomery's own companies—the True Blues, Metropolitan Guards, Montgomery Greys, Mounted Rifles, Independent Rifles, Montgomery Rifles, Winter Greys, Prattville Dragoons, and the Shorter Artillery—paraded repeatedly when not on duty at Pensacola.[137] Mustering and training at the old racecourse north of town, they performed evolutions for enthusiastic crowds in front of Montgomery Hall or down at Court Square and Welsh's Square, joined by other Alabama companies, all of whom drew crowds.[138] In their fervor, the volunteers boycotted any merchant who dismissed a clerk for enlisting, and themselves administered more than one dunking in the basin.[139] Those returned from Pensacola came with "war" stories, such as they were, including Hooper's son Willie, who got into a knife fight with a fellow volunteer over some subtle point of honor.[140] They also brought back a soldier's whimsy and exaggeration. Complaining of the terrible food at Pensacola, some of the Montgomery boys took a piece of their iron-hard, cracker-like hardtack or "army bread" and hung it outside a store with a sign identifying it to townspeople as a "Fort Morgan pain killer—instant death."[141] Already, too, citizens saw the government expanding both its buildings and their contents. At 90 Commerce Street a warehouse once used for cotton now filled with army supplies, rations of pork, flour, corn, coffee, candles, and the like.[142] None could mistake these as being preparations for peace.

If anyone sought to find one single factor that, of all others, proved that Montgomery had *become* a capital, he need look no further than that small legion of visitors whom one observer called the "ubiquitous knights of the quill."[143] As the days of the meeting of Congress wore on, more and more reporters came to Montgomery, until their own fraternity formed a small regiment when added to the newspapermen already resident. It was a young man's game, for the most part, very few of them over the age of thirty-five, and most ardently for the cause. George Shorter of the *Advertiser*, just now leaving his editorship, signed off recalling his efforts to educate its readers "into a belief in the necessity and the certainty of a separate and independent slave-holding nationality."[144] Hooper, of course, led the local pack in devotion to secession, and ironically he, too, wanted to get out of the business, hoping to relocate in New Orleans if he could find a buyer for the *Mail*. On March 14 he announced that he would sell his interest in the sheet.[145]

Indeed, as the capital's home press experienced some growing disarray with Shorter, Hooper, Whitfield, and others leaving the business, the outsiders increasingly controlled what news—or rumor—escaped the city. Some thought of starting new sheets, notably Constitution Browne. Known throughout his profession as a good writer, clear thinker, and fine gentleman, he closed his Washington *Constitution* and came to Montgomery expecting to commence anew. At one point he talked with Shorter and Reid about merging the subscription list of his old newspaper with their *Advertiser*, then later toyed with opening an entirely new paper. He had hoped at first to trade on close relations with Davis to make his publication into an administration organ, but in the end gave up and settled instead for an appointment as assistant secretary of state.[146] Just as he had in Washington before, Browne came to this new capital to capitalize personally on his connections.

Among the other more interesting newsmen in town now was Charles Stuart. Once editor of a pro-secession paper in New York called the *Volunteer*, he brought a host of eccentricities with him. He claimed descent from the royal Stuarts of England, was born in Poland and raised a Catholic, boasted a smattering of military training and experience in Europe, and occasionally maintained that he was a rightful heir to the throne of England.[147] He came to Montgomery without a newspaper or a job, looking for an appointment, but inevitably spent his time with the other journalists. "That vile Bohemian," one of Davis's official family called him, "a free lance of a fellow."[148] Stuart fancied that he looked a bit like Shakespeare with his long hair, beard, and loose-flowing garb. Yet despite all his pretensions, he had a bit of self-deprecating wit that could describe himself as one of the "conviction-burdened nobodies" then crowding Montgomery in hopes of using either pen or sword. He wanted Davis to make him a general.[149]

As March commenced, the reporters and editors visiting in the capital formed their own little society, the "Sons of the Sunny South." John Heart, a former editor of the *Mercury*, started the group and acted as moderator at their regular meetings. He engaged the room above the telegraph office in the Winter Building, and there they sang and talked, banqueted on cake, and mostly drank. All newsmen were welcome to what Stuart frankly called a "mutual admiration society," and locals like Shorter participated as well. Heart was no fool, of course. They might come to that room for fun and relaxation, but they were also within sound of the telegrapher's key, near to hand for important news.[150]

These reporters, like the townspeople themselves to some extent, found that Montgomery, like Washington, became dull when there was no Congress to report—not that this Congress gave them much. Yet it was typical of capital cities the world over that when numbers of men came to work, and their work lapsed for a time, they found other amusements to fill the time. In the days after Congress adjourned and the meager mite of news became even more paltry, the other entertainments Montgomery offered became all the more appreciated by townspeople and strangers alike. Several fraternal clubs besides the "Sons of the Sunny South" flourished, especially the several Masonic lodges, places where men like Culver took pleasure in seeing that Yankees could still be received cordially. Political and sectional animosities stopped at their front doors.[151] The Masons also had a fine two-hundred-volume library open to members. Nearby the Mechanics Library held another six hundred volumes, general fiction and nonfiction available to the public, and the supreme court library, of course, boasted fully five thousand tomes of law and reference.[152] For more avid readers, White's Bookstore under the Exchange advertised the continent's fourth largest market for old and rare European books. Often called more a library than a store, White's quickly became an informal "library of Congress" while the delegates were in Montgomery, many using it as a meeting place for talk, especially some of the South Carolinians.[153]

Many evenings lecturers held forth down at Estelle Hall, one night a traveler recently returned from adventures in China, another night a scientist discussing the latest wonders of invention.[154] More popular, of course, was the stage. From the time it opened the year before with Sheridan's "School for Scandal," the Montgomery Theatre offered some of the nation's finest artists—Edwin Forrest, Edwin Booth, and his brother John Wilkes. Attendance proved sufficient to maintain theater groups through an entire season's repertoire, and then manager M. W. Canning engaged Italian, German, and English opera groups, adding half a dozen local musicians to the traveling players.[155] Spectators attending found the Theatre cozy, rather like German theaters of the time, and every seat filled for performances that a somewhat aloof Charlestonian called "very fair," if "gotten up in a style to suit the Montgomery people."[156]

Canning brought in comedies, dramas, musicals, tableaux, and every other form of theatrical presentation for his audiences. "Lucretia Borgia" played out her villainies on the same stage that saw Dickens set to music in "Nicholas Nickleby" or a racy farce like "Hunting A Turtle."[157] Of course, Maggie Mitchell packed the house whenever she appeared. Locals regarded her as their universal favorite, though some sniffed at the way all male heads, single and married, turned when she passed. Mary Chesnut simply and contemptuously called her "the actress woman," noting that her English pronunciation was poor besides.[158] Yet even with Maggie Mitchell packing the house, profit eluded Canning. After paying his players and a $5 tax to the city for each performance, he could barely open the doors. But the people of Montgomery, taking his theater to their hearts, repeatedly gave him other compensations, a silver tea service in March, and a farewell benefit on April 12 as his season closed.[159]

Local amateurs also entertained with concerts at Hamner Hall, where teenaged ladies sang, recited poetry, and played the inevitable "Marseillaise," often with Davis, Mallory, Memminger, and other dignitaries in the audience.[160] Those seeking for more active entertainment could watch Aaron "the bruiser" Jones display his pugilistic prowess, or go to the racetrack where, in addition to the races themselves, fans might also see an unscheduled bout of fisticuffs between a judge and a spectator over a close finish.[161] Other masculine entertainments could be had at the city pistol galleries, or on Phelan's tables at the Arcade Billiard Saloon at 87 Commerce, where genial landlord G. W. Lyman also served liquor and wine along with fine cigars.[162]

Most of all Montgomeryites strolled, and even there they saw their favorite promenades now bustling with all the visitors and loungers, even their most beautiful and peaceful corners now pulpits for political speculations. "There is no walk here that even pretends to the quality of a fashionable boulevard," complained the effete Stuart.[163] Women generally preferred their carriages or an evening sitting on a verandah. After all, Montgomery was a town still rough at its edges, the more so now as it bulged with strangers. But the men all walked. Every evening after William Huddleston lit the evening lamps, they came out to promenade.[164] Even when lit and not prowled by undesirables, the streets presented something of a hazard, especially the sidewalks along Commerce and Court, where men Hooper dubbed "black-guards" in the taverns and billiard parlors habitually spat out the windows without looking first.[165] Despite mud puddles that could swallow a wagon, billows of blowing dust on dry days, the army of barking hounds, and quarts of airborne expectorant, hundreds still ambled down Commerce of an evening. Ahead of them they heard the calliope on the *Southern*

Republic playing martial airs as they strode past Government House to the river overlook. There they watched slaves tumbling great bales of cotton down the bank to the wharf below. There they mingled with other townsfolk to talk and gossip. There they found Reagan whittling and chewing, Benjamin with a lady on each arm, or the President in his gray suit, and limping along beside him his old friend Northrop, clad in a coat several sizes too great, rustling at every step thanks to the newspapers the eccentric hypochondriac stuffed inside his shirt to prevent colds.[166] There, overlooking the Alabama, the rustic society of Montgomery mingled with the elite of Charleston, New Orleans, and Atlanta, creating the first loose bonds of a new Confederate culture.

Inevitably some citizens and newcomers sought recreations representing a lower order of society that kept Sheriff W. G. Walker and his jailor R. C. Coleman well occupied, and that is perhaps what frightened Montgomery's grand dames most of all, for they all heard the stories of how people behaved in Washington.[167] Montgomery City Council defined a host of minor infractions, from flying kites in the city limits, to graffiti, to dog and cock fighting.[168] More serious misdemeanors, especially burglaries and thefts, rose dramatically as people flocked to the new capital. A Mississippi colonel returned to his room at the Exchange one day to find $132 stolen, and Hooper soon warned his readers of the pickpockets and petty thieves who came to town with the office seekers—implying that many were one and the same.[169]

Montgomery already enjoyed a reputation as a hard-drinking town, and that grew with the arrival of all thirsty politicians and hangers-on.[170] Some of the saloons, licensed only to sell lager beer, protested in fear that Congress might impose duties on their beverage, and thus "leave the field open to more intoxicating and unwholesome drinks," but men hardly needed to be forced to the wine, whiskey, and brandy counters.[171] Henry Hilliard's son unfortunately consumed more than his share regularly, which made Coleman's jail his frequent domicile. One of the Hilliard slaves became a common sight on the street, carrying a rocking chair down to the cell for the young man until he was released. Meanwhile, in an adjoining cell, often as not, sat the son of Chief Justice Abram Walker, leading one visitor to claim that he preferred to take one drink too many in order to "secure admission to select society" far better than that at the Exchange.[172] Before long Mayor Noble dealt with the younger drunks by forgiving their fines if they enlisted in a military company.[173]

Just as Montgomery turned rather an indulgent eye toward its inebriates, so it also looked only half-disparagingly on the prostitutes who
shared in the same business boom as the rest of the city's merchants.
Despite a $50 per day fine for running a bordello, the authorities gener-
ally looked the other way when passing the several establishments pur-
veying sex.[174] Some operated on the outskirts of the city, in collusion
with the stage drivers. On the road from Benton, Alabama, the driver
regularly stopped in the suburbs at a house where he recommended
male passengers would find a good meal and accommodation. Once at
the table the customer discovered that his hostess's several "daughters"
served more than food.[175] More daring proprietresses worked in the center of town, as at the Macon House just a couple of blocks from the
capitol. The "fair frail ones" could look to a lot of business from the
thousands there gathered.[176]

For the most part they went unmolested so long as they caused no
trouble. Betsey Hatton, toothless, red-eyed, red-faced, and "on the
shady side of forty," ran a house in the southwest part of town where
she gave entertainments that included blacks playing the fiddle and
rather a lot of drinking. When one of her parties got out of hand and a
row ensued, she came before the mayor on charges and was fined.[177]
Things got even rougher at another house where a man named Rolla
shot himself in the stomach, and occasionally even the women turned
pugnacious.[178] On April 1 Clara Robinson and Bell Ennes, both of
whom lived and worked near the state house, decided to settle a dispute by a duel. Bell issued the challenge, and Clara accepted, naming
"fist and skull" as the weapons. No men were to be present, and no hitting below the belt, but the police found out and brought them before
Mayor Noble. Commenting that duels were usually restricted to
"Legislators, Congressmen and *editors*," Noble decided that as there
was no precedent of women fighting a duel, and no weapons were
involved, he would discharge the antagonists with a warning not to try
it again.[179] He might have pointed out to them that their act fit the
occasion, All Fools' Day.

The same could be said for the men who went at it more in earnest.
Violence always lurked beneath the surface in Southern society, and
Montgomery was no different except that now so much of Southern
society had come to it, bringing its violence in tow. Reared in a social
ethic that condoned hot tempers and high pride and applauded the
demonstration of bravery, men took minor disputes into the streets

regularly, especially after a few hours in the taverns and brothels. At least once a week now, amid the firing of the cannon and the militia volleys for celebration, the people heard other, isolated, shots, generally on Commerce, Court, and Market. Culver twice witnessed street fights. In one, typically, each fired a shot, neither took a wound, and the major fined both $50. A man fell dead in the other, while the victor pleaded self-defense.[180] On March 14 Ryland Pollard and Isaac Watson met on Commerce, argued over a trifle, and Pollard fell dangerously wounded only after severely beating Watson. Constitution Browne witnessed the affair and protested, but other onlookers more accustomed to Montgomery manners comforted him that both combatants showed "the right temper."[181] Two weeks later A. R. Andrews and Thomas Crommelin exchanged shots with their Derringer pistols, then hammered each other over the head with the butts, both finishing unconscious and facing $50 fines when they awoke.[182]

Even Stephens's fellow boarder Moses tangled with twenty-one-year-old Edward Banks, editor of the Montgomery *Confederation*.[183] Some said it arose from a professional argument over news articles, but others suspected it just might have something to do with the attentions both paid to Sanders' daughter at the Exchange parlor. Either way, they took their quarrel out of town to Pensacola, exchanged one shot without hitting each other, and came back friends.[184] The duelists often began and ended as comrades, leading Stuart to declare the whole business "a sort of local amusement for grown children."[185]

Violence did not confine itself to the free population of Montgomery. As in every other facet of life, the city's blacks, slave and non-slave, emulated white behavior. The same day that Moses and Banks met, one of the city's free black barbers received a sentence of thirty-nine lashes for assaulting a slave.[186] In fact, whipping seemed almost commonplace as a sentence for infractions that only brought fines when committed by whites. Even using bad language or acting in "an indecent manner in the view or hearing of a white person" could result in fifty stripes. In cases of assault a hierarchy of punishments awaited, depending on the race and status of the victim. Striking a white could bring a hundred lashes for a slave, and fifty for hitting another slave. Attacking a free black could cost $10 or fifty lashes, while a free black attacking a white got the same hundred. About the cheapest fine was $10 for one free negro attacking another. Moreover, in order to affix the proper sentence, the city council also made its own legal determination of just what constituted a negro, a complex formula specifying that if a person was five-fourteenths black, then legally he or she was black. The code seemed more harsh than it was, almost all sentences of slave whippings being suspended if an owner requested. Chiefly the lash served as an admonition rather than a penalty.[187] Punishment, when they got it, came to slaves more from their owners, like the serving girl so white that Culver thought she was Irish until one morning at the Montgomery Hall table she whispered in his ear, "Massa Culver I got all whiped dis morning."[188]

Montgomery's slaves lived under a body of substantial restrictions designed in part to keep too much money out of their hands, as well as to discourage them from stealing from the cash crops of their owners. No slave could market cotton, pork, oats, meal, corn, or liquor. But since masters often allowed them their own livestock, blacks could sell milk, eggs, butter, and any fish they caught, *if* owners gave them written permission.[189] Once the frights of the past season over insurrections passed, whites eased their restrictions on slave movements, too, no longer requiring passes for slave men on one plantation to visit their wives on another.[190]

The slave business itself proceeded apace in the capital while events designed to preserve slavery swirled about. Several slave markets operated, three of them on Market Street leading to the state house, while another had just recently gone out of business on the corner opposite the future executive mansion.[191] The traders were youthful men like forty-year-old E. Murrell or thirty-six-year-old Thomas Banks.[192] City law required them to keep their blacks out of sight except when offering them at public auctions, which came every Saturday.[193] However, pedestrians walking up Market usually heard the sounds of a fiddle and dancing inside the slave showrooms. If someone stepped in a door beyond the signs that said "Negro Ware House" and "Slaves For Sale," the blacks immediately went quiet and sat on benches placed against the walls of the room.[194] Outdoor auctions attracted far more attention, some of them in front of the Exchange. "Niggers is cheap now," boasted one buyer, yet even the most ardent secessionists felt sometimes troubled, especially the women.[195] "I am my very soul sickened," Mary Chesnut felt after walking past a slave sale with Browne's wife. "If you can stand that," she told her companion, "no other Southern thing need choke you."[196]

In some ways, free blacks faced greater restrictions, chiefly because white Montgomery wanted very much to discourage them from coming into the city, where they might become layabouts, thieves, or bad influences on the slaves. Free black men owed an annual tax of $10, and free women of color $5. They could not keep shops competing with white businessmen, though they could be barbers. The city clerk maintained a register of all free blacks in the city, their occupation and residence, and changing sleeping places without notification could cost another $10 in fines. The free man was not to be on the streets after half past nine in the evening, nor to associate with slaves unless given permission, and punishment included fines or lashes. No black, free or slave, was to own a dog, and free men from outside the city could not visit for more than twenty days without a $20 fine.[197]

Interestingly enough, in spite of all this, the blacks in and around Montgomery felt—or at least manifested—almost as much enthusiasm in the mounting crisis as the whites. They may have been slaves, or free men at the very bottom of the social mountain with no hope of ascent, but still they were also native born Southerners. However much they may have been denied its bounty, still the Confederacy was *their* homeland, too, and lurid newspaper stories of expected Yankee depredations produced a minor war fever among them. William, the slave of Montgomery Doctor W. C. Rives, was among the first to subscribe to the Treasury loan, investing $150 of carefully husbanded cash. Many more followed his lead.[198] Before leaving for Florida, Patton Anderson had suggested that the army use slaves as cooks, nurses, and teamsters, confident that many would volunteer for the service if their masters gave them permission.[199] A number of slaves wished to go beyond even that. On one plantation sixty slave men gathered every evening under moonlight to practice at drill, wanting to go to Mobile to fight "the damned buckram abolitionists" whose threats had done so much, indirectly, to curtail slave privileges.[200] Already the letters came across Walker's and Davis's desks from blacks, slave and free, asking to be allowed to take arms in the defense of the South.

Impelling them as well as the whites was a growing suspicion of enemies within. In a time of crisis, any capital city feels it the more, and long since Montgomery had taken to reacting to news and rumor just as any city of state might, Indeed, the only metropolis on the continent more nervous and anxious than this one right now was Washington, and both felt keenly conscious of the difficulty of telling friend from foe. Enemies came to capitals to learn what they could, and wreak mischief if possible. A capital's people must be on guard constantly. Tom Cobb and Stephens already suspected someone in the city post office of tampering with their mail, or of reading letters before sending them on. Always paranoid, the *Mercury* reporters sent columns back to Charleston by the Adams Express Company rather than trust to the post.[201] While none yet knew with certainty of the telegrams being intercepted by Washington authorities, still some men distrusted the wires as well, and resorted to codes. Sanders, himself the object of some suspicion in Montgomery, devised his own telegraphic code for dispatches to New York. He referred to Davis as "Dot," and the Confederacy as "Sam," no doubt a borrowing from the old notion of "Uncle Sam." The Union, appropriately enough, was "Old," a musket became "bang," peace was "potatoes," and war was to be "wax." Since Toombs treated Sanders with a measure of contempt, demanding to see his passport before allowing him to remain in Montgomery, the schemer revenged himself in part by designating the stout secretary of state as "Tub."[202] Others prepared different ciphers, with even the War Department using one involving multiple copies of dictionaries, and a series of numbers designating first the page and then the line on which the encoded word appeared. With men at distant places armed with the same edition of the book, a simple string of numbers could be turned into sentences.[203]

Strangers in town attracted suspicious glances and were well advised to state their business and sympathies publicly. Known Unionists simply found it healthier to leave. Robert Tharin, one-time law partner with Yancey, injudiciously announced his desire to publish a newspaper called the *Non-Slaveholder* to speak to the interests of Alabamians opposed to secession. Men seized him, gave him a rump trial, and sentenced him to a whipping followed by banishment from Lowndes County. His flight took him first to Montgomery, where he appealed to his old school friend Miles, only to find the South Carolinian inclined to report him to the authorities for perhaps even more severe punishment. Almost hysterical, Tharin fled to Montgomery Hall, registered under an assumed name, but so aroused suspicion by his nervous manner that he had to leave once again, finally spending the night in the home of a sympathetic citizen. Only in the morning, still trembling, did he finally board the West Point cars to start his journey to safety.[204] Montgomery just now was no place for dissent.

It was, however, still the place for the Confederate capital, at least in the eyes of its leading citizens. None of them, citizens and newcomers alike, had any developed sense of what a capital city *ought* to be, yet instinctively all seemed to feel that somehow they should profit from it. Residents liked the prestige and the attention, even when protesting they did not. Merchants saw nothing but opportunity, and those who came from elsewhere arrived with nothing but opportunity on their minds. They had seen their enemy Washington, and unwittingly they had become its smaller twin. Few of them ever realized that was because in seeing their enemy, they saw themselves.

Yet for any of this to matter at all rested in the hands not of Montgomery and its citizens, but with Davis himself, with another president hundreds of miles away, and upon events taking place in a city that, despite the fears of people here, they mirrored more and more for good and ill. Even as the Congress adjourned to go home or back to the state conventions to work on ratification of the Constitution, frightening rumors coursed through the city streets that, for the moment, remained the Confederate capital. Davis and his cabinet knew something was at hand, said the gossips. Was it peace, or war?[205]

CHAPTER TWELVE

THE GAGE OF BATTLE

———◆★◆———

N O ONE LAMENTED THE ADJOURNMENT of Congress, excepting perhaps the hotel keepers. "I am delighted to leave this place," wrote one departing officer, "for it is not pleasant to loaf in a large city much less a small one."[1] Suddenly the streets seemed less crowded. Gaily dressed flocks of office hopefuls still gathered at the intersections and in the lager houses, most of them looking rather worried at their prospects now, but the hotel servants and hack drivers felt their business fall.[2] "The life of this city seems to have departed," wrote one reporter.[3] People looked a bit lost, the city quiet, rather, as one put it, like "a portrait frame, from which the beautiful picture has been removed." But for the still-sitting Alabama convention, some thought melancholia would settle over the city.[4] The cynics and critics almost rejoiced. "The Congress is not of much use, and may just as well adjourn as not," said a South Carolinian no doubt peeved at all the secret sessions,[5] while a New Orleans observer delighted that he could rest now for several weeks until "the sweet flowers of Spring fill the air with their delightful odors, and the members of Congress assemble to make buncombe speeches and attend to the grave matters of the Confederacy."[6] Those matters felt somehow a little less grave in light of the rumor sweeping the city that Davis and his cabinet had received a dispatch just before the adjournment telling them that Fort Sumter would be evacuated.[7]

In fact, to many, including the congressmen now heading home, ratification of the new Constitution seemed a more pressing concern. The President, while he took no part in the framing of the document, still thought it a good one, though with room for improvements.[8] Those could come later. Now they must get it in force. Fortunately Alabama made a good start, thanks to its convention being ready to receive the charter immediately. Men like Bob Smith and Chilton at once took the offensive, praising its wisdom while yet admitting its minor flaws.[9] On the other side, the reconstructionists like William Smith attacked the "usurpations" of "a new tribunal in the shape of a congress." It acted with no mandate or authority, they said, pleading only the flimsy excuse of urgency. No one consulted the people. "This constitution has no marble to rest upon," Smith declared. "Parchment cannot save it from the Great Destroyer."[10] But Smith and his followers cried in vain to submit the document to a popular vote, and a number of former cooperationists shifted to Chilton's side in the interest of a united South, making ratification certain.[11] Still, as a measure of the latent strength of the minority, when Fearn and Lewis both resigned their seats in Congress, the convention appointed Henry Jones and Nicholas Davis, both opponents of secession, to replace them.[12]

Georgia provided the next battleground, and one where the congressmen in Montgomery who also served as convention delegates felt anxious to take the high ground. Notwithstanding his notion that railroads should not run on the Sabbath, Tom Cobb left Sunday March 10 for the Savannah convention, soon followed by Hill, Stephens, and others.[13] Despite his disappointment in some of the document's clauses, Cobb now proclaimed full approval of the Constitution.[14] Ben Hill agreed, praising the civil service reform, and sought to appeal to the cautious conservative elements in his state by asserting that "so far from having lost our fidelity to the Constitution which our fathers made, when we sought to go, we hugged that Constitution to our bosom and carried it with us."[15]

Predictably, Stephens spoke most eloquently and to the point, though after the fact. He left Montgomery complaining half in jest of his "*big* work and *little* pay," and then labored incessantly all the way to Savannah, making speeches at every stop.[16] In Augusta he told Georgians that secession had been like the pulling of a decayed tooth—a favorite metaphor with Little Aleck—painful, but afterward a relief to the patient.[17] In Atlanta he said even more, first enunciating a theme he would make famous a few days later in Savannah. The new Constitution, he declared, "made African *inequality* and subordination, and the *equality* of white men, the chief cornerstone of the Southern Republic."[18] In Savannah on March 21 he shook North and South by going farther, saying that their new government's "foundations are laid, its cornerstone rests, upon the great truth that the negro is not equal to the white man; that slavery, subordination to the superior race, is his natural and moral condition."[19] He would have done better to stay with his other theme that their new Constitution merely sustained and upheld the principles of the original Constitution. This line of argument so provocatively asserting the Confederacy's foundation upon slavery worked against that very government's attempt to justify its plea for independence on the basis of state rights and sovereignty.[20] He would spend the rest of his life trying to back away from his "cornerstone" speech.

In fact, by the time Stephens put his cornerstone in his mouth, Georgia had already ratified the Constitution unanimously on March 16, though again there was some moodiness over the document not being put before the people in a referendum.[21] Next were Louisiana and Texas, both of which ratified with almost no objection, and then Mississippi. Here, for the first time, came serious opposition. Many in the convention at Jackson doubted their authority to adopt such a document, and favored calling a special new convention or even putting it before the people. "For some months past all power has been rapidly passing from the many into the hands of a select few," complained a Jackson editor, "and we are mistaken if this policy has not been carried about as far as the people are willing it should go."[22] Two days into their deliberations Barry wired Davis that "we are in trouble," but went on to express confidence that they would ratify in the end.[23] Wiley Harris, managing effectively as usual, ably fought submitting the Constitution to a popular vote. It required too much time, and in the event that the people rejected it, the embarrassment to the whole movement would be too great. They could not risk that much democracy.[24] In the end it swept past by 78 to 7.[25]

No one expected South Carolina to be easy, and authorities in Montgomery felt no little disquiet awaiting the outcome there.[26] Despite his own *Mercury* stating that this was the "best constitution, we believe, ever devised by man," Rhett and his supporters tried once more in convention to win all that he had lost in Montgomery.[27] He objected to the manner of admitting new states, with the possibility that free ones might gain admission. He argued against the three-fifths apportionment clause. He loathed the tariff being retained, and turned almost rabid over the abolition of the slave trade. All of his old arguments echoed once more, his goal being to make South Carolina's ratification conditional upon moving for future correcting amendments.[28] In short, Rhett sought to blackmail Montgomery by threatening the unity of the movement.[29]

Happily he stood with a distinct minority, as usual. While many in the press prayed that the radicals would not wage "a wicked and suicidal opposition,"[30] men like Chesnut stood to speak against Rhett at every turn.[31] Believing that disunion would be, or could be permanent, Chesnut had no intention of letting hotheads prejudice the movement.[32] It helped that Rhett found himself on the defensive in the convention thanks to faulty rumors that in Montgomery he maintained that only slaveholders should have the vote. In fact he argued that only slave states should be admitted, but the misrepresentation was close enough to his turn of mind that many believed.[33]

In the end Rhett lost on every point, and on April 3 the convention ratified the Constitution by 114 to 16. A few days later, in a somewhat pointless gesture, it also ratified the Provisional Constitution in order to legitimize the acts of the government to date.[34] Most South Carolinians rejoiced at the rejection of "Rhett & Co., Slave traders, free traders, fire eaters and extremists," said Hammond, "and I suppose this is an end of them."[35] In fact, "Rhett & Co." would be heard from again, and again, but for the moment news of South Carolina's passage sent a current of relief to Montgomery where few ever expected the opposition to assume such serious proportion.[36]

That left only Florida, which ratified on April 22.[37] Meanwhile, the Confederates took the good news of their new Constitution into the Border States, hoping that its conservative nature would appeal to those suspicious of the motives of the seceders. Congressmen traveled through Arkansas, Tennessee, Virginia, North Carolina, and elsewhere to promote their new government, and quickly predictions of new states came from Bob Smith and others.[38] From Montgomery Toombs almost begged Little Aleck to go to Arkansas and make speeches, though he declined, as usual.[39] Sanders unofficially—and meddlesomely—worked on Governor Beriah Magoffin of Kentucky, suggesting putting the document to a referendum in the bluegrass, while publicly boasting that thanks to the new Constitution "all discontent is gone, and the satisfaction of success beams from every face." He even said that New York ought to seek admission.[40] At the same time Davis and Walker subtly tried to woo Virginia, the latter by sending a spy to Richmond to encourage and report on secession sentiment, and the President by finding offices for prominent Virginians like John Tyler, Jr.[41]

Though Congress might be gone, the government in Montgomery still remained, and with much to do, including its own share in promoting itself to the Border States and the world. Howell Cobb ordered the printing of all of the acts and resolutions of the first session, and as soon as Wimbish & Company of Montgomery delivered the 131-page booklets, he sent copies to all of the Southern governors.[42] He also began revising the old United States statutes to suit Confederate needs, and showing a bit of nepotism—as well as an admission of his bookish legal skills—he offered the job to brother Tom, who refused to leave his home again until the next session.[43] Indeed, young Cobb determined never to accept office again, and charged Marion to keep his letter containing his vow to show to him in future in case "my vanity and self-conceit may hereafter tempt me."[44]

The several departments went on about their work, too, or those who had any. Poor Benjamin put his tiny domain in order quickly, appointed his judges and district attorneys and marshalls for each state, created an admiralty court at Key West, installed a superintendent of public printing, and then had to wait for work to come to him.[45] By the end of March he spent his days doing errands for Walker relating to raising troops in Louisiana, and issued his first legal opinion early in April on the momentous issue of the tariffs applicable to lemons, oranges, and walnuts.[46]

Reagan had almost too much to do, and even outsiders recognized that of all the departments, his was the most burdensome.[47] He oversaw the conversion and fitting out of his new offices in the Figh Block on Bibb Street. The two top floors would all be his, with twelve rooms each, all placed around a central atrium with a skylit "observatory." He should be able to take occupancy by April 15.[48] By the end of March he filled all of his positions, and local printers completed his forms and blanks and all of the bound record books necessary. Moreover, he established an informal school in his existing offices, and until he actually took control of the Confederacy's mail, he and his officials met every evening from eight until ten while experienced postal employees pirated from Washington taught them their business.[49]

By April 1 he issued a call for printing of his first stamps and postal envelopes. Selecting the grade of paper and the style of printing he wanted, he displayed samples in his offices for bidders' examination. Meanwhile the first stamp designs arrived, while he engaged other draftsmen in preparing postal maps for the new, greatly truncated, delivery routes.[50] Advertisements solicited bids for everything from mail sacks to wrapping paper, twine to sealing wax. Everything was to be in hand by May 1, as he anticipated assuming operation of the mails in June. He estimated in the end a need for thirty-eight clerks in his offices, plus a watchman for night security. In his newly revised postal system, he would have 1,305 routes operated by 1,087 contract carriers and 71 route agents, all at a cost of $56,100, a hefty saving over the expense of the United States Post Office in servicing the same region. Even the oft-critical *Mercury* complimented him on achieving so much for so little.[51] By cutting and shortening routes, eliminating the franking privilege, making fewer trips per route, reducing the weight of mail, and more, he shaved expenses by forty percent, while increasing postal rates added to revenue. Thus in his initial projected budget for Davis, he estimated only a $320,060 loss in the first year, and that should disappear as the volume of mail subsequently increased.[52]

Reagan's close management in his department lightened the burden on Memminger, who moved into newer, larger quarters of his own.[53] Besides administering customs matters, and determining—with Benjamin's help—items subject to duty, Memminger also addressed establishing ports of entry along the Confederacy's current northern border and elsewhere for trade with the Border States and, eventually, the old Union. In late March he declared one at Hernando, Mississippi, on the Mississippi Central Railroad, not realizing that the town lay more than thirty miles west of the track. A miffed Natchez editor prodded him that "a little more geographical attention would not hurt the Department."[54]

If Memminger seemed careless about the Mississippi map, he owed it to the consuming task of raising real funds in a hurry. After announcing on March 16 that the first $5 million of the $15 million loan would be offered to the public on April 17, he felt overjoyed that investors bespoke the entire issue of bonds by March 25, even before he printed the actual certificates.[55] Unfortunately, however, the actual hard cash required to pay the six percent demanded on April 17 and the balance due by the end of the month proved scarce. In the political crisis of the past winter, the South's banks had suspended payments of specie, in essence hoarding coin. Consequently, Memminger issued a circular to all banks asking that they redeem with coin any of their notes used to pay for loan bonds, and when they promptly agreed, the problem passed, though the prevalence of counterfeit notes on some banks in Mobile and elsewhere remained a difficulty.[56]

Equally encouraging, on April 2 the first shipment of new Treasury notes arrived in Montgomery. Now the government had paper of its own with which to pay its accounts. Clitherall took the first, followed by Memminger and Walker, who publicly made a show of accepting them for their salary.[57] In the hope of backing his paper with a hard currency of his own, Memminger pressed for continuing in operation the United States mint at Dahlonega, Georgia, enlisting Howell Cobb's influence in the project, and sending out solicitations for coin designs.[58]

No one worked harder than the other man who took his pay in Treasury notes. Men in Montgomery often commented that they rarely saw Walker in the War Department, and never out of it. One reporter complained that after a week in the Capital he had yet to set eyes on the secretary.[59] As March passed on and into April, Walker seemed either constantly at his desk dealing with a mountain of chores, or else closeted with Davis for hours every time the President rang the little bell on his table and sent Josselyn to fetch him.[60] In fact, Walker's preoccupation led him into confusion and delay. When he issued a troop requisition from the several states on March 8, he mailed it instead of using the telegraph, with the result that Pettus in Jackson, only two hundred miles away, did not get his for eight days, while Perry in Florida waited eleven.[61] Walker, it seems, repeatedly forgot to think about the fastest ways of doing important things.

Late in March Walker appointed Hooper his private secretary, the income proving a godsend to Jonce, who quickly presumed to call himself assistant secretary of war.[62] But his industry lifted some of Walker's burden. Better still, the general staff organization finally lay complete as Cooper, Myers, and Northrop took their offices late in March, and John Withers arrived April 3.[63] Withers, to be assistant adjutant general, was a short, direct, crisp fellow with whom some field officers almost immediately came into conflict, and more than one actually resorted to blows.[64] A few days after Withers came Josiah Gorgas, one of the officers Beauregard contacted for Walker, and now to be chief of the Ordnance Bureau.[65]

Walker oversaw a great many things, and some he found entirely pleasurable and trouble free, like notifying officers of their commissions in the Provisional Army. While Davis alone made selections for generals, Walker handled the correspondence, even in cases where the commissions came for political as well as military reasons. On March 15, for instance, he sent word to Virginia that Robert E. Lee and Joseph E. Johnston had been commissioned brigadiers, despite the fact that neither had as yet resigned from the Old Army, and their state still remained in the Union. It took little subtlety to perceive that offering high commands to prominent Border State officers added a little extra inducement to side with the Confederacy.[66]

Unfortunately Walker's diplomatic relations with state authorities already a part of the new nation fared not so well. Texas proved an immediate problem. Even after its secession it expected the Confederacy to pay for former United States property being turned over to the new government. On top of that, its congressmen lobbied repeatedly for funds and troops to man its indefensible frontiers against Indians, forcing Walker more than once to defend himself against charges of ignoring Texan security.[67]

Worst of all were the governors and the matter of raising regiments. One sympathetic Georgian lamented "so much misunderstanding" between the War Department and the states.[68] Pickens chaffed that his state militia officers like Bonham did not get equivalent commissions when they transferred to the Confederate Regular and Provisional service. Walker's plea that South Carolina and Mississippi alone had more such officers than the Confederacy needed hardly mollified the governor.[69] Then others in the Palmetto State turned to comparing its Army and Navy appointments with other states' to make certain that South Carolina got its full share.[70] Texas, at the same time that it asked for more protection, in a neat bit of contradiction refused to acknowledge that Montgomery had authority to assume control of military operations within its borders.[71]

These were all minor irritants compared to issues of terms of service, arms, and officers for regiments raised within the several states. Everyone seemed to blur the distinctions between the Regular Army, the Provisional, and the volunteer militia. Walker himself asked Attorney General Benjamin for an official interpretation of the legislation so he could repeat it to governors who quibbled.[72] Thomas Moore of Louisiana expressed his confusion in the matter by asking just which force the men he was now raising would go into, and Walker assured him they would all enter the Provisional service, and would take with them their own officers. Still Moore complained that some privately raised units like a New Orleans battalion of zouaves would be accepted directly by Montgomery without going through him.[73]

Predictably, Brown of Georgia made himself the greatest headache of all. Disingenuously protesting that "I sincerely desire to give you as little embarrassment as possible," Brown proceeded from the first to do just the opposite. For a full week in March Brown delayed raising any troops until he bullied the War Department into accepting two partially formed regiments, with their officers, even though the enabling legislation clearly specified that Montgomery would only take full strength units. He marshaled the Georgia convention behind him, and when Toombs tried to mediate, he reported that Brown's motives were good, but told Walker frankly that he could "do nothing on your basis to arrange military affairs with Governor B." Virtually blackmailed, the Secretary of War made an exception and accepted the partial units, though Brown only used that concession as a wedge to extract more in the weeks to come. Barely did he settle one dispute before he raised new quibbles over where to muster the regiments.[74] A great patriot in his own eyes, Governor Brown quickly made himself anything but that to the men in Montgomery.

Meanwhile, Walker still got a steady flow of volunteers, despite the Browns of the Confederacy. Moore sent several hundred from Louisiana as promised. Pettus in Mississippi mustered nearly forty companies by March 16. Even Indians from the western reaches of Texas offered their services as warriors.[75] Men from outside the Confederacy attempted to enlist, including the National Volunteers in the District of Columbia, a company from Memphis, and hosts of Kentuckians. Hooper actually had to turn them down diplomatically, echoing Walker's confidence that more than enough soldiers were coming forward from the seven states to justify them in declining. Davis agreed.[76]

Yet Confederate eyes certainly looked with interest beyond their own borders, and in the main that was Toombs's job. Such as it was. His growing disdain for the position became general knowledge soon enough. Applicants approaching him with letters of recommendation got an abrupt response of "Perfectly useless, sir!" When they pressed him, he took off his hat, swore, and said, "Can you get in here, sir? That's the Department of State, sir!"[77] Describing his position derisively, he told a friend that "I hold myself ready to be as polite and hospitable as I know how to my neighbors, but not one of them will even speak to me."[78] In fact, toward those "neighbors," the other nations of the world, Toombs would have adopted just about any posture to get them to recognize the Confederacy, leading Stuart to quip that "he was for an alliance with Satan himself" if it would advance the cause.[79] Unfortunately his brief included not making policy, but merely trying to communicate Davis's to other nations. Men in Montgomery saw rather soon a constrained harmony between the two men.[80] Having nearly come to the dueling field a few years before, they were hardly destined to be intimate friends. Their differing views on policy now virtually guaranteed a coolness. Toombs agreed with Stephens that they should buy every spare bale of cotton and ship it to Europe for money and credit.[81] Davis believed fervently in King Cotton, telling Stuart that the "first wail from England's manufacturing districts" would end any potential Yankee blockade and bring fleets to aid the Confederacy and renew the flow of cotton. They should keep every pound of the staple at home until then, and plant no more, to exacerbate the anticipated crisis abroad.[82]

In March about all Toombs could do was prepare the Yancey-Rost-Mann mission. He gave them copies of the new Constitution, letters of credence and introduction to Belgium, France, England, and Russia, passports, copies of the laws of the United States that prevailed in the Confederacy, and a treatise on international law. Along with their $1,000 per month allowance, he gave them instructions to study everything available during their sojourn abroad, including science, the arts, commerce, and finance. He wanted them to purchase books, maps, political tracts—anything that might be of use to the department. Their dispatches to him should be frequent and detailed, written on a specified paper so they could be bound, and sequentially numbered in order to determine if any miscarried.[83]

What Toombs could not give them were instructions to his liking. Even though the wording of their commissions stated that they would have authority to "agree, treat, consult, and negotiate of and concerning all matters and subjects . . . and to conclude and sign a treaty or treaties," their power in fact went only so far as to conclude what Davis allowed. Naturally they could initiate no policy of their own, but neither did they have any latitude for negotiation in pursuing the task set them by Montgomery.[84] They could ask for recognition, but that was all. They could propose a treaty of commerce, navigation, and friendship, promising low duties and almost free markets, but again might only act in accordance with Davis's wishes and the Constitution.[85] Given his way, when the trio left New Orleans on March 31, Toombs would much have preferred to give them wide authority to agree to almost anything in return for recognition.[86]

Progress from abroad would take months to develop. Meanwhile, everyone in the government daily looked for the latest telegrams from their other diplomatic mission. When Davis sent Crawford, Forsyth, and Roman to Washington, he armed them with a message to President-elect Lincoln that they came with a "desire to unite and bind together our respective countries by friendly ties."[87] Not many in Montgomery believed it would be that easy. Lincoln refused to receive the commissioners officially. "This will at once put the ball in motion," said one editor,[88] while many outside the capital confessed that they thought the United States would be the very last power to recognize their independence.[89] The first reports from Washington promised little. "We are feeling our way here," Forsyth confessed on March 14, "playing a game in which time is our best advocate."[90]

From the first Lincoln's Secretary of State Seward declined—politely—to meet with them. For him to do so would constitute a form of recognition.[91] Crawford quite rightly inferred that Seward wanted time, and gave it to him, refrained from pressing, and meanwhile gathered all the information he could overhear or buy, telling Stephens that he spent his money "like water" to purchase any gossip.[92] Thereafter through the balance of March he sent a steady flow of observations and inferences on the battle within Lincoln's cabinet over the line to pursue with the Confederates. Seward led the faction supporting peace, while Secretary of the Treasury Salmon Chase headed the opposite wing urging a hard line on reconstruction. Meanwhile, other foreign ministers in Washington seemed friendly, especially the Russian ambassador, who almost arranged an unofficial meeting with Seward before he backed out from fear word would leak to the press.[93]

By March 29 Roman, at least, thought Seward was winning the struggle. At the same time the envoy actually proposed foreign policy to Toombs by suggesting that the Confederacy deny—disingenuously—any designs on Cuba in order to curry favor with the Spanish foreign minister.[94] Toombs wisely ignored him, but no one could wave aside Crawford when he relayed a promise that Seward gave to the Confederates' new intermediary, Supreme Court justice John Campbell. Sumter would not be reinforced, Seward said. He wanted no confrontation, but he also wanted more time to work on the President. Lincoln, concluded Crawford, was "a poor miserable stupid ass, having no opinions of his own, drifting from one place to another."[95] Still, Crawford thought that the Confederate policy of "masterly inactivity" in Washington was working to their advantage as Lincoln's own people pushed him toward peace. Again and again Seward indirectly promised no confrontation over Sumter, and Lincoln himself appeared to be stalling for time to think.[96]

With the beginning of April the commissioners perceived a different direction to the wind. "The war wing presses hard upon [the] President," Crawford reported; "he vibrates to that side." Informants revealed Lincoln suddenly spending more time talking with military and naval officers and, significantly, engineers—men trained to attack fortresses. The commissioners suggested cutting off supplies to Sumter right away, which would force Major Anderson to evacuate in time and take matters out of Lincoln's hands. Meanwhile, they warned, "watch at all points." Seward could be lying to them about making no attempt to reinforce Sumter without first notifying the Confederates. Or "their form of notice to us may be that of the coward who gives it when he strikes."[97]

Speedily the signs turned ugly. The commissioners saw intense activity around the War and Navy departments. Even while Campbell insisted yet again that Seward did not deceive him, Crawford, Roman, and Forsyth found warships fitting out at the Navy Yard, and heard rumors that their destinations included the mouth of the Mississippi. Some stories said the ships were bound for Santo Domingo due to a minor diplomatic fray with Spain, but Crawford suspected it could be a ruse. Other gossip spoke of movements of artillery to be loaded aboard the ships for their unknown destination.[98] On April 6 a friend told Roman that Buchanan and others believed that the Union would launch an attack on Sumter or Pickens within a few days.[99] Suddenly the temperature rose exponentially. Walker hinted to a Kentuckian that he might suddenly be in a position to start accepting troops from Border States due to events "now very probable . . . at any day or hour."[100] And Toombs, while advising his Washington commissioners that "we are ready," confidentially told Little Aleck that movements by the Yankees looked increasingly hostile and he could not yet see how it was to end.[101]

Jefferson Davis read it all, and worried and worked later and later to make his little nation ready. People in Montgomery now commented that his duties were wearing him down alarmingly, and yet he would not give himself a rest.[102] He sent Campbell a confidential letter on April 6 asserting that "our policy is as you say, peace, it is our sentiment also." In words quite obviously written for Yankee eyes, and sent to the one man who could put the letter before Seward, Davis concluded that "I await the determination of a problem which it belongs to the Govt of the United States to control."[103] The President suspected that the Yankees might have been sending false telegrams to Montgomery to deceive them. He was wrong, but he did not know that far too much of his commissioners' correspondence over the wires went straight to Lincoln, revealing the Confederates' perceptions of affairs inside the White House.[104]

Thereafter the situation deteriorated almost hourly. This same April 6 Lincoln, his wavering past, notified South Carolina that he would send a fleet to resupply Fort Sumter but promised not to attempt military reinforcement if his ships passed unmolested. The next day he set in motion plans to land troops at Fort Pickens. The commissioners learned of both, and sent their secretary John Pickett to call at Seward's home on the evening of April 7 to demand on the morrow a reply to their March 12 memorandum in which they asked for a statement of Union intent and sued for official discussions. Seeing himself deceived in the end, Campbell bowed out of further participation, though still believing that Seward, at least, meant peace. At two in the afternoon on April 8 Pickett called at Seward's, where his son handed him a memorandum that the father had written weeks before on March 15, stating in sum that he could not, and would not meet with them. On his way back to their hotel, Pickett passed the State Department and saw brilliant lights glowing in the secretary's office. Surely they were coming to the last days now.[105]

When they read Seward's note, the commissioners immediately wired Toombs that their mission was over. They would reply to Seward and leave. The next day Pickett delivered a long, lecturing letter to the secretary of state declaring that provisioning Sumter constituted a declaration of war. Accepting "the gage of battle thus thrown down," they bade him a stiff farewell and started packing, with the sickening feeling that they had been duped all along, while in fact Seward shared their dismay. He had promised what he could not deliver, all the while expecting to manage Lincoln until he found that his President had a mind of his own.[106]

The news surprised few around Davis's cabinet table or in Montgomery itself. The people on the streets and in the departments seemed to welcome the final breakdown of relations. "Our people here are praying for a fight," Hooper boasted late in March.[107] By April 6, as Crawford and the rest saw their mission coming to futility, that war fever mushroomed. "People here are pleased with the prospects of a fight," one Mississippian observed, while others evidenced to a New Yorker that their only fear was that Lincoln would evade a conflict. "They are greatly pleased with the prospect of a 'brush.'"[108] Howell Cobb himself bragged to his friend Buchanan that "war with all its calamities will be welcomed with shouts of rejoicing," while at the same time he privately spoke with foolish assurance that there would be no fighting. At least he was perceptive enough to see that "the administration here are not so sanguine of peace as I am."[109] No one missed the increased activity at Government House, nor missed the talk in the War Department and at the Exchange among those in the know. "We expect every moment to hear of the commencement of hostilities," a Georgian said on April 9.[110]

Indeed the administration were not sanguine, perhaps explaining why President Davis appeared to behave kindly "but shruggingly" toward Cobb and his increasingly unrealistic hopes for peace.[111] While some of his friends like Harris still held such hopes, Davis knew it would not be, especially after news of the plan to resupply Sumter.[112] "I have not been of those who felt sanguine hope that the enemy would retire peaceably," Davis told Governor Pickens in mid-March. "His stay must soon be measured by our forebearance."[113] Convinced of what was to come, Davis had wanted ever since taking office to go to Charleston personally to look over its batteries, but the press of business in Montgomery held him.[114] Still, with Beauregard there he felt increasing confidence. The same April 6 that the hammer blow fell, a New Orleanean saw the President and found him calm, serene even, yet grave, with "a presence of mind, a chastened energy." He would be ready.[115]

The evening of March 28, the same night that Lincoln privately made his decision to resupply Fort Sumter, a white horse tied to a buggy on Bibb Street suddenly spooked and took off at a run, down Bibb to Government House, then around it into Commerce, past the Exchange, and around Court Square and on to Lawrence before it stopped.[116] The runaway seemed to symbolize something, North and South. Affairs of men had left their hands. Perhaps that poor frightened animal, like the horse of the Bible, sniffed the battle from afar, and sensed the imminent approach of another, terrible steed bearing a rider of the Apocalypse.

"The first blow must be successful, both for its moral and physical consequences," Davis told Pickens. "A failure would demoralize our people and injuriously affect us in the opinion of the world as reckless and precipitate."[117] Thus the delays in Washington actually worked to his purpose as they gave him time to build the strength of his regiments and batteries at Charleston and Pensacola. In fact, through the last of March many expected that if a first shot came, Lincoln would fire it at Fort Pickens, not Fort Sumter.[118] Rumors of several hundred Federals being ordered there in late March raised fears that were only enhanced when word came that some of Twiggs's Texas garrison were also landed there instead of being taken to New York as agreed in their paroles.[119] As of the end of March poor Bragg had a mere 1,018 soldiers in his command, prompting Cooper urgently to designate 5,000 more to be sent to him from the new levy of state regiments.[120] Within a few days of their arrival, Bragg proposed plans for attacking Fort Pickens before it could be reinforced to impregnable strength, somewhat cynically saying that he could depend for success against the intimidating fortress on the weakness of its current garrison and the "ignorance" of his own troops who would attack not knowing what they faced. Davis dissuaded him, sending Mallory to Pensacola as his messenger, and made it clear that if the first shots came there, he wanted Lincoln to fire them, especially since an attack on Fort Pickens looked much less of a certainty for success than one on Fort Sumter.[121] Meanwhile the almost daily sight of troops coming into Montgomery by rail or boat, only to embark once more on the cars for Pensacola, reinforced the popular notion that an imminent collision approached on the Gulf.[122] "There is little talked of here but Pensacola, and the prospects there," a reporter wrote. "The most absurd rumors are afloat, and men are leaving for Pensacola on the strength of them."[123]

For all the speculation about Pensacola, eyes in Montgomery never stopped straining eastward toward Charleston. On April 8, at the same time that Davis and Walker ordered Beauregard to halt any flow of local provisions into Fort Sumter, the general informed them that he had actually done so the day before upon being notified of Lincoln's intention to resupply.[124] Davis met with his secretaries for at least two hours that afternoon. Where a couple of days earlier a visit to the cabinet room found that some of the secretaries still entertained a "roseate" view of peace, matters now assumed an entirely different hue.[125] While people in town speculated on what was being said behind closed doors, everything about the War Department betrayed a bustle of excitement and activity.[126] Everyone surmised the serious import of what Davis and the rest debated, and they were right. The President pressed upon the others an aggressive policy. Seward declined to meet their ambassadors. Lincoln had been duplicitous with them. It was time to deliver an ultimatum. With the cabinet behind him, he authorized the commissioners in Washington to inform Seward that they regarded his refusal, and the announcement of an attempt to resupply Sumter, as a declaration of war. The crisis might still be averted, but only if Lincoln backed down. When the meeting adjourned, however, the cabinet unanimously expressed their opinion that "war is inevitable."[127]

That same day Davis instructed Walker to issue a call for more troops, 1,500 from Florida and 3,000 each from the rest. In the great rush, and in Walker's own haphazard manner, some notifications went out immediately, while others had to be repeated by Hooper the following day. Still Pettus only learned of the requirement from Mississippi by reading it in a Jackson newspaper on April 10, while Walker neglected to specify to Alabama's Governor Moore that he wanted infantry.[128]

The president met with his general staff supply officers, and told them that "for the infantry, men must first be fed, next armed, and even clothing must follow these; for if they are fed and have arms and ammunition they can fight." Thus their limited means would go first to Northrop for subsistence, then to Gorgas for arms, and last to Myers for clothing and other equipment.[129] From Gorgas he ordered an immediate report of the arms throughout the Confederacy, and learned that same day that somewhere over 200,000 shoulder arms of all description were available, many of them antiquated flintlocks, and only about 15,000 modern percussion rifles. Moreover, Gorgas reported less than a million rounds of ammunition, and most of that useless since he could find barely a quarter million percussion caps for firing them. They had no stores of lead, only about 60,000 pounds of cannon powder, and no field artillery to use it except a few ancient pieces that had seen service in the War of 1812. Worse, they had no machinery for making rifles, and the only cannon foundry in the South was Tredegar. He had a lot of work ahead of him.[130]

That same April 8 Walker put Forsyth in Washington to work on a new task as his old one ended. He started shopping for guns, and within two days found ninety tons of cannon powder and ten tons of rifle powder for sale by a New York firm. Walker placed the order, trying to keep it something of a secret by referring to it as "rope." Forsyth also bought 2,000 pistols and several thousand rifles.[131] More officers had to be commissioned, especially with the commandant at Fort Morgan complaining of his "deplorably ignorant" garrison and the need for instructors.[132] As newly resigned Old Army men came to Montgomery, Walker speedily assigned them to the forts at New Orleans, Mobile, and elsewhere.[133] More noted men, like the old Texan Indian fighter Ben McCulloch, got command of new regiments to be raised for frontier service, and when Davis's old friend and fellow Mississippian Earl Van Dorn arrived on April 6, the President gave him overall command in Texas, and walked him down to the bluff where he boarded the

Southern Republic amid the huzzas of the ladies on the bank. One hand on the rail and the other lifting his hat in salute, Van Dorn steamed away to the strains of the now-monotonous "Marseillaise" on the calliope.[134] He looked like so many of the other young men going off to near-certain war. "They were stalwart, handsome fellows, and had intelligent faces," wrote a Virginian then in Montgomery. "They will make the best fighting material in the world."[135]

They could measure the remaining peace by hours, now. On April 9 Walker ordered Beauregard to stop all mail into and out of Sumter. "The fort must be completely isolated," he said.[136] The braggart Wigfall, now in Charleston for the anticipated action, telegraphed a whimsical offer to give Davis a lock of Major Anderson's hair, not realizing that the major and the president were old and close friends, and that the Yankee's predicament pained Davis considerably.[137] All day long Montgomery hung suspended in anticipation. The messengers went back and forth from the War Department to the Winter Building almost hourly with their telegrams. Loungers noticed an increase in the bustle about Government House.[138] More trains came into the depots, bringing ever more soldiers for Pensacola. Crowds gathered outside the newspaper offices and the telegraph office, hoping to learn something, anything.[139] A rumor suddenly swept through the streets that the Yankee fleet had appeared off Charleston harbor, and that Beauregard even then blazed away at the ships. Confirmation that the story was a hoax dampened further speculation for a few hours as everyone sheepishly admitted how easily they had been duped.[140]

That evening President Davis sat by himself at the ladies' table in the Exchange, paying little attention to his meal as usual. Other diners left him alone, seeing him lost in deep thoughts they could only imagine.[141] Soon afterwards he called a cabinet meeting, and as the conversation lasted long into the evening, and past midnight, they struggled with their next move.[142] Confused for so long by Lincoln's "shifting and wavering," Davis now believed that he saw the Yankees' treacherous purpose all along. There was nothing left to them but to "forestall their scheming by a bold act," he said. "We, at least, mean what we say— independence or destruction." Even as he spoke fondly of Anderson, Davis argued that they should demand Sumter's immediate evacuation before the supply fleet arrived, and if Anderson refused, they should open fire and blast him out.[143]

The cabinet meetings had become increasingly tense in recent days, and none more so than the stormy one tonight. Virtually all now saw war as imminent, if not inevitable. Yet years later the formerly bellicose Toombs claimed that he, at least, shrank from making the first overt act. He feared that firing on Sumter would energize the North into rallying to Old Glory.[144] Reaching the meeting after it started, he immediately declined to advise Davis, protesting—so he said years after—that "the firing upon that fort will inaugurate a civil war greater than any the world has yet seen."[145] Now he stood and paced back and forth in the cabinet room, his hands clasped behind his back as he tried to vent his pent-up energy. "Mr. President," he told Davis, "the shot that is fired at Fort Sumpter [sic] will reverberate 'round the world." The expression may not have been very original, but its import carried no less substance. "Hasten slowly," Toombs advised, using a favorite expression of Davis's.[146] "At this time it is suicide, murder, and will lose us every friend at the North," he went on, giving in to his instinct for hyperbole. "You will wantonly strike a hornet's nest," he said. "It is unnecessary; it puts us in the wrong; it is fatal."[147]

Toombs had a wonderful hindsight that put him on the right side of issues *after* the fact. Perhaps now he did oppose overt action, though his motive for so doing is obscure, but the majority of the cabinet stood behind Davis. Outside the watchers concluded that "all the indications are that the issue of peace or war will shortly be made."[148] "This state of things cannot remain long," Hooper believed.[149] An explosion must come soon. Down at the wharf a steamboat calliope wheezed out the ever-present strains of "Dixie," now considered in Montgomery virtually a Confederate anthem.[150] With its stirring strains faintly audible at the other end of Commerce Street, President Jefferson Davis made his decision, and most of his ministers concurred. Tomorrow Beauregard should give Anderson the ultimatum. As if Davis needed any further encouragement, within a few hours Wigfall would telegraph from Charleston that "Lincoln intends war." "Let us take Fort Sumter."[151]

The next morning, April 10, Walker sent the telegram down the street to the Winter Building. Beauregard should demand an immediate evacuation. If refused, he was to commence operations to reduce the fort to surrender. A telegram also went to the commissioners in Washington from Toombs, ordering them to leave immediately after giving copies of their correspondence with Seward to foreign ministers in the hope the evident duplicity might work to Confederate advantage.[152]

In Montgomery itself anxiety only mounted when Walker posted bulletins outside Government House and the newspaper offices announcing recent events.[153] Again everyone noted intense activity in and around the War Department, and rumor now predicted that the war would commence on the morrow. "A day or two will test the truth of our prediction," said the *Advertiser*.[154] One local secession hothead actually got into Walker's office in the afternoon to berate him for not opening fire right away. People in the state still wavered on independence, he ranted, and needed the hot fire of a war to weld their resolve.[155] In the Exchange men simply stood around in the corridors, or lounged outside in the summery seventy-five degree weather.[156] Every train leaving the city took hundreds of soldiers toward Pensacola, and as the cabinet sat with Davis most of the day, a battle seemed inevitable.[157] Word came from Beauregard that he wanted to make his actual demand the next day, April 11, and when he explained that he had a special reason for doing so, Walker and Davis allowed him the delay. His reason, in fact, is that he still was not entirely ready, needing a shipment of powder due in that evening, and with a few more cannon and men to position.[158]

April 11 offered an agony of suspense for citizens and officials alike. A tense Walker spent much of the day fighting with Governor Brown once more, who now insisted that he would forward no troops directly to Montgomery for mustering, fearful that someone else would select their officers for them. All Georgia regiments must muster in Georgia, he said. His state "will insist on having her rights and interests respected." Walker really did not need this foolishness right now, and shot back a stiff reply that "you may feel satisfied that I shall regard all the courtesies." Even now Brown still delayed in obeying Congress's order that he hand over all forts and arsenals to Confederate control, leaving the War Department unable to take precautions for the defense of Fort Pulaski at Savannah. A frustrated Bartow finally wired Walker "don't wait on the Governor," as the state convention acted without him.[159] And when Hemphill complained again of Texas being ignored, the secretary almost lost his patience, begging that the Texans "concede to this Department a just allowance for the embarrassments growing out of the importance and the multiplicity of the business which has suddenly devolved upon it."[160] They were only hours away from war, and still these fools quibbled and pettifogged.

That morning Davis allowed Walker to post a new bulletin announcing Beauregard's surrender demand. "People here are delighted that the uncertainty is at an end," a New Orleans correspondent observed.[161] While the streets took on a more warlike appearance than ever before, the True Blues paraded on Market Street before an admiring crowd, and then put on a shooting competition for a silver goblet to come from the hands of the fair Maggie Mitchell. Reporters noticed that the intense excitement of the past several days so occupied the attention of all that even the number of street fights and shootings was down.[162]

The cabinet met throughout the day, chiefly now to pore over the latest telegrams from Beauregard. First word came early in the afternoon, when the general announced that Anderson had refused his demand, but then added that if the Confederates did not batter him to pieces, his garrison would be starved out in a few days anyhow. Here was a glimmer of last-minute hope for peace. Quickly Walker's messenger took a response to the Winter Building, where the wires sent out permission to hold fire if Anderson would state positively when he would have to evacuate. Montgomery felt no desire for a needless bombardment if it could get Sumter peacefully. But if the Yankees declined to state a specific date, then Beauregard was to open fire.[163]

It was well into the evening by the time Walker's last response went to Charleston. Likely they would hear nothing further until after midnight. President Davis divided his day between his apartments at the Exchange and his office in Government House. From the windows of either he could see the Winter Building, and the messengers passing to and fro with Walker's telegrams. A kind of relief, the peace of decision, settled over him now, and he talked more freely with visitors than for some time past, even waxing expansive on Confederate hopes and justifications. "He who makes the assault is not necessarily he that strikes the first blow or fires the first shot," he said in defense of their acts.[164] While well-wishers pumped his hand and offered congratulations, he predicted that the Border States must inevitably join them. "Our cause is a common cause, as our ideas and interests are common ideas and interests, all so interwoven that they are naturally adhesive," he said. The idea that state rights doctrine might carry within it the seeds of destruction was a mere plausibility, and nothing more, though Walker's problems with Governor Brown might have argued otherwise.[165]

When he turned to coming events in Charleston, the President sounded even more confidant. "Our people are a gallant, impetuous and determined people, worthy, in all respects, of their heroic sires," he told Stuart. "What they resolve to do, that, they most assuredly, mean to persevere in doing." He abhorred violence, he said, though throughout his life his temper made him quick to resort to action. He yet hoped that Anderson would make it possible for North and South not to measure swords in battle. If they must, however, then he knew his people. They were impulsive and sensitive, like himself, "but they never flinch or shrink from what an excess of either quality may superinduce." Should the Yankees challenge them, they would be met.[166]

That night another rumor went the rounds that Anderson had actually given up, but it was more than premature.[167] Sometime past midnight an anxious secretary of war wired to Charleston to ask Anderson's reply. Beauregard responded that "he would not consent."[168] Back went Walker's messenger Phillips Gayle with the order to open fire.[169] Few in the War Department slept that night waiting for the next telegram from Charleston. Dawn came, another cloudy sixty-degree morning, and new rumors circulated, one saying that Beauregard was giving Anderson until noon, or else.[170] Far more amusing was the story circulated by local character Ned Hanrick, a fellow so superstitious that he carried a heavy horse shoe in his bulging pocket. Already well along in drink, he told friends that morning that he heard that France and the United States had just declared war against each other, and that the French and the Confederates would soon be sharing Mexico between them.[171]

As it grew lighter, anxious crowds gathered in the streets, especially outside the newspaper offices, the Exchange, Government House, and in and around Court Square. Puddles in the streets outside the War office reflected gray skies, taking on the "miniature resemblance of opaque lakelets" to Hooper.[172] The Sons of the Sunny South, having nothing better to do, gathered for brandy and cake in their room above the telegrapher's office, occasionally looking out their windows at the crowds in Commerce Street. From that vantage they kept watch on Jonce going back and forth from Government House, reporter Banks of the *Confederation* and Reid of the *Advertiser* dogging his heels in the futile attempt to learn his errands. At the same time they cocked an ear for the click of the telegrapher's receiver beneath them, and occasionally went downstairs to try to persuade twenty-one-year-old William Griffith to tell them the song the wires sang. Despite his Northern birth, young Griffith kept the secrets of the Confederacy to himself. In fact, for some time Griffith found nothing to do, Walker forbidding any private telegrams in order to keep the wire open for news from Beauregard.[173]

By nine o'clock every official or government employee not at his desk stood cornered in some doorway being grilled by the curious for information he did not have. John Heart joined the Sons of the Sunny

South to debunk Hanrick's wild fantasy, and found the room filling with many who were not members, including a bombastic South Carolinian. Anxiety and frustration told on everyone by now, and soon he and Heart exchanged words. "I am a Carolinian, sir, and you are an old and lame man," shouted Heart's antagonist. Holding up his pistol hand, the newsman retorted that "this finger is young and limber." Looking on, Stuart mused to himself that "this sniffs of pistols for two." The argument stopped there forever. Outside in Court Square they all heard a great shout. Leaping to their windows they looked down to see the flag of the True Blues emerging from the balcony of the telegraph office beneath. With no prearrangement whatever, all Montgomery knew its meaning.[174]

But for the distraction of Heart and the South Carolinian they might have heard the sound of the machine below, or seen the messenger sprint to the War Department. Now as people on the streets raced to crowd the front of the building, a Doctor Weir stepped out on the balcony and announced receipt of the telegram. At half past four that morning Beauregard had opened fire on Fort Sumter. There was no more news, but it was enough.[175]

The crowd exploded. Weir asked three cheers for Beauregard, and the audience responded lustily. Then someone saw a large flag run out from the window of Government House, and they surged down Commerce in hopes of learning more.[176] As they rushed past the Exchange, some leaped up the steps and into the lobby to shout the news. E. C. Bullock stood, called for silence, and prayed "may the native hue of their resolution not be sickled o'er by the pale case of thought."[177] If any thought his words rather inappropriate for the thrill of the moment—or even wondered just what in the world he was talking about—they tarried not to quibble. In the hands of the True Blues "Old Secession" barked seven times in front of Government House, once for each state, plus an eighth for Beauregard. More cheers followed—cheers for the general, cheers for Davis, cheers for Walker, and more. The crowd shouted for their heroes to give them speeches, but already Davis and cabinet sat locked in discussion, not to emerge for hours.[178]

Rapidly the euphoria spread. Caleb Huse, just then coming into town on a stage to undertake a mission for Gorgas, met with a rider shouting to all sides that Sumter was under fire.[179] Stores closed their doors and the crowds only continued to swell, De Leon finding the "fever heat" infectious in the streets and hotel lobbies.[180] Under a now-beautiful sky with only light clouds, and the thermometer at a perfect seventy degrees, they might have thought the Almighty had sent such a day for such an occasion.[181] Almost mindlessly they milled about, first rushing the *Advertiser* office, then the *Mail*, then the Winter Building, and back again to Government House.[182] Soon the rumors mushroomed. Sumter was surrendered and the Yankee relief fleet sunk. McCulloch was going to take 25,000 soldiers and march on Washington. Lincoln and his General-in-Chief Winfield Scott would be prisoners in ten days. Only their President's refusal to accept premature congratulations dampened the wilder speculations.[183]

Finally came another telegram from Beauregard. All day the firing ran heavy. With no injury at all to his own command, he believed he had damaged several of Sumter's guns, and while the Yankee relief fleet had arrived during the bombardment, it made no attempt to come to the fort's aid. All was going well.[184] Nothing more came that day, and the thousands of men spent the balance of the afternoon in the taverns and hotel bars moistening their speculations. No one seemed even mildly interested in the other news from Pensacola that Bragg had arrested a Yankee officer who smuggled into Fort Pickens word that Lincoln would be sending reinforcements.[185] The Sons of the Sunny South returned to their club room and celebrated in brandy and wine. Over at the *Mail* offices, Hooper quickly improvised a woodblock etching of the Confederate flag and placed it at the masthead of that day's issue. Then in the early evening an impromptu assembly of half-drunk citizens, visitors, whites and blacks, men and boys gathered behind a brass band to parade through the streets and watch the True Blues come out yet again to drill on Commerce. When they all finally went to their dinners, the dining halls at the Exchange and elsewhere became a bedlam, while the streets looked suddenly deserted but for the day's inebriates unsteadily stumbling home.[186]

Their meals done, and their throats refreshed by more spirits, the throng reassembled outside the Winter Building. They pressed nearby planks into service and erected a hasty platform, then Mayor Noble officiated at an informal meeting inaugurated by a blast from a reluctant brass cannon that would not fire until Clitherall nearly scorched himself by lighting it with his cigar. In reward for his heroism Clitherall spoke first, followed by a host of others, with even Mallory and Reagan joining the audience. After some hours of this, the crowd surged to the Exchange once more, yelling for Davis and Walker to give them speeches. It was nearly midnight by now. Despite the spectacle of thousands of people illuminated by lamp and torch and bonfire, the President was too exhausted and sent his apologies. Walker came out and gave them what they wanted to hear. Sumter would fall on the morrow, he predicted, and if the Yankees did not then recognize Confederate independence, their brave new flag would fly over Washington itself in another three months, and perhaps even above Faneuil Hall in Boston.[187] Clearly, Walker lost his self-control in all the glorying, and even though Davis did not hear his speech, he would be dismayed when he learned its content. They sought to adopt a posture before the world of self-defense, not aggression. By asserting that the South might take the war into the North, Walker committed a serious diplomatic blunder that might inspirit the Yankees, and give pause to foreign powers thinking of supporting the Confederacy. Despite his words being reported identically by half a dozen correspondents in the crowd, and his virtual repetition of them almost a month later, he soon tried to deny that he ever said such things.[188]

Certainly no one in the crowd minded the secretary's indiscretion. They found it thrilling, especially when he gave the latest news from Charleston.[189] A few looked on with less than enthusiasm, Fitzpatrick groaning that "we have won a mouse to lose a mountain," while the ever-critical Stuart thought it an "exhibition of imbecility," and not just by Walker. For the rest it was what they came for. When Walker finished, others spoke. Chilton of Texas called for renewed huzzas, and Benjamin gave a talk "in a nice lispy fashion."[190]

Once the crowd extorted all the speeches it could at the Exchange, it marched on with its band to Mrs. Cleveland's, and there awoke Toombs to give them yet one more harangue.[191] Back at the hotel, a weary Davis still could not sleep. He must attend to some business. The crisis demanded that he recall the Congress earlier than planned, and at Benjamin's suggestion he drafted and signed a proclamation convening an extraordinary session on April 29.[192] A few visitors also managed to get in, though Josselyn insulated him as best he could. They found him lying on the sofa in his parlor, smoking a cigar, and showing his weariness. He confessed his regret at firing the first shot, and at the same time deprecated the posturing speeches and the mood of jollity outside. They were at an earnest business now, and the action of that day signaled either the end of their interminable political contest with the North, or else the commencement of a long war.[193]

"We are all one people now," the *Confederation* proclaimed that same evening. "No Democrat, no American—all for the new Confederacy. Let

Davis and Stephens be the war cry."[194] Only well after midnight did the cheers and the shouts finally subside in Montgomery. Their meetings and speeches done, the men caroused late into the night after everyone else went home, filling the barrooms and hotel lobbies, drinking, boasting, chewing over and over again at the news, and trying unconsciously not to let go of the euphoria that attended the greatest moment of their generation.[195]

Early with the dawn on April 13 the sleepless and the hung over stumbled out to haunt the streets for news. Davis himself escaped the Exchange briefly for a walk and a smoke, and young Culver found him at St. John's Church awaiting reports in "a brown study," troubled, reflective, more uneasy over the future than he would admit.[196] On through the morning they all waited. First came a telegram announcing that the wooden barracks inside Sumter were ablaze, and that the fort returned fire only at long intervals.[197] Then shortly after one thirty that afternoon the True Blues' flag flew from the telegraph office again, and a rush of the citizenry descended on Court Square, their shouts already rising to a roar. Once there they saw the big Confederate flag made for the Congress being unfurled from an upper story window of Government House by Capers and Charles Wagoner, and the sea of people surged down Commerce. The workers in the government departments abandoned their counting rooms and desks to join the throng. Standing in a window, Wagoner read the latest dispatches, while Davis and the cabinet stood in the other windows where the crowd could see them. "Quarters in Sumter all burned down," Wagoner slowly intoned. The crowd remained quiet, breathless. "White flag up," he went on. "Anderson surrenders."[198] Cheers interrupted him at every pause. Cooper had already ordered a fifteen-gun salute for two o'clock, and now the crowd joined in shouts for Davis, Beauregard, the cabinet, and the Confederacy.

"All honor to the gallant sons of Carolina," Davis wired Pickens.[199] To Beauregard, Walker sent congratulations. "You have won your spurs," he said, then wasted little more time on encomiums, and instead asked how many cannon could be shipped from Charleston to the next danger point, Pensacola.[200] Meanwhile the wild celebration continued outside. More bonfires charred the dusty streets, crowds gathered everywhere, the whiskey flowed with renewed enthusiasm in what Hilliard thought "splendid demonstrations of joy."[201] The only disappointed were the few Yankee sympathizers, and prudently they kept their feelings to themselves. Young Joseph Kerbey, who fancied that he might have averted all this by assassinating Davis in the Exchange a few days before, had to walk and walk to calm his nerves, and finally found himself several miles out of town along the West Point tracks before he stopped.[202]

That evening, while the great and would-be great sat in the hotel parlors and savored the narcotic of victory, some in the Exchange turned to the odd topic of past heroes who had been bastards. Washington Miller of Texas, already a disappointed office seeker with a grudge, then announced that their own president came of unmarried parents, a pure fabrication.[203] Down in suite 101, however, the "bastard" himself felt nothing but joy. "Fort Sumter is ours and nobody is hurt," he exulted in relief. "There has been no blood spilled more precious than that of a mule."[204] A man normally given neither to poetry nor to puns, he showed his own elation by relaxing his reserve and trying his hand at both. "With mortar, Paixhan and petard," he quipped, "we tender old Abe our Beauregard."[205]

CHAPTER THIRTEEN

ALL WE ASK IS TO BE
LET ALONE

———————•★•———————

THE DAY SUMTER FELL, an Alabamian's wife gave birth to twins, a
boy and a girl. The parents named them Jefferson Davis Wright
and Alexandria Stephens Wright.[1] It was the temper of the times. But
it said more than that in its implications. Now Davis and Stephens—
and by extention their government—were the heroes of the hour. They
had led the South in coming together, and now they had led it into the
face of hazard. A victory was certainly a victory, but was it a war?
Would the Yankees fight back, or would they realize that the Confederacy intended to be independent and would defend its rights at the
points of its bayonets? Now, like the Founding Fathers before them,
the Confederates had their "shot heard round the world." Could this
new government still forming contend with the mighty issue of real
war? For all of the challenges that faced those men in broadcloth in
Montgomery on April 12, two days later in the flush of triumph their
responsibilities and the dangers before them increased exponentially.

Telegrams poured into Montgomery from around the South, con-
gratulating the government on its victory. The Border States sent messages of encouragement, too, and Walker managed to stretch a point a
bit when he accepted a wagon train of supplies seized from Federals
out in Texas, declaring it contraband "under the state of war existing
between this Government & that at Washington," despite the fact
that the seizure took place several days before Fort Sumter.[2] Davis felt
almost expansive in his relief. "We are disposed to be magnanimous,"
he told Stuart. "It will leave a loophole for a more decided style of
diplomacy than Mr. Lincoln sees fit now to tolerate." They had shown
the North that they meant business by taking the fort. Forbearance
now would demonstrate "how willing we, also, are that the beginning
should be the end."[3]

319

Throughout Sunday April 14 the festive mood held in Montgomery. There could have been no more propitious time for the steamer *King* to come around the bend from Mobile, bearing the First Lady. When in sight of the city the steamer fired seven guns to announce its important passenger and the city turned out in welcome. Varina went first to the Exchange, bringing with her the French chef she hired in New Orleans, and the next day she and the President moved into the now remodeled Harrison house at Washington and Bibb.[4] With her she brought their children, her father, and her younger sister, and they rode to their new home in a fine $1,300 carriage that Davis just had imported from New Jersey, to no little comment from Montgomeryites.[5]

Varina delighted in her warm welcome. Hampers of blossoms awaited her at the house, while on all sides well-wishers waved and threw more flowers in their path. The house itself she found roomy enough for the family, and fortunately Thomas Powell had recently moved his Auction and Commission Depot for slaves out of the Dillehay House across the street, and now his wife operated it as a boardinghouse.[6] They might be about to fight over slavery, but Varina had no desire to live next to a market where they were sold. The very day after her arrival, she held her first entertainment, a small private dinner for the family, along with Toombs and the recently arrived Forsyth and Roman. Little Aleck Stephens also reached Montgomery late on April 15, and he attended as well. They all passed a most pleasant evening, even Toombs agreeing that everything seemed to be going smoothly.[7]

The mood lasted but a moment. Even as Varina joined her husband at the Exchange on April 15, a telegram arrived from Pickett, still in Washington, announcing that Lincoln had issued a call for 75,000 volunteers, summoned his own Congress to assemble on July 4, and declared the existence of a state of insurrection, giving the South just twenty days to put down its arms and abide by the laws.[8] While some rumored that President and cabinet met the proclamation with bursts of laughter, Davis resented such speculations, and in fact they took it very seriously.[9] As gossip swept Montgomery that Stephens's arrival signaled his takeover of the civil administration as Davis assumed command of an army to march on Washington, the President and his ministers turned their attention to what to do next.[10]

He made it clear immediately that he entertained no intention of taking the field himself. During a meeting of several hours on the morning of April 16, he discussed the response of the Border States, which looked promising, with rumors of imminent secession by

Virginia. They must raise more regiments at once, deciding on a call for 32,000 additional volunteers, 5,000 from each state except for 2,000 from Florida. It seemed a modest, unprovocative response to Lincoln's call, but would still give them a total army of just over 50,000.[11] It was also possible now that they might be able to raise, or accept, troops from the Border States themselves even prior to secession. Davis seemed confidant that all of the wavering slave states would now join the cause in the face of Lincoln's raising an army with the apparent intent to invade the South. "I *think* the whole South will consolidate," Stephens agreed, "but events transpire so rapidly *now* that it is useless to speculate two days ahead." Considering the probability that Lincoln would attempt to blockade Confederate ports, the cabinet also discussed giving letters of marque engaging privateers to prey on Yankee shipping, and decided that Davis should issue a call for applications.[12] Meanwhile, before any such blockade could become effective, Walker suggested that they aggressively purchase arms in Europe, perhaps up to as many as 150,000 rifles. Others, viewing the crisis more conservatively, argued that no more than 12,000 would be needed.[13] In the end, they only agreed to send Caleb Huse on the mission with flexible instructions as to quantities.

From that day on they all moved with frenzied activity. Davis frankly confessed to old friends that he had "no time for friendly correspondence," and closeted himself with Walker.[14] Explaining the obvious, that "there is every reason to anticipate the operations of both belligerents will be conducted on a much more imposing scale than this continent has ever witnessed," Walker sent his requisitions to the governors.[15] Finally learning a lesson from his earlier misjudgments, he telegraphed his request for additional regiments.[16] And he tried diplomacy, especially with Thomas Moore in Louisiana, who had a company of men armed with modern rifled muskets, the only so-equipped group in prospect at the moment. Humbly Walker asked for the men "as a courtesy to my-self." Moore willingly agreed.[17]

The President, meanwhile, concentrated on his proclamation calling for privateers. On April 16 encouraging word reached him that the British foreign minister, Lord John Russell, had told friends he expected England would recognize the Confederacy if Lincoln tried to declare a blockade.[18] Naturally Confederate privateers would honor the rights of neutral shipping, but their very existence would be a tangible reminder of any interdiction of shipping when imposed, and a suggestion as well that it was Lincoln's blockade, not Davis's policy, that kept

Southern cotton away from Europe. On April 17 Davis issued his call, and almost immediately applicants replied, the first on the next day. Thereafter they came in almost daily for ships named *Rattlesnake*, *Triton*, *Charleston*, *Jefferson Davis*, and more. In the end some four hundred applications were received. An old school friend of Josselyn's begged for his influence in getting him a letter of marque, promising no great feats, but expecting "to overhaul at least a Cincinnati flatboat."[19] Benjamin found himself somewhat embarrassed when he discovered he had no idea how to word letters of marque, and could find no examples in any of his law books. In the end he asked a British visitor for help.[20]

In time Davis would send blank letters to Europe to commission more privateers once the few available private vessels in the Confederacy had been converted and commissioned.[21] He also made certain that Yancey and the other diplomats abroad received word of his action, and the promise to observe neutrality, and at the same time sent copies of the correspondence of his commissioners to Washington to show the peaceful intent of the South, and the duplicity of the North, hoping it might help in showing Britain and France where stood the right.[22] Finally, just the day after issuing the proclamation inviting civilians to become privateers, Davis—through Mallory—summoned Semmes to go to New Orleans and take command of the refitting of the Navy vessel *Sumter*, destined to be their first armed commerce raider. Semmes hoped to have it out of the yards and on the seas by the summer.[23] Carrying out the decision of the cabinet, Gorgas and Cooper met with young Huse and gave him his instructions, as well as money to get to Europe and start buying arms and supplies of all manner on a credit of £10,000.[24]

The bustle spilled into the streets from the departments as everyone was swept up in what Benjamin told Beauregard was "the éclat of your glorious triumph."[25] The volunteers coming from the several states in response to Walker's calls marveled at all the activity. "All nature seemed palpitating in sympathy with the intensity of popular excitement," found a Georgian just arrived.[26] An aspiring young naval cadet a week after the firing on Sumter found the city's excitement boiling over. "Nobody seemed to know exactly what it was about," he discovered, "but it was the fashion to be excited." The ubiquitous "Marseillaise" thundered out the windows of every house with a piano, as well as in the Exchange parlor, where champagne flowed "like water" through crowds of freshly arrived officers clad in such a variety of gaudy militia and homemade uniforms that they looked more like a costume ball than an army in the making. The hotel parlor's chairs and windowsills brimmed with bottles and glasses, while a sweating German sat at the piano banging out the same song over and over again as the revellers sang along. "A more ridiculous sight than a lot of native-born Americans, not understanding a word of French, beating their breasts as they howled what they flattered themselves were the words of the song," said the cadet, "it was never before my bad fortune to witness." When the singers took a brief break to hiccup and listen to a speech, the exhausted foreigner left the instrument and went to a window for breath, muttering to himself "Dom the Marseillaise."[27]

The women of Montgomery stood with the men in their response. One soldier's wife wrote an open letter to Lincoln on April 17, giving it to the newspapers so she could publicly proclaim her contempt for the Union and her promise that "we are ready to meet you" and would probably march within six months to drive him from Washington.[28] The churches stayed open every day for volunteer women to gather sewing uniforms. Passersby saw and heard the laughter and song of their slave maids as they worked, too, out in the cool afternoon sun.[29] "We are living and making history every hour," a Georgian proclaimed. He might also have added that they were making a lot of myth. On April 18 a clerk yelled out the War Department window that Tennessee and Kentucky had offered to send 50,000 men, which was hardly true.[30] Others stated positively that Davis would take the field shortly, that Bragg would soon attack Fort Pickens, even that the Confederates intended to make Washington their permanent capital. "It would be an easy matter for us to fill up our whole paper with the speculations of the crowd," said the *Confederation*.[31] The fact that Jefferson Davis took his Mexican War saber to a local gun shop for sharpening certainly contributed to the stories, as it quickly became an object of curiosity for visitors who called just to look at the blade.[32]

Most of the more immediate speculation centered on Virginia. As far back as January its state assembly considered a resolution calling for unity with the seceded states if no settlement could be found.[33] The day after arriving in Montgomery at the opening of the convention, Boyce of South Carolina urged Senator R. M. T. Hunter to put his shoulder to the wheel and lead the Old Dominion out of the Union, promising that "Virginia shall have things exactly as she wants them capital included."[34] Within days, former Governor Henry Wise promised Davis to "stampede the flower of the State to the South," and the firing on Fort Sumter galvanized that sympathy to action.[35] On April 15 Confederate flags went up all over Richmond, and at the announcement of Lincoln's call for volunteers members of the Virginia convention then in session wired Toombs that the state would go out. Two days later that prediction came to pass.[36]

Davis and Stephens were meeting with Walker on April 17 when the telegram reached them. "It will probably end the war," Little Aleck speculated in a moment of uncharacteristic optimism.[37] The flag of the True Blues fluttered from the Winter Building balcony once more, a crowd gathered immediately, and as soon as the news was revealed, men in the streets started shaking hands and embracing with tears in their eyes.[38] The crowd inevitably shifted to Government House, jamming Commerce Street as Confederate flags even then started poking from every window and balcony, some even with a new star crudely sewn on the blue field.[39] Walker prudently declined to make a speech, perhaps at Davis's urging. Instead, Colonel Wagoner read the latest dispatches to the accompaniment of cheers, including one announcing that Tennessee was about to call its own state convention.[40] At once Walker ordered a salute fired from "Old Secession," John Tyler being given the honor of touching off the first shot.[41]

Predictably, that evening brought the bonfires, the fireworks, the bands, and the speeches. Virginians in town fired one hundred guns in salute from capitol hill, followed by rockets shot into the fair evening skies. The platform went up in Court Square again, and Clitherall, Tyler, the duelist Banks, and a host of others harangued the crowd, concluding with an incomprehensible brogue speech by a drunken news vendor called "Irish Billy." What De Leon now called "the invariable whiskey" came out in quantity, and most of the Border State people in town gathered at the celebrate.[42] More of the same came the next night with the arrival of Roger Pryor, one of Virginia's few fire-eaters, recently in Charleston to see the bombardment. He presented Davis with a fragment of a Confederate shell that burst inside Fort Sumter. Later three ladies from Virginia each put a flaming torch to the touch hole of a cannon in salute, and the streets blazed again in front of the Exchange as Pryor gave a thrilling speech, the first from an eyewitness to Sumter's fall. While holding them enthralled with the spectacle of it all, he neglected to add that he almost killed himself once inside the fort by taking a drink of what he took for whiskey, only to find it to be iodide of potassium. Hardly had the bonfires flickered out before a new telegram announced that earlier that day some of the first troops responding to Lincoln's call found themselves mobbed when they marched through Baltimore. Both soldiers and civilians died, seeming to promise that Maryland, too, would get off the fence and join the Confederacy. The bonfires blazed once more, and hotspurs mounted the platform again, this time to thank the Almighty that the bones of Yankees were to whiten in the Maryland sun.[43] "Nothing could exceed the enthusiasm of the people here," a Virginian just arrived declared.[44]

That evening the cabinet met in a long session on Virginia. Her Governor John Letcher announced his desire to take immediate possession of the navy yard at Norfolk and the warships there at anchor. Moreover, he expected the Federals to move soon against the just-captured arsenal at Harpers Ferry. He needed help, and quickly.[45] Already Davis had wired back that he would send whatever aid he could as soon as possible.[46] Now he discussed with his ministers Letcher's request for a commissioner to meet with the governor and his legislature to negotiate a speedy offensive and defensive alliance. Everyone expected Virginia to ratify the Constitution and apply for admission to the Confederacy, but that would take precious time. Immediately the President turned to Stephens, who just as quickly tried—as usual—to decline. Pleading his occasionally convenient ill health, and an even less convincing fear that traveling at night would give him a cold, Little Aleck in the end yielded when the cabinet stood united behind Davis in asking him to go. He left that same night on the eight o'clock train, carrying Davis's hastily written letter of credentials with him.[47]

The cabinet also discussed the Baltimore riot, in which Davis found much encouragement to hope for cooperation from Maryland. All the South, it seemed, offered a united front against Lincoln. Other Border States refused to answer the Federal call for volunteers. Such unity, he hoped, might just dissuade Lincoln from going further, while at the same time encouraging the Democratic opposition in the North to demand granting Confederate independence.[48] It was a hope, and no more than that, nor did they fool themselves. At this same moment the feeling ran unanimous in the cabinet that there would still be a fight for Fort Pickens, believing that the fleet turned away from Charleston would now sail to Pensacola. They all worried that Bragg was not nearly so well prepared as Beauregard had been.[49]

The next few days saw unbroken activity. Davis and Walker strained to rush troops to Pensacola, as well as much needed cannon and artillerists, especially siege mortars shifted from the batteries at

Charleston. Men arrived faster than Bragg could handle them, leading him to complain that he could not keep track of them all, especially when some companies went directly into camp on arrival without notifying him of their coming.[50] At the same time Davis wired Letcher that "we re-enforce you" on April 22, and to save time asked Governor John Ellis of North Carolina if he would send men and arms to defend Virginia. This governor, for a change, cooperated speedily and fully, especially after word came that the Yankees had destroyed much of Norfolk and its ships before evacuating.[51]

Unsuspected threats emerged, most of them imagined. From Mobile McRae sent Davis word of rumored Yankee troop movements in Illinois, warning him to "look out for the Mississippi River."[52] New stories surfaced of a Yankee invasion of Texas, with suspicion that Governor Houston, now deposed, might be involved, and only Reagan's direct investigation, aided by Oldham, finally quelled the rumor.[53] People worried over the presence of John Worden, the Federal naval officer taken prisoner at Pensacola, even though he was in custody while Benjamin studied the law in his case.[54] Word came that a militia captain in rural Alabama had been hanged by local tories, and another man arrested at Pensacola arrived in Montgomery for questioning at the War Department. Rumor even said that one of Walker's own employees was under suspicion, or was it one of Reagan's?[55] Sanders still aroused suspicion despite his obvious glee at Confederate success, and his open letter to the mayor of New York advising resistance to Lincoln's troop call.[56] In the effort to sift fact from fancy, Walker sent his first spy to Washington on April 20 to gather reliable information and enjoined him to use "great prudence and circumspection."[57]

Meanwhile Confederates in Montgomery exercised anything but prudence in their speculations and expectations. Predictions that Davis would lead an army on Washington commenced the same day of Virginia's secession, and for days thereafter press and pulpit urged him to assume active command and march northward. Some even reported him picking the best men from the companies then flowing through Montgomery to form his own select bodyguard.[58] Others said he would shift the capital to Richmond and from there conduct his campaigns, leaving Stephens to run the government.[59] Patriots and crackpots sent the President their promises of plans to capture Washington in twenty days, and designs for new secret weapons like airships promised to travel "at the rate of 100 miles per hour," or devices to destroy ships and forts from a distance of a mile away. Usually these patriots accompanied their proposals with protestations of selfless devotion to the cause, and requests for money.[60]

Some feared that in the dizzying rush of events, the President would act without waiting for the advice of leading men in the South, but in fact he made scarcely a move in the absence of cabinet discussion.[61] On Monday April 22 they met again in long session to go over the past week's events. Since it now looked as if several of the Border States would resist Lincoln, they determined to offer aid in that resistance. Making common cause with sister slave states would inevitably help make them into new Confederate states. As a result, Walker called for yet another 12,000 volunteers, and now for the first time he formally included Kentucky, Arkansas, North Carolina, and Tennessee in his requests. Every one came forward with the promise of a regiment.[62] Equally encouraging, the New Orleans, Jackson & Great Northern Railroad offered to transport soldiers through Louisiana and Mississippi on its lines free of charge.[63]

Montgomery renewed its appetite for spectacle when Louis T. Wigfall, the dark-haired, bearded, fiery secessionist from Texas, arrived late on April 23.[64] He went straight to the executive mansion, where he reported to Davis, and stayed the night, too exhausted to address the audience that quickly gathered at Washington and Bibb. Still he and Davis accepted their cheers, and the next night when he moved into the Exchange, he could not refuse again.[65] The crowd gathered early in the evening, and heard first from several others when word came that Wigfall was still abed from exhaustion. Stuart thought it looked more like drunkenness, as two hefty Texans had to go into his room and nearly carry him out on the portico at half past nine. But Wigfall rallied to the occasion and gave them yet another stirring account of the Sumter fight. The crowd listened intently, cheering at every gallant deed recounted in what Stuart called the "racy vehemence which poured from his limber lips."[66] The speeches were circus by now, a patriotic narcotic upon which Montgomery fed with unappeasable appetite.

That made them all the more hungry for news from Virginia. The fact of Stephens's departure already furnished what one reporter called "food for the speculative."[67] While he was away, Montgomery could only guess as to his fortune, but he kept Davis and the cabinet regularly advised of his progress. He reached Richmond April 22, finding an ardent warlike spirit all along his route, and the fiercest of all in

Virginia, where he feared "we are upon the eve of a tremendous conflict." Many even favored attacking Washington.[68] He met Letcher that same evening, and the next day called at the invitation of the state convention. In secret session he urged an immediate treaty between Virginia and the Confederacy, with adoption of the Constitution and application for statehood as soon as possible thereafter. After the meeting he thought prospects good, and so reported by telegraph to Davis, then spent the rest of the day in talks with Letcher and the commander of the state militia, Robert E. Lee, with whom he discussed strategy.[69]

Stephens privately worried that the men in the convention did not feel the heat of the citizenry at large. "The Virginians will debate & speak though war be at the gates of their city," he moaned to Linton. He signed a treaty with a committee of the convention, but the whole body must ratify it, and of that he felt not at all certain.[70] Perhaps to encourage them subtly, Little Aleck dropped hints that Davis himself might come to Richmond, the obvious inference being that the President would assume active command, even though Stephens knew of a certainty that such was not Davis's intention. But then the next day he undid whatever influence that may have had by telling others that Davis quite certainly was not coming. It caused some little dissatisfaction, especially among troops who hoped the President would lead them, their confidence in him greater than that felt for Lee.[71] Little Aleck would have done much better simply to keep quiet.

In the end it did not matter. On April 25 Stephens reported his mission a success, and two days later the Virginia convention sent Davis an invitation to move the capital to Richmond, something that Stephens hinted might be a possibility as an added inducement.[72] Within hours the Vice President was on the road south, hoping for a brief stop at Liberty Hall on his way to Montgomery. Once more, he saw everywhere the disheartening signs of war spirit. "If one general battle ensues," he feared, "it will take many more to close the strife."[73]

President Davis received the news of Virginia's action with undisguised pleasure. It came as a blessed relief amid the harrowing days in Montgomery. Now in his new home, he arose early every morning from his bed in the first floor room immediately to the right of the entrance hall. As he shaved in the mirror on the wall, a glance out his front window gave him an unobstructed look down Bibb Street to Government House, presaging where he would spend most of his day.[74] Once dressed, he stepped into the study behind his bedroom and began working even before breakfast was served in the dining room at the end of the hall.[75] Well before nine o'clock he left the house, turned right onto Bibb, and in ninety seconds walked the 180 paces in his long military stride to the door of the Executive building and went upstairs to his office. He never returned home until at least six, and often stayed at Government House to midnight or later. Even when he did return in the evening, exhausted, he ate little if anything, arguing that he had not the time, barely spoke, and then returned to his study or his bedroom. Varina complained that he overworked himself "& all the rest of mankind," seeing not all that he had accomplished but only that remaining undone. Townspeople walking by often saw the red glow of his table lamp shining out over the hedge in front of the house well into the early hours of the morning.[76]

A house guest at the time marveled at the President's patience amid all his pressures, but it was only iron will that kept Davis's nerves and temper in check.[77] He exhibited two characters, so far as Reagan could see in their daily intercourse. In his social discourse he could be pleasant and genial, especially with women and children, and a visiting editor now found him "brighter, more cheerful and in better health than we have seen him for many years."[78] But Davis felt no inclination for entertaining or frivolity. He stood an occasional informal dinner, as for Stephens or Wigfall, and sometimes invited cabinet members to working breakfasts at the mansion. But otherwise, at best he attended one of Varina's formal receptions only briefly, shook a few hands, and then returned to his work.[79]

Then the other character appeared. In his official life he was all duty, with no time for pleasantry, and no stomach for unnecessary conversation. He considered the facts available, formed his opinions, *sometimes* with the influence of his cabinet, and then refused further discussion on the matter.[80] Close friends were aware of his character and the burden of work now resting on him. Wiley Harris, who could have gained an interview at any time, took care not to interrupt Davis' day. "I perceive that you have not a moment to spare," Harris said, and sent letters instead for Davis to peruse at his convenience.[81] Even that consideration could still run athwart the President's pent-up frustration and anxiety over his responsibilities. Just two days after the firing on Fort Sumter, standing as usual with a sheaf of papers in one hand, he read a letter that set him off. "I wish people would not write me advice," he said peevishly. He tore the sheet in half. Then, his anger rising, he said it again, and ripped the two halves into tiny shreds and threw them on the floor.[82]

Observers in Montgomery believed that Davis worked wisely with his cabinet, leaving details to them while he occupied himself with the great issues, and when it came to postal, judicial, and financial affairs, they read the man correctly.[83] Unseen was the degree to which he involved himself in other affairs, most particularly the War Department. To outsiders, the executive branch of the government seemed to work with marvelous composure.[84] Certainly they all worked a little more comfortably in the days after Virginia's secession as the expansion to other buildings allowed for less crowding.[85] But some confusion as the departments rapidly grew became inevitable. A visitor to the original Government House found War and Navy department employees scurrying in every direction "very excited but doing nothing," while some confessed they did not know the way to the office of the secretary of the navy, and one attested that there "warn't no such person." Having so little else to do, Benjamin became by default the point of reference for those in doubt, directing callers to the appropriate offices. Always agreeable, his lurking smile ever evident, he charmed most who called, despite his habit of lisping out a somewhat patronizing "Thunny" when addressing young men.[86]

Davis's cabinet ministers learned their jobs to varying degrees as they struggled to keep up with events, and gained lessons, too. Within days of Fort Sumter they all assumed a new wariness toward the press, thanks to the leaks and unsubstantiated rumors that flourished, often to their embarrassment.[87] The results of their private deliberations in cabinet they kept increasingly to themselves, so that after one four-hour session April 24, not a word of its content found its way into the papers.[88] As much as possible, too, they kept their department affairs out of the press, especially Walker in the search for commanders, though Davis himself handled much of it. Immediately after the secession of Virginia, they confidentially wired Letcher to see if perhaps old General Scott, himself a Virginian, would resign with his state. The President detested the man, having had a highly publicized, quite childish feud with him back in the 1850s. But still Scott was a good soldier, if too old for the field, and would have been a valuable accession.[89] Scott stayed loyal to the Union, but at the same time Davis went directly after Lee and Joseph E. Johnston, both of whom resigned to take service in the Virginia state forces.[90] They were among the premier soldiers in the Old Army, and Davis had known and admired both back at the Military Academy. Another West Point friend was the subject of even more anxiety for the President, Albert Sidney Johnston. No one had heard from the officer, then presumed still on the far-off Pacific coast. His son came to Montgomery with an introduction from Kentucky Governor Magoffin a few days after Virginia seceded, but he knew nothing of his father's whereabouts. But then on April 26, having left the capital, he sent Davis the joyous news that a letter from the elder Johnston announced his intention to join with the Confederacy.[91] This lifted the President's heart mightily, for this was the man he believed from the first could and should lead the Confederacy's armies to victory.

The appointment of officers occupied far too much of Davis's time, especially when it came to men of lesser rank, but confidence in his own judgment so overpowered any sense of proportion in the use of his day that he could not help himself. Especially he made time to endorse recommendations from old Mexican War comrades, or promising young men he had known while secretary of war. He did not neglect looking after the interests of men of political influence, or their sons, even when they brought no military experience. When the son of Henry S. Foote, his oldest and most bitter political and personal foe in Mississippi, applied for a commission, the President gave it a hearty recommendation despite having come close to dueling with the father twice, and an enraged fistfight at least once. In this case it would be good policy to grant a commission if it should help keep the elder Foote quiet.[92] Some appointments carried a special irony, and a particular political significance, as when Davis issued a captaincy to Alexander Todd, brother-in-law of Abraham Lincoln.[93]

Yet for every happy applicant, Davis and his ministers disappointed others, men who did not forget. One recently arrived Virginian haunted the War Department, then left in a huff, complaining to General Lee that "the authorities . . . offer no adequate inducement for my remaining here."[94] Walker and Mallory, with too little time and too much to do, often gave scant attention to the sensibilities of men who came before them, and even Davis offended one naval hopeful by telling the crestfallen boy to go home and wait until the Confederacy started its Naval Academy.[95] Worst of all, disgruntled hopefuls who left empty-handed soon started rumors that their denial came not because of any lack of ability or experience, but because of prewar politics. They charged, quite absurdly, that army appointments were only going to old Breckinridge Democrats.[96]

Davis and Walker accepted more and more companies for service, meanwhile seeing their store of war materiel growing apace. Old muskets altered to the modern percussion system began to fill the basement of one of the government buildings. Finally an accurate statement of all the weapons seized from the United States arsenals revealed 159,010 pistols, carbines, rifles, and old muskets, a promiscuous variety to be certain, but still a nucleus of armament. Walker also reported some success in procuring powder and percussion caps, and the training of the volunteers progressed well enough.[97] The War Department had Barrett, Wimbish & Co. print an edition of the Articles of War to distribute to officers, and old veterans from the ranks gave out their own advice to the young volunteers on how to cope with life in the army: Let the beard grow to protect the throat and lungs, wear a hat with a high crown to allow space "for air over the brain," wash every day to prevent fevers and bowel complaints, avoid perspiring at night for fear of taking chills.[98]

Everyone, it seemed, looked upon the cause as their own. In late April Montgomery learned that five companies raised in the "Little Egypt" section of southern Illinois, where Southern sympathy ran strong, were on their way to the capital.[99] Young ladies studying at a female academy in Jackson, Tennessee, wrote to offer themselves as a military company if not enough men should volunteer.[100] Most heartening—and surprising to all except slaveholders—were the offers from the Confederacy's blacks. Two slaves in nearby Marengo County subscribed for $800 of the Treasury loan with funds saved for years, while in Montgomery one of the Bibb family slaves named Alfred contributed $100 and a fellow black, S. G. Hardaway's slave Albert, went to the Central Bank in town and cornered the president, asking to purchase bonds, and when told that he could only do so with his master's permission, speedily secured it and returned to buy $300 worth.[101]

More than that, blacks, slave and free, wanted to take arms. The day before Beauregard opened fire on Fort Sumter one Georgia regiment actually allowed a slave to "enlist" informally.[102] In the days after Virginia's secession, more than a score of requests came to Davis and Walker from blacks anxious to serve. On April 23 a company from Autauga County presented themselves to Governor Moore, to be led by a white officer.[103] A slave barber in Tennessee gave $50 toward the raising of one of the new volunteer regiments from the Volunteer State, and before the end of the month a company of blacks from Nashville offered themselves.[104] From across the South came expressions from slaves destined to accompany their masters to the war zone that if and when fighting came, they hoped to wield a weapon for their homeland, too.[105] Free blacks spoke even more stridently. Stories came to Montgomery of 1,500 of them in New Orleans organizing to present themselves as soldiers.[106] Bowman Seals, a free black in Clayton, Alabama, wrote Davis an open letter in which he attested that he fully understood "the quarrel between the two sections, and know how my own class stands affected by it." He firmly believed that the North held no love for blacks, but would simply loose all slaves, including the "lazy and lawless," to be a burden on the rest of society black and white. His arm, his rifle, and his life were the Confederacy's to command.[107]

Blacks liked Jefferson Davis. He was ever polite and respectful with them, free or slave, chiefly because in their acknowledged inferior social status they never challenged him and posed no threat to a white male. He took their offers of service as sincere patriotism, which surely many were, yet he could hardly allow them into the military. Southerners still feared placing weapons in the hands of their slaves. Thirty years after Nat Turner's "rebellion" in Virginia, the nightmare of murdering blacks storming their homes by darkness still haunted Confederates. Besides, making soldiers of blacks would grant a *de facto* recognition of some degree of equality with the white men in the ranks. The Confederacy was hardly prepared to accept that now, and might never be ready.

So many of the requests from blacks came from the Border States, perhaps because they lived in closer proximity to the Yankees and feared them the more. Hoping to capitalize on surging sentiment in those undecided states, Montgomery commenced recruiting whites as quickly as possible after Fort Sumter, and in Kentucky actually commenced work as Beauregard's guns still pounded the fort.[108] Encouragement came from North Carolina within hours of Anderson's surrender. "Come as soon as you choose," Governor Ellis wired Davis. "We are ready to join you to a man," a boast he fortified a week later with a promise to have up to 10,000 volunteers in the field in a few days.[109] "The people of my State are now thoroughly united," promised Ellis, "and will adopt the speediest method of union with the Confederate States."[110]

Davis wrote to Missouri Governor Claiborne Jackson on April 23 to say that "we look anxiously and hopefully for the day when the star of Missouri shall be added to the constellation of the Confederate States of America." Then he went further by ordering four cannon sent to use against the St. Louis arsenal, despite the fact that the state had not yet seceded. When it did—and he took that for granted—Davis wanted

Jackson prepared to move quickly and effectively. Just three days later Walker would be asking Jackson for a regiment to send to Virginia.[111] Neighboring Arkansas also got a request for a regiment, but Governor Henry M. Rector responded that his state convention would not meet until May 6 and, unlike Magoffin and Ellis, he would do nothing before then. Privately, Arkansans promised Walker that "Arkansas will go out 6th of May, before breakfast," while a privately raised regiment, unable to get state arms from Rector, left for Montgomery in hopes that Walker could equip them there.[112]

Tennessee represented a special concern thanks to its position on the immediate northern border of Mississippi, Alabama, and Georgia, and its rabidly Unionist easternmost extension thrusting like a knife between western Virginia and North Carolina. Secession sentiment in the state took a leap forward after Lincoln's proclamation, and Davis's old acquaintance General Gideon Pillow promised that he could furnish 10,000 men in three weeks if the Confederacy would accept them.[113] Governor Isham Harris reported secession sentiment growing rapidly on April 20, encouraging him to send a military envoy to Montgomery to discuss raising troops, while Walker sought permission to build forts near Memphis to guard the upper Mississippi.[114]

Deciding that Tennessee required and deserved special effort, Davis settled on an envoy. Henry Hilliard sat in his library writing letters on the afternoon of April 25 when a note arrived from Walker requesting his immediate presence at Government House to meet the President. Hilliard walked to Commerce and Bibb to find himself ushered into a chamber next to the cabinet room where Davis even then sat with his ministers. The President joined him for a few minutes and quickly outlined his wishes. Hilliard should go to Nashville, where he knew many prominent Tennesseeans. At once Hilliard agreed, whereupon Davis stood and took his hand, then ushered him into the cabinet room where they all discussed the situation in Tennessee. Hilliard proposed leaving the next day, but Davis pressed him to board a train that same evening. The Alabamian agreed, and within hours was on his way to Nashville.[115]

At that same cabinet session, Davis asked all of his ministers for reports on the status of their departments, including estimates of their financial needs for the coming year. To the President's surprise, Reagan announced on the spot that the Post Office was ready to commence operations. The Figh Block was finished, his books and forms were printed, and his staff instructed.[116] For the rest, they still needed a few days. Davis himself had to prepare an address to Congress for its meeting on April 29, and asked that they all have their reports to him beforehand. They also discussed the convention of Confederate railroad presidents due to convene in Montgomery the next day. The Memphis & Ohio, and the New Orleans, Jackson & Great Northern already offered to convey troops and munitions free of charge.[117] Now the cabinet proposed that Walker issue a request to the convention that the presidents agree among themselves on a plan for moving soldiers and materiel to any point in the Confederacy in the speediest manner, and at the most minimal cost to the government.[118] At the same time, Reagan took advantage of the executives' availability to request their indulgence in making his department run as economically as possible. Everyone got their wish. To Walker the railroaders agreed to transport everything for the government at half their rates, and soldiers at two cents per mile, and in return for Confederate bonds instead of cash, in effect postponing compensation until the Treasury redeemed the notes years hence. To Reagan they proposed to carry his mail for exactly half the rates then charged to the United States Post Office, and suggested reduction or elimination of unneeded and unprofitable mail runs. Davis rewarded them with an audience and a twenty-minute speech.[119]

More good railroad news came just then with the announcement that the Alabama & Florida line would be completed through to Pensacola by May 3, cutting the time to send troops almost in half, to a mere fourteen hours.[120] Counterbalancing this was the utter inability to ship anything by train west of the Mississippi. The great river made as good a barrier as a wall, and even once men and equipment reached the other side, rail facilities through western Louisiana were spotty, and in Texas almost nonexistent. Worse, the Texans themselves seemed almost in a panic for fear of attacks from two fronts, the Yankees and the Mexicans. Repeated rumors arrived in Montgomery that General Pedro Ampudia would lead an army across the Rio Grande in a strike to regain Texas as events in the East distracted the Confederates. While a blowhard named George Bickley promised Davis that he could provide 30,000 men from his semimythical Knights of the Golden Circle to retaliate if Ampudia should invade, Davis felt much more concern for the reaction of the Texans themselves.[121] Friends advised Governor Ed Clark that the state should respond to any incursion over the border with a campaign of their own, bent on taking and occupying the provinces of Tamalipas, Chihuahua, and Sonora.[122] Such a move would provoke the Mexicans at the very least, and perhaps the French as well, just then trying to carve a small New World empire out of the strife-torn country.

The Texans also lobbied strongly, both Oldham and Hemphill staying in Montgomery even after Congress adjourned. Of course, Reagan was there as well, and anxious to get more attention for the Lone Star State. The day after Sumter surrendered Davis sent his friend McCulloch to take command of the Indian Territory north of Texas with seven regiments, but that only promised protection—such as it was—from the Yankees.[123] Van Dorn went there too, though with only general instructions, and when Governor Clark implored Walker to help him with the defenses at Indianola in particular, the harried secretary of war replied that he had already ordered Van Dorn to do so, when in fact he did not get around to doing it until two days later.[124] Worried that Texas was being left too much to look to its own defense, north and south, Oldham and Hemphill called repeatedly on Walker and Davis, assisted by Reagan, urging them to send more of everything, and fearing that the Yankees would make this vulnerable back door to the Confederacy their first point of attack.[125]

No wonder Walker complained of "overwhelming pressure" on him as he struggled to deal with everything, plus prepare his report for Davis.[126] Indeed, while a new flag pole went up atop Government House, all of the secretaries worked hard at their reports, and all of them finished in time.[127] Naturally Walker's occupied the most immediate interest and attention. Since the organization of the department they had raised 62,000 volunteers, in addition to 5,000 South Carolinians already serving at Charleston, and even then another 15,000 began to come in. After allowing for some 25,000 spread along their seacoast and in Texas, that left more than 50,000 available to direct to interior points at hazard, chiefly Virginia. Myers estimated that it would cost $4.5 million to feed and clothe them all for the balance of the year, and should the armed forces grow to a hundred regiments, as some expected, the bill would escalate to more than $28 million.

They still needed more organization, said Walker, especially in their medical department and the Indian Bureau, and in the clerical staff of the War Department itself. Also in the field command of the growing army Walker saw a problem, noting that several states made their highest ranking militia officers major generals, while the Confederate Army currently had only brigadiers. When state and national forces mingled, then, the local major general would have the higher rank, though he might be a "rank" amateur, in fact, whereas a brigadier appointed by Davis would have been selected for experience and fitness. Walker proposed promoting their current brigadiers into full generals, thus outranking any officer encountered on any basis. They also needed to build their own powder mills and do more in erecting defenses along the Mississippi. Reacting to the pressure from the Texans, he suggested greater attention there, especially since the state provided the link to New Mexico and Arizona, territories he expected would naturally ally themselves with the Confederacy. To be certain of having God on their side, he suggested more chaplains for the army.[128]

Mallory sounded almost parsimonious by comparison, estimating a mere $278,500 in naval needs for the next ten months. They had a half-dozen modest vessels captured from the Yankees, and were putting two more in shape to become commerce raiders. But building full-scale modern warships took too long, too much money, and made no sense for the Navy, whose chief mission must be defense of the rivers and harbors, not combat on the oceans. Consequently, Mallory proposed that they turn their attention to "a class of vessels hitherto unknown." Without speaking specifically, he proposed the germ of an idea to construct ironclads.[129]

Toombs and Reagan also submitted reports, neither containing anything not already known. The mission to Washington had ended in failure; that to Virginia in success. The commission to Europe's fate remained to be seen. As for the Post Office, Reagan went on at some length about his books and forms, his appointments and contracts, and proposed to delay taking actual control of the mails until the United States suspended delivery.[130]

Armed with these, and perhaps statements from Memminger and Benjamin, Davis worked on his own message to the rapidly approaching Congress. Already men and their bags steamed toward Montgomery on trains from the East. Pritchard of the Southern Associated Press came among the earliest arrivals, checking into the Exchange on April 27 with a group of shorthand reporters. Given the newsmen's experience with the first session, their return represented a considerable triumph of hope over experience.[131] At West Point, Georgia, which most of the delegates had to pass through on their way, crowds gathered as each train came into the depot to change cars in the morning, begging speeches from any dignitaries aboard.[132] As usual, Tom Cobb traveled on a Sunday despite his religious prejudices, and rode into Montgomery in company with Keitt, Bartow, Hill, Wright, and others. He did at least decline to make speeches along the way, but when he spoke out once for five minutes against breaking the Sabbath, the silence of the crowd gave him to understand just how well it received his remarks. He was not called on to speak again that day before their arrival in Montgomery at two o'clock. Fortunately, this Sunday, April 28, the rails stayed on the ties, and the train kept to the tracks. Fate had tried once, and that was enough.[133]

They all began to gather once more around eleven on Monday, and this time the walk up Market Street required no overcoats and shawls in the warm spring air. Many of the members had not yet arrived—Stephens and Chesnut among them—but those present immediately greeted each other with smiles and handshakes, and a general hubbub of conversation filled the time until they took their seats just before noon. Much had changed since they last met a mere six weeks before. They were at war now. They had an army already grown to a size never before seen on the continent. Their envoys called at the courts of Europe, their Treasury could afford to pay for Memminger's table and Captain Deas's blankets, reimburse Capers, and still have millions to draw upon. Most of all they had a victory that put their names on the lips of the world.[134]

The gallery was packed with ladies and gentlemen waving handkerchiefs and calling out good wishes that echoed the hopes and expectations of Montgomery and the Confederacy. "The occasion is an extraordinary one," said the *Advertiser*. "We look with confidence and hope for the passage of just such measures as the exigencies of the case require." Congress must authorize Davis's previous call for privateers, address the blockade of Southern ports that Lincoln declared ten days earlier, and consider the portentous step of enacting a formal declaration of war.[135]

The Congressmen understood what was expected of them, though some scarcely knew where they were going. Cobb thought everyone "buoyant with hope" for ultimate success, and predicted there would be no war after the drubbing Lincoln took at Fort Sumter.[136] Brother Howell also tended to think they might still escape a general conflict, yet confessed after talking to his comrades in the morning that "I find that there is as much doubt about the future here, as in the country." A wide spectrum of opinion fluttered about on the floor, including a Toombs more optimistic than he had been in cabinet before the first shot at Sumter. Now he thought a peaceful settlement with Lincoln possible.[137] Over with the Louisiana delegation, DeClouet harbored a solemn resolve. "In heart and soul we are bound by the sacred cause of southern independence," he declared. "I am ready to sacrifice my all— fortune, life—in stern resistance to northern aggression."[138]

Howell Cobb called them to order precisely at noon, and turned them over to Manly for prayer. Then they called the roll, noting that several members had not arrived, yet a quorum was present and they could proceed. He recognized new members Jones and Davis of Alabama, Clayton presented Jehu A. Orr replacing the resigned William Wilson of Mississippi, Ochiltree introduced Wigfall, and the four newcomers went forward to give their credentials and take their oath, the pompous Wigfall privately seething after just learning that Major Anderson, in publishing an account of Fort Sumter, had failed to pass glowing encomiums on Wigfall's magnanimity in negotiating the surrender.[139] Finally, too, J. A. P. Campbell of Mississippi made his first appearance, having missed the entire first session. Tom Cobb moved that they notify the President they were in session and ready to receive his message, and while a committee formally left on the errand, the Congress accepted the resignation of Clitherall, who had undertaken a post as register of the Treasury.[140] They would replace him with Ferrie Henshaw.

After a few other minor formalities, Robert Josselyn appeared to announce that he bore Davis's message. Privately the President had previously showed it to Toombs, and now the Secretary of State assured the house that it contained nothing that should require them to go into secret session. On this, the first day of their sitting as a "war" Congress, they must play to the gallery, in this chamber and before the world. Josselyn handed the document to clerk Robert Dixon, who began reading slowly, distinctly.[141]

Davis started by telling them what they already knew. Every state had ratified the Constitution, and he expected more to join them in the coming weeks. Then he got to the substance of his address, and clearly he spoke not to them, but to the globe. As in so many of his speeches in the Senate in past years, he passed at length over the history of relations between the states and the federal government in Washington, over the framing of the original Constitution, and even back to the Articles of Confederation. He traced the rise of conflict of opinion and interest between North and South, the agitation over slavery, and painted a self-serving pastoral portrait of the humanitarian and benevolent nature of the institution as practiced in the South.

Likely boring his audience with a recitation they had heard from his mouth and others innumerable times in the past, he finally turned to the formation of their present confederation, and the galleries grew more hushed, the rustling of crinolines and the murmur of whispered chatter stilled. As Dixon read on, the *Mercury* reporter thought "one could have heard the ticking of a watch above all other sounds, except the voice of the Clerk."[142] They wanted peace, Davis wrote. They had tried amicable negotiations with Washington over Sumter, only to be deceived and rebuffed. "There remained, therefore, no alternative but to direct that the fort should be at once reduced." Lincoln's response in calling out 75,000 volunteers he characterized as a "declaration of war." Thus he summoned them now to help him meet the crisis. Lincoln refused to acknowledge their independence. He called them insurrectionists. He demanded that they disperse their regiments and their government and return to their homes by May 5.

At this last the silent audience erupted in hisses and howls of derisive laughter that did not soon subside. Then Dixon read on. Davis told them of his response, of his own calls for volunteers, his proclamation asking for privateers, all of which he trusted this Congress would ratify by making law. He condemned Lincoln's blockade as being one on paper only, and unenforceable, in violation of the laws of nations. When he spoke of the reaction in the South, and especially of the secession of Virginia and its subsequent adoption of the Confederate Constitution, the galleries once more erupted, this time with cheers that did not cease until Cobb repeatedly pounded his gavel.

There followed a recitation of the affairs of the several departments, and of his desire to raise their volunteers to a standing army of 100,000. He adopted Walker's proposal that the highest grade of officer in the Confederate service be full general, and suggested as well that they establish their own military academy to train the generals of the future. He congratulated the people of the South on their patriotism, their sacrifice, their anxiety to leap to the defense of their common country. The railroads did their part. The governors—he made no mention of Brown—furnished their levies of troops. The common citizens put aside their plowshares and grasped their swords.

"A people thus united and resolved can not shrink from any sacrifice which they may be called on to make," he concluded, "nor can there be reasonable doubt of their final success." Theirs was a just and holy cause. They wanted peace at any cost save honor and freedom. "We seek no conquest, no aggrandizement, no concession of any kind." In words borrowed from those Stephens had uttered more than eleven long, eventful weeks before, he told them and the North and the world that "all we ask is to be let alone." If only Lincoln would give them that, then the sword should fall from their hand and they would race to embrace once more in friendship those whom folly now threatened to make enemies. But if Lincoln wanted war, then they should give it to him, and in earnest.[143]

The floor and the gallery burst into applause as Dixon finished. "A capital document," Tom Cobb exuded.[144] Wigfall's prickly wife Charlotte found the message "an admirable one & worthy of his reputation."[145] Rhett might have been disappointed, for he had expected an outright declaration of war, the *Mercury* already complaining that "as it might have been feared, this war is regularly blundered into."[146] Any such quibbling lay with the minority this afternoon, and they kept it to themselves through the balance of the day. There were still other formalities to observe. At Rhett's motion, all those who missed signing the Constitution at the end of the last session now affixed their signatures. Toombs moved that the Foreign Affairs committee immediately consider presenting a bill authorizing the granting of letters of marque. Memminger for his part moved that Finance work on a bill excepting Virginia and all the other slave states not yet seceded from the foreign import duties, now that they were presumed about to become Confederates. Then immediately prior to adjourning, the firebrand Wigfall spoke for the first time. He introduced a bill to raise an additional military force beyond Congress's previous authorizations.[147]

Just in case Lincoln would not leave them alone.

CHAPTER FOURTEEN

WE HAVE CAST THE DIE

———•★•———

THEY COULD HAVE LOOKED ON the difficult sessions of February and March as good old days. "There is no gaiety here," Tom Cobb complained within forty-eight hours. The ladies stopped filling the galleries, he saw none of his old Montgomery acquaintances. All they did was work.[1] There was so much to be done. Each of Davis's acts during their recess had to be referred to committees to present bills authorizing them *ex post facto*, and Rhett quickly pointed out that the President, under their Constitution, had no authority to do these things unilaterally. Wright and Bartow of Georgia got into a minor dispute over a military resolution introduced by the former back in February, and which Bartow defensively confessed he had forgotten.[2] Several felt in a quibbling mood reflecting frustration at being summoned from home again so soon, while others chafed at being here instead of raising regiments of their own to lead to glory. Bartow and both Cobbs now longed to don uniforms.

On May 1 Rhett reported a bill recognizing a state of war with the United States, and as the debate began, Wigfall wrote to his son Halsey advising him not to jump into the army right away, but finish school first.[3] Significantly, in his first days in the house, the fire-eater could not be bothered to listen to others. He was accustomed to people listening to *him*. The next day Little Aleck finally arrived, as did Chesnut, Barnwell, and Boyce, and men from Alabama and Texas.[4] Patton Anderson had resigned, and Florida now sent George Ward in his place, along with Owens and Morton. The people had expected the Vice President two days before, and had gathered at the depot to welcome him and extort the inevitable speech, only to find him not on the train. When he did arrive, suffering a bad cold, he came from making a saber-rattling talk at Atlanta in which he promised that when Maryland seceded, Washington itself should revert to them by right, and they would demand it, and enforce that demand "at every hazard, and at whatever cost."[5]

"Every thing is moving on steadily and energetically," Howell Cobb delighted on May 3.[6] They voted their thanks to Beauregard for his victory. They considered a bill authorizing Davis to nationalize the Confederacy's telegraph lines, making all operators government employees in the interest of secrecy, and after some little debate passed the measure, a major step toward both security and censorship. They gladly accepted Governor Moore's offer of the state house of representatives hall for their meetings, affording considerably more room, and moved in on May 4. They dealt with measures great and small, from debating bills on raising a regiment of zouaves to their still unsettled design for a great seal. Rapidly they went through the $5 worth of stationery furnished to each member by the clerk, but it took little writing or note-making to settle their first major issue. After considerable debate and a host of proposed amendments revealing their sense of the importance of the document, on May 3 they passed their declaration of war by a unanimous voice vote. The timing was propitious, and intentional. The next day the twenty-day period of grace decreed by Lincoln expired. This declaration would be their response.[7]

"Well, Dearest Marion," Tom Cobb wrote afterward, "we have cast the die and 'accepted' the war forced upon us. . . . The issue is with God."[8] Brother Howell felt increasingly sanguine. "There continues to be great unanimity in Congress on all important questions," he wrote immediately after the passage. "It is the policy of all to press forward with the utmost energy."[9] Yet others felt less secure. Mary Chesnut, despite her loathing of Montgomery, frankly confessed to friends and family back in South Carolina that she wanted her husband to stay in the Congress and return to the capital to continue using his influence.[10] She distrusted too many of the other delegates. "Oh, if I could put some of my reckless spirit into these discreet, cautious, lazy men," she complained just before returning.[11] Yet on the streets of Montgomery the day after the declaration passed, reporters saw only confidence. Davis and Stephens evidenced no sign of fear. People laughed at the expiration of Lincoln's deadline. Even the overworked cabinet looked happy.[12]

Happier still were they when Virginia came formally onto the flag. Congress approved the convention between the Confederacy and the Old Dominion on May 6, and the following day the bill admitting her as a state passed unanimously.[13] Meanwhile, all looked anxiously for the arrival of the Virginia delegation, and some with as much suspicion as eagerness.[14] Disturbing word of the complexion of the Virginia representatives came from secessionist friends. Senator James Mason told Davis that the cast of its members revealed Union sentiment still running strong, at least in the state convention that chose the men. Most had been cooperationists, and only R. M. T. Hunter was "true" on the movement.[15] Other prominent secessionists in the state wrote to friends in Montgomery complaining of being passed over for selection. During the week just past many of the congressmen in Montgomery privately speculated on the Virginians' loyalty to the movement, and several wondered if when they arrived, they would prove to be in favor of submission.[16] "We fear they come to us for no good purposes," said Tom Cobb, "and with strong hopes for reconstruction. . . . Our Congress look with suspicion on this Virginia delegation."[17] Moreover, some resented Virginia's waiting so long, her hesitancy to be among the first. Rhett blamed her vacillation for the eruption of hostilities at Charleston. Had she joined earlier, Lincoln would certainly have backed down from confrontation.[18] Immediately after his arrival Little Aleck detected a disposition in some quarters "to give Va. the cold shoulder," which he much deplored.[19]

The first of the Virginians to arrive were John Brockenbrough and Waller Staples, the former a mild secessionist, and the latter a unionist Whig. They came on the May 6 train and took their seats the next day in time to witness Stephens presenting the bill for Virginia's admission. Brook of Mississippi held Virginia's secession ordinance in his hand as he introduced the new members, who were immediately granted their seats.[20] Two days later Hunter arrived, and took his seat on May 10. Robert Mercer Taliaferro Hunter went by his initials, which some wags said stood for "Run Mad Tom." He looked anything but the imposing statesman. Overweight, his vest perpetually riding up on his shirt and his hair apparently brushed by a hurricane, he gave what Mary Chesnut thought "a rather tumbled-up appearance."[21] Yet this man who checked into the Exchange on his arrival was believed by some to be the ideal choice for president. Boyce of South Carolina favored him above all others, and some rumored that if only Virginia had gone out earlier, Hunter might have been the man.[22] Hunter himself would not have argued. Furthermore, Jefferson Davis only held the office under the Provisional Constitution and government. In the fall there would be regular elections, and February 1862 could easily see a new man taking the oath for the first full six-year term. Why not "Run Mad Tom"?

Next to come was William C. Rives, exactly the sort of man that Cobb and others feared. He did not want to be a delegate, and at first thought of refusing the appointment or simply staying at home. Only circumstances and duty obliged him to go against his wishes, and he took his seat on May 13.[23] Gideon Camden, like Rives lukewarm on secession, simply never would come to Montgomery. Thus Virginia, the Confederacy's largest state, now had a delegation that, for the moment, was complete at four members, smaller than all the rest but Florida. Yet they exerted a powerful influence, with their state and all it represented behind them, an influence not so much legislative as geographical. Howell Cobb, at least, felt no fear of them. They were solid for the cause, he thought.[24]

Another arrival captured the attention of all, even while the Virginia delegates trickled into town. Beauregard stepped off a train the evening of May 4, accompanied by his resplendent staff and the noted English war correspondent for the *Times* of London, William H. Russell. "There is something in the wind," a reporter concluded, and the Vice President confessed his own curiosity, especially since the President had said nothing to him of summoning the general.[25] He brought trophies, including the flag that his men flew over Fort Moultrie during their bombardment of Sumter, now to be draped behind Howell Cobb's chair in the Congress hall. With it he handed Davis his reports of the operation, which in turn the President turned over to Congress.[26] Tom Cobb found him "decidedly French."[27] During the rest of his brief stay, when not accepting the admiring glances and applause of the people of Montgomery, Beauregard was to be found closeted with Walker and Davis studying maps of the Mississippi from Vicksburg north to Kentucky. Russell saw him at Government House happily measuring miles of territory on his charts "as if he were dividing empires."[28] Barely four days after he came, the general left again, so quickly that few saw him go. He returned to Charleston, but Davis and Walker kept to themselves his actual next assignment, which was to oversee the defense of the upper Mississippi Valley.[29]

Davis looked in that direction for more aid, even while Montgomery lionized Beauregard. On May 8 he made public his correspondence with Justice Campbell and the commissioners' treatment by Seward. Such evidence of duplicity ought to help persuade vital states like Kentucky, Tennessee, Arkansas, and Missouri to cross over.[30] Indications from those fronts looked somewhat equivocal. Magoffin would soon call a halt to any Confederate recruiting in his state when

Kentucky adopted an official position of neutrality. But in Missouri the Yankees stirred up a ferment when they captured on May 10 a camp of secessionist state militia outside St. Louis, and that aroused hopes that the Southern sentiment in the state might respond.[31]

The best news since the fall of Sumter came on May 7. As Little Aleck sat in a funk, depressed on the thirty-fifth anniversary of his father's death, the wires to the Winter Building buzzed with the news that Arkansas had voted to secede the day before, and almost right after breakfast as promised.[32] At once the bags of powder went to Old Secession, and nine rounds sounded to celebrate what would soon be the ninth Confederate state. Hardly had the smoke cleared when the telegraph clicked once more, this time announcing that Tennessee, too, had voted an ordinance on May 6. Though its action forced a state referendum on June 8, no one feared for confirmation. "That is good news for one day to bring," exulted the Mercury correspondent.[33] Boyce of South Carolina wrote ecstatically of their certainty of success now, their high spirits and determination, and urged a friend that "we would above all things like to receive such news of the great state of Missouri."[34] The cannon boomed almost all day. "We are all decidedly in better spirits," Tom Cobb told his wife. He even felt relief over the Virginia delegates, now that he met the first of them and measured their temper.[35]

In only a few days Congress ratified the convention that Hilliard negotiated with Tennessee on the day after her secession vote, and then on May 16 unanimously admitted Tennessee to statehood.[36] Two days later Stephens presented a bill to grant statehood to Arkansas. No one objected, of course, but old Withers, apparently uneasy again over having said and done so little, piped up to ask if the Vice President possessed actual evidence of Arkansas's action. Little Aleck displayed a copy of the ordinance of secession and also a state resolution adopting the Provisional Constitution. "I am satisfied," said Withers. "It is best always to know that the official papers are present." Having satisfied himself by getting a few words on the record, the South Carolinian sat down, the Congress unanimously accepted Arkansas, and four of her five delegates took their seats.[37] Now they were ten, and the number of visitors from North Carolina, Missouri, and Kentucky led observers to believe that "reliable information in official circles" suggested more states would follow early in June.[38]

The day after the two-state secession word arrived, Davis met with his cabinet until two in the morning or later, and he would do so again and again. In fact it became common in the days ahead for the secretaries to work all day, return to their lodgings for supper, and then go back to Government House at ten and work until midnight or later.[39] There was so much to do, and the addition of two new stars to their flag almost doubled the concerns before them. Each addition of territory meant longer borders to defend, more troops needed, more money required, and more points of danger. Privately the Vice President now estimated that they must have at least $40 million to sustain themselves in any conflict. No wonder the cabinet and Congress gave attention to little else but the preparations for war.[40]

"Independence and liberty will require money as well as blood," Little Aleck told a friend this week.[41] Toombs agreed wholeheartedly. "The revolution must rest on the treasury," he told Stephens. "Without it, *it must fail*."[42] There was plenty of money in the Treasury just then, thanks to the enthusiastic subscription to the loan and the money turned over by the several states. But it could hardly last long in the face of the estimates in Walker's report, much less the needs of the other branches of government. "How are we to get the money?" the Vice President asked a friend.[43]

Almost immediately after the convening of Congress, Memminger advised Davis that the War Department estimates required them to realize all of the $15 million loan as quickly as possible.[44] It was a cumbersome process, since every bond and its attached interest coupons required twenty-three numbers, a date, and twenty-two signatures by the controller—a total of 46,000 signatures on the first $5 million subscription alone. It took the entire Register's bureau and help from other Treasury offices to get them all prepared, one man accounting for 4,000 signatures per day.[45] The response to that first issue was staggering. Charleston alone signed for $2 million, New Orleans another $2.7 million, and Mobile for $300,000, and these all came from small investors. The capitalists waited.[46]

Memminger's call went forth on May 7, and within a few months the balance of the $15 million came in—a good start, but far from enough. They could hardly look to the tariff for much. It was still such a hot issue that Congress would never entirely agree on the best course, and Rhett continually demanded that debates on the subject be publicized so that the people could see where the delegates stood on the matter.[47] Lobbyists continued to press for low duties on imported goods, while others argued for none at all to encourage European shippers to send their vessels and cargoes through the as-yet ineffective blockade.[48] Late in the month Congress issued a heavily revised tariff schedule that levied twenty-five percent duties on only a few luxury items like bagatelle tables, liquor and tobacco, and edible delicacies. The twenty percent roll was somewhat longer, again composed of non-necessities. The largest list followed the fifteen percent heading, including virtually all day-to-day items, from alum to wagons. Ten and five percent categories applied chiefly to raw materials, and a wide range of household goods from books to guns could pass free.[49] But the tariff would be a disappointment. Memminger naively believed that it would produce $25 million in its first year. Thanks to the blockade, he would get less than $1 million.[50]

Nor would mints do him any good, for on May 14 Davis signed an act to suspend their operation indefinitely.[51] The country had neither the precious metals nor the time to develop hard currency manufacture. Honor and policy also dictated that Memminger could not accept certain captures. Merchant vessels taken in Southern ports before passage of the war declaration he ordered to be returned to their owners. "We gain more by respect for law than from the seizure of a few vessels," he said.[52] It was a wise policy, but it cost him some small addition to his coffers.

Most immediately, another loan seemed the best way. Perhaps in consultation with Memminger, Congress discussed a produce loan on May 6, under which planters would turn over to the Treasury agricultural goods—chiefly cotton—and the government could sell them and give the growers interest-bearing bonds in the amount realized from the sale. It was a way around the shortage of hard cash at the moment.[53] Davis hoped that it might yield as much as $50 million, and men like Toombs and Tom Cobb united on the importance of the measure, pushing it hard in Georgia and elsewhere. Every congressman received bond blanks to send home for distribution, and Toombs leaned hard on them all to push their planting constituents to subscribe part of their crops.[54] In the end the so-called Cotton Loan would yield almost $13 million, not nearly as much as Davis and Memminger hoped.[55]

That took them back to one of Stephens's and Toombs's early enthusiasms, the notion of the government itself buying cotton and shipping it abroad for money and to hold for credit.[56] "Samson's strength was in his locks," Little Aleck argued. "Our strength is in our locks of cotton." While the President regarded cotton as a political weapon, Stephens and others saw it only as a commercial power, and even Tom Cobb backed him on this idea.[57] It was a proposal with great promise on its face, and substantial problems beneath. For one thing, Stephens was not a substantial cotton planter, and knew rather little of the state of the most recent crop, nor how much of it was already sold and out of the country. The cotton market at the end of 1860 had been a poor one, with the quality of that new crop only "middling," as they said, or inferior. Still New Orleans was shipping 61,500 bales per week by December.[58] Overall sales were down some 660,000 bales from the year before, which presumably meant at least that much surplus on hand.[59] The most recently harvested crop ran to somewhere around two and one-half million bales, and that added to what remained of the unsold previous crop seemingly left the South with over three million as the Confederates met in February to form their government.[60]

Unfortunately, in the days leading up to February 1861, the greater portion of this crop had already been transported to seaports and shipped to foreign markets. Britain, France, the rest of Europe, and the United States accounted for at least two and one-half million bales.[61] Internal consumption used several thousand more, perhaps as many as 193,000.[62] The next crop would not come in until September, which meant that in these early days no more than two or three hundred thousand bales actually remained in the Confederacy. Planters in Appalachicola, Florida, held 20,000 in March, while a number of others held their cotton on their plantations in fear of a blockade that would simply keep it rotting on wharves in Mobile and New Orleans.[63] Then there was the problem of shipping. One large vessel might handle a thousand bales in a voyage, but that still required two or three hundred voyages for the available supply, from a Confederacy that had no merchant fleet. "The means for shipping it in large quantities were wholly wanting," attested one of Mallory's officers. Fewer than half a dozen oceangoing steamers anchored in Confederate ports as late as mid-May, and they would travel at the risk of a gradually growing blockade that concentrated first on just those major seaports from which cotton would be shipped.[64] If they waited for the September crop, the blockade would be too tight, but that lay in the future just then.

Besides, Memminger for one did not expect the "war" to last that long.[65] Though the idea came before the cabinet more than once, Memminger's notion prevailed. The President himself thought the proposal "idealistic," and most agreed on its impracticability.[66] Moreover, since the Treasury had no funds other than its loan proceeds—needed to finance the growing army and the government—how was it supposed to buy the cotton?[67] According to Memminger's reading of the Constitution, it would be unlawful for the government to go into the cotton-selling business in any case, making it a "merchant" as he put it.[68] And surely someone in the Montgomery government saw the *Times* of London occasionally, with its announcement that in the spring of 1861 Europe already had a cotton surplus of 1,433,500 bales on hand. The bumper crops of the previous year worked against Stephens's and Toombs's scheme, even if everything else did not.[69] Russell, the visiting Englishman, made no secret of his belief now that the Confederates attached far too much importance to their cotton, and that in its current position of surplus, England at least, the world's largest consumer, could do without.[70]

Memminger looked into another cotton expedient, however. He hoped to establish depots in Havana and Bermuda, where he could store bales to be released through the embargo from time to time as needed, and corresponded in April with the Charleston firm of Fraser, Trenholm and Company, hoping they might establish a private steamer line to get the cotton to his depots.[71] As luck would have it, William Trenholm left Charleston for Montgomery to discuss the matter on the same train that brought Beauregard. While they rode together, Trenholm told the general that he had just learned of ten new, fast, heavily armed vessels of the East India fleet for sale. The idea of buying a fleet, of course, had already occurred to Davis and Mallory. One of the latter's subordinates just now thought his superior "like a chieftain without a clan," and purchases would solve the problem.[72] Indeed, Mallory had already discussed acquiring an iron-sheathed clipper from Nova Scotia to come to Savannah, take on privately owned cotton, and pass through the blockade to England. And on the very day of Trenholm's arrival, May 4, Congress received a proposal for building an ironclad, while the Naval Affairs committee asked Davis to look into buying warships in Europe.[73] There was considerable support for the notion, and powerful at that, with Rhett, Stephens, and Chesnut, among others, in favor.[74]

Trenholm got before the cabinet to present a proposal for establishing the steamer line. Memminger backed it, but the others declined, probably because it bordered on being unconstitutional. After all, the Constitution forbade the government to do anything by way of appropriations or concessions to encourage private enterprise. Despite Beauregard's promises, Trenholm said nothing about his East Indies fleet idea. He did speak informally with Mallory, and probably Walker.[75] Rhett, thinking Davis hostile to him over the "hired house" affair, got another member of Congress to approach the President on the plan, or so he claimed.[76] Somehow, there the idea stopped. It never got to Davis or the cabinet, but then, given the May 4 Naval Affairs committee resolution, it need not. It could stop with Mallory. He was already about to send James D. Bulloch as agent to England charged to do exactly what Trenholm proposed, and on May 10, just days after Trenholm's meeting with the cabinet, Congress passed a bill authorizing Mallory to have Bulloch buy steamships and armaments. The East Indies vessels naturally came under Bulloch's commission, but either he forgot them, or their owners withdrew the offer before he arrived.[77]

Or Trenholm's suggestion may simply have gotten lost on someone's desk in the flurry of activity engulfing Montgomery. On every front the men running the government were pressed, rushed, and often harried. Toombs, hoping to exert some kind of influence in his State Department, promoted an alliance with Mexico, and dispatched Pickett with instructions not to press for recognition, but not to discourage it either. The Confederacy had to be careful where its southern neighbor was concerned, for as the French adventured in Mexico, an alliance with the wrong party there could prejudice a much more significant relationship with a major European power.[78] Rhett stood again to set his teeth into diplomatic grievances. Hopeful glimmers came from Yancey in England, where he met on May 3 with Lord Russell and though finding him cautious and noncommittal, still Yancey thought he made a favorable impression.[79] He reported to Montgomery that he did not doubt his eventual success.[80] Meanwhile, Toombs continued to send him whatever might be of use, from letters of marque to issue, to propaganda materials like the Campbell correspondence.[81]

Rhett wanted more, however. Trying to go around Davis, whose prerogative it was to set foreign policy, Rhett had his Foreign Affairs committee introduce a resolution empowering the commissioners to make commercial and navigation treaties. Toombs favored the idea, and appeared before the committee in advocacy. The bill reported would have allowed the diplomats to make commercial treaties guaranteeing tariff rates no higher than twenty percent on anything—and probably quite a bit less—for twenty years, virtually "most favored nation" agreements. But when it came up for debate in Congress, Perkins moved that the term be reduced to six years, which carried. Disgusted, and thinking that this offered no inducement at all to a foreign nation to risk the blockade with its merchant vessels, Rhett tabled his own bill and let it die. Somehow, in his mind it had to be Davis's fault.[82]

The President, meanwhile, worked on his army. Finally he heard from Joseph E. Johnston, who reached Montgomery May 12 to discuss Stephens's pet fear, the safety of Harpers Ferry. That was to be Johnston's charge, and Davis sent him back on his way after only three days in the capital.[83] Davis showed dual sides of his nature when he offered a generalship to William Campbell of Tennessee, a commander from the Mexican War with whom he had once engaged in a vitriolic controversy that could have led to a duel. He promised now that he had entirely forgotten their one-time animosity, but Campbell declined anyhow, being a Unionist.[84] But then Davis also gave a generalcy to an old crony, the Episcopal Bishop Leonidas Polk. They had been friends at West Point, but Polk had resigned immediately upon graduation, never wore the uniform, and never served a day in the military. He offered no experience whatever, but Davis felt confidence and gratitude for being befriended by him all those years ago, and with this President that was sometimes all it took.[85] Significantly, on May 16 when Davis used the newly enacted legislation authorizing the rank of full general, the two top ranking spots went to Samuel Cooper and Albert Sidney Johnston, the one a man who never led troops in the field and never rose above captain in the Old Army, and the other a man whose whereabouts still remained unknown. Both owed their commissions chiefly to Davis's unswerving friendship. It remained to be seen how good a rationale that made for giving men high command.[86]

The urge to see his troops in person inevitably persuaded Davis to leave Montgomery, if only for a day. Accompanied by Varina and Mallory, he left May 14 on the newly completed Alabama & Florida for the nine-hour trip to Pensacola, and there conferred with Bragg, whose crustiness some already bemoaned. There he reviewed the troops, who found him looking worn and sickly, and heard the band of the Yankee garrison inside Fort Pickens playing the "Star Spangled Banner" as a taunt.[87] Several days earlier he had complained to Governor Thomas O. Moore in Baton Rouge that "the golden opportunity has been lost at Fort Pickens." Delay and parsimony from the capital denied him the perfect time to attack the Yankee garrison. He did not say what he must have felt, that but for Montgomery's interference—or lack of it—the hero of the hour might have been he rather than Beauregard.[88] Now he complained that Walker did not send him staff officers, and when he found his own he could not get them paid or commissioned. At least the War Department sent him troops regularly, though they included several companies of dragoons, mounted soldiers quite useless on sandy beaches in operations against a masonry fort.[89] Davis's presence mollified the cantankerous general somewhat, and planted the seeds of a growing friendship based largely on the fact that for all his grousing behind the President's back, Bragg rarely complained *to* him.

Relationships assumed more and more importance as May wore on, for Davis realized that difficult men like Bragg were not the exception in his new Confederacy. Some, of course, could be a delight, and how he must have welcomed the beginning of his dealings with Isham Harris, governor of Tennessee. Hilliard's mission went as smooth as could be, thanks largely to Harris's predisposition, and when he returned to Montgomery after only a few days with an agreement in hand, the President declared "Mr. Hilliard, you have transcended my expectations."[90] When Walker first asked Harris for four regiments, he got them with no question, no condition, and no delay.[91] Better yet, his state forces contained some twenty-two infantry regiments, two of cavalry, and ten batteries of artillery, and he proposed as quickly as possible to turn all of them over to the War Department, most fully armed.[92] It was, quite literally, a small army.

If only they would all be so cooperative. Perry of Florida was happy to contribute two new regiments that Walker requisitioned, but specified that one of them had to be sent to the anticipated scene of glory in Virginia.[93] Thomas O. Moore, a staunch supporter of the Confederacy, still stood on his state rights as he saw them. Early in May, when Congress enacted new legislation authorizing the War Department only to accept regiments enlisted for three years or the term of the war, Moore, like others, balked. The three-years act made perfect sense, of course. It kept experienced men in the field instead of having to recruit whole new regiments every year. It saved time and money in training and made more efficient use of limited weapons and uniforms. And it addressed the probabilities still dawning on some that this might be a longer conflict than originally thought. But most of the governors had already raised and equipped twelve months' regiments under the old legislation, and now found that they could not turn them over because they would not be accepted. The volunteers felt cheated, their officers aggrieved, and the governors embarrassed. Moore had 8,000 such men now and he wanted Walker to take them anyhow. Walker stood by the law, at which Moore said all he could do would be to ask the men if they would switch their enlistments for the longer term. If so, fine; if not, he would disband them, and "the responsibility will not rest with me." Walker tried to be diplomatic. "You are making an objection for the troops which they will not make for themselves," he cajoled. "Try them and see." Moore refused. At the same time the governor quarreled with Benjamin on a legal issue over the arms captured from the Federal arsenal in Baton Rouge, asserting that the state had turned them over to *his* control, and not Montgomery's, and *he* would decide to grant them to Walker on request.[94]

Pettus of Mississippi also complained about the predicament of his twelve months' troops being raised. They had camped and drilled for three weeks, but now would have to go home. This governor's concern was more for the effect on morale than any affront to himself, and perhaps sensing a friendlier tone, Walker tried to find a way around the legislation to allow him to accept two of the regiments.[95] Pickens, too, caused problems, but he and the Secretary of War usually settled them amicably. At the first request he sent regiments to Virginia, but insisted on the proviso that when no longer needed there, they must not be ordered elsewhere permanently or be stationed in some tedious garrison duty. This fear of missing service in the field pervaded South Carolina's volunteer officers, one of them extracting a condition from Walker that his command would not be stuck in some fort. And despite the fact that legislation only allowed Walker to accept discrete units of infantry, cavalry, and artillery, Wade Hampton of South Carolina persisted in pressing for acceptance of his "legion," a large unit containing elements of all three. In the end, to get the men, Walker yielded.[96] At the same time, friends warned Pickens that he pressed his candidates for appointments too hard on Montgomery, and Andrew G. Magrath actually went to the capital on his behalf to smooth relations.[97] Pickens, like Pettus, in the end worked with Walker rather than against him.

Real trouble started coming from a quarter where Davis and Walker least expected it. Almost from the first, Governor Letcher and the War Department simply failed to communicate. Certainly Montgomery worked to bolster Virginia, the Confederacy's most threatened frontier. Walker made a substantial shift of heavy ordnance into the state immediately after its secession, and regiments rushed there from several of the states. Davis made certain to give Lee high rank, showing considerable delicacy toward his feelings. The May 16 legislation placing him immediately junior to Cooper and A. S. Johnston left Lee more than satisfied.[98]

But they could not seem to find the tone required for dealing with Letcher. It did not help that the man was a notorious inebriate. Repeated reports of his drunkenness came to Davis and Walker, some asserting that Letcher was so lost in the bottle that Lee should usurp authority, or Davis himself must come where he could overshadow the governor. Others seriously questioned Letcher's loyalty, suggesting that he felt at best "half-hearted" and "lukewarm" for the movement. Walker's spy in Richmond wired on May 7 that "there is treachery here," leading the secretary to tell him not to be hysterical and send only "ascertained facts, not floating rumors."[99]

Drunk or disloyal, Letcher seemed uncooperative and uncommunicative. Walker asked for a statement of Virginia's forts, arsenals, and other installations to be turned over to the Confederacy, as provided for by law, and as done by the other states. Five days later he reminded Letcher of the report, and five days after that, when still no response came, he somewhat testily asked the governor "do you desire this Government to assume any control over military operations in Virginia?"[100] Walker's spy reported that confusion seemed in charge in Richmond, and that Letcher lacked the confidence of leading men. Worse, he gave high state commands to men with drinking habits as notorious as his own.[101] Yet Davis and Walker also erred, so overjoyed at Virginia's secession that they forgot to follow it up with close consultation, apparently leaving Letcher feeling very much on his own. "I have not received a suggestion, or a recommendation of any kind from the Confederate authorities," he complained to Brockenbrough and Staples on May 11. He would be delighted to consult freely with Davis on what could and should be done, but first *someone* had to contact him.[102] Soon Letcher complained to others in Richmond about a lack of cordiality and open communication with Montgomery, the more so as he learned of Walker dealing directly with others in his state.[103] No doubt responding to the reports of the governor's intemperance and unreliability, Montgomery tried to work around him, but he was having none of that. "The authorities at Montgomery will oblige me by addressing their applications in future to the Executive of the State," he wrote petulantly on May 15, "instead of subordinates."[104] They started badly with this governor, and partly by their own doing, yet already Davis received complaints that he devoted too much time and attention to the Old Dominion. Referring to the Deep South states composing the original Confederacy, one dis-gruntled Alabamian reminded Davis that "you were elected President of them, not of Virginia."[105]

Yet for sheer obstinacy and obstructionism, none could match Joseph E. Brown of Georgia. Where other governors raised a quibble here or there, Brown seized on everything, and where nothing existed, he invented points of contention. The Georgia convention approved turning over the former Federal forts and arsenals to the national gov-ernment on March 20, yet Brown stalled the transfer for a full month in spite of inquiries from Walker. What few knew was that during the delay, he shifted all the best weapons to his own state armory in Savannah, leaving only the older and less serviceable arms to be turned over. "Under other circumstances it would be wrong," Tom Cobb grumbled, "but at present it was disgraceful."[106] When he did turn them over on April 18, after all his foot-dragging, he then immediately and peremptorily started demanding that Montgomery pay more attention to manning those forts.[107] Once Walker assumed charge of the arsenals and armories, Brown complained vigorously whenever arms from them went to other states instead of to Georgia troops. Keeping weapons and munitions in his state quickly became his mania. He forbade regiments to go into Confederate service without his per-mission. If they did so, they must leave state arms behind.[108] At Tom Cobb's urging in 1860 the state amassed nearly half a million pounds of powder.[109] Yet now when the Confederacy needed it, Brown either refused to yield it or set conditions. When the War Department ordered guns and ammunition Brown intended for Savannah to be shipped to the capital instead, he told Walker that "they are mine, not his," and countermanded the secretary's order.[110] Later when Walker very much wanted to purchase from Brown some sulphur and saltpeter for making gunpowder, the governor agreed, but only if part of the deal included some ordnance, shot, shell, and a useless old steamboat that he wanted to be rid of. When he brought Brown's response before the cabinet, Walker became livid, and Davis showed his own chagrin. The President asked Toombs to intercede, but Brown stood his ground, and to get the powder the War Department became the owner of a worth-less steamer.[111]

To Brown it became a childish game, setting conditions, pettifog-ging over technicalities, and piling up his list of little victories over the War Department. Most of Georgia's delegates came to Government House on one errand or another in which the governor enlisted their

influence. Wright came on behalf of officers appointed by Brown contrary to legislation.[112] Nisbet lobbied for appointments in Montgomery.[113] Brown even expected the Vice President to do his bidding,
lobbying for more troops in his coastal defenses, or pressuring Walker
to let him have his way.[114]

There lay the problem. They let him have his way too often, and he
liked it. Over and over Walker—and Davis—gave in. Brown naturally
turned apoplectic over the shift from twelve months' to three years'
regiments. Just two days after Virginia's secession, Walker threw up his
hands over an enlistment issue and wired Brown that "technicalities
must not stand in the way of preparation." Over and over he yielded
"for the sake of harmony."[115] Legislation called for regiments to consist
of ten companies; Brown wanted to send regiments with twelve, probably he could thereby appoint more officers. When Walker wanted to
send organized companies at Savannah—which faced no threat—to
Virginia—which did—Brown fought him at every step, even when the
soldiers themselves expressed their desire to go.[116] There was nothing
for them to do, said Tom Cobb, but guard "rice-planters and their
slaves." The whole matter put Bartow to swearing profusely whenever
it came up, and he spent considerable time with Davis trying to get an
act through Congress that would allow the President to accept the
Savannah volunteers directly without having to go through the governor.[117] Brown tried to enlist the Cobb brothers in his support, not realizing that both detested him. "I think the whole blame rests on Gov.
Brown," Tom confessed. He accused the governor of "doing all he can
to clog the Government," as if striving to "make himself hateful to all."
Howell referred to Brown as "the miserable demagogue who now dis-
graces the executive chair of Ga."[118]

Walker spent more time in correspondence with Brown than with the
rest of the governors combined, and lost more patience with him.
Making it worse was the governor's innocent posture. "I entertain no
feelings of jealousy," he told Walker. Yet for every troop or supply request he insisted that he be sent the congressional acts empowering the
secretary to make requisitions on him, or the legislation specifying the
regulations for raising and accepting troops—which Brown then
promptly ignored as it suited him.[119] Worse, to the press he was positively hypocritical. After telling an editor of all the letters he had written to
Walker and Georgia's congressmen on the matter of Savannah's
defense, Brown then enjoined editors not to publish them. "I had rather
suffer unjust censure than bring the government at Montgomery into

disrepute," he modestly pleaded.[120] Small wonder that Howell Cobb saw in mid-May "a fair prospect of a quarrel" between the governor and the President, and resolved to stand behind Davis.[121] Almost three weeks earlier brother Tom already saw that Jefferson Davis loathed the man and privately expressed his contempt for the only person in the Confederacy who had tried consistently to thwart his efforts in every endeavor.[122]

Inevitably word of the problems with the governors filtered out of the state houses and the capital offices to the people at large, and any such disillusionment over the unanimity and harmony of the leaders of the cause had to hurt. If the governors put a crack in that veneer, Congress pried it even wider during its second session. The excitement of the days of February and March was gone. They were at war, to be sure, but for Congress the work had shifted from the epic acts of creation to the endless mundane tasks of legislation. Overworked and underinterested, many quickly became bored, and it showed. Bored, too, were the spectators who no longer came to sit in the gallery only to be evicted minutes later as the doors closed. Uncharacteristically the *Mercury* reporter actually complimented the secret sessions now, for anything that appeared in the press would quickly reach the Yankees. But still he complained that the public sessions hardly gave him enough to fill a short letter.[123] Another characterized Congress's proceedings as "unimportant," and a New Orleans newsman joked that his chief experience in reporting the debates was putting on his hat and leaving.[124] Even the *Mercury* correspondent, the day after praising the secret sessions, felt abused when he walked through the rain up Market in order to hear a prayer and the appointments to fill two committee vacancies before Cobb cleared the hall. "Your reporter has thrown away his pencils in disgust," he fumed.[125]

In fact, despite all its vital enabling legislation, much of Congress's public performance seemed trivial. Their longest sustained open-session debate came over a patent bill, something even they could not pretend to find of consuming interest. It originated with Hemphill, whose incredibly wrinkled and leathery old face topped by a youthful wig only added to the sense of this being anything but vital work occupying the legislature. The bill ran to thirty-seven foolscap pages, and it took more than two hours to debate matters such as government distribution of agricultural information, the expense of publishing patent office reports, and even the mailing of free seeds, all of which they regarded as costly abuses in Washington. Withers, feeling the need to be heard again, rose to point out that no one ever read patent reports, and as for seeds, he got some from Washington's Patent Office once, and nothing grew but "a few very common turnips."[126] A growing cynicism about the legislative body would hardly be surprising.

Of course, newcomers seeing Congress for the first time still found it impressive. "The finest-looking set of men I have ever seen collected together," thought Varina Davis when she visited the hall on May 10; "grave, quiet and thoughtful-looking men, with an air of refinement."[127] It still comprised some of the oldest and most distinguished statesmen in the South, to be sure.[128] But unsettling opinions became more and more commonplace. Rumors went the rounds that their sense of unanimity was gone, replaced by an almost even split on every issue except independence.[129] Some regarded more and more of the members as "ignorant and unsavory," and Stuart, ever cynical, protested that from a newsman's point of view "there are not many of them worth a sentence."[130]

Increasingly the vanity of some, the ill-temper of others, and the sheer boorishness of a few peeked through their aura of dignity and decorum. Rhett never stopped trying to lift the veil of secrecy from their debates, that his words might get into the Charleston press.[131] Even the reporters caught on to him, a South Carolina newsman noting the removal of confidentiality from one long-winded report from Foreign Affairs "so that its author might be able to gain all the credit possible for his production through the medium of the newspapers."[132] Many barely made a pretense of listening during the debates now. Surrounded by noise and confusion on the floor, Stephens complained that he could hardly bring his thoughts to bear on the issues discussed.[133] Wigfall lowered the dignity of the house by appearing drunk far more often than his reputation could bear, bullying, braggartish, and bad tempered.[134] Old Withers became even more tiresome and indiscrete, sowing discord in his own family by complaining about watching niece Mary's husband James Chesnut "play rag dog to Jeff Davis."[135]

The attempts to exert influence, help friends, and advance family did even more to shorten their stature the longer they sat. When they debated mileage allowances for travel to and from sessions, Texans Waul and Wigfall proposed taking it from ten cents per mile all the way to forty cents, hardly unaware that, coming from Texas, they would travel the farthest and realize the greatest reimbursement.[136] The scramble to help friends and family seemed disgraceful to some. Ochiltree got his son an appointment in the army.[137] J. A. P. Campbell tried to get a young friend out of the army after he enlisted too enthusiastically.[138] Tom Cobb tried repeatedly to help friends and family, and when he failed he condemned the successful nepotism of others without seeing his own. His well-developed paranoia took over in the end, suspecting "those in authority" of dealing underhandedly with him, and when finally he did get three men appointed, he explained it by remarking that no one else had applied for the positions they sought.[139]

"I am heartily sick of this place already," he moaned on the second day of the session. "Favoritism and nepotism are controlling all public appointments." Only his pure patriotism kept him from giving in to disgust at the selfishness he saw.[140] No one complained more of the self-serving than he, yet he stood among the front rank of the selfish. Just after telling Toombs—as he kept telling everyone—that he would accept no office in the gift of the government, he heard that Davis thought about sending another minister abroad. Immediately Cobb envisioned himself in the post, asked Marion if she would like to go overseas, where he was certain he could succeed in persuading England and France to mediate between North and South. Failing that, he also thought of appointing himself an ambassador to Washington to make peace. If he did not get the appointment, with all the nepotism that he so roundly condemned in others, he suggested that he could secure it for Marion's father.[141] Adding spite to his hypocrisy, Cobb interfered in the appointments solicited by other congressmen, especially his nemesis Stephens. Learning early in May that Little Aleck sought a position for a friend in a company to be called the "Stephens Guards," Cobb told his occasional tool Bartow to try to stop it. Bartow reached the War Department just as Stephens was making his case, and somehow did manage to prevent the appointment. While the Vice President sulked through the rest of the day, Cobb boasted to his wife that "it has gratified me, I must confess."[142]

No wonder tempers flared more frequently, and occasionally beyond control. Their real arguments—when they had them—took place in secret session, and little if anything leaked to the public. On the afternoon of May 9, while debating amendments to a congressional pay bill, Crawford called for the question rather earlier than Kenan would have liked, and in responding Kenan characterized his fellow Georgian's action as "illiberal." Crawford took offense, and President Cobb had to to use his gavel repeatedly to calm the tumult that ensued. He called them to order for violating the rules of the House. Kenan afterward apologized to Cobb, but declined to do so to Crawford, and that same evening the whole matter was referred to Stephens, Wigfall, Bartow, Keitt, Toombs, and Cobb, for settlement short of a duel.[143]

Other ambitions created conflict. Now that war seemed certain, many of them wanted to be heroes on the field rather than drones in the chamber. Less than two weeks after protesting that he would like to retire to private life when this session closed, Howell Cobb dreamed of raising and commanding a regiment, despite his utter lack of military experience.[144] Bartow, too, worked actively to get his own regiment, and Toombs talked of it as well. "They are all getting ahead of me," Cobb complained.[145] Even Tom Cobb toyed with the idea, confident as usual that he knew more than enough about anything to do it better than professionals. "My efficiency is more in counsel than on the field," he confessed modestly, but "I prefer being closer to the scene of conflict." Many asked him if he did not want to raise and command a regiment, and he admitted that "*Ambition* says 'to horse!'" To Marion he wondered, "am I really doing any good here?"[146]

Meanwhile the others, the quiet, the hardworking, the ones given neither to vainglory nor ambition, simply stayed at their grinding daily chores of talk and listen, while fighting boredom, the growing heat of late spring, and the desire to stifle their more vocal colleagues. Tom Cobb confessed on May 11 that "I am worn out and broken down."[147] DeClouet complained that he was so fed up and worn out by his days in Congress that he would never seek office again.[148] A few like Clayton, who had all they could take, simply resigned before the session adjourned, and more including Withers would withdraw immediately afterward.[149]

The growing discontent rose higher than governors and Congress. As May wore on, the cabinet became the target of increasingly public criticism, most of it focused on Walker. It could not have been for want of energy, for he appeared to his staff to be working himself almost to death. Tall, thin, slightly stooped, he boasted an excellent memory but few if any administrative skills, and the larger the army grew, and the greater its demands, the more his shortcomings became manifest. He could not, or would not, delegate. Untidy in his office, instead of filing papers he threw them indiscriminately into a chair until the pile approached half a bushel in volume. More than once the President himself sat and shuffled through the hundreds of sheets to find a document he needed.[150] Despite the increasing number of clerks scurrying pell mell through the department, some business went unattended. The War Department did not have stationery until May, and then with an absence of forethought it was all printed with the year "1861" at the head, when presumably the government might last a bit longer than that.[151]

Walker worked constantly. Two clerks, Tyler and John B. Jones, opened his mail and read the letters, wrote abstracts on their backs for the secretary to read, and then acted on his scribbled pencil notes when he returned them.[152] Meanwhile, rarely less than a dozen people stood in the corridor outside Walker's door, waiting for the messenger to call them in one by one to the secretary. DeClouet saw for himself that the department was overwhelmed with applicants, and others told stories of stacks of applications in files, enough to fill five regiments just of men wanting to be surgeons.[153] So great was the press that by the middle of May Walker took to walking from his room at the Exchange to Government House by a back way three times as long as the straight stroll down Commerce, and even then applicants waylaid him en route.[154]

When Walker did meet applicants as well as other dignitaries, he could be stiff and officious, far too formal for this egalitarian young nation.[155] He offended many. A friend of Clement Clay's found him disinterested and rather impolite. Henry Wayne of Georgia came to discuss an appointment, and Walker kept him sitting beside his desk for hours while he allowed one visitor after another to interrupt them, in the end never finishing his discussion, and leaving Wayne to go back to Georgia in disgust. Another hopeful, a wealthy South Carolina rice planter offering to raise and equip a regiment, sent his card to Walker and then waited in the department lobby for days for an interview that never came. He, too, went home, a confirmed enemy.[156]

Inevitably an outcry arose. Many simply dismissed it as what the *Mercury* correspondent called "the idle tattle of the Exchange loungers," aspirants whose disappointment "sowed the seed of a discontent that ultimately grew and ripened," said Stuart.[157] Clerk Jones noted on May 20 that "the disappointed class give rise to many vexations," and by that time the complaints about Walker found their way into the press all across the Confederacy, despite defenders who argued that he was able and industrious.[158]

Almost every governor complained of him, largely for reasons entirely outside Walker's control, like the three years or the war legislation. Commanders complained that they could not get money from the War Department to pay merchants for goods. Others, when told the department could not accept a regiment because it did not meet regulations, reacted in a huff and actually discouraged theirs and other men from enlisting on any other basis. Walker hardly helped when he complained about some of his duties as being "harrassing to the judgment and annoying to the sensibilities."[159] Even in his own department Walker lost esteem, Adjutant General Cooper regarding him as at best inefficient,[160] and department employees complained of not being paid on time.[161] It got worse. Fellow cabinet ministers increasingly came to regard him with disdain, or even contempt. Toombs thought him utterly incompetent and overcautious. In an argument in Walker's office on May 22 the Georgian advocated taking the war to the North before it could mount an invasion of the Confederacy, regardless of the deplorable consequences it would have for his own ministers abroad trying to present the South as a nation seeking no conquest. Walker did not even pose an alternative, meekly saying that he had no responsibility for strategy and could only follow the dictates of Congress and the President.[162]

And the congressmen increasingly looked askance at him, having heard too many complaints from their governors, their friends and family who wanted appointments, and their constituents who wanted anything they could get. McRae tried May 6 to get in to see Walker, waiting for two hours unsuccessfully. As it happened, that same day the secretary notified Congress through Howell Cobb that he could no longer receive calls from congressmen at any and all times, as it interrupted his business too much. Henceforth they should only call on him in the morning between nine and noon.[163] It was sound time management, but poor diplomacy when dealing with congressional egos. McRae responded by writing a sarcastic letter suggesting that all he wanted was for Walker to write a letter, "not quite so big a job as the creation of the world."[164] Ever-critical Tom Cobb thought Walker unbalanced, incompetent, and probably satanic. "Feeble," "unfit," "*imbecility*," and more epithets dripped from his pen.[165] Even the ordinarily evenhanded Stephens concluded from all he saw by the end of May that Walker managed his department badly, and that the secretary himself was woefully inefficient. "He'll 'do and do and do,' and at last do nothing. . . . Toombs ought to have been there," Little Aleck concluded. "He is the brains of the whole concern."[166] Few realized yet that Walker himself felt little liking for his position. Thanks to Davis and Congress making all the real decisions, he saw himself being gradually reduced to a glorified clerkship, put in the unenviable position of target of all the animosity of the governors and the applicants, yet unable—in his eyes—to do anything about it. As May approached its close, he confessed to his son, he found himself increasingly in "an impossible position."[167]

He was not alone. Mallory, too, attracted increasing criticism, chiefly for want of energy. "Mallory," said Toombs, "is good for nothing but to squander public money," an unfair accusation given the modesty of the secretary's estimate for operations.[168] Yet men like Tom Cobb and Conrad agreed, the former ranting in rather un-Christian fashion that "if we could only get rid of Secty. Walker and Secty. Mallory and the Lord would kill that drunken Gov. Letcher, I should feel like shouting."[169] Mallory, too, could be off-putting, and at least once offended an officer by receiving him at the department "as if he had designs upon him," according to Rhett's son.[170]

In fact, dissatisfaction with the whole cabinet surfaced early in May, in part reflecting specific grievances, foiled ambitions, and a general notion that somehow everything should be going more smoothly, faster, with less uncertainty and inconvenience. The cabinet invited the criticism because they were there. "We lack efficiency," Keitt complained on May 15. "The administration has not sufficient energy." He accused them of being too much "taken up with little gratifications" to attend to their larger goal.[171] Probably reflecting her husband's prejudices more than her own, Mary Chesnut complained that "our *cabinet* [is] so dull & stupid."[172] Benjamin seemed to do nothing. Memminger did too little, and was rumored to employ embezzlers and gamblers in his department.[173] Only Reagan seemed not to offend anyone, probably because few cared about the Post Office Department, and as well because he managed to get it so well in hand. Then, too, he still was not operating, and would not until Lincoln stopped carrying the mails in the South. He got his stamps and his mail bags, set his postal rates, and announced at last on May 9 that he would assume control of the mails on June 1.[174] Even old Withers could not argue with that, though now he took to abusing other cabinet members to their faces.[175]

By May 10 rumors of trouble in the cabinet appeared in the Montgomery press, and for several days thereafter circulated through both the city and the country. Some said that Davis would appoint an entirely new group of department heads. Others maintained that it was only a subtle way of forcing Walker out of office.[176] Pundits suspected the rumors to be the work of Border State men in Montgomery who wanted to see Virginia, Tennessee, Arkansas, and the rest represented in the cabinet.[177] Conrad, for one, expected the truth lay in between,

Davis wanting both to replace Walker and Mallory, and get men from the new states in his inner circle.[178]

"The first Cabinet was a queer crowd," Toombs would say, perhaps over too much wine. Certainly he had no use for Walker or Mallory, regarded his own position as insignificant, and never expressed any great confidence in Memminger or Benjamin. He claimed later that during May he suggested to Davis that the entire group of them should go in favor of abler men. Davis, a man governed by loyalty to friends and those whom he felt served him well, said he could not do it, but agreed that not all of the departments had the best management. As senior minister, Toombs could suggest that they all resign, thus to make places for men from the new states. The Georgian says he did this, but none would agree.[179] And how could they do so, when most of them suffered growing criticism. To resign would be to accept disgrace.

The rumors, starting as hints of dissent within the cabinet and then growing to a general reorganization, disappeared almost as quickly as they arose, in little more than a week.[180] They were a symptom, for when they first hit the press, the Confederacy had just reached the end of that somehow symbolic first hundred days that in American politics signaled an emotional shift from euphoria and forbearance to discontent. Congress and cabinet all felt it, and inevitably it had to lead to the top, to the President himself.

So far Davis appeared to give universal satisfaction. By mid-May even Tom Cobb softened to approve and support his course, and another Georgian, Wright, declared that "President Davis has done all things well, and we need not fear to trust him."[181] Recent arrivals like Rives from Virginia found in him great intelligence, civility, and cordiality. Though Rives said that the President was "hardly up to the standard of merit assigned him," Davis still stood far above the average of recent presidents.[182] The clerk Jones of the War Department found him to have a clear view of the crisis at hand, and if anything, showed too much concern for consistency, which could hardly occupy high priority in times of revolution.[183] Even men far afield thought on balance that Davis was doing well. "I begin to feel that fiery as he is by nature," said Herschel Johnson, "he tempers all with good sense."[184]

But others spoke out now, for the most part privately, yet in strong terms. Stephens complained that Davis seemed slow to get things done, spending too much time on minutia. "Toombs would dispatch more in twenty minutes than he does in three hours," the Vice President carped.[185] Men close to him believed they saw a related problem in a streak of indecision, one in fact that troubled Davis most of his life. By early May he had yet to announce any definite line of policy for the impending conflict, whether to remain on the defensive, or take the war "into Africa."[186] Men who did not realize—or chose to ignore—the Herculean task before him of simply putting a government into operation and raising and equipping an army assumed that he had only the military situation to occupy his time. Even his close friend Clement Clay criticized him for having seemingly no plan of campaign, or being unable to understand or grasp the complexities of large-scale conflict.[187] Brown of Georgia, hardly an impartial observer, charged that any time Davis told a caller he was "deeply engaged," it meant that "as was usual with Mr. Davis, he was engaged in making up his mind."[188] A few even charged that the real decisions in Davis's administration came not from him but his wife, Varina.[189]

Without a doubt, Davis knew not the arts of the politician, and some feared that he would not steer a course clear of the old party hacks and their influence.[190] While he met all callers with a soothing, sometimes musical voice, the manner behind it put off too many of them.[191] Nor would he attempt to practice at diplomacy with men whose good will he needed. Varina thought that his personality could have won over many if only he relaxed enough to spend time socializing with congressmen and state officials. He used the excuse that doctors told him such activity aggravated a natural tendency to dyspepsia, but the fact was he simply had no patience for levees and receptions, and no ability to relax in the company of other powerful men.[192] In some degree, they intimidated him—or at least he felt a challenge in any strong and independent man whose opinions did not agree with his own. As a result, he could be far too uncommunicative with congressional committees who resented his aloofness.[193] Even Stephens found himself consulted less and less this May as he expressed in cabinet his emphatic views on cotton export and other such points of disagreement. "What caused a change in him I do not know," Little Aleck mused.[194] Because of the absence of free and open discussion with Congress, rumors began to circulate that Davis actually dictated to it, even drafting its bills himself.[195] It was nonsense, of course, but it fit the obstinate, autocratic image of him among his critics, and making Congress's acts seem to be his acts only made it easier for those critics to blame every ill in the country on the President.

Some of his critics were simply too foolish to be really dangerous, none more so than Withers, who simply never got over the business of the carriage with the six white horses and the $5,000 executive mansion. He never stopped ranting on the subject. "I heard that tale a thousand & one times in Montgomery," Mary Chesnut moaned.[196] Almost the only time Withers ever offered legislation was when the subject of any emolument for Davis came on the floor. When Toombs reported a bill for public buildings that included coverage of furniture for the "White House," Withers arose immediately to have that portion excluded. On a later appropriation actually specifying $987.50 for executive mansion furniture, Withers again moved to strike, and only South Carolina stood behind him.[197] The next day when Withers came to Congress, he put his hat and umbrella under his seat, walked over to Rhett—where he knew he would get a sympathetic hearing—and declared that "the fact is, Davis is venal and corrupt, and the Confederate Congress is no better." He announced his intention to resign at the end of the session.[198]

Rhett tried to dissuade the old crackpot. Withers himself would be no loss to Congress, but he represented a knee-jerk anti-Davis vote on any issue, and that was a loss to Robert Barnwell Rhett. He felt no doubt at all now that Congress had made a mistake, a terrible mistake, in electing Davis. He believed him "egotistical, arrogant, and vindictive"—character flaws that typified Rhett himself, by the way—and lacking in depth or statesmanship.[199] He charged him with "terrible incompetency and perversity," and went even farther. "Jefferson Davis is not only a dishonest man," he told his son, "but a liar."[200] Early in May the South Carolinian became quite animated in discussing the failure of Davis to take Fort Sumter sooner, and blamed that for their resulting position with the Union.[201]

Rhett, of course, had become just as irrational as Withers, only he posed a far greater danger. His venom flowed from disappointed ambition. "If the Confederacy had chosen to elect Barnwell Rhett president instead of Jefferson Davis," Mary Chesnut wrote with perception, "we might have escaped one small war, at least—the war the *Mercury* was now waging with the administration."[202] He had his newspaper to vent his spleen. Moreover, he served as a magnet for the other disaffected and disappointed, even though they might differ with Rhett on all other issues. Boyce, who had little use for Rhett, still agreed, saying "I never thought Davis was the man."[203] Bob Smith of Alabama would say shortly that "we have made a great mistake in the choice of President," citing what he took as Davis's conceit, vanity, ambition, and weakness.[204] Joe Brown, of course, characterized the act allowing Davis to call up troops from any state without the consent or authority of the governor as the action of "tyrants."[205]

Davis tried to be philosophical about the opposition of men like Rhett, but he lacked sincerity. "If we succeed, we shall hear nothing of these malcontents," he told Varina. "If we do not, then I shall be held accountable by the majority of friends as well as foes."[206] While protesting his readiness to accept whatever came to him, praise or blame alike, in fact Davis detested being opposed. It tore at him, chiefly because it affronted his own obstinate conviction of his rectitude in all matters. Even Varina admitted his being "abnormally sensitive to disapprobation," and when he felt himself misunderstood—meaning when someone failed to see that he was right—his manner could become "repellant."[207]

This applied almost equally to men whom he felt to be infringing on his prerogatives as president. Convinced that the Confederacy's very survival depended upon his involvement in all things, Tom Cobb repeatedly stuck his disapproving nose where it had no business. Fearing Walker's inefficiency, he conducted his own investigation of Confederate arms and munitions supplies, only to conclude that things did not look so bad after all.[208] At night he lay awake racking his brain "to look over the whole field of action to see our weak points to suggest to cabinet officers, and members of Congress and the President himself, for their immediate attention." Completely recovered from his brief attack of contrition and humility after the defeats of the first session, Cobb looked on himself as the saviour of the South, the only man who understood its dangers. "I doubt not many of them think me very officious," he said perceptively, "but I cannot help it."[209] Certainly the President found him officious, as he did others who flattered themselves similarly. A meddling letter he could simply shred and dismiss with an oath. A Tom Cobb, however, he could only meet with his "repellant" manner and steely glare, and that made an enemy just as surely as gaining a presidency that others thought rightfully theirs.

Inevitably these men, united chiefly by their growing hostility to Davis, from whatever cause, found their only power in joining one another. Rhett self-importantly claimed that he recognized the beginnings of a division by early April, a split not so much along policy lines as on personality. In this new nation whose founders unanimously decried continuing the old divisive and partisan system of political parties, he saw two factions in embryo—for Davis, and against Davis.[210] Gradually men polarized from a host of motives. Some like Withers

merely merged prewar notions into the new system. "What a pity—
these men have brought old hatreds & grudges & spites from the old
Union," lamented Mary Chesnut. "Already we see they will willingly
injure our cause to hurt Jeff Davis."[211] Others accused Davis himself of
fostering it by allowing the old party alignments to guide him in his
appointments. DeClouet, for instance, while granting that the former
parties ceased to exist in the Confederacy, still asserted that "old
wounds, even when healed, leave their scars behind them." Having
been a political opponent of Davis and the Democrats before the war,
he expected to have no influence now.[212]

In fact, he did not really try, nor apparently did some others. Despite
the substantial proportion of Whigs and former Unionists to whom
Davis gave positions, the notion took hold by early April that he
showed favoritism for Breckinridge Democrats.[213] "Appointments under
the new regime will be governed by the same political considerations as
in the old one," complained the pompous editor J. D. B. De Bow.
"Parties will form & are now forming in the same way & party hacks
will take the lead."[214] Vainly many protested what they thought they
saw happening. "There is no necessity for political parties," complained an editor in Davis's own Vicksburg. "The first attempt at a
party formation in the Confederate States, will be by those who have
selfish ends to promote." Doing so could only promote division and
mischief.[215] He might have been describing Rhett from a photograph,
and in time others now close to the President would join him in the
portrait. Tom Cobb saw it, unwitting that he was a player himself.
"The atmosphere of this place is absolutely *tainted* with selfish, ambitious schemes for personal aggrandizement," he complained the day
Congress reconvened.[216] And by the middle of May, one local Whig editor concluded that "it seems that secession has been accomplished
merely to make offices for aspiring Democrats."[217]

Factions were emerging, as most of any discernment could see, but
for all the wrong reasons—foiled ambitions, prewar antagonisms, imagined perceptions of favoritism based on the old parties, and of course
Davis's own personality. Thanks to the last, finding himself so widely
misunderstood only worked to make him even more distant. All of it
boded no good for a Confederacy whose only strength lay in what little
unity it could muster. Everywhere, it seemed, in the state houses, in
Congress, in the cabinet, and even in the presidency, the once apparently smooth finish of Southern harmony began more and more to take
on the crazed look of a flawed ceramic. No wonder Mrs. Fitzpatrick

found Davis looking gloomy now.[218] Just a few days before he had begged the old Union to leave him alone. Scarcely could he have imagined, when he first took his oath almost one hundred days ago in February, that a time would come when he wished that his fellow Confederates would do the same.

CHAPTER FIFTEEN

FAREWELL MONTGOMERY

———•★•———

CHARLOTTE WIGFALL FOUND THE PEOPLE OF THE CITY in fine spirits. "The streets are so lively & every one looks so happy, that you can scarcely realize the cause of the excitement." Looking out her hotel window she saw some of the city's gardens, and as she walked the streets even her snobbishness melted in the face of "as beautiful flowers as I ever saw anywhere."[1] Moreover, the people were so polite. "Everybody in Montgomery salutes everybody as if everybody knew everybody," a New Orleans visitor marveled.[2] But not everyone liked it here. The Virginia delegates worried for their health in the heat, especially Run Mad Tom Hunter with four inches of extra fat on his ribs.[3] Every day as he huffed and puffed up Market to the sittings of Congress, the steepest part of the walk took him past the Montgomery Marble Works on his left just past Decatur. Looking at the rows of yet unchiseled tombstones, he groaned repeatedly to friends that he feared he would sicken and die here in Montgomery and wind up lying beneath one.[4]

His lament spoke only a part of his real concern. Hunter came to this capital committed to seeing it moved to Richmond. For one thing, he had ambitions. There would be a fall election for president under the Permanent Constitution. Davis had told several people that he had no desire to retain the office. Others wanted Hunter for the job, and Hunter wanted it too, despite his being a rather spineless sycophant who tried to endear himself to the current president by bringing him tales of the sayings and doings of Davis's foes.[5] A meaningful step in achieving that goal would be for the national capital to be in his native state.

Debate over whether Montgomery should be the permanent capital commenced, in fact, from the very time the delegates first gathered there back in February. Advocates suggested a host of cities, starting with Tuscaloosa in March.[6] Thereafter Atlanta; Huntsville; Selma; Pendleton, South Carolina; Nashville; Memphis; Spring Hill, Alabama; and even Alexandria, Virginia, right within sight of Washington, found their advocates.[7] A host of arguments bolstered their claims. The capital should be out of the high heat and yellow fever district. It should be no more than a day from the seacoast, have excellent rail and telegraphic communications, and at least some stature and society of its own to support being the national headquarters.[8] Montgomery met some of these conditions, but not others. The secession of Virginia, however, completely threw all considerations out of balance. While Richmond had been mentioned occasionally as likely earlier, now it rapidly came to be the only spot discussed. It was all because of the war.

"If we go forty days without a conflict, there will be no war."[9] Howell Cobb still held to his optimistic outlook when he made his prediction on May 11. Indeed, his confidence grew, since only a week before he set the critical time at sixty days.[10] Brother Tom shared his rosy view, but increasingly they found themselves in the minority in Montgomery's parlors and council chambers.[11] Wigfall, who had seen a little bit of war now, expected more.[12] Harrison of Mississippi believed that "we will have our hands full, but will fight to the last extremity."[13] Boyce confessed that he expected them to have to make a "desperate resistance,"[14] and Bartow admitted a fear that they would have a long and bitter war for which they were not ready.[15] De Clouet felt even more resigned. "For us, it is a question of life or death," he warned his son. "It cannot be anything but a war of extermination."[16] Little Aleck, of course, never expected there to be anything but a war after secession. He saw a long and bloody conflict, and confessed that "I do not see the end of it."[17]

It troubled Mary Chesnut. "These men are not sanguine," she found. "I can't say without hope, exactly. They are agreed in one thing. It is worthwhile to try awhile—if only to get away from New England."[18] Some could not wait to "try awhile" personally. Bartow hoped to leave for Savannah before the end of the session in order to raise his regiment, and so did Howell Cobb, who comforted his wife that "we have all got our part to act in this war."[19] Wigfall tried earnestly to persuade his sixteen-year-old son not to quit school and enlist, while a troubled DeClouet confessed that "a father's heart is weak" when he learned of his son's decision to join a company, yet admitted his pride, too. "Young men of your age owe themselves to the country," he told son Paul.[20]

In Montgomery the people saw signs of foretelling. Viewing the high demand for surgeons, medicines, and instruments, reporters surmised that the War Department expected the medicos to have someone to work on ere long.[21] They had little doubt that the first blood would be shed in Virginia, and more than that, increasingly they expected President Davis to be leading in person, and there they got hints of the rationale for moving the capital. Within days of Virginia's secession, prominent men like Roger Pryor begged him to take command, promising that his presence would be worth 40,000, even 50,000 men to the cause.[22] As friends in the Old Dominion felt increasingly apprehensive about Letcher—and for a time, Lee—they only redoubled their pleas. "*Your presence is needed here,*" one implored. Letcher was ineffectual and Lee too cautious and despondent, warned another close associate. Only Davis could make order of the chaos. The old arch-secessionist Edmund Ruffin told him "for the salvation of our cause come immediately and assume military command."[23]

Men in Montgomery wanted him to take the field as well. To clear the way for it, on May 9 Curry introduced a resolution to amend the Constitution so that the vice president could assume the civil premiership whenever the president "shall consider that the public defense requires his absence."[24] The next day Bartow presented a resolution declaring that the emergency in Richmond required that the President go there, and even take the government with him.[25] Neither resolution went anywhere, but by May 11 rumor on the streets told of Congress asking Davis to command in the Old Dominion.[26] At the same time other gossip said that the President was already selecting one man from each of the best drilled companies of volunteers, in order to form a personal bodyguard when he donned his uniform.[27]

A few disagreed, arguing that Davis entertained no intention of joining the army, and Tom Cobb further declared that Congress would never consent to him doing so, though constitutionally the matter was out of the legislature's hands.[28] But others very close to him concurred that he would soon be in the field. On May 14 his friend and confidant Clayton, after a morning meeting with the President, assumed that Davis would take command.[29] And Stephens, by his own admission less and less in the chief executive's confidence, told friends that he expected Davis to don a uniform, and soon.[30] What Davis thought or intended, he kept to himself, though Varina later said she had hoped he would do so, both because she knew how military life suited him and also because she preferred that her family be in a less blistering climate.[31] Certainly his natural inclinations impelled him toward the field, yet he had created generals out of men in whom he felt confidence—Lee, both Johnstons, Beauregard. Moreover, he saw behind him seventy years of precedent in the old Union of the civil commander in chief never actually exercising the Constitutional prerogative of assuming field command. Regardless of the opinions and predictions of others, Davis as yet resisted the notion of breaking that precedent. He could wait to see how his generals did first, and he could still hope there would be no need for anyone to lead Confederates in battle. But if he should go to Virginia to command, how could he exercise his chief executive duties with the capital hundreds of miles away in Montgomery. With the war focus shifting inevitably to Virginia, did it not make sense for the city of state to shift there as well?

In the current Confederate capital few yet appreciated this possible eventuality. Indeed, while interest focused on Virginia, Montgomery itself settled into a lethargy, and perhaps complacency. Society tried once more to take up where it left off at the adjournment back in March, but somehow it was not the same. "There is a perfect stagnation in the way of social life in this city," Tom Cobb complained early in May.[32] He had not even heard of a party as yet, though it may only have meant that the prudish Georgian simply was not invited to any.[33] Part of the problem was the heat. In the second week of the month the temperatures soared into the nineties, and stayed there for days. Rives complained that "we are melting with heat here," and Cobb himself agreed to being "literally roasted." He survived on ice water, but drank so much that it upset his bowels. "This is a very pretty place," Varina Davis found, "and were not the climate as warm as is the enthusiasm of the people, it would be pleasant."[34] She joked that she thought she could feel her patriotism oozing from her pores in the climate. While local merchants quickly responded by advertising their latest ice chests and "refrigerators," the press speculated that perhaps the best way to defeat the Yankees would be to let them come this far south, and the sun would do the rest.[35] The streets in late spring became a nightmare of dust, and the canine population merrily barked on as always. "The city of dogs and dust," one Georgian called the place in disgust.[36] In line with its decision to halt all absolutely nonessential expenditure, the city council tabled its own suggestion to spend $150 a month watering the streets to contain the dust.[37] Strenna the confectioner had a solution, though. Those troubled by the streets should "wash the dust down" with some of his soda water, and with it to defeat the heat, he offered ice cream "which will make you dream of snow storms, sleigh bells, and Christmas days."[38]

Town rowdies hardly worried themselves over whether this would remain the capital of the Confederacy. What locals called the "spring fights" broke out as usual in the streets, this season largely Irish immigrants going at each other with knives and shears. Hooper and other editors protested yet again the "Sunday laws" that prohibited bars being open on the Sabbath, since men just took liquor home and drank it there. And some tavern keepers still flouted the statutes. Jacob Sutter went before the council charged with three offenses of selling liquor without a license. Before an increasingly frustrated Mayor Noble, councilmen dismissed one charge after another. Exasperated, Noble finally suggested sarcastically that they should give Sutter a vote of thanks for breaking the law. His motion lost 7 to 3.[39] The volunteers filled the streets, lounging in the shade of the balconies and awnings, talking pleasantly, smoking, drinking, to pass their idle hours. Indeed, a quartermaster department clerk complained of them being too noisy, even rude, and far too many lying drunk and asleep on some street corners.[40]

Stepping over the occasional prostrate soldier, townspeople and visitors promenaded up and down lovely Perry Street from Market to the West Point depot and the bluff overlooking the river. Montgomery was a city of well-tended gardens, and now the fragrance and the explosion of color compensated for the heat in some measure. Everyone loved to stand for a few moments under the shade of the massive live oaks in Yancey's yard to admire his garden.[41] Some of the city's hostesses, notably Mrs. Charles Pollard, put on the occasional ball and supper still, but not with the lavishness or enthusiasm of February and March. "The society was not smoothed down or in shape," Mary Chesnut complained, though she may have been herself partly at fault.[42] Montgomery's grand dames were a little tired of the condescension and hauteur of the Georgians and South Carolinians by now, and with the return of Congress their old fear of its influence on the morals of the town came anew. Some definitely would not have minded the government going elsewhere.

Thus the outsiders were forced to rely on themselves for their entertainment, making theirs chiefly a hotel and boardinghouse society. The Exchange, of course, always hummed, though it was chiefly the province of the men, only a few wives like Charlotte Wigfall and Mrs. Rhett, still in mourning over her child's death, being present.[43] The folk in the boardinghouses occasionally entertained, especially the gregarious Louisiana delegation, now hosting Hunter and the Virginians.[44] For some, like the Cobb brothers, the only way to find society was to look for it. They simply hired a hack for an afternoon and drove around the city making "pop" calls on their favorite hostesses from the first session.[45]

Most of the hotel society centered now at Montgomery Hall. Besides the Chesnuts, Mallory and wife and the Memmingers stayed there, Hemphill, Governor Moore, Constitution Browne and his wife, and others. They all regularly dined together, sometimes including the Florida delegates, too, and at least once Mary Chesnut held a reception. Keitt, Howell Cobb, Miles, John Campbell, and more attended. Theirs was a small circle, easily disturbed either by Wigfall's "worse than ever" bullishness, Mrs. Walker's preposterous pretensions in the presence of real society from South Carolina, and old Withers's penchant for boring everyone with endless ranting about Davis's house.[46] "What a rough menagerie we have here," Mary Chesnut confessed.[47] Yet they were laying the foundations of Confederate culture, or rather, salvaging the culture that seceded from Washington along with the states.

The chief Confederate hosts this session were the Toombses. The secretary of state doted on his wife Julia, and brought her to the capital as soon as he finally found a house. Moving in at the beginning of May, they quickly commenced a constant round of social gatherings. Little Aleck came as their first guest on May 3, then Julia held an afternoon reception on May 4 with Stephens, the Wigfalls, the Chesnuts, and others in attendance. Friday May 10 they hosted a dinner for the President at five o'clock, then another for the Virginians four days later, and yet another late evening reception on May 17 with the Wigfalls, Memmingers, Walkers, Fitzpatricks, Rives, and considerably more at their table.[48] They could serve wonderful fare now, the freshest blackberries and strawberries, ripe peas, mushrooms, honey, and oysters, lobsters, salmon, mackerel, bass, and haddock direct from Mobile or purchased from Joseph Pizzala's Rio Grande Restaurant's own seine in the Alabama. And being Toombs's house, there had to be spirits. Glackmeyer and Robinson continued to offer the finest selection, including some seventy-year-old 1790 sherry.[49]

Nowhere in Montgomery did conversation sparkle more than in the electric presence of Toombs and his friends. Little Aleck was always interesting so long as people did not get him on the subject of their future prospects, which often turned him gloomy.[50] Just the day of the dinner for the President, he told the story of his landlady Elizabeth Cleveland, who that very morning sent Livy to bring him to her. Stephens found her sobbing, and only when calmed did she tell him that her ne'er-do-well husband Charles was back in town demanding to see his children, and even threatening to take them away from her. Concluding that the man was "a great rascal scamp and knave," the Vice President of the Confederacy patiently and tenderly gave her legal advice.[51] Toombs, of course, provided most of the best conversation, whether telling amusing stories of the lovesick husband Tom Cobb, or more seriously praising the qualities of Cobb's wife Marion and vowing that "this country could never be subjugated while such women lived in our midst."[52] Better yet was Toombs's jab at old General Scott in Washington. Just recently a friend from the Yankee capital brought the Georgian a message in which the general said the rebels had better quit and go home or the blockade would starve them out. As evidence that the South would eat very well and very long despite the blockade, Toombs packed an ear of fresh corn in a box and mailed it to Scott by express, enclosing a card saying merely "R. Toombs."[53] It all delighted Mary Chesnut. "*Events*, witticisms, &c, are so rapidly following each other's heels," she crowed.[54] Rives of Virginia, encountering Montgomery and Confederate society for the first time, was less effusive. "There is no great elegance or refinement," he protested, "but this place is supplied by great cordiality & manliness."[55]

Naturally much of the new society looked to the First Family to set some tone for the rest. If left to Jefferson Davis, of course, they would look in vain. But Varina thrived on social life. After moving their furniture into the executive mansion and getting children, sister, cook, and more settled, she planned her first reception for April 30, and despite the oppressive heat, scores appeared at their invitation.[56] Callers arriving at one o'clock for the two-hour entertainment, passed through the open gate on Washington and walked across a small garden and up onto the porch. There a black butler from New Orleans who marveled at everyone's civility to him ushered the guests into the hall without ceremony, and thence through the doors on the left to the parlors.[57]

Most already knew the First Lady. Some, like Charlotte Wigfall, did not. She went as a mark of respect for the President. "I haven't yet made up my mind whether I shall like her or not," she wrote of Varina.[58] In the end, she thought her rather coarse, but then Charlotte, born to wealth in New England and raised in Charleston, came from two cultures that never really approved of anyone outside their own circles.

The rest of the guests generally took to Varina. She had her house aglow with wax candles, flowers in bouquets and vases everywhere, and a tasteful display of furniture thanks to the last minute loan of some pieces from Sophia Bibb. Varina herself met guests in a silk brocade gown with wide sleeves, and if some thought her faintly haughty, none found her less than cordial.[59]

She made these Tuesday afternoon receptions a weekly event thereafter.[60] "There was no affectation of state or ceremony," said a visitor.[61] With many of the Congress and cabinet wives having been friends in another capital and another time, much of their talk turned to old Washington gossip.[62] Politics were never far from their minds even on the most social of occasions. A congressman might corner a cabinet minister beside the dessert table to press for an appointment, or Toombs might bring along with him a potential applicant for some foreign purchasing mission. Mrs. Davis, who some called half-derisively "Queen Varina," presided over "the palace" cordially and politely, yet she did not mind unburdening herself enough to confess that she preferred Washington to Montgomery, and felt little enthusiasm at being First Lady.[63] She even quipped to one visitor that within a few weeks she should not be surprised to be presiding over a reception at the executive mansion now occupied by the Lincolns.[64] Rives of Virginia said the "Madame Presidentress" seemed clever, spirited, and educated, "but according to the custom of the country, too free & easy to be of the highest order of elegance & refinement"—proving that Charleston did not have all the snobs.[65] Varina formed—or renewed—an attachment with Mary Chesnut especially, which came much appreciated. The food at Montgomery Hall was "so repulsive in aspect" now that Mrs. Chesnut skipped dinner for two weeks. But at the executive mansion Varina always set a delicious table, thanks to her New Orleans cook.[66]

At Varina's second reception, on May 7, a guest of particular interest to Montgomery paid his respects. William H. Russell, the *Times* of London war correspondent, traveled through both North and South now, sending letters back to his paper on the spirit of the people. Widely read, and well known even here in the South, he excited the interest of the Confederates as soon as they learned from Wigfall that he was coming. Russell had readers, and influence, and from Washington on April 4, before closing down the commission, Forsyth told Davis that "we are cultivating him."[67] If Russell took to them, it could have a happy impact on his government at home.

The Englishman's arrival on May 4 coincided with the local press's publication of the first of his letters taken from the *Times*, and some feared at first that he felt a bias against the South.[68] They need not have worried. Russell's prejudice was against Americans in general, and he proved to be more than cordial in his meetings with Confederates here, though certainly condescending. "Montgomery has little claims to be called a capital," he concluded. "The streets are very hot, unpleasant, and uninteresting." Thinking he had "rarely seen a more dull, lifeless place," he concluded that it reminded him of a Russian village, rather like "a vast aggregate of small country parsonages."[69] Montgomery baffled him somewhat. In the jammed corridors of the Exchange he kept brushing against Southerners so lean he could feel their bones protruding, or so he thought until Watt told him everyone was armed and those "bones" were pistols and knives. He shared a room with five others, and paid Watt extra to get a mattress on the floor so he would not have to share a bed. Unfortunately, there everything that jumped, flew, or crawled, could get at him. Worse, one of the sleepers in the beds spit tobacco juice through the night—"a perfect liquid pyrotechny"—over the mattresses. As for food, at one restaurant he found strange fish and plants, opossums, frogs, raccoons, and more, all served "off dirty plates on a vile table-cloth."[70]

Outside beside the artesian basin he saw impromptu slave auctions that disturbed him considerably. "I tried in vain to make myself familiar with the fact that I could, for the sum of $975, become as absolute owner of that mass of blood, bones, sinew, flesh, and brains as of the horse which stood by my side," he puzzled.[71] "The native people were not very attractive, and the city has nothing to make up for their deficiency."[72] Yet he admired their spirit and enthusiasm, and when he visited Congress—aside from being disgusted at the tobacco stains everywhere, and thinking the building was "on a site worthy of a better fate and edifice"—he concluded that "an assembly of more calm, determined, and judicial-looking men could not be found."[73] "I could fancy that in all but garments they were like the men who first conceived the great rebellion which led to the independence of this wonderful country." Russell might have added that they saw themselves this way, too. When the audience filed out at the end of the open session, and Russell started to leave, Rhett, making an unaccustomed joke, said "I think you ought to retain your seat. . . . If the 'Times' will support the South, we'll accept you as a delegate." Russell probably wiped the smile from

Rhett's face when he replied that he could never sit as delegate to a congress of slave states.[74]

Montgomery met him with almost equal indifference. "Englishmen will look English," a reporter said sarcastically, "and Russell is no exception. . . . He would impress you as one who could demolish any quantity of beefsteak and onions, with a convenient capacity for throwing himself around an ordinary Englishman's allowance of 'alf and 'alf."[75] Tom Cobb regarded him as a "conceited beefy Englishman for whom I have contracted no liking," and Mary Chesnut recoiled from his snobbery and expressions of the hopelessness of their cause.[76]

Nevertheless, they courted him shamelessly. "A great deal depends upon the report [Russell] gives of our government," Cobb confessed. "He will receive marked attention I doubt not."[77] Stephens met with him first, then that same afternoon Wigfall took him to Government House for an interview with Davis. The President disappointed Russell, who found him "plain and rather reserved and drastic." At least Davis did not chew, and was neat and clean, though haggard from overwork. Disinclined as he was to explain himself to anyone, the President took pains to go on at some length about the nature of the Confederate people and the justice of their cause. The Mississippian told him that "we are a military people," speaking with pride of the rush to volunteer: "We are driven to take up arms for the defense of our rights and liberties." He summoned Walker to meet the visitor, and then allowed him to witness Beauregard and other officers pouring over maps and plans in the cabinet room while Walker drafted a somewhat sycophantish letter of safe conduct through the Confederacy, "appreciating your visit, and respecting your character."[78] Wigfall went back to the Exchange with him to expatiate further upon the unique character of Southern men. "We are a peculiar people, sir!" said the pompous Texan. "You don't understand us, and you can't understand us. . . . We have no cities—we don't want them. We have no literature—we don't need any yet. We have no press—we are glad of it. . . . We want no manufactures: we desire no trading, no mechanical or manufacturing classes. As long as we have our rice, our sugar, our tobacco, and our cotton, we can command wealth to purchase all we want."[79] While musing at Wigfall's rejection of virtually all the hallmarks of modern Western civilization, Russell dined with Benjamin and other luminaries. He thought Toombs "unquestionably one of the most original, quaint, and earnest of the Southern leaders." The attorney general he found "clever keen & well yes! What keen & clever men sometimes are," probably a veiled reference to uncertainty over Benjamin's sexuality.[80] Yet he found the Louisianian "the most open, frank, and cordial of the Confederates."[81] When finally Russell left late on May 8, Montgomery congratulated itself on what it thought a good job of impressing the visitor with its cause and its prospects.[82] Not for several weeks would they see that he said their city deserved no pretensions of being a capital.

At least Russell was news. "There seems to be a calm in the midst of the storm," Tom Cobb observed a few days after the Englishman's departure. "The news is exciting from no direction."[83] The reporters, cut off from closed sessions, diligently searched for anything to fill their columns, and even implausible rumors occupied them for awhile, if only as a diversion. Word that a stiff wind and high tide had hit Charleston harbor a few days before quickly escalated into a major Yankee attack on Fort Sumter in the rumor mill.[84] "This is a glorious city for rumors," lamented a Georgian. "We stumble over and find out more, and know less, of everything and nothing." It all centered on the Exchange, "the place to hear the news." "A visit to the Exchange every morning to hear the news, is a portion of the daily routine of life," said another Georgian. There newsmen cornered the congressmen and cabinet officials, who generally told them nothing, and in the corridor's echoes they caught hints of stories exaggerated and false. "Rumors and reports are the wharp and weft of all conversation until the evening papers appear," said one, and from them a second edition of gossip and rumor floated until morning. Real news, some complained, was such a rare commodity that reporters viewed it with disbelief.[85] No wonder some thought Montgomery seemed more and more like Washington all the time.[86]

While the newsmen waited for something to happen, and indulged their speculations on every topic, including the possibility that the capital and they might move elsewhere, they continued to jam the hotels, which once more became impossible. Without advance bookings, a visitor simply could not get in.[87] Those who did get a room had to share their beds, as Cobb and Bartow did now, resolving themselves to "grin and endure it."[88] Even then, rest presented a constant challenge. Russell found the Exchange "in a frightful state—nothing but noise, dirt, drinking, wrangling," and the incessant flow of visitors and loungers made it such a bedlam that some new arrivals found that "no one seemed to think or care about sleeping."[89] Montgomery Hall was no better. Mary Chesnut called it a "den of horrors," and said "these uncomfortable hotels will move the Congress. Our statesmen love their ease." Everywhere she found "flies and mosquitoes and a want of neatness."[90] With the spring heat and rains, the vermin took over. The mosquitoes came in clouds. At Montgomery Hall they bit clerk Jones all through the night, while when Russell stayed at the Exchange he joked that the only relief he got from the fleas came from the flies. "One nuisance neutralized the other."[91]

Just as the insects plagued them by night, the office-seekers—nearly as numerous—bedeviled them by day. Certainly they continued to operate on the belief, indeed the hope, that Montgomery would remain the seat of government. "Such crowds of applicants you never saw," Wigfall's wife wrote their son.[92] With the quantum growth of the departments and the army, and the increased money coming in from the loans and note sales, a host of new opportunists flocked to Montgomery. "These unclean birds, blinking bleared eyes at any chance bit," De Leon called them, "whetting foul bills to peck at carrion from the departmental sewer."[93] They so filled the streets that people at first did not notice that most of the young men native to the city were gone, enlisted in the volunteers.[94] It became a standing joke in the capital that the way to tell the lobbyists from the Congressmen was that the former only chewed their cigars, while the delegates smoked theirs.[95] "You can pick up any sort of man you want," joked a South Carolinian, "from a member of the Young Men's Christian Association to bearded men full of strange oaths and equivocal expressions of countenance." In any crowd of them, one wanted to be a brigadier, another a colonel, yet another a captain, and so on down the chain of command—so willing were they to accept public largesse that in the end, failing all else, many would settle simply for a drink. Not a few, failing to get anything, helped themselves to what they could find in hotel rooms, from watches to clothing, while guests were out.[96]

Wigfall complained that they almost drove him crazy, and Tom Cobb took a little perverse comfort in hearing that office seekers from Alabama and South Carolina annoyed their delegates just as much as Georgians harassed him.[97] One young South Carolinian actually managed to get into the executive mansion and take two or three meals with the Davises before they ejected him when they found that he was after a job.[98] Applicants appeared at the departments in swarms, and no sooner did the clerks dispose of one flock of them than another appeared. Hundreds of letters and applications simply sat on the department floors unopened for want of time to deal with all of them.[99] When Congress authorized appointing chaplains in the army, poor disillusioned Tom Cobb looked with dismay at the number of ministers rushing in to vie for the appointments. "Poor human nature," he groaned. "It is very hard to change."[100] The comparison to mosquitoes occurred to more than one man in Montgomery. "Kill one," they said of the applicants and lobbyists, "and a dozen will come in his place."[101] Davis told Howell Cobb that his desk groaned under letters of recommendation from every lawyer in Alabama.[102]

Of another host of strangers in town, few complained. "One cannot cross a street or turn a corner without encountering a Zouave or a Dragoon," a South Carolinian wrote on May 1.[103] The city looked gay with all the brightly colored uniforms, the rainbow of red, blue, green, gray, and more, with their red and orange hats, and even Revolutionary tricorners. As in all conflicts, the first to volunteer were the finest, and these young men behaved as perfect gentlemen, chatting with the ladies in the shade, drinking juleps with the men in the taverns.[104] Every train arriving at the depots brought more of them, and since the Montgomery & West Point line and the Alabama & Florida ran on different gauge tracks, the men and their equipment had to unload from one and march across town to board the other, taking five hours to make the change. Thus Montgomery got to see every regiment as it marched through the streets from depot to depot.[105] "No one thinks of anything but war," said a newsman, especially with all these "fine looking, dare-devil fellows" on the streets with their close-cropped hair and their constant marching.[106] In the military barracks scattered about town the volunteers cavorted mirthfully, sleeping on straw strewn on floors, and cooking their fat pork and coffee outside. Occasionally they marched out to the fair grounds, impressing the townspeople with the sight of 1,200 to 1,400 men tramping in uniform cadence. By May 14 there appeared to be 10,000 or more soldiers in and around the capital.[107] For a few it was almost too much. "The drums are beating here all the time," Charlotte Wigfall told her daughter a few days after arriving. "It really makes me heart-sick."[108]

Montgomery's own contribution to the growing army began to be felt seriously, as befit the people of a capital. So many from the fire department volunteered that Chief J. P. Stow feared he could not operate his equipment, and advertised for young men in town still remaining to come to his aid.[109] Barbecues almost every Saturday raised money and rallied men to volunteer for new companies, and when a group like Montgomery's German men could not muster to form a company entirely of their own, they cheerfully enlisted in some other local unit.[110] Siebels, now a colonel, took command of the 6th Alabama and led it off to the depot for the trip east. On April 30 Montgomery said farewell to its pet True Blues amid a flurry of cannon salutes and weeping mothers, wives, and sweethearts. The Mounted Rifles left a week later, soon to be followed by the Independent Rifles. In time the Grays and the Cadets would be on their way to the Virginia and Pensacola fronts, too, most of them volunteering for the duration of the war. Caught up in the spirit of the time, more than one teary-eyed mother told her son that if he should fall in battle, she hoped that it would be with his face toward the foe.[111]

Philanthropy quickly followed. On April 26 a citizens' meeting at Estelle Hall decided to create a Soldiers' Fund to help care for the families of men gone to the army, and by early May more than $5,000 had been subscribed. The city's Jews, always a prominent and accepted part of local society, raised $700 among themselves, prompting press and pulpit alike to praise the "Israelites" of Montgomery.[112] The city council, having planned to spend money on beautifying the artesian basin and other public property, voted instead to contribute $1,000 of its own to the fund. Furthermore, after declaring that the country would prosecute the war to a successful conclusion, thus "placing our peculiar institution upon an enduring foundation," they voted to suspend all nonessential expenditures for the duration and instead invested several thousand dollars of their funds in Confederate bonds. Moreover, all wharfage rates were to be waived for arriving munitions of war.[113]

Individual citizens did what they could in the wave of patriotism and sacrifice. Joseph Cain, clerk of the city market, loaded the St. Nicholas with donations of free vegetables and sent it off to the men at Pensacola.[114] Another man in town made a proposal that he and a thousand other Alabamians engage to pay $200 per year into the Treasury for five years or until the war ended, all of it to buy warships.[115] Montgomery's doctors offered to care for sick soldiers free of charge.[116] Henry Mittenheimer volunteered to establish a free library and reading room for congressmen and soldiers alike.[117] And the rather appropriately named Carl Schott began hand-making some eight thousand percussion caps a day to give to the War Department.[118]

The city's merchants and entrepreneurs did their part. Hooper, despite his intention to sell the Mail, tried to do his little bit of beautifying the capital by putting a new verandah on his offices. At the same time, he contracted with a Baltimore lithographer to prepare the copies of the Constitution with its signatures that thousands of enthusiastic

Confederates wanted to place on their walls.[119] Pritchard established a new telegraphic news agency in the city in order to expedite getting information out of the capital.[120] The clothiers, like Charles May, C. Pomeroy, and William Taylor, filled their windows and shelves with military apparel of every description, much of it to be worn by the civilians themselves to show their commitment to the cause.[121] Even children now walked the streets clad in the baggy trousers and colorful jackets of the zouaves.[122] The booksellers, especially White, Pfister and Company, laid in stacks of Gilham's *Manual for Volunteers and Militia*, Halleck's *Elements of Military Art and Science*, and most popular of all, William J. Hardee's *Rifle and Light Infantry Tactics*.[123] Wright's millinery at 43 Market stocked yards of red, white, and blue bunting for the ladies to make flags, and made them to order as well.[124] Once the Federals discontinued their post office in Pensacola, the liquor seller Glackmeyer volunteered to transport letters there himself.[125] Jacob Weil, a Jewish dry goods merchant in town, spoke for many when he said "this land has been good to us all. . . . I shall fight to my last breath."[126]

Perhaps most public of all was the Ladies Aid Association. On May 2 a request reached the War Department for 5,000 sandbags that Bragg needed to augment his defenses. Many in Montgomery took the telegram to signify that he faced an imminent fight.[127] Immediately that same day wives of some of the city's social elite mobilized in the local churches. At noon Gorgas got hundreds of yards of canvas to them, and with their scissors and needles they went to work. By that night 1,300 bags lay ready to ship, and on Sunday when the Alabama & Florida train left, they delivered a total of 3,000. Gorgas and others joined in the work by tying and packing the bags as the ladies handed them over, barely able to keep pace with their production.[128] Within forty-eight hours the entire requisition of sandbags stood filled.[129] Given that start, the women, led by Clitherall's sister Mrs. Eliza Moore, continued meeting in the basement of the Methodist Episcopal Church on Commerce Street every morning between half past eight and ten o'clock to sew uniforms and knit socks for the soldiers, and to receive the homemade goods of others.[130] "Needles flashed in that Ladies Aid Society," wrote the daughter of one, and "prayers arose and were knit into socks and stitched into gray jackets."[131] In time, most of the lecture rooms and church halls in town hummed to the clicking needles and whirring shears of the dedicated women.[132] When not applying their scissors to cloth, the women occasionally did duty for Memminger by trimming Treasury notes—decisively dubbed "shin-plasters"—from the huge sheets that came from the printer.[133]

The citizens' appetite for speeches sustained the same pace as their patriotism, but the high government officials seemed less and less accessible as their duties consumed all of their time. Instead, the people called on any man in town who was raising a regiment, or else organized speaking sessions of their own to celebrate the latest star added to the flag.[134] And their enthusiasm could take a more militant turn. Renewed rumors of plots surfaced, including stories of a Yankee plan to break the levees on the Mississippi and flood wide areas of the South.[135] Those suspected of being lukewarm on the movement now had to watch themselves. Antislave men like Tharin could be lashed and expelled, and lifelong friends could suddenly inform on neighbors suspected of being unreliable.[136] In the wake of Virginia's secession and Lincoln's call for volunteers, the restrictions on the movements of slaves came back into effect.[137]

A suspicious package sent north was subject to detainment and search, and when a correspondent for the New York *Herald* arrived expecting a cordial welcome thanks to his paper's sympathetic stance on secession, he discovered that while he was on the road, the firing on Sumter prompted his employers to change their tone.[138] When he signed the Exchange register and people saw who he was, he had to hide in his room for fear of being tarred and feathered. Stuart befriended the fellow journalist, and asked Toombs for a safe conduct to get the man out of Montgomery and the Confederacy, but the Georgian in typically blunt fashion said "the *Herald* man may go to hell." When asked to help, Reagan damned the "Herald pimp," and Walker and Davis refused to help either. Stuart had to bribe a railroad official to get the man safely away.[139]

When Mary Lincoln's mother and two daughters came through town again on May 7, Mary Chesnut warned "I should watch them" until the aged Mrs. Todd made it quite clear that she and her children stood with the South, and not with their "hybrid 'head of the family'" in Washington.[140] And woe to the soldier believed to be a coward. On May 18 a crowd quickly gathered outside the Exchange to watch as members of "Ben Baker's Russell County Company" took one of their own, stripped him of his stripes and buttons, and ducked him in what Russell described as the "foul, green-looking water" of the artesian well.[141] Inevitably, not a little of the ardor of the people, especially the men, came from the ample stocks of spirits in the city's bars and hotels, but usually emotions calmed in what Mary Chesnut called the "safe, sober, second thoughts of the cool, wise morning hours,"[142] Just to be safe, Memminger employed a night watchman to guard the government buildings.[143]

Everywhere around them the manifestations of a population becoming increasingly involved in war seemed evident. City council announced a halt to all but vital city expenditures. The Council of Safety called out the Home Guard to start meeting armed and equipped every Saturday, and the city council created a mounted patrol to help police the streets. Even the first "prisoners of war" came into the city, the crewmen from the recently captured *Star of the West*, while Bragg sent his prisoner Worden to be kept in the city jail. The captured Yankees hardly seemed like enemies. For two days they sat on the sidewalk in front of Government House, lounging in the heat, virtually unfettered. Yet Montgomery knew they were foemen. No citizen would bring them water, and at least one hurled taunts at the dejected seamen.[144] At last, the first word started to come from their boys in Virginia. On May 22 a letter from one of the True Blues appeared in the columns of the *Advertiser*. They were doing fine, no one was hurt, and only a few appeared on the sick list.[145] The relief could almost be seen on Montgomery's faces.

"There are no Sabbaths in revolutionary times!" exclaimed a New Orleans reporter.[146] Soldiers in town seemed to be on the streets rather than in houses of worship on Sundays. Yet the citizens paid their respects and delivered their entreaties to the Almighty with increasing frequency. The churches kept their doors open daily for nondenominational prayer meetings in support of the men in the army, while every Monday evening between five and six more of all creeds answered the summons of the bells to the lecture room of the Methodist Episcopal church to hear invocations for victory and prayers for the President, the cabinet, and Congress.[147] Davis and Varina regularly walked the three and one-half blocks from the White House to St. John's on Sunday, and Cooper, too attended the Episcopal service.[148] Certainly the President felt no doubts of the existence of a higher authority, though it came as a surprise to some who believed he admitted of no power greater than himself. Thus Tom Cobb found it "rather curious" on May 14 when the President turned to him as undoubtedly the most devout—or the most loudly proclaimed—Christian in Congress to ask for counsel on proclaiming a day of national fasting and prayer. "But many now look to god," Cobb mused, though still wondering that such a suggestion should come "from that quarter." At the President's behest, Cobb introduced a resolution formally requesting Davis to appoint such a day, which Davis later set for June 13. In reward, two days afterward Cobb received his first and perhaps only invitation to dinner at the Executive Mansion.[149]

Over that dinner, Davis and Cobb inevitably talked about Virginia, Richmond, and moving the capital. For all of Montgomery's exemplary efforts in behalf of the cause, there no longer remained a logic for keeping the capital there. Even if Davis did not take the field himself, still Virginia would be the scene of crisis, and to react quickly the government needed to be there, both to direct events and to serve as spiritual support for the Virginians who would bear the brunt of campaigning. "If there is anything in signs," Pritchard wrote in room 37 at the Exchange on April 28, "I shall not be surprised to learn that the Congress will adjourn in a few weeks to meet at Richmond."[150] Everyone gossiped about Richmond. Tom Cobb believed that Davis favored the move, and Charlotte Wigfall, whose husband had the President's confidence, told her daughter the day Congress convened that they would probably relocate to Virginia.[151] The serious inception of the idea went back to Stephens's mission to Richmond several days earlier, and even before. The Permanent Constitution authorized the government to create its own federal district, and immediately several states, including Alabama and Georgia, came forward to offer suitable tracts. After seceding and forming its alliance with the Confederacy, Virginia did the same on April 27, in a resolution presented, interestingly enough, by R. M. T. Hunter.[152]

Just two days after Congress reconvened, and well before the first of the Virginians arrived to lobby on their own, Boyce introduced a resolution calling for the relocation.[153] His act reflected the prevailing mood, for that same day many in Congress took it for granted that the move would be made.[154] Rumor said that Davis and a majority of Congress favored the idea, as well as all of the cabinet but Walker and Memminger.[155] Only the Alabama delegation, understandably enough, strongly opposed the idea.[156] Wags proposed all manner of justifications for the move. Tom Cobb thought that members wanted to be where their wives could stay near them at the healthful springs and spas west of Richmond.[157] A South Carolinian suspected that it was to get away from the exorbitant hotel rates and cost of board. "I hardly think any thriving village in Texas would receive fewer votes than Montgomery," he sniped.[158] Some said Congress just wanted to escape the office seekers.[159]

The pressure to realize the move really escalated when the Virginia members arrived, though in order not to appear self-serving, they allowed delegates from other states to champion the move. By May 9 Little Aleck thought it certain that they would adjourn to Richmond, and two days later Bartow introduced a new resolution. After considerable debate and amendment, it passed, calling for an adjournment on May 23 and reconvening July 20 in Richmond, or wherever else the President should direct.[160] As yet only Congress faced a move. The expectation that the armies would fight in Virginia, and that Davis would likely take command in person, suggested therefore that Congress ought to be close to the President. The rest of the government, however, need not necessarily leave Montgomery.[161] They referred the measure to the judiciary committee.

An outcry commenced immediately. Newsmen found opponents of the move to be "the most terrified set of individuals you ever saw."[162] Some thought they saw in it a first step toward occupying nearby Washington, moving the capitol yet again to the old Federal city, and then reconstructing the Union from there.[163] An editor in Montgomery simply turned bitter. "What!" he exclaimed. "Call this little *itinerating* concern a *permanent* government?" They would be more like a traveling grocery. "Who bids for the next squat?" he sneered.[164] As the heat rose to roasting, so did some tempers.

Judiciary returned the resolution May 15—when spring rains had cooled them all wonderfully—reporting that it found no legal obstacles to moving the Congress. That done, the measure passed and went to Davis. Two days later he took many of them by surprise when he returned it with his second veto. The bill did not go far enough, he said, and he was quite right. It was foolishness to move the executive and the Congress to one place, while leaving the rest of the government in another. "Great embarrassment and possible detriment to the public service must result," he told them. Among other objections, three of his cabinet were also members of Congress. Should they go to Richmond while wearing one hat, and ignore their other responsibilities at Government House? The attempt to override was pointless, not one state showing a majority in the voice vote.[165]

While the delegates went on about other business, Conrad quickly drafted a revised version of the bill that he submitted that same afternoon.[166] After the delegates left the hall for the day, Montgomery hummed with rumors of the veto, of the desperate measures being taken by some to relocate the capital, and of the advancing prospects of some other cities. Huntsville looked promising again, and now Nashville offered itself, as well as Opelika, Alabama.[167] Howell Cobb began to think that they might remain in Montgomery after all, and with the advent of pleasant weather some thought Congress might simply drop the idea of moving north to a better climate "unless hot weather and swarming mosquitoes change the present opinion."[168]

But Conrad and others were not dropping anything. On May 18 he and Brooke and Nisbet all offered resolutions both for adjournment and moving the capital, and they set aside Monday, May 20, for the debate.[169] Meanwhile, as the end of the session grew near and tension mounted over whether, or how, to effect the move, several of the members took advantage of an invitation from Pollard to travel to Pensacola as his guests on the newly completed rail line. That same evening about twenty-five of them boarded the cars, the President joining them for the nine-hour trip. When they arrived around midnight, they found no lodgings awaiting them, and most slept curled on the seats in their cars, but still it proved a pleasant junket, and perhaps an opportunity for Davis to lobby a bit with those wavering on relocation to Virginia.[170]

They returned Sunday, probably not rested, but ready to finish their business. Already Memminger occupied himself at Treasury with estimates of the expense of packing and moving the government departments, preparing to submit a report in secret session.[171] On Monday they went into secret session once more determined to come to some kind of final agreement. The debate lasted for hours. First they addressed once more a resolution simply reconvening Congress in Richmond, and it failed, not a single state voting in favor. Then they went on to Conrad's resolution covering the entire government, and another one similar, and after amendment reduced them to a single bill specifying that they would adjourn on Tuesday, May 21, reconvene in Richmond on July 20, and that the entire government should move with them.

This was it, the best they could do, and if it failed, the issue was dead, at least for this session. Louisiana demanded the yeas and nays, and when the vote ended Arkansas, Georgia, Texas, and Virginia agreed, while Alabama, Florida, Mississippi, and South Carolina did not. Louisiana, with the deciding vote, split, and thereby cast no vote. With no majority, the bill died. They went on to other business, but during the next half hour or so two things happened. Many of the members were absent, some having already left for home without waiting for adjournment. Only Alabama, Texas, and Virginia had full delegations in the hall. Friends started applying pressure to Ward, the new member from Florida, who thus far had voted with Owens to decide their state against the single voice of Morton. And noble old DeClouet, late arriving, now entered the hall, or someone hurriedly went to find him. Then South Carolina, at the instance of Miles who, strangely enough, was not voting, called for reconsideration of the balloting. The yeas and nays rang out again. Ward changed his vote to an affirmative, and DeClouet ended the division in Louisiana by making its ballot three to two in favor. The resolution passed, six states to three. The voice vote stood much closer, though—only twenty-four to twenty.[172] It was done. The resolution went directly to the President, and the next day he returned it with his signature.

On that last day they passed a flurry of other legislation as well, much of it done between the actions on removing the capital. Throughout the afternoon session, and again in the evening, they kept Josselyn busy hustling last-minute legislation to the President for his signature. They enacted another cotton embargo, and decreed that prisoners of war should be turned over to the War Department for them to be housed and fed the same as their own enlisted men.[173] Bills for the protection of Indian tribes, new military appropriations and larger troop levies, the increase of government clerical forces, establishment of the Patent Office, officers' pay, naval appropriations, a Library of Congress, and much more came in with the President's blessing.[174] Congress, in turn, consented to a flock of Presidential appointments of officers and judges. They even passed their one and only amendment to the Provisional Constitution, redefining judgeships in the federal districts.[175] And very much to the point of their debates that day, they began making provisions for the removal of the office equipment and archives of the government. They must sell the unexpired leases on the Executive Mansion and the government buildings, and sell all the furniture not to be transported to Richmond, and Memminger, Hunter, and Rives became a committee to see it done, though actual management of the sale of things would fall to Hooper.[176]

That done, Wigfall proposed the thanks of Congress for Howell Cobb, which passed unanimously, as did Waul's resolution of thanks to Governor Moore for the use of this hall in the state house. It only remained for Waul to move their adjournment, at which Howell Cobb arose for the last time, thanked them for their kindness and courtesy to himself, and declared them adjourned until July 20.[177]

The very next day, while most of those who remained scattered to their homes, others took care of final business. Toombs put copies of their statutes in the hands of delegates to take home and publish, while his assistant Browne sent two sets of all their acts and resolutions to Virginia.[178] Cobb tendered the thanks of Congress to Mayor Noble for the hospitality of his city.[179] Amid all the bustle, they got the happy word of North Carolina's secession. Now they were eleven, and since at the same time commissioners from Maryland were known to be traveling to Montgomery, they could hope to start the work of making the Confederate States an even dozen.[180] By that evening, the capitol itself echoed to the feverish work of the doorkeeper and a corps of burly porters packing and carrying archives and furniture. The word went to the clerks in the government departments to start packing to be ready to leave next week.[181]

Every train and boat leaving town carried congressmen toward their homes, and with them their thoughts and memories. DeClouet, who played such a pivotal role in the decision to move, departed the same night of the adjournment, bound for Mobile.[182] In no small wise disgusted, having opposed the removal to Richmond, Chesnut packed Mary and their bags and departed "that abode of Misery" Montgomery Hall the same evening, to join Hunter and Barnwell on the eastbound train. In her last conversation with Varina Davis Mary asserted that they faced a long war, and in agreeing, the First Lady suggested that hardship ahead might one day lead them all to look back fondly even on "the fare of the Montgomery hotels." Still nursing a tender stomach thanks to Montgomery Hall, Mary replied with an emphatic "Never!"[183] Howell Cobb left for Georgia, prepared already to explain the move to Richmond as an act of justice to the Old Dominion. "Her soil is to be the battle ground, and her streams are to be dyed with Southern blood," he mused on the cars. "We felt that her cause was our cause, and that if she fell we wanted to die by her."[184] Brother Tom seemed more gloomy, having finally accepted the notion that there would be a long war. "The dark clouds rise rapidly over us," he told Marion. "We are passing through the fire, but I doubt not this war, terminate as it may, will purify us as a people."[185] Rhett, bitter to the end at being thwarted at every turn, and given no credit for what he thought he had done, strove to the last minute to get secrecy lifted from their acts. "War is a period of special temptation; and therefore requires a greater vigilance and fidelity to protect the liberties of the People," he complained. "I did all I could, to bring to their knowledge all I said or did."[186] It would have crushed his already fragile ego to know that very few of them actually cared. On his way home he may already have been composing his list of grievances against Davis: the furnished house, the slave trade prohibition veto, slowness to arm the country, refusal to empower diplomats to negotiate treaties and tariffs, sloth in purchasing arms and raising the army, and the refusal to accept later twelve months' volunteers. It read like a bill of particulars for impeachment. The one thing Rhett did not include was the fact of Davis being president, not he.[187]

Little Aleck Stephens stayed in Montgomery May 22 attending to final business in the departments, and almost wore himself out by the time he returned for his last night at Mrs. Cleveland's. When he left early the next morning, he so rushed in the packing that he forgot to leave his address at the post office for mail to be forwarded.[188] Besides, there was much to preoccupy his mind as his train rumbled out of the West Point depot. With the dome of the capitol looming atop Goat Hill as he passed around north of town, then turned east, the Vice President wondered if they should be leaving Montgomery. "Whether it was wise to do so or not the future must prove," he wrote to Linton.[189] That future troubled him, as it always did. They were in for a long and bitter struggle "the end whereof no one can see."[190] He fully expected that Davis would take command in Virginia, and like everyone else he felt unbounded faith in the President's military capabilities.[191] Because of that, despite a depression of recent days, he entertained some confidence. "We can whip in this fight," he said, "but we will have to fight hard."[192] "We have the elements of independence," he believed. Spirit and energy ought to guarantee that "we cannot, I think, be conquered or subjugated under proper counsels."[193] What worried him as much as anything were those "counsels." He had seen Walker's inefficiency, Governor Brown's obstinacy, Rhett's dangerous thwarted vanity, even the President's seeming indisposition to follow good advice. "From the beginning I have considered it with us a simple question of how much *quackery* we had strength of constitution to bear and still survive."[194] He saw that quackery everywhere, alas. They were in the midst of a revolution. "Ideas are changing," he told a friend a week from now; "ideas of greatness."[195] If the Confederacy was to succeed, these men must change with those ideas. Could they? Could he?

The Congress evaporated almost without anyone noticing their leaving, and with them went the reporters and correspondents, cynical to the last. "Congress saw fit to suffer its light, hitherto kept under the bushel, to flicker out entirely," complained a South Carolinian.[196] Yet Davis and the cabinet remained, and with them their staffs, all working feverishly. At the War Department they worked until midnight, even on Sundays. Davis himself complained that he had no time to answer letters at all, and townspeople saw him and his secretaries looking "fagged" by their labors.[197] Varina held her last reception the day Congress adjourned, and that ended the First Family's entertaining in Montgomery.[198] Davis himself still received the occasional dignitary, as when Congressman Augustus Garland and his colleagues of the Arkansas delegation came for dinner on May 20. "He was as pleasant and affable, I think, as ever man was," said Garland. They talked freely of the military situation, and perhaps lobbying just a bit, he gave them his reasons for favoring the move to Richmond.[199]

The President concentrated on events elsewhere now. Despite a recent rumor that Bragg had started a fight at Pensacola, peace still prevailed, and Davis believed that the Yankee garrison in Fort Pickens could not last out the summer's yellow fever and storms. He expected there would be no need for Bragg to attack.[200] But then came word that two enemy warships briefly exchanged fire with a Confederate battery on Sewell's Point, near Norfolk, Virginia. It was not a threat—at least not yet. But it was shooting all the same. Johnston reported from Harpers Ferry the fear that Federals were on the move to force him out, and then on May 24 came the real shock. Yankees in Washington crossed the Potomac and occupied Alexandria almost without a fight, but in the aftermath each side had a man killed. Within days Rhett's *Mercury* would be asking "is this wise statesmanship? Is it efficient generalship?" There was no doubt now that Davis had a shooting war on his hands—bullets from the Yankees, and words from Rhett.[201]

Despite his anxiety to get to Richmond to be near the mounting crisis, Davis refused to leave until his cabinet were ready to go.[202] But he made his own preparations, including almost demanding that Wigfall cancel a return home to Texas and accept a position as his aide instead. He began to feel the need to have a few friends close to him as events accelerated. He thought Wigfall a friend.[203] And he may have wanted the rough, brawling Texan for more than official duties. There were threats against his person, now. Two weeks earlier came warning of a Yankee plot to abduct himself and Stephens and perhaps make of them extreme examples.[204] Now, as he worked in his study late into the night making preparations to leave, he saw an armed man standing outside peering through the window. The President grabbed a pistol and raced out into the gloom, giving chase until the stranger jumped over a hedge and disappeared into the night. And again, while walking home from Government House one evening, Davis saw a man huddled behind a wall near the gate to the executive mansion, as if laying in wait. When he saw Davis approach, he leapt up and ran into a stable at the back of the house, and by the time Davis and others searched for him, he had escaped.[205]

Varina saw his anxiety, the way he worked himself to exhaustion. He labored under constant interruption, a circumstance calculated to frustrate a man of his temperament even more. By May 24 he was almost bed-ridden from weariness and illness combined, his health worn down to a bedrock iron that alone made him survive time and again.[206] At times his only relaxation came in drawing upon his prodigious memory for poems he liked in his youth, especially Walter Scott's "Lady of the Lake," and the stanza that began "Time rolls his ceaseless course."[207]

Sunday May 26, dawned warm at sixty-four degrees and rose to ninety by noon when Davis came out of St. John's for the final time.[208] The townspeople gathered three thousand strong the night before to serenade him outside his home, extracting a speech from him despite his illness.[209] He walked down to Government House, past the lovely little houses and gardens, now filled with merrily singing birds, the china trees thick and beautiful along the streets. He went to Walker's office, where the War Department staff had all worked through the day packing and handling final business. He chatted amiably for a long time with the secretary of war, then made his final stroll down Bibb to the executive mansion.[210] Only a few knew yet that he was leaving tonight, and to them he said his farewells, and left some of them with mementoes. To Clitherall he gave a mahogany couch.[211]

In the evening the Davises took a carriage to the West Point depot, attracting little or no notice. There they boarded a rear car on the eight o'clock train, finding Cooper, Ingraham, the Wigfalls, and Toombs on the same coach. Still ill and suffering from chills, Davis took his seat so quietly that several other passengers already on the car did not notice him.[212] Bundled for warmth despite the fact that outside it was still above eighty degrees, and considerably warmer inside the train, he turned his face to the window.[213] With all the recent scares for his safety, and rumors of spies about, his friends arranged his quiet departure, and as a decoy let it be known that he expected to depart by a different train, thus ensuring that there would be no crowd gathered at the depot to say farewell.[214] Without arousing notice, they managed to get the President's gray horse to the train, and along with it his military saddle with the compass mounted in the pommel.[215] One New Orleans reporter did happen to see Davis arrive at the station, and thought to wire news of his departure back to his paper, but Toombs and Wigfall effectively persuaded him otherwise. They wanted no announcements preceding their progress, no crowds gathered at stations along the way where some assassin might lurk among the well-wishers.[216]

Then they were off into the night, each one with time for his own thoughts. The Wigfalls rode convinced now that the President would command their army, if his health improved. Why else would he bring his army saddle?[217] Toombs, whose distrust of Walker led him to make one of his final acts in Montgomery the dispatch of five thousand flint muskets to Virginia, despite its being none of his business, entertained other, darker feelings.[218] This would be his last trip with this president, he decided. He loathed his powerless portfolio at State. He regarded himself as a mere "looker on" in the government. Davis, Walker, and now the generals were the men who really made the decisions. The rest of the cabinet exerted little more influence on affairs, he believed, "than ordinary outsiders."[219] In his own department he was powerless, yet held responsible for the possible failure of plans and policies he neither made nor approved. "I shall get out of the govt. at an early day," he would tell Little Aleck. "I am of no use in it."[220] And he more and more distrusted the wisdom of selecting Davis for president. "Times look gloomy," he would say. "Davis has not capacity for the crisis & I see great troubles ahead."[221] If only *he* had been president.

The man holding the office for the present sat quietly between his suffering and his deep thoughts. He did not hear the conversation elsewhere on the car when one passenger asked another when Davis was to start for Richmond, and was told "why, he's on this train! Don't you see him lying down just behind yonder?"[222] Rather, Davis most likely heard only the clatter of the wheels on the tracks, the low hum of conversation on the car, and the echoes of his own reflections on his first ninety-eight days in an office he never wanted. He had done so much, and there was so much more to do. "Our enemies are active for our injury," he told an acquaintance a few days earlier, "but a brave and united people, like ours, cannot be conquered."[223] Yet that enemy could—and surely would—try, and the occupation of Alexandria made it certain that the attempt would come in northern Virginia. Among his last discussions with Walker before leaving was an order to reassign

Beauregard. The upper Mississippi looked secure for the moment. Davis needed his general, the Confederacy's first hero, at the head of the new army he was building north of Richmond, near Manassas and sluggish little Bull Run.[224] There might not be a battle. He hoped not. Cool heads might still reign in Washington and take the cup of war from the country. If so, his Confederacy would not be itself an aggressor. "Its policy cannot but be peace," he wrote in his very last words from Montgomery: "peace with all Nations and people."[225]

Jefferson Davis's silent departure only added to Montgomery's chagrin at the removal of the capital. Not only did Congress cast the city back into provincial obscurity, but now the president denied the townspeople their chance for one last grand demonstration of confidence and admiration. From the moment the *Weekly Montgomery Confederation* first broke the news of Congress's action, fully a day before the rest of the city press could print it, "Montgomery began to wail," as De Leon put it.[226] Indeed, the city grumbled louder over this than anything else for months, even more than about the original coming of the capital in the beginning.[227] Had the government spent up to $60,000 or more in leasing and refurbishing the executive buildings just to walk away from them? And what about the mammoth new hotel that Montgomery was practically set to start building? What waste! And all just so that delegates could enjoy a cooler climate. Southern soldiers faced hardships in the field, and were about to risk their lives. Could not a few fat, middle-aged politicians risk a little sweat and maybe a few pounds?[228]

The removal must inevitably shake public confidence in the government, and as for the other nations of the world, could they respect an administration that moved about like a "portable pedlar's wagon" for its own comfort?[229] Besides, it looked bad that Congress, having just voted itself a mileage allowance for travel to its sessions, now moved its sittings far from the center of the Confederacy, automatically increasing the reimbursements for many, and those were the thoughts of Hooper.[230] Ned Hanrick declared himself completely against all itinerant institutions, and that included the government. "Bad luck, sir," he said while fingering his ever-present horseshoe. "I can't bear your traveling circus, or menageries, or cabinets of curiosities. No more can I bear this going about of our political cabinet. Bad luck."[231] When the weather briefly took a cool cloudy turn, the disgruntled editor of the *Post* said it was "probably the effect of the decision of Congress to remove the Capitol."[232]

The removal found a few defenders, chiefly the *Confederation*, which assigned Hooper's animosity to the fact that he would lose some printing business, and asserted that it was meet that the government should share in Virginia's perils.[233] Yet elsewhere, other than Virginia of course, men met the news with much the same skepticism. Some thought that now all the patronage jobs would go to Border State men.[234] The Texans looked askance at the move, but at least seemed willing to allow that Congress should be allowed to decide for itself what was best.[235] Not so Rhett's *Mercury*, of course. If the government sat in Richmond, it could think of taking Washington, and if it took Washington it must take the rest of Maryland, and that would put the Confederacy contiguous to Pennsylvania and New Jersey, and inevitably free states would start applying for admission in the new union until reconstruction would be accomplished by the dreaded back door. Rhett prayed that Lincoln would destroy Washington himself, and remove the temptation.[236] Of Rhett's ravings few took notice. But one Montgomery editor put his pen to the most salient danger of the move. With the two opposing capitals now to be a mere hundred miles apart, they would be like two antagonists locked in the same room, too close not to fight to the knife, and the knife to the hilt.[237]

The cabinet departments started their packing the day before the President left, and no one missed the frantic activity. All archives not in daily use went on the first train, and in the interest of economy they even took with them department stationery despite its being headed "Montgomery." Clerks started at the business of selling what furniture they could, and Cooper ordered that henceforward all correspondence should be redirected to Richmond.[238] The War Department performed some of its final business that day. Fittingly enough, Walker gave in to Governor Brown one more time and agreed to accept all of the armed and equipped twelve months' regiments he had raised despite the new legislation. Having done that, there was no reason not to extend the same concession to Louisiana's Governor Moore as well. And Cooper sent a directive to Van Dorn that all remaining Federal soldiers still in Texas must be regarded as enemies now. The courtesy granted to Twiggs's command was at an end. Any man in a blue uniform was to be taken prisoner.[239] When the Washington Artillery of New Orleans came to town on its way to Virginia, Walker authorized Watt at the Exchange to give the whole company dinner at twenty-five cents per soldier.[240] And when the Maryland commissioners arrived, not expecting to find the government gone, Walker and others received them cordially with assurances that the Confederacy wanted only peace. The phrase of Stephens and Davis came into common usage now. "All we ask is to be let alone," they told the Marylanders.[241]

They continued their packing through Sunday and Davis's departure, and on into the new week. The Secretary of War declared that he would consider no more applications in Montgomery and handed a sheaf of unopened letters to his clerk Jones to take to Richmond, at the same time instructing him to leave at once and start looking for temporary quarters. Walker wrote his last letter on Monday, closed his letterbook, and departed that night.[242] Behind him people seemed astonished at the volume of paperwork until they remembered the incredible number of requests for office. Then, said Jones, "the wonder ceases."[243] Inevitably some things went overlooked. Somehow in the rush they forgot to close the government's box number 217 at the city post office.[244]

Finally it was time for the first train to leave. The depot presented an incredible jam between arriving troops and munitions, and others departing. Already extra trains ran on the tracks, and sometimes had to line up to avoid further congestion and run slowly for fear of collision.[245] The first train for the government was a long one, the boxcars bulging with packing boxes and furniture, and the passenger coaches filled with a polyglot mix of clerks and cabinet officers, reporters like Stuart, the inevitable office seekers moving on to a new field of operations, and even a fair number of the city's prostitutes who decided to go where much of their current business was going. When the engine finally strained to pull out of the depot, already the whiskey had come out, the conversation turned jolly, and they went off into the night, quite unaware that in a number of those packing boxes of archives back in the boxcars, Ned Hanrick had managed to secret innumerable horseshoes. Just in case. "Farewell Montgomery," Stuart mused. "The only consolation we can offer centres in the cold phrase—'such is life.'"[246]

The last of the government trains left at eight o'clock on the morning of May 30, at ninety-four degrees the hottest day yet that year.[247] The next day Hooper held the sale of remaining items, including some of the furniture from the executive mansion. The curious and the memento seekers paid good prices for pieces that once held the President as he sat at table, or felt the scratch of his pen as he scribbled great documents of state.[248] Navy Secretary Mallory came into town on the train from Florida, bound for Richmond, stopping only long enough to buy some dresses for his wife. With his departure on the

evening train, Montgomeryites believed that at last all of the government people were gone.[249]

How quickly the city returned to what it had been. A light rain
briefly settled the dust on the streets. The city council passed a new
tax assessment for property. On the morning of June 1 another shooting affair disturbed the peace of Commerce Street, with no one hurt.
Ironically, that same day the Confederate Post Office officially took
charge of the mails. Employees fired a salute in celebration down at
the Figh Block offices.[250] "Montgomery is no longer full of strangers. Its
streets seem almost deserted," a lingering *Mercury* correspondent
wrote. "The absorbing attractions of Government have been transferred to Richmond."[251]

Yet not every vestige was gone. For some weeks Toombs and Walker
had both worked at the business of uniting the tribes of Arkansas,
Texas, and the Indian Territory to the Southern cause. In the hope of
negotiating treaties, they invited leaders of the Chickasaw, Choctaw,
and other groups to come to the capital. Somehow in the rush to get
packed and away, everyone forgot those invitations. Everyone except
Chilly McIntosh and M. Tidman, chiefs of the Creek nation. On May
30 they stepped off a train expecting to find the throbbing nerve center
of the Confederacy. Instead they found only sleepy, slightly dazed, and
still somewhat resentful Montgomery. Confused themselves, they
remained a few days. There was no problem getting a room at the
Exchange now. They could enjoy the fresh oysters, the abundant
whiskey, the fragrance of the gardens on the river's evening breezes.
And when they were ready, they went to the West Point depot and
boarded a train to take them east, in search of a government.[252]

Epilogue, April 1886

———— ● ★ ●————

On a Tuesday evening, April 27, a train from Mobile pulled into
Montgomery. When it stopped at the platform, a band started to
play "Dixie" and the first shot of a one-hundred-gun salute boomed
out over the Alabama River. A crowd of thousands gathered around
the depot sent up a shattering shout as an old man in a plain black suit
stepped from his car. His hair was entirely gray now, his beard full and
close cropped. He wore a small white rosebud on his lapel, and in his
hand carried a polished hickory walking cane. Despite being only a few
weeks short of seventy-nine years, he stood erect and walked with the
same old, measured, military step. The Montgomery Grays and the
True Blues formed about him as he entered his carriage and started on
a procession through streets illuminated with bonfires and Chinese
lanterns. They were on their way to the Exchange. For the first time in
a quarter century, Jefferson Davis had returned to Montgomery.[1]

All along the crowded sidewalks the shouts and cheers arose as he
passed. Blossoms and bouquets flew from the ladies toward his carriage, while here and there the veterans, all of them middle-aged now,
howled out the old "Rebel yell." "Dixie" moved with the procession,
and as Davis saw the old Exchange come into view, its windows illuminated now by electric lights, he felt a sudden sense of coming home.
Once inside he found not Watt or Lanier, but a new host, a Yankee
named West, who took him to his old lodging in room 101. Tom
Watts met him here, too, and with tears in their eyes the old men
embraced. "Our hearts were young," said Davis later, "though our
heads were old."[2]

He had come to dedicate a monument on the capitol grounds for
Alabama's war dead, but to him and to Montgomery the visit meant
far more than that. At every step and every turn the sights started new
memories flooding over him. The bonfires, the familiar old uniform of

401

the True Blues, the Exchange, Watts. Not everything was the same. Now he found his room decorated with flags, both Confederate and United States, with a portrait of Robert E. Lee on the wall. Montgomery was a town of more than 25,000, with electric lights, streetcars, an electric railway, public fountains, and more. Yet there stood the Winter Building across Court Square. The artesian basin, finally cleaned up and beautified, bubbled pleasantly. Though Hooper's old *Mail* was gone, people still read the *Advertiser*. Everything was different, yet still much the same, like a new painting on an old canvas, with much of the original image showing through.

The next day the organizers had planned a ceremony for one of the city parks, but heavy rains turned it into a mire, and at the last minute they decided instead to move to the capitol grounds. It proved a happy improvisation. At noon the military companies assembled outside the Exchange, a bugle sounded on the damp April air, and a barouche drawn by four matched grays stopped at the door. Leaning on the mayor's arm, Davis came down the steps and got into the carriage as the inevitable "Dixie" brought new shouts from a new crowd. The music and the cheering followed him all the way up Market, the trip itself an echo of the one he first made all those years before. Once on Goat Hill, the True Blues and the Grays had to push back the crowds to give Davis and others room to alight. He took his hat in his hand and slowly walked up the steps and through the crowd to the portico, bowing to left and right. As a light rain commenced once more, he reached the top step, turned, and sat down between the two center columns. To his right he saw seated his daughter and only surviving child Winnie, the mayor, General John B. Gordon, the governor, and more. In front of him in the crowd, he might have recognized a middle-aged school teacher who as a teenaged girl drew the first Confederate flag up its staff on the dome. And a glance down and about a foot to the left found the spot on which he stood all those years ago and twice said "so help me, God."

The cheering never stopped from the moment he left the Exchange, and only after several more minutes of it now did the mayor finally calm the crowd. "My countrymen," he said, "with emotions of most profound reverence I introduce to [you] the highest type of Southern manhood the Hon. Jefferson Davis." Yet another shout erupted, sustained so long that the mayor feared the old hero would tire standing and waiting for it to end. Longer and longer they cheered, Davis all the while looking out over the crowd, down Market toward the Exchange, off across the housetops and spires of Montgomery, over the full Alabama, and beyond the river to the past.[3]

They lost their war. Perhaps they never had a chance of winning. For all the belief of so many that the Yankees would not stand a fight, were too parsimonious to part with the treasure and blood needed for victory, Lincoln stood the test and brought his nation up to the measure of his own resolve. King Cotton failed Davis in the end. Not a single nation granted diplomatic recognition or military intervention. Nations, like men, acted in self-interest, and the temporary shortage of cotton never came close in English and European eyes to meriting the risk of war with the United States, nor alliance with a slave power. The Confederacy simply had nothing to offer that other nations wanted that much, and at that cost. The will and resolve of Davis and his own people proved to be incredible. In the face of increasing scarcity and hardship, their economy, their industry and institutions, and in the end even many of their homes ravaged, they kept on fighting through four years of the bloodiest war of the century. They spent nearly $4 billion to keep their armies in the field, most of it loans they could never repay. From that first levy of a few thousand volunteers, more than three quarters of a million Southern men passed into and out of his armies. In the end, more than a quarter million Confederate men who went to war never came home again. Hundreds of crutches, wheelchairs, and empty sleeves in the crowd before him now attested to the ravages brought by wounds for those who survived.

They fought hard and well. Indeed, they enjoyed a second portion of victory just seven weeks after moving to Richmond, when Beauregard's army near Manassas combined with the small army that Joseph E. Johnston began building at Harpers Ferry, and together they routed a Yankee host along Bull Run. For the next two years they turned back one invasion after another. Beauregard's ego soon toppled him from favor and Johnston took over. His vanity over rank soon put him at odds with Davis, and then a Yankee bullet in 1862 took him out of the war for months. Davis put Lee in charge in Virginia, and thereby gave to the ages one of history's great captains. Davis and Lee made a perfect civil-military team, but in the end the crushing manpower losses of war saw their victories turn to defeats, the loss of Richmond itself, and the heartbreaking retreat to Appomattox. And Virginia was the Confederacy's glory theater. To the west its one great army went to Sidney Johnston when finally he arrived, but he ignored a small wound in his first real battle at Shiloh, Tennessee, and bled to death into his boot. For nearly two years Bragg commanded, unpopular with all, and making better war on his own generals than ever he did on the enemy. Joseph E. Johnston replaced him in 1864, and spent much of the balance of the war demonstrating that he, too, was no man to command an army. Like Beauregard, he fought the president most bitterly of all. For years now Davis did not speak with either of them, and refused to appear in their presence even on memorial occasions like this one in Montgomery. Even now these old Confederates, and many more, still fought their battles with each other in their memoirs.

Behind the battle lines the yeomanry of the Confederacy made sacrifices beyond expectation or measure for the cause. Yet they never fully became a Confederate *people*. The old attachments for the Union that had been so powerful—and so feared—in Alabama and Georgia in 1861 lasted through the war, and to lesser extents influenced all of the other states, especially Tennessee. Kentucky, Missouri, and Maryland never would secede thanks to this and Lincoln's speedy movement to secure them militarily. Old resentments against the wealthier planter class, coupled with opposition to slavery—or at least an indifference toward it—in the mountain regions, only further eroded the Confederate hold. In the end, every Confederate state except South Carolina would send regiments of white soldiers into the Yankee army, fulfilling Stephens's agonizing prediction that in time they would turn against themselves. By 1865 Confederate authorities actually feared to venture into some parts of their own domain, and with the ravages and cost of the war dragging on and on, civilian morale inevitably flagged in proportion. As the end approached men deserted from the armies in ever-increasing numbers, and while those remaining would have fought on indefinitely, even taking to the hills as guerrillas, the fact was that the civilian population was no longer able or willing to support them. The South did not lose its bid for independence on any one front. It lost it on all of them, military, diplomatic, civilian. In the end, perhaps its only chance of winning resided in the hope that the Union would be willing to lose.

And in some indefinable degree they failed because what they created here in Montgomery was an ending rather than a beginning. They saw themselves in a way like the early Puritans whom they so much despised, men erecting a city on a hill, one purified of the taint of the old. The delegates who gathered here so hopefully in February 1861 saw their work as the termination of decades of turmoil over the true meaning and original intent of the old Constitution. They made no pretense of being builders, or even remodelers. They were restorers, preservationists. Almost to a man they proclaimed then and ever afterward that theirs was no revolution. They sought not to overturn the Constitution, but to set it aright once more, and the principal leg to hold it up was their definition of the sovereignty of the states. Their Provisional Constitution, and the Permanent Constitution that followed, worked well for their ideological aims, but threatened to fall down under the extreme strains of war. They created not a nation but a confederation. The former can have the strength of a steel rail. And that includes the strength to defend itself even at the expedient of *commanding* the cooperation of its component parts. The latter, like the old strap-and-stringer that almost derailed the government at its start, has at best a veneer of iron attached loosely to the splinterable wood beneath. Its success depends far too much on the willing cooperation of disparate elements that quite naturally might see their own interests as coming first. That was one of the reasons the original United States found its organization under the Articles of Confederation inadequate. A nation needed more to flourish and survive, and the states then had the luxury of learning that lesson in a time of peace. Unfortunately, the seceding South, while seeing itself as the inheritor of the Constitution, patterned its organization far too much on the spirit—and the name—of the older document. Nations can win wars against greater odds; confederations under pressure more often than not disintegrate.

Observers after the war who suggested that on the Confederacy's tombstone should be engraved the epitaph, "Died of States Rights," took too simplistic a view of the problem. Hidebound state rights thinking certainly crippled the Confederacy, but then so did the absence of any true feeling of nationalism among the Southern people. State governors were not the only ones who looked out for themselves first. The South simply contained too many elements at conflict with each other for them to coalesce. Rich and poor, slaveholders and peasants, hill country and tidewater dwellers, cotton growers and tobacco men, all had their own interests, and their Southern identity simply proved too weak a branch to hold them all. Then there was the imbalance of resources, and the fact that Davis had neither the diplomatic tools nor the right lures to persuade other nations to intervene on the Confederacy's behalf. Most of all, and too often forgotten in the search for excuses for defeat, the South went up against another President and another people who had advantages where the Confederacy did not, and who were resolved to press them to victory, as long as it took.

Congress, too, contributed to defeat, and the first signs of what it was to become manifested themselves in the Alabama state house. The finest statesmen the South had to offer composed that Provisional Congress. "No body ever convened at the South was more able or more patriotic," recalled Nisbet of Georgia nine years later, and he was right. However, his recollection that "party preposition, committals, animosities and creed had no place in the deliberations of that august assembly" was at best forgiving memory.[4] Following the elections in the fall of 1861 for the regular Congress under the new Constitution, the caliber of the body began a downward plummet. Too many of the men who came to Montgomery chose to go into the army after leaving office, or not to seek reelection. Only a handful served through the entire war, and the men who replaced them brought less experience, and often even more restricted views. The problem for all of them was that for years in the old Union they had been professional opponents, an out-of-power minority focused largely on stalling the majority, and united in part by their opposition.

Once in power in their own confederation and with their enemy removed from their midst, they lost much of what once bound them together, and their Constitution and their own views worked against any new cement providing a bond. In their initial idealistic hope for a single-party nation they made the mistake of thinking that by leaving the old Union, and solving in their new Constitution all of the divisive problems like the tariff, internal improvements, and the nature of state rights, they could in future expect a democracy without issues of substance to trouble the body politic. Elections, therefore, would ideally not turn on radically differing points of view, but rather simply on which of two or more candidates was the best to act as caretaker of the single policy on which all agreed already. Indeed, there would have been no platforms even, only referenda. Just as Washington was elected president without opposition, they expected that their own future choices for chief executive would be equally without dissent.

Yet in the end, the only unity they found lay in their attitudes toward Davis and his war policy. Despite all the protestations abroad in 1861, informal parties did form, parties with no constructive platforms, no policies, no issues even, other than their support for or opposition to Davis. Not only did their division weaken the Congress and the Confederacy, but the parties themselves were less effectual because they never became more than amorphous skeletons, plagued with their own dissidents and regional factions, loose associations dependent solely on the Davis issue, while on a host of other matters the men might differ radically. In the end, the anti-Davis forces never seriously impeded the President's legislation. Every one of his vetos went through without being overturned, save one on a minor postal bill. His majority in Congress was always safe enough to get the measures and appropriations he needed, and often even his bitterest foes voted for his war legislation, their objection being to the man rather than the war.

Indeed, there lay so much of their problem, in the nature of the men themselves. Their blood, their culture and society, and their times, all conspired to make second-rate politicians of otherwise sometimes first-rate men. Doomed to be a part of a culture whose ethic accepted—even expected—a public man to be boastful, egotistical, larger than life, they inevitably did not deal well with challenges to their outsized egos. Toombs, Rhett, Tom Cobb, even Stephens in his way, and especially Davis, all represented a type who regarded opposition and disagreement as close to willful evil, men who saw so much of themselves in the issues they discussed that they could regard a challenge to one as a slap at the other. They all demonstrated in Montgomery what they would do to a much greater degree in Richmond in the years following. And for all their protestation at the excesses they left behind in Washington, in Montgomery the old inevitable scramble for patronage proved just as corrupting, only here more so, for those who failed in the quest turned against the government, or at least Davis, creating almost a new sectionalism based not upon location on the map, but on where they stood with presidential and congressional favors. They were not so much small men as large personalities confined by their times and their characters to a very limited range of reaction. The more they intended to be reformers, the more they found it was themselves who needed reforming, and that was a battle that most simply would not face, much less win. And they all suffered in some degree from a drought of the one trait that Southern leaders most desperately needed before and during the war, moderation. It simply was not in style.

All of which made Jefferson Davis stand so much above the crowd, just as now he towered above them on the portico to make his few remarks. He was a man who had no business being a president. He knew it himself, and it did not take long for him to demonstrate it to others, even before he left for Richmond. Stephens was probably a bit more intelligent, and certainly made more creative use of his intellect. Toombs had the power to charm and inspire that always eluded the Mississippian. Perhaps only Rhett and Tom Cobb were more obstinate—and Joe Brown of course—and Little Aleck was just as stubborn. Almost all of them except Stephens enjoyed better health.

Yet none of them would have made as effective a chief executive as Davis tried to be, and was occasionally. His military policy alone showed his to be a clearer perception of the nature of their cause. Where Toombs would have invaded the North, and where Rhett would have attacked Fort Sumter months before anything like a provocation gave excuse, Davis from the first here in Montgomery sensed that just as their hope of success lay so much with the outside world and the Border States, so must their posture before those audiences be one of the wronged defender. He could hardly protest that Southerners only wanted to be let alone on the one hand, and attack Washington on the other. Thus the embarrassment at Walker's ill-conceived boast after the firing on Sumter. Diplomatically he understood better than many how tenderly they must tread the slavery issue, making it not the bedrock of their cause—which in truth it was—but rather a by-product. They must first and last adopt the moral high ground of constitutional principles to justify their act, and ill-conceived statements like Stephens's "cornerstone" declaration served only to undermine their standing on the world stage.

But most of all what set Davis above the rest is that though a doctrinaire conservative in 1860, and more than a lukewarm state rights advocate in 1861, he grew into a genuine Confederate nationalist during the war. It began in Montgomery as he battled against the blinkered localism of the governors and tried to choose his top officers from men of merit rather than simply from those of means and influence. Here he saw, as others could not, that the best way to defend Joe Brown's Georgia was by sending Joe Brown's Georgians to Virginia. Unlike so many in Congress, he recognized that if their Constitution was to present them to the world as opposing the slave trade, then he could not approve a bill that made the government itself de facto a slave trader. And gradually from the first he began to see that in extraordinary times, self-preservation required some extraordinary means. He did not bend or circumvent his Constitution in Montgomery, but in days ahead, just as Lincoln overstepped his constitutional bounds during the war, so would Davis press the limits of liberty with the higher goal of independence in mind. Men who succeed are forgiven their transgressions. Men who do not succeed have failure charged to their transgressions, and so it would be with Davis. The shortcomings that he brought with him in February 1861 stayed with him throughout the war, and only victory would have made them ignorable. But the strengths that he developed as president, and most of all his sense of his nation *as a nation*, commenced here. Stephens and Toombs and Howell Cobb were great Georgians, Yancey a great Alabamian, Hunter a would-be great Virginian. Yet none of them made the cause as much a part of themselves as did their president. No one worked as hard, sacrificed as much, or endured the trial and travail that he did both during and after the war. None of them ever had the vision not of a confederation, but of a nation, none of them understood that in perilous times, to achieve the latter, they must compromise the former. In the end, Jefferson Davis proved to be the greatest *Confederate* of them all.

And thus it was somehow fitting that he should have outlasted almost all of them. Not one of his original cabinet or Congress stood out in the crowd standing quietly in the rain. Of the cabinet members themselves, only Mallory and Reagan held their portfolios throughout the war. Memminger achieved a small miracle in producing any revenue at all, given the decision to keep the Confederacy's only real asset, cotton, frozen. Frustrated and exhausted, he resigned in 1864, and returned to the law and education. Even as Davis spoke, the one-time Secretary of the Treasury had less than two years to live. Benjamin was already gone. He served briefly at the War desk before taking over State in 1862, and managed what little there was of Confederate diplomacy for the balance of the war. At the collapse, he escaped to England, and remained there the rest of his life, acquiring fame and some fortune as a Queen's Counsel, and apparently closing the door entirely on both his American and Confederate careers without looking back. He always said that he thought it a mistake to move the government to Richmond.[5]

Mallory was thirteen years dead now, never having succeeded in putting a real navy on the seas, but achieving some stunning isolated triumphs of innovation with ironclads and the commerce raiders. Leroy Pope Walker resigned his War portfolio less than four months after going to Richmond, sick of having so little influence in his own domain, and never rising to the administrative demands of such a position. He became a brigadier briefly, then returned to the bench, and died the same year as Memminger. Only Reagan proved longer-lived than them all. He went back to Congress, then the Senate after the war, and would live nearly two decades after Davis's return to Montgomery, dying in 1905. In the end he achieved his goal, and operated the only American Post Office department ever to pay its own way. He, Memminger, Benjamin, Mallory, and even Walker remained loyal to Davis to the last.

Not so Robert Toombs. He stayed in the cabinet less than two months after reaching Richmond, and though already disillusioned with Davis, to his credit he sought to make his resignation as quiet as possible. The President made him a brigadier, and for a time as he served out his term in the Provisional Congress, he divided his days between the capitol and the army camp. Thereafter until he resigned his commission in March 1863, he alternately won praise for his leadership of a brigade on the battlefield, and condemnation for his occasional drunkenness. For the last two years of the war, with no pulpit in Congress, he retired to his home and from it waged a constant sniping battle at Davis, in the end advocating his overthrow by coup, if necessary, to save the country from what he saw as a dictator's attempts to subvert the Constitution. Conscription, impressment of supplies, suspension of the writ of *habeas corpus*, and more extraordinary wartime expedients made him livid. In a Georgia already wracked with dissention thanks to Brown and others, Toombs only made matters worse. At the end he escaped to England for a time, then returned to Washington, Georgia, to live out his days in private practice and resistance to Reconstruction. In 1878 his health started a steep decline, aided by his increasing dedication to the bottle. When his beloved Julia died in 1883, he ceased entirely to resist the solace of drink. A friend described the old giant dying inch by inch, almost blind, many of his friends gone before him, living on the past: "He deliberately chose to drain full cups of purpose to sweeten bitter memories."[6] He died just four and one-half months before Davis returned to Montgomery.

Of the congressmen some few still survived, and theirs had been a lot after the war as varied as that of the states they once represented. Of the host Alabamians, Curry lived on until 1903, achieving distinction as one of America's greatest educators, as well as writing several books, all of them like his speeches in Congress, far too wordy. McRae went into exile after the war, living in Honduras until his death in 1877, his prewar fortune evaporated. Shorter succeeded Moore as governor late in 1861, but acted so staunchly in support of the Davis administration policies in his divided state that two years later he lost a bid for reelection. Thereafter he simply retired, to die in 1872. Dynamic Bob Smith served out his term, then raised the 36th Alabama

Infantry and as its colonel served briefly before bad health forced him to resign. He spent his last days in Mobile until his death in 1878. Stephen Hale left Congress for the army, too, and took a mortal wound while leading the 11th Alabama in 1862.

Of the Floridians, Patton Anderson resigned immediately after the first session adjourned to go into the army, and in the end rose to major general commanding a division in most of the greatest battles in Tennessee and Georgia, to die a few years after the surrender, in 1872. Morton simply retired when his term expired, dying in 1874, and his foe Owens did the same, only he still had three years to live as Davis stood before the Montgomery crowd. George Ward, who replaced Anderson, died leading his 2d Florida Infantry in 1862 in Virginia.

The Louisianians, the wealthy planters who had the most to lose on their way to Montgomery, generally lost the most. Conrad was one of the few who stayed in Congress throughout the war, staunchly supporting Davis all the way. He lost almost his entire estate as a result, and lived after the war until his death in 1878 entirely from the earnings of his law practice. The admirable DeClouet also stood by Davis despite their prewar differences, and kept his plantation and struggled after the war to rebuild it. He lived there still, and would until 1890. Kenner, whom Stephens found so impressive, also stayed in Congress until 1865, from which he pressed Davis late in the war to offer emancipation of the Confederacy's slaves as an inducement to gain foreign recognition. The President, willing to go to any length to preserve his nation, tentatively agreed, but it came too late. Kenner regained his wealth after the war, and became one of Louisiana's most progressive and prominent leaders. As Davis spoke from the same building where once the Louisianian had spoken so forcefully, Kenner was living out his last year at his home in New Orleans.

Barry of Mississippi followed those who went into the army when their terms expired, and it almost cost him his life with a near-mortal wound at Vicksburg. Yet he survived to practice law after the war. Brooke stood behind Davis solidly, but lost his race for the Confederate Senate, and spent the war sitting on military courts, living only four years past the surrender. Wiley Harris went back to private life when his one term expired, to become a giant at the Mississippi bar, admired and respected as Little Aleck had liked and respected him for his sound mind and sure wit. He was still active now, and would be until his death in 1891. Harrison also went home after his term, to practice law until his death in 1879. Clayton took a judgeship when he resigned his congressional seat, and thereafter worked at the law, railroading, banking, and education alike, as he did even now. He still had three years to live. Meanwhile, J. A. P. Campbell had a long time to go. The man who never quite made it to the first session of the Congress would outlive all of the others. When he failed to win reelection, he went into the army and served creditably until the surrender, and thereafter worked with distinguished success at the bar and on the bench. He lived until January 10, 1917, fifty-six years and a day after Mississippi seceded.

The tough Texans lived up to their reputations. John Gregg left Congress to become a soldier, one of Lee's finest fighting brigadiers, commanding the famed Texas Brigade. He died leading it near Richmond in October 1864. Leather-faced Hemphill did not survive the expiration of his term, dying of unspecified causes early in 1862. Ochiltree served out his term and then started to raise a regiment of his own before bad health forced him to go home, where he barely survived the war until 1867. Oldham died a year later, having spent some time in exile after the surrender, and was the only Texas delegate to serve through the entire war. Waul and Wigfall both became brigadier generals, and the former a good one serving in the oft-forgotten theater of war west of the Mississippi. He would live until 1903. Wigfall, on the other hand, went through a metamorphosis perhaps inevitable for one of his ego and stormy temperament. He held both army commission and congressional seat through the last four months of 1861, but resigned his undistinguished military career early in 1862 to serve the rest of the war in the Senate, a growing nuisance to Davis, and in the end an outright enemy. Some said that a falling out between their wives led to the estrangement between the husbands, but more likely Wigfall simply could not countenance his own fall from glory after Fort Sumter and Davis's unwillingness to include him in all his counsels. He went into brief exile after the war, but finally returned to Texas to die in 1874, ironically on the thirteenth anniversary of Davis's inauguration.

One of Wigfall's last acts had been to initiate a movement to force Davis to resign and replace him with Run Mad Tom Hunter. It took the President some time to discover the darker side of the Micawberish Virginian. He replaced Toombs at State for eight months, then took a seat in the Senate where he vacillated back and forth between support and opposition for the administration, all the while somewhat encouraging those who saw him as Davis's successor, but never quite far enough for those with ideas like Wigfall's to act. When Davis returned to Montgomery, the two were thoroughly estranged, and Hunter had but fifteen months to live.

The fortunes of the South Carolinians were those of the Confederacy itself. Barnwell served to the end in Congress, most of the time in staunch support of the President, though in the end he expressed disillusionment with Davis. After the surrender, ruined by the war, he went into education, ending his days in 1882 as librarian at the University of South Carolina. Boyce, too, remained in Congress for the duration, his antipathy toward Davis only growing with each new term. The war ruined him, too, and he removed to Washington to practice law. Now he lived in retirement in nearby Virginia, with just less than four years to live. Chesnut amounted to more than most of them. Davis liked and trusted him. The President put him on his personal staff late in 1862, and eighteen months later made him a brigadier and sent him to command South Carolina home guards. Following the war he fought carpetbag rule, then retired to his home in Camden where he died in 1885. His widow, Mary, spent much of their last years engaged in going over her wartime diaries and spinning from them a narrative of life in the Confederacy that she occasionally thought might be publishable. The engaging grandiloquent Keitt, by contrast, blazed as brightly as some of his poetry, and as briefly. When his term expired he raised the 20th South Carolina, but saw no action until June 1, 1864, when he temporarily rose to command of a brigade. That same day he fell with a mortal wound. Miles grew to be one of Davis's rocks of support as he stayed in Congress until the end. Meanwhile, charming as always, he wooed a rich woman. At war's end he went first to Virginia and then back to South Carolina and education. In his last years he moved to his wife's plantation north of New Orleans where he lived in some comfort until 1899. Old Withers barely survived the war, dying in November 1865.

That left Robert Barnwell Rhett. His portion of disappointment only grew larger as the war progressed, and with it his conviction that the source of all the Confederacy's ills—and his own—was Jefferson Davis. He finished his one term in Congress, then returned to Charleston to spend the balance of the war using the *Mercury* as a weapon against the administration and what he called "this little man—Jeff Davis." His megalomania growing with his bitterness, Rhett intrigued with anyone who would oppose the President, including Boyce and a small clique who toyed with deposing Davis at one point. In the winter of

1863–64 he proposed to Stephens that Davis should be deposed and General Lee put at the head of the government.[7] But then voters in his own district rejected his 1863 bid for Congress and the old man was shattered. His health started to deteriorate. He tried unsuccessfully to sell the *Mercury*. When the end of the war came, he was ruined and heavily in debt. Symbolically, he moved to a remote plantation called "Castle Dismal," where he lived alone in a house devoid of furniture and even books to read. He withdrew from society almost completely, and instead poured the bitterness of a lifetime of stunted ambitions into a self-righteous memoir whose half-truths and distortions of events to which he was witness and participant gave ample evidence of the blindness caused by envy. His hatred of Davis became a reason for living. No other man in the Confederacy could have destroyed it as the President did, he frothed. "He was created for this work as Judas Iscariot was for his."[8] The little bump on his nose that caused him to wear a patch in Montgomery had now become a hideously disfiguring cancer spreading over his face, emblematic of the tragic malignancy within. When he died in 1876, his own complete ruin stood as a metaphor for the disaster toward which he had so proudly led South Carolina and the South.

That left the Georgians, the giants who came to rule and left with so little. Bartow was the first to go. At Bull Run on July 21, 1861, in the first battle fought under the new flag he helped to select, he took a mortal wound in the thick of the fight and died within minutes, to be hugely mourned as the Confederacy's first martyr. Crawford raised a cavalry regiment and alternately led it and sat in Congress through much of the war, and afterwards returned to the law, and eventually a seat on the state supreme court before he died in 1883. Fiery Ben Hill died just a year before him. During the war he stayed in Congress and supported Davis staunchly, and after the war defended him just as ardently. Kenan died in June 1865 even before all of the remaining Confederates in the field took their paroles, and Nisbet only outlived the war by six years, leaving Congress in December 1861 to nurse his broken health. But Wright still lived. He served throughout the war at Richmond, gradually shifting toward Davis's opposition, and with the surrenders went home to Georgia to practice law. He would die in 1891.

The brothers Cobb gave all they had for the war, each in his own way. Howell soon moved to the fringes of Davis's opposition, and per- haps because of that actually lost a bid for reelection in 1862. Yet

Davis, bearing little or no animosity, made him a brigadier, and there-after Cobb served well, not on the battlefield, but back at home in Georgia trying to do something with Governor Brown to make him a productive citizen of the Confederacy, a vain task in the end. Barely more than three years after Appomattox he died suddenly at the age of fifty-three. Yet he survived his younger brother. Tom Cobb left the Congress in the fall of 1861 to recruit his own legion, and the next year led it in good performances in several of the great battles in Virginia. In reward Davis made him a brigadier in November, but in typical Tom Cobb fashion, he deemed the promotion almost an insult for coming too late, and with too little. He imagined that General Lee and others resented him, and plotted to hold him back and deny him recognition. He distrusted many of his own officers, and could not accept the occa-sionally wild ways of men at war. For their part, many of his men loathed the holier-than-thou martinet, and in his first battle after pro-motion, at Fredericksburg in December 1862, he took a mortal wound and died, little loved and less lamented by his command. It was a mea-sure of his standing with his own men that some actually believed—erroneously—that the offending missile had not been fired by the enemy.

Little Aleck Stephens was gone, too. He never regained the brief open relationship he had with Davis at the beginning, and the fault was largely his. Instead, as the war dragged on, he chafed in his power-less position as vice president, and more and more lent his strength to opposition to Davis's more stringent measures like conscription and suspension of the writ. In time he even joined with Governor Brown in obstructing Davis's efforts in Georgia, and in the end simply aban-doned Richmond entirely and went home, leaving his office and his seat as president of the Senate vacant. From Liberty Hill he con-demned Davis as "timid, petulant, peevish, obstinate, but not firm." For a time he tried to hide his involvement in the opposition, even denying it to himself, but there was no mistaking it. He and Toombs and the Cobbs and Rhett and so many others who would never have stood together in Montgomery found themselves uncomfortably bound by this single thread. By the end he was ardently in favor of seeking a negotiated peace, and Davis let him try in a meeting with old friend Lincoln in February 1865. It came to nothing, and after the sur-render Stephens, like Davis and several others, went to prison for a time before being released. In 1872 he started a ten-year career in the House of Representatives, and then in 1882 won the governorship. But all those infirmities over the years finally defeated him. Virtually an invalid, addicted to alcohol and to pain-killing drugs, especially morphine, he withered almost to nothing. On March 4, 1883, this littlest giant, liver of the most improbable career of all, died in a delirium aged seventy-one. His last conscious thoughts had been of politics. At his funeral in Atlanta, his dearest old friend Toombs came as chief eulogist. When he stood to address the crowd, the old man at first wept uncontrollably for five minutes or more as the crowd watched. When finally he spoke, his grief made him almost unintelligible until at last he gained command of himself.[9]

Thus they were all gone or going as their one-time President said his few words in the downpour. The faces before him were all different from those of another time. Montgomery itself had changed, though the war largely bypassed the city. Yankee raiders came near in July 1864, and then in April 1865 enemy cavalry occupied the town without resistance. Thus the first capital of the Confederacy escaped the ravages that almost erased Richmond and Atlanta. But the war took its toll in other ways. So many of the men who left for war now rested in some unmarked graves in Virginia and Tennessee and Georgia, or else beneath the headstones in the town's cemetery. Hooper died in 1862 of illness, his bid to regain his fortunes forever a dream. The year afterward Yancey, his mission a failure, died as well. Some said it was from a head injury sustained when Ben Hill hit him with an ink bottle during a heated debate in Congress in Richmond. His wife always blamed Jefferson Davis, whose letter-writing feud with the Alabamian over the appointment of a postmaster in Montgomery left them forever estranged.

So many others were gone: Josselyn, Stuart, his own sons who played as children in the executive mansion. His own life after the surrender had been one of constant struggle, first to gain freedom from imprisonment, then to get a trial at which he intended to defend not himself, but his Confederacy. For almost two decades after his release he had tried one thing after another—insurance, planting, writing—to support his family. Now at least he had a measure of physical comfort, but his peace was often disturbed by the continuing feuds between his one-time comrades in gray. None of them wore defeat gracefully, yet somehow Davis managed to do in old age what he could never have done in youth. He accepted it, without bitterness, yet without yielding his pride in what they had suffered and sacrificed. He might be beaten, but he had never been wrong, and in return now the people of the New

South, old and young, regarded him with a kind of reverence and even affection that they never felt for him as president. When he finished his speech today and another at the laying of the monument corner-stone tomorrow, he would still have another three and one-half years with them before he joined the legions who had gone before.

His brief remarks at an end, he listened to a speech by Gordon, some salutes from the artillery, then hosted a reception back at the Exchange. That night he went to the Montgomery Theatre, for drama still flourished in the city that once thrilled to Maggie Mitchell. The next day the procession came back up Market again, only this time there was less cheering as the crowd simply looked on at the ramrod-straight old man. Hats off in respect, they followed him to perform his duty on a solemn occasion. At the spot somewhat to the right of the capitol, toward the river, where the beautiful monument was to stand, he stood and carefully read a speech he had written in advance. There was nothing in it of bitterness or of sorrow, except for the dead. They were all Americans again, and must strive to be good citizens. Defeat did not make their cause any less holy in their eyes, but the result was final. He even spoke magnanimously of his old foes, especially General Grant, himself so magnanimous to Lee in defeat. At the end he became distracted and started to wander a bit, and a little of the old fire rose to the surface as he started to speak of the ravages by the Yankees in Virginia's Shenandoah Valley. But then he caught himself, and spoke his conclusion in words of love for them all.

The applause behind was deafening as Davis turned and walked into the capitol to host a small reception in the governor's office. That done, he went back down Market to the Exchange for the last time. In the old dining room where once the flower of Southern manhood and chivalry dined elbow-to-elbow with the office seekers and the news mongers, the ladies and the lobbyists, he took a little lunch. And then he left in the company of a few others for the cemetery, there to place flowers on the graves, and spend a few quiet hours with his dead.[10]

NOTES

Abbreviations Used in Notes

ADAH	Alabama Department of Archives and History, Montgomery
B & L	Robert U. Johnson and Clarence Clough Buel, eds., *Battles and Leaders of the Civil War*
GDAH	Georgia Department of Archives and History, Atlanta
LC	Library of Congress, Washington, D.C.
LSU	Louisiana State University, Baton Rouge
MCSH	Manhattanville College of the Sacred Heart, Purchaseville, New York
MDAH	Mississippi Department of Archives and History, Jackson
NA	National Archives, Washington, D.C.
OR	United States War Department, *War of the Rebellion: Official Records of the Union and Confederate Armies*
ORN	United States Navy Department, *Official Records of the Union and Confederate Navies in the War of the Rebellion*
PJD	Lynda Lasswell Crist and Mary Seaton Dix, *Papers of Jefferson Davis*
Rowland	Dunbar Rowland, comp., *Jefferson Davis, Constitutionalist*
SCHS	South Carolina Historical Society, Charleston
SCL, USC	South Caroliniana Library, University of South Carolina, Columbia
SHC, UNC	Southern Historical Collection, University of North Carolina, Chapel Hill
SHSP	*Southern Historical Society Papers*

1. Weld Them Together While They Are Hot

1. Nashville, *Daily Gazette*, February 17, 1861.
2. Martin J. Crawford to Alexander H. Stephens, April 8, 1861, Alexander H. Stephens Papers, Library of Congress, Washington, D.C. (LC)

3. William K. Scarborough, ed., *The Diary of Edmund Ruffin, Volume I, Toward Independence, October, 1856–April, 1861* (Baton Rouge, 1972), pp. 456, 463–64.

4. Robert S. Tharin, *Arbitrary Arrests in the South; or, Scenes from the Experience of an Alabama Unionist* (New York, 1863), p. 62.

5. William H. Gist to A. B. Moore, October 5, 1860, John Ellis to Gist, October 18, 1860, Moore to Gist, October 25, 1860, John Pettus to Gist, October 26, 1860, Thomas O. Moore to Gist, October 26, 1860, Joseph E. Brown to Gist, October 31, 1860, Milton F. Perry to Gist, November 9, 1860, William H. Gist Papers, South Caroliniana Library, University of South Carolina, Columbia. (SCL, USC)

6. Cobb to Marion Cobb, October 11, 1860, in "The Correspondence of Thomas Reade Roots Cobb, 1861–1862," *Publications of the Southern History Association*, XI (May 1907), p. 156.

7. Howell Cobb to James Buchanan, March 26, 1861, in U. B. Phillips, ed., *The Correspondence of Robert Toombs, Alexander H. Stephens, and Howell Cobb* (Washington, 1913), p. 555.

8. Montgomery, *Weekly Mail*, November 16, 30, 1860.

9. Charles E. Hooker to Pettus, January 12, 1861, Governor Record Group, RG 27, Volume 36, Mississippi Department of Archives and History, Jackson (MDAH).

10. Benjamin H. Hill to Herschel V. Johnson, December 3, 1860, Charles Colcock Jones, Jr., Collection of Autograph Letters and Portraits of the Signers of the Constitution of the Confederate States, Duke University, Library, Durham, N.C.

11. Montgomery, *Weekly Mail*, November 16, 1860.

12. Scarborough, *Ruffin Diary*, I, p. 448.

13. William H. Trescott to Robert B. Rhett, November 1, 1860, William H. Trescott Papers, Miscellaneous Manuscript Collection, LC.

14. Dwight L. Dumond, *The Secession Movement, 1860–1861* (New York, 1931), p. 148.

15. John G. Shorter to his daughter, December 9, 1860, John G. Shorter Letters, Alabama Department of Archives and History, Montgomery (ADAH).

16. Robert B. Rhett, Jr. to E.C. Wharton, August 2, 1886, Edward C. Wharton Papers, Louisiana State University, Baton Rouge (LSU).

17. Leroy P. Walker to Robert B. Rhett, Sr., November 1, 1860, Aiken B. Rhett Papers, Charleston Museum, Charleston, S.C.

18. New York, *Evening Post*, December 13, 21, 1860.

19. Steven V. Channing, *Crisis of Fear: Secession in South Carolina* (New York, 1970), pp. 290–91.

20. David S. Heidler, "Fire Eaters: The Radical Secessionists in Antebellum Politics" (Ph.D. diss., Auburn University, Auburn, Ala., 1985), p. 401.

21. *Ibid.*, p. 360.

22. *Ibid.*, pp. 359–60.
23. John Horsey to William Porcher Miles, December 10, 1860, William Porcher Miles Papers, Southern Historical Collection, University of North Carolina, Chapel Hill (SHC, UNC).
24. Heidler, "Fire Eaters," pp. 399–400.
25. Armand J. Gerson, "The Inception of the Montgomery Convention," *American Historical Association Annual Report* (Washington, 1910), p. 183; Charles E. Cauthen, *South Carolina Goes to War* (Chapel Hill, 1950), p. 84.
26. Charleston, *Mercury*, December 24, 1860; Rhett, Jr., to Wharton, August 2, 1886, Wharton Papers, LSU.
27. Cauthen, *South Carolina*, pp. 84–85.
28. Montgomery, *Weekly Advertiser*, January 16, 1861; Gerson, "Montgomery Convention," pp. 183–84.
29. Cauthen, *South Carolina*, p. 85.
30. George G. Henry to Jefferson Davis, May 9, 1861, in Lynda Laswell Crist and Mary Seaton Dix, eds., *The Papers of Jefferson Davis. Volume 7, 1861* (Baton Rouge, 1992), p. 156 (PJD).
31. New York, *Herald*, February 4, 1861.
32. C. Vann Woodward, ed., *Mary Chesnut's Civil War* (New Haven, Conn., 1981), April 2, 1861, p. 40.
33. Joseph E. Davis to Jefferson Davis, January 21, 1861, *PJD*, VII, p. 3.
34. U.S. War Department, *War of the Rebellion: Official Records of the Union and Confederate Armies* (Washington, 1880–1901), Series IV, volume 1, p. 28 (hereinafter cited as in OR, IV, 1, p. 28).
35. St. Louis, *Republican*, November 6, 1884.
36. Clay to Davis, October 30, 1875, in Dunbar Rowland, comp., *Jefferson Davis Constitutionalist: His Letters, Papers and Speeches* (Jackson, Miss., 1923), VII, pp. 460–61 (Rowland).
37. Robert B. Rhett, Sr., Autobiography, Robert B. Rhett, Sr. Papers, South Carolina Historical Society, Charleston (SCHS); Robert B. Rhett, Jr., "The Confederate Government at Montgomery," in Robert U. Johnson and Clarence Clough Buel, eds., *Battles and Leaders of the Civil War* (New York, 1888), I, p. 101 (B&L).
38. New York, *Herald*, January 15, 1861; OR, I, 53, p. 118.
39. New York, *Herald*, January 11, 1861.
40. Davis to Edward Bailey, January 15, 1886, Rowland, IX, p. 403.
41. Frank Moore, comp., *The Rebellion Record* (New York, 1861), I, "Rumors and Incidents," p. 39.
42. John B. Morris to Pettus, January 4, 1861, Record Group 27, Volume 36, MDAH.
43. A. H. Handy to Pettus, January 10, 1861, David Hubbard to Pettus, January 5, 1861, Record Group 27, Volume 36, MDAH.
44. Brown to Pettus, January 7, 1861, OR, I, 52, part 2, p. 3.

45. William S. Barry to William M. Brooks, January 9, 1861, OR, I, 52, part 2, p. 4; Barry to John Letcher, January 9, 1861, Executive Papers, Misc. Letters & Papers, Gov. John Letcher, Virginia State Library, Richmond.

46. Will T. Martin to Pettus, January 8, 1861, Horace Miller to Pettus, January 11, 1861, John C. Higgins to Pettus, January 18, 1861, Record Group 27, Volume 36, MDAH.

47. Jehu A. Orr, Reminiscences, MDAH; clipping, n.d. [late January–early February 1861], Josiah A. P. Campbell Papers, SHC, UNC; J.F.C. Claiborne, "The Secession Convention," J.F.H. Claiborne Papers, SHC, UNC.

48. John C. McGehee to Pettus, January 21, 1861, Record Group 27, Volume 36, MDAH.

49. Andrew G. Magrath to Andrew P. Calhoun, January 5, 1861, Andrew G. Magrath Papers, SCL, USC.

50. John C. Reed, The Brothers' War (Boston, 1906), pp. 266–67; Stephens to David B. Cotting, December 4, 1860, Joseph F. Burke Papers, Emory University, Woodruff Library, Atlanta.

51. Stephens to David B. Cotting, November 24, 1860, Burke Papers, Emory.

52. Stephens to George Curtis, November 30, 1860, in Henry Cleveland, Alex. H. Stephens in Public and Private (Philadelphia, 1866), pp. 159–60.

53. Stephens to S.J. Crawford, January 8, 1861, OR, II, 2, p. 609.

54. Reed, Brothers' War, p. 281.

55. Robert Toombs to Stephens, October 22, 1860, Alexander H. Stephens Papers, Emory University, Woodruff Library, Atlanta.

56. Heidler, "Fire Eaters," pp. 374–75; A.W. Redding to S.J. Anderson, December 1, 1860, OR, II, 2, p. 609.

57. Heidler, "Fire Eaters," p. 375.

58. Henry Hilliard, Politics and Pen Pictures at Home and Abroad (New York, 1892), p. 311; Alexander H. Stephens, The Wickedness of Secession; from the Lips of . . . (N.p., n.d. [1861]).

59. Reed, Brothers' War, p. 267.

60. Joseph E. Brown to Isham Harris, January 21, 1861, Isham G. Harris Papers, Tennessee State Library and Archives, Nashville.

61. Francis S. Bartow to John L. Branch, January 17, 1861, Margaret Branch Sexton Collection, University of Georgia Library, Athens.

62. Reed, Brothers' War, p. 267.

63. Stephens to Samuel R. Glenn, February 8, 1861, Stephens Papers, LC.

64. Michael P. Johnson, Toward a Patriarchal Republic. The Secession of Georgia (Baton Rouge, 1977), p. 120.

65. Ordinance of Secession, January 19, 1861, Record Group 27, Volume 36, MDAH; John G. Shorter to A.B. Moore, February 4, 1861, Governors Papers, Administrative Files, ADAH.

66. Cleveland, Stephens, p. 156; Myrta Lockett Avary, Recollections of A. H. Stephens (New York, 1910), p. 62.

67. Ezra J. Warner and W. Buck Yearns, Biographical Register of the Confederate Congress (Baton Rouge, 1975), p. 142.

68. Richard M. Johnston to Stephens, February 7, 1861, Stephens Papers, LC.

69. Alexander H. Stephens, A *Comprehensive and Popular History of the United States* (Raleigh, N.C., 1884), p. 588; Stephens to Cotting, February 6, 1861, Burke Papers, Emory University, Atlanta.

70. Alexander De Clouet to Paul De Clouet, January 1, 10, 1861, Alexander De Clouet Papers, Southwestern Archives and Manuscripts Collection, University of Southwestern Louisiana, Lafayette.

71. Lemuel P. Conner to Fanny Conner, January 26, 1861, Lemuel P. Conner Papers, Historic New Orleans Collection, New Orleans, La.

72. Unless otherwise cited, this and following biographical background on delegates to the Montgomery convention is drawn from Warner and Yearns, *Biographical Register*, and from Richard E. Beringer, "A Profile of the Members of the Confederate Congress," *Journal of Southern History*, XXXII, No. 4 (November 1967), pp. 518–41 *passim*, and from Thomas B. Alexander and Richard E. Beringer, *The Anatony of the Confederate Congress* (Nashville, 1972), pp. 353–87 *passim*.

73. New Orleans, *Daily Delta*, February 7, 1861.

74. Gerson, "Montgomery Convention," pp. 182, 185–86.

75. H. P. Bell to Harris, January 30, 1861, Harris Papers, Tennessee; W. S. Featherston to Pettus, January 2, 1861, Record Group 27, Volume 36, MDAH; Virginia Assembly, Joint Resolution, January 21, 1861, OR, IV, 1, p. 77.

76. Trescott to Cobb, January 14, 1861, Trescott Papers, SCL, USC.

77. Pickens to Davis, January 23, 1861, Rowland, V, p. 45.

78. Brown to Shorter, January 5, 1861, OR, IV, 1, p. 18.

79. Trescott to Cobb, January 14, 1861, Trescott Papers, SCL, USC.

80. Lowry Ware, "Letters to the *Independent Press* of Abbeville, S.C.," Malcolm C. McMillan Papers, Auburn University Library, Auburn, Ala.

81. Montgomery, *Weekly Mail*, November 9, 1860.

82. *Ibid.*, November 16, 1860.

83. Johnson Jones Hooper to John De Berniere Hooper, August 14, 1860, John De Berniere Hooper Papers, SHC, UNC.

84. William Wirt Culver, Personal Memoirs, in possession of Capt. John Culver, Portsmouth, N. H.

85. Montgomery, *Advertiser and State Gazette*, May 28, 1856.

86. Montgomery, *Weekly Mail*, November 16, 1860.

87. *Ibid.*, January 4, 1861.

88. Malcolm C. McMillan, *The Disintegration of A Confederate State* (Macon, Ga., 1986), pp. 9, 18.

89. OR, IV, 1, pp. 1ff; Moore to Letcher, December 10, 1860, Executive Papers, Virginia State Library; F. M. Gilmer, Statement, May 1880, Confederate States of America Records, Center for American History, University of Texas, Austin.

90. J. R. Powell to Moore, December 3, 1860, Records Concerning Conduct

and Loyalty of Army Officers, War Department Employees, Citizens, During the Civil War 1861–1872, Record Group 107, National Archives, Washington, D.C. (NA).

91. Lewy Dorman, *Party Politics in Alabama from 1850 Through 1860* (Wetumpka, Ala., 1935), p. 227.

92. John E. Moore to William P. Browne, March 2, 1861, William P. Browne Papers, ADAH.

93. William R. Smith to John W. DuBose, May 3, 1888, John W. DuBose Papers, ADAH.

94. Montgomery, *Weekly Mail*, January 18, 1861.

95. Robert Jemison to his daughter, January 10, 1861, Robert Jemison, Jr. Papers, Hoole Special Collections, Gorgas Library, University of Alabama, Tuscaloosa.

96. Hilliard, *Politics*, p. 309.

97. Jemison to daughter, January 10, 1861, Jemison Papers.

98. Culver, Memoirs.

99. Montgomery, *Weekly Mail*, December 21, 1860.

100. Montgomery, *Weekly Mail*, January 18, 1861.

101. Montgomery, *Weekly Advertiser*, January 9, 1861.

102. Montgomery, *Weekly Advertiser*, January 9, 16, 1861; Montgomery, *Weekly Mail*, December 28, 1860.

103. Montgomery, *Weekly Mail*, January 18, 1861.

104. Montgomery, *Weekly Advertiser*, January 9, 1861.

105. Montgomery, *Weekly Advertiser*, January 16, 1861; John Witherspoon DuBose, *The Life and Times of William Lowndes Yancey* (New York, 1892), II, p. 562.

106. W. Stanley Hoole, "The Flag of the Republic of Alabama, An Odyssey," *Alabama Historical Quarterly*, XL (Fall-Winter 1978), pp. 105–106.

107. W. H. Mitchell to Martha Mitchell, January 11, 1861, in Virginia K. Jones, ed., "Letters of Rev. W. H. Mitchell, Jan. 1861," *Alabama Historical Quarterly*, XXIII (Spring 1961), p. 186.

108. Montgomery, *Weekly Advertiser*, January 16, 1861; Basil Manly Diary, January 1861, Basil Manly to Basil Manly, Jr., January 11, 1861, Manly to his wife, January 11, 1861, Manly Family Papers, University of Alabama; E. Lewis to Mr. Kerr, January 11, 1861, ADAH.

109. Montgomery, *Weekly Advertiser*, January 16, 1861.

110. H. L. Clay to Clement C. Clay, January 11, 1861, Clement C. Clay Papers, Duke University Library.

111. William R. Smith to his wife, January 11, 1861, Easby-Smith Papers, LC.

112. Montgomery, *Weekly Advertiser*, January 8, 1911.

113. Culver, Memoirs.

114. Jeremiah Clemens to————, January 11, 1861, Montgomery, *Weekly Advertiser*, January 30, 1861.

115. H. L. Clay to Clement C. Clay, January 11, 1861, Clay Papers.

116. Smith to wife, January 12, 1861, Easby-Smith Papers.

117. William Brooks to Shorter, January 14, 1861, Shorter to George W. Crawford, January 16, 1861, John G. Shorter Papers, Duke University Library, Durham, N.C.

118. Leroy P. Walker to Moore, January 12, 1861, OR, I, 52, part 2, p. 4, Walker to C.F. Jackson, May 25, 1861, I, 3, p. 584.

119. An Ordinance to Make Provisional Postal Arrangements in Alabama, January 15, 1861, Executive Papers, Virginia State Library; Moore to J. D. Dempe, January 23, 1861, Governors Papers, Administrative Files, ADAH.

120. L. R. Davis to John B. McClellan, January 13, 1861, Robert A. McClellan Papers, Duke University Library, Durham, N.C.

121. Minority Report, Alabama Secession Convention, n.d., Robert Jemison Copybook, Robert Jemison Papers, University of Alabama.

122. William L. Barney, *The Secessionist Impulse: Alabama and Mississippi in 1860* (Princeton, 1974), pp. 303–304.

123. Smith to his wife, January 15, 1861, Easby-Smith Papers.

124. Montgomery, *Weekly Mail*, February 1, 1861.

125. I. Bragg to Colin J. McRae, January 21, 1861, Colin J. McRae Papers, ADAH.

126. "W. L. Yancey. Reminiscences of Thomas H. Watts," DuBose Papers, ADAH.

127. "In the early twilight . . . ," *Confederate Veteran*, I (March 1893), p. 80.

128. Bragg to McRae, January 21, 1861, E. S. Dargan to McRae, January 21, 1861, McRae Papers.

129. D. Salomon to McRae, February 1, 1861, McRae Papers.

130. Raphael Semmes to Stephens, January 25, 1861, Thomas Williams to Stephens, January 24, 1861, Stephens Papers, LC; Howell Cobb and T. R. R. Cobb to Joseph Brown, January 28, 1861, Howell Cobb Folder, Bartow to Brown, February 2, 1861, Francis Bartow Folder, Georgia Department of Archives and History, Atlanta (GDAH).

131. John Condon to David F. Jamison, January 11, 1861, David F. Jamison Papers, Washington and Lee University Library, Lexington, Virginia.

132. Davis to Pickens, January 20, 1861, Executive Council Journal Letter-Book, 1861, South Carolina Department of Archives and History, Columbia; Mallory to Milton Perry, January 16, 1861, OR, I, 52, part 2, p. 9.

133. Isaac W. Hayne to Pickens, January 1861, Executive Council Journal Letter-Book.

134. New Orleans, *Delta*, January 27, 1861; Commission, January 23, 1861, PJD, p. 27.

135. Vicksburg, *Weekly Whig*, February 6, 1861.

136. Wiley P. Harris Autobiography in Dunbar Rowland, *Courts, Judges, and Lawyers in Mississippi, 1798–1935* (Jackson, 1935), p. 327.

137. Memphis, *Daily Appeal*, June 21, 1870.

138. Davis to Alexander M. Clayton, January 30, 1861, *PJD*, pp. 27–28.

139. Montgomery, *Weekly Advertiser*, February 6, 1861.

140. Clemens to Leroy P. Walker, February 3, 1861, *OR*, I, 1, p. 447; Lawrence Keitt to Pickens, January 28, 1861, Francis Pickens Papers, Duke University Library, Durham, N.C.

141. James L. Pugh to Miles, January 24, 1861, Miles Papers, SHC, UNC.

142. Baltimore, *Sun*, January 10, 1861; Richmond, *Dispatch*, January 28, 1861; Washington, *States and Union*, January 24, 1861; New York, *Herald*, January 31, 1861; Junius Hillyer to Cobb, January 30, 1861, Phillips, *Correspondence*, p. 535.

143. Lemuel P. Conner to Fanny Conner, February 4, 1861, Lemuel P. Conner Papers, Historic New Orleans Collection, New Orleans, La.

144. New York, *World*, January 17, 1861.

145. Woodward, *Mary Chesnut's Civil War*, March [12], 1861, p. 25.

2. A Nice, Tidy Little Southern Town

1. Matthew P. Blue et al., *City Directory and History of Montgomery, Alabama* (Montgomery, 1878), pp. 5–8; John W.A. Sanford, *The Code of the City of Montgomery* (Montgomery, 1861), p. 1.

2. Blue et al., *Montgomery*, pp. 25, 30; Minnie C. Boyd, *Alabama in the Fifties. A Social Study* (New York, 1951), p. 15; Sanford, *Code*, p. 103.

3. New York, *Citizen*, April 13, 1861.

4. Joseph C. Kennedy, *Preliminary Report on the Eighth Census* (Washington, 1862), p. 245; Francis A. Walker, ed., *Ninth Census— Volume 1. The Statistics of the Population of the United States* (Washington, 1872), p. 81.

5. New Orleans, *Daily Delta*, February 26, 1861.

6. Sanford, *Code*, pp. 9, 17–18.

7. Blue, *Montgomery*, pp. 24, 34–35.

8. Anthony W. Dillard, "William Lowndes Yancey," *Southern Historical Society Papers*, XXI (1893), p. 151 (*SHSP*).

9. Sanford, *Code*, pp. 12, 26; Montgomery City Council Minutes, February 4, 11, 19, 1861, ADAH.

10. Montgomery, *Weekly Advertiser*, February 27, 1861; Wayne Flynt, *An Illustrated History of Montgomery* (Woodland Hills, Calif., 1980), p. 33.

11. Sanford, *Code*, p. 61; Montgomery City Council Minutes, April 22, 1861, ADAH; Montgomery, *Weekly Mail*, January 18, 1861.

12. Montgomery, *Weekly Mail*, February 15, 1861.

13. ——Ware to?, February 15, May 2, 1855, Clayton Ware Williams Papers, ADAH.

14. New York, *Citizen*, April 13, 1867; Thomas C. De Leon, *Four Years in Rebel Capitals* (Mobile, 1890), pp. 24, 28.

15. Leonard Mears and James Turnbull, *The Montgomery Directory, for*

1859–'60 . . . (Montgomery, 1859), advertisement; Boyd, *Alabama in the Fifties*, p. 42.

16. Montgomery, *Weekly Mail*, February 1, 1861; De Leon, *Four Years*, p. 24; Montgomery City Council Minutes, February 19, 1861, ADAH; United States Census, 1860, Alabama, Montgomery County, 1st District, p. 48.

17. Mears and Turnbull, *Montgomery*, pp. 84, 91; Flynt, *Montgomery*, p. 32; U.S. Census, p. 7; B. Hamilton to Stephens, May 3, 1861, Stephens Papers, LC.

18. New Orleans, *Daily Delta*, February 26, 1861; Montgomery, *Weekly Advertiser*, February 13, 1861; Mears and Turnbull, *Montgomery*, pp. 83, 84, 86–89, 91–95; Montgomery, *Daily Mail*, April 26, 1861; Culver, Memoirs.

19. William H. Russell, *My Diary North and South* (London, 1863), I. p. 165.

20. Mears and Turnbull, *Montgomery*, p. 95;——Ware to?, February 23, 1855, Williams Papers, ADAH.

21. Tharin, *Arbitrary Arrests*, p. 188.

22. New York, *Citizen*, April 27, 1861; U.S. Census, p. 69.

23. Montgomery, *Weekly Mail*, November 30, 1860; U.S. Census, p. 27; William S. Hoole, *Alias Simon Suggs: The Life and Times of Johnson Jones Hooper* (University, Ala., 1952), pp. 239n, 242n; Johnson J. Hooper to John De Berniere Hooper, August 14, 1860, Hooper Papers.

24. T. Michael Parrish and Robert M. Willingham, Jr., *Confederate Imprints. A Bibliography of Southern Publications from Secession to Surrender* (Austin, n.d.), p. 641.

25. Mears and Turnbull, *Montgomery*, pp. 104–106.

26. Montgomery, *Advertiser*, January 19, 26, November 9, 1859.

27. United States Census Office, *Statistics of the United States . . . in 1860* (Washington, 1861), n.p.

28. Sanford, *Code*, pp. 48, 49.

29. Montgomery, *Weekly Mail*, November 16, December 7, 1860.

30. Culver, Memoirs.

31. Montgomery, *Weekly Mail*, November 9, 1860.

32. *Ibid.*, November 23, 1860.

33. Culver, Memoirs.

34. Montgomery, *Weekly Mail*, January 11, 1861.

35. *Ibid.*, December 14, 1860.

36. *Ibid.*, January 11, 1861.

37. *Ibid.*, January 4, 1861; Hooper to John De Berniere Hooper, December 25, 1861, Hooper Papers.

38. Culver, Memoirs.

39. Montgomery, *Weekly Mail*, December 21, 1860.

40. *Ibid.*

41. *Ibid.*, November 30, 1860.

42. Culver, Memoirs.

43. Sanford, *Code*, pp. 11–12.

44. Culver, Memoirs.
45. Hooper to John De Berniere Hooper, December 25, 1860, Hooper Papers.
46. Montgomery, *Weekly Mail*, January 4, 11, 18, 1861; Montgomery, *Weekly Advertiser*, January 9, 1861.
47. Reid Smith, "'Dixie' on a Wall," *Inn Dixie* (July 1949), pp. 11–14, 27; Herman Arnold Band Score of Dixie, ADAH.
48. Montgomery, *Weekly Mail*, December 7, 1860.
49. Montgomery, *Weekly Mail*, December 14, 21, 1860; Frank O'Brien, "Passing of the Old Montgomery Theatre," *Alabama Historical Quarterly*, III (Spring 1941), pp. 10–11.
50. Montgomery, *Weekly Mail*, December 21, 1860, January 18, February 1, 1861.
51. *Ibid.*, January 11, 1861.
52. *Ibid.*, December 21, 1861.
53. Montgomery, *Weekly Confederation*, February 1, 1861.
54. Montgomery, *Weekly Mail*, December 7, 1860, January 4, 1861.
55. Culver, Memoirs.

3. They Are Selfish, Ambitious, and Unscrupulous

1. Montgomery, *Weekly Mail*, January 25, February 1, 8, 1861.
2. Robert H. Smith to Helen Smith, January 31, 1861, Jones, Autograph Letters, Duke; Mears and Turnbull, *Montgomery*, n.p.; Montgomery City Council Minutes, April 1, 1861, ADAH.
3. Montgomery, *Daily Post*, February 22, 1861; C. Vann Woodward and Elizabeth Muhlenfeld, eds., *The Private Mary Chesnut: The Unpublished Civil War Diaries* (New York, 1984), May 17, 1861, p. 69.
4. Montgomery, *Weekly Mail*, February 1, 1861.
5. Smith to Helen Smith, January 31, 1861, Jones, Autograph Letters, Duke.
6. Rhett to Robert B. Rhett, Jr., January 28, 1861, Robert Barnwell Rhett, Sr., Papers, SCL, USC.
7. Rhett, Autobiography, p. 25, Rhett Papers, South Carolina Historical Society (SCHS).
8. Rhett to T. Stuart Rhett, April 15, 1868, "Constitution & amendments proposed for Confederate States," Rhett Papers, SCHS.
9. Charleston, *Mercury*, February 4, 6, 1861.
10. *Ibid.*, February 6, 1861.
11. *Ibid.*, February 5, 6, 1861; Montgomery, *Weekly Mail*, February 15, 1861.
12. Russell, *Diary*, I, p. 164.
13. James P. Jones and William Warren Rogers, eds., "Montgomery as the Confederate Capital: View of a New Nation," *Alabama Historical Quarterly*, XXVI (Spring 1964), p. 8; Charleston, *Mercury*, February 5, 1861.
14. Montgomery, *Weekly Advertiser*, February 13, 1861; Montgomery, *Daily*

Post, February 22, 1861; Tharin, *Arbitrary Arrests*, p. 198; Jemison to his daughter, January 10, 1861, Jemison Papers.

15. This is, admittedly, speculation. However, it is significant that newspaper accounts detail the public lodgings of members from every state delegation except Alabama. While not every out-of-state delegate can be placed in one of the hotels, not one of them is located by the sources in a private home, other than in boardinghouses. Considering the personal and business contacts the Alabamians had in Montgomery, and the absence of any reference to their staying in hotels or boardinghouses, it seems reasonable to conclude that they boarded with friends and family.

16. Montgomery, *Weekly Mail*, February 1, 1861.

17. Charleston, *Mercury*, February 5, 1861.

18. Stephens to Linton Stephens, March 3, 1861, Alexander H. Stephens Papers, Manhattanville College of the Sacred Heart, Purchase, N.Y. (MCSH).

19. Keitt to Pickens, January 28, 1861, Pickens Papers, Duke; William Gilmore Simms to Miles, April 2, 1861, in Mary C. Oliphant, Alfred Taylor Odell, and T. C. Duncan Eaves, eds., *The Letters of William Gilmore Simms* (Columbia, S.C., 1955), IV, p. 354; Mrs. Keitt to Miss Lane, n.d. [February 1861], Lawrence Keitt Papers, Duke; Charleston, *Mercury*, February 26, 1861.

20. James E. Harvey to Stephens, December 8, 1860, Alexander H. Stephens Papers, Emory.

21. Heidler, "Fire Eaters," p. 359; Mobile, *Tribune*, n.d. [March 1861], Scrapbook #4, William T. Walthall Papers, MDAH; Magrath to Miles, February 1, 1861, Miles Papers, SHC, UNC.

22. Miles to W. T. Walthall, January 27, 1880, William T. Walthall Papers, MDAH.

23. Christopher G. Memminger to Miles, March 19, 1861, Miles Papers, SHC, UNC.

24. J. L. M. Curry, *Civil History of the Government of the Confederate States With Some Personal Reminiscences*, (Richmond, 1901), p. 48; Cauthen, *South Carolina*, p. 85 and n.; Charles R. Lee, *The Confederate Constitutions* (Chapel Hill, N.C., 1963), p. 61 and n. Curry was the only Montgomery delegate actually to attribute the plan to Memminger, but the analysis by both Cauthen and Lee leads them to accept his authorship.

25. Stephens to Linton Stephens, February 4, 1861, Stephens Papers, MCSH; Atlanta, *Daily Intelligencer*, March 12, 1861.

26. Howell Cobb to Mary Cobb, March 5, 1861, Howell Cobb Papers, University of Georgia.

27. William H. Trescott, Memoir of Feb. 1861, Trescott Papers, Miscellaneous Manuscript Collection, LC: Curry quoted in Samuel Boykin, *A Memorial Volume of the Hon. Howell Cobb of Georgia* (Philadelphia, 1870), p. 268.

28. Horace Montgomery, *Howell Cobb's Confederate Career* (Tuscaloosa, Ala., 1959), pp. 14–20.
29. Charleston, *Mercury*, February 6, 1861.
30. James Chesnut to W. T. Walthall, January 24, 1880, Walthall Papers.
31. Woodward and Muhlenfeld, *Private Mary Chesnut*, March 18, 1861, p. 42.
32. Thomas J. Kirkland and Robert M. Kennedy, *Historic Camden* (Columbia, S. C., 1905, 1926), II, p. 155.
33. S. R. Cobb to Mary Ann Cobb, February 4, 1861, Howell Cobb Papers, University of Georgia; Thomas R. R. Cobb to Marion Cobb, January 25, 1861, "Correspondence," p. 157.
34. William McCash, *Thomas R.R. Cobb: The Making of a Southern Nationalist* (Macon, Ga., 1983), pp. 19–20.
35. Woodward and Muhlenfeld, *Private Mary Chesnut*, March 10, 1861, p. 30.
36. Cobb to Marion Cobb, February 7, 1861, "Correspondence," p. 166, February 18, 1861, p. 182.
37. Montgomery, *Daily Post*, February 22, 1861.
38. Cobb to Marion Cobb, February 3, 1861, "Correspondence," p. 160.
39. Linton Stephens to Richard M. Johnston, January 30, 1861, Stephens Papers, Emory; Stephens to Linton Stephens, February 2, 1861, MCSH.
40. Thomas E. Schott, *Alexander H. Stephens of Georgia* (Baton Rouge, 1988), p. 20.
41. New York, *Citizen*, April 27, 1867.
42. Schott, *Stephens*, pp. 20–21; Columbus, Ga., *Daily Columbus Enquirer*, March 23, 1861.
43. Schott, *Stephens*, p. 20.
44. Stephens to Richard M. Johnston, February 2, 1861, in Richard M. Johnston and William Browne, *Life of Alexander H. Stephens* (Philadelphia, 1878), pp. 383–84.
45. Varina Howell Davis, *Jefferson Davis, Ex-President of the Confederate States of America. A Memoir* (New York, 1890), I, p. 410.
46. Reed, *Brothers' War*, pp. 275, 277.
47. Davis, *Jefferson Davis*, I. p. 411.
48. Avary, *Recollections*, p. 427.
49. Reed, *Brothers' War*, pp. 232, 242; De Leon, *Four Years*, p. 33.
50. Schott, *Stephens*, p. 21.
51. Cobb to Marion Cobb, February 7, 1861, "Correspondence," p. 165.
52. Stephens to Linton Stephens, March 3, 1861, Stephens Papers, MCSH.
53. *Ibid.*, February 3, 1861, p. 160.
54. Bartow to Brown, December 22, 1860, Francis Bartow Folder, GDAH.
55. Woodward, *Chesnut*, [May 6, 1861], p. 56; Woodward and Muhlenfeld, *Private Mary Chesnut*, March 12, 1861, p. 35.
56. Stephens to Linton Stephens, March 5, 1861, Stephens Papers, MCSH.
57. Chesnut to Walthall, January 24, 1880, Walthall Papers MDAH;

Stephens to the Editor, January 12, 1880, Atlanta, *Daily Constitution*, January 16, 1880; Johnston and Browne, *Stephens*, p. 389.

58. Chesnut to Walthall, January 24, 1880, Walthall Papers, MDAH.

59. Keitt to Hammond, February 13, 1861, J. D. Ashmore to Hammond, March 21, 1861, James Hammond Papers, LC.

60. Stephens to Editor, January 12, 1861, Atlanta, *Daily Constitution*, January 16, 1880.

61. Only three genuine accounts of this conversation are known (the David Twiggs Hamilton hoax memoir will be discussed later). On May 24, 1862, Stephens recalled it to Richard M. Johnston, who prepared a transcript at the time, or so he claims. (Johnston and Browne, *Stephens*, pp. 389–90). He told him that Chesnut said South Carolina looked to Georgia for a president, either Toombs or himself, and that he declined for the reasons stated in the text. Stephens reiterated his account almost verbatim in his January 12, 1880 letter (Atlanta, *Daily Constitution*, January 16, 1880), adding that they spoke of other business in forming the new government, and that Chesnut mentioned Davis's disinclination for the office. Again Stephens says that he declined being considered, but gives no specific reasons, concluding that he closed the conversation believing that not just Chesnut, but South Carolina as a whole, would go for Toombs. Upon reading this last account, Chesnut wrote his own (Chesnut to Walthall, January 24, 1880, Walthall Papers, MDAH), but it is frustratingly incomplete. Moreover, it was written well after the war, at a time when many former Confederates knowingly altered their published recollections in order to present a united front to posterity, cast a glow of harmony over their wartime actions, and counteract the embarrassing controversies then raging among a number of ranking ex-Confederates, including Davis himself. Chesnut served on Davis's staff during the war, felt loyal to him, and may have regarded defending Davis now as defending the cause. As will be shown hereafter, Chesnut certainly voted for Davis in the South Carolina delegation on February 8, and persuaded Withers to do so as well, but it is possible that he did so only *after* Stephens again, and finally, took himself out of consideration the day before. As for his 1880 letter, he very well remembers riding on the train with Stephens, but in three places claims to have no recollection of any conversation. He also states that at that time he did not know of Davis's preference for a military command, though he does say that he *might* have told Stephens of South Carolina's decision not to put forward anyone of their own. He says his own mind was made up as to Davis and Stephens for president and vice president before he left home. This may be so, or it may be merely hindsight. And then he concludes with glowing praise for Davis, Stephens, Toombs, and Cobb, adding that in his delegation Rhett and Keitt did oppose Davis, without saying whom they preferred. In short, it appears that Chesnut was trying very hard *not* to remember, and not to say anything that would offend any of the parties still living. Furthermore, he

was writing to Walthall, who was then assisting Davis in preparing his memoir *Rise and Fall*. He could not fail to realize that Davis would see his letter, nor to sense the tenor of a response that Walthall hoped to receive.

Consequently, the account here presented in the text gives those few points on which Stephens and Chesnut agree, and adds to it their known views on pressing matters as expressed to others, and which they could be expected to discuss during their talk. As for the matter of candidates for office, the discrepancies in their accounts can only be accounted for by false recollection (Chesnut, of course, claims to have none at all) on the part of one or both, or else miscommunication at the time of their talk. Hence the latter is suggested in the text as a *possibility*. But since Stephens's two accounts over a seventeen-year period are quite consistent, as well as with other sources to be presented later, and since there seems to be no sign of Johnston falsifying the transcription of his 1862 talk with Stephens, the weight of evidence—slim as it is—must tend to support the Georgian's account. As for Toombs's lack of participation, neither Stephens nor Chesnut mentions him being party to the conversation, and none of Toombs's few recollections even mention the train ride. Stephens writes of Toombs's worry over his daughter at this time to Linton, February 23, 1861, MCSH.

62. Kirkland and Kennedy, *Historic Camden*, II, p. 158.
63. Mears and Turnbull, *Montgomery*, p. 106.
64. Montgomery, *Daily Mail*, April 26, 1861.
65. Atlanta, *Daily Intelligencer*, March 12, 1861.
66. Robert C. Black, III, *The Railroads of the Confederacy* (Chapel Hill, N.C., 1952), pp. 13–14.
67. Montgomery, *Weekly Mail*, February 8, 15, 1861.
68. Thomas R. R. Cobb to Marian Cobb, February 3, 1861, "Correspondence," p. 159.
69. Savannah, *Daily Morning News*, February 7, 1861; Cobb to Marion Cobb, February 3, 1861, "Correspondence," p. 159–60; Stephens to Linton Stephens, February 4, 1861, Stephens Papers, MCSH.
70. Montgomery, *Weekly Mail*, February 15, 1861.
71. Woodward and Muhlenfeld, *Private Mary Chesnut*, March 3, 1861, p. 19.
72. Voucher, Montgomery Omnibus Co., 1861, Confederate Papers Relating to Citizens or Business Firms, Record Group 109, NA; Mears and Turnbull, *Montgomery*, advertisement, n.p.
73. Sanford, *Code*, pp. 35, 38–39.
74. New York, *Citizen*, April 13, 1867; J. Petrie Scrapbook on William L. Yancey, George Petrie Papers, Auburn University Library, Auburn, Ala.
75. Montgomery, *Weekly Mail*, February 8, 1861.
76. Montgomery, *Weekly Advertiser*, February, 27, 1861.
77. Culver, Memoirs; John Robertson to A. B. Moore, February 3, 1861, OR, IV, 1, p. 88.

78. Stephens to Linton Stephens, May 1, 1861, MCSH, places the boarding house on Montgomery. Columbus, Ga., *Daily Times*, March 1, 1861 further locates it on the corner, and a 1872 bird's eye view map of Montgomery shows only one house answering this description, and that on the southeast corner. Mrs. Cleveland's first name comes from the 1850 Census for Montgomery, p. 137. Thanks are due to Miriam C. Jones of Montgomery for finding the above.

79. Stephens to Linton Stephens, February 4, 1861, May 10, 1861, MCSH; Seaborn J. Howard to Stephens, January 31, 1861, Stephens Papers, LC; 1850 Census, Montgomery, p. 137.

80. Blue, *Montgomery*, pp. 31-32.

81. New York, *Citizen*, April 13, 1867; James F. Sulzby, Jr., *Historic Alabama Hotels and Resorts* (Tuscaloosa, 1960), pp. 124–25; John B. Jones, *A Rebel War Clerk's Diary at the Confederate States Capital* (Philadelphia, 1866), I, May 16, 1861, p. 36.

82. Augusta, Ga., *Daily Constitutionalist*, February 6, 1861.

83. Cobb to Marion Cobb, February 3, 1861, "Correspondence," p. 160.

84. New York, *Citizen*, April 13, 1867; Phoebe Frazer Edmonds, "My First Impressions of the War," *Confederate Veteran*, IX (May 1901), p. 205.

85. U.S. Census, 1860, p. 64; New York, *Citizen*, April 20, 1867.

86. U.S. Census, 1860, p. 64; Cobb to Marion Cobb, February 4, 1861, "Correspondence," p. 162.

87. Augusta, *Daily Constitutionalist*, February 7, 9, 1861.

88. Heidler, "Fire Eaters," p. 347; Woodward and Muhlenfeld, *Private Mary Chesnut*, March 7, 1861, p. 26.

89. Chesnut to Walthall, January 24, 1880, Walthall Papers, MDAH.

90. Woodward, *Chesnut*, April 27, 1861, p. 54.

91. Montgomery, *Daily Post*, February 22, 1861.

92. *Memorials of the Life and Character of Wiley P. Harris of Mississippi* (Jackson, 1892), p. 22.

93. J. F. H. Claiborne, "The Secession Convention," J. F. H. Claiborne Papers, SHC, UNC.

94. Harris, Memoir, in Rowland, *Courts*, p. 328.

95. Cobb to Marion Cobb, February 5, 1861, "Correspondence," p. 163.

96. David L. Swaim to Michael L. Woods, February 11, 1861, Michael L. Woods Papers, ADAH.

97. Cobb to Marion Cobb, February 4, 1861, "Correspondence," p. 162.

98. Charleston, *Mercury*, February 5, 1861.

99. New Orleans, *Daily Delta*, February 7, 1861.

100. Isaac Moore to Stephens, February 1, 1861, J. Seymour to Stephens, February 1, 1861, Stephens Papers, LC.

101. Stephens, *Popular History*, p. 588; Charleston, *Mercury*, February 5, 1861.

102. Charleston, *Mercury*, February 8, 1861; Keitt to Jamison, February 9, 1861, Jamison Papers.

103. Charleston, *Mercury*, February 9, 1860.
104. *Ibid.*, February 8, 1861.
105. *Ibid.*, February 5, 1861.
106. *Ibid.*
107. *Ibid.*
108. Harris, Memoir, in Rowland, *Courts*, p. 325.
109. Keitt to Jamison, February 9, 1861, Jamison Papers.
110. Robert Barnwell to James L. Orr, February 9, 1861, Orr and Patterson Family Papers, SHC, UNC.
111. New Orleans, *Daily Delta*, February 9, 1861.
112. Charleston, *Mercury*, February 9, 1861.
113. *Ibid.*, February 8, 1861.
114. Cobb to his wife, February 3, 1861, Phillips, *Correspondence*, pp. 536–37.
115. *Ibid.*, p. 537. No source specifically says that South Carolina and Mississippi delegates were the ones talking to Cobb on February 2 about the presidency of the convention, but since they were the only ones then present, besides Smith of Alabama, the conclusion seems inescapable. Similarly, in writing to his wife Cobb does not specifically name the friends who urge him to decline the appointment, but since his brother and Bartow both hoped to see him made president of the confederacy itself, they would have been first in line.
116. Cobb to Marion Cobb, February 3, 1861, "Correspondence," p. 160.
117. William M. Browne to Howell Cobb, January 28, 1861, Howell Cobb Papers, University of Georgia.
118. Savannah, *Daily Morning News*, February 7, 1861; New Orleans, *Daily Delta*, February 5, 1861; Stephens to Linton Stephens, February 5, 1861, Stephens Papers, MCSH.
119. J. L. Pugh to Miles, January 29, 1861, Edward McCrady to Miles, January 28, 1861, Miles Papers, SHC, UNC; E. S. Dargan to McRae, January 21, 1861, McRae Papers.
120. Hooper to John De Berniere Hooper, August 14, December 25, 1860, Hooper Papers, SHC, UNC.
121. Hoole, *Hooper*, p. 150; Census, 1860, p. 85.
122. Montgomery, *Daily Advertiser*, January 30, 31, 1861.
123. Stephens to Linton Stephens, February 5, 1861, Stephens Papers, MCSH.
124. Pillow to President, February 1, 1861, Cobb Papers, Georgia.
125. Cobb to Marion Cobb, February 3, 1861, "Correspondence," p. 161.
126. Simms to James Lawson, March 17, 1861, Oliphant et al., *Letters*, IV, p. 352.
127. Cobb to Marion Cobb, February 3, 1861, "Correspondence," p. 161.
128. Stephens to Linton Stephens, February 5, 1861, Stephens Papers, MCSH.
129. Cobb to Marion Cobb, February 3, 1861, "Correspondence," p. 160.
130. New Orleans, *Daily Delta*, February 9, 1861. "I am glad to see that

prominent members of the South Carolina delegation favor it," the unnamed correspondent—signing himself "Observer"—wrote of Stephens's consideration for president.

131. Augusta, *Daily Constitutionalist*, February 6, 1861.
132. Cobb to Marion Cobb, February 3, 1861, "Correspondence," p. 160.
133. Dillard, "Yancey," p. 157.
134. F. M. Gilmer and A. F. Hopkins to A. B. Moore, January 8, 1861, Governor, Administrative Files, A. B. Moore, ADAH.
135. Gilmer, Statement, May 1880, Confederate States of America Records, University of Texas.
136. Cobb to Marion Cobb, February 3, 1861, "Correspondence," p. 160.
137. Autobiography, James Patton Anderson Papers, SHC, UNC. Anderson's memoir is pathetically skimpy, but he does say that he approved of all the actions of the provisional convention, which included the selection of Davis as president.
138. Charleston, *Mercury*, February 8, 1861; New Orleans, *Daily Delta*, February 9, 1861.
139. Cobb to Marion Cobb, February 3, 1861, "Correspondence," p. 160.
140. Woodward and Muhlenfeld, *Private Mary Chesnut*, February 18, 1861, p. 6.
141. Woodward, *Chesnut*, [February 18, 1861], p. 5.
142. February 3, 1861.
143. Cobb to his wife, February 3, 1861, in Phillips, *Correspondence*, p. 537.
144. Charleston, *Mercury*, February 5, 1861; Robert B. Rhett, Sr., notes in book titled *Index Rerum*, Aiken B. Rhett Papers.
145. Rhett to Robert B. Rhett, Jr., n.d. [February 1861], 1861, Rhett Papers, SCL, USC. Rhett may have written this undated letter anytime up until February 8 or 9, but it most probably stems from the first night or two that the delegates were in Montgomery, and in any case certainly expresses his sentiments as of the end of the February 3 discussions at the Exchange.
146. Charleston, *Mercury*, February 6, 1861.

4. We Are a Congress

1. Montgomery, *Weekly Mail*, February 15, 1861.
2. Sanford, *Code*, pp. 42–43.
3. Stephens to Linton Stephens, February 4, 1861, Stephens Papers, MCSH.
4. New York, *Herald*, March 4, 1861; Jones and Rogers, "Montgomery," February 11, 1861, p. 19.
5. Montgomery, *Weekly Mail*, February 15, 1861; Mears and Turnbull, *Montgomery*, p. 102
6. Stephens to Brown, February 4, 1861, Alexander H. Stephens Folder, GDAH.

7. Jones and Rogers, "Montgomery," February 4, 1861, p. 10.

8. London, *Times*, May 30, 1861.

9. Montgomery, *Weekly Advertiser*, February 27, 1861; Montgomery, *Weekly Mail*, February 8, 1861.

10. Manly to Basil W. Manly, Jr., February 5, 1861, Manly Family Papers.

11. Montgomery, *Weekly Advertiser*, February 27, 1861.

12. Thomas L. Sweeney, "Pride of Place," *Historic Preservation News* (January 1993), p. 16; London, *Times*, May 30, 1861.

13. Jones and Rogers, "Montgomery," February 2, 1861, p. 10.

14. Montgomery, *Weekly Advertiser*, February 6, 1861.

15. *Ibid.*,

16. London, *Times*, May 30, 1861.

17. Mobile, *Daily Advertiser*, February 7, 1861.

18. New Orleans, *Daily Delta*, February 26, 1861.

19. London, *Times*, May 30, 1861.

20. Jones and Rogers, "Montgomery," February 4, 1861, pp. 11–12.

21. Stephens to Linton Stephens, March 3, 1861, Stephens Papers, MCSH.

22. James T. Harrison to Charles C. Jones, August [September] 4, 1872, Charles Colcock Jones Collection of Correspondence from Members of the Confederate Congress, University of Georgia.

23. Manly to Basil W. Manly, Jr., February 10, 1861, Manly Family Papers.

24. Alexander and Beringer, *Anatomy*, pp. 353–87; Albert N. Fitts, "The Confederate Convention," *Alabama Review*, II (April 1949), pp. 100–101; Beringer, "Profile," pp. 518–41 *passim*.

25. Montgomery, *Weekly Advertiser*, February 5, 1861. Several newspapers in the South carried telegraphic transcripts of the convention's public sessions. Not all agree, since some papers sent their own recorders. The accounts in the *Weekly Advertiser* have been found to be the fullest as a rule.

26. Manly to Basil W. Manly, Jr., February 5, 1861, Manly Family Papers.

27. Montgomery, *Weekly Advertiser*, February 5, 1861.

28. Montgomery, *Daily Post*, February 22, 1861.

29. William Stanley Hoole, ed., "The Diary of Dr. Basil Manly, 1858–1867," *The Alabama Review*, IV (April 1951), p. 146.

30. Montgomery, *Weekly Advertiser*, February 5, 1861.

31. Hoole, *Hooper*, pp. 153–54, 239n.

32. U.S. Congress, *Journal of the Congress of the Confederate States of America* (Washington, 1904), I, p. 17.

33. William C. Oates, *The War Between the Union and the Confederacy and Its Lost Opportunities* (New York, 1905), p. 57.

34. Cobb to his wife, February 6, 1861, Phillips, *Correspondence*, p. 537.

35. New Orleans, *Daily Picayune*, February 9, 1861.

36. *Ibid.*

37. James J. Deas to James Chesnut, Sr., February 12, 1861, James Chesnut, Jr., Papers, Duke University Library, Durham, N.C.

38. Cobb to Marion Cobb, February 4, 1861, "Correspondence," p. 162.

39. Columbus, Ga., *Daily Times*, February 5, 1861.

40. Trescott to Cobb, February 2, 1861, Cobb Papers.

41. Stephens to Editors, January 12, 1880, Atlanta, *Daily Constitution*, January 16, 1880.

42. Charleston, *Mercury*, February 8, 1861.

43. Vicksburg, *Daily Evening Citizen*, February 4, 1861.

44. Cobb to Marion Cobb, February 4, 1861, "Correspondence," p. 161.

45. Alexander H. Stephens, *A Constitutional View of the Late War Between the States* (Philadelphia, 1868, 1870), II, pp. 326–27, 710–12.

46. Stephens to Linton Stephens, February 5, 1861, Stephens Papers, MCSH.

47. Hoole, "Diary of Dr. Basil Manly," February 4, 1861, p. 146.

48. Montgomery, *Weekly Mail*, February 15, 1861; Stephens to Linton Stephens, February 5, 1861, Stephens Papers, MCSH.

49. Parrish and Willingham, *Imprints*, p. 62.

50. Cobb to Marion Cobb, February 5, 1861, "Correspondence," p. 162.

51. New York, *Herald*, March 4, 1861.

52. Columbus, Ga., *Daily Columbus Enquirer*, March 23, 1861.

53. Jones, *Diary*, I, May 26, 1861, p. 43.

54. Montgomery, *Weekly Advertiser*, February 13, 1861.

55. *Ibid.*

56. Cobb to Marion Cobb, February 5, 1861, "Correspondence," pp. 162–63.

57. Jones and Rogers, "Montgomery," February 6, 1861, p. 14; Mobile, *Daily Advertiser*, February 9, 1861.

58. Manly to ——, February 6, 1861, Manly Family Papers.

59. Stephens to Linton Stephens, February 6, 1861, Stephens Papers, MCSH.

60. U.S. Congress, *Journal*, pp. 20–22. In Johnston and Browne, *Stephens*, Stephens's February 9, 1861 letter to Linton is quoted as having Stephens say that Augustus R. Wright served with him from Georgia. This is a misquotation. In the original letter (MCSH), while the name is smudged, it is certainly Nisbet. Fitts, "Confederate Convention," p. 95n, accepting this misquotation, and presumably without having examined the original letters, accepts this to support his contention that "Stephens' account of the Congress contains major factual errors." Fitts compounds his own error by misreading Johnston and Browne to conclude that the February 9 letter is to Johnston, rather than Linton, and then erroneously states Wright's middle initial as H.

61. Charleston, *Mercury*, February 8, 1861; Cobb to Marion Cobb, February 5, 1861, "Correspondence," p. 163.

62. Boyce to Hunter, February 5, 1861, R. M. T. Hunter Papers, Alderman Library, University of Virginia, Charlottesville.

63. Robert H. Smith, *An Address to the Citizens of Alabama, on the Constitution of the Confederate States of America* (Mobile, 1861), pp. 6–7.

64. Rhett to Robert B. Rhett, Jr., February 11, 1861, Rhett Papers, SCL, USC.

65. Charleston, *Mercury*, February 8, 1861.
66. *Ibid*. Debate has continued for generations on just which of the editorials and reports in the *Mercury* at this time came from Dill and other reporters in Montgomery, and which Rhett himself authored. Two personalities do seem to speak. One is purely observational, as in this same issue when it says that the day passed harmoniously with dignity and "impressiveness." This is quite clearly the picture that the convention wanted the public to have, and that a reporter would have. But another voice also speaks, this one highly informed, obviously more politically motivated, and marked by a bitterness and point of view that matches Rhett's state of mind perfectly. Here and hereafter the author assumes that when *this* voice speaks, it is Rhett himself, or else Rhett speaking through one of his reporters.
67. Clipping of constitutional ratification debate in Mississippi, March 1861, Claiborne Papers, SHC, UNC; William S. Wilson to H.G. Ellett, February 9, 1861, Jones, Autograph Letters, Duke.
68. Again, Anderson's Autobiography (SHC, UNC) says nothing specific about his participation in these discussions, but his statement that he approved all of the acts of the provisional congress can be taken to constitute approval of the convention's assumption of legislative powers.
69. Smith, *Address*, p. 5.
70. Ashmore to Hammond, March 21, 1861, Keitt to Hammond, February 13, 1861, Hammond Papers.
71. Scarborough, *Ruffin*, I, April 2, 1861, p. 576.
72. Clipping, March 1861, Claiborne Papers.
73. U.S. Congress, *Journal*, I, p. 26.
74. Lee, *Constitution*, p. 61 and n.
75. Stephens to Linton Stephens, February 6, 1861, Stephens Papers, MCSH.
76. Stephens to Cotting, February 6, 1861, Burke Papers.
77. Bela Estvan, *War Pictures from the South* (New York, 1863), p. 23.
78. Montgomery *Weekly Post*, February 6, 1861.
79. Mobile, *Daily Advertiser*, February 9, 1861.
80. Cobb to Marion Cobb, February 6, 1861, "Correspondence," pp. 164–65.
81. Stephens to Linton Stephens, February 6, 1861, Stephens Papers, MCSH.
82. U.S. Congress, *Journal*, p. 22.
83. J.A.P. Campbell years later claimed that he also arrived in Montgomery on February 6, delayed by broken railroads (Campbell to Jones, October 17, 1874, Jones, Correspondence, University of Georgia). However, all other evidence—and the lack of it—suggests that Campbell in fact never made it to Montgomery at all during the first session. The *Journal* of the congress made a point of noting the presentation of credentials of all late arriving delegates, yet carries no such notice for Campbell. Moreover, neither the *Journal* nor the published transcripts of public sessions show Campbell speaking even once during this session. At the first roll call vote held on February 23 (*Journal*, p. 78), every Mississippian except Campbell

voted. And on February 15 Brooke of Mississippi asked for a leave of absence for Campbell (*Journal*, p. 54), which suggests even more strongly that he had not arrived. Campbell's own Autobiography, March 2, 1914 (J.A.P. Campbell Papers, SHC, UNC) is completely silent in the matter. This makes his 1874 claim difficult to explain, since at only forty four he could hardly be senile. More likely, he simply did not care to admit that he had missed out on the most important events of his single term. Campbell's absence from the first session is of considerable importance, as will be seen.

84. U.S. Congress, *Journal*, p. 24; Montgomery, *Weekly Advertiser*, February 13, 1861.
85. Lee, *Constitution*, p. 60.
86. Stephens to Linton Stephens, March 3, 1861, Stephens Papers, MCSH; *Memorials of the Life and Character of Wiley P. Harris*, p. 22.
87. Claiborne, "The Secession Convention," Claiborne Papers.
88. Stephens to Linton Stephens, March 3, 1861, Stephens Papers, MCSH.
89. A. B. Roman to Kenner, February 3, 1861, La Villebeuvre Family Papers, LSU.
90. Kenner to Roman, February 9, 1861, La Villebeuvre Family Papers, LSU.
91. Stephens to Linton Stephens, March 3, 1861, Stephens Papers, MCSH.
92. James T. Harrison to Susan Harrison, February 17, 1861, James T. Harrison Papers, SHC, UNC.
93. Cobb to Marion Cobb, February 12, 1861, "Correspondence," p. 174.
94. Miles to Walthall, January 27, 1880, Walthall Papers.
95. Barnwell to Orr, February 9, 1861, Orr-Patterson Papers.
96. Stephens to Linton Stephens, February 9, 1861, Stephens Papers, MCSH.
97. U.S. Congress, *Journal*, pp. 26–30.
98. Blue, *Montgomery*, p. 34; Ware, "Letters," May 2, 1855, Williams Papers.
99. Census, 1860, p. 177; Ware, "Letters," February 15, 1855, Williams Papers.
100. Woodward and Muhlenfeld, *Private Mary Chesnut*, February 27, 1861, p. 14.
101. Montgomery, *Weekly Mail*, January 4, 1861.
102. John H. Napier, III "Montgomery During the Civil War," *Alabama Review*, XLI (April 1988), p. 121.
103. Census, 1860, p. 93; Cobb to Marion Cobb, February 7, 1861, "Correspondence," p. 165.
104. New York, *Citizen*, April 20, 1867.
105. Blue, *Montgomery*, p. 34.
106. Cobb to Marion Cobb, February 10, 1861, "Correspondence," p. 170.
107. Montgomery, *Daily Post*, February 16, 1861.
108. New York, *Citizen*, April 20, 27, 1867.
109. *Ibid.*, April 20, 1867.
110. Culver, Memoirs.

111. Montgomery, *Weekly Advertiser*, February 6, 1861; Montgomery, *Weekly Mail*, February 8, 1861.

112. Woodward, *Chesnut*, March 9, 1861, p. 21.

113. New York, *Citizen*, April 27, 1861.

114. New York, *Citizen*, April 20, 1867.

115. Sanford, *Code*, p. 47.

116. Martin Crawford to the Editor, June 25, 1870, Walthall Papers; Jones and Rogers, "Montgomery," February 6, 1861, pp. 15–16; Stephens to Linton Stephens, February 23, 1861, Stephens Papers, MCSH.

117. Reed, *Brothers' War*, p. 251.

118. Miles to Pickens, February 9, 1861, William Porcher Miles Papers, LC.

119. Reed, *Brothers' War*, p. 236.

120. Herschel V. Johnson, "From the Autobiography of," *American Historical Review*, XXX (January 1925), p. 329.

121. Crawford to the Editor, June 25, 1870, Walthall Papers.

122. Stephens to Linton, February 23, March 3, 1861, Stephens Papers, MCSH.

123. Reed, *Brothers' War*, p. 279.

124. Pleasant A. Stovall, *Robert Toombs, Statesman, Speaker, Soldier, Sage* (New York, 1892), p. 365.

125. Augustin H. Hansell, Memoirs, SHC, UNC.

126. Alexander H. Stephens conversation, May 24, 1862, in Johnston and Browne, *Stephens*, p. 391.

127. *Ibid.*, p. 390; Rhett notes in *Index Rerum*, Aiken B. Rhett Papers. If such a conversation as Rhett described actually took place, it had to be either Anderson or Owens who told him this, since Morton had not yet arrived. Owens, more in line with the fire-eaters than Anderson, seems the logical choice.

128. Stephens to Linton Stephens, February 23, 1861, Stephens Papers, MCSH. Stephens, the only eyewitness authority for this episode, does not date it exactly, saying only that it happened "about two days before the election." That would place it at February 6 or 7. Since, as will appear subsequently, South Carolina is flirting again with Stephens as a candidate on the evening of February 7, this would suggest that Toombs's support in the state was gone by this point, and that the party in question took place earlier. Thus February 6 seems the most likely date that fits.

129. Henry W. Cleveland, "Robert Toombs," *Southern Bivouac*, New Series I (January 1886), p. 452.

130. Reed, *Brothers' War*, pp. 284–85; Richard M. Johnston, *Autobiography of Col. Richard Malcolm Johnston* (Washington, 1900), p. 125.

131. Stephens to Linton Stephens, February 23, 1861, Stephens Papers, MCSH.

132. Crawford to Toombs, April 1, 1861, Robert Toombs Letterbook, SCL, USC.

133. Atlanta, *Daily Intelligencer*, February 8, 1861.
134. Cobb to Marion Cobb, February 6, 1861, "Correspondence," p. 164.
135. *Ibid.*; Howell Cobb to his wife, February 6, 1861, Phillips, *Correspondence*, p. 537.
136. Cotting to Stephens, February 5, 1861, Stephens Papers, LC.
137. A. B. Roman to Kenner, February 3, 1861, La Villebeuvre Family Papers.
138. Jones and Rogers, "Montgomery," February 6, 1861, pp. 15–16.
139. Augusta, Ga., *Chronicle & Sentinel*, February 1861, in Moore, *Rebellion Record*, I, Documents, p. 30.
140. Mobile, *Daily Advertiser*, February 9, 1861.
141. John A. Cobb to Howell Cobb, February 5, 10, 1861, Howell Cobb Papers, University of Georgia.
142. Stephens to the Editor, January 12, 1881, Atlanta, *Daily Constitution*, January 16, 1880.
143. Cobb to his wife, February 6, 1861, Howell Cobb Papers, University of Georgia.
144. Cobb to Marion Cobb, February 6, 1861, "Correspondence," p. 164.
145. Charleston, *Mercury*, February 6, 1861.
146. Harris to Walthall, July 17, 1879, Walthall Papers.
147. Kenner to Walthall, July 28, 1879, Walthall Papers.
148. Charleston, *Mercury*, February 9, 1861.
149. Hammond to Simms, February 6, 1861, Hammond Papers, LC.
150. Howell Cobb to his wife, February 6, 1861, Cobb Papers, University of Georgia; Cobb to Marion Cobb, February 6, 1861, "Correspondence," p. 164.

5. The Most Momentous Event of the Century

1. Mobile, *Daily Advertiser*, February 10, 1861.
2. U.S. Congress, *Journal*, pp. 24–25; Montgomery, *Weekly Advertiser*, February 13, 1861.
3. Paul F. Ive to Stephens, Toombs, and Nisbet, February 2, 1861, Howell Cobb Papers, Georgia.
4. U.S. Congress, *Journal*, pp. 30–31.
5. Charleston, *Mercury*, February 11, 1861.
6. Vicksburg, *Daily Evening Citizen*, February 11, 1861.
7. Charleston, *Mercury*, February 9, 1861.
8. Rhett to Robert B. Rhett, Jr., February 12, 1861, Rhett Papers, SCL, USC.
9. New York, *Herald*, February 5, 1861.
10. New York, *Daily Tribune*, February 5, 1861.
11. New Orleans, *Bee*, February 6, 1861; Natchez, *Daily Courier*, February 7, 1861; Montgomery, *Weekly Confederation*, February 15, 1861.
12. New York, *Herald*, January 31, 1861.

13. Macon, *Daily Telegraph*, February 9, 1861.
14. Trescott to Miles, February 6, 1861, Miles Papers, SHC, UNC.
15. Miles to Walthall, January, 27, 1880, Walthall Papers; Rhett, "Confederate Government," p. 103.
16. Schott, *Stephens*, pp. 218–20.
17. V. M. Barnes to Stephens, February 9, 1861, Stephens Papers, LC.
18. Linton Stephens to Stephens, February 15, 1861, Stephens Papers, MCSH.
19. Stephens to Linton Stephens, February 15, 1861, Stephens Papers, MCSH.
20. Cobb to Marion Cobb, February 8, 1861, "Correspondence," p. 167, February 14, 1861, p. 177.
21. Cobb to Marion Cobb, February 7, 1861, "Correspondence," pp. 165–66.
22. Cobb to Marion Cobb, February 9, 1861, "Correspondence," p. 168. "It was with hard work that we could keep him [Stephens] from being presented for president," Cobb says in his letter. This is his only admission of any attempt to influence the election. Since Tom Cobb *had no* influence within his delegation, he can only have made his efforts outside of it, and in a manner to be discussed presently.
23. The assumption that Bartow assisted Cobb follows from the latter's statement above that "we" kept Stephens from being presented. It being unseemly for Howell Cobb to do anything in his own behalf, only Bartow's assistance would allow Tom Cobb to speak in the plural.
24. Clayton to Walthall, July 19, 1879, Atlanta, *Daily Constitution*, December 28, 1879.
25. Cobb to Marion Cobb, February 6, 1861, "Correspondence," p. 164.
26. Clayton to the Editor, June 17, 1870, Memphis, *Daily Appeal*, June 21, 1870.
27. Pettus to Davis, February 7, 1861, *PJD*, VII, p. 36. No communication from the Mississippi delegates to Pettus of this date has been found. Its sending is surmised only from the sudden urgency with which Pettus summoned Davis, and from the fact that, while his duties as commander of the Mississippi militia might require Davis's presence in Jackson, no logical contingency for Pettus's hint that Davis should be prepared to go on to Montgomery seems evident.
28. Stephens to Linton Stephens, February 8, 1861, Stephens Papers, MCSH.
29. Stephens to Samuel R. Glenn, February 8, 1861, Stephens Papers, LC.
30. Jones and Rogers, "Montgomery," April 1, 1861, p. 60.
31. Columbus, Ga., *Daily Times*, February 8, 1861.
32. U.S. Congress, *Journal*, p. 31; Mobile, *Daily Advertiser*, February 12, 1861.
33. U.S. Congress, *Journal*, pp. 31–32.
34. Cobb to Marion Cobb, February 8, 1861, "Correspondence," p. 167.
35. Paige Holliman Kemp, "Montgomery, Alabama, 1861: A Social History of the Cradle of the Confederacy" (M.A. thesis, Auburn University, Ala., 1978), p. 29.

36. U.S. Congress, *Journal*, p. 33.
37. W. S. Wilson to H. T. Ellett, February 9, 1861, Jones, Autograph Letters, Duke.
38. Alexander M. Clayton speech, n.d., Claiborne Papers, SHC, UNC.
39. Anderson et al. to President of Florida Convention, February 23, 1861, OR, IV, 1, pp. 109–10.
40. H. M. Polk to John H. Bills, February 9, 1861, Horace M. Polk Papers, LSU.
41. Jones M. Withers to McRae, February 7, 1861, McRae Papers.
42. U.S. Congress, *Journal*, p. 33.
43. *Ibid.*, p. 34.
44. Kenner to Roman, February 9, 1861, La Villebeuvre Family Papers; Stephens to Linton Stephens, March 3, 1861, Stephens Papers, MCSH
45. Keitt to Hammond, February 13, 1861, Hammond Papers, LC.
46. U.S. Congress, *Journal*, p. 35; Stephens to Linton Stephens, March 3, 1861, Stephens Papers, MCSH.
47. Cobb to Marion Cobb, February 8, 1861, "Correspondence," p. 168.
48. Mobile, *Daily Advertiser*, February 10, 1861. The reporter says this happened on the night of February 6, which must be a misprint as the constitution was not ready for printing by then.
49. Trescott to Miles, February 6, 1861, Miles Papers, SHC, UNC.
50. Vicksburg, *Daily Evening Citizen*, February 11, 1861.
51. Montgomery, *Weekly Mail*, February 8, 1861.
52. Charleston, *Mercury*, February 13, 1861.
53. U.S. Congress, *Journal*, pp. 35–36.
54. Keitt to Hammond, February 13, 1861, Hammond Papers, LC.
55. U.S. Congress, *Journal*, pp. 36–37.
56. Augusta, *Daily Constitutionalist*, February 15, 1861.
57. Stephens, *Constitutional View*, II, p. 325.
58. Stephens to Linton Stephens, February 8, 1861, Stephens Papers, MCSH.
59. Woodward, *Chesnut*, April 19, 1865, p. 786.
60. Stephens to Linton Stephens, March 3, 1861, Stephens Papers, MCSH.
61. Miles to Walthall, January 27, 1880, Walthall Papers.
62. Stephens to the Editor, January 12, 1880, Atlanta, *Daily Constitution*, January 16, 1880; Stephens conversation, May 24, 1862, Johnston and Browne, *Stephens*, p. 390. In his letter to the *Constitution* Stephens dates this conversation to February 7, but adds that it occurred when the debate on the provisional constitution was nearly through. There being no debate on February 7, it can only have occurred the next evening.
63. Mobile, *Daily Advertiser*, February 9, 1861. The correspondent "Montgomery," writing on February 6, states that "all the South Carolina delegation, except Mr. Rhett" were behind Stephens, clearly incorrect, yet adding support to the contention that at least some of them were.
64. Columbia, *Daily South Carolinian*, February 20, 1861.
65. Reed, *Brothers' War*, p. 290.

66. Kenner to Roman, February 9, 1861, La Villebeuvre Family Papers.
67. Mobile, *Daily Advertiser*, February 10, 1861.
68. While the account here given of the Keitt conversation, as well as Stephens's train conversation with Chesnut on February 3, agree in most respects with David Twiggs Hamilton, "Presidency of the Confederacy Offered Stephens and Refused," *SHSP*, XXXVI (1908), pp. 141–45, it is important to stress here that the Hamilton source has not been used. The reason is that it is completely spurious. As published, it is stated as being taken from a February 17, 1907 issue of the Richmond *Times-Dispatch*. In fact, it does *not* appear in that issue, nor in any issue within a month before or after that date. While the author is described as a colonel, no man of this name at any rank appears either in the OR or in the 1860 Georgia census. Moreover, while this account has J.A.P. Campbell calling on Stephens at the Exchange Hotel on February 8, Stephens did not board at the Exchange, and Campbell never set foot in Montgomery at all during the first session. As late as February 23 he is still in Attala County, Mississippi (Vicksburg, *Daily Evening Citizen*, February 23, 1861). Conclusive, however, is a look at a novel written by Mrs. Lafayette McLaws. *The Welding*, published in Boston in 1907, is presented as straightforward historical *fiction*, and depicts the early days of the Confederacy. Its fictional hero is David Twiggs Hamilton, and the article from *SHSP* is paraphrased almost *verbatim* from pp. 222–26. The book has the ring of authenticity because its presentation of these events is itself almost literally borrowed from Johnston and Brown, *Stephens*, and Stephens's 1880 letter to the Atlanta *Daily Constitution*. Stephens did have an acquaintance named Hanspard Dade Duncan Twiggs (T.R.R. Cobb to Brown, January 28, 1861, Cobb File, GDAH) and it is possible that this young Georgian served as the model for the fictional Hamilton. Mrs. McLaws considerably fictionalized the skeleton of history that she borrowed. By 1908 when the article appeared, the *SHSP* relied heavily on newspaper accounts from around the South for its content. Obviously a prankster refashioned this account from *The Welding* and submitted it, and the editors published it in good faith without checking to see that it really came from the *Times-Dispatch*. Unfortunately, virtually every Stephens biographer, and many others writing on the election, have accepted the fraud as authentic.
69. Stephens to S. J. Anderson, January 26, 1860, OR, II, 2, p. 605.
70. Stephens conversation, May 24, 1862, Johnston and Browne, *Stephens*, p. 390.
71. While some may be inclined to question the claim that an offer of this kind was made to Stephens, he being the only witness to record the event, and that in two places, one a year later, and the other nearly two decades in the future, still considerable contemporary evidence exists suggesting that others knew of what had happened. The Columbus, Ga., *Daily Columbus Enquirer* for February 12, 1861, states that "it is reported,

moreover, that Mr. Stephens was urged to take the first position, and declined." George Bacon of Columbus was in Montgomery at the time, or immediately afterward, and within two or three days told his son Robert that "Mr. Stephens could have been President if he had desired to" (Robert Bacon to George Bacon, February 14, 1861, Stephens Papers, LC). And on March 4, 1861, Stephens's friend A. H. Wyche (or Hyde) wrote to him saying "I regret you did not accept the first position. Your honor was the best judge in so important a matter" (Stephens Papers, LC). And Martin Crawford, in a letter to a newspaper editor on June 25, 1870 (Walthall Papers) states that "while the subject was being considered, some members of the Congress mentioned the matter to him."

72. Stephens to the Editor, January 12, 1880, Atlanta, *Daily Constitution*, January 16, 1880; Walthall to Chesnut, January 29, 1880, Walthall Papers.
73. Crawford to the Editors, June 25, 1870, Walthall Papers.
74. Cobb to Marion Cobb, February 8, 1861, "Correspondence," p. 168.
75. Cobb to Marian Cobb, February 9, 1861, "Correspondence," p. 168.
76. Cobb to Marion Cobb, February 11, 1861, "Correspondence," p. 171.
77. Congress, *Journal*, pp. 37–39.
78. Stephens to Linton Stephens, February 9, 1861, Stephens Papers, MCSH; Cobb to Marion Cobb, February 9, 1861, "Correspondence," p. 169.
79. Congress, *Journal*, p. 39; Stephens, *Constitutional View*, II, p. 328.
80. Montgomery, *Weekly Mail*, February 15, 1861.
81. Keitt to Jamison, February 9, 1861, Jamison Papers; New Orleans, *Daily Delta*, February 13, 1861.
82. Augusta, *Daily Constitutionalist*, February 15, 1861.
83. Charleston, *Mercury*, February 12, 1861.
84. Rhett to Robert B. Rhett, Jr., February 11, 1861, Rhett Papers, SCL, USC.
85. New Orleans, *Daily Delta*, February 9, 1861.
86. Crawford to the Editors, June 25, 1870, Walthall Papers.
87. Admittedly, the conclusion that Tom Cobb tried to stop Stephens, promote his brother, and influence the election by a "dirty trick," rests upon heavy interpretation of the woefully slim surviving evidence. First, Henry Cleveland, who knew both Stephens and Toombs intimately, and wrote a biography of the former, stated in 1886 in "Toombs," p. 452: "Then Thomas R. R. Cobb indiscreetly [sic] electioneered for his brother." This is the only extant direct accusation, and Cleveland was in an excellent position to have gotten it from Toombs or Stephens, or both. Stephens confirms first in 1862, and then later in 1870, that *someone* went to the other delegations with false information. "I afterward learned," he said to Johnston on May 24, 1862 (Johnston and Browne, *Stephens*, p. 390), "that the action of the States alluded to was based upon intelligence received by them the night before that Mr. Cobb would be presented by the Georgia delegation." Eight years later he said substantially the same

thing. "From all the facts I learned from others before and afterwards . . . the selection of Mr. Davis grew out of a misapprehension on the part of some of the delegates of one, or, perhaps two or three of the States, in their consultations of the night before, as to the man that the Georgia delegation had determined to present" (*Constitutional View*, II, p. 329). And further: "What I learned afterwards from others . . . was that some members of the delegations from South Carolina and Florida, and I believe Alabama too, had heard that Georgia intended to present the name of Mr. Howell Cobb" (*Constitutional View*, II, p. 331). Stephens's failure to name specifically who planted the false information may or may not be significant. He may not have known. More likely, he did, but refrained from revealing the name since Tom Cobb was dead by the time his remarks went into print, and Stephens generally observed a policy of not speaking ill of the deceased, even implacable foes.

At this point deduction must lend weight to Cleveland's scanty statement about Tom Cobb's active agency. No Georgian could seriously tell another delegation that his state intended to present Howell Cobb, and mean it. Tom Cobb himself moaned on February 9 that he, his brother, and Bartow were a powerless minority in their delegation (Cobb to Marion Cobb, February 9, 1861, "Correspondence," p. 168). While Nisbet wavered, all the rest—Hill, Kenan, Crawford, Wright—stood solidly behind either Stephens or Toombs, and forced to a choice, would have united on either of those two in preference to Cobb. Thus Howell faced at least a six-to-four majority against him, and in his February 9 letter brother Tom noted that even Nisbet was "half way over," making it more like seven-to-three. Certainly none of those six or seven against Cobb would go to other delegations and lie in an effort to influence their votes *in favor* of him. So that leaves Howell Cobb himself, whose own diffidence, if not the ethics of the time, would have forbade him from doing so, or his brother, or Bartow. While Bartow may have helped, Cleveland points directly to Tom Cobb. And it is significant that three days later Tom Cobb tells his wife that his delegation had decided for brother Howell (Cobb to Marion Cobb, February 11, 1861, "Correspondence," p. 171). Demonstrably that was impossible, unless—again—Georgia offered some *pro forma* complimentary vote to Howell, then changed its vote to Davis, as Rhett suggests. Yet if he meant to tell Marion that Georgia really backed Howell, then here he is telling the same falsehood that *someone* told the other delegations three days earlier. And from his own pen we have his testimony that he did *something* to thwart a Stephens surge. "It was with hard work that we could keep him from being presented for president," Cobb wrote to Marion on February 9, 1861 ("Correspondence," p. 168). In the absence of more, and more revealing, evidence, the above rationale seems the only one that accommodates all of the existing evidence, and that takes into account the established realities within the Georgia delegation and the assumptions common in Montgomery at the time.

88. Mobile, *Daily Advertiser*, February 10, 1861.

89. Barnwell to Orr, February 9, 1861, Orr-Patterson Papers.

90. *Ibid.* Barnwell's February 9 statement that Georgia wanted Howell Cobb is further evidence that someone did, indeed, come to him, at least, and plant the falsehood. Furthermore, writing on February 9 before the election, the Charleston *Mercury* reporter states that probably only Davis and Howell Cobb will receive votes, further evidence of the planted story about Cobb, and information that most logically came from someone on the South Carolina delegation (February 12, 1861).

91. Wilson to Ellett, February 9, 1861, Jones Autograph Letters, Duke; Stephens to Linton Stephens, March 3, 1861, Stephens Papers, MCSH.

92. Rhett notes in *Index Rerum*, Aiken B. Rhett Papers.

93. Rhett, "Government," p. 101.

94. Miles to Walthall, January 27, 1880, Walthall Papers.

95. Rhett notes in *Index Rerum*, Aiken B. Rhett Papers.

96. Woodward and Muhlenfeld, *Private Mary Chesnut*, July 30, 1861, p. 109; Woodward, *Chesnut*, February 19, 1861, p. 6, July 1861, p. 121; T. C. De Leon, "The Real Jefferson Davis in Private and Public Life," *SHSP*, XXXVI (1908), p. 83.

97. Boyce to Hammond, March 17, 1862, Rosser H. Taylor, ed., "Boyce-Hammond Correspondence," *Journal of Southern History*, III (August 1937), p. 350.

98. Chesnut to Walthall, January 24, 1880, Walthall Papers.

99. Rhett in his autobiographical writings after the war said that he, Withers, Keitt, Boyce, *and* Chesnut opposed Davis. Daniel Wallace, Political Life and Services of the Honorable Robert Barnwell Rhett, p. 8, Aiken B. Rhett Papers.

100. Miles to Walthall, January 27, 1880, Walthall Papers.

101. Rhett, "Government," pp. 101–102.

102. Woodward, *Chesnut*, August 25, 1861, p. 162.

103. Woodward, *Chesnut*, February 28, 1861, p. 12, June 27, 1861, p. 79; Woodward and Muhlenfeld, *Private Mary Chesnut*, June 27, 1861, p. 85.

104. Rhett notes in *Index Rerum*, Aiken B. Rhett Papers.

105. Trescott to Rhett, November 1, 1860, Trescott Papers, Miscellaneous Manuscript Collection, LC.; Rhett notes in *Index Rerum*, Aiken B. Rhett Papers.

106. Davis to Robert B. Rhett, Jr., November 10, 1860, Lynda Laswell Crist and Mary Seaton Dix, eds., *The Papers of Jefferson Davis. Volume 6, 1856–1860* (Baton Rouge, 1989), pp. 368–70; Rhett, "Government," p. 102.

107. Barnwell to Orr, February 9, 1861, Orr-Patterson Papers.

108. Rhett, Autobiography, Rhett Papers, SCHS.

109. *Ibid.*; Rhett to Wigfall, April 15, 1864, Louis T. Wigfall Papers, LC.; Rhett notes in *Index Rerum*, Aiken B. Rhett Papers.

110. Since Barnwell subsequently urged Memminger on Davis for secretary of

the treasury, it can at least be speculated that Barnwell was seeking to reward Memminger for his vote. Fitts, "Convention," p. 98, seems to agree. Rhett notes in *Index Rerum*, Aiken B. Rhett Papers.

111. Rhett, Autobiography, Rhett Papers, SCHS; "The Florida delegation proposed to vote for whomsoever South Carolina should support" (Rhett, "Government", p. 10).

112. Lee, *Constitution*, p. 74, says that Owens prefers Rhett, without citing a source. In his highly imaginative 1879 interview, Toombs stated that Owens was "under the influence of Rhett," but also said that Anderson had attended school with Davis (Philadelphia, *Weekly Times*, July 12, 1879). In fact, Davis was fourteen years Anderson's senior, and they did not attend any of the same schools, much less at the same time. Lee also states that Davis helped get Anderson an appointment from Pierce, again without giving a source. Davis did in the 1850's help secure an appointment for a *Robert* Anderson, now commander at Fort Sumter.

113. Johnston and Browne, *Stephens*, p. 390; Stephens, *Constitutional View*, II, p. 328; Campbell to Walthall, July 16, 1879, Walthall Papers.

114. Harris, Memoir, Rowland, *Courts*, p. 328; Harris to Walthall, July 17, 1879, Campbell to Walthall, July 16, 1879, Walthall Papers. Clayton to the Editor, June 17, 1870, Memphis, *Daily Appeal*, June 21, 1870. It needs to be stressed that any statements by Campbell in relation to the election are hearsay, since he was not present.

115. "But for the conviction of Davis' qualities as a military leader, in view of war, the position of the names might have been reversed," Kenner wrote to Roman speaking of the choice of Davis and Stephens (February 9, 1861, La Villebeuvre Family Papers).

116. Roman to Kenner, February 3, 1861, La Villebeuvre Family Papers.

117. Kenner to Walthall, July 28, 1879, Walthall Papers.

118. Montgomery, *Weekly Mail*, February 8, 1861; Montgomery, *Daily Post*, February 13, 1861.

119. Yancey to Benjamin C. Yancey, January 28, 1861, Benjamin C. Yancey Papers, SHC, UNC.

120. William P. Chilton to Davis, March 28, 1886, Rowland, IX, p. 418.

121. Gilmer, Statement, May 1880, Confederate States of America Records, Austin.

122. Withers to McRae, February 7, 1861, McRae Papers.

123. Curry, *Civil History*, p. 52, states that "the qualifications of Davis, Cobb, and Toombs were quietly canvassed."

124. Curry to Walthall, July 28, 1879, Walthall Papers. In his Philadelphia *Weekly Times* interview (July 12, 1879), Toombs says that the Alabama delegation went for Davis "by one vote, by means of what trickery I will not discuss." This may have been a mere alcoholic raving by Toombs, or it could be reference to Tom Cobb's clumsy strategy to elect his brother, which drove Alabama toward Davis instead.

125. Montgomery, *Weekly Mail*, February 15, 1861.

126. Atlanta, *Daily Intelligencer*, February 11, 1861; Charleston, *Mercury*, February 12, 1861.

127. Barnwell to Orr, February 9, 1861, Orr-Patterson Papers.

128. James T. Harrison to his wife, February 9, 1861, Jones, Autograph Letters, Duke.

129. Rhett says that Hill voted against Davis for President. Since Hill was by several accounts not present at this meeting, obviously he could not have voted at all. Rhett would not know this necessarily, and probably assumed such a vote from Hill's known preference for Stephens. Robert B. Rhett, Miscellaneous Notes, Aiken B. Rhett Collection.

130. Stephens, conversation, May 24, 1862, Johnston and Browne, *Stephens*, p. 390.

131. Stephens to the Editor, January 12, 1880, Atlanta, *Daily Constitution*, January 16, 1880; Columbus, Ga., *Sun and Times*, June 28, 1870.

132. Howell Cobb to John A. Cobb, February 10, 1861, Cobb Papers, Georgia.

133. Crawford to Stephens, April 8, 1860, Stephens Papers, LC.

134. There is some minor disagreement among the participants on details here. Tom Cobb says that Alabama, Mississippi, Florida, and South Carolina were for Davis (Cobb to Marion Cobb, February 11, 1861, "Correspondence," p. 171), though in another place in the same letter he says South Carolina was undecided between Davis and Howell. Stephens says that Cobb said Alabama, Florida, South Carolina, and Louisiana went for Davis (Stephens, conversation, May 24, 1862, Johnston and Browne, *Stephens*, p. 390). Mississippi being a known given for Davis, the only real dispute between the sources is Louisiana. Tom Cobb's statement in his February 11 letter that the Pelican state went for Howell is probably as fanciful as his claim that Georgia did as well.

135. Stephens, conversation, May 24, 1862, Johnston and Browne, *Stephens*, p. 390. "I did not understand this then," Stephens said in 1862, "but did afterwards." He gave no explanation of this cryptic remark, but taken in context with his other statements about "someone" telling delegations the night before that Howell Cobb was to be presented, it suggests that he was referring to Tom Cobb's action.

136. Crawford to the Editors, June 25, 1870, Walthall Papers.

137. Stephens, *Constitutional View*, II, p. 330.

138. Incredibly, at this juncture Tom Cobb says that his brother Howell is the one who suggests withdrawing in favor of Davis and unanimity (Cobb to Marion Cobb, February 11, 1861, "Correspondence," p. 171). This despite the fact that Howell himself writes his son John the next day that he declined to be put forward as a candidate (February 10, 1861, Cobb Papers, Georgia), and the demonstrable fact from both contemporary and later sources that Toombs, Stephens, Crawford, Kenan, and Nisbet were all against Cobb's nomination, leaving the Cobb brothers and

Bartow, as Tom Cobb admitted, in a minority. In short, Howell Cobb's name never having been brought up in the caucus, it was not his to withdraw, for unity or any other purpose. As stated earlier, Tom Cobb can only be lying or unbelievably self-deluded.

139. Cobb to Marion Cobb, February 11, 1861, "Correspondence," p. 171, says that Toombs made the nomination and Kenan and Nisbet seconded it. Stephens in his May 24, 1862, statement (Johnston and Browne, *Stephens*, p. 390) says that Kenan made the nomination, and Nisbet and Toombs seconded. The discrepancy seems hardly significant, but Cobb's account, being the earlier, is accepted here.

140. Stephens, conversation, May 24, 1862, Johnston and Browne, *Stephens*, p. 390.

141. Richard M. Johnston to Stephens, February 14, 1861, Stephens Papers, LC; O. A. Lochrane to Stephens, February 18, 1861, Stephens Papers, Emory.

142. Stephens, conversation, May 24, 1862, Johnston and Browne, *Stephens*, p. 390.

143. Howell Cobb to John A. Cobb, February 10, 1861, Cobb Papers, Georgia.

144. Cobb to Marion Cobb, February 11, 1861, "Correspondence," pp. 171–72.

145. Both Stephens and Crawford state that Toombs's nomination was unanimous, and the former also says that his own nomination met no opposition. This can only have been the case if the votes were taken *after* the Cobbs-Bartow walkout. The clue is that Stephens says "at least there was perfect unanimity on the subject, with all the delegates in attendance," which would imply that some members were *not* present at the time the Georgians voted. Stephens, *Constitutional View*, II, pp. 329–30; Crawford to the Editors, June 25, 1870, Walthall Papers.

146. Crawford to the Editors, June 25, 1870, Walthall Papers; Clayton to the Editor, June 17, 1870, Memphis, *Daily Appeal*, June 21, 1870.

147. Chesnut to Walthall, January 24, 1880, Walthall Papers.

148. Stephens, *Constitutional View*, II, pp. 330–31. A rumor would go around Montgomery, and later Richmond, that Toombs only missed the presidency by a single vote. Whether this meant the vote of one state or of a single delegate is not clear, and it is also quite possible that it was Toombs himself, when less than clearheaded, who started the story (New York, *Citizen*, April 20, July 13, 1867).

149. Crawford to the Editors, June 25, 1870, Walthall Papers.

150. Stephens, *Constitutional View*, II, p. 333.

151. Montgomery, *Weekly Mail*, February 15, 1861.

152. Cobb to Marion Cobb, February 11, 1861, "Correspondence," p. 172.

153. Rome, Ga., *Tri-Weekly Courier*, February 12, 1861.

154. U.S. Congress, *Journal*, p. 39.

155. Rome, *Tri-Weekly Courier*, February 12, 1861.
156. Cobb to Marion Cobb, February 9, 1861, "Correspondence," p. 169, February 12, 1861, pp. 173–74.
157. Rome, *Tri-Weekly Courier*, February 12, 1861.
158. Montgomery, *Weekly Advertiser*, February 13, 1861.
159. *Ibid.*
160. *Ibid.*
161. Stephens to Linton Stephens, February 9, 1861, Stephens Papers, MCSH.
162. Rhett in his autobiography states that Georgia also nominated Howell Cobb and then voted for him, afterward changing its vote to make the decision for Davis unanimous. His son, whose *Battles and Leaders* article is taken almost exclusively from the father's memoir, says the same. It is preposterous, for all of the reasons before stated. Cobb never at any time had anything close to sufficient support in his own delegation for it to agree upon nominating him. It is conceivable—but purely speculation—that Georgia might have offered some form of complimentary nomination to a less-than-favorite son for his service as president of the convention, but nothing more. Much more likely is that the embittered Rhett, writing after the war with a pen brimming with hatred for Davis, simply invented the story in the hope of tarnishing the supposed unanimity of Davis's election. Rhett, Autobiography, Rhett Papers, SCHS; Rhett, "Government," p. 103.
163. Kenner to Walthall, July 28, 1879, Walthall Papers.
164. Cobb to Marion Cobb, February 11, 1861, "Correspondence," p. 172.
165. Reed, *Brother's War*, pp. 272–73.
166. Rhett notes in *Index Rerum*, Aiken B. Rhett Papers.
167. DuBose, *Yancey*, II, p. 586.
168. Rhett to Elise Rhett, February 11, 1861, in White, *Rhett*, p. 194n.
169. U.S. Congress, *Journal*, p. 40.
170. Cobb to Marion Cobb, February 9, 1861, "Correspondence," pp. 168–69.
171. *Ibid.*, February 15, 1861, pp. 177–78.
172. Necessarily, much of the description of the electioneering in this chapter has been informed speculation, based upon all of the available sources, which are lamentably few and subject to considerable interpretation. Many are years after the fact, and obviously colored by hindsight, old grudges, and a desire to present a united face to posterity. Alexander M. Clayton spoke to this last impulse when he told Walthall on July 19, 1879, that "it would be very unwise now, in my belief, to get up strife in regard to what transpired . . . at Montgomery" (Atlanta, *Daily Constitution*, December 28, 1879). To date, no exhaustive study of the election has been done, though it is touched on in biographies of all the participants in varying degrees. Even this author's *Jefferson Davis, The*

Man and Hour (New York, 1991) contains flaws revealed by the research for this present volume. Ralph Richardson, "The Choice of Jefferson Davis as Confederate President," *Journal of Mississippi History*, XVII (July 1955), pp. 161–76, is the only discrete monograph to attempt to deal with the subject, but it is simplistic and based almost entirely on secondary sources. The subject may never be completely understood. Too much is simply missing from the record, and any presentation of the story will necessarily rely heavily upon interpretation. James Chesnut has the last word on the study of the election. "It involves an aggregation of differing recollections," he told Walthall on January 24, 1880 (Walthall Papers), "out of which, however, I think you will have no trouble in evolving the truth." As of this writing, that "truth" is still evolving.

6. Getting Along with Seven-League Boots

1. Montgomery, *Weekly Advertiser*, February 13, 1861.
2. Hoole, *Hooper*, p. 160.
3. Sanford, *Code*, p. 50.
4. Montgomery, *Weekly Mail*, February 15, 1861; Rome, *Tri-Weekly Courier*, February 12, 1861.
5. Baton Rouge, *Daily Advocate*, February 17, 1861.
6. Memphis, *Daily Memphis Avalanche*, February 13, 1861.
7. Miles to Pickens, February 9, 1861, William Porcher Miles Papers, Miscellaneous Manuscript Collection, LC.
8. Keitt to Jamison, February 9, 1861, Jamison Papers.
9. F. M. Robertson to S. J. Crawford, February 15, 1861, *OR*, II, 2, p. 612.
10. Williamson S. Oldham, Memoirs, p. 189, Center for American History, Austin. University of Texas.
11. Baton Rouge, *Daily Advocate*, February 17, 1861.
12. Harrison to his wife, February 9, 1861, Jones, Autograph Letters, Duke.
13. Stephens to Linton Stephens, February 9, 1861, Stephens Papers, MCSH.
14. U.S. Congress, *Journal*, pp. 40–41; Montgomery, *Weekly Advertiser*, February 13, 1861.
15. Charleston, *Mercury*, February 12, 1861.
16. Montgomery, *Daily Mail*, February 11, 1861.
17. Charleston, *Mercury*, February 18, 1861.
18. Columbia, *Daily South Carolinian*, February 20, 1861.
19. Charleston, *Mercury*, February 18, 1861.
20. Columbus, Ga., *Daily Columbus Enquirer*, February 16, 1861.
21. Montgomery, *Daily Mail*, February 11, 1861.
22. Rhett to "Mr. Editor," n.d. [February 1862], Rhett Papers, SCL, USC.
23. Charleston, *Mercury*, February 12, 1861.
24. Cobb to Marion Cobb, February 10, 1861, "Correspondence," p. 170, February 11, 1861, p. 172.

25. Baton Rouge, *Daily Advocate*, February 17, 1861.
26. Hoole, "Flag," pp. 111–12.
27. Toombs et al. to Davis, February 9, 1861, *PJD*, VII, p. 36.
28. Nashville, *Daily Gazette*, February 8, 1861.
29. Lee S. Daniel, "Notice to President Davis of His Election," *Confederate Veteran*, XIII (August 1905), p. 369.
30. Davis to John Callan, February 7, 1861, *PJD*, VII, pp. 34–35.
31. William C. Davis, *Jefferson Davis, The Man and His Hour* (New York, 1991), p. 8.
32. Davis, *Memoir*, II, pp. 18–19.
33. Davis to Franklin Stringfellow, June 4, 1878, *PJD, VII, p. 29n.*
34. *Robert McElroy, Jefferson Davis. The Unreal and the Real* (New York, 1937), I, p. 266. McElroy offers no source for this quote, but it is entirely in character for Davis.
35. Daniel, "Notice," p. 369.
36. Montgomery, *Weekly Mail*, February 22, 1861.
37. George Petrie to Stephens, February 10, 1861, Stephens Papers, LC..
38. Stephens to Linton Stephens, February 10, 1861, Stephens Papers, MCSH.
39. Rome, *Tri-Weekly Courier*, February 16, 1861.
40. Manly to Basil Manly, Jr., February 10, 1861, Manly Family Papers.
41. Cobb to Marion Cobb, February 10, 1861, "Correspondence," p. 171.
42. Howell Cobb to John Cobb, February 10, 1861, Cobb Papers, Georgia.
43. Stephens to Linton Stephens, February 11, 1861, Stephens Papers, MCSH.
44. Jones and Rogers, "Montgomery," February 11, 1861, p. 19; Stephens to Linton Stephens, February 11, 1861, Stephens Papers, MCSH.
45. U.S. Congress, *Journal*, pp. 42–44; Montgomery, *Weekly Advertiser*, February 13, 1861.
46. Stephens to Linton Stephens, February 10, 1861, Stephens Papers, MCSH.
47. Johnston and Browne, *Stephens*, p. 451.
48. Jones and Rogers, "Montgomery," February 11, 1861, p. 20.
49. Montgomery, *Weekly Advertiser*, February 13, 1861.
50. Cobb to Marion Cobb, February 11, 1861, "Correspondence," p. 172.
51. Manly to Basil Manly, Jr., February 11, 1861, Manly Family Papers.
52. Jones and Rogers, "Montgomery," February 11, 1861, p. 20.
53. Montgomery, *Daily Post*, February 13, 1861; Montgomery, *Weekly Advertiser*, February 13, 1861.
54. Stephens to Linton Stephens, February 15, March 3, 1861, Stephens Papers, MCSH.
55. Stephens to Linton Stephens, February 15, 1861, Stephens Papers, MCSH.
56. Wigfall to Walker, February 11, 1861, OR, I, 53, p. 124.
57. Pickens to Miles, February 11, 1861, Miles Papers, SHC, UNC; Brown to Stephens, February 12, 1861, Stephens Papers, Emory.

58. Johnson to Stephens, February 12, 1861, Johnson Papers, Duke.
59. Mobile, *Daily Advertiser*, February 12, 1861.
60. Curry to W.W. Anderson, February 20, 1861, clipping from March ——, 1884 issue of the Atlanta, *Constitution*, in Scrapbook F1, George Petrie Collection, Auburn.
61. Linton Stephens to Stephens, February 12, 1861, Stephens Papers, MCSH.
62. Hammond to M. C. M. Hammond, March 1, 1861, Hammond to J. D. Ashmore, April 2, 1861, Hammond Papers.
63. Henry S. Benning to Howell Cobb, February 13, 1861, Cobb Papers, Georgia.
64. Woodward, *Chesnut*, [April 2, 1861], p. 40.
65. New Orleans, *Daily Delta*, February 14, March 8, 1861; New Orleans, *Daily Picayune*, February 10, 1861; New Orleans, *Bee*, February 11, 1861.
66. Columbia, *Daily South Carolinian*, February 14, 19, 1861.
67. Nashville, *Daily Gazette*, February 10, 1861.
68. Natchez, *Daily Free Trader*, February 16, 1861.
69. Grove Hill, Alabama, *Clark County Democrat*, February 14, 1861.
70. James J. Deas to James Chesnut, Sr., February 12, 1861, Chesnut Papers, Duke.
71. Columbia, *Daily South Carolinian*, February 14, 1861
72. Hooper to John DeBerniere Hooper, February 22, 1861, Hooper Papers.
73. Howell Cobb to Augustus R. Wright, February 18, 1861, Stephens Papers, LC.
74. Stephens to Wright, February 18, 1861, Stephens Papers, LC.
75. Cobb to Marion Cobb, February 7, 1861, "Correspondence," p. 166, February 15, 1861, p. 178, February 18 [17], 1861, p. 181.
76. Bartow to John L. Branch, February 16, 1861, Margaret Branch Sexton Collection.
77. Curry to Anderson, February 20, 1861, George Petrie Papers, Auburn University Library, Auburn, Ala.
78. Wilson to Ellett, February 9, 1861, Jones, Autograph Letters, Duke.
79. Charleston, *Mercury*, February 13, 1861.
80. Clayton speech, Claiborne Papers.
81. Nisbet to Linton Stephens, February 19, 1861, Stephens Papers, Emory.
82. Crawford to the Editors, June 25, 1870, Walthall Papers.
83. Wilson to Ellett, February 9, 1861, Jones, Autograph Letters, Duke.
84. Rome, *Tri-Weekly Courier*, February 16, 1861.
85. Charleston, *Mercury, February 9, 1861*.
86. Barnwell to Orr, February 9, 1861, Orr-Patterson Papers.
87. Pickens to Miles, February 7, 1861, Miles Papers, SHC, UNC.
88. Miles to Pickens, February 9, 1861, Miles Papers, LC.
89. Keitt to Jamison, February 9, 1861, Jamison Papers.
90. Rhett to Robert B. Rhett, Jr., February 11, 1861, Rhett Papers, SCL, USC.

91. Clayton speech, Claiborne Papers.

92. U.S. Congress, *Journal*, p. 47.

93. Cobb to Moore, February 12, 1861, Governors Papers, Military Correspondence, ADAH; Natchez, *Daily Courier*, February 13, 1861.

94. Wigfall to Walker, February 11, 1861, OR, I, 53, p. 123; Cobb to Marion Cobb, February 18 [17], 1861, "Correspondence," p. 181.

95. Cobb to Marion Cobb, February 19, 1861, "Correspondence," pp. 184–85.

96. Deas to Chesnut, February 12, 1861, Chesnut Papers, Duke.

97. Richmond, *Daily Examiner*, July 22, 1861.

98. Deas to Chesnut, February 12, 1861, Chesnut Papers, Duke.

99. Cobb to Mary Ann Lamar Cobb, February 16, 1861, Cobb Papers, Georgia.

100. Cobb to Marion Cobb, February 12, 1861, "Correspondence," pp. 172–73.

101. Wilson to Ellett, February 9, 1861, Jones, Autograph Letters, Duke.

102. Augusta, Ga., *Daily Constitutionalist*, February 16, 1861.

103. Macon, *Weekly Telegraph*, February 21, 1861.

104. Cobb to Marion Cobb, February 13, 1861, "Correspondence," p. 175; Cobb to ?, February 13, 1861, David C. Barrow Papers, University of Georgia Library, Athens.

105. Cobb to Marion Cobb, February 14, 1861, "Correspondence," pp. 175–76.

106. Keitt to Susan Keitt, February 19, 1861, Keitt Papers, Duke.

107. Bartow to Branch, February 16, 1861, Sexton Collection.

108. U.S. Congress, *Journal*, pp. 48–51, 61; Montgomery, *Weekly Advertiser*, February 20, 1861.

109. Memminger, *Plan of a Provisional Government*, p. 6.

110. Miles to Pickens, February 9, 1861, Miles Papers, LC.

111. U.S. Congress, *Journal*, pp. 53, 55, 56–58.

112. *Ibid.*, pp. 45, 46, 52, 55.

113. Keitt to Hammond, February 13, 1861, Hammond Papers, LC.

114. U.S. Congress, *Journal*, pp. 46, 49; White, *Rhett*, pp. 196–97.

115. U.S. Congress, *Journal*, pp. 50, 51, 56, 58, 60–61, 61–62.

116. Keitt to Susan Keitt, February 19, 1861, Keitt Papers, Duke.

117. Augusta, *Daily Constitutionalist*, February 16, 1861.

118. U.S. Congress, *Journal*, p. 54.

119. New York, *Citizen*, April 27, 1867.

120. Stephens to Linton Stephens, March 3, 1861, Stephens Papers, MCSH.

121. Cobb to Marion Cobb, February 12, 1861, "Correspondence," p. 174.

122. Oldham, Memoirs, pp. 61–62.

123. Montgomery, *Weekly Advertiser*, March 6, 1861; Stephens to Linton Stephens, March 3, 1861, Stephens Papers, MCSH.

124. Brewer, W. *Alabama, Her History, Resources, War Record, and Public Men from 1540 to 1872* (Montgomery, 1872), p. 477.

125. Cobb to Marion Cobb, February 13, 1861, "Correspondence," p. 175.
126. *Ibid.*, February 16, 1861, p. 179.
127. Howell Cobb to John A. Cobb, February 15, 1861, Cobb Papers, Georgia.
128. Hooper to John DeBerniere Hooper, February 22, 1861, Hooper Papers.
129. Nisbet to Linton Stephens, February 19, 1861, Stephens Papers, Emory.
130. Rhett to Robert B. Rhett, Jr., February 11, 1861, Rhett Papers, SCL, USC.
131. Stephens to James P. Hambleton, February 22, 1861, James Pinckney Hambleton Papers, Emory University, Woodruff Library, Atlanta, Georgia.
132. Stephens to Linton Stephens, February 15, 1861, Stephens Papers, MCSH.
133. New Orleans, *Delta*, March 1, 1861.
134. Columbus, Ga., *Daily Times*, February 14, 1861.
135. Montgomery, *Weekly Montgomery Confederation*, February 15, 1861.
136. Richmond, *Daily Examiner*, July 7, 1862.
137. Mobile, *Daily Advertiser*, February 19, 1861.
138. Montgomery, *Weekly Advertiser*, February 13, 1861; Montgomery, *Daily Post*, February 18, 1861; New Orleans, *Daily Delta*, February 26, 1861.
139. Mobile, *Daily Advertiser*, February 15, 1861.
140. Curry to Anderson, February 20, 1861, Petrie Papers.
141. Yearns, Wilfred Buck, *The Confederate Congress* (Athens, Ga., 1960), p. 11. Unfortunately, Yearns gives no source for this anecdote.
142. Stephens to Linton Stephens, February 15, 1861, Stephens Papers, MCSH.
143. James Morgan to Stephens, February 11, 1861, Stephens Papers, Emory.
144. H. P. Hemenway to Stephens, March 1, 1861, Stephens Papers, Duke; Stephens to Linton Stephens, February 17, 1861, Stephens Papers, MCSH.
145. Stephens to Linton Stephens, March 3, 1861, MCSH. Stephens does not precisely date the party, but the only flag speech made by Boyce was February 13, which dates it adequately (U.S. Congress, *Journal*, p. 48).
146. Kenan and Toombs to Stephens and Hill, February 14, 1861, Stephens Papers, Emory.
147. Stephens to Linton Stephens, February 15, 1861, Stephens Papers, MCSH.
148. Cobb to Marion Cobb, February 16, 1861, "Correspondence," p. 179.
149. Stephens to Linton Stephens, February 15, 1861, Stephens Papers, MCSH.
150. Stephens to Linton Stephens, February 17, 1861, Stephens Papers, MCSH.
151. William Waddell to Howell Cobb, February 12, 1861, Howell Cobb to Howell Cobb, Jr., February 15, 1861, Howell Cobb Papers, Georgia.
152. Stephens to Linton Stephens, February 17, 1861, Stephens Papers, MCSH.

153. Cobb to Marion Cobb, February 14, 1861, "Correspondence," p. 176, February 15, 1861, p. 178.

154. Stephens to Linton Stephens, March 3, 1861, Stephens Papers, MCSH.

155. Jones and Rogers, "Montgomery," February 11, 1861, p. 21.

156. Jones and Rogers, "Montgomery," February 11, 1861, p. 21, February 12, 1861, pp. 22–23.

157. Rhett to Robert B. Rhett, Jr., February 11, 861, Rhett Papers, SCL, USC.

158. Cobb to Marion Cobb, February 12, 1861, "Correspondence," p. 174.

159. Charleston, *Mercury*, February 25, 1861.

160. *Ibid.*, February 20, 1861.

161. Trescott to Miles, February 17, 1861, Miles Papers, SHC, UNC.

162. Charleston, *Mercury*, February 27, March 1, 1861.

163. Rhett to Robert B. Rhett, February 12, 1861, and n.d. [1862], Rhett Papers, SCL, USC.

164. Woodward and Muhlenfeld, *Private Mary Chesnut*, February 26, 1861, p. 13; Wigfall to Davis, February 18, 1861, Jones, Autograph Letters, Duke.

165. New Orleans, *Daily Delta*, February 22, 1861.

166. Woodward, *Chesnut*, August 13, 1861, p. 142.

167. Macon, *Telegraph*, February 22, 1861.

168. New York, *Citizen*, April 20, 1867.

169. Harrison to Susan Harrison, February 17, 1861, Harrison Papers.

170. Montgomery, *Weekly Mail*, February 15, 1861.

171. Montgomery, *Daily Post*, February 22, 1861.

172. Jones and Rogers, "Montgomery," February 13, 1861, pp. 25–26.

173. Montgomery, *Weekly Mail*, February 15, 1861.

174. Jones and Rogers, "Montgomery," February 16, 1861, p. 29.

175. Cobb to Marion Cobb, February 8, 1861, "Correspondence," p. 168, February 13, 1861, p. 174.

176. Howell Cobb to John A. Cobb, February 15, 1861, Cobb Papers, Georgia.

177. Augusta, *Daily Constitutionalist*, February 15, 1861.

178. Haskell Monroe, "Early Confederate Political Patronage," *Alabama Review*, XX (January 1967), pp. 52–53.

179. P. G. T. Beauregard to Davis, February 10, 1861, P. G. T. Beauregard Papers, Duke University Library, Durham, N.C.

180. Wigfall to Walker, February 11, 1861, OR, I, 53, p. 124.

181. Carter Butterfield to John Forsyth, February 15, 1861, McRae Papers.

182. H. O. Brewer to McRae, February 5, 1861, McRae Papers.

183. James Conden to Davis, February 11, 1861, Confederate States of America Papers, LC; William G. Jones to McRae, February 9, 1861, McRae Papers.

184. William Shubrick to Chesnut, February 7, 1861, Williams-Chesnut-Manning Family Papers, SCL, USC.

185. Montgomery, *Weekly Montgomery Confederation*, February 22, 1861; Atlanta, *Gate City Guardian*, February 16, 1861.
186. Mobile, *Daily Advertiser*, February 15, 1861.
187. Jones and Rogers, "Montgomery," February 10, 1861, p. 18.
188. Montgomery City Council Minutes, February 14, 1861, ADAH.

7. The Man and the Hour Have Met

1. New Orleans, *Times-Democrat*, February 16, 1902.
2. Vicksburg, *Weekly Vicksburg Citizen*, February 12, 13, 1861; New York, *Times*, February 22, 1861.
3. Vicksburg, *Weekly Vicksburg Citizen*, February 20, 1861; Davis to Pettus, February 12, 1861, Rowland, V, p. 46.
4. Jefferson Davis, *The Rise and Fall of the Confederate States Government* (New York, 1881), I, p. 230.
5. Richmond, *Whig*, February 15, 1861.
6. Davis to Varina Davis, February 14, 1861, *PJD*, VII, p. 40.
7. Davis, *Rise and Fall*, I, p. 230.
8. Vicksburg, *Daily Evening Citizen*, April 4, 1861.
9. Atlanta, *Gate-City Guardian*, February 16, 1861.
10. Vicksburg, *Daily Evening Citizen*, April 4, 1861.
11. J. Norcross to Stephens, February 24, 1861, Stephens Papers, LC.
12. Charleston, *Mercury*, February 21, 1861.
13. Columbus, Ga., *Daily Times*, March 14, 1861.
14. Montgomery, *Weekly Montgomery Confederation*, February 22, 1861.
15. Montgomery, *Weekly Advertiser*, February 22, 1861.
16. Montgomery, *Weekly Advertiser*, February 20, 1861.
17. Atlanta, *Gate-City Guardian*, February 18, 1861.
18. Montgomery, *Weekly Advertiser*, February 20, 1861.
19. Columbus, *Daily Columbus Enquirer*, February 19, 1861.
20. Montgomery, *Weekly Advertiser*, February 20, 1861.
21. Thomas H. Watts, *Address of . . . on The Life and Character of Ex-President Jefferson Davis* (Montgomery, 1889), pp. 14–15.
22. Gilmer Statement, May 1880, Confederate States of America Records, Texas.
23. *Ibid.*
24. Jones and Rogers, "Montgomery," February 16, 1861, pp. 29–30; Nashville, *Union & American*, February 20, 1861; Montgomery, *Weekly Mail*, March 1, 1861.
25. Cobb to Marion Cobb, February 18 [17], 1861, "Correspondence," p. 181.
26. Columbia, *Daily South Carolinian*, February 19, 1861.
27. New York, *World*, April 28, 1886.
28. Nashville, *Union & American*, February 20, 1861.

29. Cobb to Marion Cobb, February 18 [17], 1861, "Correspondence," p. 181.
30. New Orleans, *Daily Delta*, February 27, 1861.
31. Estvan, *War Pictures*, pp. 29–30, 31, 38.
32. Cobb to Marion Cobb, February 16, 1861, "Correspondence," p. 180.
33. Stephens to Linton Stephens, February 17, 1861, Stephens Papers, MCSH.
34. Montgomery, *Weekly Mail*, March 1, 1861; Cobb to Marion Cobb, February 18 [17], 1861, "Correspondence," p. 181.
35. Cobb to Marion Cobb, February 15, 1861, "Correspondence," p. 178.
36. Montgomery, *Weekly Advertiser*, February 20, 1861.
37. Harrison to Susan Harrison, February 17, 1861, Harrison Papers.
38. Davis, *Memoir*, II, p. 919.
39. Northrop to Davis, April 17, 1879, Rowland, VIII, p. 380.
40. Davis, *Memoir*, II, p. 919.
41. Davis to Northrop, April 25, 1879, Rowland, VIII, p. 383.
42. Northrop to Davis, July 25, 1881, Rowland, IX, p. 5.
43. Davis, *Memoir*, II, p. 302.
44. New York, *Tribune*, May 20, 1861.
45. Richmond, *Enquirer*, February 15, 1861.
46. Davis, *Memoir*, II, pp. 922–23.
47. *Ibid.*, II, p. 920.
48. *Ibid.*, p. 918.
49. Richmond, *Whig*, June 3, 1861.
50. New York, *Citizen*, September 21, 1867.
51. Davis, *Davis*, is the most recent and to date most thorough biography, though the literature on the man is extensive.
52. Davis, *Rise and Fall*, I, p. 231.
53. Montgomery, *Weekly Montgomery Confederation*, February 15, 1861.
54. Augusta, *Daily Constitutionalist*, February 20, 1861.
55. William Preston Johnston to Rosa Johnston, May 22, 1862, Mason Barret Collection, Howard Tilton Library, Tulane University, New Orleans.
56. Congress, *Journal*, pp. 53–54.
57. Montgomery, *Daily Post*, February 18, 1861.
58. Montgomery, *Weekly Mail*, March 1, 1861.
59. Ellen Noyes to Mary Noyes, February 20, 1861, in Virginia K. Jones, ed., "A Contemporary Account of the Inauguration of Jefferson Davis," *Alabama Historical Quarterly*, XXIII (Fall–Winter 1961), pp. 273–74.
60. Thomas Blanchard Diary, February 18, 1861, in Etta Worsley Blanchard, *Columbus on the Chattahoochee* (Columbus, Ga., 1951), p. 274.
61. Montgomery, *Weekly Mail*, February 22, 1861.
62. *Ibid.*
63. Columbus, *Daily South Carolinian*, February 20, 1861.
64. Augusta, *Daily Constitutionalist*, February 20, 1861.
65. Montgomery, *Weekly Advertiser*, February 20, 1861.
66. Manly Diary, February 18, 1861, Manly Family Papers.

67. New York, *Herald*, February 23, 1861.
68. Montgomery, *Weekly Mail*, February 22, 1861; Montgomery City Council Minutes, March 18, 1861, ADAH; "When the Band First Played 'Dixie'," *Confederate Veteran*, XXXIV (June 1926), p. 234.
69. Confederate States of America Provisional Constitution, Museum of the Confederacy, Richmond.
70. Cobb to Marion Cobb, February 18, 1861, "Correspondence," p. 183.
71. Montgomery, *Weekly Advertiser*, February 20, 1861.
72. Montgomery, *Daily Post*, February 19, 1861.
73. Atlanta, *Intelligencer*, February 21, 1861.
74. Clipping from unidentified Vermont newspaper, September 8, 1927, in possession of Capt. John Culver; Evelyn Lovejoy, *History of Royalton, Vermont* (n.p., 1911), p. 735.
75. Peter Brannon, ed., "Some Early Montgomery Records," *Alabama Historical Quarterly*, XVIII (Spring 1956), p. 117.
76. Atlanta, *Intelligencer*, February 21, 1861.
77. Rhett notes in *Index Rerum*, Aiken B. Rhett Papers.
78. Ellen Noyes to Mary Noyes, February 19, 1861, Jones, "Account," p. 274.
79. Atlanta, *Intelligencer*, February 21, 1861; Augusta, *Daily Constitutionalist*, February 20, 1861.
80. Cobb to Marion Cobb, February 18, 1861, "Correspondence," p. 182.
81. Woodward and Muhlenfeld, *Private Mary Chesnut*, February 25, 1861, p. 12.
82. U.S. Congress, *Journal*, p. 63.
83. Charleston, *Mercury*, February 22, 1861; Woodward and Muhlenfeld, *Private Mary Chesnut*, February 25, 1861, p. 12.
84. Henry D. Capers, *The Life and Times of C. G. Memminger* (Richmond, 1893), p. 308; New York, *Herald*, February 23, 1861; Ellen Noyes to Mary Noyes, February 19, 1861, Jones, "Account," p. 274; Brannon, "Early Montgomery Records," p. 119.
85. Nashville, *Union & American*, April 26, 1861.
86. Montgomery, *Weekly Mail*, February 22 1861; Mobile, *Daily Advertiser*, February 21, 1861.
87. Barnwell to wife, February 18, 1861, Jones, Autograph Letters, Duke.
88. William B. Ochiltree to the Editor, February 18, 1861, Dallas, *Herald*, March 13, 1861.
89. Nashville, *Union & American*, February 19, 1861.
90. Rome, *Tri-Weekly Courier*, February 21, 1861; Brannan, "Early Montgomery Records," p. 118.
91. Prayer by Rev. Dr. Basil Manly, Museum of the Confederacy.
92. Charleston, *Mercury*, February 22, 1861.
93. "How Davis Took the Oath," *The Vedette*, VII (June 1886), p. 13.
94. Ochiltree to the Editor, February 18, 1861, Dallas, *Herald*, March 13, 1861.
95. Sanford, Code, p. 33.

96. George W. Halls, "Cadet Company of Alabama," *Confederate Veteran*, XXX (April, 1922), p. 130.

97. U.S. Congress, *Journal*, pp. 64–66.

98. *Ibid.*, pp. 28, 37.

99. New York, *Herald*, February 23, 1861; Blanchard Diary, February 18, 1861, Blanchard, *Columbus*, p. 275; Mobile, *Daily Advertiser*, February 21, 1861.

100. Atlanta, *Southern Confederacy*, April 2, 1861.

101. New York, *Harper's Weekly Illustrated Newspaper*, March 9, 1861.

102. DuBose, *Yancey*, p. 587.

103. Howell Cobb to his wife, February 20, 1861, Cobb Papers, Georgia.

104. Howell Cobb to Wright, February 18, 1861, Stephens Papers, LC.

105. Barnwell to his wife, February 18, 1861, Jones, Autograph Letters, Duke.

106. Ellen Noyes to Mary Noyes, February 19, 1861, Jones, "Account," p. 274.

107. Montgomery, *Weekly Montgomery Confederation*, February 22, 1861.

108. Woodward and Muhlenfeld, *Private Mary Chesnut*, February 25, 1861, p. 12.

109. Mobile, *Daily Advertiser*, February 21, 1861.

110. Manly to "Dear Children," February 26, 1861, Manly Family Papers.

111. Charleston, *Mercury*, February 22, 1861; U.S. Congress, *Journal*, p. 63.

112. Davis to Varina Davis, February 20, 1861, *PJD*, VII, p. 53.

113. Stephens to Linton Stephens, February 18, 1861, Stephens Papers, MCSH.

114. Brannon, "Early Montgomery Records," p. 118; Cobb to Marion Cobb, February 18, 1861, "Correspondence," p. 182.

115. Cobb to Marion Cobb, February 18, 1861, "Correspondence," p. 183.

116. Charleston, *Mercury*, February 22, 1861; Montgomery, *Daily Post*, February 18, 1861.

117. Montgomery, *Weekly Mail*, February 22, 1861.

118. Ellen Noyes to Mary Noyes, February 19, 1861, Jones, "Account," p. 275.

119. Hoole, *Hooper*, p. 240n.

120. Ellen Noyes to Mary Noyes, February 19, 1861, Jones, "Account," pp. 274–75.

121. Cobb to Marion Cobb, February 19, 1861, "Correspondence," p. 184.

122. Savannah, *Daily Morning News*, February 21, 1861; Augusta, *Daily Constitutionalist*, February 21, 1861.

123. Ellen Noyes to Mary Noyes, February 19, 1861, Jones, "Account," p. 275.

124. Selma, *Weekly Times*, February 19, 1861.

125. Augusta, *Daily Constitutionalist*, February 21, 1861.

126. Montgomery City Council Minutes, February 25, 1861, ADAH.

127. Montgomery, *Weekly Mail*, March 8, 1861.

128. Intercepted Telegrams, 1861, Record Group 107, Volume 399, NA.

129. Wigfall to Davis, February 18, 1861, *PJD*, VII, p. 51.

130. New York, *Harper's Weekly Illustrated Newspaper*, March 9, 1861.

8. We Are at Work

1. Mobile, *Daily Advertiser*, February 21, 23, 1861; Washington, *Evening Star*, February 19, 1861; Montgomery, *Daily Post*, February 19, 1861; Howell Cobb to his wife, February 20, 1861, Cobb Papers, Georgia; New York, *Herald*, February 20, 1861; Charleston, *Mercury*, February 23, 1861; Columbia, *Daily South Carolinian*, February 23, 1861.
2. Columbia, *Daily South Carolinian*, February 23, 1861; Mobile, *Daily Advertiser*, February 23, 1861.
3. Howell Cobb to Mary Ann Lamar Cobb, February 16, 1861, Cobb Papers, Georgia.
4. Washington, *Evening Star*, March 14, 1861.
5. Richmond, *Whig*, April 27, 1861.
6. McElroy, *Davis*, I, p. 274. McElroy gives no source for this quote, and the author has been unable to find one. While unusually humble for Davis, still it is the sort of thing he would have said without realizing that he did not mean it.
7. Davis, *Rise and Fall*, I, p. 241.
8. Mobile, *Daily Advertiser*, February 24, 1861.
9. Statement of Benjamin C. Yancey, 1886, John W. DuBose Papers, ADAH; DuBose, *Yancey*, II, p. 588.
10. Davis, *Rise and Fall*, I, pp. 241–42.
11. Barnwell to his wife, February 18, 1861, Jones, Autograph Letters, Duke.
12. Cobb to Marion Cobb, February 20, 1861, "Correspondence," p. 234.
13. Charleston, *Mercury*, March 9, 1861.
14. Cobb to Marion Cobb, February 20, 1861, "Correspondence," p. 234.
15. Stephens to Hambleton, February 22, 1861, Hambleton Papers.
16. Cobb to Marion Cobb, February 18 [17], 1861, "Correspondence," p. 181; Howell Cobb to his wife, February 20, 1861, Cobb Papers, Georgia.
17. Davis, *Rise and Fall*, I, pp. 241–42; Stephens conversation, winter 1862–63, Johnston and Browne, *Stephens*, pp. 62–63.
18. Cobb to Marion Cobb, February 19, 1861, "Correspondence," p. 184. Cobb says that as of his writing on February 19 Davis had spoken only with Stephens and Memminger leading to the inference that the meetings both took place the day before, and the logical conclusion that the interview with Memminger was to offer the Treasury post.
19. Stephens to Linton Stephens, February 19, 1861, Stephens Papers, MCSH; Cobb to Marion Cobb, February 19, 1861, "Correspondence," pp. 183–84.
20. Rhett, Autobiography; John G. Shorter to Rhett, July 25, 1866, Rhett Papers, SCHS.
21. Howell Cobb to his wife, February 20, 1861, Cobb Papers, Georgia; Cobb to Marion Cobb, February 18 [17], 1861, "Correspondence," p. 181.
22. Cobb to Marion Cobb, February 26, 1861, "Correspondence," p. 242.
23. Montgomery, *Weekly Mail*, April 12, 1861.

24. Jones and Rogers, "Montgomery," April 1, 1861, p. 59.

25. Capers, *Memminger*, p. 309.

26. Brewer, *Alabama*, p. 479n.

27. Toombs to Davis, February 19, 1861, *PJD*, VII, p. 53; Stephens conversation, winter 1862–63, Johnston and Browne, *Stephens*, p. 426; Stephens statement, November 30, 1862, Johnston, *Autobiography*, p. 165.

28. Virginia Clay-Clopton, *A Belle of the Fifties* (New York, 1905), p. 157.

29. Statement of Benjamin C. Yancey, 1886, DuBose Papers; DuBose, *Yancey*, p. 588.

30. Jones and Rogers, "Montgomery," February 20, 1861.

31. H. L. Clay to Clement C. Clay, February 11, 1861, Clement C. Clay Papers, Duke; New Orleans, *Daily Delta*, February 28, 1861.

32. Russell, *My Diary*, I, pp. 95, 174.

33. Columbus, *Daily South Carolinian*, April 1, 1861.

34. Montgomery, *Weekly Mail*, March 8, 1861.

35. New York, *Citizen*, April 13, 27, 1867.

36. Le Roy Pope Walker to Michael L. Woods, January 16, 1906, Michael L. Woods Papers, ADAH.

37. "Taps," *Southern Bivouac*, I (May–June, 1883), p. 394. Capers here erroneously dates his order as February 18, when it could not have been done before the next day, which conforms with his fuller recollections in Capers, *Memminger*, p. 309.

38. De Leon, *Four Years in Rebel Capitals*, p. 37.

39. Rome, *Tri-Weekly Courier*, March 3, 1861; Huntsville, *Democrat*, April 3, 1861. Unfortunately, not single 1861 source pinpoints exactly which corner at Commerce and Bibb the building sat on, and later recollections and secondary sources have put it variously on all four corners. Moreover, since the government later occupied two other nearby and adjacent buildings, recollections—especially Capers'—confuse one building with another. Research by Miriam Jones in 1850s plat maps and an 1872 bird's eye view map clearly establish that the Montgomery Insurance Building, the first "Government House," can only have sat on the northwest corner.

40. Rome, *Tri-Weekly Courier*, March 3, 1861. Capers's later description of the interior of the government building (*Memminger*, p. 330) is completely at odds with this, the only directly contemporary account of its layout. The most likely conclusion would seem to be that Capers described the offices as they were toward the end of Montgomery's time as capital, rather than at the beginning. He may also have been describing one of the other buildings nearby that soon came to augment the original structure.

41. Felix G. De Fontaine, *Army Letters of "Personne" 1861–1865* (Columbia, S.C., 1896), pp. 3–4.

42. Montgomery, *Advertiser*, March 6, 1881; Capers, *Memminger*, p. 310; "How Davis Took the Oath," p. 13; Montgomery, *Daily Post*, February 16, 1861.

43. Bill, February 25, 1861, Aiken B. Rhett Papers.
44. U.S. Congress, *Journal*, pp. 66–69; Montgomery, *Weekly Advertiser*, April 17, 1861.
45. Richard S. Joslyn, Biographical Sketch of Robert Josselyn, Sparta, Ga., 1992; Montgomery, *Weekly Advertiser*, March 20, 1861; New York, *Citizen*, April 20, June 22, 1867; Montgomery, *Weekly Mail*, March 22, 1861; Congress, *Journal*, p. 112.
46. Toombs to Davis, February 20, 1861, Jones, Autograph Letters, Duke; Toombs to Davis, February 20, 1861, Jefferson Davis Papers, Louisiana Historical Association Collection, Tulane University, New Orleans.
47. Johnston, *Autobiography*, p. 126.
48. Columbus, *Daily Times*, March 1, 1861.
49. Stephens to Linton Stephens, February 25, 1861, Stephens Papers, MCSH; Montgomery, *Daily Post*, February 22, 1861.
50. Charleston, *Mercury*, February 26, March 9, 1861.
51. Rhett, "Government," p. 104; Rhett to Edmund Rhett, March 5, 1861, Rhett Papers, SCL, USC.
52. Rhett notes in *Index Rerum*, Aiken B. Rhett Papers.
53. Rhett to Robert B. Rhett, Jr., February 20, 1861, Rhett Papers, SCL, USC.
54. U.S. Congress, *Journal*, pp. 72–73.
55. Mobile, *Daily Advertiser*, February 24, 1861.
56. Capers, *Memminger*, p. 310.
57. Montgomery, *Advertiser*, June 5, 1931.
58. De Fontaine, "*Personne*," p. 5.
59. "How Davis Took the Oath," p. 13; Montgomery, *Advertiser*, June 5, 1931.
60. De Fontaine, "*Personne*," p. 5.
61. U.S. Congress, *Journal*, p. 85.
62. Pierce Butler, *Judah P. Benjamin* (Philadelphia, 1907), p. 227.
63. Charleston, *Mercury*, March 4, 1861; J. B. Walton, et al., "Sketches of the History of the Washington Artillery," *SHSP*, XI (April–May 1883), p. 214.
64. Slidell to Cobb, February 25, 1861, Cobb Papers, Georgia.
65. Jones, *Diary*, May 21, 1861, I, p. 38.
66. Russell, *Diary*, I, p. 175.
67. Robert D. Meade, *Judah P. Benjamin, Confederate Statesman* (New York, 1943), pp. 123–26.
68. New York, *Citizen*, August 17, 1867.
69. Meade, *Benjamin*, 163, 396–97n.
70. Mallory to ——, March 22 [24], 1861, "Letter of Stephen R. Mallory, 1861," *American Historical Review*, XII (October 1906), p. 107; Mallory to Davis, February 26, 1861, *PJD*, VII, p. 63; Congress, *Journal*, p. 85.
71. Mallory to ——, March 22 [24], 1861, "Letter," pp. 107–108.

72. Woodward, *Chesnut*, n.d., p. 12; New York, *Citizen*, April 20, August 10, 1867.

73. Woodward, *Chesnut*, March 4, 1861, pp. 14–15.

74. Woodward and Muhlenfeld, *Private Mary Chesnut*, February 28, 1861, p. 16, April 28, 1861, p. 63.

75. Woodward and Muhlenfeld, *Private Mary Chesnut*, February 28, 1861, p. 16; Charleston, *Mercury*, March 8, 1861.

76. U.S. Congress, *Journal*, pp. 95–96.

77. Woodward, *Chesnut*, March 3, 1861, p. 14; Mallory to?, March 22 [24], 1861, "Letter," p. 108.

78. U.S. Congress, *Journal*, pp. 105–106.

79. Columbus, *Daily Times*, March 4, 1861.

80. Wirt Adams to Davis, February 28, 1861, *PJD*, VII, p. 63; Columbus, *Daily Times*, March 8, 1861.

81. Woodward and Muhlenfeld, *Private Mary Chesnut*, March 8, 1861, p. 28.

82. John H. Reagan to O. M. Roberts, March 2, 1861, John H. Reagan Papers, Benjamin H. Good Collection, Texas State Library, Archives, Division, Austin.

83. "Organization of the Confederate Post Office Department," *Confederate War Journal*, II (August 1894), p. 66.

84. Reagan to Roberts, March 2, 1861, Reagan Papers; John H. Reagan, *Memoirs, with Special Reference to Secession and the Civil War* (New York, 1906), p. 109.

85. Reagan, *Memoirs*, pp. 124–25.

86. U.S. Congress, *Journal*, p. 112; Reagan to Roberts, March 6, 1861, Reagan Papers.

87. Davis, *Rise and Fall*, II, p. 241.

88. Davis, *Memoir*, II, p. 38.

89. Charleston, *Mercury*, February 26, 1861.

90. Cobb to Marion Cobb, February 21, 1861, "Correspondence," p. 238; A. W. Redding to S. J. Anderson, March 15, 1861, *OR*, II, 2, p. 613.

91. Montgomery, *Daily Post*, March 12, 1861.

92. Columbus, *Daily Columbus Enquirer*, February 25, 1861.

93. Davis to Cobb, March 16, 1861, J. W. Eldridge Collection, The Huntington, San Marino, California; New York, *Citizen*, April 27, 1861.

94. New York, *Citizen*, April 20, 1867.

95. Butler, *Benjamin*, p. 230.

96. Hooper to John De Berniere Hooper, February 22, 1861, Hooper Papers.

97. Walker to J. F. Callan, February 21, 1861, Letter-Book of Official Correspondence of L. P. Walker, 1861, LC; Walker to John Forsyth, March 5, 1861, *OR*, IV, 1, p. 125.

98. William D. Pender to Sarah Pender, March 16, 1861, William D. Pender Papers, SHC, UNC; Rome, *Tri-Weekly Courier*, March 3, 1861.

99. Alfred Roman, *The Military Operations of General Beauregard in the War Between the States* (New York, 1883), I, p. 18.

100. Invoice, n.d., Barrett, Wimbish and Company, Confederate Papers Relating to Citizens or Business Firms, Record Group 109, NA.
101. New York, *Citizen*, April 13, 1867.
102. Vicksburg, *Daily Evening Citizen*, March 2, 1861.
103. Rome, *Tri-Weekly Courier*, March 3, 1861.
104. *Ibid.*, March 12, 1861.
105. L. Q. Washington, "The Confederate State Department," *The Independent*, LIII (September 19, 1901), p. 2222.
106. Montgomery, *Weekly Advertiser*, May 15, 1861.
107. U.S. Congress, *Journal*, p. 74.
108. New York, *Citizen*, April 27, 1867.
109. Montgomery, *Advertiser*, March 6, 1861.
110. Capers, *Memminger*, pp. 319, 322, 325–27; De Fontaine, *"Personne,"* p. 6.
111. Philip Clayton to Howell Cobb, March 25, 1861, Cobb Papers, Georgia.
112. Memminger to Howell Cobb, May 1, 1861, Christopher G. Memminger Papers, SHC, UNC.
113. Reply of Ex-Secretary Memminger, March 27, 1874, Rowland, VIII, p. 43.
114. Henry D. Capers, "Treasurer of the Confederate Government," *Confederate Veteran*, XXIV (April 1916), p. 150; De Fontaine, *"Personne,"* p. 4.
115. Barry to Pettus, February 12, 1861, RG 27, Volume 36, MDAH.
116. U.S. Congress, *Journal*, pp. 74, 87–88, 91–92.
117. Richard C. Todd, *Confederate Finance* (Athens, Ga., 1954), pp. 25–26.
118. U.S. Congress, *Journal*, pp. 116–17; Todd, *Finance*, pp. 102–104, 119.
119. Reply of Ex-Secretary Memminger, March 27, 1874, Rowland, VIII, p. 43; F. A. Nast, "History of Confederate Stamps," *Confederate Veteran*, II (March 1894), p. 77; Capers, *Memminger*, pp. 316–17; De Fontaine, *"Personne,"* p. 7.
120. De Fontaine, *"Personne,"* p. 7.
121. Todd, *Finance*, pp. 157–59.
122. Memminger to E. M. Hastings, March 5, 1861, Governors Papers, Military Correspondence, ADAH.
123. New York, *Herald*, February 20, 1861.
124. Capers, *Memminger*, p. 314.
125. Trescott to Howell Cobb, February 2, 1861, Cobb Papers, Georgia.
126. Charleston, *Mercury*, February 26, 1861.
127. Reagan, *Memoirs*, p. 147.
128. New York, *Citizen*, April 6, 1867.
129. Woodward and Muhlenfeld, *Private Mary Chesnut*, February 25, 1861, p. 16.
130. E. C. Jones to Chesnut, March 15, 1861, Chesnut-Miller-Manning Papers.
131. Walker to Bolling Baker, February 27, 1861, Walker Letter-Book, LC.
132. Atlanta, *Daily Intelligencer*, February 22, 1861.
133. A. B. Seals to Stephens, March 3, 1861, Stephens Papers, LC.

134. Davis to George Howard, April 1, 1861, Autograph File, Frederick Dearborn Collection, Harvard University, Cambridge, Mass.

135. Virginia Convention Delegates to Davis, April 2, 1861, Confederate Records Relating to Army Officers, War Department Officers, and Other Individuals, RG 109, NA; T.B.J. Hadley to Davis, April 6, 1861, Confederate States of America Records, Vol. 46, LC.

136. Columbia, *Daily South Carolinian*, February 23, 1861.

137. Woodward, *Chesnut*, February 25, 1861, pp. 8–9.

138. Mobile, *Daily Advertiser*, February 27, March 2, 1861.

139. Columbia, *Daily South Carolinian*, March 7, 1861.

140. Charleston, *Mercury*, March 14, 1861.

141. Smith to his wife, March 10, 1861, Easby-Smith Papers.

142. Mobile, *Daily Advertiser*, March 3, 1861; Augusta, *Daily Constitutionalist*, March 2, 1861; New Orleans, *Daily Delta*, March 5, 1861.

143. Charleston, *Mercury*, April 4, 1861.

144. Charleston, *Mercury*, April 2, 1861.

145. Napier, "Montgomery," p. 108n.

146. Jones and Rogers, "Montgomery," March 23, 1861, pp. 56–57.

147. Columbus, *Daily Times*, March 27, 1861.

148. Montgomery City Council Minutes, April 22, 1861, ADAH.

149. U.S. Congress, *Journal*, pp. 71–72; Charleston, *Mercury*, March 4, 1861.

150. Vicksburg, *Daily Evening Citizen*, March 2, 1861; Reagan, *Memoirs*, p. 158.

151. Jones and Rogers, "Montgomery," February 25, 1861, p. 38.

152. Mobile, *Daily Advertiser*, March 1, 1861.

153. Montgomery, *Weekly Advertiser*, May 1, 1861.

154. New York, *Citizen*, July 6, 1867.

155. "Organization of the Confederate Post Office Department," p. 67.

156. New York, *Citizen*, April 20, July 6, 1867.

9. Make Up Your Account for War

1. Russell, *Diary*, I, p. 172.

2. Edmonds, "My First Impressions," pp. 205–206.

3. New Orleans, *Daily Delta*, March 10, 1861; Stephens to Linton Stephens, March 3, 1861, Stephens Papers, MCSH.

4. Clipping, Scrapbook #4, Walthall Papers, MDAH; New York, *Citizen*, April 13, 1867.

5. Joseph O. Kerbey, *The Boy Spy* (Chicago, 1887), p. 21.

6. De Leon, *Four Years*, p. 25.

7. New York, *Citizen*, June 22, 1867.

8. Martin Crawford, *William Howard Russell's Civil War. Private Diary and Letters, 1861-1862* (Athens, Ga., 1992), May 7, 1861, p. 52; Russell, *Diary*, I, p. 172.

9. Rome, *Tri-Weekly Courier*, March 3, 1861.

10. Montgomery, *Advertiser*, October 7, 1900.

11. John W. Daniel, ed., *Life and Reminiscences of Jefferson Davis. By Distinguished Men of His Time* (Baltimore, 1980), p. 260.

12. Dating this meeting is conjectural and based on internal evidence in the only two sources covering it, both secondhand and written forty-seven years after the fact. In his *Memoirs* Reagan speaks of the "first meeting of the Cabinet after my appointment" (p. 146), which clearly suggests that this was not the actual *first* meeting of the cabinet itself. His appointment being March 6, the first meeting in question must have occurred earlier. The sources cited below agree that Benjamin figured prominently in the meeting. Since he only left New Orleans on February 27, he cannot have reached Montgomery either by boat or train before March 1 at the earliest. Mallory, Toombs, and Walker already being in Montgomery by then, the meeting could have been held anytime between March 2 and 5. The urgency that in April would see cabinet meetings lasting long into the night and on weekends as well did not yet exist at this time, so it seems reasonable to assume that Davis would not call a meeting on Saturday or Sunday, March 2–3. Furthermore, since word of Lincoln's inaugural on March 4 produced an immediate impression that war was inevitable when it reached Montgomery late the same day, a March 5 meeting at which most cabinet officers express a conviction that there will be no war seems unlikely. Consequently March 4, prior to the receipt of news of Lincoln's inaugural, seems the best fit.

13. David D. Shelby to Michael L. Woods, April 23, 1908, Woods Papers; Butler, *Benjamin*, pp. 233–34. Shelby is the source of the statement in Butler, stating what he says Walker told him years afterward. In the same collection is a letter of Woods to Shelby, April 14, 1908, giving a radically different account, but it is clear from internal evidence that Woods is confusing an account Walker gave him of an early April cabinet meeting with this early March session. The expressions assigned to others besides Benjamin and Walker in this first meeting are based upon their opinions expressed then and later, and stated and supported elsewhere in this narrative.

14. Woodward, *Chesnut*,n.d., p. 18; Woodward and Muhlenfeld, *Private Mary Chesnut*, March [7], 1861, p. 26.

15. Notes, March 16, 1861, Jefferson Davis Papers, Transylvania University, Lexington Kentucky.

16. Moore, *Rebellion Record*, I, "Poetry & Incidents," p. 24.

17. New York, *Citizen*, April 13, 1867.

18. Caleb Huse, *The Supplies for the Confederate Army* (Boston, 1902), p. 10.

19. De Leon, *Four Years*,p. 25.

20. Clipping, Scrapbook #4, Walthall Papers, MDAH.

21. Russell, *Diary*, I, p. 173.

22. Smith to his wife, March 10, 1861, Easby-Smith Papers.

23. De Leon, *Four Years*, pp. 24–25.
24. Barry to Pettus, March 11, 1861, RG 27, Vol. 36, MDAH.
25. Statement of Benjamin C. Yancey, 1886, DuBose Papers.
26. Montgomery, *Daily Post*, February 22, 1861.
27. Washington, *Evening Star*, February 19, 1861.
28. Alexander De Clouet to Charles E. A. Gayarre, February 17, 1861, Charles E. A. Gayarre Papers, Grace King Collection, LSU.
29. Slidell to Cobb, February 25, 1861, Cobb Papers, Georgia.
30. Nisbet to J.B. Lamar, February 28, 1861, Cobb Papers, Georgia; New York, *Citizen*, April 13, 1867.
31. Gayarre to Conrad, February 26, 1861, Gayarre Papers.
32. John Cripps to Miles, March 17, 1861, Miles Papers, SHC, UNC.
33. S. R. Bridgers to Pettus, February 15, 1861, Jacob Thompson to Pettus, February 25, 1861, RG 27, Vol. 36, MDAH.
34. Henry Dickenson to Pettus, February 19, 1861, RG 27, Vol. 36, MDAH.
35. U. S. Congress, *Journal*, p. 82.
36. Curry to Anderson, February 20, 1861, Petrie Scrapbook.
37. Slidell to Cobb, February 25, 1861, Cobb Papers, Georgia.
38. Stephens to Linton Stephens, March 3, 1861, Stephens Papers, MCSH; Cobb to Marion Cobb, March 3, 1861, "Correspondence," p. 250.
39. Curry to Anderson, February 20, 1861, Petrie Scrapbook.
40. Vicksburg, *Daily Evening Citizen*, February 21, 1861.
41. G. W. Yerby to Davis, March 16, 1861, Letters Received by the Secretary of War, Record Group 365, NA.
42. Forsyth to McRae, February 21, 1861, McRae Papers.
43. Vicksburg, *Daily Evening Citizen*, March 21, 1861.
44. New Orleans, *Daily Picayune*, March 13, 1861.
45. New York, *Citizen*, July 6, 1867.
46. Rhett, Autobiography, SCHS.
47. DuBose, *Yancey*, p. 599.
48. Rhett, Autobiography, SCHS; Rhett, "Government," p. 109. Here again it needs to be stressed that Rhett, "Government," is chiefly a reiteration of the older Rhett's autobiography.
49. Rhett, Autobiography, SCHS.
50. Yancey to "Fellow-Citizens," February 27, 1861, Columbia, *Daily South Carolinian*, March 3, 1861; William L. Yancey Diary, March 15, 1861, typescript, William L. Yancey Papers, ADAH.
51. James H. Stewart, My Recollections of William L. Yancey 1845 to 1862, Yancey Papers, ADAH.
52. Miles to DuBose, September 12, 1890, DuBose Papers.
53. Stephens to Linton Stephens, February 22, 1861, Stephens Papers, MCSH.
54. Crawford to George Crawford, March 1, 1861, Stephens Papers, LC.
55. Stephens to Linton Stephens, February 25, 26, 1861, Stephens Papers, MCSH.
56. John W. Forsyth to Stephens, March 1, 1861, Stephens Papers, LC.

57. Toombs to Roman, February 27, 1861, W. F.Alexander to Roman, March 20, 1861, La Villebeuvre Family Papers.
58. Mason to Davis, February 12, 1861, *PJD*, VII, p. 39.
59. Hooper to John De Berniere Hooper, February 22, 1861, Hooper Papers.
60. James C. Calhoun to Armistead L. Burt, February [March] 4, 1861, John C. Calhoun Papers, Duke University Library, Durham, N.C.
61. Jones and Rogers, "Montgomery," March 6, 1861, p. 47; Campbell to Walthall, July 16, 1879, Walthall Papers.
62. Hayne to Davis, February 18, 1861, G.A. Baker Catalog #34 (1939), p. 8.
63. Hayne to Miles, February 19, 1861, Miles Papers, SHC, UNC.
64. Barnwell to his wife, February 18, 1861, Jones, Autograph Letters, Duke.
65. John Tyler to Pickens, February 18, 1861, *OR*, I, 1, p. 257.
66. Davis to Pickens, February 20, 1861, *PJD*, VII, p. 55.
67. Davis to Pickens, February 22, 1861, *PJD*, VII, pp. 57–58.
68. Yancey to Pickens, February 27, 1861, Yancey Papers, ADAH.
69. Pickens to Miles, February 19, 1861, Miles Papers, SHC, UNC.
70. Davis to Pickens, February 20, 1861, *PJD*, VII, p. 55.
71. De Leon, *Four Years*, p. 25.
72. Toombs to Roman, March 2, 1861, La Villebeuvre Family Papers.
73. William Gwin to Davis, March 2, 1861, *OR*, I, 53, p. 128.
74. Crawford to Toombs, March 3, 1861, Toombs Letterbook, SCL, USC.
75. Wigfall to Davis, March 4, 1861, *OR*, I, 53, p. 128.
76. Memorandum "A," March 1861, Crawford to Toombs, March 6, 1861, Toombs Letterbook.
77. Crawford and Forsyth to Toombs, March 8, 12, 15, 1861, Crawford, Forsyth, and Roman to Toombs, March 20, 22, 1861, Roman to Toombs, March 25, 1861, Toombs Letterbook.
78. Vicksburg, *Daily Evening Citizen*, March 12, 1861.
79. Stephens to Linton Stephens, March 5, 1861, Stephens Papers, MCSH.
80. Act February 20, 1861, *OR*, IV, 1, p. 106.
81. Davis to Semmes, February 21, 1861, *OR*, IV, 1, p. 106.
82. Davis to Pickens, February 22, 1861, *PJD*, VII, p. 57.
83. Rhett, Autobiography, SCHS.
84. U.S. Congress, *Journal*, pp. 88–89.
85. Walker to Sam Houston, March 2, 1861, Records of the Governor, Sam Houston, Box 301-34, Texas State Library, Archives Division, Austin.
86. Braxton Bragg to Davis, February 25, 1861, *OR*, II, 1, p. 35; Charleston, *Mercury*, March 14, 1861.
87. Library of Congress Loan Record, January 30, 1861, *PJD*, VII, pp. 30–31.
88. Wigfall to Davis, February 25, 1861, *PJD*, VII, p. 60.
89. U.S. Congress, *Journal*, p. 81.
90. Mason to Davis, March 7, 1861, *OR*, IV, 1, p. 132.
91. Samuel Cooper to Charles C. Jones, May 27, 1871, copy in author's possession.
92. William Preston Johnston to Rosa Johnston, August 28, 1862, Barret Collection.

93. Lucius B. Northrop to Davis, March 16, 1861, Jefferson Davis Papers, Tulane.

94. New York, *Citizen*, July 20, 1867.

95. Cooper to Myers, February 5, 1861, Myers to Cooper, February 18, 1861, *OR*, I, 1, p. 459.

96. De Leon, *Four Years*, p. 28.

97. New York, *Citizen*, April 20, 1867.

98. Draft of speech, n.d., Chesnut-Miller-Manning Papers, SCHS.

99. Columbus, *Daily Times*, February 22, 1861.

100. Montgomery, *Weekly Advertiser*, February 27, 1861.

101. U.S. Congress, *Journal*, p. 92.

102. Davis to Howell Cobb, March 5, 1861, James D. Richardson, comp., *The Messages and Papers of Jefferson Davis and the Confederacy* (Washington, 1905), I, p. 58.

103. Reagan, *Memoirs*, pp. 116–17.

104. Davis, *Rise and Fall*, I, p. 304.

105. Davis to Bartow, March 5, 1861, Rowland, V, p. 59.

106. Act, February 28, 1861, *OR*, IV, 1, p. 117.

107. Act, March 6, 1861, *OR*, IV, 1, p. 126, Walker to Thomas O. Moore, March 8, 1861, pp. 134–35.

108. Walker to A.B. Moore, March 9, 1861, *OR*, IV, 1, p. 135.

109. Reagan, *Memoirs*, pp. 146–47.

110. Bartow to Henry C. Wayne, February 22, 1861, H. C. Wayne Papers, Duke University Library, Durham, N.C.

111. Brown to Walker, March 12, 1861, *OR*, IV, 1, p. 149.

112. Frank L. Owsley, *State Rights in the Confederacy* (Chicago, 1925), pp. 76ff.

113. *Ibid.*, pp. 87–90; Walker to Brown, April 20, 1861, Teleman Cuyler Collection, University of Georgia Library, Athens.

114. Walker to Moore, March 19, 1861, Governors Papers, Military Correspondence, ADAH.

115. U.S. Congress, *Journal*, pp. 98, 103–104; Natchez, *Daily Courier*, March 18, 1861.

116. Rhett, Autobiography, Rhett Papers, SCHS.

117. U.S. Congress, *Journal*, pp. 79, 82.

118. *Ibid.*, pp. 129–30.

119. Columbia, *Daily South Carolinian*, March 6, 1861.

120. Anderson to J. Crittenden Coleman, March 16, 1861, John J. Crittenden Papers, Duke.

121. Davis to James Lyons, April 9, 1861, *PJD*, VII, p. 98.

122. William D. Pender to Sarah Pender, March 14, 1861, William D. Pender Papers, SHC, UNC.

123. Vicksburg, *Daily Evening Citizen*, March 14, 1861; Yancey to Davis, February 27, 1861, Letters Relating to Citizens, etc., RG 109, NA; E. K. Smith to Davis, February 28, 1861, Confederate Papers Relating to Army Officers, War Department Officials, and Other Individuals, RG 109, NA.

124. Woodward and Muhlenfeld, *Private Mary Chesnut*, March 4, 1861, p. 22; New York, *Citizen*, April 20, 1867; Jones and Rogers, "Montgomery," February 13, 1861, p. 27.
125. Braxton Bragg to Perkins, February 19, 1861, *OR*, II, 1, p. 607; Thomas Compton to Walker, March 25, 1861, Governors Papers, Appointment Files, ADAH; Philip B. Spence, "Service for the Confederacy," *Confederate Veteran*, VIII (August 1900), p. 373.
126. Calhoun to Burt, February [March] 4, 1861, Calhoun Papers; Woodward and Muhlenfeld, *Private Mary Chesnut*, March 7, 1861, p. 26.
127. Pickens to Walker, March 18, 1861, Pickens Papers, Duke.
128. Walker to Pickens, March 21, 1861, Walker Letter-Book, LC
129. A. L. Humphries to Davis, April 5, 1861, Letters Received by the Confederate Secretary of War, RG 109, NA.
130. Milledge L. Bonham to Davis, March 6, 1861, *OR*, I, 1, p. 265.
131. George L. Crocket, *Two Centuries in East Texas* (Dallas, 1932), n.p.
132. W. H. T. Walker to Brown, March 10, 1861, William Palmer Collection, Western Reserve Historical Society, Cleveland, Ohio.
133. Woodward and Muhlenfeld, *Private Mary Chesnut*, March 28, 1861, p. 49.
134. Culver, Memoirs.
135. G. W. Lee to Davis, February 18, 1861, Letters Received by the Confederate Secretary of War, RG 109, NA.
136. A. Gerard et al. to Davis, February 18, 1861, Davis Papers, Tulane.
137. Vicksburg, *Daily Evening Citizen*, March 22, 1861; Walker to Wigfall, March 5, 1861, Walker Letter-Book, LC; C. K. Sherman et al. to Wigfall, March 16, 1861, *OR*, I, 53, p. 135.
138. Harris to Davis, March 31, 1861, *PJD*, VII, p. 84.
139. Vicksburg, *Daily Evening Citizen*, February 21, 1861; Semmes et al. to Conrad, February 21, 1861, *OR*, II, 2, pp. 41–43.
140. U.S. Congress, *Journal*, pp. 124–25; Rhett, Autobiography, Rhett Papers, SCHS.
141. Vicksburg, *Daily Evening Citizen*, March 26, 1861.
142. U.S. Congress, *Journal*, p. 90; Montgomery, *Weekly Mail*, March 15, 1861.
143. U.S. Congress, *Journal*, p. 144.
144. J. J. Morrison to William D. Rogers, March 25, 1861, Rogers to Ed Clark, March 1861, Records of the Governor, Ed Clark, Box 301-35, RG 301, Texas State Archives.
145. Howell Cobb to his wife, February 23, 1861, Howell Cobb Papers, Georgia.
146. Columbus, *Daily Columbus Enquirer*, March 4, 1861.
147. John Hoodless to E. Farrand, March 16, 1861, United States Navy Department, *Official Records of the Union and Confederate Navies in the War of the Rebellion* (Washington, 1894–1927), Series I, 4, p. 218; Vicksburg, *Daily Evening Citizen*, March 26, 1861.

148. Rhett, Autobiography, Rhett Papers, SCHS.

149. Charleston, *Mercury*, April 6, 1861; Mallory to A.C. Van Benthuysen, March 30, 1861, A.C. Van Benthuysen Papers, Tulane University, Howard Tilton Library, New Orleans.

150. C.W. Read, "Reminiscences of the Confederate States Navy," *SHSP*, I (May 1876), pp. 331–32.

151. Owsley, *State Rights*, pp. 8–10.

152. Requisition, February 15, 1861, Governors Papers, Military Correspondence, ADAH; Memminger to M. A. Moore, Jr., February 16, 1861, Christopher G. Memminger Papers, SCL, USC.

153. Montgomery, *Weekly Advertiser*, February 27, 1861; Columbus, *Daily Times*, March 13, 1861.

154. Semmes to Stephens, March 2, 1861, Stephens Papers, LC.

155. Walker to Brown, April 17, 1861, OR, I, 53, p. 149.

156. Walker to W. H. C. Whiting, March 9, 1861, OR, I, 53, p. 130.

157. Josselyn to Pettus, March 8, 1861, RG 27, Vol. 36, MDAH.

158. Charles H. Edwards to Davis, March 15, 1861, Letters to the Confederate Secretary of War, RG 109, NA.

159. Richard D. Goff, *Confederate Supply* (Durham, N.C., 1969), pp. 11–12.

160. Robert B. Rhett, Jr. to E. C. Wharton, August 18, 1886, Wharton Papers, LSU.

161. Statement of requisitions, March 5, 21, 23, 1861, Walker Letter-Book, LC.

162. George W. Morse to Davis, March 6, 1861, OR, IV, 1, pp. 131–32.

163. Ben McCulloch to Clark, March 31, 1861, Records of the Governor, Box 301-35, Edward Clark, Texas State Library, Archives Division, Austin.

164. Huse, *Supplies*, p. 9.

165. Walker to Davis, March 4, 1861, Walker Letter-Book, LC; Act, March 11, 1861, OR, IV, 1, p. 148.

166. C. F. Vance to Walker, March 2, 1861, OR,l IV, 1, p. 120.

167. Act, March 12, 1861, OR, IV, 1, p. 149; Davis to Howell Cobb, March 15, 1861, Richardson, *Messages*, I, p. 58.

168. Charleston, *Mercury*, March 23, 1861.

169. Davis to Whiting, February 23, 1861, Rowland, V, p. 57, Pickens to Davis, February 27, V, p. 58.

170. Roman, *Beauregard*, I, pp. 20–21. Beauregard (through ghost writer Roman) says that he pulled a map of Charleston from his pocket when Davis asked him what he knew. It seems rather too coincidental for him simply to happen to have such a map with him at the time, and also makes his claim that his assignment to Charleston took him by surprise a bit disingenuous. It seems more logical that he got a map after learning from someone—who but Walker—that he would be getting orders.

171. *Ibid*.

172. Beauregard to G.W. Smith, February 27, 1861, OR, I, 53, p. 126; Beauregard to Josiah Gorgas, February 28, 1861, Intercepted Telegrams, 1861, RG 107, Vol. 399, NA.

173. DeClouet to Paul DeClouet, February 28, 1861, DeClouet Papers, Lafayette.
174. U.S. Congress, *Journal*, pp. 96–97; Davis to Pickens, March 1, 1861, Rowland, V, pp. 58–59.
175. Natchez, *Daily Courier*, March 8, 1861.
176. U.S. Congress, *Journal*, p. 114; George Deas to Bragg, March 7, 1861, OR, I, 1, p. 448.
177. Deas to J. C. Booth, March 16, 1861, OR, I, 1, pp. 450–51; Vicksburg, *Daily Evening Citizen*, March 22, 1861; Walker to A. B. Moore, March 23, 1861, Governors Papers, Military Correspondence, ADAH; Columbus, *Daily Times*, March 23, 1861.
178. Wigfall to Davis, March 11, 1861, OR, I, 1, p. 273, Walker to Beauregard, March 15, p. 276.
179. Beauregard to Walker, March 11 [21], 1861, OR, I, 1, p. 274.
180. Atlanta, *Daily Intelligencer*, February 22, 1861; Natchez, *Daily Courier*, March 16, 1861.
181. Yulee to Davis, March 1, 1861, Confederate Papers Relating to Army Officers, RG 109, NA.
182. Montgomery, *Weekly Montgomery Confederation*, March 1, 1861; Davis to Pickens, February 22, 1861, Executive Council Journal Letter-Book, 1861, South Carolina Department of Archives and History, Columbia.
183. Charleston, *Mercury*, March 9, 1861.
184. P. Norton to Moore, February 28, 1861, Thomas O. Moore Papers, LSU.

10. A Matter of Restoration

1. U.S. Congress, *Journal*, pp. 25, 41, 42; Rhett to Robert B. Rhett, Jr., February 11, 1861, Rhett Papers, SCL, USC.
2. Lee, *Constitution*, pp. 82–83.
3. Toombs to Davis, February 20, 1861, Jones, Autograph Letters, Duke; Charleston, *Mercury*, February 16, 1861.
4. Rhett to Robert B. Rhett, Jr., February 11, 1861, Rhett Papers, SCL, USC; Charleston, *Mercury*, February 16, 1861.
5. Philadelphia, *Weekly Times*, January 24, 1880.
6. Constitution & amendments proposed for Confederate States, Rhett Papers, SCHS.
7. Rhett to T. Stuart Rhett, April 15, 1868, Rhett Papers, SCHS.
8. Philadelphia, *Weekly Times*, January 24, 1880.
9. Rhett, Autobiography, SCHS.
10. Rhett to T. Stuart Rhett, April 15, 1868, Rhett Papers, SCHS.
11. Cobb to Marion Cobb, February 14, 1861, "Correspondence," p. 176.
12. Rhett to Robert B. Rhett, Jr., February 11, 1861, Rhett Papers, SCL, USC.
13. T. R. R. Cobb notes on the Constitutional Committee, in A. L. Hull, "The Making of the Confederate Constitution," *Publications of the Southern*

History Association, IX (September 1905), p. 286. These are the only surviving notes on the Committee of Twelve's deliberations, are scanty, and were probably written by Cobb after the fact for reference during his speeches in Georgia promoting ratification of the Constitution.

14. Cobb notes, "Making of the Confederate Constitution," p. 287.
15. *Ibid.*, p. 287; Stephens, *Popular History*, p. 600; Stephens to Linton, February 17, 1861, Stephens Papers, MCSH.
16. Rhett to T. Stuart Rhett, April 15, 1868, Rhett Papers, SCHS; Cobb notes, "Making of the Confederate Constitution," pp. 287–88.
17. Cobb to Marion Cobb, February 14, 1861, "Correspondence," p. 176.
18. Cobb notes, "Making of the Confederate Constitution," pp. 288–89.
19. Rhett to T. Stuart Rhett, April 15, 1868, Rhett Papers, SCHS.
20. Cobb notes, "Making of the Confederate Constitution," p. 289.
21. Cobb to Marion Cobb, February 20, 1861, "The Correspondence of Thomas Reade Rootes Cobb, 1861–1862," *Publications of the Southern History Association*, XI (July 1907), p. 233.
22. *Ibid.*
23. *Ibid.*, February 22, 1861, p. 236.
24. *Ibid.*, February 25, 1861, p. 240.
25. Rhett, "Government," p. 105.
26. Cobb notes, "Making of the Confederate Constitution," pp. 289–90.
27. Rhett notes, Aiken B. Rhett Papers.
28. Woodward, *Chesnut*, February 25, 1861, p. 8.
29. Cobb notes, "Making of the Confederate Constitution," pp. 290–91.
30. Cobb to Marion, February 23, 1861, "Correspondence," p. 239; Lee, *Constitutions*, p. 88n; Montgomery, *Weekly Advertiser*, February 27, 1861.
31. Montgomery, *Weekly Advertiser*, March 6, 1861.
32. Rhett to Robert B. Rhett, Jr., February 12, 1861, Rhett Papers, SCL, USC.
33. Cobb to Marion Cobb, February 26, "Correspondence," p. 241.
34. Stephens to Linton Stephens, February 21, 1861, Stephens Papers, MCSH.
35. Howell Cobb to his wife, February 25, 1861, Cobb Papers, Georgia.
36. Harrison to Susan Harrison, February 17, 1861, Harrison Papers.
37. Nisbet to Linton Stephens, February 19, 1861, Stephens Papers, Emory.
38. Stephens to William H. Hidell, February 26, 1861, 1861; William H. Hidell Papers, Historical Society of Pennsylvania, Philadelphia.
39. Vicksburg, *Daily Evening Whig*, February 27, 1861; Montgomery, *Weekly Advertiser*, February 27, 1861.
40. U.S. Congress, *Journal*, pp. 44, 67, 69–70; Cobb to Marion Cobb, February 16, 1861, "Correspondence," p. 179.
41. Hooper to John DeBerniere Hooper, February 22, 1861, Hooper Papers; Montgomery, *Weekly Mail*, February 15, 1861.
42. Montgomery, *Weekly Mail*, March 22, 1861.
43. Stephens to Linton Stephens, March 3, 1861, Stephens Papers, MCSH; George Jones to Stephens, February 24, 1861, Stephens Papers, LC.

44. Cobb to Marion Cobb, February 22, 1861, "Correspondence," p. 237.
45. Montgomery, *Daily Post*, February 20, 1861.
46. Woodward and Muhlenfeld, *Private Mary Chesnut*, March 17, 1861, p. 35.
47. Cobb to Marion Cobb, February 22, 1861, "Correspondence," p. 237, February 23, 1861, p. 239.
48. W. Nelson to Miles, March 6, 1861, Miles Papers, SHC, UNC.
49. Stephens to Linton Stephens, February 27, 1861, Stephens Papers, MCSH.
50. Cobb to Marion Cobb, February 22, 1861, "Correspondence," p. 237.
51. Stephens to Linton Stephens, February 25, 27, 1861, Stephens Papers, MCSH.
52. Kirkland and Kennedy, *Historic Camden*, II, p. 158.
53. Stephens to Linton Stephens, February 27, 1861, Stephens Papers, MCSH.
54. Montgomery, *Weekly Advertiser*, March 6, 1861.
55. Woodward, *Chesnut*, February 25, 1861, p. 8; Woodward and Muhlenfeld, *Private Mary Chesnut*, February 28, 1861, p. 17.
56. Woodward, *Chesnut*, March 1861, p. 17; Woodward and Muhlenfeld, *Private Mary Chesnut*, March [7], 1861, p. 25.
57. Cobb to Marion Cobb, February 22, 1861, "Correspondence," p. 237.
58. Poem, Alexander B. Clitherall Papers, ADAH. A slight variant is to be found in Philip Clayton to Mrs. Howell Cobb, March 28, 1861, Cobb Papers, Athens. The date of the event is derived from Tom Cobb's mention of the poem in his February 22 letter cited above. U.S. Congress, *Journal*, p. 70, and the Montgomery, *Weekly Advertiser*, February 27, 1861, agree that the only date prior to February 22 on which no minister opened the session was February 21.
59. Woodward and Muhlenfeld, *Private Mary Chesnut*, March [7], 1861, p. 25.
60. Stephens to Linton Stephens, February 26, 1861, Stephens Papers, MCSH.
61. De Leon, *Four Years*, p. 3.
62. Montgomery, *Weekly Mail*, February 22, 1861.
63. U.S. Congress, *Journal*, pp. 74, 78–79; Cobb to Marion Cobb, February 23, 1861, "Correspondence," p. 239.
64. U.S. Congress, *Journal*, pp. 82–85.
65. *Ibid.*, p. 95.
66. Cobb to Marion Cobb, February 28, 1861, "Correspondence," p. 243.
67. Cobb to Marion Cobb, March 2, 1861, "Correspondence," p. 248; U.S. Congress, *Journal*, pp. 97–98; Charleston, *Mercury*, March 6, 1861.
68. Columbus, *Daily Times*, March 4, 1861.
69. Montgomery, *Daily Post*, February 21, 1861.
70. Cobb to Marion Cobb, February 21, 1861, "Correspondence," p. 238, March 1, 1861, p. 247.
71. Woodward and Muhlenfeld, *Private Mary Chesnut*, February 27, 1861, p. 17.
72. U.S. Congress, *Journal*, pp. 90, 92.

73. Stephens to Linton Stephens, February 27, 1861, Stephens Papers, MCSH; Cobb to Marion Cobb, February 28, 1861, "Correspondence," p. 245. Stephens indicates that the party was the 26th, but his reference is unclear.

74. Stephens to Linton Stephens, February 28, 1861, Stephens Papers, MCSH.

75. DeClouet to Paul DeClouet, February 28, 1861, DeClouet Papers.

76. U.S. Congress, *Journal*, pp. 94–95.

77. Lee, *Constitutions*, p. 87.

78. *Memorials of the Life and Character of Wiley P. Harris*, p. 22.

79. U.S. Congress, *Journal*, pp. 858–59; Stephens, *Popular History*, p. 599.

80. Cobb to Marion Cobb, February 28, 1861, "Correspondence," p. 245; U.S. Congress, *Journal*, pp. 859–60.

81. Stephens to Linton Stephens, March 1, 1861, Stephens Papers, MCSH; Columbus, *Daily Times*, March 4, 1861.

82. Culver, Memoirs.

83. U.S. Congress, *Journal*, pp. 860–61.

84. Stephens to Linton Stephens, March 1, 1861, Stephens Papers, MCSH.

85. U.S. Congress, *Journal*, p. 861; Cobb to Marion Cobb, March 1, 1861, "Correspondence," p. 247.

86. Stephens to Linton Stephens, March 1, 1861, Stephens Papers, MCSH.

87. Montgomery, *Weekly Advertiser*, March 6, 1861; Calhoun to Burt, February [March] 4, 1861, Calhoun Papers; Charleston, *Mercury*, March 6, 1861.

88. U.S. Congress, *Journal*, p. 97.

89. Gregg and Ochiltree to O. M. Roberts, February 23, 1861, Austin, *Weekly State Gazette*, March 9, 1861; Ochiltree to the editor, February 18, 1861, Dallas, *Herald*, March 13, 1861.

90. "To the People of Texas," March 16, 1861, Sam Houston to Sam Houston, Jr., July 23, 1861, Sam Houston Papers, Center for American History, University of Texas, Austin; Montgomery, *Weekly Advertiser*, March 20, 1861.

91. U.S. Congress, *Journal*, p. 862; Stephens to Linton Stephens, March 3, 1861, Stephens Papers, MCSH.

92. Columbia, *Daily South Carolinian*, March 6, 1861.

93. Calhoun to Burt, February [March] 4, 1861, Calhoun Papers.

94. Charleston, *Mercury*, March 6, 1861. The reporter merely says that he was told this by one of the South Carolina delegation. Rhett is, of course, the most likely candidate, especially given the pessimistic tone.

95. Stephens to Linton Stephens, March 3, 1861, Stephens Papers, MCSH.

96. Stephens, *Popular History*, p. 598.

97. Woodward and Muhlenfeld, *Private Mary Chesnut*, March 3, 1861, p. 19.

98. William Smith to his wife, n.d. "Sunday," 1861, Easby-Smith Papers. While undated, this letter's internal evidence clearly dates it as either March 3 or 10, and probably the latter.

99. De Leon, *Four Years*, p. 32.

100. Montgomery, *Weekly Advertiser*, February 20, 1861.
101. ———Prible, "Flag of the Confederate States of America," *SHSP*, XXXVIII (1910), pp. 251–52.
102. Harrison to Susan Harrison, February 17, 1861, Harrison Papers; Montgomery, *Weekly Advertiser*, February 20, 1861.
103. Davis, *Memoir*, II, p. 36.
104. Montgomery, *Weekly Advertiser*, February 20, 1861.
105. "Designs for Confederate Flags," *Confederate Veteran*, XXI (February 1913), p. 79.
106. Moore, *Rebellion Record*, I, "Rumors and Incidents," p. 23; M. E. Huger to Miles, February 7, 1861, Augustin Tarcan to Miles, April 19, 1861, J. B. D. DeBow to Miles, February 15, 1861, Miles Papers, SHC, UNC; "Editorial Miscellany," *De Bow's Review*, XXX (March 1861), p. 381; Columbia, *Daily South Carolinian*, March 13, 1861.
107. Peter A, Brannon, "The Stars and Bars," *Alabama Historical Quarterly*, XVIII (Winter 1956), p. 438; U.S. Congress, *Journal*, p. 70.
108. Prible, "Flag," p. 257.
109. U.S. Congress, *Journal*, pp. 101–102.
110. Columbus, *Daily Times*, March 6, 1861.
111. Jacksonville, Florida, *Times-Union*, May 17, 1905; Brannon, "Stars and Bars," pp. 439–40. Much controversy surrounds the original design, and the whole story certainly is not known. For one thing, there is another claimant. Jessie Randolph Smith, "About Design of the First Flag," *Confederate Veteran*, XIII (November 1905), pp. 508–10, claims that her father submitted the winning design in the second week of February. According to Brannon, "Stars and Bars," p. 427, most of the Confederate veterans' and affinity groups accepted Smith's authorship well into the 1950s. However, the claim was made so long after the fact, and coincidentally just a few months after publication of the Marschall claim, that it is suspect. Suspicious, too, is the claim in Julia Anne Cooke to "Miss Fannie," March 2, 1861, quoted in Brannon, "Stars and Bars," p. 431, that Governor Moore stayed with his daughters in Marion March 2–3 and had them make the first flag from a wedding dress. The "Miss Fannie" letter is a bit too good to be true, for in order to have prepared a lengthy speech for delivery on March 4, and moreover to have decided the day before at least to time their announcement for March 4, the flag committee must have decided on the final design at least a few days earlier, well before Governor Moore's supposed March 2–3 weekend visit to Marion. Furthermore, it is evident from Columbia, *Daily South Carolinian*, March 6, 1861, that the final design was already known in some quarters at least as early as March 2 when their reporter "Southern Confederacy" reported it precisely. And note 112 below effectively settled who made the flag, and where. At best, perhaps Moore showed the committee the Marschall design some time earlier, and came back to Marion that weekend to have one made on his own, but this is nothing

more than supposition, and it would not have been the flag that Miss Tyler raised. De Fontaine, *"Personne,"* p. 10, equally suspect in being years after the fact, says that Clitherall learned the finished design and took it on himself to have the flag prepared. This probably confuses Clitherall's certain role in procuring a much larger and more finished flag a few weeks later.

112. Montgomery, *Weekly Mail*, March 8, 1861. This is the only contemporaneous reference to the making of the flag that went up on March 4, and comes from the most authoritative source, Hooper's own newspaper.

113. Cobb to Marion Cobb, March 3, 1861, "Correspondence," p. 251.

114. Montgomery, *Weekly Advertiser*, March 6, 1861.

115. Montgomery, *Weekly Advertiser*, March 6, 1861; Marie Bankhead Owen, "Raising the First Confederate Flag," *Confederate Veteran*, XXIV (May 1916), p. 199; Jones and Rogers, "Montgomery," March 4, 1861, p. 45; Montgomery, *Weekly Mail*, March 8, 1861.

116. Montgomery, *Weekly Advertiser*, March 6, 1861.

117. Woodward, *Chesnut*, March 5, 1861, pp. 15–16.

118. Woodward and Muhlenfeld, *Private Mary Chesnut*, March 5, 1861, p. 22.

119. Columbia, *Daily South Carolinian*, March 6, 1861.

120. Montgomery, *Weekly Advertiser*, March 13, 1861. U.S. Congress, *Journal*, pp. 101–102 erroneously states that Miles made his report on March 4.

121. "The First Confederate Flag," *Confederate Veteran*, III (October 1895), p. 315.

122. Confederate States Flag, clipping, SCL, USC; Montgomery, *Weekly Mail*, April 12, 1861.

123. Montgomery, *Weekly Advertiser*, April 10, 1861; Nashville, *Union & American*, March 26, 1861.

124. Hooper to Miles, March 30, 1861, Miles Papers, SHC, UNC; U.S. Congress, *Journal*, p. 259.

125. Stephens to Linton Stephens, March 4, 1861, Stephens Papers, MCSH.

126. Kirkland and Kennedy, *Historic Camden*, II, pp. 154–55; U.S. Congress, *Journal*, p. 863.

127. Cobb to Marion Cobb, March 4, 1861, "Correspondence," p. 252.

128. Stephens to Linton Stephens, March 1, 1861, Stephens Papers, MCSH.

129. U.S. Congress, *Journal*, pp. 864–65.

130. Cobb to Marion Cobb, March 4, 1861, "Correspondence," p. 253.

131. Howell Cobb to John Cobb, March 5, 1861, Cobb Papers, Georgia.

132. John A. Cobb to Howell Cobb, March 4, 1861, Cobb Papers, Georgia.

133. E. Foullard to Stephens, March 2, 1861, Stephens Papers, LC; Woodward and Muhlenfeld, *Private Mary Chesnut*, March 8, 1861, p. 28, March 12, 1861, p. 35.

134. Stephens, *Popular History*, p. 600.

135. U.S. Congress, *Journal*, pp. 854, 865–68.

136. Hammond to F. A. Allen, February 21, 1861, Hammond Papers, LC.

137. Boyce to Hunter, February 5, 1861, R. M. T. Hunter Papers.
138. Natchez, *Daily Courier*, February 4, 1861; Ronald T. Takaki, A *Pro-Slavery Crusade. The Agitation to Reopen the African Slave Trade* (New York, 1971), p. 235.
139. James Deas to Chesnut, February 12, 1861, Chesnut Papers, Duke.
140. Smith, *Address*, p. 18.
141. U.S. Congress, *Journal*, p. 868; Cobb to Marion Cobb, March 5, 1861, "Correspondence," p. 254.
142. New Orleans, *Daily Delta*, March 12, 1861.
143. Stephens to Linton Stephens, March 5, 1861, Stephens Papers, MCSH.
144. Cobb to Marion Cobb, March 5, 1861, "Correspondence," p. 253.
145. Stephens to Linton Stephens, March 3, 1861, Stephens Papers, MCSH; Oldham Memoirs, pp. 16–17.
146. Barry to Pettus, March 6, 1861, RG 27, Vol. 36, MDAH; Cobb to Marion Cobb, March 6, 1861, "Correspondence," p. 256.
147. Cobb to Marion Cobb, March 5, 1861, "Correspondence," p. 253, March 6, 1861, p. 254.
148. Cobb to John Cobb, March 5, 1861, Cobb Papers, Georgia.
149. New York, *Citizen*, April 27, 1867.
150. U.S. Congress, *Journal*, p. 109.
151. Vicksburg, *Daily Evening Citizen*, March 8, 1861; Nashville, *Union & American*, March 20, 1861.
152. L. Q. Washington to Walker, March 17, 1861, OR, I, 53, p. 134.
153. U.S. Congress, *Journal*, p. 873.
154. Curry, *Civil History*, p. 71.
155. Scarborough, *Ruffin Diary*, February 18, 1861, p. 551.
156. "Political Quicksands," 1863, ———Curry Family Papers, ADAH.
157. Smith, *Address*, p. 14.
158. U.S. Congress, *Journal*, pp. 874–76.
159. Curry, *Civil History*, p. 63. As evidence that Curry is not the most reliable source, he also credited J. A. P. Campbell with being a very able advocate during the debates, despite the fact that Campbell was not there!
160. Charleston, *Mercury*, March 9, 1861.
161. Barry to Pettus, March 6, 1861, RG 27, Vol. 36, MDAH.
162. This is conjecture, based on the passage of Harris's motion at the end of the March 6 session and his withdrawing it first thing the next morning, and seems a likely explanation.
163. Russell, *Diary*, I, pp. 167, 182.
164. Charleston, *Mercury*, April 13, 1861.
165. New Orleans, *Daily Delta*, March 8, 1861.
166. Cobb to Marion Cobb, March 6, 1861, "Correspondence," p. 255.
167. Charleston, *Mercury*, April 13, 1861.
168. Montgomery, *Weekly Mail*, March 15, 1861.
169. Thomas Withers to Clement C. Clay, April 18, 1863, Clay Papers, Duke.
170. Congress, *Journal*, pp. 876–77.

171. Rhett to T. Stuart Rhett, April 15, 1868, Rhett Papers, SCHS; Phila-
    delphia, *Weekly Times*, January 24, 1880.
172. Stephens to Linton Stephens, March 8, 1861, Stephens Papers, MCSH.
173. U.S. Congress, *Journal*, pp. 881–83.
174. *Ibid.*, pp. 883–84.
175. New Orleans, *Daily Delta*, March 10, 1861.
176. *Ibid.*
177. Richmond, *Daily Examiner*, May 18, 1861.
178. Mobile, *Daily Advertiser*, February 23, 1861; Augusta, *Daily Constitu-
    tionalist*, March 9, 1861; Atlanta, *Gate-City Guardian*, February 28,
    1861.
179. Montgomery, *Weekly Mail*, April 5, 1861; New Orleans, *Daily Delta*,
    February 26, 1861.
180. Simms to Miles, February 20, 1861, Oliphant et al., *Letters*, IV, p. 329;
    Cobb to Marion Cobb, March 7, 1861, "Correspondence," p. 257.
181. U.S. Congress, *Journal*, p. 117; Woodward, *Chesnut*, March [12], 1861,
    p. 24.
182. Stephens to Linton Stephens, March 8, 1861, Stephens Papers, MCSH.
183. *Ibid.*
184. U.S. Congress, *Journal*, pp. 886–88.
185. Stephens to Linton Stephens, March 8, 1861, Stephens Papers, MCSH.
186. Columbus, *Daily Times*, March 9, 1861; Nashville, *Union & American*,
    March 12, 1861.
187. Augusta, *Daily Constitutionalist*, April 9, 1861.
188. Stephens to Linton Stephens, March 9, 1861, Stephens Papers, MCSH.
189. Clitherall copy of draft of Constitution, Confederate States of America
    Papers, LC; Parrish and Willingham, *Imprints*, p. 43.
190. Rhett, Autobiography, Rhett Papers, SCHS.
191. Montgomery, *Weekly Advertiser*, March 20, 1861.
192. Curry, *Civil History*, p. 74.
193. Smith, *Address*, p. 14.
194. Smith to William C. Rives, January 1, 1864, William C. Rives Papers, LC.
195. "Political Quicksands," 1863, Curry Family Papers.
196. U.S. Congress, *Journal*, pp. 889–96.
197. Stephens to Linton Stephens, March 10, 1861, Stephens Papers, MCSH.
198. U.S. Congress, *Journal*, pp. 86–87.
199. Woodward and Muhlenfeld, *Private Mary Chesnut*, March 11, 1861, p.
    33; New York, *Citizen*, April 20, 1867.
200. U.S. Congress, *Journal*, p. 896.
201. Barry to Pettus, March 11, 1861, RG 27, Vol. 36, MDAH.
202. Natchez, *Daily Courier*, March 14, 1861.
203. Columbus, *Daily Times*, March 14, 1861.
204. *Ibid.*
205. Parrish and Willingham, *Imprints*, p. 43.
206. Nashville, *Union & American*, March 15, 1861.

207. Curry, *Civil History*, p. 49.
208. Howell Cobb to his wife, March 12, 1861, Cobb Papers, Georgia.
209. Pender to Susan Pender, March 14, 1861, Pender Papers.
210. Atlanta, *Daily Intelligencer*, March 14, 1861.
211. *Ibid.*, March 12, 14, 1861.
212. U.S. Congress, *Journal*, pp. 123, 124, 128–29, 142; Natchez, *Daily Courier*, March 26, 1861; Montgomery, *Weekly Advertiser*, March 13, 20, 1861; Culver, Memoirs.
213. Montgomery, *Weekly Advertiser*, March 20, 1861.
214. Cobb to Marion Cobb, March 6, 1861, "Correspondence," p. 255; U.S. Congress, *Journal*, p. 122.
215. U.S. Congress, *Journal*, p. 131.
216. Mobile, *Daily Advertiser*, March 17, 1861; Columbus, *Daily Times*, March 18, 1861.
217. U.S. Congress, *Journal*, pp. 147, 151–52, 153; Vicksburg, *Daily Evening Sentinel*, March 18, 1861.
218. Joseph Hodgson, *The Cradle of the Confederacy, or the Times of Troup, Quitman and Yancey*, (Mobile, 1876), p. 52.
219. Jacksonville, Alabama, *Republican*, March 14, 1861; Ralph Wooster, *The Secession Conventions of the South* (Princeton, 1962), p. 60.
220. Clipping, Scrapbook #4, Walthall Papers, MDAH.
221. U.S. Congress, *Journal*, p. 150; Rhett, Autobiography, Rhett Papers, SCHS.
222. U.S. Congress, *Journal*, pp. 152–53.
223. Columbus, *Daily Times*, March 18, 1861.
224. *Ibid.*, March 14, 1861; M. Humphries to Stephens, March 19, 1861, Stephens Papers, LC.
225. Hammond to Simms, March 23, 1861, Hammond Papers, LC; Cobb to Buchanan, March 26, 1861, Phillips, *Correspondence*, p. 555.

11. One Mass of Vulgarity & Finery & Honor

1. Trescott to Miles, February 17, 1861, Miles Papers, SHC, UNC.
2. Manly to "Dear Children," February 26, 1861, Manly Family Papers.
3. New York, *Citizen*, April 13, 1867.
4. Charleston, *Mercury*, March 14, 1861.
5. Thomas Caffey to Mary Caffey, April 6, 1861, Thomas Caffey, "Letters from the Front," *Confederate Veteran*, XXVI (January 1918), p. 26.
6. Smith to his wife, March 1861, Easby-Smith Papers.
7. Read, "Reminiscences," p. 332.
8. Montgomery, *Weekly Montgomery Confederation*, March 1, 1861.
9. "Doctor Snap" [E.D. Newton] to "Sister Cricket" [Helen Newton], March 28, 1861, Carlton-Newton-Mell Collection, University of Georgia Library, Athens.
10. New Orleans, *Daily Picayune*, April 8, 1861.

11. John Luithers to Francis LeVert, April 9, 1861, LeVert Family Papers, SHC, UNC.

12. Montgomery, *Weekly Mail*, March 15, 1861.

13. Charleston, *Mercury*, March 14, 1861.

14. New Orleans, *Daily Delta*, March 10, 1861.

15. Savannah, *Daily Morning News*, March 1, 1861; Columbus, *Daily Times*, March 6, 1861.

16. Smith to his wife, March 1861, Easby-Smith Papers.

17. De Leon, *Four Years*, p. 31.

18. *Ibid.*, pp. 26, 31; New York, *Citizen*, April 20, 1867.

19. New York, *Citizen*, April 13, 20, 1867.

20. Thomas C. De Leon, *Belles, Beaux and Brains of the 60's* (New York, 1907), pp. 54, 55.

21. New York, *Citizen*, April 20, 1867.

22. *Ibid.*, May 4, 1867.

23. *Ibid.*, April 20, 1867.

24. Charleston, *Mercury*, February 22, 1861.

25. Woodward, *Chesnut*, March 19, 1861, p. 31.

26. Paige Holliman Kemp, "Montgomery, Alabama, 1861: A Social History of the Cradle of the Confederacy" (Master's thesis, Auburn University, Auburn, Ala., 1978), pp. 92–93.

27. Woodward and Muhlenfeld, *Private Mary Chesnut*, March 7, 1861, p. 25.

28. Kirkland and Kennedy, *Historic Camden*, II, p. 156.

29. Woodward and Muhlenfeld, *Private Mary Chesnut*, March 1, 1861, p. 17; March 2, 1861, p. 18; March 3, 1861, p. 20; March 4, 1861, p. 21; March 11, 1861, p. 31.

30. *Ibid.*, March 2, 1861, p. 18; Woodward, *Chesnut*, March 11, 1861, p. 21; March [12], 1861, p. 25.

31. Woodward, *Chesnut*, March 9, 1861, p. 21; Woodward and Muhlenfeld, *Private Mary Chesnut*, March 5, 1861, p. 23, March 9, 1861, p. 29, March 12, 1861, p. 35.

32. Woodward and Muhlenfeld, *Private Mary Chesnut*, March 11, 1861, pp. 31, 32, 34, March 14, 1861, p. 38.

33. Woodward, *Chesnut*, February 25, 1861, p. 9, March 3, p. 14, March 9, p. 20.

34. Woodward and Muhlenfeld, *Private Mary Chesnut*, February 25, 1861, p. 12, March 6, p. 24, March 7, p. 25, March 9, p. 29, March 12, p. 36.

35. Cobb to Marion Cobb, March 2, 1861, "Correspondence," p. 249.

36. John A. Cobb to Howell Cobb, February 23, 1861, Cobb Papers, Georgia.

37. New York, *Citizen*, April 20, 1867; Stephens to Linton Stephens, February 17, 1861, Stephens Papers, MCSH.

38. Toombs to Stephens, April 6, 1861, Stephens Papers, Emory.

39. New York, *Harper's Weekly*, March 9, 1861.

40. Montgomery, *Daily Post*, February 22, 1861.

41. Stephens to Linton Stephens, March 10, 1861, Stephens Papers, MCSH.

42. Devereux and Klapp to Stephens, April 7, 1861, Stephens Papers, LC; Stephens to Linton Stephens, March 1, 1861, Stephens Papers, MCSH.
43. Stephens to Linton Stephens, March 3, 1861, Stephens Papers, MCSH.
44. New Orleans, *Daily Delta*, March 10, 1861.
45. Louise DeClouet to Paul DeClouet, March 16, 1861, Christine DeClouet to DeClouet, February 21, 1861, DeClouet Family Papers.
46. Blanche DeClouet to Paul DeClouet, February 15, 1861, DeClouet Family Papers.
47. Woodward and Muhlenfeld, *Private Mary Chesnut*, February 26, 1861, p. 13; Culver, Memoirs.
48. Beringer, "Congress," p. 531; New Orleans, *Daily Delta*, March 10, 1861.
49. Memminger to Miles, March 19, 1861, Miles Papers, SHC, UNC.
50. Montgomery, *Weekly Mail*, March 22, 1861; De Leon, *Belles*, pp. 50–51; De Leon, *Four Years*, p. 28.
51. De Leon, *Four Years*, p. 103.
52. *Ibid.*, p. 28.
53. New Orleans, *Daily Delta*, February 26, 1861.
54. Kate Hutcheson Morrissette, "Social Life in the First Confederate Capital," Montgomery, *Journal*, March 13, 1907; Woodward and Muhlenfeld, *Private Mary Chesnut*, February 28, 1861, p. 16.
55. Morrissette, "Social Life"; ? to Charleston *Mercury*, January 12, 1861, Thomas Watts Papers, ADAH.
56. U.S. Census, 1860.
57. Hilliard, *Politics*, pp. 323–24.
58. Hilliard to Stephens, March 5, 1861, Stephens Papers, LC.
59. Stephens to Linton Stephens, March 1, 1861, Stephens Papers, MCSH; Morrissette, "Social Life."
60. Morrissette, "Social Life"; Woodward and Muhlenfeld, *Private Mary Chesnut*, February 27, 1861, p. 14, February 28, p. 16; Hilliard to Stephens, n.d., Stephens Papers, Duke; Woodward, *Chesnut*, [February 27, 1861], p. 11.
61. Stephens to Linton Stephens, March 10, 1861, Stephens Papers, MCSH.
62. Stephens to Linton Stephens, March 1, 1861, Stephens Papers, MCSH.
63. Woodward, *Chesnut*, March 1861, p. 24.
64. Montgomery, *Weekly Mail*, March 1, 1861.
65. Cobb to Marion Cobb, February 8, 1861, "Correspondence," p. 167, February 14, 1861, p. 176; Morrissette, "Social Life."
66. Woodward and Muhlenfeld, *Private Mary Chesnut*, March 7, 1861, p. 26, March 12, p. 35, March 15, p. 39.
67. Frank Maloy Anderson, *The Mystery of "A Public Man"* (Minneapolis, 1948), p. 238. While much of this diary is spurious, Anderson concluded that it is based on a "core" diary, and that the nonsensational portions—of which Montgomery women would be one—are probably genuine (pp. 175–78).
68. Woodward and Muhlenfeld, *Private Mary Chesnut*, March 3, 1861, pp. 19–20, March 6, p. 24.

69. U.S. Census, 1860, p. 94; *OR*, I, 52, 2, p. 4; Woodward and Muhlenfeld, *Private Mary Chesnut*, March 7, 1861, p. 25.

70. Woodward and Muhlenfeld, *Private Mary Chesnut*, March 7, 1861, pp. 26–27, March 9, p. 29, March 15, pp. 39–40.

71. Macon, *Telegraph*, February 22, 1861.

72. Davis to Varina Davis, February 20, 1861, *PJD*, VII, p. 54.

73. Stephens to Linton Stephens, March 3, 1861, Stephens Papers, MCSH.

74. U.S. Congress, *Journal*, p. 74.

75. Cameron F. Napier, *The First White House of the Confederacy* (Montgomery 1986), p. 2; Moore to Edmund Harrison, March 21, 1861, Governors Papers, Administrative Files, ADAH.

76. Huntsville, *Democrat*, April 3, 1861.

77. Charleston, *Mercury*, March 28, 1861.

78. Stephens to Linton Stephens, March 3, 1861, Stephens Papers, MCSH.

79. Rhett, Autobiography, Rhett Papers, SCHS.

80. Charleston, *Mercury*, February 26, 1861; Rhett, Autobiography, Rhett Papers, SCHS.

81. Davis, *Jefferson Davis*, p. 237.

82. New York, *Citizen*, May 4, 1867; clipping in Scrapbook #4, Walthall Papers, ADAH; De Leon, *Belles*, p. 48; De Leon, *Four Years*, pp. 24–25; Davis, *Memoir*, II, pp. 40, 159.

83. Columbus, *Daily Times*, March 5, 1861.

84. Davis, *Memoir*, II, p. 163.

85. Woodward and Muhlenfeld, *Private Mary Chesnut*, March 2, 1861, p. 18.

86. New York, *Citizen*, May 25, 1867.

87. Stephens to Linton Stephens, March 3, 1861, Stephens Papers, MCSH.

88. Davis to Howell Cobb, July 6, 1868, Rowland, VII, p. 243.

89. Howell Cobb to John Cobb, March 5, 1861, Cobb Papers, Georgia.

90. De Leon, *Four Years*, p. 40.

91. Columbia, *Daily South Carolinian*, March 9, 1861; Jones and Rogers, "Montgomery," March 6, 1861, p. 47.

92. Charleston, *Mercury*, March 11, 1861.

93. New York, *Times*, May 30, 1861; Woodward and Muhlenfeld, *Private Mary Chesnut*, March 5 [6], 1861, p. 23; Woodward, *Chesnut*, March 5, [6], 1861, p. 17.

94. Davis, *Memoir*, II, p. 161.

95. Montgomery, *Weekly Montgomery Confederation*, March 10, 1861.

96. William R. Smith to his wife, March 12, 1861, Easby-Smith Papers; Columbia, *Daily South Carolinian*, March 16, 1861; Vicksburg, *Daily Evening Citizen*, April 4, 1861.

97. Davis, *Memoir*, II, p. 40.

98. Davis to Memminger, March 28, 1861, *PJD*, VII, p. 83.

99. New York, *Citizen*, May 25, 1861.

100. Clipping, Scrapbook #4, Walthall Papers, ADAH.

101. Montgomery, *Weekly Montgomery Confederation*, March 29, 1861.

102. New Orleans, *Crescent*, April 4, 1861.

103. William R. Smith to his wife, March 17, 1861, Easby-Smith Papers.

104. De Leon, *Four Years*, p. 24.

105. *Ibid.*, p. 76.

106. Montgomery, *Weekly Mail*, April 12, 1861.

107. Montgomery, *Daily Post*, February 13, 1861.

108. Montgomery City Council Minutes, April 8, 1861, ADAH.

109. Montgomery, *Daily Post*, February 21, 1861; Montgomery, *Advertiser*, October 15, 1938.

110. Charleston, *Mercury*, April 11, 1861.

111. U.S. Congress, *Journal*, p. 107.

112. City Council Minutes, April 1, 22, 1861, ADAH; U.S. Census, 1860, p. 10; Sanford, *Code*, pp. 91, 92; Jones and Rogers, "Montgomery," May 9, 1861, p. 101.

113. Sanford, *Code*, pp. 34, 40, 56; Montgomery City Council Minutes, April 1, 1861, ADAH.

114. Culver, Memoirs.

115. Sanford, *Code*, pp. 69ff; Montgomery, *Weekly Mail*, March 22, 1861.

116. Receipts, March 14, 29, 1861, William S. Comstock Papers, University of Alabama; Montgomery, *Daily Post*, February 16, 1861; Montgomery, *Weekly Advertiser*, February 27, 1861; Culver, Memoirs.

117. Montgomery, *Daily Post*, February 13, 1861.

118. Montgomery, *Weekly Mail*, February 22, 1861.

119. Augusta, *Daily Constitutionalist*, March 5, 1861; Atlanta, *Southern Confederacy*, March 5, 1861.

120. Ann Easby-Smith, *William Russell Smith of Alabama, His Life and Works* (Philadelphia, 1931), pp. 119–20; Montgomery, *Weekly Montgomery Confederation*, March 29, 1861.

121. Charleston, *Mercury*, March 9, 1861; Natchez, *Daily Courier*, March 26, 1861.

122. Montgomery, *Weekly Mail*, March 8, 15, April 12, 1861; Augusta, *Daily Constitutionalist*, April 9, 1861.

123. Columbus, *Daily Times*, March 1, 1861; Jones and Rogers, "Montgomery," March 19, 1861, p. 53, March 21, p. 54.

124. Montgomery, *Weekly Mail*, March 15, 1861.

125. *Ibid.*, April 5, 1861.

126. *Ibid.*, March 15, 1861.

127. Columbus, *Daily Times*, April 10, 1861.

128. Montgomery, *Daily Advertiser*, March 21, 1861.

129. Jones and Rogers, "Montgomery," April 1, 1861, p. 60, May 1, p. 97.

130. Columbus, *Daily Times*, March 7, 1861.

131. Smith to his wife, March 5, 1861, Easby-Smith Papers.

132. Harrison to Susan Harrison, February 17, 1861, Harrison Papers; Columbus, *Daily Times*, February 27, 1861.

133. Columbus, *Daily Times*, February 27, March 2, 1861; Smith, *Address*, p. 22; Augusta Evans to Rachel Heustis, March 13, 1861, Rachel Lyons Heustis Papers, SHC, UNC.

134. City Council Minutes, February 25, March 4, April 1, 1861, ADAH.

135. Culver, Memoirs.

136. Louise DeClouet to Paul DeClouet, March 16, 1861, DeClouet Papers.

137. Napier, "Montgomery," p. 109 and n.

138. *Ibid.*, p. 107; Woodward, *Chesnut*, March 3, 1861, p. 14; Montgomery, *Daily Post*, February 19, 22, 1861.

139. Montgomery, *Daily Post*, March 12, 1861.

140. Hooper to John DeBerniere Hooper, February 22, 1861, Hooper Papers.

141. Jones and Rogers, "Montgomery," March 6, 1861, p. 48.

142. Montgomery, *Weekly Mail*, March 22, 1861.

143. Columbus, *Daily Times*, March 11, 1861.

144. Montgomery, *Weekly Advertiser*, April 10, 1861.

145. Hooper to John DeBerniere Hooper, March 23, 1861, Hooper Papers; Hoole, *Hooper*, p. 157.

146. New York, *Citizen*, June 22, 1867; New Orleans, *Daily Delta*, February 28, 1861; Charleston, *Mercury*, March 9, 1861.

147. C. E. L. Stuart to Davis, February 10, 1862, Letters Received, Confederate Secretary of War, RG 109, NA.

148. Burton Harrison to William Preston Johnston, June 29, 1867, Barret Collection.

149. New York, *Citizen*, April 27, 1867.

150. *Ibid.*.

151. Culver, Memoirs.

152. Kemp, "Montgomery," p. 78.

153. Montgomery, *Weekly Mail*, March 8, 1861.

154. New Orleans, *Daily Picayune*, April 8, 1861; Montgomery, *Daily Post*, February 19, 1861.

155. O'Brien, "Old Montgomery Theatre," pp. 8–13.

156. Charleston, *Mercury*, April 4, 1861.

157. Montgomery, *Daily Post*, February 22, 1861; Kemp, "Montgomery," p. 122.

158. Huntsville, *Democrat*, April 10, 1861; Montgomery, *Advertiser*, March 12, 15, 31, April 4, 1861; Woodward and Muhlenfeld, *Private Mary Chesnut*, March 2, 1861, p. 18.

159. Sanford, *Code*, p. 8; Montgomery, *Weekly Mail*, March 8, April 12, 1861.

160. Montgomery, *Weekly Mail*, March 29, 1861.

161. Montgomery, *Weekly Mail*, April 12, 1861; Flynt, *Montgomery*, p. 36.

162. Sanford, *Code*, p. 9; Montgomery, *Daily Post*, February 18, 1861.

163. New York, *Citizen*, April 20, 1867.

164. Montgomery City Council Minutes, April 1, 1861, ADAH.

165. Montgomery, *Weekly Mail*, April 5, 1861.

166. New York, *Citizen*, April 20, 1867.

167. U.S. Census, 1860, p. 44.
168. Sanford, *Code*, pp. 47, 49, 93.
169. Montgomery, *Weekly Mail*, February 13, March 8, 1861.
170. De Leon, *Belles*, p. 57.
171. Montgomery City Council Minutes, March 4, 1861, ADAH.
172. Culver, Memoirs.
173. Montgomery, *Weekly Advertiser*, April 3, 1861.
174. Sanford, *Code*, pp. 48–49.
175. Tharin, *Arbitrary Arrests*, pp. 192–93.
176. New York, *Citizen*, May 4, 1867.
177. Montgomery, *Weekly Mail*, March 15, 1861.
178. *Ibid.*, February 8, 1861.
179. *Ibid.*, April 2, 1861.
180. Culver, Memoirs.
181. Montgomery, *Weekly Mail*, March 15, 1861; Woodward and Muhlen-feld, *Private Mary Chesnut*, March 18, 1861, p. 42.
182. Montgomery, *Weekly Mail*, April 5, 1861.
183. U.S. Census, 1860, p. 5.
184. Columbus, *Daily Columbus Enquirer*, April 12, 1861; Augusta, *Daily Constitutionalist*, April 11, 1861.
185. New York, *Citizen*, April 27, 1867.
186. Montgomery, *Weekly Advertiser*, April 3, 1861.
187. Sanford, *Code*, pp. 27, 29, 85; Montgomery City Council Minutes, February 25, 1861, ADAH.
188. Culver, Memoirs.
189. Sanford, *Code*, pp. 85–88.
190. New York, *Herald*, February 23, 1861.
191. John H. Napier, III, "Montgomery During the Civil War," *The Alabama Review*, XLI (April 1988), p. 104.
192. U.S. Census, 1860, pp. 11, 170.
193. Sanford, *Code*, p. 89; Culver, Memoirs.
194. Culver, Memoirs.
195. Russell, *Diary*, I, p. 169.
196. Woodward and Muhlenfeld, *Private Mary Chesnut*, March 4, 1861, p. 21; Woodward, *Chesnut*, March [11], 1861, p. 23.
197. Sanford, *Code*, pp. 7, 33, 83, 89, 90.
198. Moore, *Rebellion Record*, I, "Rumors and Incidents," p. 94.
199. Anderson, Autobiography, Anderson Papers.
200. New York, *Herald*, February 23, 1861.
201. Charleston, *Mercury*, March 24, 1861.
202. Woodward and Muhlenfeld, *Private Mary Chesnut*, March 12, 1861, p. 36; Telegraphic Cypher, 1861, George N. Sanders Papers, NA.
203. New York, *Citizen*, July 20, 1867.
204. Tharin, *Arbitrary Arrests*, pp. 15, 23–24, 195, 202–14.
205. Clipping from Mobile, *Tribune*, n.d., Scrapbook #4, Walthall Papers.

12. The Gage of Battle

1. Pender to Sarah Pender, March 16, 1861, Pender Papers.
2. Columbus, *Daily Times*, March 21, 1861; Jones and Rogers, "Montgomery," March 16, 1861, p. 48.
3. New Orleans, *Daily Delta*, March 26, 1861.
4. Jones and Rogers, "Montgomery," March 19, 1861, p. 51.
5. *Ibid.*, March 16, 1861, p. 48.
6. New Orleans, *Daily Picayune*, March 20, 1861.
7. Vicksburg, *Daily Evening Citizen*, March 15, 1861.
8. Davis, *Rise and Fall*, I, p. 263; New York, *Citizen*, April 13, 1867.
9. Chilton to DuBose, October 26, 1886, DuBose Papers.
10. Easby-Smith, *Smith*, pp. 121–23.
11. Barney, *Secessionist Impulse*, pp. 305–306.
12. Jones and Rogers, "Montgomery," March 16, 1861, p. 49.
13. Woodward and Muhlenfeld, *Private Mary Chesnut*, March 10, 1861, p. 30.
14. Thomas R. R. Cobb, *Substance of an Address of . . . to His Constituents of Clark County, April 6, 1861* (N.p., 1861), *passim*.
15. Atlanta, *Southern Confederacy*, April 5, 1861; Benjamin H. Hill, Jr., *Senator Benjamin H. Hill of Georgia. His Life, Speeches and Writings* (Atlanta, 1893), p. 42.
16. Atlanta, *Daily Intelligencer*, March 14, 1861.
17. Vicksburg, *Daily Evening Citizen*, March 20, 1861.
18. Charleston, *Mercury*, March 18, 1861.
19. "Speech of A. H. Stephens," Moore, *Rebellion Record*, I, "Documents," p. 45.
20. Stephens, *Popular History*, pp. 600–601.
21. Johnson, *Patriarchal Republic*, pp. 156ff.
22. Natchez, *Daily Courier*, March 26, 1861.
23. Barry to Davis, March 27, 1861, *PJD*, VII, p. 82.
24. Harris, "Autobiography," Rowland, *Courts*, p. 325.
25. Wooster, *Secession Conventions*, p. 48.
26. Charleston, *Mercury*, April 4, 1861.
27. *Ibid.*, March 15, 1861.
28. Scarborough, *Ruffin Diary*, I, April 1, 1861, p. 575.
29. Athens, Georgia, *Southern Watchman*, April 3, 1861; Takaki, *Pro-Slavery Crusade*, p. 237; Cauthen, *South Carolina*, pp. 87, 89.
30. Columbia, *Daily South Carolinian*, March 16, 1861.
31. John Manning to his wife, April 2, 1861, Williams-Chesnut-Manning Papers.
32. George L. Pugh to Chesnut, March 16, 1861, Williams-Chesnut-Manning Papers.
33. Dallas, *Herald*, April 3, 1861.
34. Cauthen, *South Carolina*, pp. 90–91.
35. Hammond to Ashmore, April 23, 1861, Hammond Papers.

36. Charleston, *Mercury*, April 4, 1861.
37. Wooster, *Secession Conventions*, p. 74.
38. Smith, *Address*, p. 20.
39. Toombs to Stephens, April 6, 1861, Stephens Papers, Emory.
40. Sanders to Magoffin, March 21, 1861, Sanders Papers, NA; Charleston, *Mercury*, March 28, 1861.
41. John Scott to Walker, March 25, 1861, *OR*, I, 51, 2, pp. 8–9; Virginia Convention Delegates to Davis, April 2, 1861, *PJD*, VII, p. 85.
42. Parrish and Willingham, *Imprints*, p. 45; Cobb to Pettus, March 30, 1861, RG 27, Vol. 36, MDAH.
43. Cobb to Howell Cobb, March 19, 1861, Phillips, *Correspondence*, p. 551.
44. Cobb to Marion Cobb, March 2, 1861, "Correspondence," p. 249.
45. Charleston, *Mercury*, April 9, 1861.
46. Benjamin to J. W. Zacharie, March 20, 1861, *OR*, I, 52, 2, p. 28; New Orleans, *Daily Delta*, April 7, 1861.
47. Charleston, *Mercury*, March 26, 1861.
48. Montgomery, *Weekly Mail*, March 22, April 12, 1861; Charleston, *Mercury*, March 28, 1861.
49. Montgomery, *Weekly Advertiser*, April 3, 1861; Reagan, *Memoirs*, p. 125.
50. Columbus, *Daily Times*, April 3, 1861; Charleston, *Mercury*, April 4, 1861; Reagan, *Memoirs*, p. 127.
51. Reagan, *Memoirs*, p. 127; Charleston, *Mercury*, March 26, 1861.
52. Charleston, *Mercury*, March 26, 1861.
53. Charleston, *Mercury*, April 2, 1861; Capers, *Memminger*, p. 330.
54. Montgomery, *Weekly Advertiser*, March 27, 1861; Natchez, *Daily Courier*, March 28, 1861.
55. Charleston, *Mercury*, March 28, 1861.
56. Montgomery, *Weekly Advertiser*, April 3, 10, 1861.
57. New Orleans, *Daily Picayune*, April 8, 1861; Columbus, *Daily Times*, April 8, 1861.
58. Montgomery, *Weekly Advertiser*, March 6, 1861; Memminger to Brown, April 3, 1861, *The Collector*, September 1953, copy in Memminger Papers, SCL, USC.
59. Montgomery, *Weekly Advertiser*, March 27, 1861; Montgomery, *Weekly Montgomery Confederation*, April 5, 1861.
60. New York, *Citizen*, April 13, 1867.
61. Pettus to Walker, March 18, 1861, Perry to Walker, March 19, 1861, *OR*, IV, 1, p. 176.
62. Montgomery, *Weekly Montgomery Confederation*, March 29, 1861; "Mother" to Edward L'Engle, April 16, 1861, Edward M. L'Engle Papers, SHC, UNC.
63. H. E. Sterx and L. Y. Trapp, eds., "One Year of the War: Civil War Diary of John Withers, Assistant-Adjutant-General of the Confederate Army," *Alabama Historical Quarterly*, XXIX (Fall–Winter 1967), p. 145.
64. New York, *Citizen*, July 20, 1867.

65. Frank E. Vandiver, ed., *The Civil War Diary of General Josiah Gorgas* (University, Ala., 1947), p. 1.
66. Walker to Robert E. Lee, March 15, 1861, OR, IV, 1, pp. 165–66.
67. Walker to Henry Brewster, March 21, 1861, OR, I, 1, p. 614, John Hemphill and Williamson Oldham to Walker, March 30, 1861, pp. 618–20; Walker to Hemphill and Oldham, April 1, 1861, Walker to E. Sparrow, March 29, 1861, Walker Letter-Book, LC.
68. W. R. Boggs to Henry C. Wayne, April 1, 1861, Henry C. Wayne Papers, Duke.
69. Walker to Pickens, March 26, 1861, OR, IV, 1, pp. 189–90.
70. Charleston, *Mercury*, March 26, 1861.
71. E. W. Cave to Walker, March 13, 1861, OR, I, 1, pp. 611–13.
72. Walker to Benjamin, April 1, 1861, OR, IV, 1, 202.
73. Moore to Walker, March 20, 1861, OR, IV, 1, p. 181, March 30, 1861, pp. 194–95, Walker to Moore, March 25, 1861, p. 188, April 2, 1861, pp. 205–206.
74. Brown to Walker, March 18, 1861, OR, IV, 1, p. 174, April 2, 4, 1861, pp. 206–207, Walker to Brown, March 22, 1861, p. 179, March 27, 1861, p. 191, Walker to Toombs, March 22, 1861, p. 184, Toombs to Walker, March 21, 1861, p. 181, March 23, 1861, p. 184, Resolution, March 23, 1861, p. 185.
75. T. O. Moore to Walker, March 15, 1861, OR, IV, 1, p. 171, Cooper to Gaston Coppens, March 20, 1861, p. 179, Pettus to Walker, March 16, p. 174; Charleston, *Mercury*, April 11, 1861.
76. Hooper to L. Q. Washington, March 22, 1861, OR, I, 51, 2, p. 8, Hooper to John Ridley, March 29, 1861, IV, 1, p. 194, Hooper to C. H. Craige, March 26, 1861, pp. 190–91.
77. De Leon, *Four Years*, p. 33.
78. Johnston, *Autobiography*, p. 126.
79. New York, *Citizen*, July 6, 1867
80. *Ibid.*, April 20, 1867.
81. Montgomery, *Advertiser*, March 6, 1907.
82. New York, *Citizen*, April 13, 1867.
83. Toombs to Yancey, Rost, and Mann, March 16, 1861, ORN, II, 3, pp. 195–97.
84. Proclamation, March 16, 1861, ORN, II, 3, pp. 95–96.
85. Toombs to Yancey, Rost, and Mann, March 16, 1861, ORN, II, 3, pp. 191–95.
86. Vicksburg, *Daily Evening Citizen*, April 3, 1861.
87. Davis to Abraham Lincoln, February 27, 1861, Richardson, *Messages and Papers*, I, p. 55.
88. Charleston, *Mercury*, March 14, 1861.
89. Trescott to Miles, February 17, 1861, Miles Papers, SHC, UNC.
90. Forsyth to Walker, March 14, 1861, OR, IV, 1, p. 165.
91. Memorandum, March 15, 1861, Toombs Letterbook.

92. Crawford to Stephens, March 16, 1861, Stephens Papers, LC.
93. Crawford and Roman to Toombs, March 26, 1861, Toombs Letterbook.
94. Roman to Toombs, March 29, 1861, Toombs Letterbook.
95. Crawford, and Roman to Toombs, March 30, 1861, Toombs Letterbook; Crawford to Stephens, March 31, 1861, Stephens Papers, LC.
96. Crawford to Toombs, April 1, 1861, Toombs Letterbook.
97. Crawford and Roman to Toombs, April 1, 2, 1861, Toombs Letterbook.
98. Crawford, Roman, and Forsyth to Toombs, April 3, 4, 5, 1861, Toombs Letterbook; F. Perrin to Roman, April 5, 1861, La Villebeuvre Family Papers.
99. R. L. Stuart to Roman, April 6, 1861, La Villebeuvre Family Papers.
100. Walker to Luke P. Blackburn, April 4, 1861, Walker Letter-Book.
101. Toombs to Crawford, Roman, and Forsyth, April 4, 1861, ORN, I, 4, p. 257; Toombs to Stephens, April 6, 1861, Phillips, *Correspondence*, p. 558.
102. Vicksburg, *Weekly Whig*, April 17, 1861.
103. Davis to Campbell, April 6, 1861, *PJD*, VII, pp. 92–93.
104. See Intercepted Telegrams, 1861, RG 107, Vol. 399, NA.
105. Crawford, Forsyth, and Roman to Toombs, April 7, 1861, Campbell Memorandum, April 7, 1861, John T. Pickett Memorandum, April 7, 1861, Memorandum, March 15, 1861, Toombs Letterbook.
106. Crawford, Forsyth, and Roman to Toombs, April 8, 1861, Crawford, Forsyth, and Roman to Seward, April 9, 1861, Toombs Letterbook.
107. Hooper to John DeBerniere Hooper, March 23, 1861, Hooper Papers.
108. Vicksburg, *Daily Evening Citizen*, April 8, 1861; Montgomery, *Weekly Advertiser*, April 17, 1861.
109. Cobb to Buchanan, March 26, 1861, Phillips, *Correspondence*, p. 555; Howell Cobb to his wife, March 28, 1861, Cobb Papers, Georgia.
110. Nashville, *Union & American*, April 12, 1861.
111. New York, *Citizen*, April 13, 1867.
112. Harris, Memoir, Rowland, *Courts*, p. 326.
113. Davis to Pickens, March 18, 1861, Rowland, V, p. 61.
114. Pickens to Davis, March 17, 1861, *PJD*, VII, p. 70.
115. New Orleans, *Daily Delta*, April 10, 1861.
116. Montgomery, *Weekly Mail*, March 29, 1861.
117. Walker to Pickens, March 1, 1861, OR, I, 1, p. 259.
118. Nashville, *Union & American*, March 23, 1861.
119. Crawford and Roman to Toombs, March 29, 1861, Toombs Letterbook; Columbia, *Daily South Carolinian*, April 4, 1861.
120. Field return, March 31, 1861, OR, I, 1, p. 455, Cooper to Bragg, March 25, 1861, p. 454.
121. Bragg to Walker, April 6, 1861, OR, I, 1, p. 457; Davis to Bragg, April 3, 1861, *PJD*, VII, p. 85.
122. Montgomery, *Weekly Advertiser*, April 10, 1861.
123. Charleston, *Mercury*, April 11, 1861.

124. Walker to Beauregard, April 8, 1861, Beauregard to Walker, April 8, 1861, *OR*, I, 1, p. 289.

125. Basil W. Duke, *Reminiscences of General Basil W. Duke, C.S.A.* (New York, 1911), p. 44.

126. Montgomery, *Daily Advertiser*, April 9, 1861.

127. Nashville, *Union & American*, April 11, 1861; New York, *Tribune*, April 9, 1861, Vicksburg, *Daily Evening Citizen*, April 10, 1861.

128. Walker to Pickens, April 8, 1861, *OR*, IV, 1, p. 211, Hooper to A. B. Moore, April 9, 1861, p. 213, Pettus to Walker, April 10, 1861, p. 217; Hooper to Pettus, April 9, 1861, RG 27, Vol. 36, MDAH.

129. Josiah Gorgas, Extracts from My Notes Written Chiefly Soon After the Close of the War, Rowland, VIII, p. 318.

130. *Ibid.*, pp. 308–10.

131. Walker to Forsyth, April 9, 1861, *OR*, IV, 1, p. 213, April 10, 1861, p. 216, Walker to Tucker, Cooper & Co., April 9, 1861, p. 213.

132. *Ibid.*, I, 52, 2, pp. 30–31.

133. E. Kirby-Smith to his mother, April 9, 1861, E. Kirby-Smith Papers, SHC, UNC.

134. Ben McCulloch to Wigfall, April 2, 1861, Louis T. Wigfall Papers, LC; New Orleans, *Daily Picayune*, April 9, 1861; Cooper to Earl Van Dorn, April 11, 1861, *OR*, II, 1, p. 56; De Leon, *Four Years*, p. 43; *A Soldier's Honor: With Reminiscences of Major-General Earl Van Dorn. By His Comrades* (New York, 1902), p. 47.

135. Montgomery, *Weekly Advertiser*, April 10, 1861.

136. Walker to Beauregard, April 9, 1861, *OR*, I, 1, p. 291.

137. Wigfall to Davis, April 9, 1861, *PJD*, VII, p. 100.

138. Montgomery, *Weekly Advertiser*, April 10, 1861.

139. Montgomery, *Weekly Mail*, April 19, 1861.

140. Jones and Rogers, "Montgomery," April 10, 1861, pp. 65–66.

141. New York, *Citizen*, May 5, 1867.

142. Jones and Rogers, "Montgomery," April 10, 1861, p. 65.

143. New York, *Citizen*, April 13, May 4, 1867.

144. Stovall, *Toombs*, p. 226.

145. Samuel W. Crawford, *The Genesis of the Civil War* (New York, 1887), p. 421.

146. Le Roy Pope Walker, Sketch of Le Roy Pope Walker, 1906, Woods Papers.

147. Stovall, *Toombs*, p. 226. While Stovall may be imagining some of this, it is largely consistent with the account in Crawford, *Genesis*, p. 421, and Walker confirms Crawford's account in Walker to A. H. Shiplett, September 9, 1871, Joseph Rubinfine *Catalog #34* (Pleasantville, N.J., 1974), item #161, when he says Crawford does "full justice" to the story.

148. Montgomery, *Advertiser*, March 6, 1907; Montgomery, *Weekly Advertiser*, April 10, 1861.

149. Montgomery, *Weekly Mail,* April 12, 1861.
150. Augusta, *Daily Constitutionalist,* April 13, 1861.
151. Wigfall to Davis, April 10, 1861, G. A. Baker *Catalog #34,* p. 8.
152. Walker to Beauregard, April 10, 1861, OR, I, 1, p. 297; Pickett to Toombs, April 11, 1861, Toombs Letterbook.
153. De Leon, *Four Years,* p. 35.
154. New Orleans, *Daily Picayune,* April 13, 1861; Montgomery, *Weekly Advertiser,* April 17, 1861.
155. Dillard, "Yancey," p. 158.
156. Kerbey, *Boy Spy,* p. 19; Montgomery, *Weekly Mail,* April 19, 1861.
157. Charleston, *Mercury,* April 13, 1861.
158. Beauregard to Walker, April 10, 1861, Walker to Beauregard, April 10, 1861, OR, I, 1, p. 297.
159. Walker to Brown, April 10, 1861, OR, IV, 1, p. 216, Brown to Walker, April 11, 1861, p. 218, Walker to Bartow, April 11, 1861, Bartow to Walker, April 13, 1861, I, 53, 1, p. 143.
160. Walker to Hemphill, April 11, 1861, OR, I, 1, pp. 621–22.
161. New Orleans, *Daily Picayune,* April 15, 1861.
162. Columbus, *Daily Times,* April 12, 1861; Jones and Rogers, "Montgomery," April 10, 1861, p. 67; New York, *Citizen,* May 4, 1867.
163. Beauregard to Walker, April 11, 1861, Walker to Beauregard, April 11, 1861, OR, I, 1, pp. 300–301.
164. Davis, *Rise and Fall,* I, p. 292.
165. Kerby, *Boy Spy,* pp. 23–24; New York, *Citizen,* April 13, 1867.
166. New York, *Citizen,* April 13, 1867.
167. New Orleans, *Daily Picayune,* April 16, 1861.
168. Walker to Beauregard, April 12, 1861, Beauregard to Walker, April 12, 1861, OR, I, 1, p. 305.
169. "Phillips H. S. Gayle and Mary Armistead Gayle," *Confederate Veteran,* XII (March 1904), p. 126.
170. Montgomery, *Weekly Mail,* April 12, 19, 1861.
171. New York, *Citizen,* May 4, 1867.
172. Montgomery, *Weekly Mail,* April 12, 1861.
173. Jones and Rogers, "Montgomery," April 15, 1861, p. 68; New York, *Citizen,* May 4, 1867; 1860 Census, p. 65.
174. New York, *Citizen,* May 4, 1867.
175. Beauregard to Walker, April 12, 1861, OR, I, 1, p. 305.
176. New Orleans, *Daily Picayune,* April 16, 1861; Montgomery, *Daily Advertiser,* April 13, 1861; Montgomery, *Weekly Advertiser,* April 17, 1861.
177. Montgomery, *Advertiser,* January 8, 1911.
178. Montgomery, *Daily Advertiser,* April 13, 1861; Montgomery, *Weekly Advertiser,* April 17, 1861; Montgomery, *Weekly Mail,* April 19, 1861; Jones and Rogers, "Montgomery," May 1[7], 1861, p. 97; Charleston, *Mercury,* April 13, 1861.

179. Huse, *Supplies*, p. 10.

180. De Leon, *Four Years*, p. 35.

181. Montgomery, *Weekly Mail*, April 19, 1861.

182. *Ibid.*, April 12, 1861.

183. Charleston, *Mercury*, April 13, 1861; New York, *Citizen*, May 4, 1867.

184. Beauregard to Walker, April 12, 1861, OR, I, 1, p. 306.

185. John Worden to Walker, April 16, 1861, OR, I, 1, pp. 462–63.

186. New York, *Citizen*, May 4, 1867; Montgomery, *Weekly Mail*, April 12, 1867.

187. New York, *Citizen*, May 11, 1867; Baltimore, *Sun*, April 15, 1861; Montgomery, *Weekly Advertiser*, April 17, 1861; Charleston, *Mercury*, April 15, 1861; Jones and Rogers, "Montgomery," April 15, 1861, p. 68.

188. Stephens, *Constitutional View*, II, p. 421ff; Garrett, *Public Men*, pp. 508–509; Walker to James Speed, September 7, 1865, Leroy P. Walker Collection, ADAH; Russell, *Diary*, I, p. 175.

189. Montgomery, *Weekly Advertiser*, April 17, 1861.

190. New York, *Citizen*, May 11, 1867.

191. Montgomery, *Weekly Advertiser*, April 17, 1861.

192. Vicksburg, *Daily Evening Citizen*, April 13, 1861.

193. New York, *Citizen*, May 4, 11, 1867.

194. Nashville, *Union & American*, April 12, 1861.

195. New York, *Citizen*, May 4, 1867.

196. Culver, Memoirs.

197. Beauregard to Walker, April 13, 1861, OR, I, 1, p. 308.

198. Montgomery, *Weekly Advertiser*, April 17, 1861; Jones and Rogers, "Montgomery," April 15, 1861, p. 69; Beauregard to Davis, April 13, 1861, Beauregard to Walker, April 13, 1861, OR, I, 1, p. 309.

199. Davis to Pickens, April 13, 1861, South Carolina Executive Journal Letter-Book, 1861. South Carolina Department of Archives and History, Columbia.

200. Walker to Beauregard, April 13, 1861, OR, I, 1, p. 310.

201. De Leon, *Four Years*, p. 36; Hilliard, *Politics*, p. 322.

202. Kerbey, *Boy Spy*, p. 23.

203. New York, *Citizen*, May 18, 1867.

204. Davis, *Memoir*, II, p. 80.

205. Vicksburg, *Daily Evening Citizen*, April 16, 1861. Paixhan and petard were both varieties of explosives used against fortifications, though not used at Fort Sumter.

13. All We Ask Is to Be Let Alone

1. Stephens to Linton Stephens, April 17, 1861, Stephens Papers, MCSH.

2. Walker to Edward Clark, April 15, 1861, Records of the Governor, Edward Clark, 301–35, Texas State Archives.

3. New York, *Citizen*, May 4, 1867.

4. Charleston, *Mercury*, April 18, 1861; Montgomery, *Weekly Advertiser*, April 17, 1861; Napier, *White House*, pp. 2-3; Montgomery, *Weekly Montgomery Confederation*, April 19, 1861.

5. New Orleans, *Daily Picayune*, April 9, 1861.

6. Davis, *Memoir*, II, p. 37; Montgomery, *Weekly Advertiser*, February 27, 1861.

7. Stephens to Linton Stephens, April 16, 17, 1861, Stephens Papers, MCSH.

8. Pickett to Toombs, April 15, 1861, Toombs Letterbook.

9. Richmond, *Examiner*, April 25, 1861; Memphis, *Daily Memphis Avalanche*, April 27, 1861.

10. Montgomery, *Weekly Advertiser*, April 24, 1861; New Orleans, *Daily Picayune*, April 17, 1861.

11. Richmond, *Dispatch*, April 22, 1861; Montgomery, *Weekly Advertiser*, April 24, 1861.

12. Stephens to Linton Stephens, April 17, 1861, Stephens Papers, MCSH.

13. Woods to David D. Shelby, April 14, 1908, Woods Papers.

14. Davis to Beverly Tucker, April 16, 1861, Beverly Tucker Papers, University of Virginia.

15. Walker to Thomas C. Hindman, April 16, 1861, OR, I, 1, p. 685.

16. Hooper to Pettus, *Ibid.*, IV, 1, p. 223.

17. Walker to Moore, April 15, 1861, Confederate States of America Executive Papers, Louisiana Historical Association Collection, Tulane University, Howard Tilton Library, New Orleans.

18. Pickens to Davis, April 16, 1861, *PJD*, VII, p. 105.

19. Proclamation, April 17, 1861, Richardson, *Messages and Papers*, I, pp. 60–62; John Boston to Toombs, April 18, 1861, B. Sanchez to Toombs, April 18, 1861, ORN, I, 1, p. 329, John Kennedy et al. to Toombs, April 19–May 4, 1861, ORN, I, 1, pp. 330–35.

20. Russell, *Diary*, I, pp. 170, 176.

21. ORN, I, 1, pp. 342ff.

22. Toombs to Yancey, Rost, and Mann, April 24, 1861, ORN, II, 3, pp. 198–201.

23. Mallory to Semmes, April 18, 1861, ORN, I, 1, p. 613, Semmes to Mallory, April 22, 1861, p. 614.

24. Huse, *Supplies*, pp. 9–10; Gorgas, Extracts, Rowland, VIII, pp. 310–11; Cooper to Huse, April 15, 1861, OR, IV, 1, p. 220.

25. Benjamin to Beauregard, April 16, 1861, John Minor Wisdom Collection, Tulane University, Howard Tilton Library, New Orleans.

26. John B. Gordon, *Reminiscences of the Civil War* (New York, 1904), p. 13.

27. James M. Morgan, *Recollections of A Rebel Reefer* (Boston, 1917), pp. 37–38.

28. Montgomery, *Weekly Montgomery Confederation*, May 10, 1861.

29. De Leon, *Four Years*, p. 38.

30. Savannah, *Daily Morning News*, April 23, 1861.

31. Montgomery, *Weekly Montgomery Confederation*, April 19, 1861.
32. Memphis, *Daily Memphis Avalanche*, April 27, 1861.
33. Joint Resolution, January 21, 1861, OR, IV, 1, p. 77.
34. Boyce to Hunter, February 5, 1861, R.M.T. Hunter Papers, University of Virginia.
35. Henry Wise to Davis, February 22, 1861, Confederate Papers Relating to Army Officers, RG 109, NA.
36. Edward C. Anderson to Davis, April 15, 1861, OR, I, 51, 2, p. 11; Vicksburg, *Daily Evening Citizen*, April 18, 1861.
37. Stephens to Linton Stephens, April 18, 1861, Stephens Papers, MCSH.
38. Montgomery, *Weekly Montgomery Confederation*, April 26, 1861; Vicksburg, *Daily Evening Citizen*, April 20, 1861.
39. Charleston, *Mercury*, April 23, 1861.
40. Montgomery, *Weekly Montgomery Confederation*, April 26, 1861.
41. New York, *Citizen*, May 25, 1867; General Orders No. 5, April 18, 1861, OR, IV, 1, p. 224.
42. Charleston, *Mercury*, April 19, 23, 1861; Augusta, *Daily Constitutionalist*, April 23, 1861; De Leon, *Four Years*, p. 76; New Orleans, *Daily Picayune*, April 19, 1861.
43. Jones and Rogers, "Montgomery," April 22, 1861, p. 76; Scarborough, *Ruffin Diary*, April 16, 1861, p. 604; Morrissette, "Social Life"; Huntsville, *Democrat*, April 24, 1861; New York, *Citizen*, May 18, 1867.
44. J. Marshall Crawford, *Mosby and His Men* (New York, 1867), pp. 30–31.
45. Vicksburg, *Daily Evening Citizen*, April 22, 1861; Letcher to Davis, April 18, 1861, OR, I, 51, 2, p. 16.
46. Davis to Letcher, April 18, 1861, Executive Papers, Virginia.
47. Stephens to Linton Stephens, April 19, 1861, Stephens Papers, MCSH; Davis to Letcher, April 19, 1861, Huntington Miscellaneous Collection, The Huntington, San Marino, California.
48. New York, *Citizen*, May 18, 1867.
49. Stephens to Linton Stephens, April 19, 1861, Stephens Papers, MCSH.
50. Bragg to Cooper, April 14, 1861, OR, I, 1, p. 461, Walker to Bragg, April 19, 1861, pp. 463, 464.
51. Davis to Letcher, April 22, 1861, OR, I, 2, p. 773; Walker to John Ellis, April 22, 1861, Executive Papers, Richmond; G.T. Sinclair to Mallory, April 22, 1861, ORN, I, 4, p. 306.
52. McRae to Davis, April 23, 1861, *PJD*, VII, p. 121.
53. Reagan to E. B. Nichols, April 16, 19, 1861, Oldham to Clark, April 17, 1861, Governors Papers, Texas.
54. Natchez, *Daily Courier*, April 17, 1861.
55. Montgomery, *Weekly Montgomery Confederation*, April 19, 26, 1861; Charleston, *Mercury*, April 18, 1861; Jones and Rogers, "Montgomery," April 15, 1861, pp. 70–71.
56. Charleston, *Mercury*, April 18, 1861; Jones and Rogers, "Montgomery," April 15, 1861, p. 71.
57. Walker to D. G. Duncan, April 20, 1861, OR, I, 51, 2, p. 20.

58. B. F. Lum to John W. Burson, April 17, 1861, OR, II, 2, p. 375; Charleston, *Mercury*, April 23, 1861; New Orleans, *Daily Picayune*, April 24, 1861.
59. Charleston, *Mercury*, April 25, 1861.
60. N. S. Reneau to Davis, April 12, 1861, T. F. Gaszynsky to Davis, April 1, 1861, R. O. Davidson to Davis, May 11, 1861, John S. Teas to Davis, April 1, 1861, Letters Received by the Secretary of War, RG 365, NA.
61. Andrew G. Magrath to Pickens, April 21, 1861, Pickens Papers, Duke.
62. Charleston, *Daily Courier*, April 25, 1861; Mobile, *Daily Advertiser*, April 24, 1861; Walker to Magoffin, April 22, 1861, OR, IV, 1, pp. 231–32, Blanton Duncan to Walker, n.d., I, 51, 2, p. 37, Ellis to Walker, April 23, 1861, p. 235.
63. New Orleans, Jackson & Great Northern Railroad Company to Pettus, April 22, 1861, RG 27, Vol. 36, MDAH.
64. Charleston, *Courier*, April 26, 1861.
65. Montgomery, *Daily Post*, April 24, 1861.
66. Montgomery, *Daily Post*, April 25, 1861; New York, *Citizen*, May 18, 1867; Charleston, *Mercury*, April 29, 1861.
67. Columbus, *Daily Times*, April 23, 1861.
68. Stephens to Linton Stephens, April 22, 1861, Stephens Papers, MCSH.
69. Stephens to Davis, April 23, 1861, OR, I, 51, 2, p. 26, Stephens to Toombs, April 25, 1861, IV, 1, p. 242; Journal, May 30, 1861, Johnston, *Autobiography*, p. 158.
70. Stephens to Linton Stephens, April 25, 1861, Stephens Papers, MCSH.
71. Scarborough, *Ruffin Diary*, II, April 25, 1861, p. 10; Duncan to Walker, April 26, 1861, OR, I, 51, 2, p. 39.
72. Stephens to Davis, April 25, 1861, OR, I, 51, 2, pp. 32–33; John Janney to Davis, April 27, 1861, Rowland, V, p. 67.
73. Stephens to Linton Stephens, April 29, 1861, Stephens Papers, MCSH.
74. In the 1890s Varina Davis provided a description of the arrangement of the mirror and other furnishings in this room, and they are so placed in the restored White House in Montgomery today.
75. De Leon, *Four Years*, pp. 39–40.
76. De Leon, *Four Years*, pp. 39–40; Davis, *Memoir*, II, p. 40; Varina Davis to Clement C. Clay, May 10, 1861, Clay Papers, Duke.
77. Davis, *Memoir*, II, p. 40.
78. Reagan, *Memoirs*, p. 120; "Editorial," *De Bow's Review*, XXX (May–June 1861), pp. 682–83.
79. Davis, *Memoir*, II, p. 161.
80. Reagan, *Memoirs*, p. 120.
81. Harris to Davis, May 2, 1861, *PJD*, VII, p. 144.
82. Huse, *Supplies*, pp. 10–11.
83. Montgomery, *Daily Post*, May 28, 1861.
84. Memphis, *Daily Memphis Avalanche*, April 23, 1861.
85. New York, *Citizen*, May 25, 1867.

86. Morgan, *Reefer*, p. 38.
87. Jones and Rogers, "Montgomery," April 22, 1861, pp. 75–76.
88. Charleston, *Mercury*, April 26, 1861; Montgomery, *Weekly Montgomery Confederation*, April 26, 1861.
89. Howell Cobb to Letcher, April 20, 1861, Executive Papers, Virginia.
90. Davis to Letcher, April 22, 1861, Executive Papers, Virginia.
91. Beriah Magoffin to Davis, April 17, 1861, *PJD*, VII, p. 108, William Preston Johnston to Davis, April 26, 1861, p. 128.
92. John G. Hancock to Davis, April 15, 1861, Jefferson Davis Papers, RG 109, Henry Heth to Davis, April 17, 1861, Henry S. Foote, Jr., to Davis, April 29, 1861, Confederate Papers Relating to Officers, RG 109, Henry Wise to Davis, May 15, 1861, Letters Received by the Secretary of War, RG 365, NA.
93. Montgomery, *Weekly Montgomery Confederation*, April 19, 1861.
94. Richard Gott to Lee, n.d. [April 1861], Executive Papers, Virginia.
95. Morgan, *Reefer*, p. 38.
96. Andrew Dawson to Stephens, April 18, 1861, Stephens Papers, LC.
97. Montgomery, *Weekly Advertiser*, April 17, 1861; Goff, *Confederate Supply*, pp. 11–12, 13–16; Jones and Rogers, "Montgomery," May 15, 1861, p. 106; Statement of arms, April 20, 1861, *OR*, IV, 1, pp. 227–28, May 7, 1861, p. 292, Walker to Howell Cobb, May 7, 1861, p. 292; Walker to Letcher, April 27, 1861, Executive Papers, Virginia.
98. Parrish and Willingham, *Imprints*, p. 222; Montgomery, *Daily Post*, May 2, 1861.
99. Vicksburg, *Daily Evening Citizen*, April 26, 1861.
100. Mariane Jones et al. to Davis, April 23, 1861, Letters Received by the Secretary of War, RG 365, NA.
101. Montgomery, *Weekly Mail*, April 19, 24, 1861; Montgomery, *Weekly Advertiser*, April 24, 1861.
102. Atlanta, *Southern Confederacy*, April 11, 1861.
103. Montgomery, *Weekly Advertiser*, April 24, 1861.
104. Nashville, *Union & American*, April 26, 1861; Vicksburg, *Daily Evening Citizen*, May 6, 1861.
105. Montgomery, *Weekly Advertiser*, April 24, 1861.
106. Montgomery, *Weekly Montgomery Confederation*, May 3, 1861.
107. Montgomery, *Weekly Mail*, April 26, 1861.
108. Cooper to Thomas Taylor, April 13, 1861, *OR*, I, 52, 2, p. 44.
109. Ellis to Davis, April 17, 1861, *OR*, I, 51, 2, p. 14, Ellis to Walker, April 24, 1861, IV, 1, pp. 237–38.
110. Ellis to Davis, April 25, 1861, *PJD*, VII, p. 125.
111. Davis to Claiborne Jackson, April 23, 1861, *OR*, I, 1, p. 688, Walker to Jackson, April 26, 1861, p. 689.
112. Walker to Henry M. Rector, April 22, 1861, *OR*, I, 1, p. 687, Rector to Walker, April 23, 1861, p. 687, S. P. Cockrell to Walker, April 21, 1861, p. 686, T. B. Flournoy to Walker, April 24, 25, 1861, pp. 688–89.

113. Natchez, *Daily Courier*, April 19, 1861.
114. Nashville, *Union & American*, April 21, 1861; Walker to Harris, April 19, 1861, *OR*, I, 52, 2, p. 56, April 22, 1861, p. 63; Harris to Davis, April 20, 1861, Autograph File, Frederick Dearborn Collection, Harvard University, Cambridge, Mass.
115. Hilliard, *Politics*, p. 325. While Hilliard's memoir does not date this meeting, a reporter noted his departure on April 25 (Charleston, *Mercury*, April 26, 1861). Evans C. Johnson, "A Political Life of Henry W. Hilliard" (M. A. thesis, University of Alabama, 1947), p. 154, somewhat mysteriously dates Hilliard's departure in May.
116. Reagan, *Memoirs*, pp. 126–27; Charleston, *Mercury*, April 29, 1861.
117. Walker to H. J. Ranney, April 24, 1861, *OR*, IV, 1, pp. 236–37, J. P. Wood to Walker, April 18, 1861, p. 224.
118. Walker to Railroad Presidents, April 25, 1861, *OR*, IV, 1, p. 238.
119. Parrish and Willingham, *Imprints*, p. 245; Reagan, *Memoirs*, pp. 133–34; Resolution, April 30, 1861, *OR*, IV, 1, p. 269; Montgomery, *Weekly Advertiser*, May 1, 1861.
120. Montgomery, *Daily Mail*, April 26, 1861; Jones and Rogers, "Montgomery," May 4, 1861, p. 91.
121. George Bickley to Davis, April 3, 1861, Sam Richey Collection, Miami University, Miami, Ohio.
122. C. E. Brame to Clark, April 12, 1861, Records of the Governor, Ed Clark, 301-35, Texas.
123. McCulloch to Clark, April 14, 1861, Records of the Governor, Ed Clark, 301-35, Texas.
124. Walker to Clark, April 27, 1861, *OR*, I, 1, p. 629, Cooper to Van Dorn, April 29, 1861, p. 630.
125. Oldham to Clark, April 20, 1861, Records of the Governor, Ed Clark, 301-35, Texas; Oldham to the Secretary of War of Texas, April 19, 1861, Austin, *Weekly State Gazette*, May 4, 1861.
126. Walker to Pickens, April 30, 1861, *OR*, IV, 1, p. 271.
127. Montgomery, *Weekly Montgomery Confederation*, April 26, 1861.
128. Walker to Davis, April 27, 1861, *OR*, IV, 1, pp. 247–54.
129. Mallory, Report, April 26, 1861, *ORN*, II, 2, pp. 51–57.
130. Toombs to Davis, Reagan to Davis, April 29, 1861, *PJD*, VII, p. 143.
131. Augusta, *Daily Constitutionalist*, April 17, 1861.
132. Howell Cobb to his wife, April 29, 1861, Cobb Papers, Georgia.
133. Cobb to Marion Cobb, April 29, 1861, "Correspondence," p. 259.
134. Montgomery, *Weekly Advertiser*, May 1, 1861; Charleston, *Mercury*, May 2, 1861.
135. Montgomery, *Weekly Advertiser*, May 1, 1861.
136. Cobb to Marion Cobb, April 29, 1861, "Correspondence," p. 259.
137. Howell Cobb to his wife, April 29, 1861, Cobb Papers, Georgia.
138. DeClouet to Paul DeClouet, May 1, 1861, DeClouet Papers.
139. Woodward and Muhlenfeld, *Private Mary Chesnut*, April 29, 1861, p. 64.

140. Clitherall to Howell Cobb, April 29, 1861, Cobb Papers, Georgia.
141. Montgomery, *Weekly Advertiser*, May 1, 1861.
142. Charleston, *Mercury*, May 2, 1861.
143. U.S. Congress, *Journal*, pp. 160–68.
144. Cobb to Marion Cobb, April 29, 1861, "Correspondence," p. 259.
145. Charlotte Wigfall to Halsey Wigfall, April 29, 1861, Wigfall Papers.
146. Charleston, *Mercury*, April 30, 1861.
147. U.S. Congress, *Journal*, pp. 169–70.

14. We Have Cast the Die

1. Cobb to Marion Cobb, May 1, 1861, "Cobb Correspondence. (Continued)," *Publications of the Southern History Association*, XI (September–November 1907), p. 316; Cobb to Marion Cobb, May 9, 1861, Thomas R. R. Cobb Papers, Georgia.
2. Charleston, *Mercury*, May 3, 1861; Montgomery, *Weekly Advertiser*, May 8, 1861.
3. U.S. Congress, *Journal*, p. 173; Rhett, Autobiography, Rhett Papers, SCHS; Wigfall to Halsey Wigfall, May 1, 1861, Wigfall Papers.
4. Montgomery, *Weekly Montgomery Confederation*, May 3, 1861.
5. Nashville, *Union & American*, May 4, 7, 1861; Jones and Rogers, "Montgomery," May 1, 1861, p. 85; Stephens to Linton Stephens, May 3, 1861, Stephens Papers, MCSH.
6. Howell Cobb to his wife, May 3, 1861, Cobb Papers, Georgia.
7. U.S. Congress, *Journal*, pp. 174–81, 183–84, 202–203; Charleston, *Mercury*, May 7, 1861; Richmond, *Daily Dispatch*, May 4, 1861.
8. Cobb to Marion Cobb, May 4, 1861, "Correspondence," p. 320.
9. Howell Cobb to his wife, May 3, 1861, Cobb Papers, Georgia.
10. John Manning to his wife, April, 1861, Williams-Chesnut-Manning Papers.
11. Woodward and Muhlenfeld, *Private Mary Chesnut*, April 27, 1861, p. 63.
12. Jones and Rogers, "Montgomery," May 1, 1861, p. 82, May 4, 1861, p. 90.
13. U.S. Congress, *Journal*, pp. 187, 193.
14. Stephens to Letcher, May 3, 1861, Executive Papers, Virginia.
15. Mason to Davis, May 6, 1861, *PJD*, VII, p. 151.
16. H. McLeod to Clark, May 29, 1861, Records of the Governor, 301–35, Texas.
17. Cobb to Marion Cobb, May 4, 1861, "Correspondence," p. 321.
18. Charleston, *Mercury*, April 30, 1861.
19. Stephens to Linton Stephens, May 4, 1861, Stephens Papers, MCSH.
20. U.S. Congress, *Journal*, p. 192; Stephens to Linton Stephens, May 7, 1861, Stephens Papers, MCSH; Natchez, *Daily Courier*, May 8, 1861.
21. Montgomery, *Daily Post*, May 10, 1861; Woodward, *Chesnut*, [May 18, 1861], p. 61.

22. Montgomery, *Weekly Montgomery Confederation*, May 17, 1861; Boyce to Hunter, February 5, 1861, Hunter Papers; Garnett, T.S. "Address of . . . ," *SHSP*, XXVII (1899), p. 154.

23. William C. Rives to William C. Rives, Jr., May 6, 1861, William C. Rives Papers, LC; Duncan to Walker, May 6, 1861, *OR*, I, 51, 2, p. 69; U.S. Congress, *Journal*, p. 214.

24. Howell Cobb to his wife, May 10, 1861, Cobb Papers, Georgia.

25. Columbus, *Daily Columbus Enquirer*, May 9, 1861; Stephens to Linton Stephens, May 5, 1861, Stephens Papers, MCSH.

26. Charleston, *Mercury*, May 21, 1861; U.S. Congress, *Journal*, p. 201.

27. Cobb to Marion Cobb, May 6, 1861, "Correspondence," p. 327.

28. Russell, *Diary*, I, p. 175.

29. Beauregard to Walker, April 30, 1861, *OR*, I, 53, p. 159, Special Orders NO. 57, May 23, 1861, I, 52, 2, p. 106; Russell, *Diary*, I, pp. 174–75; Woodward and Muhlenfeld, *Private Mary Chesnut*, May 8–9, 1861, p. 68.

30. Montgomery, *Weekly Advertiser*, May 15, 1861.

31. Magoffin to Davis, May 19, 1861, *OR*, I, 52, 2, pp. 102–103.

32. Stephens to Linton Stephens, May 7, 1861, Stephens Papers, MCSH.

33. Charleston, *Mercury*, May 10, 1861.

34. Boyce to Thomas C. Reynolds, May 8, 1861, J. W. Eldridge Collection, Huntington.

35. Cobb to Marion Cobb, May 7, 1861, Thomas R. R. Cobb Letters, University of Georgia, Athens.

36. U.S. Congress, *Journal*, pp. 223–24, 235.

37. Montgomery, *Weekly Mail*, May 22, 1861; U.S. Congress, *Journal*, p. 244.

38. Nashville, *Union & American*, May 11, 1861.

39. Clipping, Scrapbook #4, Box 25, Walthall Papers; New Orleans, *Daily Crescent*, May 14, 1861.

40. Stephens to Linton Stephens, May 5, 1862, Stephens Papers, MCSH.

41. Stephens to Johnston, May 14, 1861, Johnston and Browne, *Stephens*, p. 403.

42. Toombs to Stephens, July 5, 1861, Robert Toombs Papers, Duke University Library, Durham, N.C.

43. Stephens to Johnston, May 14, 1861, Johnston and Browne, *Stephens*, p. 403.

44. Memminger to Davis, May 2, 1861, *OR*, IV, 1, p. 274.

45. Charleston, *Mercury*, April 23, May 13, 1861.

46. Nashville, *Union & American*, April 20, 1861.

47. Jones and Rogers, "Montgomery," May 18, 1861, p. 108.

48. Charleston, *Mercury*, May 4, 1861; Natchez, *Daily Courier*, May 22, 1861.

49. Nashville, *Union & American*, May 31, 1861.

50. Todd, *Finance*, p. 125.

51. U.S. Congress, *Journal*, p. 223.

52. Nashville, *Union & American*, May 4, 1861; Vicksburg, *Daily Evening Citizen*, April 29, 1861.

53. U.S. Congress, *Journal*, pp. 186–87, 227–29.
54. Toombs to Stephens, July 5, 1861, Toombs Papers, Duke; Conrad to W. T. Palfrey, May 31, 1861, Palfrey Family Papers, LSU.
55. Todd, *Finance*, p. 63.
56. New York, *Citizen*, April 27, 1867.
57. Reed, *Brothers' War*, pp. 286–87; Journal, June 11, 1862, Johnston, *Autobiography*, p. 159.
58. Montgomery, *Weekly Mail*, December 14, 1860.
59. *Ibid.*, February 15, 1861.
60. All of these figures are approximate and subject to error and interpretation. Joseph C. Kennedy, ed., *Preliminary Report of the Eighth Census, 1860* (Washington, 1862), p. 201, says that the 1860 crop totaled 5,196,944 bales. However, this is for *two* crops, which would argue that the last one of the year here under discussion would be no more than half that. Other estimates—flawed by hindsight and defensiveness on the part of Davis and others—put the available total crop at 4 million or less ("The Confederate Collapse," Rowland, VIII, pp. 50–51; "Reply of Ex-Secretary Memminger," March 27, 1874, Rowland, VII, pp. 42–43).
61. *American Annual Cyclopaedia, 1861* (New York, 1864), p. 252, gives an 1860 total of 4,666,940 bales shipped, but again this constitutes both crops.
62. "The Confederate Collapse," 1877, Rowland, VIII, pp. 50–51.
63. H. E. Owens to Walker, March 9, 1861, OR, I, 1, p. 448; William Tayloe to B. O. Tayloe, February 3, 1861, Rives Papers, LC.
64. James D. Bulloch, *The Secret Service of the Confederate States in Europe* (Liverpool, 1883), I, pp. 104–105.
65. Memminger to Stephens, September 17, 1867, Avary, *Stephens*, p. 66.
66. Davis to Northrop, October 15, 1882, Rowland, IX, p. 189; Reagan, *Memoirs*, p. 115.
67. "Reply of Ex-Secretary Memminger," March 27, 1874, Rowland, VIII, pp. 42–43.
68. Statement of Stephens, winter 1862, Johnston and Browne, *Stephens*, p. 427; Hammond to Davis, May 26, 1861, Hammond Papers.
69. London, *Times*, May 8, 1862.
70. Duncan Johnston to Hammond, May 2, 1861, Hammond Papers.
71. Memminger to Davis, September 25, 1877, Rowland, VIII, p. 26.
72. Bulloch, *Secret Service*, I, p. 20.
73. Andrew Low to Walker, April 24, 1861, OR, IV, 1, p. 237; Robert Gamble to Congress, May 4, 1861, ORN, II, 2, pp. 59–61; U.S. Congress, *Journal*, p. 182.
74. Stephens statement, May 30, 1861, Johnston and Browne, *Stephens*, p. 405; Woodward, *Chesnut*, May 20, 1861, p. 62.
75. Memminger to Davis, November 27, 1878, Rowland, VIII, p. 288. This proposition, like so many things relating to Davis and the loss of the war, became a hotly contested issue after the fact. Rhett makes possibly the earliest mention of it thus far found in his Autobiography, written prior to

his death in 1876. No one brought it up until the 1870s and 1880s, when it surfaced in memoirs by Beauregard, Stephens, and other enemies of Davis, all of whom sought to embarrass him. To that extent, their assertions can be assumed to be tainted by prejudice. Walker, himself given to a variable memory, claimed never to have heard of the idea (Walker to Davis, December 10, 1878, Rowland, VIII, p. 296), and so did Memminger (Memminger to Davis, November 27, 1878, Rowland, VIII, p. 288). Reagan also says it never came up in cabinet (John H. Reagan, "Judge Reagan on Davis," clipping, n.d., Dallas Historical Society, Dallas, Texas). Davis himself asserted that he never heard of it (Davis to Trenholm, July 14, 1889, Rowland, X, p. 128), and Trenholm's own recollections varied (Trenholm to Beauregard, September 18, 1878, Rowland, VIII, p. 303, Trenholm to Davis, December 28, 1878, p. 301). Charles Prioleau, Liverpool agent of Fraser, Trenholm and Company, confirmed that the ten steamers had indeed been available, and that he mentioned them in a letter to William Trenholm's father George, but concluded that probably the offer never got to Davis or the cabinet (Davis, *Memoir*, II, pp. 902–904). The story is so blurred by latter-day recollections, prejudice, and a complete lack of direct contemporary evidence that the truth is probably lost. Probably the best argument that the idea never did get before the cabinet, and perhaps even Mallory, is that the inventive Secretary of the Navy consistently showed himself to be just the man to jump at any such proposition.

76. Rhett, Miscellaneous Notes, Aiken B. Rhett Collection.
77. Bulloch, *Secret Service*, I, pp. 41–42; U.S. Congress, *Journal*, pp. 207–208; Mallory to Bulloch, May 9, 1861, ORN, II, 2, pp. 64–65.
78. Toombs to Pickett, May 17, 1861, ORN, II, 3, p. 202ff.
79. Yancey Diary, May 3, 1861, Montgomery, *Advertiser*, January 31, 1954.
80. Natchez, *Daily Courier*, May 25, 1861.
81. Toombs to Yancey, Rost, and Mann, May 18, 1861, ORN, II, 3, pp. 208–13.
82. Rhett, Autobiography, Rhett Papers, SCHS; DuBose, *Yancey*, II, p. 600.
83. Davis to Joseph E. Johnston, May 2, 1861, Executive Papers, Virginia; Joseph E. Johnston, *Narrative of Military Operations* (New York, 1874), p. 13; Charleston, *Evening News*, May 16, 1861; Johnston to Walker, May 15, 1861, OR, I, 53, p. 167.
84. J. C. Cummings to William B. Campbell, May 1, 1861, Campbell Family Papers, Duke University Library, Durham, N.C.
85. Leonidas Polk to Davis, May 14, 1861, *The Collector*, XLVII (November 1932), n.p.
86. Cooper to Charles C. Jones, May 27, 1871, author's possession.
87. Richmond, *Dispatch*, May 20, 1861; New York, *Times*, May 22, 1861; De Leon, *Four Years*, pp. 69–70.
88. Bragg to Moore, May 2, 1861, Thomas O. Moore Papers, LSU.
89. Nashville, *Union & American*, May 2, 7, 1861.
90. Hilliard, *Politics*, pp. 326–29.

91. Walker to Isham Harris, May 20, 1861, Harris to Walker, May 25, 1861, Isham Harris Letterbook, Isham Harris Papers.
92. Harris to Davis, July 2, 1861, Letterbook, Tennessee.
93. Perry to Jackson Morton, May 20, 1861, *OR*, I, 53, p. 174.
94. Moore to Walker, May 7, 1861, *OR*, IV, 1, p. 295, Walker to Moore, May 7, 1861, p. 296, Moore to Walker, May 8, 1861, p. 307; Moore to Davis, May 9, 1861, *PJD*, VII, pp. 157–58.
95. Pettus to Walker, May 18, 1861, Walker to Pettus, May 18, 1861, *OR*, IV, 1, p. 334.
96. Pickens to Walker, April 23, 1861, *OR*, IV, 1, pp. 235–36; Charleston, *Mercury*, May 7, 9, 1861.
97. Montgomery, *Weekly Advertiser*, April 24, 1861; Magrath to Pickens, April 21, Pickens Papers, Duke.
98. Cooper to S. Bassett French, April 30, 1861, Walker to Letcher, April 29, 1861, Executive Papers, Virginia; Lee to Davis, May 7, 1861, *OR*, I, 51, 2, p. 69.
99. A. T. Bledsoe to Davis, May 11, 1861, Dearborn Collection; Cobb to Marion Cobb, May 10, 1861, Thomas R. R. Cobb Papers, Georgia; Mason to Davis, May 6, 1861, *PJD*, VII, p. 150; Duncan to Walker, May 7, 1861, *OR*, I, 51, 2, p. 71, Walker to Duncan, May 12, 1861, p. 87.
100. Walker to Letcher, April 26, May 1, 6, 1861, *OR*, I, 2, pp. 783, 792, 805.
101. Duncan to Walker, May 5, 1861, *OR*, I, 51, 2, pp. 65–66.
102. Letcher to John Brockenbrough and Waller Staples, May 11, 1861, Executive Papers, Virginia.
103. Duncan to Walker, May 15, 1861, *OR*, I, 51, 2, p. 91.
104. Letcher to Gorgas, May 15, 1861, Executive Papers, Virginia.
105. Spencer Adams to Davis, May 1, 1861, *PJD*, VII, P. 143.
106. Cobb to Marion Cobb, May 3, 1861, "Correspondence," p. 318.
107. Ordinance, March 20, 1861, *OR*, I, 53, p. 150, Brown to Walker, April 18, 1861, p. 140, May 4, 1861, pp. 160–61.
108. Brown to Walker, May 17, 1861, *OR*, IV, 1, p. 332, General Orders No. 8, May 14, 1861, I, 52, 2, p. 97.
109. Cobb to Marion Cobb, May 9, 1861, Thomas R. R. Cobb Papers, Georgia.
110. Brown to H. C. Wayne, April 22, 1861, Joseph E. Brown Papers, typescripts, University of Georgia Library, Athens.
111. Montgomery, *Advertiser*, March 6, 1907; Brown to Walker, May 13, 1861, *OR*, IV, 1, p. 316, Walker to Brown, May 22, 1861, p. 348.
112. Wright to Brown, May 8, 1861, Wright Papers, Georgia.
113. Nisbet to Brown, April 19, 1861, E. A. Nisbet Folder, GDAH.
114. Brown to Stephens, May 4, 1861, Stephens to Brown, April 18, 1861, Stephens Papers, Emory.
115. Walker to Brown, April 19, 1861, *OR*, IV, 1, p. 226.
116. Cobb to Marion Cobb, April 29, 1861, "Correspondence," p. 260; Brown to Walker, May 17, 1861, *OR*, IV, 1, p. 332; Brown to James Jackson, May 4, 1861, Brown Papers.

117. Cobb to Marion Cobb, May 10, 12, 1861, Thomas R. R. Cobb Papers, Georgia.
118. Cobb to Marion Cobb, May 2, 1861, "Correspondence," p. 317; Cobb to Marion Cobb, May 10, 16, 1861, Thomas R. R. Cobb Papers, Georgia; Howell Cobb to his wife, May 18, 1861, Cobb Papers, Georgia.
119. Brown to Walker, April 27, 1861. OR, IV, 1, p. 254.
120. Brown to editor of the Brunswick Advocate, May 11, 1861, Brown Papers.
121. Howell Cobb to his wife, May 18, 1861, Cobb Papers, Georgia.
122. Cobb to Marion Cobb, April 29, 1861, "Correspondence," p. 260.
123. Charleston, Mercury, May 18, 1861.
124. Montgomery, Daily Post, May 7, 1861; New Orleans, Daily Picayune, May 17, 1861.
125. U.S. Congress, Journal, pp. 213–14; Charleston, Mercury, May 16, 1861.
126. U.S. Congress, Journal, pp. 230–33; Woodward, Chesnut, p. 58; Montgomery, Weekly Advertiser, May 22, 1861.
127. Varina Davis to Clement C. Clay, May 10, 1861, Katherine M. Jones, Heroines of Dixie (New York, 1955), pp. 27–28.
128. John D. C. Atkins to Harris, August 13, 1861, Harris Papers.
129. Charleston, Mercury, May 7, 1861.
130. Edward A. Pollard, The First Year of the War (New York, 1863), p. 351; New York, Citizen, April 27, 1861.
131. U.S. Congress, Journal, p. 244.
132. Jones and Rogers, "Montgomery," May 13, 1861, p. 103.
133. Stephens to Linton Stephens, May 14, 1861, Stephens Papers, MCSH.
134. Cobb to Marion Cobb, April 30, 1861, "Correspondence," pp. 312–13; Cobb to Marion Cobb, May 15, 1861, Thomas R. R. Cobb Papers, Georgia.
135. R. W. Winston, High Stakes and Hair Trigger. The Life of Jefferson Davis (New York, 1930), p. 179.
136. U.S. Congress, Journal, p. 201.
137. Charlotte Wigfall to Halsey Wigfall, April 29, 1861, Wigfall Papers.
138. Campbell to Pettus, May 16, 17, 1861, RG 27, Vol. 36, MDAH.
139. Cobb to Marion Cobb, May 3, 1861, "Correspondence," p. 319, May 4, 1861, p. 324; Cobb to Marion Cobb, May 11, 1861, Thomas R. R. Cobb Papers, Georgia.
140. Cobb to Marion Cobb, April 30, 1861, "Correspondence," p. 312.
141. Cobb to Marion Cobb, April 30, 1861, "Correspondence," p. 314; Cobb to Marion Cobb, May 1, 10, 1861, Thomas R. R. Cobb Papers, Georgia.
142. Cobb to Marion Cobb, May 4, 1861, Thomas R. R. Cobb Papers, Georgia.
143. Kenan to Crawford, May 9, 1861, Crawford to Stephens et al., May 9, 1861, Stephens Papers, LC; Howell Cobb to his wife, May 10, 11, 1861, Cobb Papers, Georgia.
144. Atlanta, Southern Confederacy, May 10, 1861; Cobb to Marion Cobb, May 8, 1861, Thomas R. R. Cobb Papers, Georgia.

145. Cobb to Marion Cobb, May 8, 1861, Thomas R. R. Cobb Papers, Georgia; Howell Cobb to his wife, May 15, 1861, Cobb Papers, Georgia.

146. Cobb to Marion Cobb, May 6, 8, 15, 1861, Thomas R. R. Cobb Papers, Georgia.

147. Cobb to Marion Cobb, May 11, 1861, Thomas R. R. Cobb Papers, Georgia.

148. Yvonne Pavy Weiss, "Alexandre Etienne DeClouet" (Masters thesis, Louisiana State University Baton Rouge, 1937), pp. 36–37.

149. Congress, *Journal*, p. 211.

150. Jones, *Diary*, I, May 20, 1861, p. 38, May 26, p. 44, June 22, p. 54.

151. Walker to Harris, May 20, 1861, Harris Papers.

152. Jones, *Diary*, I May 17, 1861, pp. 36–37.

153. Charleston, *Mercury*, May 14, 1861; DeClouet to Paul DeClouet, May 12, 1861, DeClouet Papers.

154. Rhett, "Government," p. 108.

155. Jones, *Diary*, I, May 20, 1861, p. 38.

156. T. O. Chestney to Clay, May 11, 1861, Clay Papers; Henry C. Wayne to Davis, May 10, 1861, *PJD*, VII, p. 162; Rhett, "Government," p. 108.

157. Charleston, *Mercury*, May 16, 1861; New York, *Citizen*, May 25, 1867.

158. Jones, *Diary*, I, May 20, 1861, p. 38.

159. P. N. Luckett to Clark, June 12, 1861, McCulloch to Clark, May 4, 1861, Records of the Governor, 301-35, Texas; Walker to Brown, May 4, 1861, OR, IV, 1, pp. 280–81.

160. New York, *Citizen*, July 20, 1867.

161. Henry S. Figures to Dear Pa, May 3, 1861, Henry S. Figures Papers, Civil War Miscellaneous Collection, United States Army Military History Institute, Carlisle, Pa.

162. Jones, *Diary*, I, May 22, 1861, p. 39.

163. Walker to Howell Cobb, May 6, 1861, Walker Letter-Book, LC.

164. McRae to Walker, May 6, 1861, OR, I, 52, 2, p. 87.

165. Cobb to Marion Cobb, April 30, 1861, "Correspondence," p. 312, May 2, 1861, p. 317, May 4, 1861, p. 322.

166. Stephens statement, May 30, 1861, Johnston and Browne, *Stephens*, p. 405.

167. Walker, Sketch of LeRoy Pope Walker, Woods Papers.

168. Toombs to Stephens, July 5, 1861, Toombs Papers, Duke.

169. Cobb to Marion Cobb, May 7, 1861, Thomas R. R. Cobb Papers, Georgia; Conrad to Palfrey, May 31, 1861, Palfrey Family Papers.

170. Rhett, "Government," p. 107.

171. Keitt to Hammond, May 15, 1861, Hammond Papers.

172. Woodward and Muhlenfeld, *Private Mary Chesnut*, May 3, 1861, p. 65.

173. John Finney to Walthall, April 23, 1861, Walthall Papers; "Orthan" to Howell Cobb, April 20, 1861, Cobb Papers, Georgia.

174. Proclamation, May 9, 1861, Records of the Governor, 301-35, Texas.

175. Woodward, *Chesnut*, [May 7–8, 1861], p. 56.

176. Charleston, *Mercury*, May 29, 1861.
177. *Ibid.*, May 16, 1861.
178. Conrad to Palfrey, May 31, 1861, Palfrey Family Papers.
179. Clipping, 1881, Toombs Papers, Duke. This article, like all expressions by Toombs in his later years, especially in newspapers, must be regarded with considerable skepticism. Aging, given up increasingly to drink and bitterness at Davis, he gave frequent interviews filled with hyperbole, inaccuracies and flights of imagination. Yet, considering the rumors in May 1861, it is possible that some germs of truth dwell in his account. Certainly, at least, it seems to fit the situation.
180. Montgomery, *Daily Post*, May 16, 1861; Montgomery, *Weekly Confederation*, May 17, 1861; Montgomery, *Weekly Advertiser*, May 22, 1861; Charleston, *Mercury*, May 16, 1861.
181. Cobb to Marion Cobb, May 12, 1861, Thomas R. R. Cobb Papers, Georgia; Montgomery, *Weekly Advertiser*, May 8, 1861.
182. Rives to his wife, May 18, 1861, Rives Papers.
183. Jones, *Diary*, I, May 17, 1861, pp. 36–37.
184. Johnson to Stephens, May 8, 1861, Johnson Papers, Duke.
185. Stephens statement, November 30, 1862, Johnston, *Autobiography*, p. 164.
186. Charleston, *Mercury*, May 3, 1861.
187. Clay to E. D. Tracy, May 4, 1861, Clay Papers.
188. Untitled typewritten sketch, n.d., Joseph E. and Elizabeth C. Brown Collection, University of Georgia Library, Athens.
189. New York, *Citizen*, May 25, 1867.
190. J. B. D. De Bow to Gayarre, August 28, 1861, Gayarre Papers.
191. Woodward, *Chesnut*, May 20, 1861, p. 62.
192. Davis, *Memoir*, II, p. 161.
193. Davis, *Memoir*, II, p. 162.
194. Stephens statement, winter 1862, Johnston and Browne, *Stephens*, p. 426.
195. De Leon, *Four Years*, p. 39.
196. Woodward and Muhlenfeld, *Private Mary Chesnut*, November 11, 1861, p. 198.
197. U.S. Congress, *Journal*, pp. 234, 247–48.
198. Rhett, Autobiography, Rhett Papers, SCHS.
199. Rhett, "Government," p. 102.
200. Rhett to Wigfall, April 15, 1864, Wigfall Papers; Rhett to Robert B. Rhett, Jr.,———17, 1861, Rhett Papers, SCL, USC. The latter document is unclear in its date, and may be May, August, or December.
201. Woodward and Muhlenfeld, *Private Mary Chesnut*, May 7, 1861, p. 67.
202. Woodward, *Chesnut*, October 3, 1861, p. 206.
203. Boyce to Hammond, March 17, 1862, Taylor, "Boyce-Hammond Correspondence," p. 350.
204. Smith to Jemison, December 1, 1861, Jemison Papers.

205. Brown to Jared Whitaker, May 20, 1861, Brown Papers, Georgia.
206. Davis, *Memoir*, II, p. 164.
207. *Ibid.*, II, p. 163.
208. Cobb to Marion Cobb, May 3, 1861, "Correspondence," p. 318.
209. Cobb to Marion Cobb, May 10, 1861, Thomas R. R. Cobb Papers, Georgia.
210. Rhett, "Government," p. 104.
211. Woodward and Muhlenfeld, *Private Mary Chesnut*, February 28, 1861, p. 17.
212. DeClouet to Gayarre, February 20, 1861, Jones Autograph Letters, Duke.
213. Montgomery, *Weekly Montgomery Confederation*, March 29, April 5, 1861.
214. De Bow to Gayarre, August 28, 1861, Gayarre Papers.
215. Vicksburg, *Daily Evening Citizen*, March 30, 1861.
216. Cobb to Marion Cobb, April 29, 1861, "Correspondence," p. 257.
217. Montgomery, *Daily Post*, May 16, 1861.
218. Woodward and Muhlenfeld, *Private Mary Chesnut*, May 17, 1861, p. 69.

15. Farewell Montgomery

1. Charlotte Wigfall to Halsey Wigfall, April 26, May 6, 1861, Wigfall Papers.
2. Montgomery, *Weekly Advertiser*, April 17, 1861.
3. Cobb to Marion Cobb, May 11, 1861, Thomas R. R. Cobb Papers, Georgia; Jones, *Diary*, I, May 26, 1861, p. 43.
4. Montgomery, *Daily Post*, April 27, 1861; Jones, *Diary*, I, May 24, 1861; p. 41.
5. Jones, *Diary*, I, May 24, 1861, p. 41; Davis to Francis R. Lubbock, January 19, 1878, Francis R. Lubbock Papers, Center for American History, University of Texas, Austin.
6. Montgomery, *Weekly Montgomery Confederation*, March 29, 1861.
7. Shofner and Rogers, "Montgomery to Richmond," pp. 158–59.
8. Montgomery, *Weekly Advertiser*, April 17, 1861.
9. Howell Cobb to his wife, May 11, 1861, Cobb Papers, Georgia.
10. *Ibid.*, May 3, 1861.
11. Cobb to Marion Cobb, May 14, 1861, Thomas R. R. Cobb Papers, Georgia.
12. Charlotte Wigfall to Halsey Wigfall, May 8, 1861, Wigfall Papers.
13. Harrison to Susan Harrison, May 14, 1861, Harrison Papers.
14. Boyce to Reynolds, May 8, 1861, Eldridge Collection.
15. Bartow to Josiah Tattnall, May 9, 1861, Jones Autograph Letters, Duke.
16. DeClouet to Paul DeClouet, May 3, 1861, DeClouet Papers.
17. Stephens to Linton Stephens, May 4, 6, 1861, Stephens Papers, MCSH.

18. Woodward, *Chesnut*, [May 18, 1861], p. 61.
19. Bartow to John L. Branch, May 1861, Margaret Branch Sexton Collection, Georgia; Cobb to William Cobb, May 11, 1861, Cobb Papers, Georgia.
20. Charlotte Wigfall to Halsey Wigfall, May 13, 1761, Wigfall Papers; DeClouet to Paul DeClouet, April 24, May 6, 1861, DeClouet Papers.
21. Jones and Rogers, "Montgomery," May 11, 1861, pp. 102–103.
22. Pryor to Davis, April 25, 1861, Davis Papers, Tulane; George Deas to Davis, May 14, 1861, *OR*, I, 51, 2, p. 90; Richmond, *Dispatch*, May 4, 1861.
23. O. P. Baldwin to Davis, May 4, 1861, Pritchard von David Collection, Center for American History, University of Texas, Austin; Albert T. Bledsoe to Davis, May 10, 1861, *PJD*, VII, pp. 159–60; Ruffin to Davis, May 16, 1861, *OR*, I, 51, 2, p. 92.
24. U.S. Congress, *Journal*, p. 200.
25. *Ibid.*, pp. 208–209.
26. Charleston, *Daily Courier*, May 14, 1861; Jones and Rogers, "Montgomery," May 11, 1861, p. 102.
27. Vicksburg, *Daily Evening Citizen*, May 4, 1861.
28. Richmond, *Whig*, May 6, 1861; Cobb to Marion Cobb, May 10, 1861, Thomas R. R. Cobb Papers, Georgia.
29. Clayton to Walker, May 14, 1861, *OR*, I, 52, 2, p. 98.
30. Stephens to Johnston, May 14, 1861, Johnston and Browne, *Stephens*, p. 403; Stephens to William H. Hidell, May 14, 1861, Hidell Papers, Philadelphia.
31. Varina Davis to Clay, May 10, 1861, Clay Papers.
32. Cobb to Marion Cobb, May 9, 1861, Thomas R. R. Cobb Papers, Georgia.
33. Cobb to Marion Cobb, May 4, 1861, "Correspondence," p. 322.
34. Varina Davis to Clement C. Clay, May 10, 1861, Clay Papers, Duke.
35. Rives to his wife, May 14, 1861, Rives Papers; Cobb to Martion Cobb, May 12, 1861, Thomas R. R. Cobb Papers, Georgia; Varina Davis to Clay, May 10, 1861, Clay Papers; Montgomery, *Daily Mail*, April 26, 1861; New York, *Times*, May 1, 1861.
36. Montgomery, *Daily Mail*, April 26, 1861; Savannah, *Republican*, May 11, 1861.
37. Montgomery, City Council Minutes, May 13, 27, 1861, ADAH.
38. Montgomery, *Daily Post*, May 29, 1861.
39. Montgomery, *Daily Post*, May 7, 1861; Montgomery, *Weekly Mail*, April 26, 1861; Montgomery City Council Minutes, May 20, 1861, ADAH.
40. Figures to Dear Pa, May 3, 1861, Figures Papers.
41. Montgomery, *Daily Mail*, April 26, 1861; Montgomery, *Weekly Confederation*, May 3, 1861; Charleston, *Evening News*, May 16, 1861.
42. Woodward, *Chesnut*, May 24, 1861, p. 347.
43. Cobb to Marion Cobb, May 10, 1861, Thomas R. R. Cobb Papers, Georgia.
44. DeClouet to Paul DeClouet, May 12, 1861, DeClouet Papers.

45. Cobb to Marion Cobb, May 16, 1861, Thomas R. R. Cobb Papers, Georgia.

46. Woodward and Muhlenfeld, *Private Mary Chesnut*, April 28–29, 1861, p. 63, April 30, p. 64, May 8–9, pp. 67–68, May 19 [10–12], p. 68, May 18, p. 69, May 19, p. 70.

47. Woodward, *Chesnut*, May 20, 1861, p. 62.

48. Stephens to Linton Stephens, May 4, 1861, Stephens Papers, MCSH; Woodward and Muhlenfeld, *Private Mary Chesnut*, May 6, 1861, p. 66; Toombs to Stephens, May 1861, Stephens Papers, Emory; Cobb to Marion Cobb, May 11, 1861, Thomas R. R. Cobb Papers, Georgia; Sterx and Trapp, "Diary of John Withers," May 17, 1861, p. 146.

49. Montgomery, *Daily Post*, April 23, 30, 1861; Montgomery, *Daily Mail*, April 26, 1861; Jones, *Diary*, I, May 15, 1861, p. 35.

50. Woodward, *Chesnut*, [May 6, 1861], p. 56.

51. Stephens to Linton Stephens, May 10, 1861, Stephens Papers, MCSH.

52. Cobb to Marion Cobb, May 11 1861, Thomas R. R. Cobb Papers, Georgia.

53. Montgomery, *Daily Post*, June 6, 1861.

54. Woodward and Muhlenfeld, *Private Mary Chesnut*, May 26–28, 1861, p. 72.

55. Rives to his wife, May 15, 1861, Rives Papers.

56. New York, *Times*, May 1, 1861.

57. Varina Davis to Clay, May 10, 1861, Clay Papers; Columbus, *Daily Times*, May 2, 1861; New Orleans, *Daily Crescent*, May 24, 1861.

58. Charlotte Wigfall to Louly Wigfall, April 29, 1861, Wigfall Papers.

59. Montgomery, *Advertiser*, November 14, 1930.

60. Columbus, *Daily Times*, April 30, 1861.

61. Russell, *Dairy*, I, p. 177.

62. Woodward, *Chesnut*, [May 6, 1861], p. 56.

63. Russell, *Diary*, I, p. 177; Leonora Clayton to Stephens, May 20, 1861, Stephens Papers, Emory; Edward C. Anderson Diary, n.d. [May 1861], Volume 5, pp. 4–5, Edward C. Anderson Papers, SHC, UNC; Harrison to Susan Harrison, May 14, 1861, Harrison Papers; Woodward and Muhlenfeld, *Private Mary Chesnut*, May 18, 1861, p. 69.

64. Montgomery, *Weekly Advertiser*, April 24, 1861.

65. Rives to his wife, May 18, 1861, Rives Papers.

66. Woodward, *Chesnut*, May 20, 1861, p. 62.

67. Forsyth to Davis, April 4, 1861, Toombs Letterbook.

68. Charleston, *Mercury*, May 10, 1861.

69. Russell, *Diary*, I, p. 165.

70. *Ibid.*, p. 164.

71. London, *Times*, May 30, 1861.

72. Russell, *Diary*, I, p. 183.

73. London, *Times*, May 30, 1861; Russell, *Diary*, I, p. 167.

74. Russell, *Diary*, I, p. 168.

75. Columbus, *Daily Columbus Enquirer*, May 9, 1861.
76. Cobb to Marion Cobb, May 9, Thomas R. R. Cobb Papers, Georgia; Woodward and Muhlenfeld, *Private Mary Chesnut*, May 7, 1861, p. 67.
77. Cobb to Marion Cobb, May 5, 1861, "Correspondence," p. 325.
78. Stephens to Linton Stephens, May 6, 1861, Stephens Papers, MCSH; Russell, *Diary*, I, pp. 173–74; London, *Times*, May 30, 1861; Crawford, *Russell* p. 52; Walker to William H. Russell, May 8, 1861, Letter-Book.
79. Russell, *Diary*, I, p. 179.
80. *Ibid.*, pp. 179, 181; Crawford, *Russell*, p. 52.
81. Russell, *Diary*, I, p. 175.
82. Charlotte Wigfall to Halsey Wigfall, May 8, 1861, Wigfall Papers; Nashville, *Union & American*, May 11, 1861.
83. Cobb to Marion Cobb, May 14, 1861, Thomas R. R. Cobb Papers, Georgia.
84. New Orleans, *Daily Picayune*, May 11, 1861.
85. Columbus, *Daily Times*, May 16, 1861, Savannah, *Daily Morning News*, May 11, 1861.
86. Chestney to Clay, May 11, 1861, Clay Papers.
87. Charleston, *Mercury*, April 29, 1861.
88. Cobb to Marion Cobb, April 29, 1861, "Correspondence," p. 259.
89. Jones, *Diary*, I, May 16, 1861, p. 36; Russell, *Diary*, I, p. 171; Bulloch, *Secret Service*, I, p. 41.
90. Woodward and Muhlenfeld, *Private Mary Chesnut*, May 20, 1861, p. 71; Woodward, *Chesnut*, May 20, 1861, p. 62, July 9, 1861, p. 94.
91. Jones, *Diary*, I, May 14, 1861, p. 55; Charlotte Wigfall to Halsey Wigfall, May 6, 1861, Wigfall Papers; Sterx and Trapp, "Diary of John Withers," May 14, 1861, p. 146.
92. Charlotte Wigfall to Halsey Wigfall, April 26, 1861, Wigfall Papers.
93. De Leon, *Four Years*, p. 26.
94. Huntsville, *Democrat*, May 8, 1861.
95. Yearns, *Congress*, p. 12.
96. Columbus, *Daily Columbus Enquirer*, May 6, 1861.
97. Charlotte Wigfall to Halsey Wigfall, April 26, May 13, 1861, Wigfall Papers; Cobb to Marion Cobb, May 10, 1861, Thomas R. R. Cobb Papers, Georgia.
98. Richmond, *Daily Dispatch*, May 8, 1861.
99. Savannah, *Daily Morning News*, May 11, 1861.
100. Cobb to Marion Cobb, May 3, 1861, "Correspondence," p. 319.
101. Columbus, *Daily Columbus Enquirer*, May 9, 1861.
102. Cobb to Marion Cobb, April 30, 1861, "Correspondence," p. 313.
103. Jones and Rogers, "Montgomery," May 1, 1861, p. 86.
104. *Ibid.*, May 9, 1861, p. 100.
105. Black, *Railroads*, p. 74.
106. *Ibid.*, April 28, 1861, pp. 78–79.
107. Jones and Rogers, "Montgomery," April 28, 1861, pp. 79–80, May 14, p. 105.

108. Charlotte Wigfall to Louly Wigfall, April 29, 1861, Wigfall Papers.

109. Montgomery, *Daily Post*, May 9, 1861.

110. *Ibid.*, April 26, May 6, 13, 1861.

111. *Ibid.*, April 30, May 2, 4, 8, 20, 24, 27, 1861; Montgomery, *Weekly Advertiser*, May 8, 15, 1861; Montgomery, *Daily Mail*, April 26, 1861.

112. Montgomery, *Daily Mail*, April 26, 1861; Nashville, *Daily Gazette*, May 25, 1861; Charleston, *Mercury*, May 8, 1861.

113. Montgomery City Council Minutes, April 22, 29, May 9, 1861, ADAH.

114. Montgomery, *Daily Post*, May 25, 1861.

115. Nashville, *Union & American*, April 21, 1861.

116. Montgomery, *Weekly Advertiser*, April 17, May 29, 1861; Montgomery, *Daily Post*, May 24, 1861.

117. Montgomery, *Daily Post*, May 27, 1861.

118. *Ibid.*, May 15, 1861.

119. City Council Minutes, May 13, 1861, ADAH; Jones and Rogers, "Montgomery," May 8, 1861, p. 99.

120. Atlanta, *Southern Confederacy*, May 14, 1861.

121. Montgomery, *Daily Post*, April 26, May 8, 1861.

122. Russell, *Diary*, I, p. 177.

123. Montgomery, *Daily Post*, June 5, 1861; Montgomery, *Daily Mail*, April 26, 1861.

124. Montgomery, *Daily Mail*, April 26, 1861.

125. Montgomery, *Weekly Advertiser*, May 29, 1861.

126. Jacob Weil to Josiah Weil, May 16, 1861, Jacob Weil Papers, ADAH.

127. Charleston, *Mercury*, May 7, 1861.

128. Montgomery, *Weekly Montgomery Confederation*, May 10, 1861.

129. Jones and Rogers, "Montgomery," May 1 [7], 1861, p. 97.

130. Montgomery, *Daily Post*, May 4, 1861; Mary Phelan Watt, "The Women of Alabama in the War," *Confederate Veteran*, XXIV (May 1916), p. 225.

131. Anne Warren Jones, "The First Soldiers' Hospital," *Confederate Veteran*, XXXVI (July 1928), p. 262.

132. Clipping, Belle Johnston Scrapbook, ADAH.

133. Watt, "Women," p. 225.

134. *Ibid.*, May 27, 1861; Columbus, *Daily Times*, May 11, 1861.

135. Vicksburg, *Daily Evening Citizen*, May 13, 1861; Anonymous to Davis, February 20, 1861, RG 27, Vol. 36, MDAH.

136. Tharin, *Arbitrary Arrests*, pp. 148–50.

137. Montgomery, *Daily Mail*, April 26, 1861.

138. Montgomery City Council Minutes, May 13, 1861, ADAH.

139. New York, *Citizen*, May 25, 1867.

140. Woodward and Muhlenfeld, *Private Mary Chesnut*, May 6, 1861, p. 66; Montgomery, *Weekly Advertiser*, May 8, 1861; Kemp, "Montgomery," p. 128.

141. Charleston, *Mercury*, May 21, 1861; London, *Times*, May 30, 1861.

142. Woodward, *Chesnut*, October 20, 1861, p. 220.

143. U.S. Congress, *Journal*, p. 205.
144. Montgomery, *Weekly Advertiser*, May 1, 1861; Montgomery, *Daily Mail*, April 26, 1861; Montgomery City Council Minutes, April 29, 1861, ADAH; Walker to Montgomery Jailor, May 19, 1861, Walker Letter-Book; New York, *Citizen*, May 25, 1867.
145. Montgomery, *Weekly Advertiser*, May 22, 1861.
146. New Orleans, *Daily Picayune*, May 2, 1861.
147. Jones and Rogers, "Montgomery," April 28, 1861, p. 81, May 1 [7], 1861, p. 97; Montgomery, *Daily Post*, May 25, 1861.
148. Jones, *Diary*, I, May 26, 1861, pp. 42–43.
149. Cobb to Marion Cobb, May 15, 1861, Thomas R. R. Cobb Papers, Georgia; U.S. Congress, *Journal*, p. 218; Proclamation, May 28, 1861, *ORN*, II, 3, p. 102.
150. Augusta, *Daily Constitutionalist*, May 1, 1861.
151. Cobb to Marion Cobb, April 29, 1861, "Correspondence," p. 259; Charlotte Wigfall to Louly Wigfall, April 29, 1861, Wigfall Papers.
152. U.S. Congress, *Journal*, p. 206.
153. *Ibid.*, pp. 173–74.
154. Wigfall to Halsey Wigfall, May 1, 1861, Wigfall Papers; DeClouet to Paul DeClouet, May 1, 1861, DeClouet Papers; Jones and Rogers, "Montgomery," May 1, 1861, p. 82.
155. Jones and Rogers, "Montgomery," May 1, 1861, p. 83.
156. Columbus, *Daily Times*, May 3, 1861.
157. Cobb to Marion Cobb, May 1, 1861, "Correspondence," p. 316.
158. Charleston, *Mercury*, May 3, 1861.
159. Jones and Rogers, "Montgomery," May 9, 1861, p. 101.
160. Stephens to Linton Stephens, May 9, 1861, Stephens Papers, MCSH; U.S. Congress, *Journal*, pp. 211–12.
161. Columbus, *Daily Times*, May 14, 1861.
162. Jones and Rogers, "Montgomery," May 11, 1861, p. 102.
163. Charleston, *Mercury*, May 7, 1861.
164. Atlanta, *Southern Confederacy*, May 14, 1861.
165. U.S. Congress, *Journal*, pp. 225, 241–43.
166. *Ibid.*, p. 244.
167. Columbus, *Daily Times*, May 20, 1861; Jones and Rogers, "Montgomery," May 18, 1861, p. 111; Nashville, *Union & American*, May 9, 1861; Confederate States of America, Location of Capital, University of Georgia Library, Athens.
168. Howell Cobb to his wife, May 18, 1861, Cobb Papers, Georgia; Charleston, *Mercury*, May 21, 1861; Savannah, *Daily Morning News*, May 11, 1861.
169. U.S. Congress, *Journal*, p. 245.
170. Charleston, *Mercury*, May 25, 1861; New Orleans, *Daily Picayune*, May 22, 1861.
171. Charleston, *Mercury*, May 25, 1861.

172. U.S. Congress, *Journal*, pp. 254–55.
173. Act, May 21, 1861, *OR*, IV, 1, pp. 341–42, Act, May 21, 1861, II, 3, pp. 680–81.
174. U.S. Congress, *Journal*, pp. 263–64.
175. *Ibid.*, p. 909.
176. *Ibid.*, pp. 264–65; Natchez, *Daily Courier*, May 23, 1861; Hoole, *Hooper*, p. 158.
177. U.S. Congress, *Journal*, pp. 264–65.
178. Toombs to George Munford, May 22, 1861, Browne to Letcher, May 22, 1861, Executive Papers, Virginia.
179. Howell Cobb to Noble, May 22, 1861, Montgomery City Council Minutes, May 27, 1861, ADAH.
180. Ellis to Davis, May 20, 1861, *OR*, I, 51, 2, p. 96; Coleman Yellott to Davis, May 22, 1861, *PJD*, VII, p. 175.
181. Jones and Rogers, "Montgomery," May 22, 1861, pp. 118–19.
182. DeClouet to Paul DeClouet, May 23, 1861, DeClouet Papers.
183. Woodward and Muhlenfeld, *Private Mary Chesnut*, May 21, 1861, p. 70; Woodward, *Chesnut*, May 20, 1861, p. 62.
184. Montgomery, *Daily Post*, May 29, 1861.
185. R. K. Porter, "Sketch of General T. R. R. Cobb," *Land We Love*, III (July 1867), p. 188.
186. Rhett to "Mr. Editor," n.d. [February 1861], Rhett Papers, SCL, USC.
187. List of grievances against Jefferson Davis, n.d., Aiken B. Rhett Papers.
188. Stephens to Linton Stephens, May 22, 1861, Stephens Papers, MCSH; Stephens to David G. Cotting, June 5, 1861, Burke Papers, Emory.
189. Stephens to Linton Stephens, May 22, 1861, Stephens Papers, MCSH.
190. Stephens to Johnston, May 25, 1861, Johnston and Browne, *Stephens*, pp. 403–404.
191. Tuscaloosa, *Independent Monitor*, May 31, 1861.
192. Journal, May 30, 1861, Johnston, *Autobiography*, p. 158.
193. Stephens to Johnston, May 14, 25, 1861, Johnston and Browne, *Stephens*, pp. 402, 404.
194. Stephens to Hilliard, September 12, 1864, Hilliard Papers, University of Alabama.
195. Journal, May 30, 1861, Johnston, *Autobiography*, p. 158.
196. Jones and Rogers, "Montgomery," May 22, 1861, p. 118.
197. Jones and Rogers, "Montgomery," May 18, 1861, pp. 109–10; Davis to Bledsoe, May 18, 1861, *PJD*, VII, p. 169; Richmond, *Examiner*, May 24, 1861.
198. Sterx and Trapp, "Diary of John Withers," p. 147.
199. Daniel, *Jefferson Davis*, p. 152.
200. Jones and Rogers, "Montgomery," May 15, 1861, p. 106; Davis to Bragg, May 23, 1861, *PJD*, VII, pp. 175–76.
201. Duncan to Davis, May 16, 1861, *PJD*, VII, p. 168; Charleston, *Mercury*, June 2, 1861.

202. Richmond, *Examiner*, May 28, 1861.
203. Charlotte Wigfall to Halsey Wigfall, May 23, 1861, Charlotte Wigfall to Louly Wigfall, May 23, 1861, Wigfall Papers.
204. R. M. Smith to Davis, May 9, 1861, *PJD*, VII, p. 159.
205. Davis, *Memoir*, II, pp. 74–75; *PJD*, VII, p. 177n.
206. *Ibid* II, p. 74; Davis to Bragg, May 23, 1861, *PJD*, VII, p. 175.
207. Davis, *Memoir*, II, p. 303.
208. Montgomery, *Weekly Mail*, June 7, 1861; Jones, *Diary*, I, May 26, 1861, pp. 42–43.
209. Montgomery, *Weekly Post*, June 8, 1861.
210. Jones, *Diary*, I, May 26, 1861, p. 44.
211. Napier, *White House*, p. 14.
212. Charleston, *Mercury*, May 30, 1861.
213. Jones, *Diary*, I, May 26, 1861, p. 44.
214. *Ibid.*, May 27, 1861, p. 45; New York, *Citizen*, June 1, 1867.
215. Augusta, *Daily Chronicle and Sentinel*, May 30, 1861.
216. J. Cutler Andrews, *The South Reports the Civil War* (Princeton, 1970), p. 61.
217. Charlotte Wigfall to Halsey Wigfall, May 30, 1861, Wigfall Papers.
218. George W. Lacy to Letcher, May 26, 1861, Executive Papers, Virginia.
219. Toombs to Brown, July 12, 1861, Telemon Cuyler Collection, University of Georgia, Athens.
220. Toombs to Stephens, July 5, 1861, Toombs Papers, Duke.
221. Toombs to Crawford, February 20, 1861, Robert Toombs Papers, Miscellaneous Manuscript Collection, LC.
222. Charleston, *Mercury*, May 30, 1861.
223. Davis to John J. Byrd, May 9, 1861, Palmer Collection.
224. Beauregard to Walker, May 26, 1861, OR, I, 53, p. 176; Roman, *Beauregard*, I, pp. 64-66.
225. Davis to McKaig, Yellot, and Harding, May 25, 1861, Rowland, V, p. 101.
226. Montgomery, *Weekly Montgomery Confederation*, May 24, 1861; De Leon, *Four Years*, p. 76.
227. Jones and Rogers, "Montgomery," May 22, 1861, p. 118.
228. Montgomery, *Weekly Advertiser*, May 22, 1861.
229. Montgomery, *Daily Post*, May 15, 22, 1861.
230. Montgomery, *Weekly Mail*, May 23, 1861.
231. New York, *Citizen*, June 1, 1867.
232. Montgomery, *Daily Post*, May 22, 1861.
233. Montgomery, *Weekly Montgomery Confederation*, May 17, 24, 1861.
234. Jones, *Diary*, I, May 24, 1861, p. 41.
235. H. McLeod to Clark May 29, 1861, Records of the Governor, 301-35, Texas.
236. Charleston, *Mercury*, May 22, 17, 1861.
237. Montgomery, *Daily Post*, May 31, 1861.
238. De Leon, *Four Years*, p. 75; Montgomery, *Weekly Advertiser*, May 29, 1861.

239. Walker to Brown, May 25, 1861, Walker to Thomas O. Moore, May 25, 1861, *OR*, IV, 1, p. 355, Cooper to Van Dorn, May 25, 1861, II, 1, p. 60.

240. Invoice, Watt, Lanier & Co., June 23, 1861, Confederate Papers Relating to Citizens, RG 109, NA.

241. New Orleans, *Daily Picayune*, May 30, 1861.

242. Jones, *Diary*, I, May 28, 1861, p. 45; Walker to Phelan, May 27, 1861, Walker Letter-Book; Walker to Thomas O. Moore, May 25, 1861, *OR*, IV, 1, p. 355.

243. Jones, *Diary*, I, May 27, 1861, p. 45.

244. Voucher, Edwin Belsa, July 3, 1861, Confederate Papers Relating to Citizens, RG 109, NA.

245. De Leon, *Four Years*, p. 77.

246. New York, *Citizen*, June 1, 1867.

247. Sterx and Trapp. "Diary of John Withers," May 30, 1861, p. 147. Montgomery, *Weekly Mail*, June 7, 1861.

248. Montgomery, *Daily Advertiser*, June 1, 1861.

249. Stephen R. Mallory Diary, May 30, 1861, Stephen R. Mallory Papers, SHC, UNC; Montgomery, *Daily Post*, May 31, June 1, 1861.

250. Montgomery, *Daily Post*, June 1, 1861; Montgomery City Council Minutes, May 27, 1861, ADAH.

251. Charleston, *Mercury*, May 30, 1861.

252. Montgomery, *Daily Post*, May 31, 1861.

Epilogue

1. "Mr. Davis at Montgomery," *Southern Bivouac*, New Series, II (July 1886), p. 130.

2. Speech of Jefferson Davis at Montgomery, Rowland, IX, p. 434.

3. *Ibid.*, pp. 426–29.

4. Boykin, *Cobb*, p. 187.

5. Meade, *Benjamin*, p. 173.

6. Reed, *Brothers' War*, p. 280.

7. Rhett, Miscellaneous Notes, Aiken B. Rhett Papers.

8. Rhett notes in *Index Rerum*, Aiken B. Rhett Papers.

9. Thompson, *Toombs*, p. 255. Unless otherwise noted, the details included in these sketches of the postwar careers of the members of Congress are derived from Warner and Yearns, *Biographical Register*.

10. Speech of Jefferson Davis at Montgomery, Rowland, IX, pp. 430–31, 433–38.

BIBLIOGRAPHY

Manuscripts

Edward C. Anderson Papers, Southern Historical Collection, University of North Carolina, Chapel Hill

James Patton Anderson Papers, Southern Historical Collection, University of North Carolina, Chapel Hill

Herman Arnold, Band Score of "Dixie," 1860, Alabama Department of Archives and History, Montgomery

Mason Barret Collection, Tulane University, New Orleans, Louisiana

David C. Barrow Papers, University of Georgia, Athens

Francis Bartow Folder, Georgia Department of Archives and History, Atlanta

P. G. T. Beauregard Papers, Duke University, Durham, North Carolina

Matthew P. Blue Papers, Alabama Department of Archives and History, Montgomery

Thomas Bragg Diary, Southern Historical Collection, University of North Carolina, Chapel Hill

Joseph E. Brown Papers, typescripts in University of Georgia, Athens

Joseph E. and Elizabeth G. Brown Collection, University of Georgia, Athens

William P. Browne Papers, Alabama Department of Archives and History, Montgomery

Mary Elizabeth Buckner Papers, Tennessee State Library and Archives, Nashville

Joseph F. Burke Papers, Emory University, Atlanta, Georgia

John C. Calhoun Papers, Duke University, Durham, North Carolina

Josiah A. P. Campbell Papers, Southern Historical Collection, University of North Carolina, Chapel Hill

Campbell Family Papers, Duke University, Durham, North Carolina

Carlton-Newton-Mell Collection, University of Georgia, Athens

Anna Ella Carroll Papers, Maryland Historical Society, Baltimore

James Chesnut Letter Book, 1862, Miscellaneous Manuscripts Collection, Library of Congress, Washington, D.C.

James Chesnut, Jr., Papers, Duke University, Durham, North Carolina

Chesnut-Miller-Manning Papers, South Carolina Historical Society, Charleston

J. F. H. Claiborne Papers, Southern Historical Collection, University of North Carolina, Chapel Hill

Clement C. Clay Papers, Duke University, Durham, North Carolina

Alexander B. Clitherall Papers, Alabama Department of Archives and History, Montgomery

Howell Cobb Folder, Georgia Department of Archives and History, Atlanta

Howell Cobb Papers, University of Georgia, Athens

Thomas R. R. Cobb Folder, Georgia Department of Archives and History, Atlanta

Thomas R. R. Cobb Letters, University of Georgia, Athens

William S. Comstock Papers, William S. Hoole Special Collections, Gorgas Library, University of Alabama, Tuscaloosa

Confederate Constitution Drafts, Confederate States of America Papers, Library of Congress, Washington, D.C.

Confederate Papers Relating to Army Officers, War Department Officials, and Other Individuals, Record Group 109, National Archives, Washington, D.C.

Confederate Papers Relating to Citizens or Business Firms, Record Group 109, National Archives, Washington, D.C.

Confederate States of America Executive Papers, Louisiana Historical Association Collection, Tulane University, New Orleans, Louisiana

Confederates States of America, Location of Capital, 1861, University of Georgia, Athens

Confederate States of America Records, Center for American History, University of Texas, Austin

Confederate States Flag clipping, South Caroliniana Library, University of South Carolina, Columbia

Lemuel P. Connor Papers, Historic New Orleans Collection, New Orleans, Louisiana

Samuel Cooper Letter, copy in possession of William C. Davis, Mechanicsburg, Pennsylvania

John J. Crittenden Papers, Duke University, Durham, North Carolina

Martin J. Crawford Folder, Georgia Department of Archives and History, Atlanta

Samuel W. Crawford Papers, Library of Congress, Washington, D.C.

Cross Collection, University of Florida, Gainesville

William Wirt Culver, Personal Memoirs of . . . , in possession of Captain John Culver, Portsmouth, New Hampshire

Jabez L. M. Curry Papers, Duke University, Durham, North Carolina

Jabez L. M. Curry Family Papers, Alabama Department of Archives and History, Montgomery

Telemon Cuyler Collection, University of Georgia, Athens

Jefferson Davis Collection, Chicago Historical Society, Chicago, Illinois

Jefferson Davis Collection, Museum of the Confederacy, Richmond, Virginia

Jefferson Davis Letter, March 1, 1861, in possession of Gary Hendershott, Little Rock, Arkansas

Jefferson Davis Miscellaneous Papers, Jefferson Davis Association, Rice University, Houston, Texas

Jefferson Davis Papers, Duke University, Durham, North Carolina

Jefferson Davis Papers, Emory University, Atlanta, Georgia

Jefferson Davis Papers, The Huntington, San Marino, California

Jefferson Davis Papers, Schoff Collection, University of Michigan, Ann Arbor

Jefferson Davis Papers, Record Group 109, National Archives, Washington, D.C.

Jefferson Davis Papers, Transylvania University, Lexington, Kentucky

Jefferson Davis Papers, Louisiana Historical Association Collection, Tulane University, New Orleans, Louisiana

Jefferson and Varina Davis Collection, Series 2, Private Manuscripts, Mississippi Department of Archives and History, Jackson

Frederick Dearborn Collection, Harvard University, Cambridge, Massachusetts

Alexander De Clouet Papers, T. B. Favrot Collection, Dupre Library, Southwestern Archives and Manuscripts Collection, University of Southwestern Louisiana, Lafayette

Paul De Clouet Papers, Southern Historical Collection, University of North Carolina, Chapel Hill

Designs for Confederate Flags, Treasure Room, Volumes TR-4, Record Group 109, National Archives, Washington, D.C.

John Witherspoon DuBose Papers, Alabama Department of Archives and History, Montgomery

Easby-Smith Papers, Library of Congress, Washington, D.C.

J. W. Eldridge Collection, The Huntington, San Marino, California

John Ellis Papers, Southern Historical Collection, University of North Carolina, Chapel Hill

Executive Council Journal Letter-Book, South Carolina Department of Archives and History, Columbia

Executive Papers, Miscellaneous Letters and Papers, Governor John Letcher, Virginia State Library, Richmond

Henry S. Figures Papers, Civil War Miscellaneous Collection, United States Army Military History Institute, Carlisle, Pennsylvania

Foster Family Papers, Southern Historical Collection, University of North Carolina, Chapel Hill

Charles E. A. Gayarre Papers, Grace King Collection, Louisiana and Lower Mississippi Valley Collections, Louisiana State University, Baton Rouge

William H. Gist Papers, South Caroliniana Library, University of South Carolina, Columbia

Goodyear Collection, Yale University, New Haven, Connecticut

Gorgas Family Papers, Hoole Special Collections, University of Alabama, Tuscaloosa

Governors Papers, Administrative Files, Alabama Department of Archives and History, Montgomery
Governors Papers, Appointment Files, Alabama Department of Archives and History, Montgomery
Governors Papers, Administrative Files, Alabama Department of Archives and History, Montgomery
Governors Record Group, Record Group 27, Volumes 36 and 37, Mississippi Department of Archives and History, Jackson
James Pinckney Hambleton Papers, Emory University, Atlanta, Georgia
James Hammond Papers, Library of Congress, Washington, D.C.
Augustin H. Hansell Memoirs, Southern Historical Collection, University of North Carolina, Chapel Hill
Isham Harris Papers, Tennessee State Library and Archives, Nashville
James T. Harrison Papers, Southern Historical Collection, University of North Carolina, Chapel Hill
Rachel Lyons Heustis Papers, Southern Historical Collection, University of North Carolina, Chapel Hill
William H. Hidell Papers, Historical Society of Pennsylvania, Philadelphia
Henry W. Hilliard Papers, Hoole Special Collections, University of Alabama, Tuscaloosa
John De Berniere Hooper Papers, Southern Historical Collection, University of North Carolina, Chapel Hill
Sam Houston Papers, Center for American History, University of Texas, Austin
R.M.T. Hunter Papers, University of Virginia, Charlottesville
Huntington Miscellaneous Collection, The Huntington, San Marino, California
Intercepted Telegrams, 1861, Record Group 107, Volume 399, National Archives, Washington, D. C.
David F. Jamison Papers, Washington and Lee University, Lexington, Virginia
Robert Jemison, Jr., Papers, Hoole Special Collections, University of Alabama, Tuscaloosa
Herschel V. Johnson Papers, Duke University, Durham, North Carolina
Belle Johnston Scrapbook, Alabama Department of Archives and History, Montgomery
Charles Colcock Jones, Jr., Autograph Letters and Portraits of the Signers of the Constitution of the Confederate States, Duke University, Durham, North Carolina
Charles Colcock Jones, Jr.., Correspondence from Members of the Confederate Congress, University of Georgia, Athens
Edmund Kirby-Smith Papers, Southern Historical Collection, University of North Carolina, Chapel Hill
Laurence M. Keitt Papers, Duke University, Durham, North Carolina
La Villebeuvre Papers, Louisiana State University, Baton Rouge
Edward M. L'Engle Papers, Southern Historical Collection, University of North Carolina, Chapel Hill

Letters Received by the Confederate Adjutant and Inspector General, Record Group 109, National Archives, Washington, D.C.

Letters Received by the Confederate Secretary of War, Record Group 109, National Archives, Washington, D.C.

Letters and Telegrams Received by Robert E. Lee, Record Group 109, National Archives, Washington, D.C.

Letters Received by the Secretary of War, Record Group 365, National Archives, Washington, D.C.

Le Vert Family Papers, Southern Historical Collection, University of North Carolina, Chapel Hill

E. Lewis Letter, Alabama Department of Archives and History, Montgomery

Francis Lubbock Papers, Center for American History, University of Texas, Austin

Andrew G. Magrath Papers, South Caroliniana Library, University of South Carolina, Columbia

Stephen R. Mallory Diary, Southern Historical Collection, University of North Carolina, Chapel Hill

Manly Family Papers, Hoole Special Collections, University of Alabama, Tuscaloosa

Robert A. McClellan Papers, Duke University, Durham, North Carolina

Malcolm C. McMillan Papers, Auburn University Library, Auburn, Alabama

Colin McRae Papers, Alabama Department of Archives and History, Montgomery

Christopher G. Memminger Papers, South Caroliniana Library, University of South Carolina, Columbia

Christopher G. Memminger Papers, Southern Historical Collection, University of North Carolina, Chapel Hill

Messages of the President to Congress, Record Group 109, National Archives, Washington, D.C.

William Porcher Miles Papers, Miscellaneous Manuscript Collection, Library of Congress, Washington, D.C.

William Porcher Miles Papers, Southern Historical Collection, University of North Carolina, Chapel Hill

William H. Mitchell Papers, Alabama Department of Archives and History, Montgomery

Montgomery City Council Minutes, September 1860–December 1866, Alabama Department of Archives and History, Montgomery

Thomas O. Moore Papers, Louisiana State University, Baton Rouge

E. A. Nisbet Folder, Georgia Department of Archives and History, Atlanta

Williamson S. Oldham, Memoirs of a Confederate Senator, Center for American History, University of Texas, Austin

Orr and Patterson Family Papers, Southern Historical Collection, University of North Carolina, Chapel Hill

Jehu A. Orr Reminiscences, Mississippi Department of Archives and History, Jackson

Palfrey Family Papers, Louisiana State University, Baton Rouge

William H. Palmer Collection, Western Reserve Historical Society, Cleveland, Ohio

William Dorsey Pender Papers, Southern Historical Collection, University of North Carolina, Chapel Hill

George Petrie Papers, Auburn University Library, Auburn, Alabama

Philip Phillips Papers, Library of Congress, Washington, D.C.

Francis Pickens Papers, Duke University, Durham, North Carolina

Horace M. Polk Letters, Louisiana State University, Baton Rouge

Provisional Constitution of the Confederate States of America, February 1861, Museum of the Confederacy, Richmond, Virginia

John H. Reagan, "Judge Reagan on Davis," clipping, Dallas Historical Society, Dallas, Texas

John H. Reagan Papers, Benjamin H. Good Collection, Texas State Archives, Austin

Records Concerning Conduct and Loyalty of Army Officers, War Department Employees, Citizens During the Civil War 1861–1872, Record Group 107, National Archives, Washington, D.C.

Records of the Governor, Edward Clark, Box 301-35, Texas States Archives, Austin

Records of the Governor, Sam Houston, Texas State Archives, Austin

Aiken B. Rhett Papers, Charleston Museum, Charleston, South Carolina

Robert Barnwell Rhett, Sr., Papers, South Carolina Historical Society, Charleston

Robert Barnwell Rhett, Sr., Papers, South Caroliniana Library, University of South Carolina, Columbia

Sam Richey Collection, Miami University, Miami, Ohio

William C. Rives Papers, Library of Congress, Washington, D.C.

George N. Sanders Papers, National Archives, Washington, D.C.

Margaret Branch Sexton Collection, University of Georgia, Athens

John G. Shorter Letters, Alabama Department of Archives and History, Montgomery

John G. Shorter Papers, Duke University, Durham, North Carolina

Alexander H. Stephens Folder, Georgia Department of Archives and History, Atlanta

Alexander H. Stephens Papers, Duke University, Durham, North Carolina

Alexander H. Stephens Papers, Emory University, Atlanta, Georgia

Alexander H. Stephens Papers, Library of Congress, Washington, D.C.

Alexander H. Stephens Papers, Manhattanville College of the Sacred Heart, Purchase, New York

Alexander H. Stephens Papers, Historical Society of Pennsylvania, Philadelphia

Robert Toombs Letterbook, South Caroliniana Library, University of South Carolina, Columbia

Robert Toombs Papers, Duke University, Durham, North Carolina

Robert A. Toombs Papers, Miscellaneous Manuscript Collection, Library of Congress, Washington, D.C.

Townsend Collection, The Huntington, San Marino, California

William H. Trescott Papers, Miscellaneous Manuscript Collection, Library of Congress, Washington, D.C.

William H. Trescott Papers, South Caroliniana Library, University of South Carolina, Columbia

Beverly Tucker Papers, University of Virginia, Charlottesville

United States Census, Alabama, Montgomery County, 1st District, National Archives, Washington, D.C.

A.C. Van Benthuysen Papers, Louisiana Historical Association Papers, Tulane University, New Orleans, Louisiana

Pritchard von David Collection, Center for American History, University of Texas, Austin

Leroy P. Walker Collection, Alabama Department of Archives and History, Montgomery

Letter-Book of Official Correspondence of L.P. Walker, 1861, Confederate States of America Papers, Library of Congress, Washington, D.C.

William T. Walthall Papers, Mississippi Department of Archives and History, Jackson

Thomas H. Watts Letterbook, Alabama Department of Archives and History, Montgomery

H.C. Wayne Papers, Duke University, Durham, North Carolina

Jacob Weil Papers, Alabama Department of Archives and History, Montgomery

Edward C. Wharton Papers, Louisiana State University, Baton Rouge

Wigfall Family Papers, Library of Congress, Washington, D.C.

Louis T. Wigfall Letter, Southern Illinois University, Carbondale

Louis T. Wigfall Papers, Center for American History, University of Texas, Austin

Clayton Ware Williams Papers, Alabama Department of Archives and History, Montgomery

Williams-Chesnut-Manning Family Papers, South Caroliniana Library, University of South Carolina, Columbia

John Minor Wisdom Collection, Tulane University, New Orleans, Louisiana

Anita Dwyer Withers Diary, Southern Historical Collection, University of North Carolina, Chapel Hill

Michael L. Woods Papers, Alabama Department of Archives and History, Montgomery

Augustus R. Wright Papers, University of Georgia, Athens

Benjamin C. Yancey Papers, Southern Historical Collection, University of North Carolina, Chapel Hill

William L. Yancey Papers, Alabama Department of Archives and History, Montgomery

Newspapers

Athens, Georgia, *Southern Watchman*, 1861
Atlanta, *Daily Constitution*, 1879, 1880
Atlanta, *Daily Intelligencer*, 1861
Atlanta, *Gate-City Guardian*, 1861
Atlanta, *Intelligencer*, 1861
Atlanta, *Southern Confederacy*, 1861
Augusta, Georgia, *Daily Chronicle and Sentinel*, 1861
Augusta, Georgia, *Daily Constitutionalist*, 1861
Austin, Texas, *Weekly State Gazette*, 1861
Baltimore, *Sun*, 1861
Baton Rouge, *Daily Advocate*, 1861
Charleston, *Daily Courier*, 1861
Charleston, *Evening News*, 1861
Charleston, *Mercury*, 1861
Columbia, *Daily South Carolinian*, 1861
Columbus, Georgia, *Daily Columbus Enquirer*, 1861
Columbus, Georgia, *Daily Times*, 1861
Dallas, *Herald*, 1861
Grove Hill, Alabama, *Clarke County Democrat*, 1861
Huntsville, Alabama, *Democrat*, 1861
Jacksonville, Alabama, *Republican*, 1861
Jacksonville, Florida, *Times-Union*, 1905
London, *Times*, 1861
Macon, Georgia, *Daily Telegraph*, 1861
Macon, Georgia, *Weekly Telegraph*, 1861
Memphis, *Daily Appeal*, 1861, 1870
Memphis, *Daily Memphis Avalanche*, 1861
Mobile, *Daily Advertiser*, 1861
Montgomery, *Advertiser*, 1859
Montgomery, *Advertiser and Mail*, 1881
Montgomery, *Advertiser and State Gazette*, 1856
Montgomery, *Daily Mail*, 1861
Montgomery, *Daily Post*, 1861
Montgomery, *Weekly Advertiser*, 1861
Montgomery, *Weekly Montgomery Confederation*, 1861
Montgomery, *Weekly Mail*, 1861
Nashville, *Daily Gazette*, 1861
Nashville, *Union & American*, 1861
Natchez, Mississippi, *Daily Courier*, 1861
Natchez, Mississippi, *Daily Free Trader*, 1861
New Orleans, *Bee*, 1861
New Orleans, *Daily Crescent*, 1861
New Orleans, *Daily Delta*, 1861

New Orleans, *Daily Picayune*, 1861
New Orleans, *Sunday Delta*, 1861
New Orleans, *Times-Democrat*, 1902
New Orleans, *True Delta*, 1861
New York, *Citizen*, 1867
New York, *Daily Tribune*, 1861
New York, *Harper's Weekly Illustrated Newspaper*, 1861
New York, *Herald*, 1861
New York, *Times*, 1861
New York, *Tribune*, 1861
New York, *World*, 1861
Philadelphia, *Weekly Times*, 1879–1880
Richmond, *Daily Dispatch*, 1861
Richmond, *Dispatch*, 1861
Richmond, *Enquirer*, 1861
Richmond, *Daily Examiner*, 1861
Richmond, *Whig*, 1861
Rome, Georgia, *Tri-Weekly Courier*, 1861
Savannah, *Daily Morning News*, 1861
Selma, Alabama, *Weekly Times*, 1861
Tuscaloosa, Alabama, *Independent Monitor*, 1861
Vicksburg, *Daily Evening Citizen*, 1861
Vicksburg, *Weekly Whig*, 1861
Washington, *Evening Star*, 1861
Washington, *States and Union*, 1861

Theses and Dissertations

Halperin, Rick. "Leroy Pope Walker and the Problems of the Confederate War Department, February–September, 1861." Ph.D. diss., Auburn University, Auburn, Ala., 1978.

Heidler, Davis S. "Fire Eaters: The Radical Secessionists in Antebellum Politics." Ph.D. diss., Auburn University, Auburn, Ala., 1985.

Johnson, Evans C. "A Political Life of Henry W. Hilliard." M.A. thesis, University of Alabama, University, Ala., 1947.

Joslyn, Rick. "Biographical Sketch of Robert Josselyn." Sparta, Ga., 1992.

Kemp, Paige Holliman. "Montgomery, Alabama, 1861: A Social History of the Cradle of the Confederacy." M.A. thesis, Auburn University, Auburn, Ala., 1978.

Rucker, Brian R. "Jackson Morton: West Florida's Soldier, Senator, and Secessionist." N. p., n. d.

Weiss, Yvonne Pavy. "Alexandre Etienne DeClouet." M.A. thesis, Louisiana State University, Baton Rouge, 1937.

Wible, Hazel Butler. "History of Montgomery, Alabama, 1860–1865." M.A. thesis, Auburn University, Auburn, Ala., 1939.

Young, Hugh Peter. " A Social and Economical History of Montgomery, Alabama, 1846–1860." M.A. thesis, University of Alabama, University, Ala., 1948.

Official Publications

Confederate States Congress. *Constitution of the Confederate States of America.* Milledgeville, Georgia: 1861.

Kennedy, Joseph C. *Preliminary Report on the Eighth Census 1860.* Washington: 1860.

Matthews, James M., ed. *The Statutes at Large of the Provisional Government of the Confederate States of America.* Richmond: 1864.

Ordinances and Constitution of the State of Alabama . . . Provisional Government. N. p.: n.d.

Richardson, James D., comp. *The Messages and Papers of Jefferson Davis and the Confederacy.* 2 vols. Washington: 1905.

United States Census Office. *Statistics of the United States . . . in 1860.* Washington: 1861.

United States Congress. *Journal of the Congress of the Confederate States of America.* 7 vols. Washington: 1904.

United States Government Printing Office. *List of Staff Officers of the Confederate States Army, 1861–1865.* Washington: 1891.

United States Navy Department. *Official Records of the Union and Confederate Navies in the War of the Rebellion.* 31 vols. Washington: 1894–1927.

United States War Department. *War of the Rebellion: Official Records of the Union and Confederate Armies.* 128 vols. Washington: 1880–1901.

Walker, Francis A., ed. *Ninth Census—Volume 1. The Statistics of the Population of the United States.* Washington, 1872.

Wierenga, Theron, comp. *Official Documents of the Post Office Department of the Confederate States of America.* 2 vols. Holland, Michigan: 1979.

Articles

"Beautiful Reception at First White House of the Confederacy." *Alabama Historical Quarterly,* XVIII (Spring 1956), pp. 126–30.

Beringer, Richard E. "A Profile of the Members of the Confederate Congress." *Journal of Southern History,* XXXII, No. 4 (November 1967), pp. 518–41.

Brannon, Peter A., ed. "Some Early Montgomery Records." *Alabama Historical Quarterly,* XVIII (Spring 1956), pp. 1–130.

———. "The Stars and Bars." *Alabama Historical Quarterly,* XVIII (Winter 1956), pp. 427–42.

Caffey, Thomas. "Letters from the Front." *Confederate Veteran*, XXVI (January 1918), pp. 26–27.

Capers, Henry D. "Treasurer of the Confederate Government." *Confederate Veteran*, XXIV (April 1916), pp. 150–51.

Cheshire, R. M. "Official Seal Maker of the Confederacy." *Confederate Veteran*, XX (October 1912), p. 471.

Cleveland, Henry W. "Robert Toombs." *Southern Bivouac*, New Series, I (January 1886), pp. 449–59.

"The Correspondence of Thomas Reade Rootes Cobb, 1861–1862." *Publications of the Southern History Association*, XI (May 1907), pp. 148–85; (July 1907), pp. 233–60; (September–November 1907), pp. 312–28.

Daniel, L. S. "Notice to President Davis of His Election." *Confederate Veteran*, XIII (August 1905), p. 369.

De Leon, Thomas C. "The Real Jefferson Davis in Private and Public Life." *Southern Historical Society Papers*, XXXVI (1908), pp. 74–85.

"Designs for Confederate Flags." *Confederate Veteran*, XXI (February 1913), p. 79.

Dillard, Anthony W. "William Lowndes Yancey." *Southern Historical Society Papers*, XXI (1893), pp. 151–59.

"Editorial." *DeBow's Review*, XXX (May–June 1861), pp. 682–83.

"Editorial Miscellany." *DeBow's Review*, XXX (March 1861), p. 381.

Edmonds, Phoebe Frazer. "My First Impressions of the War." *Confederate Veteran*, IX (May 1901), pp. 205–208.

"The First Confederate Flag." *Confederate Veteran*, III (October 1895), p. 315.

Fitts, Albert N. "The Confederate Convention." *Alabama Review*, II (April 1949), pp. 83–101.

Garnett, T. S. "Address of. . . ." *Southern Historical Society Papers*, XXVII (1899), pp. 151–55.

Gerson, Armand J. "The Inception of the Montgomery Convention." *American Historical Association Annual Report* (1910), pp. 179–87.

Halls, George W. "Cadet Company of Alabama." *Confederate Veteran*, XXX (April 1922), pp. 129–30.

Hamilton, David Twiggs. "Presidency of the Confederacy Offered Stephens and Refused." *Southern Historical Society Papers*, XXXVI (1908), pp. 141–45.

Hardaway, Roger D. "The Confederate Constitution: A Legal and Historical Examination." *Alabama Historical Quarterly*, XLIV (Spring–Summer 1982), pp. 18–31.

Hoole, William Stanley, ed. "The Diary of Dr. Basil Manly, 1858–1867." *The Alabama Review*, IV (April 1951), pp. 127–49.

———. "The Flag of the Republic of Alabama, An Odyssey." *Alabama Historical Quarterly*, XL (Fall–Winter 1978), pp. 105–18.

"How Davis Took the Oath." *The Vedette*, VII (June 1886), pp. 12–13.

Hull, A. L. "The Making of the Confederate Constitution." *Publications of the Southern History Association*, IX (September 1905), pp. 272–92.

"In the early twilight. . . ." *Confederate Veteran*, I (March 1893), p. 80.

Johnson, Herschel V. "From the Autobiography of. . . ." *American Historical Review*, XXX (January 1925), pp. 311–36.

Jones, Anne Warren. "The First Soldiers' Hospital." *Confederate Veteran*, XXXVI (July 1928), pp. 262–63.

Jones, James P., and William Warren Rogers, eds. "Montgomery as the Confederate Capital: View of a New Nation." *Alabama Historical Quarterly*, XXVI (Spring 1964), pp. 1–125.

Jones, Virginia K., ed. "A Contemporary Account of the Inauguration of Jefferson Davis." *Alabama Historical Quarterly*, XXIII (Fall-Winter 1961), pp. 273–77.

———. "Letters of Rev. W. H. Mitchell." *Alabama Historical Quarterly*, XXIII (Spring 1961), pp. 180–87.

"Last Survivor of the Original Confederate States Congress." *Confederate Veteran*, XXV (February 1917), p. 54.

"Letter of Stephen R. Mallory, 1861." *American Historical Review*, XII (October 1906), pp. 103–108.

McCaleb, Walter F. "The Organization of the Post-Office Department of the Confederacy." *American Historical Review*, XII (October 1906), pp. 66–74.

Monroe, Haskell. "Early Confederate Political Patronage." *Alabama Review*, XX (January 1967), pp. 45–61.

Morrissette, Kate Hutcheson. "Social Life in the First Confederate Capital." *Our Women of the War*, supplement, Montgomery, *Journal*, March 13, 1907.

"Mr. Davis at Montgomery." *Southern Bivouac*, New Series, II (July 1886), pp. 129–30.

Napier, John H., III. "Martial Montgomery: Ante Bellum Military Activity." *Alabama Historical Quarterly*, XXIX (Fall-Winter 1967), pp. 107–32.

———. "Montgomery During the Civil War." *Alabama Review*, XLI (April 1988), pp. 103–31.

Nast, F. A. "History of Confederate Stamps." *Confederate Veteran*, II (March 1894), pp. 77–78.

O'Brien, Frank. "Passing of the Old Montgomery Theatre." *Alabama Historical Quarterly*, III (Spring 1941), pp. 8–14.

"Organization of the Confederate Post Office Department." *Confederate War Journal*, II (August 1894), pp. 66–67.

Owen, Marie Bankhead. "Raising the First Confederate Flag." *Confederate Veteran*, XXIV (May 1916), p. 199.

"Phillips H. S. Gayle and Mary Armistead Gayle." *Confederate Veteran*, XII (March 1904), pp. 125–27.

Pickett, Mrs. George E. "Words from Jefferson Davis." *Confederate Veteran*, XXI (March 1913), p. 108.

Porter, R. K. "Sketch of General T. R. R. Cobb." *Land We Love*, III (July 1867), pp. 183–97.

"Prayer at Inauguration of President Davis." *Confederate Veteran*, XXIX (June 1921), p. 203.

"Prayer at the Jefferson Davis Inaugural." *Confederate Veteran*, XXXVII (July 1929), p. 275.

Prible,————. "The Flag of the Confederate States of America." *Southern Historical Society Papers*, XXXVIII (1910), pp. 243–61.

Read, C. W. "Reminiscences of the Confederate States Navy." *Southern Historical Society Papers*, I (May 1876), pp. 331–62.

Rhett, Robert Barnwell, Jr. "The Confederate Government at Montgomery." Robert U. Johnson and Clarence C. Buel, eds., *Battles and Leaders of the Civil War*. New York: 1888. I, pp. 99–110.

Richardson, Ralph. "The Choice of Jefferson Davis as Confederate President." *Journal of Mississippi History*, XVII (July 1955), pp. 161–76.

"Seals, Stamps and Currency." *Southern Historical Society Papers*, XXXIII (1905), pp. 188–90.

Shofner, Jerrell H. and William Warren Rogers. "Montgomery to Richmond: The Confederacy Selects A Capital." *Civil War History*, X (June 1964), pp. 155–66.

Smith, Jessica Randolph. "About Design of the First Flag." *Confederate Veteran*, XIII (November 1905), pp. 509–10.

Smith, Reid. "'Dixie' on A Wall." *Inn Dixie* (July 1949), pp. 11–14, 27.

Spence, Philip B. "Service for the Confederacy." *Confederate Veteran*, VIII (August 1900), pp. 373–74.

Stephens, Alexander H. "Reminiscences of Alexander H. Stephens vs. Those of General Richard Taylor." *International Review*, V (March 1878), pp. 145–54.

Sterx, H. E. and L. Y. Trapp, eds. "One Year of the War: Civil War Diary of John Withers, Assistant-Adjutant-General of the Confederate Army." *Alabama Historical Quarterly*, XXIX (Fall–Winter 1967), pp. 133–84.

Sweeney, Thomas W. "Pride of Place." *Historic Preservation News* (January 1993), pp. 16–17.

"Taps." *Southern Bivouac*, I (May–June 1883), p. 394.

Taylor, Rosser H., ed. "Boyce-Hammond Correspondence." *Journal of Southern History*, III (August 1937), pp. 348–54.

Walton, J. B., et al. "Sketches of the History of the Washington Artillery." *Southern Historical Society Papers*, XI (April-May 1883), pp. 210–22.

Washington, L. Q. "The Confederate State Department." *The Independent*, LIII (September 19, 1901), pp. 2218–2224.

Watt, Mary Phelan. "The Women of Alabama in the War." *Confederate Veteran*, XXIV (May 1916), pp. 225–27.

"When the Band First Played 'Dixie'." *Confederate Veteran*, XXXIV (June 1926), p. 234.

Williams, Edward F., III, ed. "John Reagan's Own Account of Confederate

Post Office Operations." *Confederate Philatelist*, XVII (May 1972), pp. 42–46; (July 1972), pp. 66–69.

Books

A Soldier's Honor: With Reminiscences of Major-General Earl Van Dorn. By His Comrades. New York, 1902.

Alexander, Thomas B., and Richard E. Beringer. *The Anatomy of the Confederate Congress*. Nashville, 1972.

American Annual Cyclopaedia and Register of Important Events of the Year 1861. New York, 1864.

Anderson, Frank Maloy. *The Mystery of "A Public Man."* Minneapolis, 1948.

Andrews, J. Cutler. *The South Reports the Civil War*. Princeton, 1970.

The Annual Directory to the Inhabitants, Institutions, Incorporated Companies, Manufacturing Establishments, Business, Firms, etc., etc., in the City of Montgomery, for 1873. Montgomery, 1873.

Avary, Myrta Lockett. *Reminiscences of A. H. Stephens*. New York, 1910.

Barney, William L. *The Secessionist Impulse: Alabama and Mississippi*. Princeton, 1974.

Black, Robert C., III. *The Railroads of the Confederacy*. Chapel Hill, N.C., 1952.

Blanchard, Etta Worsley. *Columbus on the Chattahoochee*. Columbus, Ga., 1951.

Blue, Matthew P., et al. *City Directory and History of Montgomery, Alabama*. . . . Montgomery, 1878.

Boyd, Minnie C. *Alabama in the Fifties. A Social Study*. New York, 1931.

Boykin, Samuel, ed. *Memorial Volume of the Hon. Howell Cobb of Georgia*. Philadelphia, 1870.

Brannon, Peter A. *The Organization of the Confederate Post Office Department at Montgomery*. Montgomery, 1960.

Brewer, W. *Alabama, Her History, Resources, War Record, and Public Men from 1540 to 1872*. Montgomery, 1872.

Bulloch, James D. *The Secret Service of the Confederate States in Europe*. 2 vols. Liverpool, 1883.

Butler, Pierce. *Judah P. Benjamin*. Philadelphia, 1907.

Capers, Henry D. *The Life and Times of C. G. Memminger*. Richmond, 1893.

Cauthen, Charles E. *South Carolina Goes to War*. Chapel Hill, 1950.

Channing, Steven A. *Crisis of Fear: Secession in South Carolina*. New York, 1970.

Clay-Clopton, Virginia. *A Belle of the Fifties*. New York, 1905.

Cleveland, Henry. *Alex. H. Stephens in Public and Private*. Philadelphia, 1866.

Cobb, T. R. R. *Substance of an Address of . . . to His Constituents of Clark County, April 6, 1861*. N. p., 1861.

Crawford, J. Marshall. *Mosby and His Men*. New York, 1867.

Crawford, Martin. *William Howard Russell's Civil War. Private Diary and Letters, 1861–1862.* Athens, Ga., 1992.

Crawford, Samuel W. *The Genesis of the Civil War.* New York, 1887.

Crist, Lynda Lasswell and Mary Seaton Dix, eds. *The Papers of Jefferson Davis. Volume 6, 1856–1860.* Baton Rouge, 1989.

———. *The Papers of Jefferson Davis. Volume 7, 1861.* Baton Rouge, 1992.

Crocket, George L. *Two Centuries in East Texas.* Dallas, 1932.

Curry, J. L. M. *Civil History of the Government of the Confederate States, With Some Personal Reminiscences.* Richmond, 1901.

Daniel, John W., ed. *Life and Reminiscences of Jefferson Davis. By Distinguished Men of His Time.* Baltimore, 1890.

Davis, Jefferson. *The Rise and Fall of the Confederate Government.* 2 vols. New York, 1881.

Davis, Varina. *Jefferson Davis, Ex-President of the Confederate States of America. A Memoir.* 2 vols. New York, 1890.

Davis, William C. *Jefferson Davis, The Man and His Hour.* New York, 1991.

De Fontaine, Felix G. *Army Letters of "Personne" 1861–1865.* Columbia, S. C., 1896.

De Leon, Thomas F. *Belles, Beaux and Brains of the 60's.* New York, 1907.

———. *Four Years in Rebel Capitals.* Mobile, 1890.

Denman, Clarence P. *The Secession Movement in Alabama.* Montgomery, 1933.

DeRosa, Marshall L. *The Confederate Constitution of 1861.* Columbia, Mo., 1991.

Dorman, Lewy. *Party Politics in Alabama from 1850 Through 1860.* Wetumpka, Ala., 1935.

DuBose, John W. *The Life and Times of William Lowndes Yancey.* 2 vols. New York, 1892.

Duke, Basil W. *Reminiscences of General Basil W. Duke, C. S. A.* New York, 1911.

Dumond, Dwight L. *The Secession Movement, 1860–1861.* New York, 1931.

Durkin, Joseph T. *Stephen R. Mallory, Confederate Navy Chief.* Chapel Hill, 1954.

Easby-Smith, Ann. *William Russell Smith of Alabama, His Life and Works.* Philadelphia, 1931.

Estvan, Bela. *War Pictures from the South.* New York, 1863.

Flynt, Wayne. *Montgomery, An Illustrated History.* Woodland Hills, Calif., 1980.

Goff, Richard D. *Confederate Supply.* Durham, N. C., 1969.

Gordon, John B. *Reminiscences of the Civil War.* New York, 1904.

Harris, William C. *Leroy Pope Walker, Confederate Secretary of War.* Tuscaloosa, Ala., 1962.

Hill, Benjamin H., Jr. *Senator Benjamin H. Hill of Georgia. His Life, Speeches and Writings.* Atlanta, 1893.

Hilliard, Henry. *Politics and Pen Pictures at Home and Abroad.* New York, 1892.

Hodgson, Joseph. *The Cradle of the Confederacy, or the Times of Troup, Quitman and Yancey*. Mobile, 1876.

Hoole, William S. *Alias Simon Suggs: The Life and Times of Johnson Jones Hooper*. University, Ala., 1952.

Huse, Caleb. *The Supplies for the Confederate Army*. Boston, 1904.

Johnson, Michael P. *Toward a Patriarchal Republic. The Secession of Georgia*. Baton Rouge, 1977.

Johnston, Joseph E. *Narrative of Military Operations*. New York, 1874.

Johnston, Richard M. *Autobiography of Col. Richard Malcolm Johnston*. Washington, 1900.

———, and William Browne. *Life of Alexander H. Stephens*. Philadelphia, 1878.

Jones, John B. *A Rebel War Clerk's Diary at the Confederate States Capital*. 2 vols. Philadelphia, 1866.

Jones, Katherine M. *Heroines of Dixie. Confederate Women Tell Their Story of the War*. New York, 1955.

Kerbey, Joseph O. *The Boy Spy*. Chicago, 1887.

Kirkland, Thomas J., and Robert M. Kennedy. *Historic Camden*. 2 vols. Columbia, S. C., 1905, 1926.

Lee, Charles R. *The Confederate Constitution*. Chapel Hill, 1963.

Lovejoy, Evelyn. *History of Royalton, Vermont*. N. p., 1911.

McCash, William B. *Thomas R. R. Cobb: The Making of a Southern Nationalist*. Macon, Ga., 1983.

McElroy, Robert. *Jefferson Davis. The Unreal and the Real*. 2 vols. New York, 1937.

McLaws, Mrs. Lafayette. *The Welding*. Boston, 1907.

McMillan, Malcolm C. *The Disintegration of A Confederate State*. Macon, Ga., 1986.

Meade, Robert D. *Judah P. Benjamin, Confederate Statesman*. New York, 1943.

Mears, Leonard, and James Turnbull. *The Montgomery Directory, for 1859–'60. Containing the Names of the Inhabitants, A Business Directory, Street Directory. . . .* Montgomery, 1859.

[Memminger, Christopher G.]. *Plan of a Provisional Government for the Southern Confederacy*. Charleston, 1861.

Memorials of the Life and Character of Wiley P. Harris, of Mississippi. Jackson, Miss., 1892.

Montgomery, Horace. *Howell Cobb's Confederate Career*. Tuscaloosa, Ala., 1959.

Moore, Frank, comp. *The Rebellion Record*. 12 vols. New York, 1861–1868.

Morgan, James M. *Recollections of A Rebel Reefer*. Boston, 1917.

Muskat, Beth. *The Way It Was*. Montgomery, n.d.

Napier, Cameron F. *The First White House of the Confederacy*. Montgomery, 1989.

———. *The Struggle to Preserve the First White House of the Confederacy*. University, Ala., 1983.

Oates, William C. *The War Between the Union and the Confederacy and its Lost Opportunities.* New York, 1905.

Oliphant, Mary C. Simms, Alfred Taylor Odell, and T. C. Duncan Eaves, eds. *The Letters of William Gilmore Simms.* 5 vols. Columbia, S. C., 1955.

Owsley, Frank L. *King Cotton Diplomacy.* Chicago, Second Edition, 1959.

———. *State Rights in the Confederacy.* Chicago, 1925.

Parks, Joseph H. *Joseph E. Brown of Georgia.* Baton Rouge, 1977.

Parrish, T. Michael, and Robert M. Willingham, Jr. *Confederate Imprints. A Bibliography of Southern Publications from Secession to Surrender.* Austin, Texas, n.d.

Pearce, Haywood J., Jr. *Benjamin H. Hill, Secession and Reconstruction.* Chicago, 1928.

Phillips, Ulrich B., ed. *The Correspondence of Robert Toombs, Alexander H. Stephens, and Howell Cobb.* Washington, 1913.

———. *Life of Robert Toombs.* New York, 1913.

Pollard, Edward A. *The First Year of the War.* New York, 1863.

———. *The Lost Cause.* New York, 1866.

Reagan, John A. *Memoirs, with Special Reference to Secession and the Civil War.* New York, 1906.

Reed, John C. *The Brothers' War.* Boston, 1906.

Roman, Alfred. *The Military Operations of General Beauregard in the War Between the States.* 2 vols. New York, 1884.

Rowland, Dunbar. *Courts, Judges, and Lawyers in Mississippi, 1798–1935.* Jackson, Miss., 1935.

———, comp. *Jefferson Davis, Constitutionalist: His Letters, Papers and Speeches.* 10 vols. Jackson, Miss., 1923.

Russell, William H. *My Diary North and South.* 2 vols. London, 1863.

———. *Pictures of Southern Life, Social, Political, and Military.* New York, 1861.

Sanford, John W. A. *The Code of the City of Montgomery.* Montgomery, 1861.

Scarborough, William K., ed. *The Diary of Edmund Ruffin, Volume I, Toward Independence, October, 1856–April, 1861.* Baton Rouge, 1972.

———. *The Diary of Edmund Ruffin, Volume II, The Years of Hope, April, 1861–June, 1863.* Baton Rouge, 1976.

Schott, Thomas E. *Alexander H. Stephens of Georgia.* Baton Rouge, 1988.

Smith, Robert H. *An Address to the Citizens of Alabama, on the Constitution of the Confederate States of America.* Mobile, 1861.

Smith, William R. *The History and Debates of the Convention of the People of Alabama, 1861.* Montgomery, 1861.

Stephens, Alexander H. *A Comprehensive and Popular History of the United States.* Raleigh, N.C., 1884.

———. *A Constitutional View of the Late War Between the States.* 2 vols. Philadelphia, 1868, 1870.

———. *The Reviewers Reviewed.* New York, 1872.

———. *The Wickedness of Secession: From the Lips of. . . .* N. p., [1861].

Stovall, Pleasant A. *Robert Toombs, Statesman, Speaker, Soldier, Sage*. New York, 1892.

Sulzby, James F., Jr. *Historic Alabama Hotels and Resorts*. Tuscaloosa, 1960.

Takaki, Ronald T. *A Pro-Slavery Crusade. The Agitation to Reopen the African Slave Trade*. New York, 1971.

Tharin, Robert S. *Arbitrary Arrests in the South; or, Scenes from the Experiences of an Alabama Unionist*. New York, 1863.

Thian, Raphael P. *Register of the Confederate Debt*. Boston, 1972.

Thomas, Emory. *The Confederate Nation, 1861–1865*. New York, 1979.

Thompson, William Y. *Robert Toombs of Georgia*. Baton Rouge, 1966.

Todd, Richard C. *Confederate Finance*. Athens, Ga., 1954.

Vandiver, Frank E., ed. *The Civil War Diary of General Josiah Gorgas*. University, Ala., 1947.

Walther, Eric H. *The Fire-Eaters*. Baton Rouge, 1992.

Warner, Ezra J., and W. Buck Yearns. *Biographical Register of the Confederate Congress*. Baton Rouge, 1975.

Watts, Thomas H. *Address of . . . on the Life and Character of Ex-President Jefferson Davis*. Montgomery, 1889.

White, Laura A. *Robert Barnwell Rhett: Father of Secession*. Washington, 1931.

Winston, R. W. *High Stakes and Hair Trigger. The Life of Jefferson Davis*. New York, 1930.

Woodward, C. Vann, ed. *Mary Chesnut's Civil War*. New Haven, Conn., 1981.

————, and Elizabeth Muhlenfeld, eds. *The Private Mary Chesnut: The Unpublished Civil War Diaries*. New York, 1984.

Wooster, Ralph A. *The Secession Conventions of the South*. Princeton, 1962.

Wright, Louise. *A Southern Girl in '61*. New York, 1905.

Yearns, Wilfred Buck. *The Confederate Congress*. Athens, Ga., 1960.

Catalogs

Baker, G. A. *Catalog #34*. 1939.

The Collector, XLVII (November 1932).

The Collector. #871. Hunter, N. Y., 1980.

Goodspeed's Catalog #373, 1943.

Rubenfine, Joseph. *Catalog #34*. Pleasantville, N. J., 1974.

Sotheby's Sale Catalog. New York, May 21, 1993.

INDEX

Note: Subentries appear in chronological order for the most part, separated by semi-colons following their main entry. In the case of individuals, after the general listing, subtopics appear in this order: personal information, if any, then activities in Montgomery, relations with and opinions of other delegates, and last, post-Montgomery careers.

537